Venetian Academy of Indian Studies Series
No. 4

General Editor
Gian Giuseppe Filippi

Venetian Academy of Indian Studies (VAIS)

As a prestigious instrument of the Department of East Asian Studies, University "Ca' Foscari" of Venice, Italy, the Venetian Academy of Indian Studies has, since its inception, been involved with organisation of symposia, missions in field, publications, and cultural programmes that have some kind of relevance to Indological studies.

Foremost among its other academic/researach concerns, however, is the VAIS' aim to promote scientific interaction and mutual understanding between Indian and European scholars, institutions, media and enterprises.

Guru
The Spiritual Master
in Eastern and Western Traditions
Authority and Charisma

गुरुर्ब्रह्मा गुरुर्विष्णुः गुरुर्देवो महेश्वरः ।
गुरुः साक्षात् परब्रह्म तस्मै श्री गुरवे नमः ॥

gururbrahmā gururviṣṇuḥ gururdevo maheśvaraḥ ।
guruḥ sākṣāt parabrahma tasmai śrī gurave namaḥ ॥

The *Guru* himself is Brahmā [the Creator], Viṣṇu [the Preserver] and Śiva [the Destructor]. He is the embodiment of the Supreme Spirit. I bow down to that *Guru* ॥

Venetian Academy of Indian Studies Series, no. 4

Guru
The Spiritual Master
in Eastern and Western Traditions
— Authority and Charisma —

Edited by
Antonio Rigopoulos

Venetian Academy of Indian Studies
Venice, Italy

D.K.Printworld (P) Ltd.
New Delhi, India

Cataloging in Publication Data — DK
[Courtesy: D.K. Agencies (P) Ltd. <docinfo@dkagencies.com>]

National Conference on Guru, the Spiritual Master in Eastern and Western Traditions : Authority and Charisma (2002 : Venice, Italy)
Guru, the spiritual master in Eastern and Western traditions : authority and charisma / edited by Antonio Rigopoulos. — 1st Indian ed. 2007.
iv, 564 p. 23 cm. — (Venetian Academy of Indian Studies series ; no. 4)
Papers presented at the National Conference on Guru, the Spiritual Master in Eastern and Western Traditions : Authority and Charisma, held at Venice during 18-20 April 2002.
Includes bibliographical references.
ISBN 8124603901

1. Gurus — Congresses. I. Rigopoulos, Antonio, 1962- II. Title. III. Series: Venetian Academy of Indian Studies series ; no. 4.

DDC 206.1 22

ISBN 81-246-0390-1
First appeared as *Indoasiatica* no. 2/2004 Venezia (Italy)
First Indian Edition, 2007

Published by:
Venetian Academy of Indian Studies
Department of East Asian Studies
"Ca' Foscari" Venice University
Ca' Soranzo, San Polo 2169
30125 Venice (Italy)

and

D.K. Printworld (P) Ltd.
Regd. office : *'Sri Kunj'*, F-52, Bali Nagar
New Delhi - 110 015
Phones : (011) 2545-3975; 2546-6019; *Fax* : (011) 2546-5926
E-mail: dkprintworld@vsnl.net
Web: www.dkprintworld.com

Printed by: D.K. Printworld (P) Ltd., New Delhi.

Preface

This volume comprises most of the papers which were presented at the National Conference "*Guru*. The Spiritual Master in Eastern and Western Traditions: Authority and Charisma", held in Venice, 18-20 April 2002, organized by the Venetian Academy of Indian Studies (VAIS) in collaboration with the Department of East Asian Studies of the University of Venice, Ca' Foscari, and the Cultural Center Palazzo Cavagnis. These twenty-seven essays are grouped according to the different cultural and religious traditions involved, moving from West to East and circularly coming back to the West. In a crossing of boundaries which sharpens the comparative exchange, we move through the following civilizations and worldviews: Ancient Greece, Judaism, Christianity, Islām, Hinduism, Indian Shamanism, Buddhism, Confucianism and Daoism, Native Americans. Two final articles on the *guru* as mediator of healing and on the figure and role of the master between East and West bring the volume to a close.

Though the majority of papers are devoted to the religions and philosophies of India and the manifold expressions of its *guru* institute – the main focus of the Conference – all other traditions are fairly represented, each scholar aiming at rigorously placing in context the nature and function of the master. I must stress that an interdisciplinary and truly sophisticated comparative interest animated the Conference, especially during the lively debate sessions. The essays mirror two basic formats, as per their authors' wish: they either reflect, with minor modifications, one's speech as it was originally delivered and thus are often short contributions meant for discussion, or else they are expanded, revised versions of one's paper i.e. full-fledged articles with critical note apparatus.

The thirty-two Italian scholars who participated in this rich and intense three-day meeting open to the public (which attracted hundreds of people to the Waldensian and Methodist Church of Venice, where the Conference took place, making it an 'event' of sorts) were: Attilio Andreini, Stefano Beggiora, Paolo Bettiolo, Giuliano Boccali, Pier Cesare Bori, Michele Botta, Luca Caldironi, Piero Capelli, Claudio Cicuzza, Chiara Cremonesi, Thomas Dähnhardt, Fabrizio Ferrari, Gian Giuseppe Filippi, Gaetano Lettieri, Franco Macchi, Massimo Makarovic, Monia Marchetto, Giangiorgio Pasqualotto, Gianni Pellegrini, Cinzia Pieruccini, Corrado Puchetti, Claudia Ramasso, Massimo Raveri, Paolo Ricca, Fabian Sanders, Angelo Scarabel, Maurizio Scarpari, Francesco Sferra, Francesco Spagna, Aldo Tollini, Giovanni Torcinovich, and myself. The Conference was also honoured by the presence of a most distinguished guest (himself a *guru*!): the Sanskrit *ācārya* Pandit Vidya Nivas Mishra from Vārāṇāsī who delivered a short, momentous *pravacana* or speech.

The theme of the *guru* institute and, more broadly, of the master/disciple relationship, is certainly crucial within all religious traditions. In Italy, important monographs have been dedicated to the subject in recent years, especially with reference to classical and late antiquity, Judaism, early Christianity and Christian monasticism.[1] De-

[1] Significant, recent publications are: M. CATTO – I. GAGLIARDI – R. M. PARRINELLO (eds.), *Direzione spirituale tra ortodossia ed eresia. Dalle scuole filosofiche antiche al novecento*, Brescia, Morcelliana, 2002; G. FILORAMO (ed.), *Maestro e discepolo. Temi e problemi della direzione spirituale tra VI secolo a.C. e VII secolo d.C.*, Brescia, Morcelliana, 2002. See also

voted to this same issue and the crucial theme of education, *paideia*, is the latest, stimulating book written by George Steiner, *Lessons of the Masters* (Cambridge and London, Harvard University Press, 2003), outcome of the *Charles Eliot Norton Lectures* held in Harvard in 2001-2002. From the outset, our Conference was thought of as an exploration concerning the sources of legitimation of religious authority within any given tradition and as a critical examination of the special charisma which the spiritual master exhibits or is in any case attributed to him/her by any given community. The focus of attention has been directed upon India and Eastern traditions, cultivating an approach of 'dialogical', comparative openness towards all other traditions.

The idea was that of avoiding a purely phenomenological approach (typically focused upon theological/philosophical speculation and doctrinal issues), in an effort to promote a veritable 'sociology of knowledge' so as to uncover the dynamism of the ideological, social, even political network of discourses governing each case in its own context. The *guru* and the master/disciple relationship are indeed of crucial significance for a discussion of the various ways institutional *power* (religious as well as political, social as well as economical) is constructed, acquired, enacted, transacted, transferred, and, eventually, lost.

In particular, the fabrication of 'spiritual' power (and authority/charisma) and the potential acquisition of freedom *in* it and *through* it (even allowing one to free himself/herself from all temptations of exercising an individual/egotistical power!), appears to be linked to the active building of one's subjectivity, to the very notion of education and the 'taking care of oneself' by means of 'working upon oneself'. On these issues, most precious and thought-provoking are the recently published lessons of Michel Foucault (1926-1984) at the *Collège de France*, relative to the techniques and practices of 'shaping the self' in Greek and Roman antiquity (particularly within

G. FILORAMO (ed.), *Carisma profetico. Fattore di innovazione religiosa*, Brescia, Morcelliana, 2003.

Stoicism and Cynicism, but also in Platonism and Christian monasticism).

Indeed especially in his last years Foucault, himself influenced by the writings of Pierre Hadot,[2] dedicated special attention to the theme of the unending search for wisdom and the perfecting of the self through the detaching from oneself. For Foucault, such transformation is to be understood as an ongoing process of discovery, implying an 'ethics of unsettlement' (*contra* any juridical foundation of a 'perennial' ethics), never established once for all: what he called a transformative or 'ethopoietic' wisdom, an unending search to be aimed at through exerting one's critical eye *in primis* upon oneself and one's fixed conventions. A critical investigation which the philosophers of classical antiquity cultivated precisely through the practice of asceticism and spiritual exercises. Foucault's study focused upon an in-depth analysis of figures such as Socrates, Plato, Marcus Aurelius, Epicurus up to a final consideration of the *meditatio mortis* to be found in the writings of Seneca and Epictetus.[3]

The understanding of philosophy as a 'taking care of oneself' and as a practical, 'performative' tool is nowadays more and more emphasized: one is here reminded of the seminal work of Gerd B. Achenbach, *Philosophische Praxis* (Köln, Dinter, 1984).[4] In Italy,

2 For an assessment, see the following works by P. HADOT: *Philosophy as a Way of Life: Spiritual Exercises from Socrates to Foucault*. Edited and with an Introduction by Arnold I. Davidson. Oxford, Blackwell, 1995; *Qu'est ce-que la philosophie antique,* Paris, Gallimard, 1995; *La philosophie comme manière de vivre. Entretiens avec Jeannie Carlier et Arnold I. Davidson,* Paris, Albin Michel, 2001; *Exercices spirituels et philosophie antique,* Paris, Albin Michel, 2002.

3 M. FOUCAULT, *L'herméneutique du sujet. Cours au Collège de France 1981-1982*, Paris, Seuil-Gallimard, 2001.

4 See also, among others, R. LAHAV – M. DA VENZA TILLMANNS (eds.), *Essays on Philosophical Counseling*, Lanham, New York and London, University Press of America, 1995; P. B. RAABE, *Philosophical Counseling: Theory and Practice*, Connecticut and London, Praeger, 2001; T. CURNOW (ed.), *Thinking through Dialogue: Essays on Philosophy in Practice*, Oxted, Practical Philosophy Press, 2001; L. MARINOFF, *Philosophical Practice*, San Diego,

along the same lines, an important contribution has been recently offered by Romano Màdera and Luigi Vero Tarca, *La filosofia come stile di vita. Introduzione alle pratiche filosofiche* (Milano, Bruno Mondadori, 2003).[5] To be sure, the religious and philosophical traditions of India and of Asia in general have much to say and to offer concerning this fundamental orientation towards a practical, experiential wisdom (characterized by the primacy of oral teaching and the dialectical method versus any written form of transmission of knowledge). From ancient times, these traditions have conjugated sophisticated ideologies and worldviews *and* the practical application of the same to man, never divorcing pure intellectual theory from its necessary existential implementation.

I think that looking at the *guru* figure and master/disciple relationship in any concrete, given context requires the capacity to *simultaneously* take into consideration the issue of power *both* in its 'spiritual', transformative model and function (basically, the ideological level of wisdom) *and* in its overt-covert links with the 'institutional' realm of (again!) Foucaultian punishment and sanction/control, the very worldly socio-political and economical interests which *guru*-ship or master-ship inevitably entails and attracts. Unfortunately, these two directions of research have for too long remained separate or even opposed, almost inimical one to the other. The ideological sphere has typically been monopolized by historians of religions, philosophers and theologians, whereas the more institutional sphere has been the specific field of research of sociologists, anthropologists, and the social sciences in general. In order to make further progress and focus attention on the broader picture, I would argue that we need to create more occasions of inter-disciplinary exchange, being always ready to redefine one's positions and critical constructs. I'm happy to say that at least some of the essays in this collection

Ca., Academic Press, 2002; P. B. RAABE, *Issues in Philosophical Counseling*, Westport, Greenwood/Praeger, 2002.

5 Very useful is also the study by N. POLLASTRI, *Il pensiero e la vita. Guida alla consulenza e alle pratiche filosofiche*, Milano, Apogeo, 2004.

and especially the debate which followed the Conference presentations ventured in these avenues of research.

As VAIS, we think of this Conference as an initial exploration of a most important, rich and intricate field, too often subject to superficial analyses or naïve simplifications (one is here reminded of the use and abuse of the very term *guru*). These proceedings should promote further debate and a deeper probing into the complexity of the issues involved, with a growth in multi-disciplinary openness and sophisticated hermeneutic analysis: I hope this collection of essays may represent the first, tentative steps in the right direction.

Antonio Rigopoulos

ACKNOWLEDGMENTS

I would like to thank the many people and institutions that helped to organize this National Conference in April 2002. In the first place, the Waldensian and Methodist community of Venice and its Minister Gregorio Plescan, for allowing us to hold our three-day Conference in their nice Church. The committee of the Cultural Center Palazzo Cavagnis and its President, Franco Macchi, offered wonderful hospitality. Their sensibility and competence, both logistic and intellectual, in preparing the Conference were invaluable and the key to its success.

I also thank Prof. Maurizio Scarpari, head of the Department of East Asian Studies of the University of Venice, Ca' Foscari, for his unflinching support and cooperation.

Prof. Giuliano Boccali of the University of Milan and Prof. Gian Giuseppe Filippi of the University of Venice, both heads of the Venetian Academy of Indian Studies, were enthusiastic promoters of the Conference: without their advice and supervision it would never have seen the light of day. As always, all members and staff of VAIS offered generous assistance, our untiring General Secretary, Guido Zanderigo, setting the example.

It's both an honour and a pleasure to remember the patronage of the Indian Embassy of Rome, the Ministry of Foreign Affairs, the Regione Veneto, the Comune and Provincia of Venice, and UNESCO.

Finally, I wish to thank my mother, Sally Rigopoulos, for her precious work of proofreading the entire volume.

Antonio Rigopoulos

NOTE ON TRANSLITERATION

In view of the difficulties and even impossibility of using a single system of transliteration for all articles in the book, individual authors' decisions as to the method of transliteration have been respected. They were only asked to maintain consistency.

CONTENTS

Guru. *The Spiritual Master in Eastern and Western Traditions: Authority and Charisma*

Michele Botta
Socrates and the Maieutic Enterprise 15

Chiara Cremonesi
Apollonius of Tyana or the Spectacle of Wisdom 27

Piero Capelli
Kinds of Doctrinal Transmission in Late Ancient Judaism 45

Franco Macchi
The Master-Disciple Relationship in Christianity: Some Introductory Observations 61

Pier Cesare Bori
The Interior Master in the Understanding of the First Friends 81

Angelo Scarabel
Master and Disciple in the Islamic Sufi Tradition in the Writings of ʿAbd al-Qādir al-Jīlānī 91

Thomas Dähnhardt
Encounters with Khiḍr: Saint-Immortal, Protector from the Waters, and Guide of the Elected Ones Beyond the Confluence of the Two Oceans 105

Gian Giuseppe Filippi
The guru *and Death* 121

Giovanni Torcinovich
The Custodians of Truth 137

Cinzia Pieruccini
Authority, Devotion, and Trials: Teachers and Pupils in the Mahābhārata 157

Antonio Rigopoulos
The Guru-gītā *or "Song of the Master" as Incorporated in the* Guru-caritra *of Sarasvatī Gaṅgādhar: Observations on Its Teachings and the* guru *Institute* 169

Monia Marchetto
The Function of the guru *in Tantric Traditions* 227

Corrado Puchetti
The Twenty-four guru-*s of Dattātreya* avadhūta 235

Fabrizio Ferrari
The Jewel of the Secret Path or the Neglected guru? *Some Remarks on the* guruvāda *among the Bāuls of Bengal* 247

Claudia Ramasso
The Master Architect in the Corporations of India 285

Gianni Pellegrini
The Figure of the paṇḍita *as* guru 305

Stefano Beggiora
The Subtle Teacher. Typologies of Shamanic Initiation: Trance and Dream among the Lanjia Saoras of Orissa 327

Francesco Sferra
Teaching and Spiritual Counselling in Indian Buddhist Traditions. Some Considerations on the Role of the kalyāṇamitra 345

Claudio Cicuzza
The Spiritual Teacher in Theravāda Buddhism: Inner Motivations and Foundations of Mindfulness 373

Fabian Sanders
Tulku, *the* guru *by Birth* 409

Aldo Tollini
Dōgen zenji, a Buddhist Master in 13th Century Japan 419

Maurizio Scarpari
Zi yue, *"The Master said...", or Didn't He?* 437

Attilio Andreini
The Paradoxical Virtue (de) *of the Sage in the* Laozi 471

Massimo Makarovic
The Master in Dan *Taoism* 509

Francesco Spagna
A Wordless Teaching: Native American Spiritual Masters 519

Luca Caldironi
The guru *as Mediator of Healing* 529

Giangiorgio Pasqualotto
Figure and Role of the Master Between East and West 539

Socrates and the Maieutic Enterprise

Michele Botta

As long as consciousness maintains the distinction between master and pupil, between the truth of the first and the imperfection of the latter, no form of knowledge is possible. In the learning of truth there are neither masters nor pupils, neither experts nor beginners. Truth is learning *what is*, moment after moment, free from what was in the past and what can still exercise its influence in the present.

(J. Krishnamurti, *Questions and Answers*, 1983)

We ourselves must be our own masters and our own disciples. There is no other guide, no other saviour, no other master. We must transform ourselves by ourselves, and thus we must learn to watch ourselves and know ourselves. It's a fascinating discovery which brings pure joy.

(J. Krishnamurti, *Talks with A. S.*, 1977)

1. Masters and Disciples

We might ask ourselves whether the provocation present in these statements should be taken seriously or not, since Krishnamurti (1895-1986) taught for many years and with great public resonance:

no doubt, this preacher of freedom from all religious ideologies exercised and still exercises great influence. On the other hand, however, his teaching cannot be taken in a dogmatic sense without contradicting it; since in fact it stimulates us to free ourselves from prejudices and encourages us to change.

I don't think it is inappropriate to recall a contemporary master in order to introduce my paper on an ancient master who lived about two thousand and four hundred years ago, since both of them denied being masters and encouraged people to cultivate autonomy and self-responsibility.

2. The Character: A Silenus Who Contradicts the Hellenic Ideal and a Torpedo Fish

The task to which Socrates (469-399 BCE) faithfully dedicated himself up to his death was philosophical research, understood as an untiring examination of himself and others, and certainly not as an academic or theoretical enterprise. He disregarded all other activities and lived in poverty along with his family.

His personality, totally devoid of those conventional tracts which tradition attributes to other sages, such as Thales (c. 624-547 BCE) or Democritus (460-371 BCE), appears to have been strange (ἀτοπον) and disquieting: at least, in this way it was perceived by the ones who came in touch with him and who wrote about him. In the *Symposium* (215, 221) we are told that his physical appearance – similar to that of a Silenus – contradicted the Hellenic ideal of harmony between the wisdom of the soul and the beauty of the body (καλόσ καὶ ἀγαθός). Indeed, his ugly appearance didn't 'correspond' to his moral integrity and to the marvellous self-control which he exhibited under all circumstances, even the most dramatic.

Plato (427-347 BCE) compared him to a torpedo fish (*Meno*, 80) which benumbs whoever touches it, and with this expression he wanted to allude to the feeling of dismay and doubt which Socrates aroused in whoever approached him.

3. Socrates' Dialectics

Socrates, who remains to this day the very icon of Greek philosophy and – *tout court* – of philosophy itself, never wrote a single word. This to be sure constitutes the major paradox of Greek philosophy. The fundamental reasons for the absence of any Socrates' writings are hinted at in two of Plato's texts:

> And you offer your pupils the appearance of wisdom, not true wisdom, for they will read many things without instruction and will therefore seem to know many things, when they are for the most part ignorant and hard to get along with, since they are not wise, but only appear wise.[1]
>
> (*Phaedrus*, 275 A-B)

> There does not exist, nor will there ever exist, any treatise of mine dealing therewith. For it does not at all admit of verbal expression like other studies, but, as a result of continued application to the subject itself and communion therewith, it is brought to birth in the soul on a sudden, as light that is kindled by a leaping spark, and thereafter it nourishes itself. Notwithstanding, of thus much I am certain, that the best statement of these doctrines in writing or in speech would be my own statement; and further, that if they should be badly stated in writing, it is I who would be the person most deeply pained. And if I had thought that these subjects ought to be fully stated in writing or in speech to the public, what nobler action could I have performed in my life than that of writing what is of great benefit to mankind and bringing forth to the light for all men the nature of reality?[2]
>
> (*Epistle VII*, 341 C-D)

1 H. N. FOWLER, *Plato with an English Translation. Euthyphro, Apology, Crito, Phaedo, Phaedrus.* Introduction by W. R. M. Lamb. The Loeb Classical Library. London – Cambridge, William Heinemann – Harvard University Press, 1966, pp. 563-565.

2 R. G. BURY, *Plato with an English Translation. Timaeus, Critias, Cleitophon, Menexenus, Epistles.* The Loeb Classical Library. London – Cambridge, William Heinemann – Harvard University Press, 1966, pp. 531-533.

4. Socrates' Peculiar Wisdom

> The fact is, men of Athens, that I have acquired this reputation on account of nothing else than a sort of wisdom. What kind of wisdom is this? Just that which is perhaps human wisdom. For perhaps I really am wise in this wisdom; and these men, perhaps, of whom I was just speaking, might be wise in some wisdom greater than human, or I don't know what to say; for I do not understand it, and whoever says I do, is lying and speaking to arouse prejudice against me.[3]
>
> (*The Apology*, 20 D-E)

> For of my wisdom – if it is wisdom at all – and of its nature, I will offer you the god of Delphi as a witness. You know Chaerephon, I fancy. ... Well, once he went to Delphi and made so bold as to ask the oracle this question; and, gentlemen, don't make a disturbance at what I say; for he asked if there were anyone wiser than I. Now the Pythia replied that there was no one wiser. ... When I heard this, I thought to myself: "What in the world does the god mean, and what riddle is he propounding? For I am conscious that I am not wise either much or little. What then does he mean by declaring that I am the wisest? He certainly cannot be lying, for that is not possible for him." And for a long time I was at a loss as to what he meant; then with great reluctance I proceeded to investigate him somewhat as follows.[4]
>
> (*The Apology*, 20-21 A-B)

The enquiry is aimed at contradicting the oracle so as to say: "See, this one is wiser than me, whereas before you maintained that I was the wisest."

> So examining this man – for I need not call him by name, but it was one of the public men with regard to whom I had this kind of experience, men of Athens – and conversing with him, this man seemed to me to seem to be wise to many other people and especially to him-

[3] FOWLER, *Plato with an English Translation. Euthyphro, Apology, Crito, Phaedo, Phaedrus*, *op. cit.*, pp. 79-81.

[4] *Ibid.*, p. 81.

> self, but not to be so; and then I tried to show him that he thought he was wise, but was not. As a result, I became hateful to him and to many of those present; and so, as I went away, I thought to myself, "I am wiser than this man; for neither of us really knows anything fine and good, but this man thinks he knows something when he does not, whereas I, as I do not know anything, do not think I do either. I seem, then, in just this little thing to be wiser than this man at any rate, that what I do not know I do not think I know either." From him I went to another of those who were reputed to be wiser than he, and these same things seemed to me to be true; and there I became hateful both to him and to many others.[5]
>
> (*The Apology*, 21 C-E)

> For know that the god commands me to do this, and I believe that no greater good ever came to pass in the city than my service to the god. For I go about doing nothing else than urging you, young and old, not to care for your persons or your property more than for the perfection of your souls, or even so much; and I tell you that virtue does not come from money, but from virtue comes money and all other good things to man, both to the individual and to the state. If by saying these things I corrupt the youth, these things must be injurious; but if anyone asserts that I say other things than these, he says what is untrue. Therefore I say to you, men of Athens, either do as Anytus tells you, or not, and either acquit me, or not, knowing that I shall not change my conduct even if I am to die many times over.[6]
>
> (*The Apology*, 30 A-C)

Socrates promotes in others this recognition of their fundamental ignorance, truly the prerequisite of philosophical research (and of all research), through the means of irony. Irony is necessary in order to unveil one's ignorance and lead a person to a condition of uneasiness and restlessness, a state of spiritual darkness, so as to force him/her to commit himself/herself to research.

5 *Ibid.*, p. 83.
6 *Ibid.*, pp. 109-111.

In such a way, the person will be able to unmask the inconsistency of all beliefs – i.e. of all forms of fictitious knowledge – and recognize his/her ignorance, which everyone likes to hide through a false knowledge made up of words and concepts, being incapable of admitting one's limits.

Irony operates like the shock of the torpedo fish. It provokes doubt which kindles one's investigation. Irony is what frees one from fictitious certainties and what is commonly believed to be knowledge or science, as S. Kierkegaard (1813-1855) explained in his *Concept of Irony*: it is evidently a negative function, a limiting and destructive one, and yet – precisely for this reason – it constitutes a liberating force, inseparable from an authentic intellectual and ethical freedom.

Socrates constantly declares that he does not know. This means that he has not found anything which may truly allow one to know: not the rules set down by the law, not family traditions and customs, not religious beliefs, not ethical principles, and not even philosophical doctrines since all these – if subject to a penetrating inquiry – prove to be unfounded or contradictory and are thus not to be accepted as incontrovertible knowledge, that is, as truth.

The affirmation or recognition of not knowing entails that no assertion, no principle, no convention known to Socrates presents the character of truth, including those assertions which are proposed as the rejection or negation of all truths.

Socrates' critique was even more radical than that of the Sophists. This is so true that the society of Athens perceived it as dangerous and threatening, and for this reason sentenced him to death.

I don't know, but I know of not knowing, says Socrates, whereas all others ignore the fact that they don't know and precisely *this contrast* brings to the surface that truth which is his sole and profound interest. Knowing of not knowing doesn't simply mean having truth as one's target, but *to be in truth* i.e. to use a term which is dear to existential philosophers to abide in authenticity, even though this is, as E. Severino has observed,

> a poor truth ... but it is also a truth which predisposes itself to become rich, in the sense that it leads one to turn himself/herself in

search of that true knowledge which now we realize we do not possess.[7]

5. The Maieutic Enterprise

Socrates does not know and he knows of not knowing. He also knows that truth cannot be transmitted to us by others or communicated to us from outside, and Gorgias (c. 480-376 BCE) had already shown the inability of language to reveal and communicate that about which it speaks.

> Then Socrates sat down, and – "How fine it would be, Agathon," he said, "if wisdom were a sort of thing that could flow out of the one of us who is fuller into him who is emptier, by our mere contact with each other, as water will flow through wool from the fuller cup into the emptier.[8]
>
> (*Symposium*, 175 D)

But things are not at all like this. Instead, Socrates tells us that his peculiar art of maieutics, of 'midwifery',

> differs ... in being practised upon men, not women, and in tending their souls in labour, not their bodies. But the greatest thing about my art is this, that it can test in every way whether the mind of the young man is bringing forth a mere image, an imposture, or a real and genuine offspring. For I have this in common with the midwives: I am sterile in point of wisdom, and the reproach which has often been brought against me, that I question others but make no reply myself about anything, because I have no wisdom in me, is a true reproach;

7 E. SEVERINO, *La filosofia antica. I grandi temi del pensiero greco dai presocratici a Plotino*. Milano, Biblioteca Universale Rizzoli, 2002 (1a ed. 1984), p. 73. The translation from Italian is mine.

8 W. R. M. LAMB, *Plato in Twelve Volumes. With an English Translation.* III *Lysis, Symposium, Gorgias*. The Loeb Classical Library. London – Cambridge, William Heinemann – Harvard University Press, 1967, p. 93.

> and the reason of it is this: the god compels me to act as midwife, but has never allowed me to bring forth. I am, then, not at all a wise person myself, nor have I any wise invention, the offspring born of my own soul; but those who associate with me, although at first some of them seem very ignorant, yet, as our acquaintance advances, all of them to whom the god is gracious make wonderful progress, not only in their own opinion, but in that of others as well. And it is clear that they do this, not because they have ever learned anything from me, but because they have found in themselves many fair things and have brought them forth. But the delivery is due to the god and me. … The spiritual monitor that comes to me forbids me to associate with some of them, but allows me to converse with others, and these again make progress. Now those who associate with me are in this matter also like women in childbirth; they are in pain and are full of trouble night and day, much more than are the women; and my art can arouse this pain and cause it to cease.[9]
>
> (*Theaetetus*, 150 B-151 B)

It's precisely for this reason that Socrates constantly admonishes whoever listens to him that he has nothing to teach them. He can only help them to uncover the truth but only because they already possess it in themselves, since they themselves generate it. Thus, he can help them in their giving birth to it in the same way as his mother, as midwife, used to do with women in labour.

The art of maieutics is the way through which Socrates helps those who do not yet abide in truth. To these people, he asks for the meaning and justification of what they think they know. Typically the interlocutor answers in a way which is conditioned by his/her education and culture up to a point when, pressed by Socrates, the person is reduced to silence since he/she realizes the impossibility of offering any adequate answer to what Socrates' asks.

This particular way of posing questions is termed ἔλεγχειν in Greek (*confutatio* in Latin), that is, the ability to test oneself and the

9 H. N. FOWLER, *Plato with an English Translation. Theaetetus, Sophist.* The Loeb Classical Library. London – Cambridge, William Heinemann – Harvard University Press, 1961, pp. 35-37.

interlocutor. Truth dawns once one realizes that all the knowledge he/she believed to possess has actually no real truth to it, and that the latter springs out only when a person comes to know of not knowing.

The figure of Socrates in some way calls to mind that of the Zen master. The latter, just as Socrates, does not transmit any preconceived doctrine nor does he ask the disciple to accept it. He rather tests whoever confronts him through the dialogic experience of the *kō-an* and the *mon-dō*. This practice is not aimed at demonstrating anything whatsoever. Its function is the dismantling of all prejudices and of the logical, discursive way of thinking of the disciple. In time, this brings about a kind of bewilderment or shock (similar to that of the torpedo fish!) from which the *ken-shō*, the inner vision, may originate.

Socrates does not utilize Gorgias' thesis of the incommunicability of truth in order to reach conclusions of a sceptic or nihilistic kind, as the Sophists did. Rather, his maieutic art is directed to the uncovering of that truth which abides in a dimension different from that of language and which resides in our conscience, as the inscription "know thyself" of the Delphi temple suggests.

Kierkegaard has rightly noticed – both in his *Diary* and in his *Concept of Irony* – how in Socrates thought affirms itself as freedom from all that blocks/hinders life by defining and immobilizing the multiplicity of experience in rigid schemes. Socrates' maieutic enterprise is constantly aimed at reaffirming life's authenticity. His dialectic is a smiling yet most serious unmasking of all, recurrent forms of thought which pretend to be exhaustive. According to Kierkegaard, only Jesus would have succeeded in responding to Socrates' challenge, by proposing himself as the living answer, the incarnated truth.

6. The Socratic Demon

> Something divine (θεῖόν) and spiritual (δαιμόνιον) comes to me … I have had this from my childhood; it is a sort of voice that comes to

> me, and when it comes it always holds me back from what I am thinking of doing, but never urges me forward.[10]
>
> (*Apology*, 31D)

> My dear Hippias, you are blessed because you know the things a man ought to practise, and have, as you say, practised them satisfactorily. But I, as it seems, am possessed by some accursed fortune, so that I am always wandering and perplexed, and, exhibiting my perplexity to you wise men, am in turn reviled by you in speech whenever I exhibit it. For you say of me, what you are now saying, that I busy myself with silly little matters of no account; but when in turn I am convinced by you and say what you say, that it is by far the best thing to be able to produce a discourse well and beautifully and gain one's end in a court of law or in any other assemblage, I am called everything that is bad by some other men here and especially by that man who is continually refuting me; for he is a very near relative of mine and lives in the same house. So whenever I go home to my own house, and he hears me saying these things, he asks me if I am not ashamed that I have the face to talk about beautiful practices, when it is so plainly shown, to my confusion, that I do not even know what the beautiful itself is.[11]
>
> (*Greater Hippias*, 304 B-D)

The δαίμων motif is strictly linked and, actually, interdependent with the "know thyself" and the "knowing of not knowing" sayings, since precisely the unmasking of false knowledge, the deconditioning operated by the Master, allows one to hear the voice of the δαίμων, the voice of the god who – according to Severino – is "the voice of faith, according to which whoever doesn't possess truth

10 FOWLER, *Plato with an English Translation. Euthyphro, Apology, Crito, Phaedo, Phaedrus*, *op. cit.*, p. 115.

11 H. N. FOWLER, *Plato with an English Translation. Cratylus, Parmenides, Greater Hippias, Lesser Hippias*. The Loeb Classical Library. London – Cambridge, William Heinemann – Harvard University Press, 1963, pp. 421-423.

must regulate himself/herself",[12] but which perhaps is even more than this.

It is much more than this if the δαίμων is understood – as in Xenophon (b. 480 BCE) – as a veritable divine inspiration, the voice through which the deity commands what is to be done and what is not to be done, to the point of confusing itself with divination (*Memorabilia* I, 1, 2-3). Indeed, the expression "something divine (θεῖόν) and spiritual (δαιμόνιον) comes to me" appears to suggest this ulterior meaning.

7. Socrates' Vision

We have noticed how the maieutics and irony of Socrates have the function of de-conditioning his interlocutors so as to purify their inner life (the mind-heart complex, as one would say utilizing a Buddhist parlance). This is done in order to predispose them to a more profound vision and to an understanding which transcends the domain of language.

As one gathers from reading the *Symposium*, such a supreme understanding seems to have been allowed to Socrates, who experienced the transcending of the phenomenal world:

> It is a habit he has. Occasionally he turns aside, anywhere at random, and there he stands. He will be here presently, I expect. So do not disturb him; let him be.[13]
>
> (*Symposium*, 175 B)

> Immersed in some problem at dawn, he stood in the same spot considering it; and when he found it a tough one, he would not give it up but stood there trying. The time drew on to midday, and the men began to notice him, and said to one another in wonder: "Socrates has

12 SEVERINO, *La filosofia antica*, *op. cit.*, p. 79. The translation from Italian is mine.

13 LAMB, *Plato in Twelve Volumes*, *op. cit.*, p. 91.

> been standing there in a study ever since dawn!" The end of it was that in the evening some of the Ionians after they had supped – this time it was summer – brought out their mattresses and rugs and took their sleep in the cool; thus they waited to see if he would go on standing all night too. He stood till dawn came and the sun rose; then walked away, after offering a prayer to the Sun.
>
> (*Symposium*, 220 C-D)

And I wish to conclude in this spirit, by quoting the following passage of S. Natoli:

> There comes a time when, in a disposed mind, the divine rushes in. At that point, one keeps silent and irony has no more place, since it subsides when confronted with the vision. And the absorbed Socrates, what does he see? To quote Heraclitus, he sees the God, the Lord of Delphi "who does not reveal (οὔτε λέγει) and does not hide (οὔτε κρύπτει), but offers a sign (αλλά σεμάνει)" (DK, fr. 93). The god hints at: he ensnares, he calls for decipherment. It's the same as saying: Socrates beholds, dismayed, the world's enigma.[14]

14 S. NATOLI, *Stare al mondo*, Milano, Feltrinelli, 2002, p. 183. The translation from Italian is mine.

APOLLONIUS OF TYANA OR THE SPECTACLE OF WISDOM

CHIARA CREMONESI

> Where has the Sage disappeared to, where is he hiding? / After so many miracles (the renown of his preaching / spread throughout many, many people), suddenly, he has concealed himself. What has happened to him / no-one knows for sure, / and no-one has ever seen his tomb. / ... Perhaps the time is not yet come / for him to appear again in the world, / or perhaps, unknown, he wanders among us / in a strange metamorphosis. – He will appear one day / as he was, in the act of teaching the truth: then / he will certainly restore the worship of our gods, / our exquisite Hellenic rites.

Thus runs the melancholic evocation of the poet Cavafy, a Greek from Alexandria, who saw in Apollonius the signs of a time past but not lost and wondered in the coded language of dreams whether the "Sage" would ever return. Cavafy alludes to his "disappearance", a death not followed by a burial, echoing Philostratus's final words in the *Vita Apollonii* (*VA*) or *Life of Apollonius*:

> With any tomb, however, or cenotaph of the sage I never met, that I know of, although I have traversed most of the earth, and have listened everywhere to stories of his divine quality. And his shrine at Tyana is singled out and honoured with royal officers: never have

> the Emperors denied to him the honours of which they themselves were held worthy of.[1]

His disappearance is nothing more than the *coup de théâtre* of a sage whose life was one continuous performance. Born a few decades later, Philostratus,[2] an intellectual associated with the circle of the Severus clan, recorded the story of his life under the instructions of the Empress Julia Domna: in this way, he rescued his memory from the oblivion of time. He turned this man born in Tyana, Cilicia, on the very edge of the Greek world, into a champion of "Greek-ness".

Apollonius lived in the 1st century A.D. and was a sage, or perhaps a miracle-worker, a magician, a Pythagorean philosopher, or maybe a charlatan. There have been numberless interpretations of this figure, often accompanied by ethical judgments or ideological glosses, with typically apologetic or disparaging – rarely neutral – agendas. Perhaps this was an inevitable fate for one who was in the position, probably in spite of himself, of competing with Christ and acting as the instrument of a nostalgic revival of paganism. To be sure, paganism was becoming extinct in the corridors of power: not surprisingly, Apollonius was therefore also turned into the symbol of the defeat of paganism for those celebrating the spread of Christ's message in the *oikoumene*.

Ancient historiography has handed down to us myriad different readings of Apollonius and modern interpretations have added their

1 Philostr., *VA* VIII 31, 41-46: τάφῳ μὲν οὖν ἢ ψευδοταφίῳ τοῦ ἀνδρὸς οὐδαμοῦ προστυχὼν οἶδα, καίτοι τῆς γῆς, ὁπόση ἐστίν, ἐπελθὼν πλείστην, λόγοις δὲ πανταχοῦ δαιμονίοις, καὶ ἱερὰ Τύανάδε βασιλείοις ἐκπεποιημένα τέλεσιν οὐδὲ γὰρ βασιλεῖς ἀπηξίουν αὐτὸν ὧν αὐτοὶ ἠξιοῦντο.

2 The *Life of Apollonius of Tyana* is attributed to the second of four authors named Philostratus, all of whom belonged to a single family from Lemnos and lived between the 2nd and 3rd century A.D. To this second Philostratus (ca. 165-170 to ca. 244-249) are attributed the *Lives of the Sophists*, the *Imagines*, the *Gymnasticus*, the two dialogues *Eroicus* and *Nero,* and a collection of seventy-three erotic "Love Letters"; see F. SOLMSEN, s.v. *Philostratos* 9-12, in A. PAULY – G. WISSOWA, *Realencyclopädie der classischen Altertumwissenschaft*, XX, 1, 1941, coll. 125-177.

own. In an effort to reach a kernel of truth, modern scholars have provided portraits of the 'real' Apollonius which, in fact, have probably little to do with the man from Tyana. Perhaps, he too has been a victim of the peculiarly Western tendency of superimposing its own models when relating across time to the 'other' in antiquity.[3] When it has not destroyed, most of the time it has 'comprehended'[4] and incorporated the other, legitimating it in virtue of its assimilation through a *reductio ad unum* which has turned Apollonius himself into a subject worthy of study, to the extent that "the spirit of his asceticism and teaching" has come to suggest "a certain consonance with the interpretation of human existence and with the conception of the divine expressed at the same time but with a different outcome by the Gospels."[5]

The underlying leitmotiv of these interpretations is the 'crisis' of late antiquity, which has become a kind of myth within a historiography constantly in search of areas of "high emotional temperature", without considering, as Peter Brown pointed out, that if the invisible world was reputed to be as real as the visible one, there was certainly no need for a stronger emotional effort in order to relate oneself to a deity.[6]

It thus seems unfair to purge Philostratus' biography of the waste of the "marvellous"[7] – considering it the mere literary accident of a decadent rhetorician – in order to arrive at the *realia*, reassuring

3 See E. DE MARTINO, *La fine del mondo. Contributo all'analisi delle apocalissi culturali*. A cura di C. Gallini. Torino 2002, p. 395 ff.

4 See T. TODOROV, *La conquête de l'Amérique. La question de l'autre*, Paris 1982.

5 D. DEL CORNO (ed.), *Filostrato. Vita di Apollonio di Tiana*, Milano 2002, p. 46. The English translation from the Italian is mine.

6 P. BROWN, *Genesi della tarda antichità*. Traduzione italiana di P. Guglielmotti. Torino 2001, pp. 14-15: "A study of the religious evolution of late antiquity principally based on the search of areas of high emotional temperature, is conceived in an erroneous way" (my translation).

7 The expression is taken from A. VAUCHEZ, *Santi, profeti e visionari. Il soprannaturale nel medioevo*. Traduzione italiana di R. Ferrara. Bologna 2000, p. 10.

though they may be, by means of an ideological operation which divests Apollonius of his historical identity. The deconstruction and reconstruction of Philostratus' *Life* leads to the risk of writing a new hagiography following a sort of 'positivist faith', in which the 'real' Apollonius is assessed in terms of how plausible he appears in the light of our own ideological and symbolic framework.

I therefore believe we should consider not so much 'things' but rather representations, in the sense of Wittgenstein's *Übersicht Darstellung*[8] or "clear sight". It is especially useful to explore the representation of Apollonius provided by Philostratus, in which in my view the author's depiction of Apollonius actually represents Philostratus himself. It is precisely through an ongoing representation, i.e. the spectacle of his *persona*, that Philostratus' Apollonius acts as *a guide*, for the crowds who follow him and perhaps later for his disciples as well. Fundamentally, he relies on a visual code as his means of guaranteeing the transmission of knowledge – the final outcome of his assumed inner quest – rather than on any oral communication.

This is the distinctive code of Philostratus' narrative. In his effort to present Apollonius' 'Pythagoreanism', he has been accused of operating a superficial and empty rhetorical exercise.[9] I rather think that Philostratus is moving on a plane which is simply different from that of theoretical and theological reflection. It is the *bios*, the Pythagorean way of life, which is here represented, and not the doctrinal system, which is rather its corollary: Apollonius is said to have built a consensus around himself by assuming a lifestyle that guaranteed him the gods' approval, and therefore the possibility of becoming a mediator between them and mankind, and, as such, to make miracles and foretell the future.

8 See L. WITTGENSTEIN, *Tractatus logico-philosophicus*, London 1961. See also his *Notebooks 1914-1916*, Oxford 1961.

9 See M. DZIELSKA, *Apollonius of Tyana in Legend and History*, Rome 1986, p. 191: "However, one thing is clear: Philostratus' Pythagoreanism as presented in *VA* is very superficial and does not square with the Pythagorean speculations of his time."

This is especially evident in a passage of Philostratus' *Life*, in which Apollonius' first public appearance is described. After following the teachings of Euxenus of Heraclea in Pontus, who did not practise "in his conduct the philosophy he taught; for he was the slave of his belly and appetites, and modelled himself upon Epicurus"[10], Apollonius abandons his master and 'goes beyond' him. While Euxenus "knew the principles of Pythagoras just as birds know what they learn from men"[11], and merely communicated them orally, Apollonius is said to turn himself into a Pythagorean, refusing the spoken word and opting for an altogether different way of communicating.

He takes leave from his master[12] and decides to move to the temple of Asclepius at Aegae. Here he begins his process of purification, which has little to do with spiritual purification. He refrains from eating any living beings (ἔμψυχα), which were regarded as impure and causing dullness; instead, he eats dried fruit and vegetables, because they are products of the earth; he gives up wine, because it affects the mind's balance; he discards footwear and wears linen clothes, rejecting any items made from animal skins, and lets his hair grow unchecked.

This behaviour takes the guardians of the temple of Asclepius by surprise and wins them over, thus achieving the legitimating of a place of worship. In this way, he is said to gain the god's favour, who informs his minister he is pleased to heal the sick with Apollonius as his witness. This divine promise brings huge popularity to Apollonius: "Such was his reputation", says Philostratus, "that the

10 Philostr., *VA* I, 7, 27-29
... οὐδὲ ἐνεργῷ τῇ φιλοσοφίᾳ χρώμενος, γαστρός τε γὰρ ἥττων ἦν καὶ ἀφροδισίων καὶ κατὰ τὸν Ἐπίκουρον ἐσχημάτιστο.

11 *Ibidem* I, 7, 30-32
... τὰς δὲ Πυθαγόρου δόξας ἐγίγνωσκεν, ὥσπερ οἱ ὄρνιθες ἃ μανθάνουσι παρὰ τῶν ἀνθρώπων ...

12 *Ibidem* I, 7, 48.

Cilicians themselves and the people all around flocked to Aegae to visit him."[13]

Apollonius founded, or rather restored, a Pythagorean orthopraxis, even before revealing any truths, and in this way he became a guide and a master. It is no accident that the first mention of an act of healing is linked to a dietary injunction: by offering the example of an appropriate lifestyle to a dissolute young man and providing rules of proper behaviour, he performed a nomothetic function in a context in which disease is never to be reduced to a purely natural event.

Thus, in the treatise in which he responds to the celebration of Apollonius of Tyana contained in Philostratus' *Life* and in the *Philalethes* by Sossian Hierocles, Eusebius emphasizes the Neo-Pythagorean's iatric function, while belittling him when compared to Christ and also denying his superhuman nature. Recognizing Apollonius' skill in everyday matters, the Bishop of Caesarea mentions his healing activities, admitting his ability to cure a young man suffering from dropsy by prescribing a suitable diet. Above all, Eusebius praises him for refusing to look after a wealthy man, well known for his wickedness (κακία)[14], even expelling him from the temple. This man had committed incest – Eusebius does not mention this, but the accusation is made in Philostratus' biography, the real target of *Against Hierocles* – and, in rejecting him, Apollonius is shown to uphold social and family values.[15]

13 *Ibidem* I, 8, 19-20
... ξυνῄεσαν ἐς τὰς Αἰγὰς ἐφ' ἱστορίᾳ Κίλικές τε αὐτοὶ καὶ οἱ πέριξ ...

14 *Hierocl.* 381, 14-24
ἔστω δ' ἐπὶ τούτοις ἐντρεχὴς καὶ τὰ κοινά, ὡς τὸν εἰς Ἀσκληπιοῦ θεραπείας χάριν ἀφιγμένον διὰ γνώμης ἀρίστης ἀπαλλάξαι τῆς ἀρρωστίας, νοσοῦντι γὰρ δὴ ὑδέρου πάθει κατάλληλον ἐγκρατείας ὑποθέσθαι δίαιταν τῷ κάμνοντι καὶ ταύτῃ αὐτὸν ὑγιᾶ καταστῆσαι καὶ τούτῳ γε τῆς φρονήσεως ἀποδεκτὸν τὸ μειράκιον, καὶ ὡς τὸν πολυτελῶς θύειν παρεσκευασμένον εἶρξεν οἷα εἰκὸς ἐπὶ κακίᾳ διαβεβοημένον, καὶ γὰρ δὴ τῶν ἐγχωρίων ἁπάντων πλουσιώτατόν τε καὶ περιφανέστατον αὐτὸν ὑποτίθεται.

15 Besides, this position taken by Eusebius follows the general tendency of Christian authors to restore the 'ethical' portrait of Apollonius: in this regard, see

On the other hand, Apollonius sees himself as a legislator and, like Pythagoras, he is not indifferent to men's lives. His asceticism does not lead him to withdraw from the world, but, on the contrary, makes him a leading figure in social and political life: as he repeatedly states, a sage should behave "as a legislator"; his job is therefore to give his convictions "the form of orders for the masses".[16]

By carrying out a constant purification of himself, he overturns the "Homeric lifestyle".[17] By eliminating the constraints of ritual purification, linked to sacred time and space, he turns his own *persona* into a sacred space. A legislator and religious reformer,[18] he also becomes a soothsayer when, in the footsteps of Asclepius and Apollo, he directs human behaviour and re-establishes the natural 'order of things' by curing illnesses.

DEL CORNO, *Filostrato. Vita di Apollonio di Tiana*, *op. cit.*, p. 39: "This tendency to emphasize the ethical aspect of Apollonius' experience is especially evident in all those who, though being part of the now triumphant church, are still sensitive to the charm of the classic past" (my translation). Here, reference is made to Apollinaris Sidonius (*Letters* VIII, 3, 4), Jerome (*Letters* 53, 1, 4), and Augustine (*Letters* 138, 4, 18).

16 See Philostr., *VA* I, 17, 12-19
ἐρομένου δὲ αὐτὸν τῶν στενολεσχούντων τινός, ὅτου ἕνεκα οὐ ζητοίη, ὅτι" ἔφη μειράκιον ὢν ἐζήτησα, νῦν δὲ οὐ χρὴ ζητεῖν, ἀλλὰ διδάσκειν ἃ εὕρηκα." πῶς οὖν, 'Απολλώνιε, διαλέξεται ὁ σοφός;" πάλιν ἐπερομένου αὐτὸν ὡς νομοθέτης," ἔφη δεῖ γὰρ τὸν νομοθέτην, ἃ πέπεικεν ἑαυτόν, ταῦτα ἐπιτάγματα ἐς τοὺς πολλοὺς ποιεῖσθαι.
"And when a certain quibbler man asked him why he asked no questions, he replied: 'Because I asked questions when I was a stripling; and it is not my business to ask questions now, but to teach people what I have discovered.' 'How then,' the other asked him afresh, 'O Apollonius, should the sage converse?' 'Like a law-giver,' he replied, 'for it is the duty of the law-giver to deliver to the many instructions, of the truth of which he has persuaded himself.'"

17 Plat., *Rp*. 600a.

18 Within the corpus of works attributed to Apollonius, there is also a treatise on *teletai* and sacrifices (Τελεταὶ ἢ περὶ θυσιῶν) and one on divination through the study of stars (Περὶ μαντείας ἀστέρων); cf. Philostr. *VA* III, 41; IV, 19; Eus. *PE* IV, 13, 1; *DE* III, 3, 11.

Absorbing all different functions within his own person, and moulding it as *the* veritable sacred space, he no longer needs to refer to external sacred places in order to heal and foretell the future, or in order to manifest himself.

His wisdom is not so much transmitted individually as it is enacted. It is a wisdom which is not communicated through the *logos* but through a ritual re-proposition, since it is a kind of wisdom which is founded on myth. Conforming to De Martino's definition of myth, he seems to turn himself into a meta-historical paradigm, able to direct the course of ritual practice: he appears as a cultural hero civilizing the world by retracing the footsteps of Pythagoras and Heracles, meeting the wise men of India and Ethiopia, and re-establishing ancient rites and sacrifices (not beliefs, as it is still sometimes wrongly argued). He restores value systems, not faiths, subsuming myth within his own person and enacting it ritually through the theatrical staging of himself as a sage.

Apollonius does not seek 'truth' since it is already within him; he does not communicate it since he rather represents it, placing himself as it were on stage. He thus chooses a lifestyle, the Pythagorean *bios*. The transmission of wisdom belongs more properly to his encounter with the crowds, rather than to his relationship with his disciples, and it involves semantic codes that include the "marvellous".

The definition of philosophy which Philostratus has him put forward is particularly important in this sense, and it also backs up the definition of his *persona* as a meta-historical paradigm:

> And yet the gratification of a well-staged tragedy is insignificant, for its pleasures last a day, as brief as the season of the Dionysiac festival is; but the gratification of a philosophic system devised to meet the requirements of Pythagoras, and also breathing the inspiration in which Pythagoras was anticipated by the Indians, lasts not for a brief time, but for an endless and incalculable period. It is then not unreasonable on my part, I think, to have devoted myself to a philosophy so highly elaborated, and to one which - to use a metaphor derived

> from the stage - the Indians mount, as it deserves to be mounted, upon a lofty and divine mechanism, and then wheel it forth on stage.[19]

Referring to the Brahmins of India, who, like Pythagoras, appear to establish models rather than imitable examples, Apollonius, defined by Porphyry as "a man adorned by all forms of wisdom",[20] represents philosophy as a permanent enactment which is not limited to the space and time of 'holidays' but becomes part of the sage's *persona*. This *persona* takes the place of the Athenian stage; it becomes a stage and theatrical mechanism itself, and the sage's words re-establish a new ritual performance.

What is redefined are the frontiers of space: whereas the Athenian theatre was a ritual performance within the cult of Dyonisus (the reference to the Dyonisiacs is explicit), Philostratus' Apollonius finds himself having to act as the dramatist - in this case, Aeschylus - the magistrate who must decide which tragedy is to be performed, the actor (or, rather, the mask), and the hero himself, whose vicissitudes are described in the ancient tragedies.

There seems to be here no sign of the affirmation of the primacy of inner religiosity over and above the mythical and ritual components of traditional religions,[21] or of the cancellation of mythical and

19 Philostr., *VA* VI, 11, 132-137
καίτοι τραγῳδίας μὲν εὖ κεκοσμημένης ὀλίγη χάρις, εὐφραίνει γὰρ ἐν σμικρῷ τῆς ἡμέρας, ὥσπερ ἡ τῶν Διονυσίων ὥρα, φιλοσοφίας δὲ ξυγκειμένης μέν, ὡς Πυθαγόρας ἐδικαίωσεν, ὑποθειαζούσης δέ, ὡς πρὸ Πυθαγόρου Ἰνδοί, οὐκ ἐς βραχὺν χρόνον ἡ χάρις, ἀλλ᾽ ἐς ἄπειρόν τε καὶ ἀριθμοῦ πλείω. οὐ δὴ ἀπεικός τι παθεῖν μοι δοκῶ φιλοσοφίας ἡττηθεὶς εὖ κεκοσμημένης, ἣν ἐς τὸ πρόσφορον Ἰνδοὶ στείλαντες ἐφ᾽ ὑψηλῆς τε καὶ θείας μηχανῆς ἐκκυκλοῦσιν.

20 Porph., *Chr.* fr. 60 Harnack: ... Ἀπολλώνιον τὸν Τυανέα ... ἄνδρα φιλοσοφίᾳ πάσῃ κεκοσμημένον.

21 See G. SFAMENI GASPARRO, *Le religioni del mondo ellenistico*, in G. FILORAMO (ed.), *Storia delle religioni* I. *Le religioni antiche*, Bari 1994, p. 443: "Philostratus, however, considers essential for the definition of Apollonius' *ethos* his work as a reformist of beliefs and cult practices, in order to af-

ritual features. On the contrary, mythical and ritual links are in fact re-established, and the limitations – πείρατα – of the spatial and temporal context of the rite are redefined. These links are no longer those of the religious holidays, but those of the philosopher's *persona*, a spatial and temporal entity, which through its dialectical relationship between the inner and the outer – between the space of Greek-ness and that of the 'Greek-ized' other, Indian and Ethiopian – bursts onto the historical scene as "an outsider from within".[22] His philosophy is first and foremost enacted: Apollonius' own use of technical stage vocabulary confirms it.

This provides the basis for Apollonius' asceticism, inasmuch as it represents the code through which he achieves and communicates his condition of purity, determining the necessary consensus in order to legitimate his function as saviour. The wisdom of the Indians – and therefore wisdom *tout court* – "uses the same ornaments as the Pythia",[23] he avers.

Philosophy utilizes ornaments precisely because it is a spectacle, a visible performance to be seen. It is 'staged' and displayed, finding substance and meaning from its very staging. As such, it does not put itself forward only as *bios* for the individual, but as the fountainhead of meaning for those who see the philosopher, for those who are present at his performances. In this sense, this 'outer' rather than 'inner' philosophy is religious; it exists inasmuch as it is seen, and its meaning and significance is ensured by the audience present at the performance.

Indeed, speaking to his disciple Damis, Apollonius says:

firm the primacy of inner religiosity over the mythic-ritual components of traditional religions" (my translation).

22 This expression is used by F. Hartog. See F. HARTOG, *Memoria di Ulisse. Racconti sulla frontiera nell'antica Grecia*. Traduzione italiana di A. Perazzoli Tadini. Torino 2002, pp. 271-286.

23 Here the reference is to the expression used by Apollonius to identify the wisdom of the Indians: of them, he says that "they are divine and use the same ornaments as the Pythia" (Philostr., *VA* VI, 11, 218-219: οἱ μὲν γὰρ θεῖοί τέ εἰσι καὶ κεκόσμηνται κατὰ τὴν Πυθίαν).

> But you perhaps imagine that it is a lesser thing to go wrong in Babylon than to go wrong in Athens or at the Olympian or Pythian games; and you don't reflect on the fact that a wise man finds Hellas everywhere, and that a sage will not regard or consider any place to be a desert or barbarous, because he, at any rate, lives under the eyes of virtue, and although he only sees a few men, yet he is himself looked at by ten thousand eyes.[24]

The stress laid by Philostratus on the visual code, on recalling Apollonius' "spectacle" on the one hand and his beauty on the other, is significant. The constant and repeated references to his way of dressing and to his appearance are thus anything but superficial.

Philostratus mentions that when Apollonius came to cities which were oppressed by internal divisions, often caused by unseemly exhibitions,[25]

> he would advance and show himself, and by indicating something of his intended rebuke through a hand gesture or by a look on his face, he would put an end to all the disorder, and people hushed their voices, as if they were engaged in the mysteries.[26]

Those who had been arguing about dancers or horses blushed and took hold of themselves "at the sight of a man worthy of the name", easily regaining their reason. Philostratus underlines the power of

[24] Philostr., *VA* I, 34, 31-37
σὺ δ' ἴσως ἡγῇ τὸ ἐν Βαβυλῶνι ἁμαρτεῖν ἧττον εἶναι τοῦ Ἀθήνησιν ἢ Ὀλυμπίασιν ἢ Πυθοῖ, καὶ οὐκ ἐνθυμῇ ὅτι σοφῷ ἀνδρὶ Ἑλλὰς πάντα, καὶ οὐδὲν ἔρημον ἢ βάρβαρον χωρίον οὔτε ἡγήσεται ὁ σοφὸς οὔτε νομιεῖ, ζῶν γε ὑπὸ τοῖς τῆς ἀρετῆς ὀφθαλμοῖς, καὶ βλέπει μὲν ὀλίγους τῶν ἀνθρώπων, μυρίοις δ'ὄμμασιν αὐτὸς ὁρᾶται.

[25] *Ibidem* I 15, 5-6
πολλαὶ δὲ ἐστασίαζον ὑπὲρ θεαμάτων οὐ σπουδαίων ...

[26] *Ibidem* I 15, 6-9
παρελθὼν ἂν καὶ δείξας ἑαυτὸν καί τι καὶ μελλούσης ἐπιπλήξεως τῇ χειρὶ καὶ τῷ προσώπῳ ἐνδειξάμενος ἐξῄρητ' ἂν ἀταξία πᾶσα καὶ ὥσπερ ἐν μυστηρίοις ἐσιώπων.

Apollonius' silence, successful in restoring order and calm in a city suffering from famine much more than any persuasive speech.[27]

So, when he became an advocate of the poor of the city of Aspendos, in Pamphylia – who had risen in fury and were on the point of assaulting the governor and "burning him alive" (since in times of famine the rich would hoard their grain and sell it elsewhere) – he, turning himself towards the bystanders, beckoned them that they should listen: and they put down the brands they had kindled on the altars which were there.[28]

Obliging them "with gestures" to refrain from attacking the estates of the rich, Apollonius forestalled *stasis*. These episodes occurred in the five-year period when Apollonius chose to keep silent, and although this was meant to be an exercise in asceticism, it seems to have been mainly a channel for the expression of divine power.[29] Silence was also imposed on his disciples, and this seems to have been more like the acceptance of an all-embracing order rather than an occasion for the transmission of esoteric truths. Through silence Apollonius reinforced his superior role as 'legislator' and arbiter between contending parties, being the mediator between the wielders of power and the crowds, between gods and men.

His self-enactment alone, his 'epiphany', enables him to resolve conflicts and restore order, the same order he is able to re-establish through his healing powers after illness has disrupted it.

In this sense, philosophy is a stage performance since it provides a system of values through the *mise-en-scène* it makes of itself. Although Apollonius criticizes the 'stories' staged in theatre i.e. the

27 *Ibidem* I 15, 16-17
ἀλλ' Ἀπολλωνίῳ καὶ ἡ σιωπὴ πρὸς τοὺς οὕτω διακειμένους ἤρκει.

28 *Ibidem* I 15, 32-36
μετεστράφη τε εἰς τοὺς περιεστηκότας ὁ Ἀπολλώνιος καὶ ἔνευσεν ὡς χρὴ ἀκοῦσαι, οἱ δὲ οὐ μόνον ἐσιώπησαν ὑπ' ἐκπλήξεως τῆς πρὸς αὐτόν, ἀλλὰ καὶ τὸ πῦρ ἔθεντο ἐπὶ τῶν βωμῶν τῶν αὐτόθι.

29 See P. SCARPI, "The Eloquence of Silence. Aspects of a Power without Words", in M. G. CIANI (ed.), *The Regions of Silence. Studies on the Difficulty of Communication*, Amsterdam 1987, pp. 19-40.

mythical tales told by poets following the well-established codes of classical tradition, he recognizes the function that theatre exercises. He is appalled by the orgiastic events which take the place of tragedies, and represents himself into a myth and a ritual at one and the same time.

It is perhaps no accident that Philostratus refers to the most astonishing example of Apollonius' healing, the victory over the plague in Ephesus of the man from Tyana, the new Heracles, saying that he gathered all the citizens together in the theatre, where the statue of the tutelary god stood. It was highly appropriate that he should choose a theatre to wage his war against the demon of disease, 'staging' himself once again and ritually performing the myth. Philostratus goes on to say that he saw the plague in "the form of a poor old man"[30] and having seen it, he defeated it.

Apollonius' wisdom is 'enacted' not mainly through the language of words, but in the first place through that of outward appearance. This acquires such an importance that it becomes his identifying code, both for the crowds seeking him and for the Imperial power set against him. The immutability of his appearance becomes a visible 'proof' of his condition of purity and of his power. The philosopher's impassibility, his unchanging appearance, is a reflection of the hieratic solemnity expressed in physical stillness, rather than in a 'stoic' impassibility. To achieve an invariable self, revealing himself through the absence of changes, is the absolute imperative of Apollonius, whose interest appears to be other than a scrutiny *in interiore homine*:

> For when he came down from Ethiopia he made a long stay on the sea-board of Egypt, and then he returned to Phoenicia and Cilicia, and to Ionia and Achaia, and Italy, never failing anywhere to show himself the same as ever. For, hard as it is to know oneself, I myself consider it still harder for the sage to remain always himself; for he

30 Philostr. *VA* VIII, 7, 413-414
τὸ γὰρ τοῦ λοιμοῦ εἶδος, πτωχῷ δὲ γέροντι εἴκαστο ...

> cannot ever reform evil natures and improve them, unless he has first trained himself never to alter in his own person.[31]

On the basis of these considerations, the stress which Philostratus places on the image Apollonius projects of himself does not seem so superficial, particularly since it is precisely on the issue of his 'visibility' that he battles against the powers that be, as we learn from the text. Tyrannies, we are reminded, are especially suspicious of all figures in the public eye,[32] whereas they are less severe with those who prefer to lead obscure lives.

So it is by no mere chance that, when Apollonius was attacked during Domitian's tyranny, the charge of having sacrificed a boy in order to foretell the future was given equal weight to others regarding his attire and lifestyle, and the cult which had formed around him.[33]

These were the "many and varied" charges of which Apollonius was informed by Aelian, the prefect of the *praetorium*:

> The counts of the indictment… are as varied as they are numerous; for your style of dress is assailed in them and your way of living in general, and your having been worshipped by certain people, and the fact that in Ephesus you once delivered an oracle about the famine; and also that you have uttered certain sentiments to the detriment of

31 *Ibidem* VI, 35, 1-13
... περί τε γὰρ τὴν ἐπὶ θαλάττῃ Αἴγυπτον καταβάντι αὐτῷ ἐξ Αἰθιοπίας διατριβὴ πλείων ἐγένετο, περί τε Φοίνικας καὶ Κίλικας Ἴωνάς τε καὶ Ἀχαιοὺς καὶ Ἰταλοὺς πάλιν οὐδαμοῦ ἐλλείποντι τὸ μὴ οὐχ ὁμοίῳ φαίνεσθαι. χαλεποῦ γὰρ τοῦ γνῶναι ἑαυτὸν δοκοῦντος χαλεπώτερον ἔγωγε ἡγοῦμαι τὸ μεῖναι τὸν σοφὸν ἑαυτῷ ὅμοιον, οὐδὲ γὰρ τοὺς πονηρῶς φύντας ἐς τὸ λῷον μεταστήσει μὴ πρότερον ἐξασκήσας τὸ μὴ αὐτὸς μεθίστασθαι.

32 *Ibidem* VII, 12, 62-64
αἱ γὰρ τυραννίδες ἧττον χαλεπαὶ τοῖς φανεροῖς τῶν ἀνδρῶν, ἣν ἐπαινοῦντας αἴσθωνται τὸ μὴ ἐν φανερῷ ζῆν.

33 *Ibidem* VII, 11, 36-38
... ἣν τὰ νεαρὰ τῶν σπλάγχνων φαίνει, πρόσκειται δὲ τῇ γραφῇ καὶ περὶ ἀμπεχόνης καὶ διαίτης καὶ τὸ ἔστιν ὑφ᾽ ὧν προσκυνεῖσθαί σε.

> the sovereign, some of them openly, some of them obscurely and privately, and some of them on the pretence that you learned them from heaven ... that you ... cut up an Arcadian boy ... For if the accuser attacks your dress and your mode of life and your gift of foreknowledge, it is only by way, I assure you, of leading up to this charge; these peculiarities prompted you to commit the crime of conspiring against the Emperor, so he says, and emboldened you to offer such a sacrifice.[34]

Apollonius' clothing and appearance were so distinctive that they came to head the charges pronounced by the Emperor himself. Choosing from among the counts which "he regarded as the most serious and hardest to refute", Domitian asked the sage questions such as the following:

> What induces you..., Apollonius, to dress yourself differently from everybody else, and to wear this peculiar and singular garb?[35]

His clothing and lifestyle in general were the most important accusations, because they carried a powerful symbolic charge, acting as a power that dared set itself up as an alternative to that of the tyrannical Emperor.

34 *Ibidem* VII, 20
αἱ μὲν ἰδέαι τῆς γραφῆς ποικίλαι τε" ἔφη καὶ πλείους, καὶ γὰρ τὴν ἐσθῆτα διαβάλλουσι καὶ τὴν ἄλλην δίαιταν καὶ τό ἐστιν ὑφ' ὧν προσκυνεῖσθαί σε καὶ τὸ ἐν 'Εφέσῳ ποτὲ ὑπὲρ λοιμοῦ χρῆσαι, διειλέχθαι δὲ καὶ κατὰ τοῦ βασιλέως τὰ μὲν ἀφανῶς, τὰ δ' ἐκφάνδην, τὰ δ' ὡς θεῶν ἀκούσαντα ... τεμεῖν παῖδα 'Αρκάδα ... ὁ γὰρ λαμβανόμενος τοῦ σχήματος καὶ τῆς διαίτης καὶ τοῦ προγιγνώσκειν ἐς τοῦτο δήπου ξυντείνει καὶ ταῦτά γε καὶ τὴν παρανομίαν τὴν ἐς αὐτὸν δοῦναί σοί φησι καὶ τὸ ἐς τὴν θυσίαν θάρσος.

35 *Ibidem* VIII, 5, 6-8
τί γὰρ μαθών," ἔφη Απολλώνιε, οὐ τὴν αὐτὴν ἔχεις ἅπασι στολήν, ἀλλ' ἰδίαν τε καὶ ἐξαίρετον;

Apollonius, in contrast to the performances of a Nero[36] – whose songs were more dangerous for the Greeks than Xerxes' fires[37] and who cast aside the robes of Augustus and Julius putting on the clothing of Amebeus and Terpnus – displays his own face and the attire of the sage. As noted, his *persona* takes the place of the show on the Athenian theatre: here, he identifies himself both with the stage as well as with the theatre's mechanism.[38]

The contest between Apollonius and tyranny is acted out as a show, a game which our sage knows very well, as when Philostratus recalls the reactions of the audience of Ipola before the performance of a tragic actor:

> But when he appeared in Ipola, they showed fear of him before he even opened his lips upon the stage, and they shrank in dismay for his appearance when they saw him striding across the stage, with his mouth all agape, mounted on extra-high buskins, and clad in the most wonderful garments; but when he lifted up his voice and bellowed out loud, most of them took to their heels, as if they had a demon yelling at them. Such and so old-fashioned are the manners of the barbarians of that country.[39]

36 Speaking with young Menippus, Apollonius examines the performances of Nero (Philostr. *VA* VIII, 7, 25-27): αὐτοφυὲς καὶ γυμνὰ πάντα, τὸν δὲ νικᾶν, ἃ χρὴ ἐγκαλύπτεσθαι, καὶ τὴν Αὐγούστου τε καὶ Ἰουλίου σκευὴν ῥίψαντα μεταμφιέννυσθαι νῦν τὴν Ἀμοιβέως καὶ Τερπνοῦ τί φήσεις;

37 Philostr. *VA* VIII, 7, 47-48
τοῖς δὲ Ἕλλησι τίνα ἡγῇ, ὦ Μένιππε; πότερα Ξέρξην καταπιμπράντα ἢ Νέρωνα ᾄδοντα;

38 It is significant that Philostratus' Apollonius refers, albeit by an antithesis, to tragedy. Philostratus himself bears witness in *Lives of the Sophists* to the close relationship between the Second Sophistic and archaic and classical Greek poetry, where he mentions that Nicagoras defined tragedy as the "mother of the sophist" (II, 27, 620): Νικαγόρου δὲ τοῦ σοφιστοῦ μητέρα σοφιστῶν τὴν τραγῳδίαν προσειπόντος ..
On this issue, see M. CIVILETTI (ed.), *Filostrato. Vite dei Sofisti*, Milano 2002, pp. 448-449.

39 Philostr. *VA* V, 9, 12-21

Indeed, Apollonius knows the theatre's semantic code so well that he can even afford to appear naked, beardless, and shaven-headed at his trial. He stages his 'disappearance' during the proceedings, vanishing before the Emperor. And once the curtain has come down, he also performs his disappearance from the world.

Lucian himself, to whom we owe the first reference to Apollonius, underlines this side of the sage's 'wisdom': on the subject of Alexander of Abonuteicus' master and lover, in the polemical tract *Alexander or the False Prophet* (ca. 180 A.D.), he writes: ἦν δὲ ὁ διδάσκαλος ἐκεῖνος καὶ ἐραστὴς τὸ γένος Τυανεύς, τῶν Ἀπολλωνίῳ τῷ πάνυ συγγενομένων καὶ τὴν πᾶσαν αὐτοῦ τραγῳδίαν εἰδότων.[40]

With his τραγῳδία, Apollonius of Tyana thus seems to master a wisdom in which the ethical and aesthetic dimensions coincide. He becomes the *guru* of a *sophia* which is not confined to the *logos* but achieves its own special fulfilment in the ascetic and enacting dimension which bears on *phantasia*.[41]

παρελθὼν δὲ ἐς τὰ Ἴπολα φοβερὸς μὲν αὐτοῖς ἐφαίνετο καὶ ὃν ἐσιώπα χρόνον ἐπὶ τῆς σκηνῆς, καὶ ὁρῶντες οἱ ἄνθρωποι βαδίζοντα μὲν αὐτὸν μέγα, κεχηνότα δὲ τοσοῦτον, ἐφεστῶτα δὲ ὀκρίβασιν οὕτως ὑψηλοῖς τερατώδη τε τὰ περὶ αὐτὸν ἐσθήματα, οὐκ ἄφοβοι ἦσαν τοῦ σχήματος, ἐπεὶ δὲ ἐξάρας τὴν φωνὴν γεγωνὸν ἐφθέγξατο, φυγῇ οἱ πλεῖστοι ᾤχοντο, ὥσπερ ὑπὸ δαίμονος ἐμβοηθέντες. τοιαῦτα μὲν τὰ ἤθη τῶν ταύτῃ βαρβάρων καὶ οὕτως ἀρχαῖα.

40 Luc., *Alex.* 5.
A. M. Harmon translates this passage as follows: "This teacher and admirer of his was a man of Tyana by birth, one of those who had been followers of the notorious Apollonius, and who knew his whole bag of tricks."

41 He represents the type of wisdom despised by Marcus Aurelius (I, 16), who boasted that he had never been a man given to *askesis* or who enjoyed disguises in general. Indeed, Marcus Aurelius praised Antoninus Pius' ἀτραγῴδως behavior. On this issue, see M. TASINATO, "Marco Aurelio: vane speranze per un'estetica", in *Simplegadi. Rivista di Filosofia Orientale e Comparata*, 7/19 (2002): 33-45.

KINDS OF DOCTRINAL TRANSMISSION IN LATE ANCIENT JUDAISM*

PIERO CAPELLI

In this paper I shall deal briefly with transmission of doctrine, authority, and charismata within Palestinian Jewish groups in the 1st

* Sources are translated from the originals according to the following editions: *Dead Sea Scrolls*: *The Dead Sea Scrolls Electronic Reference Library*, 2 (Leiden, Brill, 1999). *Damascus Covenant*: *Documents of Jewish Sectaries* (S. SCHECHTER, ed.; Cambridge, Cambridge University Press, 1910 [Repr. New York, Ktav, 1970]). *Josephus*: Josephus, *Jewish Antiquities. Books XVIII-XIX* (L. FELDMAN, ed.; Cambridge, Mass. – London, Harvard University Press – Heinemann, 1981 [Loeb Classical Library]). *Mishnah*: *Šišah sidre Mišnah*, vols. 1-6 (H. ALBECK – H. YALON, eds.; Yerushalayim – Tel Aviv, Mosad Ha-Rav Kook – Dvir, 1952-1959). *Talmud Babli*: *Talmud bavli*, vols. 1-20 (Bene Beraq, Tevel, 1960). *Mekhilta de-Rabbi Ishmael: Mechilta d'Rabbi Ismael* (H. S. HOROVITZ – I. A. RABIN, eds.; Frankfurt a.M., 1931 [Repr. Yerushalayim, Bamberger & Wahrmann, 1960]). *Genesis Rabba*: *Bereschit Rabba mit kritischem Apparat und Kommentar*, vols. 1-3 (J. THEODOR – H. ALBECK, eds.; Berlin, 1903-1936 [Repr. Yerushalayim, Wahrmann, 1965]). *New Testament*: *The Greek New Testament*, 3rd ed. (K. ALAND – M. BLACK – C. M. MARTINI – B. M. METZGER – A. WIKGREN, eds.; United Bible Societies, 1975).

century BCE and 1st CE: Pharisees, Sadducees, Essenes, and Jesus' group.

1. Discipleship among the Pharisees and the Rabbis

In the period taken into consideration, the Pharisees were a Jewish fundamentalist group, generally stemming out of the craftsmen class (but also of the peasants' and merchants' and particularly of the bureaucrats' class). They had elaborated a set of ritual rules of their own (called *halakhah*, "the way") out of the Mosaic Law contained in the Torah. Starting from this *halakhah* they constituted an ideology centred on rectitude of daily lifestyle, and gradually organized themselves in synagogues and mutual aid groups called *haburoth* ("companionships"). At least up to the 2nd century CE, *halakhah* was worked out of its Scriptural basis in a loose way, aiming at a functional updating of the Law more than at faithfulness to the source.[1]

Even before the national disasters of the wars against Rome (1st century BCE-1st century CE) the Pharisees and their leaders, i.e. the teachers of the Law, had begun to attribute to their *halakhah* the same status of truth revealed by God to Moses on the Sinai that had long been the main feature of Torah. The result was a sole Torah divided into two parts equal in dignity and relevance; these are defined in rabbinic documents of the first centuries CE as the "written Torah" (*Torah she-bi-ketab*) and the "oral Torah" (*Torah she-be-ʿal-peh*). It therefore became necessary to show that Pharisean-Rabbinic *halakah* had been transmitted orally from revelation on the Sinai up until the present along an absolutely trustworthy succession. Thus a sequence of transmitters was conceived—starting from Moses down to the rabbis—that had to serve as a pedigree of the Oral Law. This

[1] See H. L. STRACK - G. STEMBERGER, *Introduction to the Talmud and Midrash*, Edinburgh, T. & T. Clark, 1991, pp. 142-145; J. LE MOYNE, *Les sadducéens*, Paris, Lecoffre, 1972, pp. 372-379 (about Rabbi Yose ben Yoʿezer's saying in Mishnah *Hagigah* 2:2).

"chain of tradition" (*shalsheleth ha-qabbalah*) is listed in chapter 1 of the Mishnah tractate *Aboth* ("Fathers"), a text including ancient material albeit redacted only in the 7th-8th century CE.[2] The same chapter also includes a series of sayings attributed to the most authoritative among the rabbis of the first generations, stating the doctrinal and ethical tenets of post-Pharisean piety. Among these, a major standing is given to setting a large number of disciples:

> Moses received Torah on the Sinai and transmitted it to Joshua; Joshua to the Elders; the Elders to the Prophets; the Prophets to the men of the Great Synagogue.[3] They stated three things: "Be moderate in judgement, make yourself many disciples, and make a hedge around the Torah" (1:1).[4]
>
> Yose ben Yo'ezer from Tzeredah and Yose ben Yohanan of Jerusalem received [the tradition] from them. Yose ben Yo'ezer says: "Let thy house be a place of meeting for the Sages; get dusty with their feet's dust and drink their words with thirst (1:4).
>
> Yehoshua' ben Perahyah and Nittay from Arbela received [the tradition] from them. Yehoshua' ben Perahyah says: "Get yourself a

2 About a possible Gnostic origin of the idea of legitimacy through tradition (Gk. *paradosis*) see further, as well as the bibliography quoted in G. FILORAMO, *A History of Gnosticism*, Cambridge, Mass. – Oxford, Blackwell, 1992, p. 159, note 42.

3 This otherwise mysterious institution – which other rabbinic sources date back from Ezra's time – is called an "empty holder" in recent historiography; see e.g. A. MELLO, *Detti di rabbini. Pirqè Avot con i loro commenti tradizionali* , Bose, Qiqajon, 1993, p. 18.

4 The risk of infringing the basic precepts of the Law had to be averted through the elaboration of lots of secondary precepts. The result was a huge proliferation of casuistry that was soon perceived as a problem: see the saying of Rabbi Hiyya (2nd century CE) in *Genesis Rabba* 19:3: "Make not the secondary precept greater than the basic one, lest it fall and cut off the buds" (that is, lead to hostility towards religion).

> teacher, get yourself a companion, and judge everyone according to the scale of merit" (1:6).[5]

> Rabban Gamaliel says: "Get yourself a teacher, get out of doubt, and do not set tithes aside repeatedly without precision" (1:16).

The reiterated exhortation to "get oneself a teacher" means in substance "learn our *halakhah* (and put it into practice)". Besides such exhortations, rabbinical literature of the first centuries CE supplies evidence of the institution of a precise *curriculum* in rabbinical studies, which Rabbi Yehudah ben Tema formulated as follows:

> He used to say: "At five Scripture; at ten Mishnah; at thirteen the precepts (*mitzwoth*); at fifteen Talmud" (*Aboth* 5:21).

From such a statement originated also a pedagogic theory: "(Hillel) used to say: '(…) One who is bashful cannot learn; one who is impatient cannot teach" (*Aboth* 2:5). A great Christian expert in Judaism like Jerome informs us that even for studying the Jewish mystical tradition the precisely defined age of thirty was required;[6] other requirements were a solid grounding in Scripture and its exegesis, both normative (*halakhah*) and homiletic (*haggadah*), and a proven rectitude in lifestyle.[7]

Already in the period between the two wars a precise ordination ritual, the *semikhah* (from the verb *samakh*, "to unite"), was in force in Palestine. Until the 4th century at least the *semikhah* was effected by imposing hands, but did not include anointing—which was uniquely peculiar to the priestly class (*Exodus* 29:7.21; 30:22-23).[8]

5 The scales of judgement – when no evidence for attributing responsibility is available – must be tipped in favour of innocence.

6 Thus Jerome in the prologue to his *Commentary on Ezekiel*; compare his *Epistles* (53:8:16).

7 See *Hekhaloth Rabbati* 20:1.

8 On the formal opposition between the ritual of priestly ordination and rabbinical *semikhah*, see R. DE VAUX, *Ancient Israel: Its Life and Institutions*, New York, McGraw-Hill, 1961, p. 347.

Also in the Jewish communities of the Babylonian diaspora a defined investiture formula was in use, in which the main functions of the rabbi-to-be were summarized. Most relevant among these functions was teaching doctrine to other candidate rabbis, then followed the faculty of judging and deciding autonomously on religious matters:

> "Can he teach?" "He can teach".
> "Can he judge?" "He can judge".
> "Can he allow (slaughtering of) firstborn cattle?" "He can allow (it)"
> (Babylonian Talmud, *Sanhedrin* 5a).[9]

The ritual and formula of the *semikhah* apparently fell out of use from the 5th century on, with changes in structure and function of the rabbinate. In Talmudic times rabbis could keep holding a secular job (in fact they were exhorted to do so)[10] and still had no definite leading role within the community.[11]

In 1952 the "chain of tradition" in *Aboth* 1 became the object of a masterly, enlightening inquiry by Elias J. Bickerman,[12] pointing out the major features that *Aboth* shared with different traditions of the late ancient Greek-Roman world. Most relevant among these are the following:

9 He can act as the priest once did, declaring that such cattle (which according to *Deuteronomy* 12 had to be consumed within the Temple precincts) have no blemishes that render them unclean.

10 Mishnah, *Aboth* 1:10 ("Love working!"); 2:2 ("Seemly is the study of Torah along with a worldly activity, for busying oneself with both of them makes one forget transgression").

11 Rabbinical teaching was gradually given an academic structure in Babylonian schools; see D. GOODBLATT, *Rabbinic Instruction in Sasanian Babylonia*, Leiden, Brill, 1975. On rabbinical education and investiture, see in detail G. STEMBERGER, *Das klassische Judentum. Kultur und Geschichte der rabbinischen Zeit (70 n.Chr. bis 1040 n.Chr.)*, München, Beck, 1979, pp. 84-90.

12 E. BICKERMAN, "La chaîne de la tradition pharisienne", *Revue Biblique* 59, 1952, pp. 44-54; Repr. in ID., *Studies in Jewish and Christian History*, vol. II, Leiden, Brill, 1980, pp. 256-269.

i) *Aboth* 1 lists fourteen intermediaries in Torah transmission; fourteen are also the high priests from Aaron to Azariah and fourteen those from Azariah to Jaddua according to *1 Chronichles* 6:3-10 and *Nehemiah* 12:10, and thrice fourteen are Jesus' forefathers according to his genealogy in *Matthew* 1:17. Similarly, number fourteen recurred also in the succession lists of Hellenistic scholarchs (see e.g. the entry *Epicurus* in the Byzantine lexicon called *Souda*);
ii) Jewish intellectuals had already applied the Hellenistic model of succession lists to the succession of the prophets (*diadoche ton propheton*), complaining of its absence in the period of Persian rule (so Josephus in the 1st century CE: *Against Apion* 1:41).

Pharisees proved thus to be far less averse to influences from Hellenistic culture than they pretended to be. According to Bickerman, by following Hellenistic models the Pharisees meant precisely to establish the spiritual genealogy of the doctrines of the two main Pharisean schools in the 1st century CE, Hillel's school and Shammai's school. Such a well assured chain of tradition of the Oral Law made it possible not to have to account for each and every *halakhic* conclusion by means of a thorough listing of every transmitter of it, starting from Moses onwards. This was different from the Pythagorean *ipse dixit*,[13] and also from the subsequent case of Islam, where each *hadith* related to the Prophet required the complete listing (*isnad*) of all of its transmitters.

After the wars against Rome, the rabbinic movement became the direct continuator of the Pharisean movement under many respects—transmission of doctrine being most relevant among them.[14] The underlying principle that oriented all of rabbinic *haggadah*, and backed *halakhah* too, was that Scripture had to be read as a totally syn-

13 See Cicero's *On the Nature of the Gods* 1:10.

14 On the limits of this assumption, see G. STEMBERGER, *Jewish Contemporaries of Jesus: Pharisees, Sadducees, Essenes*, Minneapolis, Fortress Press, 1995, pp. 141-147.

chronic whole, so that between two or more of its parts there could be neither differences nor insoluble contradictions, as can be read in the midrash *Mekhilta de-Rabbi Ishmael*: "There is neither before nor after in Torah" (*Shirata* 7). Therefore, at least in the homiletic approach, the Bible had first to be explained by means of the Bible itself, according to precise rules through which the growth of tradition could be verified. Hints of formalized hermeneutical rules can already be found in the Qumran texts.[15] The rabbinic school system accepted certain rules (the so-called *middoth*, "measures") that display remarkable kinship to those of Hellenistic rhetoric (borrowed by Roman law as well).[16] Rabbinic tradition states that these rules were codified in different sets and numbers by different rabbis: there were seven rules according to Hillel (1st century BCE), thirteen according to Rabbi Ishmael (1st-2nd century CE), and thirty-two according to Rabbi Eliezer (2nd century CE).[17]

Transmission of rabbinical lore and doctrine mainly through discipleship did not rule out the possibility that some sons of rabbis followed in their fathers' steps. Instances are known of dynasties of rabbis, such as the important one of the Gamaliels during the 1st and the 2nd century CE: Gamaliel I, member of the Sanhedrin according to *Acts* 5:34-39, whom Paul mentions as his teacher; his son Simon; Simon's son Gamaliel II; Gamaliel II's son Simon; and the latter's son, who was no less than the Patriarch Yehudah ha-Nasi himself, to whom rabbinical tradition attributes the initiative of having the *halakhah* put down in writing in the form of Mishnah around 200 CE. Besides, Origen in the 3rd century relates to have consulted "a learned Jew who has among them the title of 'son of a Sage' and who

15 See G. STEMBERGER, "Hermeneutik der jüdischen Bibel", in Ch. DOHMEN – G. STEMBERGER (eds.), *Hermeneutik der jüdischen Bibel und des Alten Testaments*, Stuttgart, Kohlhammer, 1996, pp. 23-132, especially § 1.3.

16 See D. DAUBE, "Rabbinic Methods of Interpretation and Hellenistic Rhetoric", *Hebrew Union College Annual* 22, 1949, pp. 239-264; Repr. in ID., *Collected Works*, I, Berkeley, The Robbins Collection, 1992, pp. 333-355.

17 For an outline of all the *middoth*, see STRACK – STEMBERGER, *Introduction*, *op. cit.*, pp. 17-34.

had been educated in such a way that he could become his father's successor" (*Epistle to Africanus* 11[7]).[18] Nonetheless, especially when compared to Sadducean teaching, the Pharisean transmission of doctrine was mainly grounded in dialectical discussion of the Law, as can be seen in its later transcripts found in the Mishnah. No authority could assert itself but by virtue of a greater skill in applying the *middoth*. Pharisean and Rabbinic mastership and discipleship resulted in the actual *democratisation* of the transmission of lore and doctrine, and determined the formation of a new ruling class which would lead Israelite society and piety up to the modern age.

2. Transmission of Doctrine among the Sadducees

Sadducees were the Jerusalem Temple's hierocracy together with their acolytes in aristocratic and monarchic circles. Had they a way of their own to transmit doctrine? In case they had one, what were its forms? We already see in the prophetical books of the Bible that teaching (etymologically *torah*) was among the priests' statutory duties.[19] In his *Jewish Antiquities*, Josephus relates that they differed from the Pharisees in that they did not acknowledge any "tradition (*paradosis*) of the fathers" as legally binding (13:297) and "had no observances whatsoever apart from that of the laws", i.e. of written Torah; "indeed they deem a virtue to dispute with teachers (*didaskaloi*) about the wisdom (*sophia*) they follow" (18:16). Disputation was in origin an oral genre. Jean Le Moyne—whose essay on the Sadducees is still seminal after more than thirty years—believed that these "teachers" were Sadducees too, and that the "wisdom" they dealt with was *haggadah*.[20]

18 This passage is discussed by N. DE LANGE in Origène, *Philocalie, 1-20. Sur les Écritures et la Lettre à Africanus sur l'Histoire de Suzanne* (M. HARL – N. DE LANGE, eds., Paris, Cerf, 1983, pp. 538-539, note 2).

19 *Jeremiah* 18:18; *Ezekiel* 7:26; *Micah* 3:11; *Hoseah* 4:6.

20 LE MOYNE, *Les sadducéens*, *op. cit.*, p. 42. The *scholium* to the *Megillat Ta'anith* (12), a post-Talmudic Jewish text, while stating that the rabbis refused

Since the function, ideology, and existence of the Sadducean movement were mostly centred around the worship ministered in the Jerusalem Temple and around the thereby linked economy, the destruction of the Temple by the Romans in 70 CE meant a start-off to the movement's quick extinction.

3. Didactic Figures in the Qumran Community

The Qumran site is deemed to have been the mother-house, so to speak, of the Essene movement, founded by a group of priests who had moved away from Jerusalem already in the 2nd century BCE since they refused that the offices of king and high priest be unified as the Hasmonean monarchs were doing. More generally, the Essenes also disagreed to the many compromises that the Hasmonean dynasty and the Sadducees then in power made with foreign powers (Rome first) and their culture, both of which, being pagan, were perceived as unholy and impure.

The Dead Sea Scrolls have provided evidence of the Essenes' hard-line ideology and organization structure, which can be defined as monastic. The quasi-mythical figure of the group's founder is identified by such a 'didactic' appellation as "Teacher of Righteousness". The texts ascribe to this otherwise unnamed character the role of a moral guide to the group's initiates: "to direct them in the way of his heart" (*Damascus Covenant* 1:11). The Teacher of Righteousness is also deemed to be the recipient of a God-given and therefore authentic but secret interpretation of the eschatological meaning of the

(at least until drawing up the Mishnah) to put *halakhah* into writing (*'yn kwtbym hlkwt bspr*), mentions a Sadducean "book of decrees" (*spr gzrwt*); see *ibid.*, pp. 219-220. It is also possible that some passages in the Mishnah preserve remains of Sadducean *halakhah*: compare *Makkoth* 1:6 and *Terumoth* 11; see P. CAPELLI, "Alcune note al trattato *Terumot* della Mishnà", *Egitto e Vicino Oriente*, 9, 1986, pp. 165-173. In Josephus' passage, Daube perceives the influence of Hellenistic philosophical schools and their dialectic method; see DAUBE, *Rabbinic Methods*, *op. cit.*, p. 243.

prophecies in the Bible: "God made known to him all the meanings of the words of his servants the prophets" (*Pesher Habakkuk* 7:4-5). The *Damascus Covenant*, one of the sect's codes, institutes a further priest "to keep watch on the Many"—i.e. the community's assembly. This priest had to be "learned in the Book of *Hagu* and in every Torah norm (*mishpatim*) as to tell them according to their norms" (14:7-8), that is, in the Torah and in teaching it. Of this teaching, the otherwise mysterious *Book of Hagu* could have possibly been some sort of handbook.[21]

Another character invested with an even more detailed role as a doctrinal guide within the Qumran community was the so-called "Instructor" (*maskil*). This has been identified by Julio Trebolle Barrera with a further leading figure, the *mebaqqer* or "Inspector", a sort of father guardian who will be "between thirty and fifty years old, mastering every secret and every tongue of men" (*Damascus Covenant* 14:9-10). The Instructor's functions too were almost identical to those of the Inspector's in transmitting the group's doctrines, especially its eschatological interpretation of history: "Let him instruct and teach every Son of Light about the history of all the sons of men, about the classes of their spirits, about their deeds in their generations and about the visitation of their scourge and the time of their reward" (*Rule of the Community* 3:13-15).[22] That such a transmission of doctrine was esoteric and secretive, can be inferred by Josephus' autobiographical account. Herein, he states that he himself—a priest by birth—had adhered to the Essene movement for some time (*Life* 10-11), and that the Essene novices were forbidden to disclose either

21 On Qumran *halakhah*, see L. H. SCHIFFMAN, *The Halakhah at Qumran*, Leiden, Brill, 1975. On the *Book of Hagu*, see M. GOSHEN-GOTTSTEIN, "*Sefer Hagu*: The End of a Puzzle", *Vetus Testamentum*, 8, 1958, pp. 286-288; I. RABINOWITZ, "The Qumran Authors' *SPR HHGW/Y*", *Journal of Near Eastern Studies*, 20, 1961, pp. 109-114.

22 J. TREBOLLE BARRERA in J. TREBOLLE BARRERA – F. GARCIA MARTINEZ, *The People of the Dead Sea Scrolls: Their Writings, Beliefs and Practices*, Leiden, Brill, 1995, p. 57.

the secrets of the sect or its codes or other books to outsiders (*Jewish War* 2:141-142).

The text called *Canticles of the Sage* (4Q510 and 4Q511, dated to the 1st century BCE on palaeographical grounds), reveals that the Instructor was also acknowledged as one possessing charismatic powers and as an exorciser and wondrous healer:

> I, the Instructor, proclaim his (i.e. God's) splendour's majesty so as to frighten and terri[fy] all the spirits of the angels of destructions and bastard spirits, demons, Lilith, owls and [desert wild] beasts (...) and those who smite suddenly in order to lead astray the spirit of knowledge and to make their hearts desolate and (...) at the time of domination by the wicked and in times of abasement for the Sons of Light, in the guilt of the times of the smitten by iniquity; not to eternal destruction, but for the time of the abasement of sin (...) (4Q510 1:4-8).

Other Qumran texts also supply evidence of the continuing presence of the archaic notion of illness as a consequence of impurity in Essene ideology. In early Jewish thought, impurity had been considered as a natural, physical condition; at the time we are dealing with—and especially in Essene thought—many had come to deem it a moral, ontological stain that one could normally identify with sin.[23] In the *Epistle of Enoch*, the most recent (1st century BCE) stratum of the *Ethiopic Book of Enoch* (*1 Enoch*) (chaps. 91-104)—which is a text related to the Enochic tradition and therefore not far removed from Essene ideology—we read:

> Sin has not been exported into the world. It is the people who have themselves invented it. (...) Why is a woman not given (a child)? On

[23] See *Isaiah* 6:5-7; *Zechariah* 13:1. On the evolution of the category of impurity in ancient and late ancient Jewish thought, see P. SACCHI, "Sacro profano, impuro puro: una categoria ebraica perduta", in *I segni di Dio. Il Sacro-Santo: valore, ambiguità, contraddizione*, Cinisello Balsamo, Paoline, 1993, pp. 25-53.

> account of the deeds of her own hands would she die without children (98:4-5).[24]

The two explanations for impurity—either the physical or the ontological one—did not necessarily exclude one another: in both cases impurity could be blamed upon an intervention by an evil spirit. The synoptic Gospels repeatedly mention "impure spirits" exorcized by Jesus, especially in *Matthew* 10:1 (// *Luke* 9:1-2), where both exorcism and thaumaturgic healing are shown as comparable and almost equivalent activities.[25] In the *Prayer of Nabonidus* (4Q242), a Dead Sea scroll roughly contemporary to the *Epistle of Enoch*, we see at work the same conception of sin as the cause of illness: Nabonidus, King of Babylon, is healed by remitting his sins:

> I was oppressed [by a malignant inflammation] for seven years (…) and my sin was forgiven (vb. *shabaq*) by an exorciser (*gazar*), a Jew of [those of the diaspora] (frgs. 1:2-4).

This very same identification between sin, exorcism of an evil spirit, and the recovering from illness can be seen at work in Jesus' and his disciples' thaumaturgic activity, as I will show further.[26]

The first war against Rome (66-73 CE) brought about the destruction of the Qumran settlement and is likely to have started the mostly violent extinction of the Essene movement. As for Sadducees, it was history to determine that the pre-eminent Jewish pattern of transmission of doctrine, authority, and charisma would be the Pharisean-Rabbinic one.

24 J.H. CHARLESWORTH (ed.), *The Old Testament Pseudepigrapha*, vol. I, Garden City, NY, Doubleday, 1983, p. 78. On this passage, so important in the development of Jewish apocalyptical doctrines, see P. SACCHI, *Jewish Apocalyptic and Its History*, Sheffield, Sheffield Academic Press, 1997, pp. 114-115, 242-243; J.J. COLLINS, *Apocalypticism in the Dead Sea Scrolls*, London – New York, Routledge, 1997, p. 23.

25 See also *Mark* 5:8.

26 See H.C. KEE, *Medicine, Miracle, and Magic in New Testament Times*, New York – Cambridge, Cambridge University Press, 1986.

4. Authority and Charisma in Jesus' Discipleship

As said before, in the activity of charismatic healers such as the Instructor at Qumran, or Jesus, the natures of illness—which we deem physical—and of sin—which we deem moral—came to coincide within the category of impurity (*Zachariah* 13:1 already stated that both sin and impurity can be removed through ablution). It is precisely in this sense that in the so-called "longer ending" of Mark's Gospel the risen Jesus invests the apostles with special charismata in addition to the intellectual and spiritual authority to preach the Gospel, that is, the coming of the Kingdom of God:

> Go into all the world and proclaim the gospel to the whole creation. He who believes and is baptized will be saved, but he who does not believe will be condemned. And these signs will be together with those who believe: by using my name they will cast out demons, speak new tongues, pick snakes in their hands, and if they drink any deadly poison, it will not hurt them; they will lay their hands upon the sick, and these will recover (*Mark* 16:15-18).[27]

An investiture of such a kind requires three observations:

i) This is certainly not an authentic saying of Jesus, but rather a doctrinal formulation from the early Church, "a collage of a series of resurrection traditions" as C. S. Mann has called it,[28] which most scholars date back to the 2nd century.[29] In the other versions of the synoptic Gospels, the bestowal of charismata to the apostles includes subjugating demons (*Mark* 3:15; *Luke* 9:1; *Matthew* 10:1),

27 Compare with the other accounts of bestowal of charismata to his disciples in *Luke* 10:19-20 (being immune to snakes + subjugating demons), *Matthew* 10:1 (// *Luke* 9:1-2) (subjugating demons + healing the sick), and *Mark* 3:13-15 (subjugating demons).

28 C.S. MANN, *Mark*, New York, Doubleday, 1986, p. 673.

29 See J. HUG, *La finale de l'évangile de Marc (Mc 16,9-20)*, Paris, Gabalda, 1978 (half of 2nd century); R. PESCH, *Das Markusevangelium*, vol. II, Freiburg – Basel – Wien, Herder, 1980, p. 544 (beginning of 2nd century).

being immune to snakes (*Luke* 10:19), and healing the sick (*Luke* 9:1-2; *Matthew* 10:1) but not glossolalia;

ii) The purpose of such an investiture is not to create new teachers, with an authority of their own in discussing the Law and teaching it. Such an investiture is different from the rabbinical one, and it is thus historically incorrect to ascribe to Jesus the title of rabbi—as nowadays is so fashionable in inter-religious dialogue. The technical meaning of the title *rabbi*—apart from the merely honorific one as in Jesus' case—is developed in Israel only after 70 CE;[30]

iii) The power of speaking unknown languages will emerge for the first time at the Pentecost (*Acts* 2:1-13). The apostles themselves will afterwards confer the "spirit" on others by means of imposing their hands upon them (*Acts* 8:18). On being immune from snake bite, a comparison can be made with Paul who was bitten by a viper in Malta and suffered no damage, and also with the Galilean healer Hanina ben Dosa, a contemporary of Jesus.[31] A narrative which is found in several rabbinic compilations, presents Hanina being bitten by a poisonous snake. Nothing, however, happens to him. Rather, it is the snake that dies, and Hanina takes it in his hand (thus incurring in a double impurity, because

30 On this, see M. PESCE, "Discepolato gesuano e discepolato rabbinico. Problemi e prospettive della comparazione", in W. HAASE (ed.), *Aufstieg und Niedergang der römischen Welt*, vol. II.25.1, Berlin – New York, De Gruyter, 1982, pp. 351-389 (especially 366-378), and STEMBERGER, *Das klassische Judentum*, *op. cit.*, pp. 83-85. On Jesus' discipleship in general and compared to Pharisean-Rabbinic discipleship, see G. THEISSEN – A. MERZ, *Der historische Jesus*, Göttingen, Vandenhoeck und Ruprecht, 1997, especially § 8.5; B. GERHARDSSON, *Memory and Manuscript*, Lund – Copenhagen, Gleerup – Munksgaard, 1964; R. RIESNER, *Jesus als Lehrer*, Tübingen, Mohr, 1984; G. VERMES, *Jesus the Jew: A Historian's Reading of the Gospels*, London, SCM Press, 2001, chap. 1; M. HENGEL, *The Charismatic Leader and His Followers*, New York, Crossroad, 1981, especially §§ III.3-4.

31 Most charismatic healers and exorcizers came from Galilee, where the observance of the Law was quite loose; see VERMES, *Jesus the Jew*, *op. cit.*, pp. 53-63.

> of the snake as such and its corpse) and goes around the village crying: "It is not the snake that kills, rather it is sin" (Talmud Babli, *Berakhoth* 33a).[32] Thus, Hanina put himself in open dispute with the traditional interpretation of impurity according to Mosaic Law as then represented by the Pharisees and Sadducees. And Hanina's polemic attitude was thoroughly akin to that of his contemporary and fellow countryman Jesus'.

According to Jesus' and Hanina's interpretation, the most ruinous forms of impurity were those caused by being possessed by an "evil spirit", or, even worse, because of the sins committed by one's ancestors. A strong criticism of this idea had been aroused by the prophet Ezekiel already in the 6th century BCE (*Ezekiel* 18:1-4). Nonetheless, such a conception had clearly remained popular among the Israelites, since Jesus' disciples still asked their master in front of the man born blind: "Who sinned, this man or his parents, that he was born blind?" (*John* 9:2).[33]

Hence, in the *Prayer of Nabonidus* from Qumran and in the Instructor's activity as well as in Jesus' thaumaturgic acts, the recovering from illness or handicap is obtained either through exorcism or by means of remitting the patient's sins. The clearest instance of this latter 'method' is the healing of the paralytic man in Capernaum, when a disputation is aroused between Jesus and the scribes—certainly Pharisees—who call him a blasphemer as their doctrine stated that the faculty of remitting sins pertained only to God (*Mark*

[32] Compare Mishnah, *Baba Qamma* 7:7; Tosefta, *Berakhoth* 2:20; Talmud Babli, *Ta'anith* 25a; Talmud Yerushalmi, *Berakhoth* 9a.

[33] Jesus himself reproaches his disciples in this circumstance, though in an earlier instance, after healing a paralytic, he told him: "Here you are healed; do not sin any more, lest something worse happens to you" (*John* 5:14). It is likely, however, that in this latter case Jesus intended damnation after death; see R. SCHNACKENBURG, *The Gospel according to St. John*, vol. II, New York, Seabury Press, 1982.

2:1-2.7; *Matthew* 9:1-8; *Luke* 5:18-26).[34] And this is precisely what sounded outrageous in the investiture in *Mark* 16:17, stating that Jesus had bestowed upon his disciples the charismata of driving out demons, speaking unknown languages, being immune to snakes and poisons, and healing others by mere touch *in Jesus' own name* (not in God's name). Indeed, the early Church declared that Jesus *was* God.[35]

[34] On the identification of sin and disease in Jesus' thought, see also *Matthew* 9:10-32.32-33.

[35] E. P. SANDERS, *Jesus and Judaism*, London, SCM Press, 1985, pp. 273-274, notes that in other more likely authentic sayings, Jesus does not state explicitly to take God's place in forgiving sins. He rather speaks as God's representative but, actually, he is not God. The most important advocates of the opposite perspective (i.e. Jesus presents himself as God, therefore he is a blasphemer) are listed in *ibid.*, p. 402, notes 9 and 14.

THE MASTER-DISCIPLE RELATIONSHIP IN CHRISTIANITY: SOME INTRODUCTORY OBSERVATIONS

FRANCO MACCHI

The subtitle to this paper offers a necessary key for interpreting my contribution. Indeed, for the Western non specialists, any paper concerning different, alien cultures is looked at with interest and as an original source of knowledge, even if partial and geographically as well as chronologically circumscribed to a specific cultural context. On the other hand, to deal with such a topic from the point of view of our own local tradition, that is, Western Christianity, may appear inevitably reductive, also given the fact that it is generally believed to be quite widely known. For this reason, after a short examination of the master-disciple relationship as it can be gathered from the canonical texts of the *New Testament*, I shall consider some peculiar cases of this relationship in the history of Western Christianity, so as to evidence some of its peculiar and even problematic traits. I will focus attention on distinct, autonomous points, which I hope will help clarify some of the fundamental issues involved in the master-disciple relationship.

Preliminary Considerations

My paper moves along the lines traced by professor Paolo Ricca in his presentation,[1] which I consider essential. The first, important observation evidenced by Ricca is the following: Jesus was called a *master* (*rabbi* in Aramaic), even though this title is not widely attested to in the texts of the *New Testament*. The attribution of this title to Jesus, in fact, is fairly frequent in the synoptic Gospels of *Matthew*, *Mark*, and *Luke*, and especially in *Matthew* as well as in the Gospel of *John*. Interesting is the datum that Paul in his *Letters* never attributes such title to Jesus, nor is it ever found in the *Letters* of the Apostles or in the *Apocalypse*. Apart from the Gospels, whenever the title master is utilized in the *New Testament*, it's a title which is applied to persons who in different ways have a magisterial function, who offer teachings of a didactic, doctrinal, or ethical nature (see *Romans* 2, 20; *Titus* 3, 3; *Hebrews* 5, 12; *James* 3, 1).

When in the Gospels Jesus is referred to as *master*, the term bears the meaning it had in the Rabbinic tradition of his times. Exemplary in this regard is what we read in the first chapter of *John*'s Gospel. Two disciples of John the Baptist, whom they had heard addressing Jesus as the *Lamb of God*, start following him:

> When he turned and saw them following him, he asked, 'What are you looking for?' They said, 'Rabbi' (which means a teacher), 'where are you staying?' 'Come and see', he replied.
>
> (*John* 1, 38-39)[2]

This text makes us understand very clearly how the figure and the public activity of Jesus fit in quite well with the Rabbinic tradition contemporary to him. He acts as a Rabbi, behaves like other Rabbis,

[1] Unfortunately, professor Ricca's contribution could not be included in the volume given his precarious health conditions, which prevented him from presenting a written text for publication.

[2] All quotes from the *New Testament* are taken from *The New English Bible. New Testament*, Oxford University Press and Cambridge University Press, 1961.

and his followers are his disciples. All this has already been effectively described by Piero Capelli in his paper.

On the other hand, Ricca has strongly underlined how in the Gospels Jesus is presented as a Rabbi who is very different from all others. This is indicated by some traits which make of Jesus a unique case for his times, so original and anomalous that he aroused astonishment, curiosity and, at the same time, profound enthusiasm as well as hatred. The main, peculiar characteristics of Jesus as *master* which the Gospels highlight may be summarized thus: a) he does not limit himself to expound the Law, but he renews and changes it; b) he teaches *with authority*: he forgives sins, he dispels demons; c) he is a Rabbi who does not ask people to serve him: rather, he himself is the one who serves. He is a master who washes his disciples' feet.

A disquieting question emerges from Ricca's overall observations. Should the fact that the title *master* attributed to Jesus soon disappears already within the corpus of the writings of the *New Testament* – and even more so in posterior Christian literature – be interpreted as purely a lexical, statistical datum or rather as something much more revealing and significant? The question becomes even more problematic if one considers the history of Christianity: whereas on the one hand the frequency with which Jesus is called and considered a master rarefies itself, on the other hand the concept of the teaching of the Church, that is, of ecclesiastical authority, affirms itself to very high levels of ambiguity. Thus, *Jesus the master* risks being suffocated by the *Ecclesia magistra*, which in fact takes his place.

Jesus' First Disciples (*John* 1, 35-51). The Nature of the Master-Disciple Relationship: The Central Place of Testimony

Ricca's paper has underlined the difference between Jesus of Nazareth and the Rabbis who were his contemporaries. It is precisely this difference that characterizes the peculiar master-disciple relationship which lies at the root of Christianity. Diversity, at least in this context, does not imply superiority nor inferiority. It simply means distinction, a specific characteristic. The fact that the contemporaries of Jesus realized that he changed the law, taught with authority, served his disciples instead of having them honour and serve him, expresses the peculiarity of his teaching activity. Let me try to present such peculiarities through some Biblical texts which are especially significant, in particular *John* 1, 35-51.

The Jewish Rabbis had to undergo a long formative period in order to be recognized as teachers. Moreover, their disciples, once admitted to their schools, had to dedicate themselves totally to study, in order to assimilate their wisdom. In this way, a strong tie was established which often entailed the sharing of a profound common experience. This, in any case, was essentially based on the acquisition of an in-depth knowledge of doctrines and norms, as well as on the elaboration of well defined religious and theological concepts. At the time of Jesus, this could lead to forms of communal life, as the existence of a community such as that of Qumran testifies.

What distinguishes from the outset the peculiarity of the relationship of the Rabbi Jesus with his disciples is the will to communicate and receive a special kind of knowledge which is not merely conceptual, i.e. rational and theoretical, but rather existential, being founded upon *faith*. From the beginning, his followers don't see in Jesus simply a well-prepared master, as one could find many in Israel, but they recognize in him a person in whom resides a fullness of life and a contagious strength and energy, bearing characteristics which go beyond natural human limitations. By the same token, the prerequisites in order to be admitted to the inner circle of Jesus' disciples were not the same as those which were required by all other Rabbis. Indeed, these latter ones required that their pupils come from high social strata and that they were fit for a life of research, what we nowadays would classify as a specialized and qualified elite.[3]

[3] On this issue, see P. A. CAROZZI, "L'ebraismo biblico come religione e civiltà", in P. REINACH SABBADINI (ed.), *La cultura ebraica*, Torino, Einaudi, 2000, pp. 64-91.

The anomaly of the Rabbi of Nazareth manifests itself from the very beginning of his activity and is perceived in such a strong way, that it immediately determines violent reactions. Among other texts, chapter 4 of the Gospel of *Luke* bears testimony to this situation. Here, and we are at the very beginning of Jesus' public life, we read:

> Then Jesus, armed with the power of the Spirit, returned to Galilee; and reports about him spread through the whole countryside. He taught in their synagogues and all men sang his praises.
>
> (*Luke* 4, 14-15)

The text goes on telling us that, when he was invited to comment upon a Biblical passage in the synagogue of his home town, as according to the local custom, initially

> there was a general stir of admiration; they were surprised that words of such grace should fall from his lips. 'Is not this Joseph's son?' they asked.
>
> (*Luke* 4, 22)

However, when he finished his speech, the reaction was quite different:

> At these words the whole congregation was infuriated. They leapt out, threw him out of the town, and took him to the brow of the hill on which it was built, meaning to hurl him over the edge. But he walked straight through them all, and went away.
>
> (*Luke* 4, 29-30)

The abrupt change in the mood of the inhabitants of Nazareth, according to *Luke*, verifies itself when Jesus, after reading a Biblical passage as according to traditional custom, applies with authority the contents of the Biblical words to himself and the present situation. The normal listening of texts which were studied, commentated upon and perhaps exalted from a literary point of view, is thus made disturbing by Jesus' authoritative charisma. Indeed, he presented himself as the one about whom the text referred to and pronounced judgments which tended to judge and modify the listeners' behaviour. This kind of attitude went beyond the function which was typically recognized to Rabbis, being rather linked to the characteristics of prophetic preaching which had disappeared from the institutions and praxis of Jewish society:

> Then Jesus said, 'No doubt you will quote the proverb to me, "Physician, heal yourself!", and say, "We have heard of all your doings at Capernaum; do the same here in your own home town." I tell you this,' he went on: 'no prophet is recognized in his own country'.
>
> (*Luke* 4, 23-24)

We have already seen how in its first chapter the Gospel of *John* narrates the encounter between Jesus and his first disciples. I wish to come back to this text, since from it emerge some special characteristics of the master-disciple relationship, which are typical of the way of thinking of the author of the fourth Gospel. From the outset of the narration, one understands that the relationship of Jesus with his disciples will be of an existential kind, rather than strictly theoretical, doctrinal or ethical. Of extreme interest is the chapter's conclusion. To Nathaniel, who marvels at the fact that Jesus saw him under a fig-tree before Philip spoke to him, Jesus says:

> 'Is this the ground of your faith, that I told you I saw you under the fig-tree? You shall see greater things than that.' Then he added, 'In truth, in very truth I tell you all, you shall see heaven wide open, and God's angels ascending and descending upon the Son of Man.'
>
> (*John* 1, 50-51)

Jesus as the master is presented not only as *he who knows* but, first of all, as *he who is* (the awaited Messiah)[4] and as *he who sees*, and who allows whomever has faith in him to *see*.[5]

[4] In verse 41 of the first chapter of the Gospel of *John* – within the narration of the calling of Jesus' first disciples – Andrew says to his brother Simon: "'We have found the Messiah (which is the Hebrew for 'Christ')."'

[5] The identification of faith and vision is very frequent in *John*. To believe is to see; cf. John 1, 39; 1, 46; 1, 51; 3, 3; 3, 36; 8, 56; 9, 39; 12, 45; 17, 24. Various other passages in the *New Testament* equate the act of faith with the act of see-

The teaching of the master Jesus will be in the first place the showing within himself and beyond himself "the heaven wide open, and God's angels ascending and descending upon the Son of Man". It will be focussed on a profound personal experience, at once religious and mystic. The verb which is most insisted upon is indeed *to see*. Of course, this *vision* will also need to be re-elaborated and transmitted, described and moulded into a new way of understanding the human world and its history. In other words, it will need to be translated into a comprehensible human language in order to be conceptually transmissible. Still, it will not be possible to comprehend it if he who speaks and those who listen don't share in a common faith. The believers must situate themselves in the condition of *seeing* what the disciples – who later became themselves masters – saw and the master Jesus allowed them to see.[6]

Therefore, the Christian master, *before being a teacher, is a witness*: *if faith is vision, its transmission is testimony*. The first disciples of Jesus, of whom *John* 1, 35-51 tells us about, *first* had news about him through the word of witnesses who had recognized him as the along waited for Saviour and Messiah. Then, only *after* this, they met him in person and they *saw and believed*. The tie between the master and each individual disciple establishes itself through a chain of people who, after having witnessed personally, have in turn invited others to meet Jesus and to directly experience him in person. In this way, a special relationship of each single disciple with the

ing: see, for instance, *Matthew* 13, 16; 18, 10; 24, 30; *Luke* 11, 33; *Acts* 7, 55-56.

6 This is what in chapter 3 of *John*'s Gospel Jesus tells Nicodemus in his nocturnal meeting with him: "'In truth, in very truth I tell you, unless a man has been born over again he cannot see the kingdom of God.'" The whole episode is important in order to understand this point. Jesus recognizes Nicodemus as a "famous teacher of Israel", but until he will continue to try to understand and teach according to the criteria of human science and language alone ("But how is it possible for a man to be born when he is old?") he will never be able to grasp Jesus' teaching: "'Is this famous teacher of Israel ignorant of such things? In very truth I tell you, we speak of what we know, and testify to what we have seen, and yet you all reject our testimony'" (*John* 3, 10-11).

master Jesus originates, determined by personal trust. The encounter with Jesus has then revealed to the believer what others could have never seen with their natural eye.[7] One could argue that this passage of the Gospel of *John* expresses the principle of *fides ex auditu* (*Romans* 10, 17) as vouched by the apostle Paul, albeit in a different terminology and literary genre. Paul will express the content of faith, which in *John* is the vision of God which illumines and destroys all darkness, with the expression *justice of God*:

> For I am not ashamed of the Gospel. It is the saving power of God for everyone who has faith – the Jew first, but the Greek also – because here is revealed God's way of righting wrong, a way that starts from faith and ends in faith; as Scripture says, 'he shall gain life who is justified through faith'.
>
> (*Romans* 1, 16-17)

This salvation which is transmitted through faith, as Paul writes, is not due to the fascinating and persuasive capacity of the witnesses: it does not function this way. It is rather said to be sustained and made vital in all its 'passages' and in all people involved thanks to the presence and power of the Holy Spirit, which after Jesus' Resurrection and ascent to heaven, the Father, in the name of Christ, sends upon those whom he loves, as promised (*John* 14, 26).

The conclusion of the passage, which quotes the words which Jesus told to his first disciples, is even more explicit in underlining how the teaching of the Christian master is grounded upon his testimony of faith, rather than on the words he pronounces:

> In truth, in very truth I tell you all, you shall see heaven wide open, and God's angels ascending and descending upon the Son of Man.
>
> (*John* 1, 51)

7 On faith understood as a sort of 'third eye' which allows to see human existence in a radically new way, see R. PANIKKAR, *La pienezza dell'uomo. Una Cristofania*, Milano, Jaca Book, 1999, p. 35 ff.

All this, as we have seen, means that the believers i.e. the disciples, as it happened in the case of John the Baptist, can only testimony to the light and divine life which they recognized in Jesus of Nazareth. In turn, the contact with the Father, the God in heaven, can be established only through the mediation of the Son, the Christ, in whom, thanks to the Holy Spirit's power, the fullness of divinity reveals itself. After all, it is again *John* who has Jesus say:

> He who puts his faith in the Son has hold of eternal life, but he who disobeys the Son shall not see that life; God's wrath rests upon him.
>
> (*John* 3, 36)

> When a man believes in me, he believes in him who sent me rather than in me; seeing me, he sees him who sent me.
>
> (*John* 12, 44-45)

> I am the way; I am the truth and I am life; no one comes to the Father except by me.
>
> (*John* 14, 6)

Peculiarity of the Dialectics Master-Teaching of the Church in Christianity: Existential Experience is Prior to Rational Knowledge

Even a superficial reading of the first writings of Paul and the *Pastoral Letters* enables one to notice the different kind of theological atmosphere which characterizes them. The *Pastoral Letters* reflect problems of the Christian communities, in which a process of institutionalisation has already started.[8] It is in this context that the reason for the disappearance of the title *master* for Jesus must be searched for. Indeed, it is precisely here that we find an evident preoccupation

[8] On this well-known evolutive process, see G. A. DENZER, *Le lettere pastorali*, in R. E. BROWN – J. A. FITZMYER – R. E. MURPHY, *Grande Commentario Biblico*, Brescia, Queriniana, 1973, pp. 1283-1285 (in the Italian translation by A. BONORA – R. CAVEDIO – F. MAISTRELLO).

for the definition and defence of the *depositum fidei* received from the apostles and which must be faithfully transmitted to future believers. The Christian movement, as any other movement, once the first phase of creative effervescence linked to the personality and charisma of the founder had passed, felt the need to organize itself through precise rules, defining the essential nucleus of its fundamental religious conceptions. This is a process which is common to all movements which originate from an action of profound cultural, social, and religious renewal. The rising church could not escape such process. With the disappearance of the direct witnesses of the life, teachings, and death of Christ (*cum* resurrection and ascent to heaven), a period of 'normalization' and codification ensued. This developed also from the necessity for the church to confront itself with new situations and problems, determined by the contact with other worldviews and cultures, and due to the evolution and change in the societies in which Christians lived.

Christianity, in its long history, has passed through profound crises, often salutary, which, in order to be overcome, has seen many important figures and intellectuals ask themselves up to what point the church of their times reflected the roots and origins of the first Christian experience. History is replete and enriched by the constant emergence of reformers, whose major concern has been that of making Christianity more faithful to its origins. It must be noted, however, that Christianity, in its need to revert to its supposed pristine origins, must always take into account a specific peculiarity. Within a given philosophical movement, for instance, one can try to better understand what the founder said by studying his writings, his relationship with other philosophical movements, with the society in which he operated in, etc. All this, of course, is valid also for Christianity, but it is still not enough. The figure of Jesus as master is in fact not reducible to that of an author who elaborated and imparted teachings and ethical precepts. To revert to the school of Jesus the master requires the reestablishment of a personal, direct relationship with him, with his person. It is then simple to understand how whoever bears institutional responsibilities, at whatever level, mistakes the pretence of possessing certain and reliable knowledge of Jesus' teaching with the pretence of judging the authenticity of the relationship of the believers with the master, who, however, had told to Nicodemus:

> You ought not to be astonished, then, when I tell you that you must be born over again. The wind blows where it wills; you hear the sound of it, but you do not know where it comes from, or where it is going. So with everyone who is born from spirit.
>
> (*John* 3, 7-8)

In those who have responsibilities in the church, as well as in each and every Christian, the dialectics between faithfulness to the master and faithfulness to the teaching of the church may stiffen to such an extent that the preoccupation for defending the completeness and orthodoxy of the doctrine may lead to not recognize, to condemn, and even to persecute the ones who have established a vital relationship with Jesus of Nazareth, based upon faith. In the course of the history of Christianity, it is not difficult to document these cases.

The case of Saint Francis of Assisi...

I will here mention the single case of a giant in the history of Christianity, admired by all Christians as well as by all people belonging to whatever cultural orientation: Francis of Assisi. Francis rediscovered the essential nature of Christianity and its demands not after an in-depth study of history, philosophy, or theology, nor – though being a diffused phenomenon in his times – through a critique of the church motivated by ethical or even political reasons. He rather discovered the original force of Christianity in his encounter with the sick and the excluded, especially the lepers, in whom he recognized the suffering Christ, with whom he established a personal, direct relationship, which he strengthened and developed through the constant reading of the scriptures. But the peculiarity of Francis, as of many other important testimonies of Christianity, lies precisely in their will to read the Gospels *sine glossa*. The text for Francis served as an intermediary through which he entered into a direct dialogue with the master Jesus. His experience was so contagious that he himself was immediately recognized and sought for as a master by numerous disciples. Francis achieved in his own experience all the special features which were the characteristics of the Rabbi of Nazareth and his disciples. Around him a relationship of profound existential solidarity originated, which he prevented from degenerating into a personality cult. He and his disciples lived a life of profound fraternity, grounded on the principle, as evidenced in the Gospel of *John*, that the Christian master is not served but rather serves. This principle was well understood by Dante Alighieri, who, in *The Divine Comedy* (*Paradise*, Canto XI), after accusing the Church of having forgotten poverty (*Madonna povertà*) on the cross, first exalts the figure of Francis – since, after "a thousand and a hundred years" of guilty forgetfulness on the Church's part, fell madly in love with *Madonna povertà* – and then underlines the power of attraction which the saint exercised on his first followers as well as the atmosphere of profound religious experience which cemented their communal life. The author of *The Divine Comedy* has Thomas Aquinas put forward the following, beautiful and incisive verses:

> La lor concordia e i lor lieti sembianti,
> amore e maraviglia e dolce sguardo
> facìeno esser cagion di pensier santi;
> tanto che'l venerabile Bernardo
> si scalzò prima, e dietro a tanta pace
> corse e, correndo, li parve esser tardo.
> Oh ignota ricchezza! oh ben ferace!
> Scalzasi Egidio, scalzasi Silvestro
> dietro allo sposo, sì la sposa piace.
> Indi sen va quel padre e quel maestro
> con la sua donna e con quella famiglia
> che già legava l'umile capestro.
>
> (*Paradise*, Canto XI, 76-87)

With these words the poet renders in a magnificent way the extraordinary force and charisma of Francis, who attracts disciples to himself and who – as an exemplary Christian master – causes their falling in love not with his persona but rather with his spouse, that is, poverty i.e. Christ, the poor, who died on the cross and whose sacrifice raised him as the victorious saviour of all humanity.

Such an experience was in fact so disruptive that it inevitably caused tensions of an institutional nature. This is shown by the difficulties Francis found in having the church authorities and even his own disciples accept his choice, his *forma vitae*. The ecclesiastical authorities didn't accept the original project Francis had conceived for giving a rule to his movement. Indeed, Francis refused the very concept of rule and his first idea was simply that of gathering and put together passages from the Gospels: only the Gospels would be the *magna charta* for anyone who aspired to become his disciple. However, half-heartedly he had to accept a rule which was prepared in a formal and juridical language. However, he was never fully convinced by its formulations, to the point that in the last hours of his life he dictated a *Testament* to his closest disciples, in which he tried to recover his initial ideas. His position determined profound divisions within his own order, between those who wanted to remain faithful to the original intentions of the founder and who thought it necessary to give a well-organized structure to the movement, which by now had become quite large in numbers. In the end, Francis didn't recognize himself in the features his movement took, to the point that he resigned from his office as father general and lived the last years of his life at the margins of the order he had founded. Despite all appearances and an atmosphere of triumphant sacredness which was implemented with great skill, he was rather tolerated than actually listened to and followed by the majority of his disciples.[9]

9 The bibliography on Francis of Assisi is vast. I'll here recall only the following works: G. MICCOLI, "Francesco d'Assisi e l'ordine dei minori", in R. ROMANO – C. VIVANTI (eds.), *Storia d'Italia*, Torino, Einaudi, vol. 2, pt. 2, 1974, pp. 734-793; Ch. FRUGONI, *Francesco, un'altra storia*, Genova, Marietti, 1989; Ch. FRUGONI, *Francesco e l'invenzione delle stimmate*, Torino, Einaudi, 1993; Ch. FRUGONI, *Vita di un uomo*: *Francesco d'Assisi*, Torino,

… and that of Kierkegaard

Inevitably, I think it useful to recall here some of the considerations put forward by Kierkegaard, by all recognized as a brave Christian, who in the 19th century took up questions and proposed themes on which the debate is still ongoing. Among the many issues which the Danish thinker took into consideration, we find a central theme: that of the possibility or impossibility of becoming disciples along the path of Jesus the master. Is it possible, after nineteen centuries, to live as contemporaries of the master of Nazareth and to establish with him a relationship of profound existential commitment? Leaving aside all issues of a theoretical kind linked to this question (for instance, the relationship between time and infinity, human will and divine grace, etc.), I here concentrate on what has direct bearing on the master-disciple subject. In this regard, I must mention the strong call which Kierkegaard addressed to the Danish church and to Christianity as a whole with respect to the need to place *first* – if anyone wishes to consider himself/herself a true Christian – the direct, existential relationship with Christ, as his disciples experienced it. The fundamental premiss of Kierkegaard's convictions is condensed in his assertion that

> the contrary of sin is not at all virtue … no, what is the opposite of sin is faith, as it is said in *Romans* 14, 23.[10]

This is precisely the re-proposal of what was affirmed in the passages we analysed previously, especially in the Gospel of *John*. In the fifth article published in *The Instant*, the Danish thinker wrote:

Einaudi, 1995; J. LE GOFF, *San Francesco d'Assisi*, Bari, Laterza, 2002 (1st French edition, Paris, Gallimard, 1999).

10 See S. KIERKEGAARD, *La Malattia per la morte* (a cura di E. ROCCA), Roma, Donzelli, 1999, p. 84. All English translations from the Italian editions of Kierkegaard's texts are mine.

> Because he loves you and wants to be loved by you, in both cases moved by love; but as soon as you desire something you don't think of him anymore, just as when you fear something.[11]

This fundamental need of love, which from the master is poured on the disciple, is such a radical requirement that, contrary to what is commonly thought:

> To become Christians in the sense of the *New Testament* entails such a radical change that, from a simply human point of view, we must say that the stronger pain for any family is that one of its members become Christian.[12]

This is deemed as an unavoidable outcome since

> you must make the 'exemplary model' present in such a way that you suffer as if you'd recognize him for what he is in the contemporary world ... this is the Christian demand.[13]

In the light of this direct and contemporary way of conceiving the master-disciple relationship, the believer must live as if the 1,800 years of Christianity had never existed.[14] Moreover, according to Kierkegaard, Christianity, in order to reach maximum expansion, has in fact edulcorated the original message of the *New Testament* mak-

11 See S. KIERKEGAARD, *L'Istante* (a cura di A. GALLAS), Genova, Marietti 1820, 2001, p. 150.

12 *Ibid.*, p. 222.

13 *Ibid.*, p. 243.

14 "I do not define myself a Christian ... No, I cannot change my assertion, I don't want to and I don't dare to; I cannot serve these legions of rascal hacks, I mean the ministers, who have falsified the very definition of 'Christian' and have – for the sake of their own interests – produced millions and millions of Christians... The point of view which I must make clear and which I make manifest is so particular that in the 1,800 years of Christianity I literally don't find anything similar to it, nothing equivalent to which I may address myself. Even in this sense – precisely facing these 1,800 years – I stand literally alone"; *ibid.*, p. 287.

ing it palatable, pleasing, poetically and artistically attractive and interesting, to the detriment of its authenticity and its exacting demands. All this has determined a close and suffocating alliance with political power which, in order to improve its capacity to control its subjects, has transformed bishops and ministers – who ought to be the appointed masters institutionally responsible for transmitting the message of the Gospels – into officials at its direct dependence. Here is the very core of our subject-matter. Those who ought to be the masters, or, better, the witnesses of the Gospels' message and the exemplary disciples of the master of Nazareth, are in fact the first traitors of the primitive church.

> Until here in Denmark there will exist a thousand salaries for the masters of Christianity, the best will have be achieved in order to obstacle Christianity.[15]

> Most of these people lack the calling to announce Christianity, and view all this simply as a means to earn their bread.[16]

This is not simply the radical reporting of a particular situation which is to be found at a particular place. What Kierkegaard highlights is a fundamental aspect of the nature of Christianity which from its very beginnings has been left unsolved, to the point that our author ventures to say that Christianity has never really entered history:

> The matter takes a different aspect when one realizes that to be Christians is such an elevated ideal that – instead of blabbing about the 1,800 years of Christian history and on the perfectibility of Christianity – we should probably state that Christianity has never really entered the world; that it has not gone beyond its model or the apostles; moreover, even these latter ones have announced it aiming so

15 *Ibid.*, p. 128.
16 *Ibid.*, p. 129.

> strongly at its diffusion that it can be said that the fraud originates already from here.[17]

We are faced with an unprecedented, radical statement. Indeed, Kierkegaard not only rejects as false the idea that Christianity is in fact Christian, but comes to suspect that the unfaithfulness to Jesus the master is already present and at work in the apostles, in his first disciples. Thus, the suspicion is insinuated that even allegiance to the apostolic tradition is not capable of linking anyone to the authentic Jesus of Nazareth.

Can we then conclude that, for our Danish theologian, there have never been true disciples of the master of Nazareth from the time of his death and ascent to heaven? Actually, according to Kierkegaard, there have been true disciples, but these have been limited to isolated figures or few persons, typically unknown and often even persecuted by Christianity:

> Within the enormous 'population' of Christians, in this swarming of 'Christians', there can be found from time to time single cases of true Christians. For a true Christian the road is narrow – as it is said in the *New Testament*; everyone hates him – to kill him is thought to be a pious act, as reported in the *New Testament*. The *New Testament* is really an odd book, though absolutely right and true: yes, precisely this single person or these single people alone were true Christians.[18]

These statements of Kierkegaard were not the words of an academician but expressed his profound existential anguish. He demonstrated this with his life choices. Thus, in the final phases of his existence he refused the so called religious solaces and ordered that at his funeral no minister be present, nor any official representative of the Danish church. The authenticity or non authenticity of his discipleship knew no mediation but was rather direct: it could be verified only by the

17 *Ibid.*, p. 153.
18 *Ibid.*, p. 101.

paradigmatic model, that is, by Jesus the master. All other mediations – social, cultural, or even religious – were to be excluded.

Jesus the Master versus his Disciples Today: Not a Necessarily Intra-ecclesial Relationship Only

The case of Kierkegaard is exemplary in order to understand in which terms – for certain aspects new – the relationship between master and disciple poses itself in Christianity. Certainly, the various Christian churches are sufficiently aware of the ways in which they must predispose themselves and their believers in order to establish contact with the master Jesus. It seems nonetheless clear, at least in Western Christianity, that the number of people who address themselves directly to the master of Nazareth i.e. bypassing the judgement and overall control of clerical authorities, has grown enormously. In our contemporary society, the number of 'Christians without church' is constantly increasing. To be sure, Kierkegaard went too far when he stated that just a few, rare persons – who remained anonymous and were opposed by the institutions – succeeded in being true disciples of the master of Nazareth. I also think he went too far when, in *The Instant*, he condemned without appeal all ecclesiastic authorities bearing magisterial functions in their respective churches as being – both as an institutional body and single individuals – corruptors and traitors of the Gospels.

The history of Christianity proves that a great number of disciples have followed the rabbi Jesus loyally and 'existentially'. In turn, these disciples have become true masters of Christian life, being the inspirers of collective experiences and a variety of Christian movements.

It would thus be unfair to radically condemn all Christian institutions, which took pains to elaborate rules and regulations for a well ordained life conduct for all Christians and to safeguard the doctrinal nucleus of Christian revelation. Nonetheless, nowadays it is clear – as it was never before – that the person of Jesus of Nazareth and his teaching is not an exclusive patrimony of Christian churches, nor is it the patrimony of those churches or Christian institutions which affirm to be the sole, faithful custodians of Jesus' legacy. The magisterial authority of Jesus is recognized both by Christians as well as by people belonging to different religious traditions, by believers and non believers: each and everybody may arrive at his teaching, even though in a partial way i.e. comprehending it only up to a certain extent. Indeed, if, according to the Gospels, in Christ the fullness of truth is revealed, no human being, although capturing authentic fragments of it, can ever say to have realized it in its entirety.[19] Perhaps, the words which Jesus addresses to Nicodemus have never been as significant as in our own times:

> The wind blows where it wills; you hear the sound of it, but you do not know where it comes from, or where it is going. So with everyone who is born from spirit.
>
> (*John* 3, 8)

These notes evidence how easily in Christianity the weight placed on the central role of the master may shift to that of magisterial authority. The two do not necessarily exclude each other, but certainly the disciple can never reduce himself/herself to a simple learner, and he/she can never be deprived of the direct and personal relationship with Jesus the master, a relationship grounded upon faith and which allows the disciple to *see* in him the *revelation of the fullness of truth*. On the other hand, every true disciple of Christ becomes automatically a master. His function, however, is not so much that of teaching some truths, but rather that of testifying and indicating to

[19] J. DUPUIS, in his recent study *Verso una teologia cristiana del pluralismo religioso* (Brescia, Queriniana, 1998, 2nd ed.), has bravely faced this problem especially with respect to other religions. One of the theological presuppositions upon which the Jesuit scholar bases his theses is the following: "As the human conscience of Jesus as the Son could not, in and of itself, exhaust the divine mystery, thus leaving God's revelation incomplete, in a similar way the event-Christ does not exhaust – nor it could – the saving power of God" (p. 403; the English translation is mine).

the faithful the necessity to deepen one's own experience of faith in Christ. This will bring the human master to gradually disappear, while the disciple will reinforce and deepen his/her personal experience of Jesus. The same principle was taught by John the Baptist, who told his followers:

> You yourselves can testify that I said, 'I am not the Messiah; I have been sent as his forerunner.' It is the bridegroom to whom the bride belongs. The bridegroom's friend, who stands by and listens to him, is overjoyed at hearing the bridegroom's voice. This joy, this perfect joy, is now mine. As he grows greater, I must grow less.
>
> (*John* 3, 28-30)

It is clear that the magisterial function of whichever church, though surely legitimate, cannot pretend to expand itself to the point of encompassing the *priority* of the direct and existential relationship disciple-master, that is, faithful-Christ. Moreover, it cannot be negated that such a vital relationship may extend itself outside the boundaries of the singular churches, comprising people belonging to different religions and even non believers or simply people who do not recognize themselves in any organized religion.

THE INTERIOR MASTER
IN THE UNDERSTANDING OF THE FIRST FRIENDS

PIER CESARE BORI

Friends or Quakers: this twofold denomination of the protagonists of a prophetic movement which arose in England around the middle of the forties of the 17th century deserves an explanation, which already constitutes an introduction to our topic.

1. "Friends", "Friends of the Truth", and later, in a somewhat more bureaucratic fashion, "Society of Friends", is the preferred self-designation. It comes from the Gospel of *John* (15, 14-15), in which it is said:

> You are my friends, if you do what I command you. I call you servants no longer; a servant does not know what his master is about. I have called you friends, because I have disclosed to you everything that I heard from my Father.[1]

[1] All quotes from the *New Testament* are taken from *The New English Bible. New Testament*, Oxford University Press and Cambridge University Press, 1961.

INDOASIATICA 2/2004, [81-89]

This is a text which speaks about a lord and about servants, of a master and of disciples (the terms in the context of our passage are reversible; see *John* 15, 9). But it is also said that the servants become friends, thanks to a new and different relationship based upon knowledge and love, *gnosis* and *agape*.

"Quaker", instead, is an ironic definition, labelled from outside the movement, which makes reference to the shaking, the tremor which the Friends experience at the time when they speak moved by the spirit and feel the emotion of the master's presence.

The topic of the inner light or of the spiritual master who lies within, is central in the Quakers' first mission. Here is how George Fox presents himself, preaching in 1652 in a public place in Ulverston:

> O People consider, who be within the parish of Ulverston; I was moved of the Lord to come to your public places to speak among you, being sent of God to the directing of your minds to God, that you might know where you might find your teacher; that your minds might be stayed alone upon God, and you might not gad abroad without you for a teacher; for the Lord God alone will teach his people; and he is coming to teach them [...].
> God hath given to every one of you a measure of his spirit according to your ability ... This is the measure of the spirit of God that shows you sin, evil and deceit ... Therefore mind your measure ... and prize your time while you have it. Therefore love the light which Christ hath enlightened you withal who saith, 'I am the light of the world', and doth enlighten every one that cometh into the world [...].
> Your teacher is within you; look not forth; it will teach you lying in bed, going abroad, to shun all occasion of sin and evil.[2]

This text, which Rex Ambler places first in his anthology, shows how the two great presuppositions of the Quakers' vision join and

2 J. L. NICKALLS (ed.), *Journal*, Cambridge, Cambridge University Press, 1952, p. 142 ff. See also R. AMBLER, *Truth of the Heart*, London, Quaker Books – Friends House, 2001, 1, 1.

unite themselves together: *Matthew* 18, 20 and *John* 1, 9. The master is in the midst of his disciples, gathered around him in his name.

> Christ Jesus [...] you may see the beginning of his setting up his meetings, when he saith: 'Where two or three are gathered together in my name, I am in the midst of them'.[3]

The "Christ Prophet" present at this very moment in the midst of the community is the fulfilment of the prophecy of *Deuteronomy* 18, 15. According to L. Benson, the key-phrase "Christ has come He himself to teach his people" appears at least forty-two times in the writings of Fox.[4]

But this is possible thanks to the light within, which illumines all men (*John* 1, 9),[5] and which in the Quaker vision leads to interpret the problem of those who are not reached by the preaching in an original way. But let us now consider in the first place the issue of the master.

2. The position of the Quakers has certainly a strong critical dimension against the Catholic rite, but also against the central place of the scriptures. It affirms that the spirit which dictated the scriptures is *in the believers*, and that the *interior* Christ is much more important than the sacramental bread and wine.

> You need no mass to teach you, for the spirit that gave forth the scripture teacheth us how to pray, sing, praise, rejoice, honour and worship God, and in what, and how to walk and to behave ourselves to God and man, and leadeth us into all truth, in which is our unity; and it is our comforter and guide and leader.[6]

3 Ep. 249, 1667; *Works* 7, 298; AMBLER, *op. cit.*, 2, 8.

4 See P. C. BORI, *Un profeta come me. I Quaccheri*, in www.spbo.unibo.it/pais/bori.

5 See P. C. BORI, "'La luce che illumina ogni uomo' (*Gv.* 1, 9) in George Fox e Robert Barclay", *Annali di storia dell'esegesi* 11/1 (1994): 119-144.

6 Ep. 171, 1659; AMBLER, *op. cit.*, 1, 28.

> And know you not yourselves how that Christ is you, except you are reprobates; and if he be witnessed within and known within when he is come, then what need you have of bread and wine to put you in remembrance of him?[7]

3. The revolution does not consist in radically modifying the contents of faith, but rather in placing the believer at the centre, and, at the believer's centre, the interior, spiritual master.

> Keep within. And when they shall say: 'lo here', or 'lo there is Christ', go not forth; for Christ is within you [...]. For the measure is within, and the light of God is within, and the pearl is within you, which is hid; and the word of God is within you, and ye are the temples of God; and God hath said, he will dwell in you and walk in you. And then what need ye go to the idols' temples without you?[8]

It is noteworthy, as R. Ambler observes, that the message of the first Friends does not insist so much on what truth is, but rather on *how* and *where* to find it:

> If you would them come to the knowledge of truth, let them know it, and where it is to be found.[9]

4. A fundamental instrument in this research is the meeting, the Friends' silent assembly.

> So every spirit comes to have a particular satisfaction and quietness in his own mind, and here the weary come to have rest in Christ [...]. Such shall find mercy of God when their minds are quieted in silent waiting upon God. In one hour they have more peace and satisfaction

7 *To the King of France*, 1660; *Doctrinals*, *Works* 4, 237; AMBLER, *op. cit.*, 1, 103.

8 Ep. 19, 1652; AMBLER, *op. cit.*, 1, 23.

9 Ep. 405, 1685; *Works* 8, 293; AMBLER, *op. cit.*, 3, 24.

> than they have had from all other teachers of the world all their lifetime.[10]

Fox also recalls an interesting episode which took place in 1653: a Friend who, amidst the silent assembly, stood up for talking and then sat down again without having spoken a single word: "no need of words" when one sits at the feet of the master, in his vine (*John* 15).

> We came through that country into Cumberland again where we had a general meeting of many thousands of people atop a hill, near Langlands. Heavenly and glorious it was and the glory of the Lord did shine over all, and there where as many as one could well speak over, there was such a multitude. Their eyes were kept to Christ their teacher and they came to sit under their vine and afterwards a Friend in the ministry, Francis Hogwill, went amongst them, and when he was moved to stand up amongst them he saw they had no need of words for they were all sitting down under their teacher Christ Jesus; so he was moved to sit down again amongst them without speaking anything.[11]

5. The spirit teaches to each and every person, individually.

> Mark and consider in silence, in lowliness of mind, and thou wilt hear the Lord speak unto thee in thy mind.[12]

> Be still and cool in thy own mind and spirit from thy own thoughts, and then thou will feel the principle of God to turn thy mind to the Lord God, whereby thou will receive his strength and power from whence life comes, to allay all tempests, against blusters and storms [...]. Therefore be still a while from their own thoughts, searching, seeking, desires and imaginations, and be stayed in the principle of

10 *An Epistle to All People on the Earth*, 1657; *Doctrinals*, *Works* 4, 125; AMBLER, *op. cit.*, 1, 65.

11 NICKALLS, *op. cit.*, p. 168; AMBLER, *op. cit.*, 1, 66.

12 ELLWOOD (ed.), *Journal*, 1650, in *Works* 1, 1008; AMBLER, *op. cit.*, 1, 60.

God in thee, to stay thy mind upon God, up to God; and thou wilt find strength from him and find him to be a present help in time of trouble, in need, and to be a God at hand.[13]

Be still and silent from thy wisdom, wit, craft, subtlety of policy that would arise in thee, but stand single to the Lord, without any end to thyself.[14]

But you that be in your wisdom and in your own reason, you tell that silent waiting upon God is famine to you; it is a strange life to you to come to be silent, you must come into a new world. Now you must die in the silence, die from the wisdom, die from the knowledge, die from the reason, and die from the understanding.[15]

So every spirit comes to have a particular satisfaction and quietness in his own mind, and here the weary come to have rest in Christ [...]. Such shall find mercy of God when their minds are quieted in silent waiting upon God. In one hour they have more peace and satisfaction than they have had from all other teachers of the world all their lifetime.[16]

Much more might I write concerning these things but they are hard to be uttered, or to be borne; for there has so much strife and foolishness entered the minds of people, and a want of stillness and quietness in the pure spirit of God, in which things are revealed that have been veiled; in which things are opened that have been hid, and uncovered that have been covered.[17]

13 *Letter to Lady Claypole*, 1658: NICKALLS, *op. cit.*, p. 346 ff.; AMBLER, *op. cit.*, 1, 61.

14 *Letter to Oliver Cromwell*, 1655: NICKALLS, *op. cit.*, p. 194; AMBLER, *op. cit.*, 1, 62.

15 *An Epistle to All People on the Earth*, 1657; *Doctrinals*, *Works*, 4, 132; AMBLER, *op. cit.*, 1, 63.

16 *An Epistle to All People on the Earth*, 1657; *Doctrinals*, *Works*, 4, 125; AMBLER, *op. cit.*, 1, 65.

17 Ep. 313, 1674; *Works*, 8, 72 ff.; AMBLER, *op. cit.*, 1, 67.

6. There remain two important issues to be dealt with. The first concerns those who cannot be reached by the preaching, "the real light which enlightens every man" (*John* 1, 9). I here recall the reasoning, dated around 1675, of R. Barclay in his *Apology* (p. 181):

> How many have been wounded due to Adam's fall, without ever knowing he existed in the world, and that he ate the forbidden fruit? Why can't they be saved from the gift and grace of Christ within them, which renders them just and saint, even if they ignore that all this comes to them from the death and sufferings of Jesus who was crucified in Jerusalem, especially considering the fact that God has simply made this knowledge impossible for them to acquire? As many people can be killed by some poison placed in their food – even though they don't know which kind of poison it is and who put it – similarly, on the other hand, many people can be cured of their illnesses without knowing how the medicine was prepared, its ingredients, and often even without knowing who brought it.

According to this same author, the historical knowledge of Christ is useful but not essential: what counts above all is the "mystery", which can be manifested even without "history" (p. 141):

> The history then is profitable and comfortable with the mystery, and never without it; but the mystery is and may be profitable without the explicit and outward knowledge of the history.[18]

Many pagan philosophers somehow perceived the presence of an original fault or sin, even though the biblical story was not known to them (p. 141):

> Many of the heathen philosophers were sensible of the loss received by Adam, though they knew not the outward history.

[18] The Latin version runs as follows: *Historia igitur prodest, et consulabunda est, cum mysterio conjuncta, sed non sine illo; et mysterium est, et prodesse potest sine esplicita et externa cognitione historiae* (p. 86).

As for instance Plato, when he talked about the cave ("man's soul had fallen into a dark cave, where it only conversed with shadows", *Rep.* VII), or Pythagoras, who spoke about man as wandering in the world as a stranger, banned from God's presence ("man wandereth in this world as a stranger, banished from the presence of God"), or Plotinus, who spoke of the human soul as a sort of ash or extinguished fire. Moreover, observes Barclay, some say that the wings of the soul were cut (p. 188). Seneca mentions a "sacred spirit, which treats us as we treat him" (*Ep.* 41). Cicero, in his *De re publica* quoted by Lactantius (*Inst.* 6), speaks of an "innate light". Even Plotinus speaks of this light, which he calls "Wisdom" (*Pr.* 1, 20-33; 8, 9-34). Focilides declared that the best word is that which comes out of divine wisdom, and Justin spoke of Socrates as being a Christian. Statements along these lines can also be found in Clement of Alexandria (*Apol.* 2, and *Strom.* I) and Augustine (*De civitate Dei*, XVIII, 47).[19]

7. The second issue concerns a well-known objection: don't we in this way unduly confuse the natural light of conscience with the divine one? Thus, for instance, argues the puritan Richard Baxter in *The Quakers' Catechism*, of 1655. To this, Fox will always answer by reading *John*'s *Prologue*, from which context it can be shown that the light which illumines all men is "divine and spiritual".

It should be added that Barclay does not uphold the automatism of salvation: for each and all there is always a specific, unique *kairos*. God offers to all men "a time when He visits them":

> God ... hath given to every man, whether Jew or Gentile, Turk or Scytian, Indian or Barbarian, of whatsoever nation, country or place,

[19] See Lodovico Vives who, in this regard, quotes *John* 1, 9. With reference to the study of Platonic texts, see also Augustine (*Conf.* I, 9) as well as the Arab Ibn Tufayl and his work *Hayy ben Yaqdhân* (XXVII), recently translated with the title *Philosophus autodidactus*.

a certain day or time of visitation; during which day or time it is possible for them to be saved.[20]

[20] Cf. the Latin version: [*Quod*] *Deus certum diem et visitationis tempus dederit, quo die et tempore possibile est illis servari, et beneficii Christi mortis participes fieri* (p. 79).

MASTER AND DISCIPLE IN THE ISLAMIC SUFI TRADITION IN THE WRITINGS OF ᶜABD AL-QĀDIR AL-JĪLĀNĪ

ANGELO SCARABEL

There are two very good reasons to take into account the writings of ᶜAbd al-Qādir al-Jīlānī (1077-1166) as a guide to the understanding of the relationship between master and disciple in Sufism. The first one is the Sufi tradition itself, which recognizes him as the founder of the first organized *ṭarīqa*.[1] ᶜAbd al-Qādir is the most popular saint among Muslims, the exemplary miracle-maker, the intercessor between the faithful and the Lord, the helper in the troubles

[1] G. MAKDISI, *Ibn ᶜAqīl et la resurgence de l'Islam traditionaliste au Xᵉ siècle (Vᵉ siècle de l'Hégire)*, Damas 1963, p. 383; J. S. TRIMINGHAM, *The Sufi Orders in Islam*, Oxford University Press, 1973, pp. 32, 37-42, denies this antecedence, ascribing the birth of the Qādiriyyah to a later period and thus attributing this antecedence to the Rifaᶜiyyah, a *ṭarīqa* that always rivalled the Qādiriyyah or has often been described as such (see, e.g., L. MASSIGNON, "La dernière querelle entre *Rifâᶜyîn* et *Qâdiryîn*", *Revue du Monde Musulman* 6 (1908): 454-461; cf. also *Revue du Monde Musulman* 7 (1909): 316-317). A. SCHIMMEL, *Mystical Dimensions of Islam*, Chapel Hill, 1996, pp. 244-249, seems to place the Suhrawardiyyah first, and then discusses the issue of the birth of the Qādiriyyah; the Rifaᶜiyyah comes third.

INDOASIATICA 2/2004, [91-103]

of life, and hope in the depths of despair: his *ṭarīqa* is perhaps the most widespread one in the Muslim world.

The second good reason concerns the issue of ʿAbd al-Qādir al-Jīlānī's belonging to Sufism and his connection to the *ṭarīqa* with which the Islamic tradition links him.[2] The *Kitāb ġunya ṭālibi ṭarīq al-ḥaqq* is the work of ʿAbd al-Qādir on whose authorship nobody has cast doubt so far.[3] We can take its pages concerning the master-disciple relationship as proof of his Sufi identity as well as an authoritative presentation, written by a figure that the Islamic traditions recognize as a representative of Sufism at its highest level of spirituality.[4] I might also add that this is a work of great doctrinal significance. As we will see, if the texts usually ascribed to ʿAbd al-Qādir al-Jīlānī are very far from the doctrinal treatises of Tirmiḏī Ḥakīm (d.

2 The whole issue is analyzed by A. DEMEERSEMAN, *Nouveau regard sur la voie spirituelle d' ʿAbd al-Qādir al-Jīlānī et sa tradition*, Paris 1988.

3 Two other books, the *Futūḥ al-ġayb* and the *Fatḥ al-rabbānī,* are the saint's sermons collected on his order – or on his behalf – respectively by: 1) a son of his, *šayḫ* ʿAbd ar-Razzāq (d. 1207) – see the beginning of the Arabic text, in margin to ŠAṬṬANAWFĪ's *Bahja al-asrār* ..., Cairo 1330 h., p. 2 (for other sons proposed by some scholars, see DEMEERSEMAN, *op. cit*., pp. 10-11) – and, 2) ʿAfīf, to be likely identified with ʿAfīf b. al-Mubārak al-Jīlī (cited by ŠAṬṬANAWFĪ, pp. 94 and 115). J. CHABBI, "ʿAbd al-Ḳâdir al-Djîlânî personnage historique. Quelques éléments de biographie", *Studia Islamica* 38 (1973): 75-106, acknowledges only the authenticity of the *Kitāb Ġunya* and the *Futūḥ al-ġayb*: "*L'autenticité de ce dernier recueil ... ne paraît pas faire de doute, puisque* Ibn Taymiyya *lui même en a fait un commentaire*" (p. 103). What I find difficult to understand is how come the fact that Ibn Taymiyya wrote a commentary on this work of ʿAbd al-Qādir is a good reason to accept it as authentic, whereas the fact that Ibn Taymiyya says that this same ʿAbd al-Qādir was a Sufi is not: see J. R. MICHOT, *Musique et danse selon Ibn Taymiyya*, Paris 1991, pp. 72, 96, 121. There are many doubts on the authenticity of the *Fatḥ al-rabbānī,* even though J.-CL. VADET, "L'inspiration du Shaykh al-Jīlānī dans le *Fath al-Rabbânī*", *Revue d'Études Islamiques* 51 (1983): 51-62, seems to think it is a work of ʿAbd al-Qādir.

4 See A. SCARABEL, "Considerazioni su *silsila* e genealogia in ʿAbd al-Qādir al-Jīlānī", *Rivista degli Studi Orientali* 51 (1977): 83-84.

905/10),[5] Ibn ᶜArabī (d. 1240),[6] or ᶜAbd al-Karīm al-Jīlī (d. 1408 >),[7] and are hardly estimated to go beyond the juridical treatises or the collections of Friday noon service's sermons, there are nonetheless many passages in his work which disclose at first glance unsuspected doctrinal dimensions. Moreover, these passages shed light on whether or not ᶜAbd al-Qādir al-Jīlānī was a Sufi and the founder of a *ṭarīqa*.[8]

ᶜAbd al-Qādir al-Jīlānī's *Kitāb ġunya li-ṭālib ṭarīq al-Ḥaqq* ("*The Book of Riches for the Seeker on the Path to Truth*"), is a treatise on religious law which includes in its last section a *Kitāb ādāb al-murīdīn*, dealing with the rules, manners, and customs of the people of the Path, i.e. the Sufis and their disciples. It is precisely in the second chapter of this section, "*On What is First of All Necessary for the Beginner on this Path*" that the figures of master and disciple and the rules of their mutual relationship are discussed.[9]

The Arabic word for "*path*" is *ṭarīqa*, a technical term meaning the Sufi path. Here, with the demonstrative *hāḏihi 'ṭ-ṭarīqa*, "*this path*", it refers to the path of ᶜAbd al-Qādir al-Jīlānī. Just a little brick in the wall of the Sufi tradition, which has the saint of Baghdad

5 Two works of his have been recently translated into English by B. RATDKE & J. O'KANE, *The Concept of Sainthood in Early Islamic Mysticism*, Richmond 1996.

6 On his work, see O. YAHYA, *Histoire et classification de l'oeuvre d'Ibn ᶜArabī*, Damas 1964.

7 On him, see the article by H. RITTER in the *Encyclopaedia of Islam*, CD-Rom Edition 2000 (I: 70 b).

8 Deserving note are the passages concerning the Qādiriyyah in three works on Sufism: TRIMINGHAM, *The Sufi Orders in Islam, op. cit.*, pp. 40-44; SCHIMMEL, *Mystical Dimensions of Islam, op. cit.*, pp. 246-248; TH. ZARCONE, "La Qâdiriyya" in A. POPOVIC & G. VEINSTEIN (eds.), *Les Voies d'Allah*, Paris 1996, pp. 460-467.

9 *Bāb fī mā yajbu ᶜalā 'l-mubtadiʾfī hadihi 'ṭ-ṭarīqa awwal*[an], pp. 163-169, in the Cairo 1375/1956[3] edition.

as the founder of the Qādiriyyah.[10] But I will come back to this point later on.

Šayḫ ᶜAbd al-Qādir, or, as he is more commonly known in the non-Arabic Muslim world, *Hazrat* ᶜAbdul Qādir, exhorts all seekers along the path to conform themselves to the tradition of the Prophets and Envoys, Companions and Followers, Saints and Sincere ones.[11] He then stresses the need to find a spiritual master, whose characteristics are defined by a number of terms.[12]

The first one, *hidāya*, is an infinitive and a substantive at the same time; here it is employed as an infinitive: the root means "*to direct somebody*" and then "*to direct somebody aright*".[13] *Iršād* is also an infinitive, with the meaning of "*making or causing somebody to follow a right way or direction*" i.e. the right path in this case.[14] Ibn Manẓūr[15] establishes an identity of meaning between the two terms. None of them is quranic as such, though *hidāya* is usually identified with *hudā*, a quranic infinitive derived from the same root with the same meaning.[16]

Iršād too has a strong quranic tie through the active participle of the same form, *muršid,* usually synonymous with spiritual master, which is an 'ἅπαξ λεγόμενον in an interesting passage of the *Quran* relative to the sleepers in the cave:

10 Of course, it is possible to suppose an interpolation of the text. However, this has not been demonstrated so far.

11 These latter ones are those who strictly adhere to truth; see E. W. LANE, *Arabic-English Lexicon*, Cambridge 1984, 2.1668. The *ṣiddīqūn* are referred to by ᶜAbd al-Qādir al-Jīlānī as a category of saints placed between the *awliyāʾ* and the *substitutes* (*abdāl*); see A. SCARABEL, "Remarques sur le Fatḥ al-baṣāʾir de ᶜAbd al-Qādir al-Jīlānī", *Journal of the History of Sufism* 1-2, 2000, Special Issue, *The Qādiriyyah Order*, p. 10.

12 *Ġunya* 2,163.

13 LANE, *op. cit.*, 2.3042.

14 *Ibid.*, 1.1089.

15 IBN MANẒŪR, *Lisān al-ᶜArab*, Beirut, n. d., 3, 175.

16 *Ibid.*, 15, 354.

> And you will see the sun departing from their cave, to the right when it is rising, and [you will see it] coming to their left when it is setting ā. That is one of the signs of God. And whomever God guides is the rightly guided, and whomever He misleads, you shall not find any guide (*muršid*) for him.[17]

Dalīl is derived from a root meaning "*to direct, to guide*", or "*to cause to follow the right way*".[18] The person imbued with the characters of a guide at a very high degree is called a *dalīl*. It is a quranic term, also found as an 'άπαξ λεγόμενον in *Quran* 25, 45, where God says He established the sun as a pointer to the shade, in order to separate day from night.

A master is also a *qāʾid*. *Qāʾid* is an active participle which indicates the leader who leads his flock marching in front of them, and thus opening the road, or even pushing them on from behind.[19] This suggests the image of the perfect master, who at the same time stands *in front* of the disciples on account of his own enlightened experience and *behind them* on account of his care and love for them. The term is not quranic.

The spiritual master is then defined a *muʾannis*, "*a tamer*": this is an active participle of the causative verbal form derived from the same root as *ins*, "*humanity*", and *insān*, "*man, human being*". *Muʾannis* is the master who transforms his disciple from the status of wild beast, prey to all the instincts and whims of the individual soul, to the status of a man. What this means becomes clearer when we learn that *muʾannis* is a synonym of *mubṣir*, "*he who makes people see*", "*he who allows perception and knowledge*"[20] of the true nature of man and of his relationship to the Lord.

Finally, the spiritual master is said to be a *mustarāḥ*. As a substantive the term may be translated as "*place of rest*", and this is the meaning it has in the following passage:

17 *Quran* 18, 17.
18 LANE, *op. cit.*, 1.900-901.
19 See IBN MANẒŪR's *Lisān al-ʿArab*, *op. cit.*, 3, 370.
20 *Ibid.*, 6,16.

> A place of rest in which to take rest when he [= the disciple] is exhausted and pained, in darkness amidst the whirling of passions and pleasures and the negative characters of his soul.[21]

Moreover, *mustarāḥ* is also a passive participle of a verb which means "*to take rest*" as well as "*to trust*", which explains what this passage really means.

Thus the disciple is called to find a master whom he must trust under all circumstances, even when he may go against one's own certainties, one's own points of view.

From this understanding of the spiritual master derives the first rule with which the chapter on the disciple's behaviour towards his master begins:[22] it's a rule which has the scent of experience, along with a deep knowledge of Sufi doctrines which goes far beyond the limits of a mere compiler. Though various sources and scholars have depicted ᶜAbd al-Qādir al-Jīlānī mainly as a famous preacher and a skilled jurist, he was certainly also a spiritually inclined person. [23]

What the disciple must absolutely avoid is to dissent with his master outwardly (*tarak muḫālafa šayḫihi fī 'ẓ-ẓāhir*) as well as criticize him inwardly (*tarak al-iᶜtirāḍ ᶜalayhi fī'l-bāṭin*). Even if there is a remote possibility that the disciple did in fact witness a mistake committed by his master,[24] he must avoid all judgements since he doesn't possess the means for recognizing the truth. Indeed, what his senses and mind tell him could be false: the disciple, being incapable of any correct evaluation of what is taking place, would therefore be led astray. To be able to know what is right and what is wrong, the disciple should share in his master's spiritual attainment, which of course is not the case. It is common wisdom that no disciple or subordinate can correctly judge a master or superior since he doesn't be-

21 *Ġunya* 2,163: *wa mustarāḥ^{an} yastarīḥa ilayhi fī ḥāla iᶜyāʾihi wa naṣabihi wa ẓulmatihi ᶜinda ṯawrān šahwātihi wa laḏḏātihi wa hanāt nafsihi.*

22 *Ġunya* 2,164-165.

23 *Vide supra*, notes 2-4.

24 The Arabic text is much more cautious: *wa iḏā ẓuhira lahu min aš-šayḫ mā yakrahu fī'š-šarᶜ ... fa-in lam yajid lahu ᶜuḏr^{an}.*

long to the latter's 'horizon': thus, it is impossible for any disciple to understand a master's behaviour.[25] The horizon of the disciple is said to be limited to the world of phenomena in which he lives and which is the dominion of materiality as well as of the Law, since this one applies to the gross bodies and the natural world. The horizon of the master is clearly and necessarily beyond these limitations.

It is just what ᶜAbd al-Qādir al-Jīlānī stresses in the following lines, when he explains the reasons of the apparent infringements of the Law by the spiritual master: what the disciple witnessed was an unmindful condition (*ġafla*), a temporal accident (*ḥadaṯ*), a by-product of the interval between two states[26] during the master's spiritual journey. This interval is called by ᶜAbd al-Qādir "*a coming back to the indulgences of the Law*": it's a very interesting definition, which accords with the nickname of *ᶜulamāʾ ar-rusum*, "*doctors of the traces*" [of the real world], which almost all Sufi writers use for the Doctors of the Law. Our material world is indeed the world of indulgences. Thus, its rules cannot be but relative, especially in comparison with the superior world of the *aḥwāl*, the "*states*": as such, all rules *are* in fact indulgences, since they meet the human weaknesses and failings, upon which the mercy of the Lord spreads out its wings.[27] But the world which the master inhabits is the *ᶜazīma*, lit. "*determination*", which this passage of the *Ġunya* clearly sets against that of indulgences,[28] and the meaning of which acquires a nuance of rigor.

25 This epistemological principle is clearly established by M. AL-GHAZALI. See D. B. BURRELL & N. DAHER (trans.), *The Ninety-nine Beautiful Names of God*, Cambridge, The Islamic Texts Society, 1992, pp. 36-44.

26 *Faṣl bayna al-ḥalayn*; on *ḥāl* and *maqām*, see JUNAYD, *Enseignement spirituel*. Par Roger Deladrière, Paris, Sindbad, 1983, pp. 191-196.

27 On the principle of *ruḫṣa*, "*indulgence*" in Muslim Law, see the article written by R. PETERS in the *Encyclopaedia of Islam*, CD-Rom Edition 2000 (VIII: 505 b).

28 There is also a kind of indulgence (*ruḫṣa*) in the world of the *ṭarīqa*, an indulgence which is, of course, of the same nature as the indulgence of the world of the *šarīᶜa*, but at a very different level.

The Arab term for "*coming back*" is *rujūᶜ*, which means "*coming back to the point of departure*"[29] i.e. "*coming down*" to a world the master has left behind and which he no more regards as his abode: to him, it is just an interval between two states - *dārayn*, "*two abodes*" says ᶜAbd al-Qādir - of which the next one is higher and nobler (*aᶜlā wa ašraf*) than the previous one was, every new abode (= state) being closer to God. During an interval, the master is full of regret for the abode he has left, and full of greed and expectation for the next one. His mood is the one described by this verse of Abū Bakr Šiblī (d. 945):

> I forgot my prayer today on account of my love, and I cannot tell my nightfall-meal from my breakfast.[30]

The term Šiblī employs for "*love*" in this verse is *ᶜišq*. Abū'l-Ḥasan Nūrī (d. 907)[31] remarks that *ᶜišq* means a kind of love which is different from *maḥabba*. The former is the love which has not yet attained its goal, and is still on the way, the latter is the love of the nearness (*qurb*) to the Beloved.[32]

It is because the master belongs to the world of *ᶜazīma*, the world of realities that are far beyond the disciple's horizon, that this latter one cannot but perceive the lower, material reality of carelessness (= *ġafla*). Beyond this, there is said to be another reality, with far more comprehensive values and rules. In order to penetrate into this higher world, the disciple needs a master who will be able to guide him

29 LANE, *op. cit.*, 1.1038.

30 *nasītu 'l-yawma min ᶜišqī* • *fa-lā adrī ᶜašā'ī min ġadā'ī*. Abū Bakr Šiblī too is among the saints frequently quoted by ᶜAbd al-Qādir al-Jīlānī; see DEMEERSEMAN, *Nouveau regard, op. cit.*, p. 16: The verse is quoted from ᶜABD AL-WAHHĀB AŠ-ŠAᶜRĀNĪ, *aṭ-Ṭabāqāt al-kubrā*, Cairo 1373/1954, 1, 104.

31 Also styled Abū'l-Ḥusayn; he was a friend of al-Junayd. See SCHIMMEL, *Mystical Dimensions of Islam, op. cit.*, pp. 59-62.

32 See P. NWYIA, *Exégèse coranique et langage mystique. Nouvel essai sur le lexique technique des mystiques musulmans*, Beyrouth 1970, pp. 317-320. "*Excess of love*" is the definition of the *Lisān al-ᶜArab* (10, 251).

therein: just as any would-be courtier needs the help of a relative or favourite of the king in order to learn the rules and behaviour his status requires, as ᶜAbd al-Qādir observes.[33]

The master-disciple relationship is profoundly ingrained in the very nature of human beings: there's no exception, ᶜAbd al-Qādir stresses, because this is precisely the custom (*ᶜāda*) God established on earth: that there should be a master and a disciple (*šayḫ wa murīd*), a protector and a protected (*ṣāḥib wa maṣḥūb*), a follower and a followed (*tābiᶜ wa matbūᶜ*) from Adam's time till the Last Day.[34] Adam was the first one: the first master as well as the first disciple.

Adam became the first master when God taught him the names of all creatures, and ordered him to teach them to the Angels, as is stated in the *Quran* (2, 31-33). ᶜAbd al-Qādir partially quotes these verses inserting them in a kind of report, which might be viewed as a short commentary: Adam is placed in front of God just as a schoolboy in front of his teacher or a disciple in front of his master. He learns *all* the names of *all* the creatures of God: not only the names of the heavens, of the animals and plants, but also of all things created by man (such as bowls and the like):[35] this reflects the uniqueness of creation and its Creator. Indeed, for al-Ġazālī (d. 1111), in whom the theological tradition of al-Ašᶜarī and Sufi doctrines converge, "*inventor*" and "*creator*" are attributes that can be ascribed to man only metaphorically (*mujāz^{an}*).[36]

33 *Ġunya* 2,165.

34 *Ibidem*.

35 *qaṣᶜa wa quṣayᶜa*: *Ġunya* 2, 165. To be compared with MUḤ. AṬ-ṬARAFĪ's *Qiṣaṣ al-anbiyāʾ*: see R. TOTTOLI (trans.), *Storie dei Profeti*, Genova 1997, p. 35. In the *Sunna* I have found no hint of any symbolic meaning of the word (which is not quranic).

36 This is the translation proposed by BURRELL & DAHER, *The Ninety-nine Beautiful Names of God, op. cit.*, p. 72. For the Arabic text, see F. A. SHEHADI (ed.), *Maqṣad al-asnāʾ*, Beyrut 1971, p. 84. The term, which is a passive participle, was usually employed to designate a disciple who had obtained an *ijāza* i.e. a document certifying his competence in a specific field of science or in an art (*ṣināᶜa*).

Then God ordered Adam to teach these names to the Angels,[37] which he did, and so became the first master among creatures, and the Angels the first disciples, and – as ᶜAbd al-Qādir tells us – Adam disclosed his superiority (*faḍl*) before them.

In his Sufi commentary to these verses, Al-Qušayrī (d. 1074) states that what God gave to Adam was the knowledge of the names of creatures – the name of every thing He created – and, at the same time, the knowledge of the names of His Reality (*asmāʾ al-Ḥaqq subḥānaHu*).[38] The order to teach them to the Angels was the answer to the objection they raised when God announced His decision to establish a vicar on earth,[39] which marks the beginning of human history. This showed to the Angels the superiority of Adam (*rujḥānuhu ᶜalayhim*), and paved the way for the subsequent order God gave them, that is, to prostrate themselves before His new creature and vicar.[40]

The superiority of Adam over the Angels is not a superiority of nature. In fact, all human beings were created out of clad or mud.[41] This is a base material, even if it is described as the best of clad.[42] Humans have sprung up from the earth, whereas Angels are made of light, being the purest manifestation of fire:[43] this is the reason for the rebellion of Iblīs, who refused to prostrate before Adam as his Lord had ordered him to do. Al-Qušayrī writes that Iblīs' crime lies in his

37 *Quran* 2, 33.

38 ᶜABD AL-KARĪM AL-QUŠAYRĪ, *Tafsīr al-Qušayrī, al-musammā bi Laṭāʾif al-išārāt*, Beyrut 1420/2000, 1, 35.

39 *Quran* 2, 30: *Innī jāᶜil fī 'l-arḍi ḫalīfan*.

40 *Quran* 2, 34.

41 "*Clad*" (*ṭīn*) in *Quran* 6, 2; 7, 12; 17, 61; 23, 12 (*sulāla min ṭīn*); 32, 7; 37, 11; 38, 71-76. "*Mud*" (*ḥamaʾ masnūn*; see LANE 2.1711) in *Quran* 15, 26-27 and 33 (in which Iblīs speaks): the term is associated with *ṣalṣāl*, "*dry clay*" or "*clay mixed with sand*".

42 On this understanding of *sulāla min ṭīn* - *Quran* 23, 12 - see A. SCARABEL, "Il sangue e la tradizione islamica" in A. AMADI (ed.), *Mysterium sanguinis. Il sangue nel pensiero delle civiltà dell'Oriente e dell'Occidente*, Venezia 2000, pp. 32-33.

43 On the theory of the elements, see *ibid.* and the bibliography therein.

fallacious use of analogical reasoning (*qiyās*): he wished to constrain the Lord and His will (*qismah*) within the limits of the world of creatures and its rules.[44] What makes Adam superior to the Angels is clearly explained in the *Quran*:

> [The] Lord said to the Angels: "I'm going to create a human from dry clay, from black mud, and when I have shaped him well and blown into him My spirit, come and prostrate before him".[45]

The *qismah* or God's blowing His spirit into Adam counterbalanced the inferiority of man's nature. Whether this unnatural albeit deep rooted superiority is peculiar to Adam as a Prophet or is a common heritage of humanity as a whole is not explicitly stated in this passage of the *Ġunya*. Nonetheless, we can say that it is the whole humanity which partakes in this superiority, even though under certain conditions. Undoubtedly, ᶜAbd al-Qādir al-Jīlānī sides with the Sufi masters who recognize the superiority of the Prophets over the Angels.[46] But we also see that in ᶜAbd al-Qādir's text Adam is understood as the paradigm, the *locus imitationis*, for *both* the master and the disciple. Every human being has the faculty of acquiring *ᶜilm*, which is the "*knot*" of his/her superiority,[47] the consequence of the spirit of God being blown into him/her. This faculty, however, can only be activated through a strenuous training under the guidance of a spiritual master. The one who acquires this superiority is the saint: he has attained Adam's pristine condition.

44 ᶜABD AL-KARĪM AL-QUŠAYRĪ, *Tafsīr*, *op. cit.*, 1, 325. On the issue of the admissibility of *qiyās*, see I. ZILIO-GRANDI, *Il Corano e il male*, Torino 2002, pp. 79-85.

45 *Quran* 15, 28-29.

46 On the historical development of this issue in Sufism, see ᶜA. AL-HUJWIRĪ *Kašf al-maḥjūb fī arbāb al-qulūb* (in the French translation by Dj. MORTAZAVI, *Somme spirituelle*, Paris 1988, pp. 280-283) and A. B. KALĀBĀDHĪ *Kitāb at-taᶜrruf li-madhab ahl at-taṣawwuf*, Cairo 1380/1960, pp. 50-51. See also P. URIZZI, *Il Sufismo,* Palermo 2002, pp. 123-124.

47 See A. SCARABEL, "Il sangue tra fisiologia e simbolo" in G. CANOVA (ed.), *Scienza e Islam. Quaderni di Studi Arabi.* Studi e Testi n. 3 (1999): 23-24.

And this is what ᶜAbd al-Qādir seems to allude to when he goes on to say that when Adam was thrown onto earth his status was changed,[48] and he felt lost and afraid. He felt hunger, thirst, heat and pain, and was unable to deal with his new situation: he needed a guide. This guide was the archangel Gabriel, the first of his disciples when Adam was the master in the Garden. Gabriel instructed him in sowing, reaping, winnowing, grinding, cooking and eating, and then taught him how he should utilize his body's basic functions.

ᶜAbd al-Qādir stresses this fundamental point i.e. that the master of old has become a disciple, and that the disciple of old has become a master.[49] On earth, Adam seems to have lost his knowledge. Here, the only nature he shares is the human, earthly nature, which is lower than the enlightened one of the Angels.

After the training Adam became a master of his son Šīṯ, who in turn became the master of his sons. These latter ones were masters of their own sons, and so was Ibrāhīm to Yaᶜqūb, Mūsā to Hārūn, ᶜĪsā to his disciples,[50] and so on up to the present time. The Angel was the means through which God fulfilled His promise to help the offspring of Adam with the Revelation sent to the Prophets. This Revelation includes the law as well as the knowledge of all names, which proves the superiority of Adam – the perfect human being – over the Angels. ᶜAbd al-Qādir refers to this knowledge and its transmission precisely through the master-disciple relationship, when he points out that every Prophet has his own disciples, and cites the Apostles (*ḥawāriyīn*) in the case of ᶜĪsā, and the four Caliphs, the Companions, the saints (*awliyā*) and the *abdāl* in the case of Muḥammad.[51] Here we find a clear indication of the knowledge possessed by a

48 What happened to him is explained in *Ġunya* 2, 165 (*intiqāl fī ḥāla uḫrā wa manzil ġayrihi*).

49 *Ġunya* 2, 165: *Fa-ṣāra Ādam ᶜalayhi's-salām tilmīḏ li-Jibrīl, wa Jibrīl ᶜalayhi's-salām ustāḏahu wa šayḫahu, baᶜda an kāna Ādam šayḫahu ... wa aᶜlamahum kullu ḏalika li-taġyīr al-ḥāl bihi wa al-intiqāl min manzil ilā aḫir.*

50 *Ġunya* 2, 165-166: *ḥawāriyīn*, "*companions*" i.e. disciples as well as apostles.

51 *Ġunya* 2, 166. On the *abdāl*, see D. GRIL, "Doctrine et croyance" in POPOVIC & VEINSTEIN, *Les Voies d'Allah*, *op. cit.*, p. 135.

spiritual master, and in a context which leaves no room for any kind of transmission of such knowledge outside a master-disciple relationship.

These passages of the *Ġunya* reveal a profound, experienced understanding of Sufi doctrine, as well as of the practical issues involved in the relationship between the spiritual master and his disciples. All this brings me to postulate a direct involvement of its author in the Sufi teachings and ortho-praxis.

ENCOUNTERS WITH KHIḌR: SAINT-IMMORTAL, PROTECTOR FROM THE WATERS, AND GUIDE OF THE ELECTED ONES BEYOND THE CONFLUENCE OF THE TWO OCEANS

THOMAS DÄHNHARDT

Among the many extraordinary characters we encounter in the vast universe of the Islāmic world, the enigmatic figure of Khiḍr (as he is known in Turkish and Persian sources as well as in the indigenous traditions of the Indian subcontinent) or al-Khaḍir (in the Arab world), both terms meaning "the green one", holds a pivotal position due to his multiple functions as protector of mankind at large and spiritual guide of the intellectual elite. His importance in the traditional perspective is reflected on one side in the manifold forms of popular devotion that live on in numerous cults, festivals, and sanctuaries dedicated to Khiḍr all over the Near East and Middle East and, on the other, in his frequent appearance in the esoteric traditions perpetuated by the great Sufi authorities within the context of the orthodox *ṭuruq* (pl. of *ṭarīqa*).

Perhaps the element most commonly associated with Khiḍr, who is known for his extreme mutability and transient features, is water in its manifold aspects. On a popular level, we find a myriad of local and regional cults and customs, which bear witness to this mythical figure's association with the sea, rivers, lakes, and fluvial estuaries, as well as with islands, rocks, reefs, and atolls emerging from the waters of the ocean. We know, for instance, that it was a long-established custom among the inhabitants of Baghdad struck with illness to dip small oil-lamps fixed on date-palm wood into the current of the river Tigris at sunset, accompanied by a prayer to al-Khaḍir that he may free them from their disease. In the Indian subcontinent, Khwāja Khiḍr is venerated as a fluvial deity and benign spirit by both Hindus and Muslims, acting also as a custodian of wells, springs, and other places bearing a relation with water. The fishermen of coastal Bengal pay homage to him before embarking on their daily journeys into the vast open space of the Indian Ocean, many of their boats bearing the name of the revered saint and protector. In the great fluvial plains of Northern India, the ancient custom still survives of honouring Khiḍr on the day of the "festival of the raft" (*beṛā*) celebrated in the course of the month of Bhadon, which falls in the midst of the Indian monsoons. On such occasion, people leave thousands of small rafts and other kinds of craft illuminated by oil lamps to the current of the river Ganges, so as to ensure a safe passage to the other shore. Inshā Allāh Khān 'Inshā' (d. 1233/1818), the celebrated poet at the court of the Nawabs of Lucknow, mentions in his verses the annual boat-festival held along the banks of the river Gumti, in honour of Khwāja Khiḍr.

The main sanctuary (*dargāh*) dedicated to the 'green man' in mainland India is found on a small island along the river Indus, in the proximity of the old fortress of Bhakkar, identified with the ancient settlement of Sogdi which is said to have been established by Alexander the Great during his campaigns in the Sind region of what is now southern Pakistan. Here, both Hindus and Muslims used to pay their respects to the saintly patron of the waters, before the compound was almost entirely washed away by the floods of the mighty river in the early 1990's. Elsewhere, on the southern island of Sri Lanka, associated by the Arabs since time immemorial with paradise, we find an important sacred complex dedicated to al-Khiḍr, mentioned by the famous North African traveller Ibn Battuta in the fourteenth century. Situated on the slopes of Mount Sarandib (nowadays popularly known as "Adam's Peak"), where according to a widely diffused myth Adam first set his foot on earth the day of his departure from the celestial garden of Eden, the sanctuary spreads around a large rock formation associated with the appearance of Khiḍr to a shaikh of the Qadiri order during a nocturnal vision (*ru'ya*).

Among other sacred places in the Islāmic world which are linked to Khiḍr's cult, it is worth mentioning the town of Samandağ located at the mouth of the river Orontes on the coasts of the eastern Mediterranean sea, at the border between Anatolia and Syria. Ritual sites and places built to the memory of the mysterious 'green man' can be found in several locations in this tiny town. The most important among these is situated on the local beach, consisting of a recently rebuilt sanctuary which incorporates a rock formation bearing a clear phallic resemblance. According to local tradition, the site corresponds to the location of Moses' encounter with al-Khaḍir, a belief that draws the pious crowds of pilgrims to perform a reverent triple circumambulation in anti-clockwise direction (*ṭawāf*) around this sacred place.

But what do we really know about the identity of this mysterious figure venerated by many Muslims as the saint of waters, protector of fishermen, patron of sailors and seafarers, and supreme guardian of confluences?

According to the canons of orthodox esoteric science, al-Khaḍir is one of the ancient saint-prophets mentioned in the Holy Qur'ān, along with Idris (Enoch), Ilyās (Elias), and 'Isā (Jesus), who are considered "immortal" (*khālid*) and "long-lived" (*mu'ammar*). Free in their essential function from the limitative conditions of time and space that characterise God's creatures, including humans, the mission entrusted to these special individuals by Allāh - who in the cosmological doctrines represent the four cornerstones, *awtād*,[1] of the interior edifice of the Islāmic *Dīn* - extends over the entire human

1 More precisely, in the context of ancient Arabia's predominantly nomadic population, this term refers to the wooden 'tent pegs' used to fix the tent to the ground at its four corners.

cycle up until the day of resurrection (*yawm al-qiyāmat*).[2] Their essentially spiritual nature does not, however, prevent them from playing a role in the world's destiny also in historical terms, in a way similar to the first and last in the chain of prophets, Adam and Muḥammad. Thus, they assume now and then the shape of human beings so as to directly intervene at the appropriate time in the dominion of mankind (*insāniyat*). As a matter of fact, numerous traditions mention the name of al-Khiḍr in a genealogical line of descent derived from (or even identifying the 'green man' with) the prophet Noah, the lord of the ark, who crossed the waters of the universal deluge with the blessings of the Almighty. These traditions confer on Khiḍr both a historical and human dimension, emphasizing his tangible, concrete function albeit somewhat remote in time.

Among the various legends concerning al-Khiḍr that have been passed down over many generations in the regions of the *dār al-Islām* from ancient times, one of the best known narrates the story of how he attained immortality after quenching his thirst at the source of eternal life (in Arabic: *'ain al-khuld* or *'ain al-hayawān*; in Persian: *chashma-yi āb-i ḥayāt*).[3] The variants of this story in Arabic and

2 Although not explicitly named in the Holy Text, al-Khaḍir appears frequently in association with Ilyās or Elias (*Koran* XXXVII, 123-132), the prophet of the desert mentioned in the Old Testament (*Book of Kings* I, 17-22; II, 1-2) whose twofold nature, heavenly and earthly, is attested to by his ascent to heaven in a chariot of fire or a horse of fire. Here, one should note the complementary symbolism of water and fire represented respectively by Khiḍr and Elias, especially with regard to posthumous destiny.

3 According to another popular version of the story, Khiḍr attained immortality following a promise made by Allāh to concede this special boon to those among His creatures who would bury the corpse of His first servant Adam; see ABŪ HĀTIM AL-SIJISTĀNĪ, *Kitāb al-mu'ammarīn* (I. GOLDZIHER, ed., 1982). Here, we detect obvious similarities with the ancient Syrian-Aramaic myth of Melchizedek, an incarnation of celestial priesthood mentioned in the book of *Genesis* (XIV, 18-20). The story goes that Noah ordered his son Shem to follow Melchizedek on the way leading to the centre of the world, Mount Golgotha, to bury Adam's corpse. Once the task had been successfully accomplished, God raised Melchizedek to the rank of high priest and perpetual guardian of that sacred place. We can see how these versions in a way complement each other,

Persian sources[4] show evident similarities with the ancient Greek, Hebrew, and Syrian versions of the epic cycle which developed around the ancient world sovereign, Alexander (Ar./Pers.: Iskandar). These tales inform us that Khiḍr (or, alternatively, in pre-Islāmic versions of the story, the cook of Alexander) reached the fountain of eternal life at the vanguard of an expedition organised by King Dhū'l-Qarnain. This 'two-horned' sovereign is mentioned in the same chapter of the Holy Qur'ān which tells the story of the mysterious Khiḍr, Dhū'l-Qarnain being identified by many Muslims with Alexander the Great himself! Apparently, Khiḍr recognised the fountain's miraculous properties after witnessing a pickled fish turning back to life through contact with it.

Although Khiḍr is nowhere explicitly mentioned with his name in the Holy Qur'ān, he can nevertheless be identified on the basis of the numerous hints made by prophet Muḥammad (*aḥādīth*, pl. of *ḥadīth*) to the mysterious figure mentioned in the *Chapter of the Cavern* (*Sūrat al-kahf*, *Koran* XVIII, 60-82). Among other important events, this chapter tells the episode of Khiḍr who appears as the authoritative guide of the prophet Moses. Moses entrusts himself to him so as to receive from Khiḍr the knowledge of crossing the "straight path" (*rushd*).[5] In a way, this tale constitutes the prototype of the innumer-

making explicit the real meaning of the fountain of immortality by using the symbolism of the centre of the world, from where it is possible to have access to the superior worlds located on the celestial plane.

4 See IBN BĀBOYE, *Kamāl al-Dīn wa tamām al-n'ima*, Teheran, 1958; 'ABD AL-MALIK AT-TA'ĀLIBĪ, *Ghurār akhbār mulūk al-Fars*, Paris, 1963; ILYĀS b. YŪSUF NIẒĀMĪ, *Sikandar-nāma, Qiṣṣat al-Iskandar*. For a detailed study of many of these legends of both the pre-Islāmic and Iṣlāmic period, see I. FRIEDLANDER, *Die Chadirlegende und der Alexanderroman: eine sagengeschichtliche und literaturhistorische Untersuchung*, Berlin-Leipzig, 1923.

5 According to a tradition of the Prophet reported by al-Bukhārī in his *Ṣaḥīḥ*, the recital on a Friday of this particular *sūra* – which also narrates the story of the Sleepers in the cave (XVIII, 1-31) and of the enigmatic sovereign Dhū'l-Qarnain including details about his building a dam to withhold the hordes of Yā'jūj and Mā'jūj (Gog and Magog; XVIII, 82-98) – bears the capacity of pro-

able encounters with Khiḍr which are documented in the course of the centuries both in the exoteric and esoteric tradition. But in order to get a better understanding of the story told in the Holy Qur'ān, we must put it in context by turning our attention to the teachings imparted by the prophet of Islām outside of the Qur'ānic revelation. In other words, we must turn to the *aḥādīth,* some of which comment upon the tale told in the *Chapter of the Cavern* thus providing a frame to the story. In his collection of prophetic traditions (*al-Ṣaḥīḥ*), al-Bukhārī (d. 356/870) reports a *ḥadīth* according to which Muḥammad narrated that one day, when Moses was preaching to the people of Israel, a man appeared to him and asked: "Do thou know anybody whose knowledge by far excels the degree of your own [knowledge]?" To which Moses, overconfident about his own wisdom, replied firmly: "Indeed not!" God then revealed Himself to His prophet and said to him: "Well then, there is a servant of Ours, called Khaḍir, who possesses a knowledge yet unknown to you!" And when Moses enquired with His Lord about the possibility of meeting this unknown holder of a superior wisdom, Allāh gave him a fish in token of His guidance accompanied by the warning: "Follow the way [indicated by this fish]! But proceed carefully and stop at the place where thou will have lost [it] from your sight! From there, retrace your steps immediately [till you will reach the rock] ... there thou shall meet him [= al-Khaḍir]!"[6]

tecting the faithful (*mu'minīn*) from the evil influences of the activities of al-Dajjāl, the anti-Christ, who will appear at the time of final dissolution at the end of the present human cycle.

6 Al-Bukhārī: *Ṣaḥīḥ, kitāb al-'ilm, bāb* 16, 19, 44; *kitāb al-anbiyā', bāb* 27; *kitāb tafsīr al-Qur'ān*. See also: Muslim: *Fadhā'il*, 17-74; al-Tirmidhī: *bāb* 1. It should be noted that other traditions expressly mention that the fountain of immortality gushes out from a rock identified with the "confluence of the two oceans" (*majma' al-baḥrain*) which, in turn, is said to be the same rock where Moses and his companion stopped to rest on their journey to meet the mysterious wise man mentioned by Allāh. Moreover, the story goes that after coming in contact with a few drops of water gushing out from that fountain, the fish given to Moses as his guide disappears into the ocean: see *Ṣaḥīḥ al-Bukhārī, kitāb al-tafsīr al-Qur'ān, bāb fa-lammā jāwazī qāla li-fatūhu.*

Based upon these premises, the episode of Moses and Khaḍir continues with the explicit intention of Moses to undertake a long and difficult journey, in the company of his faithful servant, with the aim of reaching the "confluence of the two oceans" (*majma' al-baḥrain*) in order to attain the highest degree of wisdom. In this undertaking, the two wayfarers are guided by the fish, agile agent of the divine will, which leads Moses and his companion along the [initiatory] path until they eventually reach a rock - demarcating the place where the two oceans meet - where their fish guide suddenly disappears, diving into the deep waters of the ocean (*saraban*). After a moment of initial distraction following their night rest - during which the two travellers direct their steps beyond that place - they come back to the rock in search of the fish and ultimately meet "one of the humble servants of Allāh" (*'abdan min 'ibādinā*), to whom "God had conceded His mercy" (*raḥmata min 'indinā*) and to whom He had taught a "science sprung from His intimate presence" (*wa 'allamnāhu min ladunnā 'ilman*). Looking back to the story of pre-Islāmic origins, there appears a striking similarity between the journey covered by Khiḍr himself and the one followed by Moses as revealed by the prophet Muḥammad in the Holy Book, as if the leader into the promised land was to follow in the footsteps of his archetypical predecessor.

In short, the Qur'ānic episode ends as follows: Moses requests Khiḍr to accept him as his follower so as to receive from him the instructions regarding the "secret science" (*'ilm al-ladunnī*). Moses solemnly promises to remain patient and obedient at the side of his mysterious guide. Khiḍr, though well aware of Moses' ultimate inability to stick to his pledge due to his limited comprehension and insight, nonetheless accepts to lead him along the journey through the stations of the divine mysteries. Moses must never question the actions and deeds of his guide. However, after three enigmatic and apparently nonsensical and cruel acts performed by Khiḍr - the hidden sense of which baffles Moses, inducing him to openly criticise his companion - their common journey comes to an end: Moses having failed to fulfil his initial promise, Khiḍr bids him farewell not without revealing the hidden sense of his actions to the remorseful prophet (verses 78-82).

From the descriptions given in verse 65 of the Qur'ānic chapter, it becomes clear that the main characteristics that distinguish Khiḍr in his guiding role are those of being endowed with two special qualities conceded to him in virtue of his intimate relationship with Allāh, that is, mercy (*al-raḥma*) and knowledge, which he received from the "intimate presence of Allāh" (*'ilm al-ladunnī*). And it is precisely because of this latter aspect related to divine knowledge that the figure of Khiḍr, beginning with the episode told in the *Chapter of the Cave*, will assume fundamental importance in the esoteric tradition of *taṣawwuf* or Sufism, since knowledge constitutes the prime modality for the realization of the divine mysteries pertaining to the invisible world (*'ālam al-ghaib*). On the other hand, it is important to underline that, from an Islāmic point of view, this aspect is intimately linked with and, in a sense, issues from divine mercy (*raḥmat Ilāhī*), for it is through His mercy that the Most Exalted Allāh offers mankind - the crown among His creatures (*taj al-makhlūqāt*) - the possibility to take part in His Omniscience (*al-'Alīm*). For this purpose, He sends His envoys in the shape of messengers (*rusul*), prophets (*anbiyā'*), and intimate friends (*awliyā'*) into whom He infuses His own mercy. Therefore, in virtue of their intrinsic quality these exalted ones act as living examples of the magnitude and almightiness of Allāh for all world creatures.

We learn from the Qur'ānic exegete al-Qushairī (d. 465/1074) that to all creatures who are especially close (*qurb*) to their Lord i.e. saints and intimate friends, Allāh concedes to take part in His intimate science, for the sake of all creatures. According to the explanatory comments made by al-Qushairī, this science can be obtained through direct divine inspiration (*ilhām*), without the need of any effort or activity on the part of the chosen individual. Nor can this sort of wisdom be contested to those who truly possess it, since the knowledge resulting from this inspiration is of an extremely subtle nature and, therefore, essentially beyond the need for any proof.[7]

Another famous exegete, Fakhr al-Dīn al-Rāzī (d. 606/1209), commenting upon verse 18:65, adds the following: "The expression 'from my intimate presence' (*min ladunnī*) indicates that the knowledge possessed by Khiḍr has been transmitted to him directly by Allāh. It cannot possibly be learned or acknowledged if not through intuitive revelation (*mukāshafa*) - hence the venerated shaikhs of *taṣawwuf* call it the 'ladunic science' (*'ilm al-ladunnī*)."[8]

And the renowned shaikh and scholar Abū Ḥamīd al-Ghazālī (d. 506/1111) points out in his treatise *Al-risāla al-ladunniya* - which, as the title suggests, is entirely devoted to the divinely revealed science - that the knowledge possessed by humans can be of two kinds: one can be acquired through the means of instruction by another fellow human being, the other one must be imparted through direct divine instruction. In its turn, this latter one can be further distinguished into two different types of science or, rather, transmitted knowledge: *waḥy*, that is, knowledge acquired through infallible divine revelation, an exclusive prerogative of Allāh's prophets and messengers and no longer possible since the prophets' epoch has been brought to conclusion by Muḥammad's mission (*khatimat al-nubuwwa*); and *ilhām*, that is, celestial intuition, a special characteristic of the "intimate friends of Allāh" (*awliyā' Allāh*), which refers to that "hidden science" (*al-'ilm al-ghaibī*) of which Khiḍr is the natural custodian. This secret science is understood to flow from its source in the realm of the Transcendent directly into the heart of the *walī*, without any need of intermediaries (*bi lā wāsiṭa*) or of sheikhs belonging to initiatory lineages (*silsila*).

From these descriptions the intimate relationship subsisting between Khiḍr and the concept of *ilhām* appears evident. It is in this role of transmitter of a science of an extremely sublime nature that Khiḍr transcends the attributes of his historical and human condition

7 *Laṭā 'if al-ishārat*, Cairo, Basyuni, pp. 78-84.
8 *Al-tafsīr al-kabīr* XXI:149.

(on which subject some exegetes among the *ahl al-ẓāhir*, such as the historian al-Ṭabarī, have so extensively commented upon), thus assuming the dimension of a super-human, universal archetype, of an essentially spiritual nature. Khiḍr presents himself as the mediator between the divine realm and the human world, in a way similar to the angels. In special moments in the history of mankind, through Khiḍr's intervention, one or more individuals said to have been chosen by Providence to receive a certain kind of instruction will become the receptacles of Its mercy. These persons are believed to receive a most secret knowledge, pertaining to the intimate nature of the Most Sublime Principle. Thus, he who receives initiation and instruction from Khiḍr will himself be introduced into the transcendent order (*tasbīḥa*) which lies beyond time and space, allowing him to dominate over the immanent realm (*tanzīha*).

In this function as the spiritual agent of divinity, Khiḍr can play a double role: he appears as a 'spontaneous guide' conferring the type of initiation known as '*uwaysī* (which takes its name from the Yemenite saint 'Uways al-Qaranī, d. 18/639, reputedly an intimate companion of the prophet Muḥammad and an ardent follower of his message without ever meeting him physically), which is characterised by a sudden irruption, similar to a 'lightning out of blue sky', into the life of an individual. Such individual is thought to be chosen by divine Providence so as to snatch him from his ordinary condition and offer him a special teaching: this spiritual doctrine is always thought to be adapted depending on the different periods in the history of mankind. This type of spiritual rapture is known as *jadhba* and those saints who benefit from it are known as *majdhūb*.[9]

Alternatively and by far the most commonly encountered case in Sufi literature, Khiḍr appears in the role of the "most sublime teacher" or "master of masters" (*shaikh al-shuyūkh*). Those to whom he appears in an extraordinary vision (*ru'ya*) must regard his com-

9 This being the true, superior meaning of the term. More frequently, it is used in common parlance to designate those people apparently afflicted with mental disorders, the so-called 'mad-men'.

pany as a great privilege, sign of outstanding qualification and spiritual rank which, as al-Ghazālī explains, remains an exclusive prerogative of "those who possess the heart" (*arbāb al-qalb*). The sublime degree of esoteric realization attained to by these most sincere ones, leads them to "feel with purity of heart" and to "see with the eyes of the heart". It is said that Khiḍr blows the subtle knowledge of Allāh's intimate science into the "ears of the heart" of these extraordinary individuals, once they have accomplished the degree of spiritual perfection corresponding to what is known in Sufi circles as the stage of "major sainthood" (*wilāyat al-kubrā*). In these cases, Khiḍr acts as a substitute of the regular, outer shaikh and takes up the role of interior master, waiting for the initiate at the 'isthmus' of the heart to conduct him along the journey through the inner spaces of the Self (*sair al-anfusī*).

The Sufi authorities who have largely contributed to the teachings of the esoteric science (*'ilm al-bāṭin*) perpetuated until today within the *khānaqahs* all over the Muslim world, provide us with several examples of encounters with the 'green man', during which he appears to have poured streams of divine wisdom into the calyx of men's purified hearts. There are many examples of authoritative shaikhs in both orthodox and heterodox Sufi orders who claim to have received precise instructions regarding the metaphysical doctrine, the science of cosmology, and the modalities and methods of the initiatory path from Khiḍr himself. Here, it shall be sufficient to mention the elaborate metaphysical teachings of Shaikh al-Akbar Ibn al-'Arabī (d. 638/1240), synthesized in the doctrine known as *waḥdat al-wujūd* ("oneness of existence"), which from its formulation between the twelfth and thirteenth centuries CE continues to represent the basis of spiritual education in the entire Muslim world. The great master affirms that this doctrine is the outcome of his repeated meetings with the inner guide al-Khaḍir. Shaikh Aḥmad Sirhindī (d. 1034/1624), the renowned leader of the *Naqshbandiyya* order in India, largely owes the title of "Renovator of the Second Millennium of Islām" (*mujaddid alf-i thānī*) because of his vision culminating in the doctrine known as *waḥdat al-shuhūd*, based on the wisdom which he acquired thanks to his 'meetings' with Khiḍr. Yet another celebrated example is that of the Persian shaikh and poet Maulānā Jalāl al-Dīn Rūmī (d. 672/1273), who recognised in his spiritual guide Shams al-Tabrīzī the "Khiḍr of his time" (*Khiḍr-i zamān*), thereby developing the concept of the lover and the beloved of Khiḍr whose heart is inflamed by the heat of his passionate desire to meet him (*'ishq*): an image which has inspired generations of "searchers for Truth" (*murīdīn bar Ḥaqq*) in an effort to describe their spiritual longings, their wish to passionately 'dive' themselves into the sea of Khiḍr.

It is said of Khwāja 'Abd al-Khāliq al-Gujdawānī (d. 575/1220), one of the chief authorities of the *ṭarīqa-yi khwājagān* later known as *Naqshbandiyya*, that he received the instructions regarding the silent *dhikr* (*dhikr-i khafī*) - a technique peculiar to this *ṭarīqa* - as well as the eight principles upon which the order's spiritual path rests, from Khiḍr himself who taught him to recite the *dhikr* with the tongue of his heart, while remaining immersed under water for ever longer periods of time.[10]

But let us return to the symbolism of water, which so frequently accompanies the presence of our enigmatic guide, be it in the shape of the "fountain of immortality" (*chashma-i āb-i ḥayāt*) which appears in the tales relative to the Alexandrine cycle, be it in the image of the "confluence of the two oceans" (*majma' al-baḥrain*) as in the episode told in the *Sūrat al-kahf*. Besides its generative power (is it not water that turns a barren desert into a green field?), water seems to bear an intimate relation with the symbolism of the polar axis representing the ascending and descending planes of universal existence. According to a tradition of the prophet transmitted through the authority of Ka'b al-Aḥbar, Khiḍr is said to have once expressed the desire to be immersed into the waters of the ocean of existence tied to a rope, so as to explore the secrets of its deepest abysses. After a journey which lasted several days and nights, he eventually met an angel who informed him of the futility of his undertaking. However, on the insistence of Khiḍr, the angel agreed to teach him the secrets

10 See, for instance, 'Abd al-Raḥman Jāmī's *Nafaḥāt al-uns* and 'Alī ibn al-Ḥusain al-Kashīfī's *Rashahāt-i 'ain al-ḥayāt*.

which lie hidden in the ocean's depth. Khiḍr thus learned that the entire world rests upon the back of a giant fish (once again!), the 'breath' of which causes regular water tides. Similarly, the seven insular continents of the world (*ṭabaqāt al-sab'a*) are said to rest on a single rock which, in turn, leans on the palm of the hand of an angel who firmly stands upon that very fish.[11] According to another tradition going back to Ka'b al-Aḥbar, Khiḍr is said to have appeared behind a radiating pulpit situated between the inferior and superior oceans, from where he instructed all creatures of the sea gathered around him.[12]

Apart from the episode of the above-mentioned encounter between Moses and Khiḍr, there are numerous other passages in the Holy Book that quite explicitly mention these two oceans. Verse 12 of chapter 35 (the *Sūra of the Originator of Creation*) tells us that "the two seas are not alike; one is palatable, sweet, and pleasant to drink, the other one is salty and bitter to the tongue." Another verse (XXV:53, the *Sūra of the Criterion*) specifies: "It is He Who has let free the two bodies of flowing water: one palatable and sweet, and the other salty and bitter; yet He has made a barrier between them, a partition that is not to be passed."

This barrier mentioned in the Qur'ānic verse, called *barzakh*, constitutes a fundamental tenet of Islāmic cosmology. It marks the boundary between the two oceans of cosmic existence, representing from an esoteric point of view a barrier between two dominions of different nature (sweet and salty). At the same time, however, the

11 From Ibn Abī Dunyā's *al-'Uqubāt*, pp. 205 ff. It should be noticed that among the Muslims of the Indian subcontinent one commonly encounters the image of Khiḍr riding on the crest of a fish. The fish symbolism was adopted by the Shi'a rulers of Awadh in their dynastic insignia: it can still be seen on numerous buildings in the cities of Faizabad and Lucknow, as well as on the coins that were in circulation during their reign (1722-1856). Hence, the possible association with the *matsya-avatāra* of the Hindū god Viṣṇu, who pulls the ark with the seeds of this world through the great ocean of universal deluge onto the shores of a new cycle of existence.

12 From Ibn Hajar al-'Asqalānī: *Zahr* 29.

barrier is also understood as a juncture or meeting point and hence, in a way, a sort of passage - narrow though it may be - from one domain to the other. In Sufi terminology, these two oceans together represents the macrocosm (*'ālam al-kabīr*), which is divided into two parts, an inferior and a superior one. The inferior part corresponds to the "world of creation" (*'ālam al-khalq*), pertaining to the formal dominion in which live all creatures inhabiting the world as we know it. The superior part, referred to as the "world of order" (*'ālam al-amr*), includes all the informal potentialities of the spiritual dominion: herein, we find the "world of spirits" (*'ālam al-arwāḥ*) and the "world of celestial archetypes" (*'ālam al-mithāl*), known only to Allāh the Most Exalted One and to a select few of His intimate friends. This latter dominion corresponds to the celestial waters, of a sweet and agreeable quality from which all future generations will be born. For this reason, it is also known as the "radiant world" (*'ālam al-nūr*). It stands in stark contrast to the former dominion, characterised by the sterility of its salty waters populated by beings who are imprisoned in the cage of their bodily sheaths which can either be of a gross nature, as that of common creatures, or of a subtle nature as that of angels.

The point of contact which links and, at the same time, separates these two universal dominions consists of that very *barzakh* that certainly appears insurmountable to the ignorant ones whose uncultivated soul is dominated by lower, egotistic instincts. However, it is accessible to those who have progressed significantly in the purification of their hearts, to the extent of turning them into an immaculate mirror capable of reflecting the radiance of the celestial abode. It is believed that once the initiate has reached this stage of the esoteric path (*sulūk*) corresponding to the full realization of "major sainthood" (*wilāyat al-kubrā*), the external teacher (*shaikh* or *murshid*) is substituted by the interior master, the luminous *pīr* of supra-human nature to be identified with Khiḍr. He is the guide of the elected ones among the initiates, he conducts them through the heavenly abodes. These abodes are like a chain or series of islands in the celestial sea of the worlds to come. To use an image which is common among the authorities of the *Naqshbandiyya*, and which reflects a microcosmic perspective, this is a journey through the intimate essence of the spiritual seeds contained in the subtle centres (*laṭā'if*, pl. of *laṭīfa*) sown by divine Providence into the sacred abode of the human heart (*maqām-i sīna*).

To conclude this brief presentation concerning some aspects of the multi-faceted, fascinating figure of al-Khiḍr, I would like to quote a vision of this mysterious master-guide as described in the renowned work by 'Abd al-Karīm al-Jīlī (d. 832/1428), titled *Al-insān al-kāmil* ("The Perfect Man"). Herein, Khiḍr himself informs us about his function. According to the author, this passage - which is part of an elaborate commentary on the cosmological theories exposed by the *Shaikh al-Akbar* Ibn al-'Arabī (d.1240 CE) in his Meccan revelations (*Fuūḥāt al-Makkiya*) - is itself the outcome of an encounter with al-Khiḍr, proving the role played by this extraordinary character. In the description given by al-Jīlī, Khiḍr appears as the ruler of a marvellous region called Yūh, situated somewhere in the farthest north of the world. At its centre there is a city described as being whiter than milk, where the air is sweeter than musk, the alleys of which are covered with a dust whiter than flour and above which there extends a firmament that glows in a shade of emerald green. This is the residence of the "hidden men" (*rijāl al-ghaib*), among whom Khiḍr bears the highest rank. Questioned by the wandering spirit of an intimate friend of Allāh concerning his real nature, Khiḍr agrees to unveil the secrets of his identity:

> I am the sublime reality (*al-ḥaqīqa al-'āliya*) and the subtlety that descends [from the heights of the heavens to the earth], I am the intimate mystery of the *wujūdī* man, I am the fountainhead of all esoteric wisdom, I am the path of the interior realities and the abyss of the dominion of the subtle, I am the shaikh qualified by the nature of the divine (*lāhūtī*), I am the guardian of the world of mankind (*ḥafiḍ al-'ālam al-nasūtī*). I can assume every possible shape in the interior spaces of human beings, I can appear in every place at every time, I can change my appearance so as to appear in every possible shape. My dominion is the "world of the interior realities" (*al-bāṭin*), marvellous and mysterious, my abode is the mountain Qāf ... I am the radiant full moon, I am the supreme guardian of the confluence of

the two oceans, I am he who plunges himself into the sea of omnipresence, I am He who draws from the fountain of all fountains, I am the guide of the fish in the sea of divine presence. I am the goal of those who have chosen to follow the path of inner research, I am the dot of the first and the last ... only a perfect man can discern my features and only the unified spirit (*al-rūḥ al-wāṣil*) is capable of reaching me, to him alone I will concede access to my abode ... since he alone is the possessor of the knowledge of the Almighty Allāh.[13]

13 *Al-insān al-kāmil* II, 42-46.

THE *GURU* AND DEATH[1]

GIAN GIUSEPPE FILIPPI

It is very unusual for a disciple, a *śiṣya*, to have a definite awareness regarding the function and role of the *guru*. In fact, the first impulse which leads a young human being to a spiritual master is the desire for a new, secret knowledge, reserved to an elite. The background of this quest, apart from any sincere aspiration for deeper knowledge, is generally an egotistical drive, led by pride in one's own mental and intellectual capacities. Thus, we read:

1 Initiation, *dīkṣā*, either in the *śrauta* or in yogic traditions, is always understood as a radical and irreversible transformation of the inner essence of the disciple. In some texts, it has been declared as a third birth for the human being. The *upanayana*, on the contrary, defined in all Hindū texts as a second birth, marks the entrance of the child into his own caste. A confusion between these two rites has sometimes been generated within circles of historians of religions, with odd consequences. Indeed, in ancient times the *dīkṣā* was celebrated immediately after the *upanayana*, mostly in the families of *śrauta brāhmaṇa*-s, and this may have determined the above-mentioned misunderstanding. On these issues, see R. B. PANDEY, *Hindu Samskaras*, Delhi, Motilal Banarsidass, 1976, pp. 111-133; G. G. FILIPPI, *Mṛtyu: The Concept of Death in Indian Traditions*, New Delhi, DK Printworld, 1996, pp. 70-76.

> When Śvetaketu was twelve years old he went to a master. Being twenty-four, with the knowledge of all the *Veda*-s, he came back to the house proud of himself, haughty of his science, full of himself.[2]

It is not by chance that the present contribution starts with an episode concerning Śvetaketu: the young *brāhmaṇa* had the fortune of being the son of one of the most celebrated *guru*-s of the Vedic tradition, Uḍḍālaka Āruṇi. In a tale reported in the *Kaṭha Upaniṣad*,[3] he appears as the father – or just the *guru*? – of another boy, Naciketas. Here also Uḍḍālaka Āruṇi plays an enigmatic part of paramount importance. Coming back to the *Chāndogya Upaniṣad* episode, Uḍḍālaka Āruṇi questions Śvetaketu about his acquired knowledge. The pupil's answers betray his ignorance and the talk ends with the humbling of proud Śvetaketu. Śvetaketu first blames his *guru*-s for his lack of true gnosis:

> My venerable *guru*-s didn't know anything about it. Even if they knew something they didn't tell me a word.[4]

During the discussion between father and son, it is evident that Śvetaketu had gotten from his *guru*-s the full scholastic formation on the *Veda*-s. But his egotism and self-conceit obstructed his comprehension. The humbling of the young man's vanity is the instrument utilized by Uḍḍālaka so as to move him away from mere theory.

The tale of the *Chāndogya Upaniṣad* is useful in order to understand that the disciple often needs to spend a period of illusion. In such period, he is attracted by the doctrine of the *guru* as a means to become wiser and more powerful in his individuality, without imagining that this opinion is opposite to the truth. Actually, the ego is the

2 *Chāndogya Upaniṣad* VI.I.2. All English translations from the original Sanskrit as well as from Italian are mine.

3 See G. G. FILIPPI, *Dialogo di Naciketas con la Morte. Kaṭha-upaniṣad, Taittirīya-brāhmaṇa (III.11.8)*, Venezia, Cafoscarina, 2001.

4 *Chāndogya Upaniṣad* VI.I.7.

feeling of *I and mine*, in Sanskrit called *asmitā*. On it, there is the following statement:

> Ignorance, *asmitā*, attraction, repulsion and the will to live are the five obstacles.[5]

Therefore, egotism is the illusion of the individual who presumes to be one with the Supreme Self, the *ātman*. When, however, their natures have been understood and discriminated they are known as separate.[6] For this reason, the *Kaṭha Upaniṣad* declares:

> When the Supreme Good and the will to live appear in front of men, the wise man, after an effort at discrimination, distinguishes between them and chooses the Supreme Good and not the will to live; instead, the foolish one chooses the will to live with the aim of preserving and saving [his own individuality].[7]

It can be said that egotism and the desire for self-achievement constitute the basic impulse which leads most candidates to initiation, *dīkṣā*, on the quest for a *guru*. The *guru*, by accepting the candidate as disciple, draws him into a mortal trap. Actually, the path of initiation inevitably leads to the removal of individuality. The ego is thrown into the fire of dissolution as the victim of a sacrifice:

> They burn themselves with the *dīkṣā*[8] and cook themselves with the *upasad*-s [a kind of sacrifice].[9]

5 *Yoga-sūtra* II.3.

6 On this issue, see *Yoga-sūtra* II.6.

7 *Kaṭha Upaniṣad* I.II.2.

8 Concerning the term *dīkṣā*, the most satisfactory etymology is from the desiderative of Sanskrit root *dah*, "to burn"; see M. MAYRHOFER, *Kurzgefassest etymologisches Wörterbuch des Altindischen*, Heidelberg, Carl Winter-Universitätsverlag, 3 vols., 1957. See also Ch. MALAMOUD, *Cuocere il mondo*, Milano, Adelphi, 1994 (1st ed. Paris, 1989), p. 66. *Dīkṣā* as the 'burning' of the individual is thus the first step towards *nirvāṇa*.

9 *Taittirīya Saṃhitā* VII.4.9.

To all intents and purposes, initiation is a human sacrifice, a *puruṣa-medha*, the result of which is liberation of the true being from all the tinsels of individuality. *Dīkṣā* is not only the opening ritual to self-realization, but it is also the very path which ends with initiatory death. Along the way the initiated person, *dīkṣita*, realizes the direction towards which he is heading and can choose between two opposite behaviours: he can understand the significance of his own sacrifice and its absolute goal, and thus follow the instructions of his *guru*; or rather the *dīkṣita* may become afraid to loose his own individuality and slow down on the path to self-realization. As it is said in the *Bhagavad-gītā*:

> The Blessed One said:
> Evidently *yoga* is hard to attain for a man of uncontrolled ego; but it can easily be attained by him who has subdued his ego.
> Arjuna said:
> An unsuccessful striver who is endowed with faith, whose mind is distracted from *yoga*, having failed on the path of *yoga*, what goal does he attain, o Kṛṣṇa?[10]
> ...
> The Blessed One said:
> Having attained the heavenly worlds and having dwelt there for endless years, who failed on the path of *yoga* is reborn in a pure and illustrious house.[11]

Here we are not especially interested in the destiny of those who fail along the path.[12] I rather wish to emphasize how the fear of the annihilation of one's individuality is similar to the terror of dying. Indeed, such fear is the same since the removal of one's individuality coincides with death. We read:

10 *Bhagavad-gītā* VI.36-37

11 *Bhagavad-gītā* VI.41.

12 Regarding the posthumous destiny of the *yogin* who either fails or is successful along the initiatory path, see my *Post-mortem et libération d'après Shankarâchârya*, Milano, Archè, 1978.

> A man dies thrice: he dies a first time when his father emits the seed in the matrix ... he dies a second time when he is consecrated at the *dīkṣā*.[13]

Of course, the aware and doctrinally well prepared *dīkṣita* should have a different behaviour and should rather feel attraction, not fear for that death which is offered by the *guru*:

> Who knows the Impassible, Firm, Immortal, Self-subsistent, Blissful, Perfect, Good, Imperishable, Powerful Lord, such a wise man is not afraid of death.[14]

With reference to the above-mentioned concept, the initiatory death, along with the resulting process of the annihilation of individual features, is a sacrificial ritual in which the human individual plays the part of the victim and the Gods perform the sacrifice as the actual executors:

> That is to say, in ancient time the Gods offered the man as victim. After his offering, the sacrificial power got out from him and entered in the horse. Then they offered the horse. After its offering, the sacrificial power got out from it and entered in the ox. Then they offered the ox. After its offering, the sacrificial power got out from it and entered in the ram. Then they offered the ram. After its offering, the sacrificial power got out from it and entered in the billy goat. Then they offered the billy goat. After its offering, the sacrificial power got out from it and entered in the earth. They sought it and excavated the earth. They found it as rice and barley. For this reason even at the present day they gather these two [cereals] after digging. This is why

13 The third death is the one concluding one's earthly life; *Jaiminīya Brāhmaṇa* III.11.3.

14 *Atharva Veda* X.8.44.

> for the man who knows the doctrine this oblation has the same efficacy of every animal victim sacrificed in his stead.[15]

I've quoted this long passage from the *Śatapatha Brāhmaṇa* since here the analogy between the primordial sacrifice of Puruṣa performed by the Gods, as related in *Ṛg Veda* X.90,[16] and the initiatory death of a human being, *puruṣa*, emerges clearly. In the cosmic sacrifice, the divine unity was split into multiplicity. Conversely, ritual death aims at reintegrating the individual back to its original source.[17]

We must now consider another problem. Having ascertained that the *dīkṣita* is both the sacrificer and the victim, as it is stated in the *Aitareya Brāhmaṇa* - whoever performs the *dīkṣā* is the victim, *paśu*, which all the Gods sacrifice[18] - how are we to understand the Gods' function: are they the beneficiaries or the performers of the sacrifice? Another passage of the *Aitareya Brāhmaṇa* states:

> Whoever performs the *dīkṣā* becomes food offered to the Gods.[19]

There is the need to explain what the *śruti* calls Gods in this context. It is clear that we are not dealing with the *devatā*-s, the celestial inhabitants of the heavens:

> Then Bhārgava Vaidarbhi asked him: "O Venerable, how many are the *deva*-s who maintain the beings, who make them visible, and among them who is the highest?" The master replied: "The ether is

15 *Śatapatha Brāhmaṇa* I.2.3.6-7. We are here faced with the gradual substitution of the Vedic sacrificial victims, starting from the perfect, human oblation down to vegetable oblations. Possibly, this passage hints at a historical truth.

16 "When the Gods were preparing the sacrifice having Puruṣa as victim..." It is well known that in the *Brāhmaṇa*-s the figure of Puruṣa is substituted with that of Prajāpati: "The sacrificer offered himself to the Gods as Prajāpati offered himself to the Gods..."; *Śatapatha Brāhmaṇa* VIII.6.1.10.

17 "In front of him there was the abyss: afterwards one offered him a vehicle to come back"; *Ṛg Veda* X.135.6.

18 *Aitareya Brāhmaṇa* II.3.

19 *Śatapatha Brāhmaṇa* III.3.4.21.

indeed this God, and the air, the fire, the water, the earth, the speech, the *manas*, the sight and the hearing. Having manifested it, they declared: "Having supported it, we maintain that empty cane" [the body].[20]

Also Śaṅkara maintains the same principle:

We must underline that the single *prāṇa*-s [the *indriya*-s] in the body of the sacrificer become Indra and others, taking a form similar to the Gods.[21]

Now it is clear that the individual is the food of his own subtle prāṇic faculties. This is well described by the following Upaniṣadic statement:

Then they become food and there the Gods eat them.[22]

From all the previous scriptural quotes a doctrine derives, according to which the *dīkṣita*, being both the sacrificer and the victim, feeds upon himself. His self-cannibalism is a true consummation or dissolution of his own individuality, the process leading to the ego's death. This self-consummation ritually becomes the fast, which occupies a central place in the performance of the *dīkṣā*. Thus, we read:

When he begins the fast he offers himself to the Gods ... therefore he becomes an oblation to the Gods.[23]

When a man refuses to swallow food, he lives by feeding himself upon himself, consuming the alimentary supplies stored in his body. Therefore, regarding the initiate, the ritual texts say:

20 *Praśna Upaniṣad* II.1-2. This *śruti* goes on to explain that all the Gods are but differentiations of the one, vital *prāṇa*.
21 *Bṛhadāraṇyaka-upaniṣad-bhāṣya* VI.2.9.
22 *Bṛhadāraṇyaka Upaniṣad* VI.2.16.
23 *Śatapatha Brāhmaṇa* XI.1.8.4.

> The *dīkṣita* must become dry, no food has to remain in him, he must become skin and bone.[24]

By fasting to his utmost limits man reaches death, as it is stated in the well-known aphorism:

> Hunger is death.[25]

We have now gathered all the necessary elements in order to understand the details of the *śrauta* tale of Naciketas, which is an accurate description of the ritual experience of initiatory death:

> He [Naciketas] said to his father: "And me, o Father, to whom will you give me?" As [his father] did not reply, he repeated the question a second and a third time. Getting angry, his father cried out: "I will give you to Death!" Regarding this, when he was standing up after the conclusion of the sacrifice, a voice told him: "Do not forget your son, Gautama!" Then he said: "Go to the abode of Death … you will stay three nights in His abode without swallowing food".[26]

The threefold question, as I will analyse later, hints at the three days spent in the realm of death. Naciketas' three days of fast, waiting for the arrival of death, are the mythical transposition of the ritual process of initiation, when the fasting *dīkṣita* awaits for the experience of death in life. During the initiatory rituals the *guru* is the human aid of the god of death:

> Therefore, I am the disciple of Death who requests the soul from the body [as an offering] to Yama.[27]

24 *Āpastamba Śrauta-sūtra* X.14.9.10.
25 *Śatapatha Brāhmaṇa* X.6.5.1; *Bṛhadāraṇyaka Upaniṣad* I.2.1.
26 *Taittirīya Brāhmaṇa* III.11.8.
27 *Atharva Veda* VI.133.3.

This means that the *guru* leads the disciple along the initiatory path towards ritual death, to the annihilation of his human frame. He is the sacrificer and the 'killer' of the *śiṣya*'s ego. Pleased, Yama-Mṛtyu, the personification of Death, addresses Naciketas in the following way:

> May we have other disciples such as you, o Naciketas!"[28]

In fact, the *guru* is death since he already suffered the experience of the initiatory annihilation of individuality. He has explored the path before his disciples and, for this very reason, he is entitled to be their guide towards death. Similarly, Yama was the first man to die. He explored the path towards the afterlife and was the first to discover the realm of the ancestors. This is why he became the king of the *pitṛ-loka*, the guide of the dead to his kingdom, and the god of death. Thus it is said:

> Sacrifice to King Yama, son of Vivasvān, the gatherer of men, who travelled to the deep abyss above us, finding that trail which now he shows to the multitude.
> Yama first found the route for us toward that pasture we cannot avoid. Our ancient ancestors walked on his footprint, as well as all who are born proceed along their path.[29]

He who knows this truth, follows in the steps of his *guru* with full trust, because the spiritual teacher leads him on a path which he has already tested. The disciple dies under the supervision of his master, obtaining a rebirth to immortality:

> When he who has this knowledge leaves the world, he pierces this envelope and becomes immortal because death is his *ātman*.[30]

28 *Kaṭha Upaniṣad* I.2.9.
29 *Ṛg Veda* X.14.1-2.
30 *Śatapatha Brāhmaṇa* X.5.2.23.

From this last statement of the *śruti* we derive some important consequences. First of all the *guru* is death, as I have already pointed out. In the second place, death is the very self of the *dīkṣita*, his own inner *guru*. Indeed, the human *guru* is but the empiric, exterior representative of the true master, the *sad-guru*, the *ātman* which resides in the heart of every being. The *sad-guru* is dormant in the profane, whereas in the *dīkṣita*

> he wakes up and, as from a blazing fire, the sparks flash all around; in the same way, from this *ātman* get out the faculties [the *indriya*-s], each towards its own seat. From the *prāṇa*-s get out the Gods, and from the Gods the objects [of the senses].[31]

The function of the *guru* is to transmit the *dīkṣā* to the disciple through an authoritative lineage, a *guru-paramparā*. When his *śiṣya* is spiritually ready he leads him to death, so as to bring him in touch with his inner *sad-guru*. This is the golden rule from the very beginning of time: the first men, who could not count upon human *guru*-s, gained their knowledge directly from the *sad-guru*. As it is stated in the *Yoga-sūtra*-s:

> The very Lord has been the teacher of the primordial Seers, because He is not limited by time [as human beings are].[32]

Concerning primeval times, we also read:

> In the beginning there was nothing here, indeed: all this [world] was covered by death, by hunger. Hunger indeed is death. [Mṛtyu] manifested the mind, thinking: "May I have a body!"[33]

The *sad-guru*, whose abode is in the heart of all beings, is thus the Lord of the universe and is also death. Likewise, the human *guru* i.e.

31 *Kauṣitakī Upaniṣad* IV.20.

32 *Yoga-sūtra* I.26.

33 *Bṛhadāraṇyaka Upaniṣad* I.2.1.

in our case Uḍḍālaka Āruṇi, coincides with the *sad-guru* and with death.[34]

Another consequence to be derived from the last quote from the *Śatapaṭha Brāhmaṇa* is that initiatory death leads towards immortality, to the overcoming of one's mortal condition. In other words, initiatory death is thought to be conducive to a new birth leading to immortality. The *guru* is then viewed as the spiritual mother who gives birth to his disciple:

> When the master accepts a disciple he carries him into his lap as a foetus. He bears him three nights in his womb.[35]

Three days are precisely the time spent by Naciketas in the abode of death. However, the disciple is led by his *guru* to experience a *regressus ad uterum*:

> And imposing his right hand on his head, the master becomes pregnant of him.[36]

The experience of death transforms the disciple. By dying, he becomes an embryo:

> He who becomes a disciple becomes an embryo.[37]

The coincidence of the experience of death with the transformation into a foetus has also been seen in a previous quote, when it has been noticed how the seed of the father dies when it is emitted in the matrix.[38] Analogously, from a cosmic point of view:

[34] FILIPPI, *Dialogo di Naciketas con la Morte*, *op. cit.*, pp. 38-44.

[35] *Atharva Veda* XI.5.3.

[36] *Śatapatha Brāhmaṇa* X.5.4.12.

[37] *Śatapatha Brāhmaṇa* XI.5.4.16.

[38] See footnote 13. The Kumbakonam version of the *Mahābhārata* (XI.215.7) calls the matrix *naraka-garta* i.e. an infernal grave for the embryo.

> Prajāpati is pregnant with all beings. While they were in his matrix they met their death.[39]

The seed dies to its previous condition of existence and obtains its first birth in a human body when the new-born baby is ejected from the mother's womb. His second birth will take place on the tying of a girdle of *muñja* grass, and the third at the time of initiation with the performance of a *śrauta* sacrifice.[40] The first is the biological birth, the second is the psychological birth, and the third is the spiritual birth. The second as well as the third death and rebirth bear a ritual dimension. About the third rebirth it is said:

> These who lead him to perform the *dīkṣā* are the sacrificers who transform him once again in an embryo. They sprinkle him with waters and the waters are seed. Having identified him with seed they initiate him ... They lead him into the hut of initiation; the hut of initiation is the womb for the initiate ... They cover him with a garment; the garment is the omentum of the initiate ... They put upon it a skin of black antelope; this is the placenta which covers the omentum, and they truly cover him with the placenta.[41]

The ritual achieves the new birth of the initiate:

> At last, he goes for a bath getting out from the black antelope skin.[42]

But the new birth is not just a return to ordinary life. One is now led towards immortality, that is, liberation, *mokṣa*:

39 *Śatapatha Brāhmaṇa* VIII.4.2.1.

40 See R. C. PRASAD, *The* upanayana*: The Hindu Ceremonies of the Sacred Thread*, Delhi, Motilal Banarsidass, 1997, p. 149. "In ancient times, the *upanayana* and the *dīkṣā* could be performed simultaneously. This happens even nowadays, when the boy is a *brāhmaṇa* by caste and his father is both an *ācārya* and a *guru*"; FILIPPI, *Dialogo di Naciketas con la Morte*, *op. cit.*, p. 19.

41 *Aitareya Brāhmaṇa* I.3.1-3.

42 *Aitareya Brāhmaṇa* I.3.5.

> Agni and Soma take between their jaws the one who is performing the *dīkṣā* ... the performer of *dīkṣā* becomes food for the Gods; in this way, they have taken him between their jaws ... Therefore, he gets out saying: "Hurrah, I'm freed from the noose of Varuṇa".[43]

Once Yājñavalkya, one among the most celebrated masters of the *Upaniṣad*-s, wanted to abandon his householder's life for becoming a forest-dweller, a *vāna-prasthin*. He had two wives living with him who were also his disciples:

> He said: "Maitreyī, now I will leave my present condition in the human community, so I want to make the division of my goods between you and Kātyāyanī." Maitreyī replied: "If , o my Lord, the whole earth belonged to me with all its riches would I be immortal on account of this?" Yājñavalkya answered: "Certainly not! Your life would be similar to the life of the rich people; immortality cannot be reached through wealth." Then Maitreyī said: "If it does not lead to immortality, what could I do with it?" At last Yājñavalkya replied: "You, my beloved, say words which I like very much. Then sit down, I will teach you: listen carefully to my teachings."[44]

The *guru* puts to test his or her disciple with the luring of wealth, power, and honours. The disciple who chooses these things invariably fails along the spiritual path. On the contrary, he who is willing to face death is said to become immortal. Regarding this point, when Naciketas asks supreme knowledge to his *guru*, which is Death personified, the latter replies:

> [Yama said:] "Ask for children and nephews living up to a hundred years, request numerous cattle and elephants, gold, horses and land, and may you live as long as you wish! If you are able to imagine a similar gift, request wealth and longevity, and be a great man in the world, o Naciketas! I make you capable of enjoying every delight.

43 *Śatapatha Brāhmaṇa* III.6.3.19-20. The Gods are always the individual faculties. Here Varuṇa, as all strangling deities, is a figure of death.

44 *Bṛhadāraṇyaka Upaniṣad* II.4.1-4.

> All desirable things which are difficult to reach in the world of mortals, request them as you prefer! Here you have such maidens that human beings cannot possess ... I give them to you, get their service. Naciketas, do not investigate death!"[45]

Although similar to the previous example of Yājñavalkya, here the master is clearly tempting his disciple. Mṛtyu endeavours to persuade Naciketas to abandon all interest in spiritual knowledge, and tries to corrupt him. But the qualified disciple is worthy of supreme knowledge and repels the tempter:

> Man cannot be satisfied by wealth ... The only one gift of great value is what I have requested.[46]

The transmission of the doctrine of the Absolute *brahman*, which is the content of Yama's reply to the request of Naciketas, is thus evoked in the *Chāndogya Upaniṣad*:

> Brahmā taught this doctrine to Prajāpati, Prajāpati to Manu, Manu to his progeny. The father taught *brahman* to his elder son Uḍḍālaka Āruṇi. The father teaches *brahman* to his elder son and to some qualified disciple.[47]

Uḍḍālaka Āruṇi, father and *guru* of Naciketas in the tale of the *Kaṭha Upaniṣad*, is therefore none other than the god of death himself. The *guru* is identified with Yama precisely since his task deals with the disciple's experience of initiatory death. Through the ritual, the *śiṣya* is believed to win over death, along with the whole chain of rebirths and re-deaths:

45 *Kaṭha Upaniṣad* I.1.23-25.
46 *Kaṭha Upaniṣad* I.1.26.
47 *Chāndogya Upaniṣad* III.12.4-5.

> Naciketas obtained from Mṛtyu this teaching and the integral method of *yoga*; freed from passions and death, he reached *brahman*.[48]

The victory over death guarantees freedom from transmigration:

> Who obtains It [*brahman*] wakes up here before the arrival of his own death. Otherwise, he gets ready to take up another body in the manifested worlds.[49]

The issue of overcoming death is a leitmotif in Indian thought and mythology. One is here reminded of the attributes of the great god Śiva: Mṛtyuñjaya, Yamāntaka, Kālāntaka, etc. This is a necessary stage along the way leading to self-realization, which entails the following steps: quest for a *guru* and attainment of initiation; access to the teachings and powers; vision of death; renouncing wealth as well as all powers and facing initiatory death; victory over death and attainment of immortality. Significantly, even the tale of the Buddha's enlightenment ends up with the following, solemn words:

> While Death [Māra] and his defeated army fled with their flag of flowers, the Blessed one, freed from all passions, having won over darkness, triumphed.[50]

Indeed, how could the Buddha ever attain *nirvāṇa* without Māra's temptations?[51]

48 *Kaṭha Upaniṣad* II.3.18.

49 *Ibid.*

50 Aśvaghoṣa, *Buddha-carita* XIII.72.

51 In the Hindū tradition, the temptations of Death are also expressed through the descent to the hells, as in Naciketas' tale.

THE CUSTODIANS OF TRUTH

GIOVANNI TORCINOVICH

Hinduism presents itself as a religion of tradition, in which the presence of masters as vehicles of transmission of the teachings is necessary for the acquisition of knowledge, for the achievement of both material and spiritual aims.

Already the Vedic religion, which may be regarded as the starting point and the heart of what will later be known as Hinduism, presents analogous characteristics. Vedic religion, as it has reached us, that is, in a written form, is the result of a practical and doctrinal tradition and thus of a transmission of the teachings by ancient masters, teachings which in the beginning were imparted through words and acts.

In Hinduism there is much insistence on the issue that in order to develop oneself spiritually, with the aim of achieving liberation, the teachings of a master are necessary. In the Hindū tradition the most common term, and surely the best known in the West as well, to indicate the master, the spiritual guide, is *guru*.

The term *guru*, meaning spiritual master, appears for the first time in the *Chāndogyopaniṣad* (8.15.1). According to Jan Gonda[1] the Sanskrit adjective *guru* would have the same etymology as Latin *gravis* and *gravitas* and thus in origin it meant "heavy", "ponderous", "grave", "efficacious", "powerful", "influent", etc. In time, as a noun it came to denote a "solemn, circumspect, influent, authoritative person" in the spiritual field, and, more in general, in all cultural fields in which the learning of various kinds of knowledge and techniques is of fundamental importance.

The *Mānavadharmaśāstra* (2.140-142) calls the brahman who acts as a teacher an *ācārya*, if, after having initiated the disciple, he teaches him the *Veda*-s, the sacrificial rules, and the *Upaniṣad*-s. The text calls an *upādhyāya* the brahman who teaches only a part of the *Veda*-s, or the auxiliary sciences, the *Vedāṅga*-s; whereas *guru* is the brahman who performs the rites of the ceremony of conception and who gives to the child his first nourishment of rice.

In fact, the same text makes a more general use of the term *guru* as spiritual master, as is done in other texts and in common usage as well. In particular, it designates with this same term the *ācārya* himself. Thus, the *guru* is he who teaches the *Veda*-s, the rituals, and the behaviour which the disciple must keep, depending upon his caste (see *Mānavadharmaśāstra* 2.69, 71-73, 164, 175). The *guru* is thus he who imparts the teaching of the *Veda*-s or of their essence.

Starting from conception, the future Hindū belonging to the first three castes or social categories (*varṇa*-s),[2] is the recipient, directly or through other people, of private rites, called *saṃskāra*-s, "sacraments" or "consecrations", of which one of the most important is certainly the *upanayana*, homologous to the rite of initiation into puberty which is found in various ancient civilizations.

1 See J. GONDA, *Change and Continuity in Indian Religion*, London, Mouton & Co., 1965, p. 238 ff.

2 To these three upper castes belong the priests (*brāhmaṇa*), the warriors (*kṣatriya*), and the merchants (*vaiśya*). A fourth caste or category is represented by the servants (*śūdra*).

The term *upanayana* is derived from the Sanskrit verbal root *nī* + *upa*, which means "to bring close to oneself", "to guide", and indicates the act with which the *guru* brings close to himself, receives and accepts the future disciple in order to instruct him with his first teachings. It can thus be translated as "introduction" or "initiation". The term echoes or is in any case very close to the term *upaniṣad*, meaning "secret doctrine", "esoteric teaching". *Upanayana* evokes the situation in which the disciple sits near to his master in order to receive from his very voice the secret teachings.

In the *Atharvaveda* (11.5.3) it is said that the teacher "having received" (*upanayamāna*) the disciple, transforms him into an embryo and guards him for three nights in his womb. The *Śatapatha-brāhmaṇa* (11.5.4.12) specifies that the teacher conceives at the precise moment when he places his hand on the disciple's shoulder, and that on the third day the latter is reborn in the condition of a brahman. The second birth is evidently of a spiritual kind and entails initiation through the *sāvitrī* formula, taken from the *Ṛgveda*[3] and solemnly taught by the master to his pupil.

With the *upanayana* the period of studentship began, the so-called *brahmacarya*, during which the disciple would typically live in the house of his master. This system of education, known as *guru-kula* or *ācāryakula*, was a system of global education, in which the disciple was educated in a variety of ways. Through his personal relation with the *guru*, the young disciple came to know his religious tradition, practiced the rituals, grew spiritually.

Listening to the teachings from the very mouth of the master, who at times was his father himself, constituted the first and most elementary aspect of learning, but it also resulted as the first, essential stage, since without it there could be no access to the oral tradition and to the knowledge of the Absolute, the *ātman-Brahman*, and thus to liberation.[4]

In this regard, it is useful to recall that Vedic literature is also designated with the word *śruti*, which means "that which was heard". The written form of the *śruti* is none other than the fixation of a pre-

3 *Ṛgveda* 3.62.10. It is also known as *gāyatrī*.

4 See, for instance, *Bṛhadāraṇyakopaniṣad* 2.4.5 and *Kaṭhopaniṣad* 1.2.13.

vious transmission of teachings, to which the orthodox brāhmaṇical circles tried to be faithful, not only with regard to their contents but also with regard to their form, that is, to the sound of all words and syllables, viewed as essential and through which those same contents were expressed and preserved.

The student who started studying the *Veda*-s was made to recite the first hymn of the *Atharvaveda*, in order to obtain the perfect knowledge of all sounds of the Sanskrit language. Moreover, the teacher would tie to the pupil's neck the tongues of three birds known for their ability in imitating sounds and especially the human voice. These tongues were subsequently eaten by the student, so that he might magically acquire the capacity of repeating correctly all that he had heard (*śrutam*) from his master.[5]

Together with the faithful repetition of the sacred formulas (*mantra*), an analogous care was dedicated to the correct transmission of all ritual acts. This detailed accuracy in the exact repetition of sounds/words and in the performance of all ritual acts at their proper time, etc. - which came to be almost an obsession - gave rise to fundamental works of exegesis as we may find in the *Vedāṅga*-s and the *Śulva*- and *Dharma-sūtra*-s. This same sense of fidelity and of belonging to a doctrinal and ritual tradition is at the origin of the frequent reference to the teachers and their lines of succession which we find in the *śruti*. Perhaps in all this there is also the preoccupation of giving to one's knowledge a recognition of authenticity and quality, which in the end amounts to a recognition of the genuineness of the teaching.

Thus the *śruti*, as it has reached us i.e. in written form, is the result of a long tradition of teachings of ancient masters, which were imparted for centuries directly through words and acts. In general, scholars widely accept the idea of subsequent stages and layers in the compilation of the various hymns which are found in the *śruti*. The *Ṛgveda*, the oldest of the Vedic collections (*saṃhitā*), appears to present an older nucleus, comprising *maṇḍala*-s[6] 2 through 8,

5 See Ch. ORLANDI – S. SANI (eds.), *Atharvaveda. Inni magici*, Milano, TEA, 1997 (1st ed. 1992), pp. xiv-xv.

6 Lit. "wheel". The main sections in which the *Ṛgveda* is divided up.

and a more recent collection of hymns, represented by *maṇḍala*-s 1, 9, and 10. Even the brāhmaṇical tradition admits the existence of lineages of Vedic poets, of patriarchs, who were also ancient teachers of wisdom and sacrificial rites.[7] For instance, the composition of the hymns comprised within the 2nd and the 7th *maṇḍala*-s is attributed to poets belonging to distinct families. Ancient sacrificers such as Manu, the Aṅgirasa-s, the Bhṛgu-s, and the Atharvāṇa-s are at times mentioned by the composers of Vedic hymns as their fathers or ancestors.[8] Śunaḥśepa and his story are remembered in the fifth *maṇḍala* of the *Ṛgveda* (5.2.7).[9] The poet and sacrificer Kakṣīvat, son of Dīrghatamas, is well known to the composers of hymns, some of which are found in portions of the *Ṛgveda* which are

7 C. Kunhan Raj argues that poetry, wisdom, and ritualism are the essence of Vedic religion: "Although we cannot disentangle ritualism from wisdom, yet, these are two distinct currents. Manu is most prominently connected with the institution of the system of rituals. The Aṅgirases, including Bṛhaspati who also belongs to the Aṅgiras family, are chiefly connected with the winning of light. Ritualism is connected with orderly life and wisdom is connected with the understanding of the origination and the process of the evolution of the world from the Absolute. Manu is essentially the founder of the religion and the others are the founders of the philosophy. But the philosophers were connected with ritualism and the ritualists were also poets, wise persons. We see in the *Ṛgveda* more wisdom and philosophy than ritualism. The civilisation that developed in India is the incorporation of wisdom into ritualism, the development of wisdom within a ritualistic environment, the organisation of ritualism with a high element of wisdom in it. All three are the same. There is not a single poem that is not connected with a ritualistic situation. This combination is the essence of Vedic culture; this continued throughout the ages, when the ancient thoughts remained a living force in the nation"; C. KUNHAN RAJ, *Poet-philosophers of the Ṛgveda, Vedic and Pre-Vedic*, Madras, Ganesh & Co., 1963, p. xxiii.

8 See *Ṛgveda* 1.62.2; 1.71.2; 2.33.13; 10.14.6; 10.62.2; 10.80.16.

9 To Śunaḥśepa are attributed the *Ṛgvedic* hymns 1.24 through 1.30.

judged to be quite old.[10] The son of Atharvan, Dadhyañc, is mentioned various times in the *R̥gveda.*[11]

Thus, the Vedic poets invoke Agni as in old times did the Bhr̥gu-s, the Manu-s, the Aṅgirasa-s[12] and as Aurva Bhr̥gu and Apnavāna did.[13] In the *R̥gveda* it is said that Yama was the first mortal to discover the path to the hereafter.[14] To Manu, his younger brother, is attributed the institution of religious rites.[15] It is said that Atharvan was the first to establish certain ritual foundations, and to show the path to follow through sacrifice.[16] It is also said that Aṅgiras was the one who discovered the sacrificial fire.[17] Therefore, with their statements the Vedic poets make us understand that they perceived themselves as belonging to the same religious tradition and to a shared cultural context.

To the composers of the Vedic hymns and more in general of the *śruti* as well as to the ancient patriarchs, to whom they refer to, the brāhmaṇical tradition has given the honorific title of *r̥ṣi*-s, "seers". This term possibly derives from the Sanskrit verbal root *dr̥ś*, meaning "to see", "to observe", "to perceive", etc. Yāska, who refers himself to the authority of Aupamanya, underlines that one is a *r̥ṣi* "thanks to his capacity to see" (*r̥ṣirdarśanāt*),[18] hinting with this expression to

10 *R̥gveda* 1.18.1; 1.51.13; 1.112.11; 4.26.1; 5.41.5; 8.9.10; 10.25.10; 10.61.16. To Kakṣīvat probably refer even hymns 1.112.4 and 10.40.5. An allusion to Dīrghatamas, who was a composer of Vedic hymns just like his son, is found in *R̥gveda* 4.4.13.

11 See *R̥gveda* 1.8.13; 1.8.16; 1.116.12; 1.117.22; 1.120.10; 1.139.9; 6.16.14; 9.108.4; 10.48.2.

12 *R̥gveda* 8.43.13.

13 *R̥gveda* 8.91.4.

14 *R̥gveda* 10.14.2.

15 *R̥gveda* 10.63.7; see also 1.76.5.

16 *R̥gveda* 1.83.5; 10.92.10.

17 *R̥gveda* 10.67.1.

18 YĀSKA, *Nirukta, naighaṇṭukakāṇḍam* 2.11. In this passage, in which he explains how Devāpi came to know the will of the gods, Yāska attributes to Aupamanya the expression *stomāndadarśa*, with which it is clear that he is referring to the vision of hymns and formulas of praise (*stoma*), in the deities' honour.

the vision of the Vedic *mantra*-s,[19] that is, to the hymns contained in the *saṃhitā*-s. It is clear that, in the case of these seers, what is at stake are visionary experiences of a mystical kind, an inner vision which goes beyond the mere seeing with one's physical eyes. These were mystical experiences, extraordinary spiritual attainments which only special gifted people could ever attain.[20] According to the brāhmaṇical tradition, these visions, though being reached through ascetic practices (*tapas*), are to be understood as spontaneous revelations of divine origin, or, in any case, non human.[21] For this reason, the *ṛṣi*-s are not to be considered the authors of the Vedic hymns, but rather those who 'cognised' them.

Even the *Brāhmaṇa*-s, in accordance with their sacrificial perspective, attribute to specific *ṛṣi*-s the discovery of special *mantra*-s and their use in the sacrificial context, as well as the vision of sacrifices or particular aspects and ways of performing the sacrificial rites.[22]

It is claimed that the *ṛṣi*-s saw in their hearts the transcendent reality through the 'eye of the mind', and that they gave form to their visions by composing *mantra*-s and by establishing all sacrificial acts and their appropriate rules. The outcome of their meditative experiences, the *mantra*-s, from the simplest mono-syllabic sounds up to the most elaborated hymns, were transmitted orally to their disciples, so that they may use them in their meditations and during the performance of the sacrifices, the modalities of which, known during their ecstatic experiences, were by themselves seen established.

19 *ṛṣiṇām mantradṛṣṭayo bhavanti, ibid., daivakāṇḍam*, VII. 3.

20 Concerning the process of 'seeing' and its various meanings in connection with the religious experience of the Vedic *ṛṣi*-s, see J. GONDA, *The Vision of the Vedic Poets*, New Delhi, Munshiram Manoharlal, 1984 (1st ed. 1963), pp. 25-36.

21 See YĀSKA, *Nirukta, naighaṇṭukakāṇḍam* 2.11.

22 Some examples can be found in J. E. MITCHINER, *Traditions of the Seven Ṛṣis*, Delhi, Motilal Banarsidass, 1982, pp. 177-180. The author takes into account the *Sūtra*-s as well as the *Brāhmaṇa*-s. However, I don't agree with his statement that "the role of the Ṛṣis as sacrificers is by no means to be entirely separated from their role as seers of hymns", *ibid.*, p. 177.

Thus, the *ṛṣi*-s inaugurated the recitative and sacrificial traditions which were to be preserved by their disciples and descendents.

The awareness of belonging to an unbroken tradition of wisdom, transmitted through chains of masters, appears in the *Upaniṣad*-s in all of its importance. In these texts, the *ṛṣi*-s are represented as knowers of the identity *ātman-Brahman*, the realization of which freed the individual from the cycle of rebirths. Some passages represent them as masters in the act of instructing their disciples. Other passages present the lineages of the masters through whom such extraordinary knowledge has been passed on to the following generations. These lists mention the masters' names from the latest ones to the first ones, so as to reach the original source of the teaching i.e. the god Brahmā or the *Brahman* itself. Also in this case, the revelatory nature of the wisdom transmitted by the masters is implicitly confirmed.

From what has been said above, it appears clear that already in the Vedic period there existed generations of *ṛṣi*-s, who had the aim of guaranteeing the transmission of the revealed truth and the genuineness of the teachings. The Vedic *ṛṣi*-s gave a sensible form to their inner visions and, as masters, transmitted orally to the following generations those same *mantra*-s and all other teachings which are encoded in the *śruti*.

To the ancient *ṛṣi*-s the Hindū tradition also attributes the transmission of the *smṛti*: the second, vast category of religious texts which constitutes, together with the *śruti*, the very heart of Hinduism. In the *smṛti* the awareness of belonging to different schools and lineages of masters articulates itself in a doctrine of the custody and transmission of Vedic knowledge and of the behaviour prescribed by the *śruti*, linked to the cyclical doctrine of time and to the theory of the progressive decadence of humanity, subsequent to cyclical periods of reconstituted fullness and integrity. In other respects, this doctrine also combines itself with the doctrine of transmigration and of the *avatāra* i.e. the belief in the descent of the divine on earth for the good of mankind. This latter doctrine, which is articulately dealt with in the *Purāṇa*-s, presents some discrepancies between one work and the other and even some inconsistencies or obscurities within a same text. Still, all in all it appears sufficiently clear and coherent.[23]

In what follows, I shall present some major points concerning the doctrine of the cyclical nature of time, which illustrates among other things the function which classes of *ṛṣi*-s perform as masters. It also helps to clarify what is the function of the spiritual master in general, although it doesn't exhaust all aspects covered by such concept. Moreover, it throws light on some doctrinal aspects of Hinduism, in particular of brāhmaṇical orthodoxy, which proposes itself as the expounder and interpreter of the truth contents of the *śruti*.[24] In dealing with such doctrine, I will obviously limit myself to those aspects which are especially relevant to our issue.

A *kalpa*, one day of Brahmā, is the period of time comprised between a manifestation and an annihilation of the universe. To this corresponds a night of Brahmā i.e. an equal period of latency or non-manifestation. A *kalpa* is subdivided into fourteen temporal intervals, known as *manvantara*-s, each of which lasts seventy-one *caturyuga*-s i.e. groups of four ages (*yuga*). A thousand *caturyuga*-s make up a *kalpa*. Since *kalpa*-s are infinite, even the *manvantara*-s as well as the *caturyuga*-s and the *yuga*-s are infinite. And like each *kalpa* presents structural characteristics which are identical to those of the other *kalpa*-s, in the same way each temporal group presents within itself many structural characteristics which are identical to those of the corresponding groups.[25] The same can be said for the periods of time which separate one *kalpa* from the next. Therefore, when the

23 The *Purāṇa*-s are encyclopaedic works in harmony with tradition, which gather materials of different provenance and which took centuries to assume their actual written form. Although taking care to expound correctly all doctrines and teachings, they are religious texts which do not aim towards any 'scientific' precision but rather aim at transmitting their message successfully. Therefore, they often utilize a poetic language, more easily assimilated by the minds of simple readers and of the often illiterate hearers.

24 Among its tasks, the *smṛti* has that of transmitting the truths contained in the *Veda*-s to those who cannot have access to the *Veda*-s, that is, women and all people who do not belong to the first three *varṇa*-s, adapting the teachings to their capacity of comprehension.

25 *Vāyupurāṇa* 1.58.116-122.

Purāṇa-s describe what happens in the Svāyaṃbhuva *manvantara*, the first of the fourteen *manvantara*-s which make up a *kalpa*, they also aim at describing what will happen in the following *manvantara*-s.[26] Analogous considerations can be made for the *caturyuga*-s and for each single *yuga*.

The *Purāṇa*-s, considering the various ups and downs of humanity in the course of cosmic cycles, assign to classes of *ṛṣi*-s whose personalities during a *kalpa* change with the advent of each *manvatara* or of each *dvāpara* age, the fundamental task of preserving the *dharma* and of transmitting it in a comprehensible way to all men. *Dharma* remains a fundamental tenet and reference point in Hindū society. This is thus the function of the seven seers (s*aptarṣi*), the Manu-s, and the Vedavyāsa-s.

One *caturyuga* is made up of the *yuga*-s of *kṛta* or *satya*, *tretā*, *dvāpara*, and *kali* or *tiṣya*, which, one after the other, have a decreasing temporal length. Before or after each *yuga*, there is a period of passage or conjunction, known as *saṃdhyā* if it precedes the *yuga* to which it belongs and *saṃdhyāṃśa* if it follows it. These periods of conjunction each have a length which is proportionate to the *yuga* from which they depend. To this temporal decrease corresponds a progressive physical, intellectual, and ethical-religious decline of humanity, which determines a progressive diminishing in the understanding of the Vedic teachings and a progressive distancing from the rules and regulations established in the *śruti* and in the *smṛti*, that is, a distancing from the *śrauta* and *smārta dharma*.

In the first *kṛta* age, at the beginning of a *kalpa*, there is no difference between *dharma* and *adharma*, no distinction between what is good and right and its opposite. As in all other *kṛta* ages, human beings are all equally beautiful, long-lived, free from pain, and happy.[27] They are said to obtain everything they wish for without any effort. In the *kṛta* age everything is good, natural, spontaneous, and innocent. Following the *Vāyupurāṇa*, one can say that in this age *dharma*

[26] *Vāyupurāṇa* 1.61.127; 1.61.147.
[27] *Brahmāṇḍapurāṇa* 1.2.7.43; 1.2.7.56.

is natural,[28] which means that everyone practises it naturally i.e. adopting appropriate rules of life both in general as well as according to the special position which each individual occupies within society. There is not yet a systematic classification of castes and stages of life (*āśrama*),[29] even though the differences between human beings are said to exist. These latter ones prelude to the future division in social categories or *varṇa*-s and to the codification of the rules concerning each of them, which will be formulated in the following *yuga*. The distinction among human beings is based upon the predominating qualities (*guṇa*) of their respective nature. According to the *Mārkaṇḍeyapurāṇa*, from the mouth of the creator god Brahmā emerged a thousand pairs, in whose nature the *guṇa sattva* predominated; from his eyes came out another thousand pairs, the predominant quality of which was represented by the *guṇa rajas*; from Brahmā's thighs another thousand pairs originated, characterized by a mixture of *rajas* and *tamas*; and finally, from Brahmā's feet another thousand pairs emanated, in which the *guṇa tamas* was predominant.[30]

With the *tretā yuga* and the decline of pure spontaneity the distinction between *dharma* and *adharma* emerges as well as the issue of spirituality. *Dharma*, which in the *kṛta* age rested upon four legs, now rests only upon three.[31] Even at the beginning of the *tretā yuga*, all beings perform their duties, have offspring and riches and live a happy life.[32] Humans are endowed with a fine intellect, are healthy and live in righteousness.[33] Their expected life-span is quite long, even though shorter if compared to the preceding age, and humans

28 *Vāyupurāṇa* 1.58.5.

29 *Brahmāṇḍapurāṇa* 1.2.7.55.

30 *Mārkaṇḍeyapurāṇa* 49.3-7; however, 48.29 states that mankind was created at the beginning of the *kalpa*, when the *tretā* age begins.

31 On the four phases of *dharma* deterioration and the four *yuga*-s, see *Matsyapurāṇa* 144.5-6. On the 'feet' and 'legs' of *dharma* and its progressive decay in the four *yuga*-s, see *Matsyapurāṇa* 165.1-15. See also *Bhāgavatapurāṇa* 3.11.21 and *Mānavadharmaśāstra* 1.81-82.

32 *Vāyupurāṇa* 1.57.51; *Matsyapurāṇa* 142.51.

33 *Vāyupurāṇa* 1.57.54.

die surrounded by their sons and nephews, according to the natural order of things.[34] In the *tretā* age sacrifice (*yajña*) is instituted.[35] All activities are though to be propitious, especially the rites and duties which are proper to each caste and stage of life.[36] It's precisely in the *tretā* age that Brahmā establishes the rules which regulate all castes and stages of life (*varṇāśramadharma*).[37] People live according to the rules of one's own *varṇa*.[38] The *kṣatriya*-s obey to *brāhmaṇa*-s, the *vaiśya*-s to *kṣatriya*-s, and the *śūdra*-s follow the commands of the *vaiśya*-s. All people are expected to mutually collaborate.[39] The general rules of *dharma* in life are veracity (*satya*), the repetition of sacred formulas (*japa*), asceticism (*tapas*), and charity (*dāna*).[40] Therefore, in this age the *varṇāśramadharma* becomes operative.[41] Yet, under the negative influence of time people distance themselves from it more and more, weakening it. The rules of conduct for the different castes and stages of life established by Brahmā are lost. People make discussions and quarrel. Humans commit all sorts of evil actions and thus rigid laws for guaranteeing justice are instituted and the divisions of caste are definitely sanctioned.[42]

In the *dvāpara* age, *dharma*, which now rests on two feet only, is profoundly injured. In the beginning, people are said to acquire the same perfections (*siddhi*) as in the *tretā* age, but as the *yuga* advances all good qualities and moral and spiritual attainments disappear and a series of vices and negative qualities take their place, such as craving, violence, etc.[43] More and more people divide themselves due to such confusion regarding *dharma* and what is true and right,

34 *Vāyupurāṇa* 1.57.84.

35 *Vāyupurāṇa* 1.57.61.

36 *Vāyupurāṇa* 1.57.53.

37 *Matsyapurāṇa* 142.55; *Mārkaṇḍeyapurāṇa* 49.76.

38 *Matsyapurāṇa* 142.51.

39 *Vāyupurāṇa* 1.57.52.

40 *Matsyapurāṇa* 142.58; *Vāyupurāṇa* 1.57.63.

41 *Vāyupurāṇa* 1.57.81.

42 *Vāyupurāṇa* 1.57.55-60. Concerning the administration of justice (*daṇḍanīti*), see *Vāyupurāṇa* 1.57.82.

43 *Matsyapurāṇa* 144.1-4; *Vāyupurāṇa* 1.58.2-4.

and from all this a situation of complete chaos is determined.[44] Greed grows, together with the desire to accumulate material things and to fight one against the other.[45] The *varṇa*-s inevitably get mixed and the whole system of *varṇa*-s and *āśrama*-s is ruined. Lust and enmity, desire and hatred predominate (*kāmadveṣau*).[46] Even the *śrauta* sacrifices are modified and performed in different ways.[47] Humans progressively enter into the dark age of *kali*, in which the distance from *dharma* is greatest.

In this fourth age, violence (*hiṃsā*), theft (*steya*), untruth (*anṛta*), fraud (*māyā*), arrogance (*dambha*) and many other vices and evil and unlawful behaviour come to prevail.[48] Caste rules and regulations are destroyed and the discipline of the stages of life is disrupted and in a state of confusion.[49] As in the *kṛta* age, at the end of this *kaliyuga* one sole *varṇa* is to be found, and all humans are identified as *śūdra*-s.[50] And when the *śrauta* and *smārta dharma*-s are abandoned, men fall prey to all sorts of vices and end up killing one another.[51] Sometimes the *Purāṇa*-s, in order to underline the state of desolation and perversion of the whole of humanity, even state that *dharma* in this *kali* age extinguishes itself, since men don't practise it anymore.[52] It's precisely in this cyclical drama that the seven seers, the Manu-s, and the Vedavyāsa-s unfold their specific functions.

Despite some contradictions, the texts indicate the *tretā* age as the *yuga* in which the seven seers and one Manu begin their action of promulgating and transmitting the *dharma*. They manifest themselves as genuine knowers and interpreters of truth, as masters of doctrines and techniques of spiritual realization, as the founders of doctrines and ethical and religious behaviour, which constitute the

44 *Matsyapurāṇa* 144.9.
45 *Matsyapurāṇa* 144.25.
46 *Matsyapurāṇa* 144.4; 144.26.
47 *Matsyapurāṇa* 144.15-16.
48 *Matsyapurāṇa* 144.30; 144.35-37.
49 *Vāyupurāṇa* 1.58.6.
50 *Matsyapurāṇa* 144.78.
51 *Brahmāṇḍapurāṇa* 1.2.31.95.
52 *Vāyupurāṇa* 1.58.5; *Matsyapurāṇa* 144.5-6.

foundations upon which Hinduism is grounded and will develop itself. More specifically, in the first *tretā* age of the Svāyaṃbhuva *manvantara*, the seven seers Marīci, Atri, Aṅgiras, Pulastya, Pulaha, Kratu, and Vasiṣṭha reveal the Vedic *mantra*-s i.e. the *ṛc*, *yajus*, *sāman* and *atharvan*, whereas Svāyaṃbhuva Manu reveals the *mantra*-s which make up the *smṛti* and their corresponding rites.[53] Together with Manu, the seven seers establish the *śrauta* and *smārta dharma*-s which were revealed to them by Brahmā. While they institute marriage, the *agnihotra*, and other *śrauta dharma*-s on the basis of the *ṛc*, *yajus*, and *sāman* formulas, Svāyaṃbhuva Manu indicates the conduct which each individual must keep according to the *smārta dharma*.[54]

In each of the six following *manvantara*-s other groups of seven seers and other Manu-s will perform an analogous function. With the progressive distancing from *dharma*, in the *tretā* age also progressively diminishes the understanding of the sacred scriptures. It's precisely in this age that the first doubts regarding the contents of the *śruti* and the *smṛti* arise. Due to a minor or only partial comprehension of the nature of *dharma* taught in the *śruti* and in the *smṛti*, divergent interpretations of the teachings are put forward.[55]

Besides some minor incoherence, mainly formal,[56] various Purāṇic passages state that in the *tretā* age there exists just one *Veda* which is divided up in four portions, most probably corresponding to the four different types of *mantra*-s i.e. the *ṛc*, *yajus*, *sāman* and *atharvan*. This fourfold *Veda*, after repeated modifications, in the *dvāpara* age came to be divided up in four parts or collections (*saṃhitā*-s).[57] And with the composition of the *Purāṇa*-s and of the *Mahābhārata* the *smṛti* was developed. This twofold intervention is said to be the work of a *ṛṣi* called Vedavyāsa i.e. the "Arranger of the *Veda*". His main task was that of adapting the *Veda* to men's diminished capacities of

53 *Matsyapurāṇa* 142.47; *Vāyupurāṇa* 1.57.46.

54 *Matsyapurāṇa* 142.40-43; *Vāyupurāṇa* 1.57.39-41; *Brahmāṇḍapurāṇa* 1.2.29.43-46.

55 *Matsyapurāṇa* 144.7-9.

56 *Vāyupurāṇa* 1.57.47; 1.57.83; 1.58.10; *Matsyapurāṇa* 142.47; 142.76; 144.10.

57 *Matsyapurāṇa* 144.10-11.

comprehension.[58] Moreover, he expounded once more the *smārta dharma*. In each *dvāpara* age, a different Vedavyāsa manifests on earth in order to gather and arrange the four types of Vedic *mantra*-s and to divide the one *Veda* into the four distinct portions of the present *saṃhitā*-s of the *Ṛgveda*, *Yajurveda*, *Sāmaveda*, and *Atharvaveda*. According to Purāṇic tradition, in the present Vaivasvata *manvantara* there have already existed twenty-eight Vedavyāsa-s, the last of whom has been Kṛṣṇa Dvaipāyana to whom even the composition of the *Mahābhārata* is attributed.[59] In some *Purāṇa*-s, this tradition is combined with a variant understanding of the *avatāra* doctrine. Thus, Parāśara in the *Viṣṇupurāṇa* teaches Maitreya that Viṣṇu, for the good of all creatures in the *kṛta* age, revealed the supreme knowledge in the guise of Kapila and other masters; in the *tretā* age he restrained all evil people and protected the three worlds as universal monarch; in the *dvāpara* age, as Vedavyāsa, he divided up the one *Veda* into four parts and distributed it in various sections; finally, in the *kali* age, as Kalkin, he will once again establish *dharma* and the right path.[60] Several textual passages agree in saying that Kṛṣṇa Dvaipāyana, after having apportioned the *Veda*, transmitted one of the four collections to each of his four disciples. He also gathered the ancient stories (*itihāsapurāṇa*) so as to constitute one sole *Purāṇa*, which he then taught to a fifth disciple. These five disciples are said to have passed on the received teachings to their own pupils, thus originating the vast Vedic and Purāṇic corpus as well as numerous theological orientations.[61] As a consequence, in the *dvāpara* age various Vedic schools emerged and, with them, different

58 *Viṣṇupurāṇa* 3.3.4-7.

59 *Viṣṇupurāṇa* 3.3.8-19; 3.4.1-5. The same *Purāṇa* tells us that in the next *dvāpara* age of the present *manvantara* the name of the twenty-ninth Vedavyāsa will be Drauṇi.

60 *Viṣṇupurāṇa* 3.2.54-57. On Kṛṣṇa Dvaipāyana as *avatāra* of Nārāyaṇa (= Viṣṇu) see *Viṣṇupurāṇa* 3.4.5; *Kūrmapurāṇa* 1.51.48-49; *Bhāgavatapurāṇa* 1.3.21.

61 *Viṣṇupurāṇa* 3.4.7-26. Similar versions may be found in *Kūrmapurāṇa* 1.52.12-21 and *Bhāgavatapurāṇa* 1.4.14-24. For the attribution of the *Mahābhārata* to Kṛṣṇa Dvaipāyana, see *Bhāgavatapurāṇa* 1.4.25.

versions of the *Veda*-s. Then the confusion over doctrinal matters or even mistakes modified the *saṃhitā*-s and the musical tones (*svara*), determined interpolations and the addition of commentaries. Precisely at this time the *Brāhmaṇa*-s, the *Kalpasūtra*-s, and the *Bhāṣya*-s were written i.e. the first literature relative to the *Veda*-s and the *śrauta dharma*.[62] The final consequence is that many doubts originated concerning all other doctrinal treatises (*śāstra*),[63] the *dvija*-s didn't study or didn't understand the *Veda*-s anymore, they didn't perform the required sacrifices and didn't follow the rules of conduct of their own *varṇa*-s. Many *śūdra*-s became kings and heretical religious movements came to the fore.[64]

At the end of the *kali* age and in the following *saṃdhyāṃśa* humanity reaches its bottom line, both in terms of its material conditions of life and of its spiritual life. Precisely this ultimate state of degradation and the residual strength born out of sheer necessity brings the few survivors of the *kali* age to ponder over their terrible condition and to spiritually awaken. They are thus able to attain self-realization and to follow *dharma*. In this way the foundations for the future *kṛta* age are placed, with the advent of a new generation of human beings. In the *kṛta* age, people are once more naturally happy and enjoy life with equanimity and the seven seers can again practise and teach the *śrauta* and *smārta dharma* among the pious, righteous, and spiritually realized persons, who practise the rules codified in the *śruti* and the *smṛti*.[65] In the following *tretā* age they will reformulate and complete their teachings, adapting them to the characteristics of the age. All cycles of time unfold one after the other according to this general scheme.

To be sure the Purāṇic stories of the passage from one *caturyuga* to the next and from one *manvantara* to the next are often obscure. Even the transmission of the teachings by the seven seers and by Manu and their collective destiny at the end of each and all *manvan*-

62 *Matsyapurāṇa* 144.11-14; *Vāyupurāṇa* 1.58.12-14.

63 *Matsyapurāṇa* 144.22.

64 *Matsyapurāṇa* 144.38-41.

65 *Brahmāṇḍapurāṇa* 1.2.31.99-108. See also *Matsyapurāṇa* 144.85-97.

tara-s of a *kalpa* is not clear. Nonetheless, the textual passages may be interpreted as follows. Each *manvantara* is governed by a group of seven seers[66] and by one Manu[67], who function as spiritual guides bearing all religious authority. As seen in the case of the first *tretā* age of the Svāyaṃbhuva *manvantara*, which is also the first of a *kalpa*, these enlightened beings propagate their teachings. At the end of the *manvantara* they survive together with a restricted group of human beings practising and spreading *dharma* in the following *kṛta* age. When their authority wanes, they ascend to the *maharloka*, together with the 'personified' *mantra*-s.[68] Then, in a subsequent *tretā* age, a different group of seven seers and another Manu will appear on earth, the first in order to once again teach the Vedic *mantra*-s known by the previous (*pūrva*) masters and the latter in order to transmit the teachings of the *smṛti* of the past *manvantara*, of which he bears memory,[69] in a process which will repeat itself in a similar way in each future *manvantara* of the *kalpa*.

At the end of the fourteen *manvantara*-s of the *kalpa* all seven seers and fourteen Manu-s will meet in the *maharloka*. Then they will stop performing the functions for which they had manifested on earth.[70] When the flames of the *saṃvartaka* fire will envelop the three worlds and will lick the *maharloka*, they, together with the other inhabitants of this world, will take refuge in the *janaloka*, where they will reside for the entire period of the universe's dissolution.[71] At the time of a new manifestation, the inhabitants of this *loka*

66 For a presentation of the Purāṇic lists of the seven seers in each *manvantara* and a critical evaluation, see MITCHINER, *Traditions of the Seven Ṛṣis*, *op. cit.*, pp. 51-60.

67 Practically all *Purāṇa*-s agree on the names of the Manu-s of the past *manvantara*-s and on the name of the Manu of the present *kalpa*. They are: 1) Svāyaṃbhuva, 2) Svārociṣa, 3) Auttami, 4) Tāmasa, 5) Raivata, 6) Cākṣuṣa, 7) Vaivasvata, 8) Sāvarṇi, 9) Dakṣasāvarṇi, 10) Brahmasāvarṇi, 11) Dharmasāvarṇi, 12) Rudrasāvarṇi, 13) Raucya, 14) Bhautya.

68 *Vāyupurāṇa* 1.61.128.

69 *Matsyapurāṇa* 145.32-33.

70 *Brahmāṇḍapurāṇa* 3.4.2.2-5.

71 *Viṣṇupurāṇa* 1.3.23-25; *Brahmāṇḍapurāṇa* 3.4.2.47-53; *Mārkaṇḍeyapurāṇa* 46.39-40.

who haven't yet exhausted the fruits of actions done in previous lives, will be reborn. Among them there will be the future Manu-s and the future seven seers, who will appear in the same order as in all preceding *kalpa*-s.[72] They will be responsible for the performance of the same functions.

With this Purāṇic doctrine we pass from the simple awareness of belonging to a tradition to a theoretical reflection regarding one's identity. We witness a shift from an individual to a collective plane: it is now an entire society which recognizes itself as part and parcel of a shared tradition. Moreover, this doctrine evidences a peculiar, perhaps unique characteristic of Hinduism. Besides considering itself as a religious tradition with no end, it considers itself as a tradition with no beginning given the transcendent nature of what is transmitted and the cosmic conception of time, construed as an infinite succession of cycles and sub-cycles.

The *Brahmāṇḍapurāṇa*, the *Matsyapurāṇa*, and the *Vāyupurāṇa* refer to *dharma* as *śrauta* and *smārta* i.e. the conduct of life based upon the rules of the *śruti* and *smṛti*. They also call it *śiṣṭācāra*, the conduct (*ācāra*) of the ones who have remained/survived (*śiṣṭa*). From the point of view of the rules of ethical-religious behaviour, the *śiṣṭa*-s are the *sant*-s and *sādhu*-s. In this case, the word *sant* refers to those who have realized *Brahman* and the word *sādhu* to those who belong to the first three *varṇa*-s and who adhere to the appropriate rules of conduct (*āśramadharma*). From a temporal point of view, the *śiṣṭa*-s are those who survive at the end of a *caturyuga* or of a *manvantara* and who, in the *kṛta* age of the following cycle, practice *dharma*. More specifically, the word *śiṣṭa* indicates those who have survived at the end of a *manvatara* and thus the seven seers and the Manu-s, who practise and teach the *śiṣṭācāra* in all *yuga*-s and *manvantara*-s. They teach the eternal *dharma* that will be handed down in the infinite successive *kalpa*-s, the same which was taught in the infinite preceding *kalpa*-s.

Hinduism presents itself as a tradition without beginning and end, the contingency of which concerns its adepts and the *corpus* of

72 *Brahmāṇḍapurāṇa* 3.4.2.22; 3.4.2.54-57.

teachings on which it is grounded, but not its truth, thought to be eternal and immutable, of which historical Hinduism represents only the 'outer' form. It's the special function of the seven seers and Manu-s to be the custodians and masters of this truth, assuring the continuity of its presence on earth and guaranteeing the genuineness of the teaching leading towards liberation.

AUTHORITY, DEVOTION, AND TRIALS: TEACHERS AND PUPILS IN THE *MAHĀBHĀRATA*

CINZIA PIERUCCINI

According to the most ancient and traditional Indian conception, the *guru* is the teacher of the Vedic science. He is a Brahman, thus his person is holy and inviolable by nature. He is one with the sanctity of his teachings. Surely the Indian figure of the *guru* and, more generally, all the Indian Brahmanical class owe the origins of their prestige to this primary, intimate link with the sacred Revelation (*śruti*). With this Brahmanical *guru*, young men spend their stage of life called "studentship", *brahmacarya*, during which, accordingly, they study the *Veda*. During this period, teachers and pupils are tied by a very special relationship, implying peculiar attitudes, rules, and beliefs. Of this, the narrative as well as the didactic sections of the *Mahābhārata* epic provide a good documentation. I shall here consider three important passages, adding the necessary remarks.

It is the sixth day of the great battle and Bhīṣma, the ancient and wise hero, is wounded by the shower of arrows shot by Arjuna and Śikhaṇḍin. But he has the faculty to choose the moment of his own death, so he decides to postpone it until the sun will begin its northern course, that is, until his spirit will be able to ascend the path of the gods. For fifty-eight days, Bhīṣma will lie on his bed of arrows; and from there, inspired by Kṛṣṇa, he will teach the fundamentals of morality, of *dharma*. Among the teachings of Bhīṣma which constitute, as it is well-known, nearly the totality of books XII and XIII of the *Mahābhārata*, the theme of the *guru* appears almost at the beginning (XII, 109).[1] The passage, full of echoes of the Brahmanical law-texts, and of course conceived to be normative, describes in an exemplary way the absolute respect that must surround the figure of the *guru*.

The passage opens with the words of Yudhiṣṭhira, who asks Bhīṣma which duty, among all (*sarvadharmāṇāṃ*, 2), he reputes to be the most important. Bhīṣma replies that, in his opinion, of the greatest value is devotion (*pūjā*, 3) towards the parents and the *guru*; and he declares at once that one should accomplish everything they command, be it in accordance with *dharma* or not (*dharmyaṃ dharmaviruddhaṃ vā*, 4). Already a kind of hierarchy emerges, since Bhīṣma specifies that he who serves the father obtains this world, he who serves the mother obtains the other world, and he who honours the *guru* obtains the Absolute *Brahman*. With a similar or identical wording, these last statements (6-8) also occur in the law-codes of Manu (II, 230-233).[2]

Then Bhīṣma says that one should never eat before them or offend them, and that one should always devote himself to them: in this way, merit, honour, and happiness will be gained. On the contrary, disregarding these precepts will bring calamity, and will also spoil the fruit of other good deeds. He observes that, as a reward for his own devotion, he has received one hundred times more, even one thousand times more, and thus has attained all the three worlds.

1 The *Mahābhārata* is quoted according to its Critical Edition: *The Mahābhārata*, For the First Time Critically Edited by V. S. SUKTHANKAR *et al.*, 19 vols., Poona, Bhandarkar Oriental Research Institute, 1933-1966.

2 *Mānava Dharma-Śāstra. The Code of Manu*, Critically Edited by J. JOLLY, London 1887. Compare also *Mahābhārata* XII, 109, 5 with Manu II, 229.

But, as he has already anticipated, these three objects of devotion (father, mother, *guru*) are not in fact equal, and now the great hero explains this point in some detail. First, there exists a hierarchy among teachers: a good *ācārya* is superior to ten [Brahmans] well versed in the *śruti*, and an *upādhyāya* is superior to ten *ācārya*-s. However, parents are even more important, because the father is said to be worth more than ten *upādhyāya*-s, and the mother, in her turn, is said to be superior to ten fathers or even more important than the whole earth: there is no *guru* equal to the mother (*nāsti mātṛsamo guruḥ*, 16). Then Bhīṣma contradicts this assumption declaring that, in his opinion, the *guru* is more important even than the mother and father, since parents give bodily life but the *guru* gives celestial life, which is not subject to old age and death (*jātiḥ sā divyā sājarāmarā*, 17). Though reversing the positions of the *ācārya* and the *upādhyāya*, Manu again has a very similar passage (II, 145-148). More precisely, Manu clarifies that the *ācārya* teaches the entire *Veda* to his pupil, while the *upādhyāya* teaches only a part of it (Manu II, 140-141). The *guru* is said to be the giver of sacraments (Manu II, 142), or, better, the man who teaches the *Veda* to a small or greater extent (Manu II, 149).

Bhīṣma reminds us that the greatest respect is due to the father and mother, even if they should make errors. He also speaks of the *guru* and discusses the importance of the father and mother, all together or in a comparative way. Whoever imparts a teaching of truth, explaining the *ṛta* (= *dharma*) and giving immortality, he is himself father and mother (19; cf. Manu II, 144; *Vāsiṣtha-dharma-śāstra* II, 10; *Viṣṇu-smṛti* XXX, 47).[3] He bestows the real knowledge, *vidyā*; the devotion which is due to him has a counterpart in his duty towards his disciples: "As they must be treated with attention by the teachers, so they must revere the teachers" (*yathaiva te gurubhir bhāvanīyās tathā teṣāṃ guravo'py arcanīyāḥ*,

[3] *The Dharma Śāstras, Text and Translation of the Twenty Samhita's*, Edited by M. N. DUTT, 3 vols., Calcutta 1907-1908.

20; see also, though with a different meaning, *Vāsiṣṭha-dharma-śāstra* II, 11). Though insisting that all of them – father, mother, and teacher – must be greatly revered, and that they should never be blamed for anything, Bhīṣma again strongly underlines that the *guru* deserves a greater devotion than the parents (*mātṛtaḥ pitṛtaś caiva tasmāt pūjyatamo guruḥ*, 23; *na ca mātā na ca pitā tādṛśo yādṛśo guruḥ*, 24).

The whole passage is a remarkable instance of the epic/normative style. It really seems the answer to a question i.e. a rather improvised and not very systematic speech. It is full of quotations of famous works. The speaker goes back again and again to the concept he views to be fundamental: absolute devotion. But the most interesting feature of the passage is surely the constant link, under the guiding thread of devotion, of the precepts concerning the *guru* and the parents.

This approach reflects the mingling of the religious and psychological motives which make the *guru*, in every respect, a parental figure. Parents and *guru* have an analogous function for the son/disciple: if parents give physical life, the *guru*, celebrating the investiture with the sacred thread (*upanayana*) which inaugurates the study of the *Veda*, makes the disciple a "twice-born" (*dvi-ja*), who, as Bhīṣma reminds us, can move beyond the limits of earthly life through the knowledge of Revelation. More importantly parents are the social and emotional models of authority, or of the educational role, of the given and received affection, which are the essential requisites of the *guru*:[4] Bhīṣma's joined treatment leaves no doubt and indeed this fundamental affinity parents/*guru* is clearly recognized in the sources.

Leaving doctrinal aspects aside, a couple of narrative passages of the first book of the *Mahābhārata* present other interesting indications of the relationship of the Brahmanical *guru* with his dis-

4 See R. M. STEINMANN, *Guru-śiṣya-sambandha. Das Meister-Schüler-Verhältnis im traditionellen und modernen Indien*, Stuttgart, Steiner Verlag Wiesbaden GMBH, 1986, chapter I, 4.

ciples. The great poem is still at the beginning – the poet is explaining the facts leading to the great snake sacrifice of Janamejaya, during which the *Mahābhārata* itself is narrated by Vaiṣampāyana – when a teacher and his pupils appear on the scene (I, 3 19, ff.). The teacher is Āyoda Dhaumya, who, at the beginning of the passage, is said to be a *ṛṣi* (19), but later in the text is commonly called an *upādhyāya*; his pupils (*śiṣyās*, 20) are Upamanyu, Āruṇi Pāñcālya (= coming from the Pañcāla country), and Veda. Each of them must undergo a trial.

First of all, Āruṇi is ordered to go and repair the breach in a dam controlling the water in a certain field. Not knowing how to do it, the pupil resolves to lie down on the breach and stop the water with his own body. Later on the teacher starts looking for him, and when Āruṇi sees him coming he stands up to pay him homage, thus letting the water run off. The teacher declares that from then onwards, in order to honour the memory of his action, he will be called Uddālaka (= "he who makes something burst", from the Sanskrit verbal root *dal* + *ud*). Thanks to the obedience he has shown, he will get to know the *Veda*-s and the *Dharmaśāstra*-s (*sarve ca te vedāḥ pratibhāsyanti sarvāṇi ca dharmaśāstrāṇīti*, 30). Now the pupil can go free. Here, the reference is obviously to Uddālaka Āruṇi, the well-known upaniṣadic teacher, father of Śvetaketu and perhaps of Naciketas.[5] The text offers a fanciful etymology of his name.

The second pupil, Upamanyu, is faced with a more complicated trial. Āyoda Dhaumya sends him to tend the cattle. At the end of the first day, when he comes back, the teacher asks him how come he has such a healthy aspect. Upamanyu explains that he has obtained some food by begging. Āyoda Dhaumya then reproaches him, since, before eating, he should have offered the food to his teacher. At the next round of begging, Āyoda Dhaumya is offered all the food. Thus, one day after the other,

5 See C. DELLA CASA (ed.), *Upaniṣad*, Torino, UTET, 1976, p. 580.

imposing more and more prohibitions upon him, the teacher forces Upamanyu to fast.

Terribly hungry, Upamanyu eats a poisonous plant, becomes blind, and falls into a well. Not seeing him come back, the teacher with his other disciples go in search of him in the forest. Finding him at the bottom of the well, he tells him to invoke the Aśvin-s in order to recover his sight. Upamanyu recites a long hymn to the divine Twins, who, very pleased, appear to him and offer him a cake, inviting him to eat it. Upamanyu insists that he would like to offer it to his teacher first, against the will of the Aśvin-s themselves. The gods remark that Āyoda Dhaumya, having received the same gift from them in the past, had not offered anything to his own teacher. In the end the Twins, extremely happy with Upamanyu's devotion, announce that while his teacher has iron teeth (here evidently presumed to be the meaning of *āyoda*)[6] he will have golden ones (*upādhyāyasya te kārṣṇāyasā dantāḥ / bhavato hiraṇmayā bhaviṣyanti*, 75): in short, they repute him superior to Āyoda Dhaumya himself and promise that he will regain back his sight and obtain good luck.

No more blind, Upamanyu returns to his teacher and tells him everything that had happened. Āyoda Dhaumya confirms that he will certainly acquire the prosperity announced by the Aśvin-s and promises him the knowledge of all the *Veda*-s (*sarve ca te vedāḥ pratibhāsyantīti*, 77). "This was Upamanyu's trial", concludes the text (*eṣā tasyāpi parīkṣopamanyoḥ*, 78).

Now is the turn of the third disciple, Veda. Āyoda Dhaumya asks him to stay for some time in his house and serve him: this will bring him good luck (*bhavatā madgṛhe kaṃ cit kālaṃ śuśrūṣamāṇena bhavitavyam / śreyas te bhaviṣyatīti*, 80). Veda obeys and, for quite a long time, he serves in his *guru*'s house

6 Cf. the compounds *ayo-daṃṣṭra* (*Ṛg-veda*) and *ayo-datī* (see Pāṇini, *Kāśikā-vṛtti*): M. MONIER-WILLIAMS, *A Sanskrit-English Dictionary,* Delhi-Varanasi-Patna, Motilal Banarsidass, 1981 (1st ed. Oxford University Press, 1899), p. 85.

"like an ox always yoked to heavy burdens, bearing the pain of cold, heat, hunger and thirst, without ever objecting" (*gaur iva nityaṃ guruṣu dhūrṣu niyujyamānaḥ śītoṣṇakṣuttṛṣṇāduḥkhasahaḥ sarvatrāpratikūlaḥ*, 81). At last, Āyoda Dhaumya is satisfied and, as a consequence, Veda obtains fortune and universal knowledge. This is Veda's trial (*tatparitoṣāc ca śreyaḥ sarvajñatāṃ cāvāpa / eṣā tasyāpi parīkṣā vedasya*, 82).

When he has concluded his studies (*samāvṛtta*-s, 83), Veda enters the stage of a householder and, in turn, becomes the teacher of three pupils. However, after his own experience, he prefers to entertain a different relation with them. Indeed, "to his disciples he never said to do works, or to serve the *guru*: he knew the suffering of staying in the teacher's house, and he did not want to inflict torments on his pupils" (*sa śiṣyān na kiṃ cid uvāca / karma vā kriyatāṃ guruśuśrūṣā veti / duḥkhābhijño hi gurukulavāsasya śiṣyān parikleśena yojayituṃ neyeṣa*, 84).

Veda then receives the visit of two *kṣatriya*-s, Janamejaya and Pauṣya, who appoint him as their *upādhyāya*. When Veda has to leave for certain sacrificial duties, he entrusts the care of the house to his pupil Uttaṅka. While Veda is away, Uttaṅka is tempted by the beauty of the women of the house. In particular, he is tempted to have intercourse with the *upādhyāya*'s wife, that is, the *upādhyāyinī* (89 and *passim*) who is in her fertile period. Uttaṅka resists his strong passion, and when Veda comes back and learns everything he is pleased by his disciple's virtuous behavior and promises him every achievement (*sarvām eva siddhiṃ prāpsyasi*, 92). He then bids him farewell from his house.

But Uttaṅka wants to offer his *guru* a fee (*gurvartham*, 95 etc.). After some hesitation, Veda advises him to speak to his wife and receive instructions from her. The *upādhyāyinī* requests him to go to King Pauṣya, and ask for his queen's earrings: she wants to wear them some days later, for a certain occasion. We can now leave Uttaṅka to his journey, supernatural encounters and strange visions. I shall only remember that, at the end of the *ādhyāya*, after having adventurously satisfied his last obligation towards the teacher and his wife, he will reach Janamejaya's court to inflame his anger against Takṣaka, the King of Snakes, who had opposed him in various ways and had killed Janamejaya's father. The story lends itself to some interesting remarks.

First of all, we should note how the relationship between teachers and pupils inspires narrative plots which are developed through the promotion of the Brahmanical ideals of obedience and devotion. The disciple must cultivate an attitude of absolute devotion towards the master. Thus, the knowledge of the Vedic science obtained by the pupil at the end of his training does not seem to depend on any particular study, but rather on a kind of grace received from the teacher. The *guru* bestows it as a reward after submitting his pupil to all sorts of trials. Indeed, the latter must give proof of complete subservience. It is, in many respects, a magic conception. Very concrete, on the other hand, is the acknowledgement of how service to the *guru* can be hard, almost cruel. Veda's words sound almost like an accusation. Lastly, let me remark the prestige of the *upādhyāyinī*, who can impose a very hard task on Uttaṅka for what appears to be an extremely futile (revengeful?) purpose. But perhaps in the wearing of the earrings we should see the acquisition of a kind of magical power, or, at least, some strong symbolic value.

The last passage of the *Mahābhārata* I will deal with stands right at the centre of the epic's main action, and the teacher in question is an important character of the poem, namely Droṇa. At the beginning I noticed how in the Brahmanical conception the *guru* is, in the first place, the teacher of the *Veda*. Now we meet with a patent exception. The text calls Droṇa a *guru* or *ācārya* (for instance, I, 122, 47; I, 123, 52). Nevertheless, he does not teach the Pāṇḍava-s and Kaurava-s the sacred Revelation, but the very practical science of the use of weapons and, more generally, the science of war. Here and there, the text defines this subject as *dhanur-veda*, literally "science of the bow", "archery". The term sounds rather reductive, but underlines the supremacy attributed to this ability. Obviously, this science consists in a sum of technicalities belonging to the *kṣatriya* or warrior culture; and Droṇa's pupils are, indeed, *kṣatriya*-s. But, very notably, Droṇa is a Brahman (and a Brahman is also his brother-in-law, Kṛpa, who plays a similar role). It is clear that the Brahman condition is felt as intrinsic to the identity of the true teacher, to the point that, even if the science he teaches is remote from the classical priestly occupations, he must belong to that social category.

Thus Droṇa, who has found in Arjuna his favourite pupil, instructs him in every sort of fighting (I, 123, 7 ff.). Amazed by the skill he has reached, many kings and princes come to ask for Droṇa's teachings. Among them, a rather despised character appears: Ekalavya, prince of the *niṣāda*-s, son of their King Hiraṇyadhanus. In the *niṣāda*-s of the *Mahābhārata* we must probably see (and the same holds good for various other people mentioned in the poem) a social and perhaps also ethnical group separate from the *ārya*-s, initially seen as a potential foe though soon confined, for its cultural difference, to an inferior status: the status of a tribe of hunters living at the fringes of civilized society, or of a 'mixed tribe'.[7] As we shall see, both attitudes – contempt and the acknowledgement of a potential danger – coexist in the passage under scrutiny.

Ekalavya asks Droṇa to instruct him, but receives a refusal. Droṇa, "who knew the *dharma*, as he [Ekalavya] was a *niṣāda* did not accept him as a disciple in archery, out of respect for them (i.e. his other pupils)" (*na sa taṃ pratijagrāha naiṣādir iti cintayan / śiṣyaṃ dhanuṣi dharmajñas teṣām evānvavekṣayā*, 11). But Ekalavya does not give up. He bows down, touching Droṇa's feet with his head, then leaves him and goes to the forest, and there, with some earth, he moulds an image of the Brahman (*kṛtvā droṇaṃ mahīmayam*, 12). To this image he performs all the acts of devotion which are due to a teacher (*ācāryavṛttiṃ ca paramām*, 13), and, in front of it, he starts to train himself with care. As a result of his intense faith and strong efforts (*parayā*

[7] See J. BROCKINGTON (ed.), *The Sanskrit Epics*, Leiden-Boston-Köln, Brill, 1998, pp. 211-212.

śraddhayā yukto yogena paramena ca, 14), he soon acquires a great skill.

The conception of the 'magic' transfer of sciences has gone far. Now, the bodily presence of the teacher, and even his direct will, are not deemed necessary. In order to operate the transmission of knowledge, his 'virtual' image is enough. Devotion automatically operates the desired effects and forces all results, according to the same process which, in Brahmanical thought, governs the fruits of sacrifice or of penance.[8]

The story goes on with the Kaurava-s and Pāṇḍava-s setting out to the forest on a hunting expedition, together with a servant and a dog. Wandering around, the dog comes upon Ekalavya. Seeing this black, dirty man dressed in a dark antelope skin, the animal starts barking. Ekalavya's repulsive appearance, which we will see again pointed out later, is linked to his being a *niṣāda*. It also qualifies him as an ascetic who lives in the forest, engrossed in his *yoga* (13, 14).

With the dog in front of him, and willing to prove his ability, Ekalavya shoots seven arrows, succeeding in hitting the animal's mouth with all of them. When the wounded dog comes back, the Pāṇḍava-s are amazed: who is that wonderful archer, whose skill is superior even to theirs? They find him in the woods, and on their request Ekalavya introduces himself, saying he is a disciple of Droṇa who has put all his efforts in the science of archery (*droṇaśiṣyaṃ ... dhanurvedakṛtaśramam*, 24).

Back to town, the Pāṇḍava-s go to visit Droṇa and tell him everything. Arjuna, to whom the teacher has promised special favour, protests with him in private: why is another of Droṇa's disciples superior to him? Droṇa ponders over these words and decides to enter the forest with Arjuna in order to trace Ekalavya. They find him dirty, with matted locks, dressed in rags, constantly

8 Jan Gonda remarks that the episode of the image shows "the increasing deification of the 'teacher'": J. GONDA, *Change and Continuity in Indian Religion*, Delhi, Munshiram Manoharlal, 1985 (1st ed. The Hague, Mouton, 1965), p. 252.

shooting with his bow. When he sees the man whom he regards as his teacher, he shows him all his respect. But Droṇa tells him: "if you are my disciple, give me at once my salary" (*yadi śiṣyo 'si me tūrṇaṃ vetanaṃ saṃpradīyatām*, 33). Ekalavya replies that he is ready to give anything his *guru* asks (34, 35): then Droṇa, as "sacrificial salary" (*dakṣiṇa*, 35), asks him the thumb of his right hand.[9] At these cruel words (*vaco droṇasya dāruṇam*, 36) Ekalavya obeys with serenity cutting off his thumb. Naturally, when he later tries to shoot an arrow with his bow, he discovers that his exceptional ability is lost. At this point, Arjuna's envy is calmed.

Droṇa takes back what had been given against his own will, due to the extraordinary power of Ekalavya's devotion. He takes it back through an unavoidable order, as unavoidable is any request coming from a *guru*. As we have seen, the authority of the teacher is always on the verge of becoming a form of tyranny. In this case, as the text itself admits, Droṇa's decision appears authentically cruel. Indeed, if the difficulty of the trials which a disciple must face may have a deep meaning in connection with the excellence of the teachings he is supposed to receive, quite a different thing is to instantly destroy that very excellence as it happens in Ekalavya's case. In a Brahmanical perspective Droṇa's action may be partly justified by the status of the *niṣāda* (though certainly not by Ekalavya's behaviour, which is extremely noble), as well as by the promises he had made to Arjuna, given Droṇa's declared predilection for him. Moreover, we should not forget that other episodes in the *Mahābhārata* notoriously involve tricks and seemingly non-*dharmic* behaviours. These, however, can also be interpreted as being directed to a superior *dharmic* outcome, that is, the final victory of the Pāṇḍava-s. Still, I cannot avoid thinking that all the quoted passages also express the idea that we should not expect perfection even from a *guru* (at least, a perfection

9 The name Ekalavya itself refers to this episode. Derived from the Sanskrit verbal root *lū*, it can be interpreted as meaning "he who must be cut off of one [thing/part]".

which humans can understand). Bhīṣma himself admits that a teacher may give orders which are against *dharma*. But in the end, this is totally unimportant: the *guru* is not to be discussed. Nothing in his actions and decisions can lessen his charisma nor alleviate the hardships a disciple must endure.

THE *GURU-GĪTĀ* OR "SONG OF THE MASTER" AS INCORPORATED IN THE *GURU-CARITRA* OF SARASVATĪ GAṄGĀDHAR: OBSERVATIONS ON ITS TEACHINGS AND THE *GURU* INSTITUTE

ANTONIO RIGOPOULOS

mānasa-bhajare guru-caraṇam /
dustara-bhava-sāgara-taraṇam //

Worship in thy mind the *guru*'s feet:
[these alone] carry over the ocean of existence, hard to overcome!
(Satya Sāī Bābā's first *bhajan* - Ūravākoṇḍa, 20 October 1940)

My interest in the *Guru-gītā* – celebrated Sanskrit hymn (*stotra*) exalting the figure of the authoritative spiritual master, popular in the whole of the Indian subcontinent – was prompted by a study of the Marāṭhī *Guru-caritra* ("The Deeds of the Master"), the foundational text of the *Datta-sampradāya* ("The tradition [of the followers] of Datta/Dattātreya")[1] in the Marāṭhī cultural area, when I

1 Presented in the *Mārkaṇḍeya Purāṇa* as well as in other *Purāṇa*-s as a partial descent of Viṣṇu, Dattātreya became very popular in the Marāṭhī cultural area where to this day he is revered as the paradigm of the eternal master (*guru*), the supreme renunciant (*yogin*, *avadhūta*), and the full manifestation (*pūrṇa-avatāra*) of Brahmā, Viṣṇu, and Śiva in one. On the elusive yet fascinating figure of Dattātreya, see my monograph *Dattātreya*: *The Immortal Guru, Yogin, and Avatāra*. A Study of the Transformative and Inclusive Character of a Multi-Faceted Hindu Deity, Albany, N.Y., State University of New York Press, 1998. On the *Datta-sampradāya*, see R. C. ḌHERE, *Datta Sampradāyācā Itihās*, Puṇe, Nīlakanṭh Prakāśan, 1964. For a beautiful, short poem eulogizing Dattātreya in *kāvya* style – written by one of his allegedly oldest devotees – see DALĀDANAMUNI, *Dattalaharī. L'onda di Datta*. A cura di Antonio Rigopoulos. Venezia, Cafoscarina, 1999.

INDOASIATICA 2/2004, [169-226]

realized that in some of its editions the work incorporates as its 49th chapter (*adhyāya*) a version of this eulogy of the master.

In Mahārāṣṭra, the advent of the modern *Datta-sampradāya* is traced back to two figures venerated as the first historical *avatāra*-s[2] of Dattātreya: Śrīpāda Śrīvallabha (circa 1323-53) and Nṛsiṃha Sarasvatī (circa 1378-1458). This latter one was an ascetic belonging to the brāhmaṇical caste ordained in the *sarasvatī* branch of the *daśanāmī* renunciants. Nṛsiṃha Sarasvatī was truly the founder of the tradition once he settled at Gāṇagāpūr[3] – where he spent the last twenty-three (or perhaps twenty-four) years of his life – a locale in the north of today's State of Karṇāṭaka (Afzālpūr *tāluk*, Gulbarga District) at the border with Mahārāṣṭra. The miraculous lives of Śrīpāda Śrīvallabha and Nṛsiṃha Sarasvatī, together with the places which they sanctified with their presence (especially Gāṇagāpūr, Narsobāvāḍī, and Audumbar: all locales which have become important pilgrimage sites[4] and where the wooden sandals or *nirguṇa*-

[2] The peculiar belief in the manifestation of *avatāra*-s of an *avatāra* is not unusual. It is actually institutionalized in the *guru-paramparā* or uninterrupted "succession of masters" of the *Datta-sampradāya*. Dattātreya, being magnified as eternal *avatāra*, is believed to manifest himself from time to time under a variety of different guises (natural and animal, as well as human). Having the "sight" (*darśana*) of Dattātreya in his typical iconographic form, bearing three heads and six arms, or in the guise of one of his manifestations, as well as having the capacity or gift of being able to recognize him, are considered to be a rare privilege. As a Marāṭhī saying goes: "To appear all of a sudden like Datta" (*datta mhaṇūna ubhā rahāṇeṃ*), it is commonly believed that he may manifest all of a sudden and in unpredictable ways and circumstances. On the other hand, he is believed to be always present everywhere, albeit in an invisible form. On the notion of *avatāra*, tightly linked to the institute of sacred kingship, see M. BIARDEAU, "Études de mythologie hindou IV", in *Bulletin de l'École Française d'Extrême-Orient*, tome LXIII, Paris, 1976, pp. 111-200.

[3] For a presentation of Gāṇagāpūr, also known as Gandharvapūr and Gāṇagābhavana, certainly the most important pilgrimage center of the *Datta-sampradāya*, see M. S. MATE, *Temples and Legends of Maharashtra*, Bombay, Bharatiya Vidya Bhavan, 1988 (1st ed. 1962), pp. 79-101.

[4] On the practice of pilgrimage in the Marāṭhī area, a classic is the account of her going to Paṇḍharpur of I. KARVE, "'On the Road': A Maharashtrian Pilgrimage", in E. ZELLIOT – M. BERNTSEN (eds.), *The Experience of Hinduism.*

pādukā-s[5] of these masters, recognized as the receptacle of their power and grace, are worshipped), are narrated in the *Guru-caritra* (circa 1550)[6] of Sarasvatī Gaṅgādhar,[7] a Marāṭhī hagiography in 51 *adhyāya*-s for a total of more than 7,000 *ovī*-s,[8] emphasizing

Essays on Religion in Maharashtra, Albany, N.Y., State University of New York Press, 1988, pp. 142-171. See also D. B. MOKASHI, *Palkhi*: *An Indian Pilgrimage*, Albany, N.Y., State University of New York Press, 1987 (1st ed. 1964).

5 The feet and sandals are *par excellence* the repository of the saint's *śakti*. Devotees are always eager to massage or even simply touch the feet of an ascetic or *guru*. Sandals, at the same time, are the emblem of royal dignity and spiritual authority, especially in a *vaiṣṇava* context. The *pādukā*–s are also the symbol of being constantly on the way. Dattātreya, as supreme ascetic, is the paradigm of *homo viator*: said to be omnipresent – although incognito – a popular belief has it that he bathes daily in the Gaṅgā in Kāśī (or, according to others, in Haridvār, or even in the Godāvarī near Pañcāḷeśvara), begs his food at noon in Kolhāpur (the ancient Karvīr, important *śakti-pīṭha* dedicated to Mahālakṣmī), and finally reaches Mahur (the ancient Mātāpur, another important *śakti-pīṭha*) where he spends the night. It is also believed that Dattātreya meditates every day in the area of Girnār. The *Kulārṇava Tantra* (12.12) solemnly proclaims that the supreme *pādukā-mantra* is *pādukāṃ pūjayāmi*: "I venerate the sandals [of the master]!" On the crucial importance of the veneration of feet and sandals, see H. BAKKER, "The Footprints of the Lord", in D. L. ECK – F. MALLISON (eds.), *Devotion Divine*: *Bhakti Traditions from the Regions of India*. Studies in Honour of Charlotte Vaudeville, Groningen – Paris, Egbert Forsten – École Française d'Extrême-Orient, 1991, pp. 19-37. See also the recent monograph of J. JAIN-NEUBAUER, *Feet & Footwear in Indian Culture*, Toronto, The Bata Shoe Museum Foundation, 2000.

6 A short presentation of the *Guru-caritra* is offered by S. G. TULPULE in his *Classical Marāṭhī Literature*. From the Beginning to A.D. 1818, Wiesbaden, Otto Harrassowitz, 1979, pp. 352-353. To this day, the most accurate edition of the text is the one by R. K. KĀMAT (ed.), *Śrīgurucaritra*, Mumbāī, Keśav Bhikājī Ḍhavḷe Prakāśan, 1990 (1st ed. 1937). See also S. SARASVATĪ (ed.), *Śrīgurucaritra*, Indore, Dharmajñān Prakāśan, 2000. For a summary of the work, see D. D. JOSHI, *Śrī Gurucaritra Kathāsār*, Puṇe, Ādarś Vidyārthī Prakāśan, 1986. On the *Guru-caritra*, see also my *Dattātreya*, *op. cit.*, pp. 109-134.

7 He was the first to promote the ideal of a *Mahārāṣṭra-dharma*, prior to the time of the poet-saint Rāmdās (1608-1681). Curiously, Sarasvatī Gaṅgādhar's mother-tongue seems to have been Kannaḍa and not Marāṭhī.

8 The term *ovī* derives from the verb *ovaṇẽ*, " to interlace". The *ovī* meter, which in its original form was recitable and singable, consists of six or eight syllables,

brāhmaṇical ritual orthodoxy and venerated as a veritable 'Bible' by all devotees of Dattātreya. Tradition has it that Sarasvatī Gaṅgādhar belonged to a *śaiva* clan (*gotra*) going back to Kauṇḍinya and that he was a disciple of 4th generation of Nṛsiṃha Sarasvatī, in the line of Sāyaṃdev (direct disciple of Nṛsiṃha Sarasvatī), Nāgnāth (son of Sāyaṃdev, he also personally knew Nṛsiṃha Sarasvatī), and Devrāv (son of Nāgnāth). From Devrāv Gaṅgādhar was born and, from this latter one, Sarasvatī. Tradition subdivides the *Guru-caritra* into three sections (*kāṇḍa*): *jñāna-kāṇḍa* (chapters 1-24), *karma-kāṇḍa* (chapters 25-37), and *bhakti-kāṇḍa* (chapters 38-51). Only the first *adhyāya*-s are dedicated to a presentation of Śrīpāda Śrīvallabha's life, especially the 5th and the 9th, which ends with the description of his 'disappearance' at Kuravapur, on the banks of the Kṛṣṇā. The major part of the work, chapters 11 to 51, are devoted to the extraordinary life of Nṛsiṃha Sarasvatī, the great *guru* and founder of the *Datta-sampradāya*, a *brāhmaṇa* descendant of the Vājasaneyin branch, whose birthplace was Karañjā in the Akolā District of Mahārāṣṭra.[9]

To this day, these *adhyāya*-s are read by devotees as a sacred and powerful *mantra*, healing both physical as well as spiritual ailments. On the other hand, the *Guru-caritra* does not particularly excel as a literary work. It is the simple narration in the form of a dialogue between the *yogin* Siddhamuni (an ascetic having made vow of silence, a direct disciple of Nṛsiṃha Sarasvatī) and the pilgrim-devotee Nāmdhārak of the most relevant episodes – always emphasizing the

the quantity of the syllable being usually long. Each syllable has the length of a musical time unit (*tāla-mātrā*). The origin of the *ovī* meter is to be traced to popular songs, as it is indicated by the following stanza: "In Mahārāṣṭra, the *ovī* is sung while pounding [corn]" (*mahārāṣṭreṣu yoṣidbhiḥ ovīgeyā tu kaṇḍane*).

9 For a presentation of Nṛsiṃha Sarasvatī as depicted in these chapters, see my *Dattātreya*, *op. cit.*, pp. 110-115. In the *Guru-caritra* the figure of Śrīpāda Śrīvallabha – though being the first *avatāra* of Datta – is subordinated to that of Nṛsiṃha Sarasvatī: he is presented according to hagiographic patterns which are practically the same as the ones utilized to present the latter. Vājasaneyin is the name of the Upaniṣadic teacher Yājñavalkya, founder of the white (*śukla*) Yajurveda school.

miraculous – of Nṛsiṃha Sarasvatī's life. The whole work is interspersed with stories clearly echoing major purāṇic themes and is replete with sacred spells and *mantra*-s.[10] Contrary to the more open and liberal outlook of the *Vārkarī-sampradāya* (the popular movement of the Marāṭhī poet-saints devoted to Viṭṭhala/Viṭhobā[11] of Paṇḍharpur),[12] the main objective of Nṛsiṃha Sarasvatī was clearly that of awakening brāhmaṇical orthodoxy, then in decline due to the Islāmic domination of the Bahāmāni rulers (the *Guru-caritra* mentions more than once the Islāmic kingdom of Bīdar as well as that of other Deccan sultanates). This awakening of brāhmanism was implemented by insisting upon the observance of caste rules and regulations (*cāturvarṇya*)[13] and the practice of sacrifices (*yajña*) and rituals, such as the ceremony in honor of the ancestors (*śrāddha*) or the initiation rite into the study of the four *Veda*-s (*mauñji-bandhana*). All this was meant to contrast and counter both Muslim rule as well as the excesses of tantrism.

In more recent times, another important master in the tradition of the *Datta-sampradāya*, Śrī Vāsudevānanda Sarasvatī (1854-1914, also known as Ṭembe Svāmin), took pains to translate the *Guru-caritra* into Sanskrit.[14] During the 20th century, the *Guru-caritra* has

10 On the origin and function of *mantra*-s in the religious traditions of India, see H. P. ALPER (ed.), *Mantra*, Albany, N.Y., State University of New York Press, 1989.

11 On the sanctuary of Viṭṭhala/Viṭhobā in Paṇḍharpur, see the classic monograph of G. A. DELEURY, *The Cult of Viṭhobā*, Poona, Deccan College Post-Graduate and Research Institute, 1960. On the all-important pilgrimage site of Paṇḍharpur, see MATE, *Temples and Legends of Maharashtra*, *op. cit.*, pp. 188-220.

12 On the *Vārkarī* movement from the time of its founder Jñāndev onwards, see TULPULE, *Classical Marāṭhī Literature*, *op. cit.*, pp. 329 ff.

13 For an introduction to the caste system, see L. DUMONT, *Homo Hierarchicus: The Caste System and Its Implications*, Chicago, University of Chicago Press, 1980 (1st ed. 1966). See also B. K. SMITH, *Classifying the Universe: The Ancient Indian* varṇa *System and the Origins of Caste*, New York, Oxford University Press, 1994.

14 This work, in two thousand verses, is known as *Dvi-sahasrī* and was written in 1889 in the village of Māṅgāon, Mahārāṣṭra, when Vāsudevānanda was still a *gṛhastha*: according to tradition, he completed his *opus* in just twelve days. An-

been translated into various Indian languages and, more recently, it has also been rendered into English.[15]

The *Guru-gītā* or "Song of the Master" is a short Sanskrit poem of vedāntic, non-dual (*advaita*) inspiration, magnifying the figure of the spiritual master as the supreme Absolute (*brahman*), paradigm of devotion (*bhakti*) and knowledge (*jñāna*). The *Guru-gītā* presents itself as a divine revelation, in the form of a dialogue between lord Śiva, the Benevolent, and his spouse Pārvatī.[16] The fundamental

other Sanskrit work of his based upon the *Guru-caritra* is the *Guru-saṃhitā* (lit. "The 'Collection' of the Master", in nearly 6,500 *śloka*-s), also known as *Sama-ślokī* being a stanza-for-stanza translation. This was composed in 1902 at Brahmavarta, near Kanpur, on the banks of the Ganges, in less than two months. On his writings, see Vāsudevānanda Sarasvatī, *Datta-Purāṇa and Other Works, together with his Biography Gurudeva-caritra*, Puṇe, 1954. For a more detailed presentation of this important figure, see L. N. JOŚĪ, *Śrīvāsudevānandasarasvatī (Ṭembesvāmīmahārāj). Caritra va śikavaṇ*, Puṇe, Śrīgajānan Books, n.d. See also my article "Il *Dattāparādhakṣamāpanastotra* di Vāsudevānanda Sarasvatī" in R. PERINU – V. AGOSTINI (a cura di), *Atti del decimo convegno nazionale di studi sanscriti* (Biella, 15 ottobre 1999), Torino, Associazione italiana di studi sanscriti, 2003, pp. 119-139.

15 For the English translation, see A. E. BHARADVAJA (trans.), *Sree Guru Charitra*. By Gangadhar Saraswati. Ongole, Sai Baba Mission, 1985. For an English summary of the text, see B. R. SHENOY, *Sri Guru Charitra*, Bombay, Bharatiya Vidya Bhavan, 1994, and also K. V. R. RAO, *Guru Charitra*, Apta, Panvel, Shree Swami Samarth Vishwa Kalyan Kendra, 1995.

16 For an overview of Śiva's figure and mythology, see W. D. O'FLAHERTY, *Asceticism and Eroticism in the Mythology of Śiva*, London, Oxford University Press, 1973; A. K. RAMANUJAN, *Speaking of Śiva*, Harmondsworth, Penguin, 1973; J. GONDA, *Viṣṇuism and Śivaism: A Comparison*, New Delhi, Munshiram Manoharlal, 1976; C. DIMMITT – J. A. B. VAN BUITENEN, *Classical Hindu Mythology: A Reader in the Sanskrit Purāṇas*, Philadelphia, Temple University Press, 1978, pp. 147-218; S. KRAMRISCH, *The Presence of Śiva*, Princeton, Princeton University Press, 1981. See also M. PIANTELLI's introduction to his *Īśvaragītā o "Poema del Signore"*. Introduzione, traduzione e note di Mario Piantelli, Parma, Luigi Battei, 1980, pp. 21-105. For a useful bibliography on Śaivism, see A. PELISSERO, *Il riso e la pula. Vie di salvezza nello śivaismo del Kaśmīr*, Alessandria, Edizioni dell'Orso, 1998, pp. 163-178. On Pārvatī and her indissoluble link with Śiva, see D. R. KINSLEY, *Hindu Goddesses. Visions of the Divine Feminine in the Hindu Religious Tradition*, Berkeley, University of California Press, 1986, ch. 3, pp. 35-54.

question which she asks at the very beginning is how is it possible for the individual soul to attain union with the Absolute. Śiva answers by establishing an equivalence between *brahman* and the authoritative master, since "*brahman* is none other than the master" (*guruṃ vinā brahma nānyat*). Typically, the *Guru-gītā* presents itself as part of the vast *Skanda Purāṇa* (*Sanatkumāra-saṃhitā, Uttara-khaṇḍa*) or, more rarely, of the *Padma Purāṇa* or even of the *Brahma Purāṇa*. Presenting itself also as a *Tantra*, the *Guru-gītā* is said to be part of the *Rudra-yāmala Tantra* as well as of the *Viśva-sāra Tantra*, and a collection of its verses can also be found in the *Kulārṇava Tantra* and other tantric sources.[17] Inspired by the exemplary model of the celebrated *Bhagavad-gītā* – a frequent imitative phenomenon in purāṇic literature[18] – the *Guru-gītā* is in fact an

[17] On the elusiveness of the *Rudra-yāmala* ascription in tantric literature, see T. GOUDRIAAN – S. GUPTA, *Hindu Tantric and Śākta Literature*, Wiesbaden, Otto Harrassowitz, 1981, pp. 47-48. For an appreciation of these various purāṇic and tantric attributions, see G. V. DEVASTHALI, *A Descriptive Catalogue of the Saṃskṛta and Prākṛta Manuscripts* (*Bhagvatsinghji Collection & H.M. Bhadkamkar Collection*) *in the Library of the University of Bombay*, Bombay, The University of Bombay, 1944, Book I (Volume I & Volume II: Parts I-III), p. 511; P. K. GODE, *Descriptive Catalogue of the Government Collections of Manuscripts Deposited at the Bhandarkar Oriental Research Institute*, Poona, Bhandarkar Oriental Research Institute, 1950, Vol. XIII, Part III, Stotras etc., pp. 71-76; J. FILLIOZAT, *Catalogue du fonds sanscrit*, Paris, Bibliothèque Nationale, Département des manuscrits, 1970, Fascicule II, no. 9, 11; K. KUNJUNNI RAJA, *New Catalogus Catalogorum. An Alphabetical Register of Sanskrit and Allied Works and Authors*, Madras, University of Madras, 1971, Vol. 6, pp. 64-66; V. VARADACHARI, *Catalogue descriptif des manuscrits – Descriptive Catalogue of Manuscripts*, Pondichéry, Institut Français d'Indologie (Publications de l'Institut Français d'Indologie No. 70.I), 1986, Vol. I, Mss. 1-115, pp. 110-111.

[18] The *Guru-gītā* is but one among many extant *gītā*-s present on Indian soil, the *gītā* label comprising hundreds of specimens. An important phenomenon within the literature of both *Itihāsa*-s and *Purāṇa*-s, the flourishing of these *gītā*-s developed as a deliberate attempt to reproduce or imitate (at least ideally) the celebrated *Bhagavad-gītā*. In the *Mahā-bhārata*, the *Bhagavad-gītā* is flanked by the *Anu-gītā* and fourteen other *gītā*-s of various content. In purāṇic texts, special sections, either devotional or doctrinal in content, receive the appellation of *gītā*-s, even if independent treatises or portions of larger scriptural frameworks.

autonomous *stotra*, certainly composed in a vedāntic milieu. Even though tradition ascribes it to Vyāsa, its author is unknown and it is presumably rather late: the oldest manuscript of the *Guru-gītā* which I was able to examine – presenting itself as part of the *Uttara-khaṇḍa* of the *Skanda Purāṇa* – dates to 1705 (*saṃvat* 1761) and comprises a total of 168 verses.

Many *Guru-stotra*-s or *Guru-stuti*-s are abbreviated forms of the *Guru-gītā*. Having said this, one must immediately add that the *Guru-gītā* is an extremely porous and fluctuating 'text', since the number of its verses varies widely (and wildly) in the hundreds of manuscript copies as well as in its more recent printed editions. To cite but a few examples, some manuscripts present versions of just 45 or 52 verses, other manuscripts present versions of 140, 168 or

Indeed, even isolated collections of teachings, usually of an anonymous character, often bear the *gītā* title. Thus, a *gītā* typically takes the form of a dialogue (*saṃvāda*) between a sage or deity and a disciple or devotee, in which a teaching (*upadeśa*) is expounded, supposed to reveal a supreme metaphysical truth. These *gītā*-s may be divided into two main groups: the *gītā*-s in which the various teachings are expounded by divine masters or *ṛṣi*-s (such as the *Īśvara-gītā*, the *Vyāsa-gītā*, the *Agastya-gītā*, the *Sūta-gītā*, the *Kapila-gītā*, the *Aṣṭāvakra-gītā*, the *Vasiṣṭha-gītā* and the *Avadhūta-gītā*) and the *gītā*-s in which the central figure is a deity (such as the *Śiva-gītā*, the *Brahma-gītā*, the *Uddhava-gītā*, the *Devī-gītā*, the *Lalitā-gītā*, the *Sūrya-gītā*, the *Gaṇeśa-gītā*, the *Rāma-gītā*, and the three *Yama-gītā*-s). Given so many *gītā* collections, one might be induced to conclude that there exists a definite literary genre, inaugurated by the extraordinary popularity of the *Bhagavad-gītā*. After all, this would not be an isolated case: the poetic genre of the *dūta-kāvya*-s, for instance, was first inaugurated by Kālidāsa's celebrated poem *Megha-dūta*. In the case of these various *gītā*-s, however, the situation is different. Just a few of these texts, such as the *Īśvara-gītā*, follow the exemplary structure of the *Bhagavad-gītā*. Most *gītā*-s are wholly detached or entirely different in scope and content from the *Bhagavad-gītā* model. Thus, in these works the *gītā* titling basically refers to the metric structure in which the teachings are expressed. Though the popularity of these *gītā*-s, given their often sectarian character, cannot match the *Bhagavad-gītā*'s fame and renown, a certain number of these texts have played in the past and still play today a considerable role within many *sampradāya*-s and devotional circles. On the subject of *gītā*-s, see chapter XV ("Gītās, Māhātmyas, and other Religious Literature") of J. GONDA, *Medieval Religious Literature in Sanskrit*, Wiesbaden, Otto Harrassowitz, 1977, pp. 271-286.

201.[19] Concerning printed editions, Varadachari mentions two main variants: one in 134 *śloka*-s and another one in 351 *śloka*-s. He suggests that the *Guru-gītā* as part of the *Rudra-yāmala Tantra* constitutes a more synthetic version of the *Guru-gītā* as part of the *Skanda Purāṇa*.[20] However, even a cursory examination of the sources I have scrutinized shows the weakness of such a thesis. Given the great variety of *stotra*-s denominated *Guru-gītā* (despite the fact that they typically share a sensible amount of verses), it would appear more sensible to examine each of these in its own, specific cultural and regional context.

The reasons that make the *Guru-gītā* especially noteworthy are at least three: 1) It is perhaps the most paradigmatic *summa* of the irreplaceable importance of the spiritual master in the Hindū tradition, given the absence of any organized institutions such as the Church in the West.[21] The text presents a portrait of the ideal *guru* that equates

19 See GODE, *op. cit.*, pp. 71-76. Only the manuscript in 140 verses presents itself as part of the *Padma Purāṇa*. The other four all present themselves as part of the *Skanda Purāṇa*.

20 VARADACHARI, *op. cit.*, pp. 110-111. For an English translation of a version of the *Guru-gītā* in 352 *śloka*-s – also presenting itself as part of the *Skanda Purāṇa* (*Sanatkumāra-saṃhitā*, *Uttara-khaṇḍa*) – see SWAMI NARAYANANANDA (trans.), *Sri Guru Gita*, Shivanandanagar, The Divine Life Society, 1999 (1st ed. 1972). For other recent editions of versions of the *Guru-gītā* with English translation (also with commentaries), see H. v. STIETENCRON – K.-P. GIETZ – A. MALINAR – A. KOLLMANN – P. SCHREINER – M. BROCKINGTON (eds.), *Epic and Purāṇic Bibliography* (*up to 1985*) *Annotated and with Indexes*. Compiled under the Chairmanship of Heinrich von Stietencron, Wiesbaden, Otto Harrassowitz, 1992, Part II, S – Z, Indexes, pp. 1167-1169 (n. 6973, 6977, 6982).

21 On the subject of the master, of his 'weight' and social role as well as of his functions – in the first place, that of conferring initiation (*dīkṣā*) either by means of a sacred spell (*mantra*) or a teaching (*upadeśa*; in some cases, it can be purely non verbal consisting of a simple gesture, such as touching the hand or foot or throwing a glance) – there exists a wide range of literature, even though not always of first rate or scholarly level. To begin with, still deserving attention are the observations put forward by M. WEBER in his *The Religion of India: The Sociology of Hinduism and Buddhism*. Translated and Edited by Hans H. Gerth and Don Martindale, New York, The Free Press, 1958 (especially chap. IX: "The Orthodox Restoration in India"). On the term *guru*, linked

with Sanskrit *giri* (lit. "mountain") and corresponding to Latin *gravis* (lit. "heavy", "important"), see J. GONDA, "À propos d'un sens magico-religieux de skt. "*guru-*", in *Bulletin of the School of Oriental and African Studies* 12 (1947), pp. 124-131; J. GONDA, *Change and Continuity in Indian Religion*, Delhi, Munshiram Manoharlal, 1997 (1st ed. The Hague, Mouton, 1965), pp. 229-283. On the term *ācārya*, other name for the teacher who shows the correct conduct (*ācāra*), see P. V. KANE, "The Meaning of Ācāryāḥ", in *Annals of the Bhandarkar Oriental Research Institute* 23 (1942), pp. 206-213. On both *guru* and *ācārya*, see M. HARA, "Hindu Concepts of Teacher: Sanskrit *guru* and *ācārya*", in M. NAGATOMI *et al.* (eds.), *Sanskrit and Indian Studies: Essays in Honor of Daniel H. H. Ingalls*, Dordrecht, Reidel, 1980, pp. 93-118. For a fine overview, see R. M. STEINMANN, *Guru-śiṣya-sambandha. Das meisterschüler-verhältnis im traditionellen und modernen hinduismus*, Stuttgart, Steiner Verlag Wiesbaden GMBH, 1986; D. GOLD, *The Lord as a Guru*, Oxford, Oxford University Press, 1987; A. MICHAELS (ed.), *The Pandit. Traditional Scholarship in India*, New Delhi, Manohar, 2001. See also G. S. GHURYE, *Sadhus of India*, Bombay, Popular Prakashan, 1953; A. BHARATI, "The Hindu Renaissance and its Apologetic Patterns", *Journal of Asian Studies*, 29, 2 (1970), pp. 267-288; P. BRENT, *Godmen of India*, London, Allen Lane, 1972; A. MENEN, *The New Mystics*, London, Thames & Hudson, 1974; K. SINGH, *Gurus, Godmen, and Good People*, Bombay, Orient Longman, 1975; J. D. MLECKO, "The Guru in Hindu Tradition", *Numen* XXIX, Fasc. 1 (1982), pp. 33-61; D. G. WHITE, "Why Gurus are Heavy", *Numen* XXXI, Fasc. 1 (1984), pp. 40-73; J. P. WAGHORNE – N. CUTLER – V. NARAYANAN (eds.), *Gods of Flesh, Gods of Stone: The Embodiment of Divinity in India*, New York, Columbia University Press, 1985; L. A. BABB, *Redemptive Encounters. Three Modern Styles in the Hindu Tradition*, Berkeley, University of California Press, 1986; R. HUMMEL, *Les gourous*, Paris – Montréal, Cerf/Fides, 1988; P. VAN DER VEER, *Gods on Earth: The Management of Religious Experience and Identity in a North Indian Pilgrimage Centre*, London, Athlone, 1988; G. FEUERSTEIN, *Holy Madness. The Shock Tactics and Radical Teachings of Crazy-wise Adepts, Holy Fools, and Rascal Gurus*, New York, Arkana, 1990; R. L. GROSS, *The Sadhus of India: A Study of Hindu Asceticism*, Jaipur, Rawat Publications, 1992; S. S. UBAN, *The Gurus of India*, London, Fine Books, 1997; A. COPLEY (ed.), *Gurus and Their Followers: New Religious Reform Movements in Colonial India*, New Delhi, Oxford University Press, 2000. A bibliographic guide on the subject is offered in C. J. FULLER, *The Camphor Flame: Popular Hinduism and Society in India*, Princeton, Princeton University Press, 1992, p. 277. For a bibliography of the most popular ancient and modern *guru*-s in the Marāṭhī area, see ZELLIOT – BERNTSEN, *The Experience of Hinduism*, *op. cit.*, pp. 358-361. A very useful inside account on the role and function of the *guru* is offered by S. CHANDRASEKHARENDRA, *The Guru*

him to the Absolute (*brahman*), and illustrates the special relationship that the disciple must develop with him, grounded in devotion and focused on the attainment of knowledge as pathway to liberation (*mokṣa*); 2) This short poem or a collection of its verses continues to be piously recited every day, generation after generation, in the monasteries founded by Śaṅkara (8th century CE), the celebrated teacher of non-dual Vedānta.[22] In this tradition, the Absolute is said to manifest Itself as a triad: God (Īśvara), the *guru* and the Self (*ātman*). The master is believed to teach, through his words or even through his silence (as in the case of the divine *guru* Dakṣiṇāmūrti,[23] a form of Śiva), the eternal truth of the *Veda*-s and *Upaniṣad*-s. The fact that the *Guru-gītā* is highly esteemed in these more elitist, traditional brāhmaṇical environments reflects the veneration of which it is ob-

Tradition, Bombay, Bharatiya Vidya Bhavan, 1991. For an appreciation of the peculiar phenomenon of Christian *guru*-s in contemporary South India, see W. HOERSCHELMANN, "*Christian Gurus*". *A Study of the Life and Works of Christian Charismatic Leaders in South India*, Chennai, Gurukul Lutheran Theological College and Research Institute, 1998. For an assessment as well as a bibliography of the social and political role played by *guru*-s in contemporary India, see J. ASSAYAG, "L'économie politique de la spiritualité: renoncement et nationalisme chez les gourous hindous depuis les années 1980", *Bulletin de l'École Française d'Extrême-Orient* 84 (1997), pp. 311-319. On the place of *guru*-s in modern times, see also the recent study by D. SMITH, *Hinduism and Modernity*, Cornwall, Blackwell, 2003, pp. 167-180.

22 For an introduction to Śaṅkara's teachings, see K. H. POTTER (ed.), *Advaita Vedānta up to Śaṅkara and His Pupils*, Princeton, Princeton University Press, 1982 (Vol. III of the *Encyclopedia of Indian Philosophies*). On the internal organization and daily routine of Śaṅkara's monastic orders, see W. CENKNER, *A Tradition of Teachers: Śaṅkara and the Jagadgurus Today*, Delhi, Motilal Banarsidass, 1983; W. DAZEY, "Tradition and Modernization in the Organization of the Daśanāmi Sannyāsins", in A. CREEL – V. NARAYANAN (eds.), *Monastic Life in the Christian and Hindu Traditions: A Comparative Study*, Lewiston, N.Y., Edwin Mellen Press, 1990; Y. SAWAI, *The Faith of Ascetics and Lay Smārtas: A Study of the Śaṅkaran Tradition of Śṛṅgeri*, Vienna, Sammlung De Nobili, 1992.

23 For an appreciation of Dakṣiṇāmūrti's divine icon in the Vedānta milieu, see A. MAHADEVA SASTRY (trans.), *Dakshinamurti Stotra of Sri Sankaracharya and Dakshinamurti Upanishad with Sri Sureswaracharya's Manasollasa and Pranava Vartika*, Madras, Samata Books, 1978.

ject.[24] The text also exhibits a poetic quality, rich as it is of beautiful, vivid metaphors and symbolic elements; 3) The *Guru-gītā*, on the other hand, is not a sectarian text. Just like Dattātreya is a 'honey-bee' *yogin*, in the sense that he has been appropriated by a variety of yogic schools as their fountainhead and patron (brāhmaṇical, tantric, *śākta*, Mahānubhāva, etc.), in the same way the *Guru-gītā* is appealing to a great variety of ascetics and religious groups as well as to the laity. Precisely because of its contents, as it can be appreciated by its incorporations in purāṇic texts as well as in tantric esoteric texts, the *Guru-gītā* in one of its many variants is popular in the whole of the

24 See M. PIANTELLI, *Śaṅkara e la rinascita del brāhmanesimo*, Fossano, Editrice Esperienze, 1974, pp. 158-159, where a hymn composed with verses taken from the *Guru-gītā* is quoted. This hymn is piously recited every morning by all monks (the source is ŚRĪ CANDRAŚEKHARENDRA SARASVATĪ, "Daiva-bhakti and Gurubhakti", in *The Call of the Jagadguru*, Madras, 1958, 2nd ed., p. 32). In a hagiography on Śaṅkara by Govindanātha, the *Śrī-śaṅkarācārya-carita* (probably composed in Keraḷa around the 17th century), we find a stanza (3.37) certainly adapted from the *Guru-gītā*: "Real abode in a sanctuary is the abiding close to the Master, and real sacred ford is the water which wets His feet! Here alone you must stay, and not go anywhere else!" See GOVINDA-NĀTHA, *Il poema di Śaṅkara* (*Śrīśaṅkarācāryacarita*). A cura di Mario Piantelli, Torino, Promolibri, 1994, pp. 44, 50. In *kevala-advaita-vedānta*, the most celebrated hymn in praise of the *guru* is certainly the *Gurvaṣṭakam* attributed to Śaṅkara. Its first verse reads thus:

śarīraṃ surūpaṃ tathā vā kalatraṃ
yaśaścāru citraṃ dhanaṃ merutulyam /
manaścenna lagnaṃ guroraṅghripadme
tataḥ kiṃ tataḥ kiṃ tataḥ kiṃ tataḥ kim //
"One's body may be handsome, wife beautiful,
fame excellent and varied, and wealth like unto Mount Meru;
but if one's mind be not attached to the lotus feet of the *guru*,
what thence, what thence, what thence, what thence?"

For an English rendering, see T. M. P. MAHADEVAN, *The Hymns of Śaṅkara*, Delhi, Motilal Banarsidass, 1997 (1st ed. 1980), pp. 27-32. For an appreciation of the *guru*'s invaluable role in the words of a celebrated contemporary Vedānta master, see ABHINAVA VIDYATHEERTHA MAHASWAMIGAL, *Divine Discourses*, Chennai, Sri Vidyatheertha Foundation, 1994, pp. 59-160. See also SRI SATHYA SAI BABA, *Sree Gurucharanam. A Compilation of Divine Discourses of Bhagavan Sri Sathya Sai Baba during Guru Poornima (1956-1998)*, Prasanthi Nilayam, Sri Sathya Sai Books & Publications Trust, 1999.

Indian subcontinent since it 'cuts across' traditions (*sampradāya*), be they *śaiva*, *vaiṣṇava* or *śākta*: it is truly conceived as a 'classic' of Hindū piety (as the *Guru-gītā* itself proclaims, for instance in verse 151). Herein, the *guru* is celebrated as the "chosen deity" (*iṣṭa-devatā*) to whom all acts of worship and one's whole life must be consecrated. D. R. Brooks rightly observes:

> Some important Siddha Yoga scriptures curiously stand between the exoteric sources of Revelation and Recollection and esoteric Tantric categories. The most important of these is the *Gurugītā* (...). But the *Gurugītā* itself has a less than certain origin whether it be as a portion of the *Skanda Purāṇa*, as a section of another text known as the *Gurucaritra*, or as an independent quasi-Tantric text. This status is similarly not unusual for sources belonging to traditions of mystical yoga; they may have multiple "stations" in the larger canon, sometimes belonging to the exoteric Recollections and sometimes associating with the esoteric Tantras. This is due largely to the fact that Tantric sources seek frequently to *include* themselves as esoteric forms of exoteric works, in other words, as secrets concealed or appearing within more public resources.[25]

Even today in many *maṭha*-s, especially *śaiva* but also *vaiṣṇava*,[26] the *Guru-gītā* is sung at the feet of the *guru* or in his honor, and this *stotra* remains one of the most frequently utilized texts in daily recitation (*svādhyāya*).[27]

25 D. R. BROOKS – S. DURGANANDA – P. E. MULLER-ORTEGA – W. K. MAHONY – C. R. BAILLY – S. P. SABHARATHNAM, *Meditation Revolution. A History and Theology of the Siddha Yoga Lineage*, South Fallsburg, N.Y., Agama Press, Muktabodha Indological Research Institute, 1997, pp. 290-291.

26 On the hypothesis, perhaps chronologically too daring, that the recitation of the *Guru-gītā* or of a collection of its verses was performed at the *āśrama* of Rāmānanda (1299-1410), and that this text was also known to his disciples Kabīr and Raidās, see P. CARACCHI, *Rāmānanda e lo yoga dei sant*, Alessandria, Edizioni dell'Orso, 1999, p. 221.

27 On this, see R. B. S. C. VIDYARNAVA, *The Daily Practice of the Hindus. Containing Morning and Midday Duties*, Delhi, Oriental Books Reprint Corporation, 1979 (4th ed.), pp. 8-9.

Given the impossibility (and also perhaps the uselessness) of trying to reach back to the *ur-text* of what is a hymn/prayer which fluctuates in an essentially oral dimension, or even of tracing its main developments in order to put forward a tentative critical edition, I think it more useful to consider the particular form and function which this 'text' has historically come to assume in each specific regional environment of the subcontinent. Here, I will focus attention on the *Guru-gītā* as it is attested within the Marāṭhī cultural milieu. In his seminal preface to his edition of the *Guru-caritra* of 1937, R. K. Kāmat evidenced how the first versions of the *Guru-caritra* incorporating the *Guru-gītā* are linked to the so-called edition of Kaḍgañcī (a village not far from Gāṇagāpūr, nowadays in Karṇāṭaka, in the Aland *tāluk*, Gulbarga District), according to tradition the hometown of the author Sarasvatī Gaṅgādhar. Among the twenty-four different versions of the *Guru-caritra* which Kāmat analyzed, the oldest incorporating the *Guru-gītā* which he identified dates to 1847.[28] The *Guru-caritra* versions *cum* the *Guru-gītā* are all understood to be copies of an original Kaḍgañcī edition which, unfortunately, despite claims to the contrary, has never been unearthed.

Concerning chronology, what are usually given are the dates when the copies were written from a supposed original (or from other copies of the same text). Actually, some copies – such as the first Kaḍgañcī version found by Kāmat – do not even bear a date. The oldest, datable copy studied by Kāmat was written in 1769, which he refers to as the Kengerī version (named after another town in Karṇāṭaka): this traditional (*vādī*) version did *not* include the *Guru-gītā*. However, among the twenty-four versions of the *Guru-caritra* which Kāmat analyzed *five* do *include* the *Guru-gītā* chapter and the oldest of these copies, as noted, dates to 1847. Although these five versions do *not* materially come from the village of Kaḍgañcī, the Marāṭhī scholar labelled these copies as Kaḍgañcī versions, since they were either copied down from the original Kaḍgañcī

28 R. K. Kāmat first discovered the *Guru-gītā* chapter within the *Guru-caritra* around 1920. For his important preface, see KĀMAT, *Śrīgurucaritra*, *op. cit.*, pp. 7-21.

edition or from a copy thereof. Subsequently, in Gāṇagāpūr, Kāmat came across one more version of the *Guru-caritra* including the *Guru-gītā*. This sixth copy, which dates to 1909, he also labeled as Kaḍgañcī. It must be underlined that the oldest date of 1847 as well as the latter of 1909 refer to the dates when each version was copied down or transcribed from a prior version or supposed original (which has never been found). It may reasonably be assumed that though the first traced copy of the *Guru-caritra cum Guru-gītā* chapter dates to 1847, this particular form of the text originated at an earlier date. Possibly, *Guru-caritra* copies including the *Guru-gītā* insertion may have coexisted with the more traditional *Guru-caritra* versions lacking the *Guru-gītā* from as early as the second half of the 18th century, or even prior to this period.

In all *Guru-caritra*-s including the *Guru-gītā*, the latter always figures as its 49th *adhyāya*. In order to maintain the total number of the *Guru-caritra*-s *adhyāya*-s to 51, a reordering of *adhyāya*-s 41-49 was devised. In traditional versions of the *Guru-caritra not* comprising the *Guru-gītā* chapter, the important subject of the *Kāśī-yātra* covers chapters 41 and 42. In the so-called Kaḍgañcī versions *cum Guru-gītā* discovered by Kāmat, these two chapters are always combined into one i.e. chapter 41 (bringing the Gāṇagāpūr chapter, with the illustrative stories of the Jalandhara demon and the miraculous cure of Ratnabāī, to be counted as *adhyāya* 48). Following Kāmat's edition of the text (listing its main variants), the *Guru-gītā* as 49th *adhyāya* of the *Guru-caritra* presents a total of 176 *śloka*-s (182 with the addition of 6 more verses according to variant readings). It is preceded by the "firm resolution", *saṃkalpa*, and the "consacration" of the adept's limbs, *nyāsa*, plus another 34 Marāṭhī verses in *ovī* metre, 13 placed at the beginning and 21 at the end of the Sanskrit *stotra*.

In his preface, Kāmat also mentions other, more recent versions of the *Guru-gītā* which he was able to identify: in particular, a manuscript edition belonging to one Dhūpkar Śāstrī in 140 *śloka*-s, a printed edition of 1915 edited by the Bhārat Dharma Mahāmaṇḍal in 221 *śloka*-s, and a Tamiḷ translation by V. Kuppuswami of the Shri Sharangvila Press of Tanjāvur in 352 *śloka*-s. Moreover, he signals four Marāṭhī commentaries of the *Guru-gītā*: the *Svānanda-laharī* of C. Cidānandasvāmin, edited in 1911 (*śaka* 1833), based on a version of the *Guru-gītā* in 193 *śloka*-s; the *Jñāna-śikhā* of Nṛsiṃha Māṇikprabhu, edited in 1921, based on a version of the *Guru-gītā* in 137 *śloka*-s; the *Guru-gītā-stotra-cintāmaṇi* of Nityānanda Sarasvatī, edited in 1929, based on a version of the *Guru-gītā* in 187 *śloka*-s; and, finally, a commentary ascribed to one Raṅganāthsvāmī Nigḍīkar, based on a version of the *Guru-gītā* in 105 *śloka*-s (recently re-edited by the Ādarś Vidyārthī Prakāśan of Puṇe, n.d.). The essential data concerning the tradition of the *Guru-gītā* in the Marāṭhī cultural area can be summarized thus:

1) Given the original autonomy and 'textual porousness' of this *stotra* – the date of which, although fundamentally late, cannot be established with certainty – its insertion within the *Guru-caritra* has certainly contributed to popularize it within the framework of its 176 (or 182) *śloka*-s;
2) Most separate editions and versions of the *Guru-gītā* prevalent in the Marāṭhī area are dependent upon it to the largest extent. In this regard, and to limit myself just to some recent printed editions, I cite the following: *The Nectar of Chanting*. South Fallsburg, N.Y., SYDA Foundation, 1972 (in 182 verses);[29] *Sri Guru Gita*. Commentary by Parama Pujya Sri Swamiji. English Translation by Dr. P. G. Krishna Murthy. Mysore, Sri Ganapati Sa-

[29] This is the version which Svāmin Muktānanda (1908-1982) of Gaṇeśpurī recently popularized within his neo-Hindū yogic and devotional milieu, counting many Western followers. As Swami Durgānanda notes: "In 1972, he replaced the *Bhagavadgītā* with a chant that has remained the main scriptural text of Siddha Yoga: the *Gurugītā*, "Song of the Guru". Muktananda found this philosophical poem on the guru-disciple relationship quoted within the *Gurucaritra*, a medieval (ca. 1500) hagiographic text on the primordial guru, Dattatreya, from the Maharashtrian yogic tradition. Muktananda himself had chanted it privately for many years. The *Gurugītā* became the core of the ashram morning recitation" (BROOKS *et alia*, *op. cit.*, p. 60). Rather emphatically, Swami Durgānanda, in a note, adds: "Swami Muktananda can be credited with bringing the *Gurugītā* out of obscurity. After he began chanting it publicly, other spiritual groups discovered and incorporated portions of it in their practice;" *ibid.*

chchidananda Avadhoota Datta Peetha, 1988 (in 142 verses); *Śrī Gurugītā*. Artha evaṃ vyākhyā Svāmī Śivomtīrtha. Mumbaī, Devātmaśakti Society, 1990 (in 182 verses); Shree Maa, *The Guru and the Goddess*. The Complete Text and Translations of Kaśyapa Sūtra and Śrīgurugītā and Lalitā Triśatī. Translated by Swami Satyananda Saraswati. Saṃskṛt and Transliteration by Viṭṭalananda Saraswati. USA, Devi Mandir Publications – Delhi, Motilal Banarsidass, 1996 (in 182 verses); *Śrī Gurugītā*. Puṇe, Anmol Prakāśan, 2000 (in 176 verses); *Śrī Gurucaritrāntārgata Śrī Gurugītā*. Mumbaī, 2000 (in 182 verses);

3) Leaving aside those synthetic editions of the *Gurugītā* of just a few dozen verses, it is useful, especially for the modern period, to distinguish the *Gurugītā* in 176 or 182 verses most diffused in the Marāṭhī milieu – always presenting itself as part of the *Uttara-khaṇḍa* of the *Skanda Purāṇa*, even when integrated within the *Guru-caritra* – from a sensibly longer version of the *Gurugītā* in 351 or 352 verses (which incorporates, widening it, the preceding one), of which I have found trace in an edition in Tamiḻ Nāḍu and also in Uttar Prades;[30]
4) If the *Guru-caritra* dates around 1550, the insertion in some versions of it of the *Guru-gītā* – towards the end of the poem, as its 49th *adhyāya* – is certainly later. How much later, however, is hard to say. As noted, Kāmat found the first specimen of this insertion in a copy of the *Guru-caritra* dated 1847. Kāmat's linking of the versions of the *Guru-caritra cum Guru-gītā* chapter to the '*ur*' Kaḍgañcī edition, if correct, favors the hypothesis that such an appropriation was operated within a tradition and perhaps even a lineage going back to the venerable figure of Sarasvatī Gaṅgā-dhar. Possibly, *Guru-caritra*-s with *Guru-gītā* chapter were circulating already sometime around the middle or second half of the 18th century. Nonetheless, at the state of our present knowledge, it cannot be proved that the insertion of the *Guru-gītā* in some versions of the *Guru-caritra* predates the 19th century.

[30] See SWAMI NARAYANANANDA, *Sri Guru Gita*, *op. cit.*

The 49th *adhyāya* of the *Guru-caritra* begins like most other chapters with a question posed by the virtuous and well-qualified disciple Nāmdhārak to the narrator Siddhamuni, a *rāja-yogin*, a knower of *brahman* (*brahma-jñānī*), the graceful *guru* who has revealed the sacred *Guru-caritra* to the world. After the initial salutations to Gaṇeśa,[31] the lord of wisdom and remover of obstacles, Sarasvatī,[32] the goddess of learning, and Śrī Guru (= Nṛsiṃha Sarasvatī), the first thirteen Marāṭhī stanzas present Nāmdhārak extolling the *guru* and surrender to him as the only means to achieve liberation from this unending round of transmigration (*saṃsār*), otherwise impossible to cross. Only the *guru* possesses that medicine which will cure once and for all the ailment of existence (*bhav*): this is said to be the doctrine propounded by the wise ones throughout the ages. The teacher is magnified as the mythic cow of plenty which grants all desires (Kāmadhenu, the first of the 'treasures' produced from the churning of the ocean or *samudra-manthana* operated by *deva*-s and *asura*-s). Through selfless dedication to him sages such as Śukamuni and the *ṛṣi* Vasiṣṭha, who knew the very essence of scriptures, are said to have attained *mokṣa*. Since the path of the *guru* is what leads to liberation, and precisely this was elucidated in a purifying and felicitous dialogue of Śiva with Pārvatī, Nāmdhārak prays Siddhamuni to tell him, for the uplift of all people, how Pārvatī questioned Lord Śiva and how Lord Śiva responded. This query of the disciple is said to mightily please Siddhamuni, who declares:

> Oh my child, who are ever diligent in the service of the *guru*, your life is indeed blessed! You have sought the eternal knowledge that

31 For an excellent introduction to the elephant-headed god Gaṇeśa, see P. COURTRIGHT, *Gaṇeśa: Lord of Obstacles, Lord of Beginnings*, Oxford, Oxford University Press, 1985. See also R. L. BROWN (ed.), *Ganesh: Studies of an Asian God*, Albany, N.Y., State University of New York Press, 1991; J. A. GRIMES, *Gaṇapati: Song of the Self*, Albany, N.Y., State University of New York Press, 1995.

32 For an overview of the goddess Sarasvatī, at the time of the *Veda*-s primarily celebrated as a grand river, see D. KINSLEY, *Hindu Goddesses*, *op. cit.*, pp. 55-64.

> will awaken you from the stupor of ignorance to the sunlight of truth! Listen with concentration, oh servant of the *guru*, the answer to your well-conceived question! Long long ago, Lord Śaṅkar [lit. "Benefactor", a name of Śiva], the Vanquisher of Tripura [= the city of the *asura* demons destroyed by Śiva], was seated on the peak of Mount Kailās [= a mountain in the Himālaya, north of the Mānasa lake, believed to be the abode of Śiva's paradise] when His consort, the Daughter of the Mountain [= Himālaya], Pārvatī, asked Him a question for the upliftment of humanity.

Precisely at this point, the Sanskrit *Guru-gītā* begins.[33] The 176 verses of the *Guru-caritra*'s *Guru-gītā* do not present a coherent and clear-cut structure. After the traditional, introductory stanzas comprising *saṃkalpa* and *nyāsa*, at the initial question posed by Pārvatī on how it is possible for the embodied soul to attain identity with the Absolute *brahman* (verse 3) Śiva's reply follows (verses 4-65). References are made in verses 57-58 to the yogic practice of visualizing and incorporating the divine form in the *cakra*-s i.e. the "circles" of one's subtle body according to tantric mystical physiology, and to the all-important yogic *mantra so 'ham* (lit. "That I [am]", expressing one's identity with the Absolute *brahman*, as reflected in verse 114). This *mantra*, together with its interchangeable form *haṃsaḥ*, is technically known as *ajapa-kriyā* i.e. "practice of the un-muttered *mantra*", since it is thought to be constantly performed through the natural breathing in and breathing out process. From verse 66, Śiva explains how to practice meditation (*dhyāna*) on the *guru*, and especially from verse 87 onwards he outlines the contemplative exercise which the adept must carry out in an effort to internalize the "*guru* principle". More references are made to the yogic practice of visualizing the *guru* within the *cakra*-s (verses 91-92, 95, 113). In verses 115-122, Śiva presents the effects produced upon the *yogin* or *bhakta* who has perfectly interiorized the *guru* as his own *puruṣa* or *sad-*

33 I have followed Kāmat's standard edition. In his sixty-six footnotes to the *Guru-gītā* chapter, more than half highlight slight variants based on all the editions and commentaries which he was able to gather and compare. The English translation of the *Guru-gītā* verses is mine.

guru. In other popular versions of the *Guru-gītā* there are three additional verses after verse 119, offering an explanation of the meditative planes of *piṇḍa* (lit. "massiveness"; in various yogic and tantric texts, *piṇḍa* or *piṇḍāṇḍa* refers to the microcosm of the human body: herein, it specifically identifies the potency or *śakti* of the *kuṇḍalinī* energy[34]), *pada* (lit. "position", here relative to the spontaneous repetition of the *haṃsaḥ / so 'ham mantra*), *rūpa* (lit. "form", the realm of form), and *rūpa-atīta* (lit. "superior-to-form", the transcendent realm or state beyond form).[35] From verse 123 up to the end, Śiva expounds the traditional *phala-śruti*, that is, the extraordinary results – both in the worldly as well as in the spiritual sphere – which one can derive from the pious recitation of the *Guru-gītā*. Again to be noted is that in other versions of the *Guru-gītā*, Śiva, in two additional verses after verse 133, offers advice on meditative postures and sittings, presenting the positive and negative effects to be derived. Śiva also presents the auspicious places where the *Guru-gītā* should be recited (verses 147-150; in verse 169 the most auspicious place is said to be absorption in the *guru* himself i.e. in his heart). In verse 173, Śiva instructs his spouse never to reveal this secret teaching and to guard it carefully. Its esoteric quality is such that, in verse 174, Śiva admonishes Pārvatī not to reveal it even mentally to the other gods (be it Viṣṇu or their sons Gaṇeśa and Skanda!). Eventually, the *Guru-gītā* may be taught only to those rare, mature (and orthodox! i.e. *astika*) adepts who are full of faith (*śraddhā*) and devotion (*bhakti*; see the final verses 175-176). In one last, additional verse closing other separate versions of the hymn, Śiva himself honors the *Guru-gītā* with these solemn words:

> To [that] unique *mantra* which saves [man] from
> the ocean of rebirth,

[34] On *kuṇḍalinī* in tantric yoga, see the monograph of L. SILBURN, *La Kuṇḍalinī ou l'énergie des profondeurs*, Paris, Les Deux Océans, 1983.

[35] On these tantric meditative planes and their various equivalences in the *Kubjikāmata Tantra* (ch. XIV-XIX), see GOUDRIAAN – GUPTA, *Hindu Tantric and Śākta Literature*, *op. cit.*, p. 54.

to [that] perfect *mantra* which is venerated by all
the gods beginning with Brahmā as well
as by all ascetics having made the vow of
silence,
to [that] *mantra* which annihilates poverty, pain,
fear, and anguish (or: the disease of mundane existence),
to that *mantra* which is the most excellent of
Masters, which removes the great fear
[of transmigration], I render honor!

As noted, the *Guru-gītā* chapter inserted within the *Guru-caritra* explicitly presents itself as a dialogue between Īśvara (= Śiva) and Pārvatī derived from the *Uttara-khaṇḍa* of the *Skanda Purāṇa*. Not surprisingly, herein the *Guru-gītā* is concluded by declaring that the *stotra* is offered to the Venerable *guru*-God Dattātreya (*śrī-guru-deva-dattātreya-arpaṇam-astu*), in the *Datta-sampradāya* revered along with his *avatāra*-s as the supreme paradigm of the divine Master.

The Sanskrit *stotra* is followed by twenty-one more Marāṭhī stanzas (verses 14-34, reconnecting with verses 1-13 introducing the *Guru-gītā*), which bring this 49th *adhyāya* of the *Guru-caritra* to an end. In sum, these twenty-one verses reaffirm the essential doctrines highlighted in the poem and their special relevance in the present *kali* age. In stanzas 25-28, it is stated that *śrī-guru-mūrti*, identified with the "king of ascetics" (*avadhūt-rāy*) Dattātreya, in the present age first incarnated in the pure, *sātvik* human form of Śrīpāda Śrīvallabha, thus opening the phase of Datta's 'historical *avatāra*-s'.

The *Guru-gītā* is thus a devotional hymn, a *stotra* in which each verse has a force of its own and is often loosely connected to the following one. Some of its verses also bear a distinctive upaniṣadic flavor (see, for instance, verse 40, echoing the *Kena Upaniṣad*; verse 82, echoing *Bṛhadāraṇyaka Upaniṣad* 2.3.6; as well as verses 63 and 89[36]). Rather than presenting an analytic study of each verse or delv-

[36] For a contemporary, word-for-word interpretation of this *Guru-gītā* verse, see SRI SATHYA SAI BABA, *Sree Gurucharanam*, *op. cit.*, pp. 38-49.

ing into the technicalities of the suggested yogic meditative absorptions on the highest *cakra*-s, I will here focus attention on three main stages which the disciple is ideally called by the *guru* to practice and experience. Given the overall unsystematic nature of this *stotra* (despite its purported '*sāṃkhya*' structure, see verse 162) the isolation of these subsequent stages or conditions has a purely heuristic value i.e. reflects my own understanding of the *guru-śiṣya* relation as I think it can be derived from reading the *Guru-gītā*. What follows is therefore a kind of 'rationalization' of the overall 'path' which the *guru* adept is ideally called to embark upon.

1) Couched within a vedāntic framework, the emphasis of the text is constantly placed on the unflinching, total faith and surrender a disciple must cultivate towards his physical master in words, thoughts, and deeds. In principle, nothing else is needed to achieve final emancipation (*mokṣa*) since there is nothing superior to one's *guru* who is the actual, concrete proof of the reality of *brahman*. If he didn't exist, the entire universe would not exist: indeed, he is said to be the one responsible for the making, maintenance, and destruction of the worlds. As the one fixed in *brahman* and who *is brahman*, he illumines all states of consciousness: the waking state, the dream state, the dreamless state, as well as the "fourth" (*turīya*; see verse 38, echoing the *Māṇḍūkya Upaniṣad*). To quote but a few yet significant verses:

(18) Always remember the *guru*'s form!
Constantly repeat the [divine] name given by the *guru* (or: of the *guru*)!
[Always] follow the *guru*'s command!
Think of nothing other than the *guru*!

(22) In the three worlds openly proclaim
the gods with their retinues, the demons and snakes:
"The knowledge lying on the tongue of the *guru*
is obtained only through devotion to the *guru*!"

(28) Through actions, mind and speech
one should constantly worship the *guru*!
Prostrate fully on the ground
before the *guru* without reserve!

(32) The *guru* is Brahmā, the *guru* is Viṣṇu,
the *guru* is [Śiva] Maheśvara (lit. "the Great Lord")!
The *guru* is indeed the Absolute *brahman*:
adoring salutations be paid to this Venerable *guru*!

(34) The eye of one who is blinded by the cataract of ignorance
with the stick soaked in the collyrium of knowledge
is opened thanks to Him:
adoring salutations be paid to this Venerable *guru*![37]

(35) You are my father and my mother,
my brother and my God,
with the aim of awakening me from [the nightmare of] transmigration:
adoring salutations be paid to this Venerable *guru*!

(36) From His Reality (= the Master as *brahman*) the world derives its reality,
thanks to His Light this [world] shines forth,
and because of His Bliss [creatures] rejoice:
adoring salutations be paid to this Venerable *guru*!

(44) If Śiva[38] is angry the *guru* protects you,
but if the *guru* is angry, even Śiva cannot save you!
Therefore, with every effort,
take refuge in the Venerable *guru*!

(47) He is [Śiva], the Witness of all, [but] without the three eyes,
he is [Viṣṇu], the Imperishable, [but] without the four arms,
he is Brahmā, [but] without the four faces:
thus the Venerable *guru* is declared to be, oh Dear [Pārvatī]!

(50) The pair of the feet of the Venerable Lord
in whatever direction they may shine,
precisely in that very direction one should prostrate himself
in devout adoration, every day, oh Beloved [Pārvatī]!

37 The *guru* is here extolled as the giver of supreme, liberating gnosis (*jñāna*, *vidyā*): this is indeed his fundamental role! As a popular hagiography extolling Śaṅkara declares: "May the Light of that Jewel which is the Master shine in the palace of my mind! Such Jewel, having dispelled the darkness of ignorance, reveals the inner meaning of the words of all sacred texts!" (*Śrī-śaṅkarācārya-carita* 1.4).

38 Verse 79 is identical to this one, only Viṣṇu takes the place of Śiva.

(76) The root of contemplation is the *guru*'s form!
The root of worship is the *guru*'s foot!
The root of the *mantra* is the *guru*'s word!
The root of liberation is the *guru*'s grace!

I could continue quoting similar verses for several more pages. The fundamental message that the *Guru-gītā* is eager to convey is that only selfless devotion and surrender to the will of one's master is *the* pathway to salvation from worldly pain and rebirth: the *guru* alone is said to be the giver of both material welfare (*bhukti*) as well as liberation (*mukti*; see verses 72, 87, 160-161), this being a common refrain in tantric literature.[39] Surrender to the master is the cornerstone teaching of the whole *stotra*, and, in a way, its '*alfa* and *omega*' since even in the following phases or stages this principle is never forgotten but rather deepened and sublimated. This phase, especially for what concerns the prime, crucial steps in the *bhakti-mārga*, is to be understood as a cleansing, purifying process, a cathartic *praeparatio*: one's complete faith in the *guru* is expected to naturally bear the fruits of pure ethical behavior, brāhmaṇical ortho-praxis. The psychological[40] and even physical dependence of the disciple upon his *guru* is total: the latter exercises full power and authority over the former, whose ego and individuality is to be obliterated, being called to a life of perfect obedience, humility, and submission to the master as his/her veritable God even if the *guru* be strange, whimsical, and should appear not to behave properly (verse 102; the *guru*, being equal to *brahman*, is the paradigm of perfect freedom: he is thus ul-

[39] For a general introduction to tantric ideology and practice, see A. BHARATI, *The Tantric Tradition*, London, Rider & Co., 1975; S. GUPTA – D. J. HOENS – T. GOUDRIAAN, *Hindu Tantrism*, Leiden, Brill, 1979; D. G. WHITE (ed.), *Tantra in Practice*, Princeton, Princeton University Press, 2000.

[40] On the psychology of the relationship between the *guru* and his disciple, based upon the complete surrender of the latter to the former, see the insightful study by S. KAKAR, *The Analyst and the Mystic: Psychoanalytic Reflections on Religion and Mysticism*, New Delhi, Viking, 1991, pp. 52-60. By the same author, see also *The Inner World: A Psychoanalytic Study of Childhood and Society in India*, New Delhi, Oxford University Press, 1978.

timately unpredictable, a law unto himself).[41] In other words, once the choice of the *guru* has been made, the 'spiritual parent' should be as fixed as any other kin. Thus, the disciple must never challenge the master: any ill-behavior towards the *guru* is said to condemn the adept to a hellish rebirth since his curse is dreadful and most powerful, and not even the gods can subvert it (verses 103-104, 106). Only if the *guru* is satisfied with the disciple the latter's prayers, vows, and penances will bear fruit (verse 166). Since everything belongs to the master, the adept must always be ready to offer him his material possessions as well as his own wife (verses 26-29). The heart of the *guru* or full contemplative absorption upon him is declared to be the supreme pilgrimage place, as the big toe of his right foot is the receptacle of all sacred places (verse 169). It is clearly stated that only through such devotion and service to the master can liberating knowledge (*jñāna*, *vidyā*) arise, since only if the pupil submits himself/herself totally to the master can the *guru*'s grace be showered (see verses 48, 55-56, 83, 110). In this regard, the three verses which – following a time-honored tradition – purport to explain the true meaning of the term *guru* are noteworthy:

(23) The syllable *gu* is darkness, and
the syllable *ru* is said to be light!

41 The master's behavior is believed to be perfect and holy at all times and under all circumstances. The *guru* is often expected to speek and act in strange, unpredictable ways. His seemingly *a-dharmic*, antinomian character borders sometimes with madness and, indeed, as a popular Marāṭhī saying goes, "a saint who is not mad is not a saint"! On the behavior of saints as if mad, see D. KINSLEY, "'Through the Looking Glass': Divine Madness in the Hindu Religious Tradition", *History of Religions* 13 n. 4 (May 1974), pp. 270-305. See also A. FELDHAUS, *The Deeds of God in Ṛddhipur*, New York, Oxford University Press, 1984; J. McDANIEL, *The Madness of the Saints: Ecstatic Religion in Bengal*, Chicago, University of Chicago Press, 1989; FEUERSTEIN, *Holy Madness*, *op. cit.* For an appreciation of the subtle ties between madness and saintliness in the Marāṭhī milieu of the last century, see W. DONKIN, *The Wayfarers: An Account of the Work of Meher Baba with the God-Intoxicated, and also with Advanced Souls, Sadhus and the Poor*, San Francisco, Sufism Reoriented, 1969 (2nd printing).

The *brahman* which swallows [the darkness] of ignorance
is solely the *guru*, there is no doubt!
(24) The first syllable *gu*
evidences the attributes [which are intrinsic to Nature] such as cosmic illusion (= *māyā*) and so on.
The second syllable *ru* [evidences] *brahman*,
which destroys the error [generated from the only apparent reality] of cosmic illusion.
(46) The syllable *gu* indicates that which is beyond the attributes [which are intrinsic to Nature] and
the syllable *ru* that which is without form.
He who bestows [on the disciple] the [realization of his]
true identity, beyond [all] attributes [and forms], that one is said to be the *guru*!

Curiously enough, the first part of verse 24, where *gu* is interpreted to stand for the *guṇa*-s i.e. the attributes or qualities of the material world (*prakṛti*), is contradicted by the first part of verse 46, where *gu* is said to stand for *guṇa-atīta* i.e. that Principle (= the *guru* as *brahman*) which is beyond all attributes. Despite being opposite, both interpretations are common and coexist within devotional circles. The two syllables which make up the term *guru* are proclaimed to be the supreme *mantra* (verse 107). Precisely in order to predispose himself/herself to be the fitting recipient of the *guru*'s gift of *jñāna*, the disciple is instructed to plunge into yogic, meditative exercises, which may be regarded as the second, fundamental step.

2) Whereas the first, 'dualistic' phase can be defined – to a lesser or greater degree of maturity – a popular one, given the preponderance of the emotional element attracting masses of devotees to the *guru*, this second one is reserved only to the spiritual *virtuosi*, typically represented by the inner-circle of the *guru*'s pupils. The ideal, traditional Hindū setting is that of the peaceful life at the monastery or hermitage (*āśrama*), where the *guru*, surrounded by his disciples (*yogin*-s, renouncers, etc.), guides them in all ritual and meditative practices. At this stage, the disciple is called to practice a strong and constant effort in order to achieve the *interiorization* of the '*guru*

principle', that is, he/she must come to realize the master's spiritual essence, which is exactly the same as the one which lies within oneself. The discovery through various yogic and meditative techniques of the inner *sad-guru*, coincides with the realization of one's true being, which is the *ātman*. Thus, in a vedāntic perspective, the *guru* who is *brahman* is eventually discovered to be none other than one's own *ātman*. Such final interiorization of the *guru* marks a definite turning point: the outer, physical appearance of the human *guru* – although persisting – is now transmuted, transcended. The ordinary subject-object dichotomy, as well as all past dualisms, are utterly obliterated. The previous dependent relationship to the human *guru* leaves space to the recognition of a pure identity, a spiritual non-otherness (*ananyatā*).

Even before verse 66 – at which point Śiva explicitly says he will explain to Pārvatī how to practice true meditation – we find references to the practices of interiorization and inner absorption:

(9) The *guru* is none other than the conscious Self:
This is the truth, this is the truth, there is no doubt!
In order to attain It, an effort
should certainly be made by the wise!
(15) Having drunk the water of the *guru*'s feet,
one should eat the food that has been left by the *guru*!
One should constantly meditate on the divine form of the *guru*,
and always repeat the *guru*'s *mantra*!
(54) Mental absorption on the physical form of one's *guru*,
is mental absorption on the Infinite Śiva (= *brahman*),
and the singing glorifying the names of one's *guru*,
is the singing in praise of the Infinite Śiva!

Verses 57 and 58 refer to the lotus feet of the *guru*, paradigm of the '*guru* principle', being situated in the highest "circle of the thousand rays" (*sahasrāra-cakra*), and verse 61 proclaims the *so 'ham* to be the king of *mantra*-s, the repetition of which in the inhaling (*so*) and exhaling (*ham*) process is believed to purify the adept and protect from death itself. Once the adept's Self reflects that bliss which has the form of Consciousness i.e. the 'guru principle', he/she comes to recognize in a flash the *ab aeterno* identity with *brahman*, which is conveyed by the semantic meaning of *so 'ham* (verse 114).

Especially from verse 87 onwards, Śiva teaches Pārvatī the meditative exercises to be practiced in order to interiorize the *guru*. Verses 91 and 113-114 locate the divine form of the *guru* as seated in the heart lotus, that is, in the *anāhata-cakra*: the adept is called to visualize the form of the master seated herein, imagined as holding the *Veda*-s (lit. "the book of Consciousness", *cit-pustika*) in his left hand and conferring blessings with his right hand fixed in the "seal of Consciousness" (*cin-mudrā*): such an idealized portrait of the *guru* is quite popular and it especially calls to mind the way Śaṅkara, paradigm of the perfect master in the *kevala-advaita-vedānta* tradition, is represented. Again, verse 95 advises the yogic adept to contemplate the *guru* as seated in the white lotus at the top of his/her head, that is, in the highest *sahasrāra-cakra*: here, the master, supremely serene, with one hand bestowing his blessings (*varada-mudrā*) and the other one bestowing the gift of non-fear (*abhaya-mudrā*), is revered as the supreme Śiva or *brahman*.

Through the contemplative and breathing technique of *so 'ham* as *ajapa-kriyā* (verse 114), Śiva goes on presenting the effects produced upon the *yogin* who has perfectly interiorized the *guru* as his own spirit (*puruṣa*). The experience which characterizes one's achievement of perfect interiorization of the *sad-guru* is solemnly proclaimed in verses 115-116:

(115) In whom contemplates the thumb-sized Puruṣa,[42]
who is Consciousness, [residing] in the heart (= one's Self),
listen to that [particular] condition which then arises:
I'm now going to tell you!
(116) Indeed, That is to be recognized as the Transcendent, the Inaccessible [to thought],
That which is without name and form,
[Pure] Silence:
[such] is *brahman*, Its intrinsic nature, oh Pārvatī!

42 The *aṅguṣṭha-mātra-puruṣa* or "thumb-sized Puruṣa" refers to the presence of the Self or *ātman* within one's body/heart; *loci classici* in upaniṣadic literature are *Kaṭha Upaniṣad* 4.12-13, 6.17 and *Śvetāśvatara Upaniṣad* 3.13, 5.8.

As verse 119 declares, the *yogin* or adept who has properly undertaken the contemplation of the *guru* (*guru-dhyāna*) *becomes brahman* (*svayaṃ brahma-mayo bhavet*)! And verse 153 establishes that a disciple who is fully devoted to his master, precisely in virtue of such identification and interiorization process, *becomes* the master (*sa eva ca guruḥ sākṣāt*). In the same way as water merges in the ocean, so the individual soul reunites and dissolves itself into the Supreme (verses 157-158).

3) The final state coincides with the spontaneous, innate awareness, beyond thoughts and words, of the *guru*'s or *brahman*'s omnipresence everywhere and in everyone in the 'outer world'. Once the discovery within oneself of the '*guru* principle' i.e. of the identity *ātman-brahman* has been definitely achieved, the disciple acquires the status of a *jīvanmukta* or of one "liberated while living",[43] and may in turn be regarded as a *guru*. This state is perfectly natural and no introspective efforts are anymore needed: he/she does not need to embark in formal meditative sessions. The adept has by now realized that there is only *brahman*, and that the ordinary experiences of worldly life are but illusory appearances or partial manifestations of that Absolute. This state, which is the pinnacle of liberating *gnosis* (*jñāna*), might be referred to as the universalization or 'maximization' of divine presence: wherever the realized soul goes or looks, whoever he or she sees, whatever he or she does, it is always the *guru* i.e. *brahman* that he or she experiences. Indeed, there is no one, no place, no thing which is not *brahman*! In final analysis, this state is the natural outcome of the perfect achievement of the previous processes of interiorization and 'minimization'/annihilation of one's ego (*ahaṃkāra*).

[43] On the notion of *jīvanmukti*, see G. OBERHAMMER, *La délivrance, dès cette vie* (*jīvanmukti*), Paris, de Boccard (Collège de France – Publications de l'Institut de Civilisation Indienne, Fasc. 61), 1994; A. O. FORT – P. MUMME (eds.), *Living Liberation in Hindu Thought*, Albany, N.Y., State University of New York Press, 1996; A. O. FORT, *Jīvanmukti in Transformation*: *Embodied Liberation in Advaita and Neo-Vedānta*, Albany, N.Y., State University of New York Press, 1998.

In theistic terms, it might be argued that the adept lives now fully and spontaneously absorbed in God's presence, at all times: both within and without, he/she is enveloped and engrossed in the '*guru*-God principle'. Such discovery of the oneness of all (*ekatva*) *in* God brings peace (*śānti*) and equanimity (*samatva*), even while engaged in the worldly activity of daily life. Formal reverence to the name and form (*nāma-rūpa*) of one's human *guru* is maintained, although by now all dichotomies and dependent relations have simply evaporated. The former disciple has achieved perfect freedom and autonomy (*svātantrya*). In order to reach this ultimate goal, the passing through the first stage of intense devotion and being utterly dependent from the *guru* is viewed as a necessary prerequisite. The *Guru-gītā* illustrates the achievement of such final liberation (*mokṣa*) in a variety of ways. Thus, at various points in the *stotra*, Śiva proclaims:

(62) It [the *guru* principle] moves and moves not,
It is far as well as near!
It is inside everything
as well as outside everything!
(71) [The entire universe], the movable and the immovable,
the animate and the inanimate,
by Him is pervaded:
adoring salutations be paid to this Venerable *guru*!
(75) My Lord is the Venerable Lord of the universe!
My Master is the Master of the three worlds!
My Self is the Self of all beings!
Adoring salutations be paid to this Venerable *guru*!

The realization of *brahman*'s omnipresence is echoed in the following verse:

(97) This, indeed, is Śiva! And this too, is also Śiva!
And this other one is also Śiva! And this other one too is Śiva!
This is My teaching! This is My teaching!
This is My teaching! This is My teaching!

Verse 109 explicitly declares that everything is *brahman*: though being without any exterior appearance i.e. Imperceptible, *brahman* as Light illumines all individual souls (*sarvaṃ brahma nirābhāsaṃ dīpo dīpāntaraṃ yathā*). Verses 111 and 112 solemnly equate *brahman* and the *guru*:

(111) To the One in Whom all things are included, from Brahmā down to a blade of grass,
Whose nature is that of the supreme Self,
to the One of Whom the entire universe is made, the movable and the immovable,
I prostrate myself!
(112) I bow always to the *guru*, Who is Being-Consciousness-Bliss,
Who transcends all differences!
He is Eternal, Perfect, Formless,
Attributeless, established in His own Self!

In verse 118, Śiva underlines the freedom and joy of the enlightened adept. He or she may now abide anywhere (see also verses 154-156, 158), since at all places and times his/her identity with *brahman* or fusion with the *guru* – who is recognized as the intimate essence of all things – is full and perfect:

(118) After having attained such State (= one's identity with *brahman*),
one may live anywhere!
Wherever one is,
one's contemplation [on the *guru*] will be like that of the worm on the wasp!

This metaphor reflects the teaching conveyed by the 24th and last master of Dattātreya, as narrated in a celebrated purāṇic tale.[44] As K. V. R. Rao observes:

[44] The *locus classicus* for this story is *Bhāgavata Purāṇa* 11.7.24-11.9.33 (corresponding to *Uddhava-gītā* 2-4), where we find a dialogue between King Yadu and a young *avadhūta*, which tradition identifies with Dattātreya. The *avadhūta* teaches the secret of happiness, which lies in detachment (*vairāgya*), acquired

As per the Brahmara-Keetaka [*bhramara-kīṭa*, *Vespa solitaria*] Nyaya, whereby the (ugly looking) beetle gets metamorphosed and transfigured into the beautiful Bhramara itself, so also the Jiva, striken with ignorance and all the afflictions of worldly life, attains enlightenment, blossoms forth and begins to shine in his Atmic (Divine) splendour, just like his Guru, through Nidhidhyasana [*nidi-*

through the careful observation of the laws of nature. The twenty-four masters comprise the five elements, the sun and moon, the sea, twelve animals (the pigeon, the python, the moth, the bee, the elephant, the honey gatherer, the fallow deer, the fish, the osprey, the snake, the spider, and the wasp), the prostitute Piṅgalā, a child, a young girl, and an arrow maker. A parallel text in which a sage (*jñānin*) presents six masters of his - Piṅgalā, the osprey, the snake, the bee, an arrow maker, and a young girl – is found in *Skanda Purāṇa* VI, *Nāgarakhaṇḍa* 184.11-185.91. The idea is that the real *guru* one must rely upon is nature, saturated with God. The connection between the renouncers' milieu and the animal kingdom has always been very strong. The woods is typically presented as the ideal *habitat* of the ascetic, from which he learns all that he needs to know and through which he 'deconstructs' his limited ego together with all his ideological and cultural conditionings. Already in *Mārkaṇḍeya Purāṇa* 43.48-58, Dattātreya points at various animals (ants, mice, lizards, sparrows, deer, etc.) as masters of detachment and other virtues. As the well-known contemporary *guru* Satya Sāī Bābā of Puṭṭaparthi (b. 23 November, 1926) cogently notes: "There is no need to wander in search of a *Guru* (preceptor). Learn lessons from every living being, everything that you find around you. Learn faithfulness and gratitude from the dog, patience and fortitude from the donkey, perseverance from the spider, farsightedness from the ant and monogamy from the owl;" SRI SATHYA SAI BABA, *Sree Gurucharanam*, *op. cit.*, p. 6. Moreover: "The world itself is a great teacher, a constant guide and inspiration. That is the reason why man is surrounded and sustained by the world. Every bird, every animal, every tree, mountain and star, each tiny worm, has a lesson for man, if he has but the will and the thirst to learn. These make the world a veritable university for man; it is a *Gurukul* (sacred commune of preceptor with disciples) where he is a pupil from birth to death;" *ibid.*, p. 14. On the *Bhāgavata Purāṇa* tale, see my *Dattātreya*, *op. cit.*, pp. 40-42. For a modern interpretation of Dattātreya's twenty-four masters, see Y. H. YADAV, *Glimpses of Greatness*, Bombay, Bharatiya Vidya Bhavan, 1991 (3rd ed.), pp. 33-55; S. SIVANANDA, *Hindu Fasts and Festivals*, Shivanandanagar, Yoga-Vedanta Forest Academy Press, 1987, pp. 65-70; S. S. KESHAVADAS, *Sadguru Dattatreya*, Oakland, Vishwa Dharma Publications, 1988, pp. 8-16.

dhyāsana, intense meditation] on the Guru and the Guropadesa [= the teaching of the master].[45]

Indeed, no more special abode is recognized for *brahman* or the '*guru* principle'. In this perspective i.e. *sub specie brahman*, everything is holy and sacred:

(120) Having become one with everything,
may [the adept] perceive the Highest Truth!
There is nothing higher than the Highest!
All this is without [any particular] abode (= *brahman* is all-pervasive)!

Such transforming awareness should spontaneously lead the disciple to a condition of pure detachment, equanimity, and peace:

(121) Having experienced It (= *brahman*),
remain free from all attachments,
in solitude, without desires, pacified,
in virtue of His (= the *guru*'s) grace!

Oneness with all things brings with itself the adept's omniscience and perfect bliss (*ānanda*). The place where he or she – now the archetype of the *guru* – happens to be, is revered as the receptacle of merit (*puṇya*):

(123) "The condition of omniscience – so say
the sages – is that in which the embodied soul
becomes one with everything."
Being ever-blissful, ever-peaceful,
who has achieved such state abides in perfect
joy wherever [he may be]!
(124) Wherever he lives,
that place becomes a receptacle of merit!
Oh Goddess, the distinctive feature of the liberated one
I have thus described to you in full!

45 RAO, *Guru Charitra*, *op. cit.*, p. 153.

All actions – bodily, vocal, and mental – performed by the liberated while living, being totally selfless and without attachment, are believed to be free of *karman* and thus not at all binding (see verse 127, echoing the *naiṣkarmya* doctrine of the *Bhagavad-gītā*).

The insertion of the Sanskrit *Guru-gītā* into the Marāṭhī *Guru-caritra* is clearly aimed at ennobling the latter, emphasizing its tie to the brāhmaṇical 'great tradition' and elevating its sectarian figures to the status of supreme *guru*-s, mirroring Dattātreya's paradigmatic model. Such phenomenon of inter-textuality is not at all rare, being commonly resorted to, especially in medieval devotional literature. Echoes of the *Guru-gītā* can be found also in other *adhyāya*-s of the *Guru-caritra*, notably in the 2nd chapter, in the so-called *Kali-Brahmā saṃvād*, the dialogue between Brahmā and the present Kali age personified, where the essential theme (*upakram*) of the *Guru-caritra* is spelled out. Herein, Brahmā expounds the importance of the *guru* to Kali while dispatching him to the earth. This dialogue, like most other stories in the *Guru-caritra*, is a re-elaboration of a purāṇic account.[46] In the *Guru-caritra*'s 2nd chapter we find quoted a few Sanskrit *śloka*-s (131, 133, 136, 138, 140, 145, 204, 276) and to be sure some of its verses resemble, both thematically and verbally, *Guru-gītā* verses. Thus, verses 128-130, with their symbolic interpretation of the term *guru*, call to mind *Guru-gītā* 23, Sanskrit verse 133 is similar to *Guru-gītā* 35, Sanskrit verse 136 is almost identical to the famous verse of *Guru-gītā* 32 ("The *guru* is Brahmā, the *guru* is Viṣṇu, the *guru* is [Śiva] Maheśvara! The *guru* is indeed the Absolute *brahman*: adoring salutations be paid to this Venerable *guru*!"),[47]

46 A possible source is the late *Brahma-vaivarta Purāṇa*. For an overview of this text, see L. ROCHER, *The Purāṇas*, Wiesbaden, Otto Harrassowitz, 1986, pp. 160-164.

47 This often quoted, celebrated verse has been interpreted in a number of ways. For instance, Satya Sāī Bābā observes: "*Gurur-Brahma*: The Brahma referred to here is not the creator. It refers to *Vaak*. *Gurur-Vishnu* refers to the all-pervasive mind, which is present in all beings. This is the *Vishnu* principle. *Gurur-devo Maheswarah*: This refers to the seat of the heart. *Guru-saakshaath Para Brahma*: This means that the unity of speech, mind and heart represents the Supreme *Atma*, which should be revered as *Guru*;" SRI SATHYA SAI BABA, *Sree Gurucharanam*, *op. cit.*, pp. 1-2.

and other Sanskrit verses such as 138 and 145 closely recall our *stotra*. Besides the above-mentioned *śloka*-s in chapter 2, the occurrence of Sanskrit verses is rare in the *Guru-caritra*. I may here recall a couple of *śloka*-s in *adhyāya* 13 (verses 83-85), relative to the encounter between Śrī Guru and one Mādhavāraṇya at Mañjarikā, on the banks of the Godāvarī.[48] Also, worthy to be mentioned are a few Sanskrit *śloka*-s in *adhyāya* 41 (verses 187, 264, 312-313, 391, 428), where the *saṃkalpa* and *samarpaṇa mantra*-s of the various processions (*yātrā*-s) to holy Kāśī[49] are cited. Close to the end of this chapter, especially significant are the eight Sanskrit verses of the *stotra-aṣṭaka* (401-408). With reference to the *guru* issue, it should be noted that some of the many Marāṭhī verses praising Nṛsiṃha Sarasvatī in the *Guru-caritra* could well be interpreted as free renderings of Sanskrit *śloka*-s which are found in the *Guru-gītā*.

If the *Guru-gītā* is to be viewed as the ideal presentation of the divine *guru* leading to enlightenment, the *Guru-caritra*, by incorporating it, aims at representing its highest *exemplum*, through the narration of the lives of Śrīpāda Śrīvallabha and especially of Nṛsiṃha Sarasvatī. Indeed, Siddhamuni's recounting of the *Guru-gītā* to Nāmdhārak is obviously meant to affirm Nṛsiṃha Sarasvatī's role as supreme *guru*: precisely *he* is the one the *Guru-gītā* is extolling and depicting! The path of *bhakti* (*bhakti-mārga*) finds here its fulfillment. The identification of the major *tīrtha*-s of Gāṇagāpūr as *śaiva* in the preceding 48th *adhyāya* as well as of Nṛsiṃha Sarasvatī (after all, an *avatāra* of Viṣṇu!) with Śiva, should not surprise us: in fact, not only "the synthesis of Shaivism and Vaishnavism (...) is the

48 On the Godāvarī, the Ganges of Mahārāṣṭra, as well as on the beliefs concerning rivers, confluences, and sacred fords in the Marāṭhī cultural area, see the excellent monograph of A. FELDHAUS, *Water and Womanhood*: *Religious Meanings of Rivers in Maharashtra*, New York – Oxford, Oxford University Press, 1995.

49 For a thorough introduction to Kāśī (lit. "the Luminous", nowadays called Vārāṇasī), revered as the holiest of places by all Hindū-s, see the monograph of D. L. ECK, *Banaras, City of Light*, New York, Alfred A. Knopf, 1982. See also Ch. JUSTICE, *Dying the Good Death*: *The Pilgrimage to Die in India's Holy City*, Albany, N.Y., State University of New York Press, 1997.

hallmark of Maharashtrian Hinduism",[50] but also the cult of Dattātreya exhibits in an exemplary way this integrative force, with a typical prevalence of the *śaiva* element.[51]

Theology aside, the appropriation of this Sanskrit *stotra* affirming the *guru* as the highest authority is clearly meant to further legitimize and qualify the *sampradāya*'s brāhmaṇical status, re-enforcing the social weight of the movement of the Datta adepts who consider the *Guru-caritra* as their sacred text. The *Guru-gītā*'s intrinsic authority is understood as a glorification of Dattātreya as supreme master, and is further utilized for affirming the brāhmaṇical *auctoritas* of the *Datta-sampradāya*, a social as well as religious movement aiming at vigorously reaffirming a Hindū ritualistic ethos, particularly in an anti-Islāmic function. In all this, Nṛsiṃha Sarasvatī's belonging to the *daśanāmī* order of the great Śaṅkara must have played a significant role. Differently from the more popular *Vārkarī-sampradāya* – a basically inter-sectarian movement open to all and diffused especially in rural environments – the *Datta-sampradāya* along with its various branches (among these, the important *Ānanda-sampradāya*) will develop as an essentially ascetic and increasingly chauvinistic brāhmaṇical movement, with growing diffusion in urban environments and among the more intellectual, conservative Hindū *élites*.

There is thus no doubt that the *Guru-gītā*'s insertion reinforces the weight of the sacred, foundational text of the *Datta-sampradāya*. Within a regional narrative aimed at glorifying the lives of two historical *guru*-s, the addition of the holy *Guru-gītā* is instrumental in determining a series of equivalences: Śiva = Dattātreya = Śrīpāda Śrīvallabha & Nṛsiṃha Sarasvatī (Śrī Guru / Guru Nāth). Such a reinforcement via the *Guru-gītā*'s insertion may have possibly played a non negligible role in the movement's expansive phase, when the

50 E. ZELLIOT, "Introduction", in ZELLIOT – BERNTSEN, *The Experience of Hinduism*, *op. cit.*, p. xvii.

51 On the tendency towards a *śaiva-vaiṣṇava* synthesis in the Marāṭhī cultural area, see Ch. VAUDEVILLE, "The Shaiva-Vaishnava Synthesis in Maharashtrian Santism", in K. SCHOMER – W. H. McLEOD (eds.), *The Sants. Studies in a Devotional Tradition of India*, Berkeley, Berkeley Religious Studies Series, 1987, pp. 215-228.

sampradāya started organizing itself at the main pilgrimage sites of Gāṇagāpūr, Narsobāvāḍī, and Audumbar, gathering patronage and social support from the upper castes, and developing a network of alliances and affiliations. The proclamation of Gāṇagāpūr and its *saṃgama* as highest *tīrtha* and pilgrimage site in *adhyāya* 48 is functional to this objective. The equivalence Gāṇagāpūr = *Dattātreya-puṇya-tīrtha* = Kāśī and Bhīmā-Amarajā = Prayāga, is a typical hagiographic device aimed at legitimating the *kṣetra* as the perfect paradigm of sanctity (*sarva-tīrtha*).[52] It is clear that the insertion of the *Guru-gītā* as *adhyāya* 49, near the very end of the *Guru-caritra*, serves the aim of extolling the masterly figure of Nṛsiṃha Sarasvatī. The narration of the glory of Gāṇagāpūr's *tīrtha*-s in chapter 48 *cum* the recitation of the *Guru-gītā* in chapter 49 are texts which support and reinforce each other well. In other words, the insertion of the *Guru-gītā* precisely at this point of the *Guru-caritra* is not casual: it is meant to gloriously crown Nṛsiṃha Sarasvatī's descent unto earth, almost a kind of spiritual testament before his final "great departure" (*mahā-prasthāna*) as described in the last 51st *adhyāya*.

In order to better appreciate such textual appropriation, it is not out of place to offer a short summary of the 48th *adhyāya* of the *Guru-caritra*, which immediately precedes the *Guru-gītā* chapter, as well as a summary of the two last *adhyāya*-s i.e. 50 and 51. After the detailed presentation in chapter 47 of a miracle of Nṛsiṃha Sarasvatī – who granted a poor peasant having full faith in him the grace of reaping a rich harvest when all surrounding fields were devastated by bad weather – in *adhyāya* 48 the central theme is Gāṇagāpūr's sanctity. It begins with the following question: why, asks Nāmdhārak to Siddhamuni, did Nṛsiṃha Sarasvatī love this place so much to the point of electing it as his permanent abode? Moreover: what is the merit of Gāṇagāpūr, declared to be *Dattātreya-puṇya-tīrtha* (lit. "the

52 On the ubiquitous notion of *sarva-tīrtha*, see ECK, *Banaras*, *op. cit.*, p. 144 and *passim*. For a recent study of various hagiographic models, with a rich and up-to-date bibliography, see F. MALLISON (ed.), *Constructions hagiographiques dans le monde indien. Entre mythe et histoire*, Paris, Librairie Honoré Champion, Bibliothèque de l'École des Hautes Études – Sciences historiques et philologiques, Tome 338, 2001.

ford of Dattātreya's religious merit")? Siddhamuni answers by offering the same explanations which were once given by Nṛsiṃha Sarasvatī to these questions. The story which Siddhamuni recalls tells of a meeting of Nṛsiṃha Sarasvatī, Guru Nāth, with a group of devotees who had come to Gāṇagāpūr for the holiday of *āśvayuja bahula caturdaśī* (the fourteenth day of the dark half of the lunar month of *āśvina*, in September-October), preceding *dīpāvali*.[53] Guru Nāth proposes to the group to embark on a pilgrimage to Kāśī, Gayā, and Prayāga (= Allāhābād, where the Gaṅgā and the Yamunā – and, according to myth, also the ancient Sarasvatī in an invisible form – merge).[54] The devotees, all thrilled at the idea, ask for permission to leave, so as to make provisions and organize themselves for the journey. But Guru Nāth, laughing, reveals to them that Kāśī, Gayā, and Prayāga are all already at hand precisely where they stand i.e. within the sacred *kṣetra* (lit. "[holy] land") of Gāṇagāpūr, and promises to

53 Lit. "row of lights", the popular festival of lights as symbol of good and of its victory over the powers of evil symbolized by darkness: it occurs during the lunar month of *kārttika* (October-November), on the fourteenth day of the waning moon.

54 *Dharma*, in this dark age of *kali*, is said to be based upon the four pillars of *tīrtha-kṣetra-vrata-dāna*: going to sacred fords and holy places, together with the performance of religious vows and the pious giving of alms. For a general introduction to the practice of pilgrimage to holy sites (*tīrtha-yātrā*), see A. BHARATI, "Pilgrimage in the Indian Tradition", *History of Religions* 3 (1963), pp. 135-167; S. M. BHARDWAJ, *Hindu Places of Pilgrimage in India: A Study in Cultural Geography*, Berkeley, University of California Press, 1973; D. L. ECK, "India's Tīrthas: 'Crossings' in Sacred Geography", *History of Religions* 20 (1981), pp. 323-344. For a bibliography on pilgrimage, see FULLER, *The Camphor Flame*, *op. cit.*, pp. 277-278, 281-282. For the relevance which the *saṃgama* has in the myths relative to Dattātreya, I may mention a well-known tale narrated in the *Skanda Purāṇa* as well as in other *Purāṇa*-s concerning the great penances which the mother of Datta, Anasūyā (lit. "the Non-envious", wife of the *ṛṣi* Atri), performed at the confluence of the Narmadā with the Airaṇḍī. Very pleased with her arduous austerities, the *trimūrti* of Brahmā, Viṣṇu, and Śiva consented to her wish that the three gods be born as her sons: so it was that Soma, Datta, and Durvāsas came into existence, 'descents' of Brahmā, Viṣṇu, and Śiva respectively. On this episode, see S. V. KUMAR, *The Paurānic Lore of Holy Water-places with Special Reference to Skanda Purāṇa*, New Delhi, Munshiram Manoharlal, 1983, p. 68.

show them the entire sacred site that very day. Thus, Guru Nāth leads them to the confluence of the Bhīmā with the Amarajā, proclaiming that *saṃgama* to be Prayāga. He then adds that, since here the river flows in the northern direction, the site is sacred as Kāśī itself. He proceeds to indicate eight holy *tīrtha*-s located all around the place. Of these, he says, not even the great snake bearing a thousand tongues Śeṣa or Ādiśeṣa (lit. "Remainder", the cosmic serpent representing the infinite) would be able to adequately describe the power and the glory. Interestingly, these *tīrtha*-s are all clearly identifiable as *śaiva*. In this regard, it must be remembered that Nṛsiṃha Sarasvatī – as the 12th *adhyāya* of the *Guru-caritra* informs us – was ordained in the *sarasvatī* branch of the Śaṅkara *daśanāmī* order of monks at the age of nine or ten years old.

The devotees then ask the master to please tell them the origin of the sacred river Amarajā. Guru Nāth reveals that it is thus described in the *Jalandhara Purāṇa*:[55] once upon a time, the demon (*asura*) Jalandhara succeeded in overwhelming all the gods. The *asura* was made invincible thanks to a mysterious power: if he was beheaded in battle, a new head would immediately spring up upon his neck; if a drop of blood was to fall on the ground, instantaneously from it a new demon would originate.[56] His army thus multiplied incessantly, overpowering that of the *deva*-s. It so happened that the gods were defeated and forced to abandon their heavenly abode. Then Indra, the king of the *deva*-s (*deva-rāja*), came to Śiva and told him all that had happened, praying him to save them. Śiva, moved by compassion, created for him a vessel containing the miraculous water *saṃjīvanī*

[55] Actually, no *Purāṇa* is known with this name. The story of Jalandhara, the mighty son of the Ocean who came to challenge Śiva and was ultimately killed by him, is narrated in the *Śiva Purāṇa* (*Rudra-saṃhitā*, *Yuddha-khaṇḍa*).

[56] The multiplication of demonic beings bursting out from spilled blood – the prime symbol of life and vital energy – is a recurring motif. One is here reminded of the well-known episode in which the goddess Kālī kills the demon Raktabīja, as narrated in *Devī-māhātmya* 88.52 ff. On this, see my article "Il sangue e la Dea nel contesto mitologico hindū", in A. AMADI (ed.), *Il sangue nel mito. Il sangue purificatore nel sacrificio del bufalo nell'Asia meridionale*, Venezia, Grafica L'Artigiana, 2002, pp. 101-112.

(lit. "animating", "enlivening"). He gave it to Indra saying that, if the water be sprinkled on the corpses of the *deva*-s who had died in battle, these would instantaneously come back to life: in this way, the gods would certainly win against the demon. Now it so happened that, just when Indra was on his way carrying the vessel bearing the miraculous water, he inadvertently spilled[57] some of it upon the earth. This water became the river Saṃjīvanī, which later came to be known as Amarajā (lit. "Born from the immortal").

Nṛsiṃha Sarasvatī underlines how taking a bath in the waters of this river at the time of solar or lunar eclipses, or even on full moon nights or at the time of *ekādaśī* (= the 11th day of the lunar calendar), is especially sanctifying and brings great merit. He also mentions other important *tīrtha*-s located around Gāṇagāpūr, among which the *manohara-tīrtha* (lit. "the ford of the Stealer of minds" [= Śiva]; *manohara* is also a name of Nṛsiṃha Sarasvatī's *pādukā*-s), the *aśvattha* tree (*Ficus religiosa*) not far from the main Dattātreya temple, the *śaṅkara-bhuvana-tīrtha* (lit. "the ford of the Benefactor of the world", *śaṅkara* being one of Śiva's most sacred names[58]), the *saṃgameśvara-tīrtha* (lit. "the ford of the Lord of the confluence" [= Śiva]), and the *nandikeśvara-tīrtha* (lit. "the ford of the Lord of Nandin", this latter one being the bull, Śiva's mighty vehicle).

At this point, Siddhamuni tells another anecdote narrated to the pilgrims by Guru Nāth. Once upon a time, there lived a *brāhmaṇa*

57 The motif of spilling or dropping a most precious substance is again a paradigmatic one. The most celebrated mythic tale is relative to the supposed origin of the popular *Kumbha-melā* festival: the gods and demons once fought a great battle for a pitcher (*kumbha*) containing the nectar of immortality (*amṛta*). During the fight four drops of the precious nectar were spilt on the earth: these gave origin and fame to the holy towns of Allāhābād, Haridvāra, Nāsik, and Ujjayinī. On the *Kumbha-melā* festival, a tradition which dates back to at least 644 C.E. as certified by the Chinese Buddhist pilgrim Xuanzang, see D. K. ROY – I. DEVI, *Kumbha. India's Ageless Festival*, Bombay, 1955.

58 The name *śaṅkara* is found in the invocation known as *Śrī-rudra*, which for all *śaiva*-s is the ideal center of the *Veda*-s. The formula *śaṅkarāya namaḥ* – "Adoring salutations be paid to the Benefactor" – precedes the famous *śivāya namaḥ*, the solemn five-syllabled spell (*pañcākṣara-mantra*); see *Śatapatha-brāhmaṇa* 9.1.1.41.

named Gosvāmin, a very devout and pious man belonging to the Bhāradvāja *gotra*. He lived in the village of Nāgeśa, not far from Gāṇagāpūr. Perfectly detached from all worldly allurements, he spent his time absorbed in the contemplation of Śiva. Gosvāmin had two older brothers, Īśvara and Pāṇḍuraṅga. One day, both his brothers planned to make a pilgrimage to Kāśī and invited Gosvāmin to come along with them. But Gosvāmin replied declaring that in Gāṇagāpūr only is the abode of Śrī Viśveśvara (lit. "Lord of all"; the name of the "*liṅga*[59] of light" or *jyotir-liṅga* which is venerated in Kāśī), and that Gāṇagāpūr *is* in fact Kāśī. His brothers, being totally unable to perceive the place's sanctity, asked him to offer proof of what he affirmed. Then Gosvāmin prayed to Śiva asking him to manifest all the *tīrtha*-s of Kāśī in that very spot, so that his brothers could have a clear vision of them and convince themselves of the greatness of Gāṇagāpūr. Immediately, the *mūrti* of Śiva Viśveśvara was seen coming out of one of the nearby water pools (*kuṇḍa*). Following this, they saw the waters of the Bhagīrathī (one of the Ganges' epithets,[60] from the name of the ascetic-king Bhagīratha who obtained its descent from the sky unto earth) oozing out from a spring. The two brothers, overwhelmed with emotion, could thus contemplate with their very eyes all the Kāśī *tīrtha*-s in holy Gāṇagāpūr.

To the convened pilgrims, Nṛsiṃha Sarasvatī describes then in some detail the sanctity of the *saṃgama-mahimā-tīrtha* (lit. "the great ford of the confluence [of the Bhīmā with the Amarajā]"), not at all inferior to that of Kāśī. From there, he leads the devotees to the *pāpa-vināśinī-tīrtha* (lit. "the ford which annihilates sin"), located a few miles away, and explains the merit to be derived from taking a

59 The sacred *liṅga* (lit. "mark", "sign") is the symbol of phallic origin representing Śiva in all of his temples, as a smooth cylindrical shaft set on a pedestal. In Śaivism, the most sacred *liṅga*-s are twelve and one of these is precisely the *viśveśvara-liṅga*. On the cosmic symbolism and iconography of the *liṅga*, which is truly the mark of Śiva's transcendence, see T. A. GOPINATHA RAO, *Elements of Hindu Iconography*, Madras, 1914-1916, vol. 2, pp. 39-102.

60 For an appreciation of the Ganges' rich and complex mythology, see S. PIANO, *Il mito del Gange* (*Gaṅgā-māhātmya*). Con una prefazione di Mario Piantelli. Torino, Promolibri, 1990.

bath in that holy spot. He solemnly declares that the waters of the *pāpa-vināśinī-tīrtha* have the power of purifying the embodied soul (*jīva*) from all sins accumulated in previous births, and concludes by proclaiming once again that Gāṇagāpūr *is* indeed Kāśī.

Siddhamuni proceeds to extol the greatness of the *pāpa-vināśinī-tīrtha* to Nāmdhārak by narrating another short story in the life of Nṛsiṃha Sarasvatī. Guru Nāth had a younger sister, Ratnāī by name. Due to a sin she had committed in her previous life, she had contracted leprosy. Her sin is thus described: a female cat once gave birth to five kittens inside a kitchen vessel. The woman, being unaware of the presence of the newborn kittens, poured some water in the vessel and started boiling it. As a consequence, all kittens died a horrible death. Precisely because of this fault, Ratnāī had to suffer leprosy in her present life. Terribly afflicted, she went to her brother praying him that he free her from her illness. Nṛsiṃha Sarasvatī first reminded her of the sin she had done, though inadvertently, in her previous life. Then, moved by compassion by seeing the sister's great pain and intense devotion, he instructed her to go to the *pāpa-vināśinī-tīrtha* and to reside there for some time, bathing daily in its holy waters. She obeyed his command and was soon cured of leprosy.

The narration continues with Nṛsiṃha Sarasvatī taking the pilgrims to the *koṭi-tīrtha* (lit. "the lofty ford"), of which he magnifies the greatness. He then takes them to the *rudrapāda-tīrtha* (lit. "the ford of the foot of Rudra" i.e. Śiva), which he equates for merit and power to the *tīrtha* of Gayā. From there, Guru Nāth leads the group to other holy places, such as the temple of Kāleśvara – perhaps the oldest in Gāṇagāpūr – and the *manmatha-tīrtha* (lit. "the ford of love" or "the ford of Kāma", Eros personified). He invites all pilgrims to perform the ablutions (*abhiṣeka*) to the idol of Kāleśvara (lit. "Lord of time": a name of Śiva as well as of a *liṅga* celebrated in the *Skanda Purāṇa*[61]) during the entire lunar month of *śravaṇa* (July-August), and to dedicate themselves to the deity's cult through the

61 Śrī Mahākāleśvara is the name of the *jyotir-liṅga* venerated in the Mālava region, in Ujjayinī, along the river Śiprā in Madhya Prades.

offerings of lights (*dīpārādhana*) in the lunar month of *kārttika* (October-November). In this way, Nṛsiṃha Sarasvatī explained to them in detail the power and the glory of Gāṇagāpūr and of all its eight, wondrous *tīrtha*-s (*aṣṭa-tīrtha*): this, in sum, the contents of the *Guru-caritra*'s 48th *adhyāya*.

After the *Guru-gītā* chapter, the 50th *adhyāya* illustrates the merit which may be derived from visiting saints (*mahā-puruṣa-saṃdarśana*): a Muslim *navāb* of the kingdom of Bīdar – who in his previous life had been a poor Hindū washerman devoted to Śrīpāda Śrīvallabha, now reborn into a royal family thanks to the latter's blessings – is afflicted by a painful ulcer that no doctor is able to cure. He is then advised to seek the *darśana* of Nṛsiṃha Sarasvatī. After meeting the saint he is miraculously cured from his illness and finally, again thanks to Guru Nāth's grace, he attains liberation. It is noteworthy how in the *Guru-caritra* several miracles of Nṛsiṃha Sarasvatī are aimed at helping as well as impressing Muslim rulers of the Deccan sultanates. The equanimity and religious universalism attributed to this Muslim king devoted to Guru Nāth are especially stressed: a trait which – despite the often intolerant[62] brāhmaṇical re-

62 Also in recent times, there have been cases of open clash between brāhmaṇical circles devoted to Datta and the untouchable community (and one should here remember that, starting from 1955, the *Untouchability* (*Offenses*) *Act* has made the practice of untouchability illegal). For a well documented instance relative to the seventies of the past century, see K. SAPTARSHI (trans. M. BERNTSEN), "Orthodoxy and Human Rights: The Story of a Clash" in ZELLIOT – BERNTSEN, *The Experience of Hinduism*, *op. cit.*, pp. 251-263. T. LUBIN of the Washington and Lee University has studied the politico-religious connections of the *Datta-sampradāya*, especially with the more conservative brāhmaṇical sectors. In the contemporary Marāṭhī context, he has examined the reconfiguration of a peculiar form of 'Vedic' ritual, which has been rendered palatable to a Westernized and rationalist Hindū middle class. On this significant issue, see his article "Science, Patriotism, and Mother *Veda*: Ritual Activism in Maharashtra", from which I quote the abstract: "Over two decades, a holy man from eastern Maharashtra (Marathwada) has made it his mission to reestablish the archaic, multi-fire Vedic sacrificial system as an important element in public religious life in India. Drawing his inspiration from Dayananda Saraswati's idealized and abstract vision of Veda as the original and pure piety, this 'saint', Ranganath Selukar Maharaj, innovates in his attempt to revive the

vivalism characterizing the *Datta-sampradāya* – is present in several saintly figures who are assimilated to this tradition, whose biography and teaching are highly eclectic mixing a Hindū background with Islāmic elements and vice-versa[63] (in modern times, one is here reminded of the charismatic figure of the Sāī Bābā of Śirḍī (d. 15 October, 1918),[64] who is venerated as an *avatāra* of Dattātreya by hundreds of thousands of followers and whose official biography/hagiography, the *Śrī-sāī-satcarita*,[65] imitates the *Guru-caritra* model). As K. V. R. Rao synthesizes with reference to the Muslim *navāb*:

full Vedic *shrauta* sacrificial cult (minus the animal victims) as a vehicle for unifying and reempowering Hindus – religiously, socially, and politically – whose culture and society has been weakened by centuries of 'foreign' rule. Simultaneously evoking Vedantic renunciant ideals, Maharashtrian regional bhakti traditions, and nationalist heroism (citing Selukar's participation in the movement to liberate Marathwada from the Muslim state of Hyderabad in the late forties), his movement has been effective in attracting support from a range of social groups through the annual multi-week Vedic festivals he organizes. While his revival of priestly ritual vividly affirms the value of traditional piety, he argues that the ritual is essentially scientific and rational, and will have salutary effects on Hindu society, the Indian state, and the natural environment. This combined appeal to prestigious, pan-Indian traditional authority, regional sympathies, and scientistic rationalism, all articulated both in preaching and in print, and dramatized by spectacular public acts of piety, seems calculated to persuade the educated and professional middle castes (a sort of middle class) while repackaging archaic Brahmanical ritual in a way that appeals also to an illiterate, rural clientele" (http://home.wlu.edu/~lubint/AAS2000.htm).

63 On this subject, see N. K. WAGLE, "Hindu-Muslim Interactions in Medieval Maharashtra", in G. D. SONTHEIMER – H. KULKE (eds.), *Hinduism Reconsidered*, New Delhi, Manohar, 1989, pp. 51-66.

64 For an introduction to the Sāī Bābā of Śirḍī, among modern saints certainly the most beloved and popular all across the Indian subcontinent, see my monograph *The Life and Teachings of Sai Baba of Shirdi*, Albany, N.Y., State University of New York Press, 1993. More recently, see M. WARREN, *Unraveling the Enigma. Shirdi Sai Baba in the Light of Sufism*, New Delhi, Sterling Paperbacks, 1999.

65 The full text has been translated into English. See G. R. DABHOLKAR (HEMAD PANT), *Shri Sai Satcharita. The Life and Teachings of Shirdi Sai Baba.* Translated from the Original Marathi by Indira Kher. New Delhi, Sterling Publishers, 1999.

When he became the ruler, he was very kind to all the subjects, treating the Hindus and the Muslims alike and all the subjects as his own children. He used to respect brahmins very much. The Maulwis [= holders of Islāmic religious instruction; *'ālim*, *mullāh*] used to feel envious and jealous of this. They tried to turn him against the Hindus, but the king never heeded them. He was very spiritual-minded and believed that all the religions – even so Hinduism and Islam – are but different pathways to the same God. He firmly believed all the Hindu Gods are but different facets of the same Allah and that the various idols and forms which Hindus worship are but an aid for purifying and to bring the mind to one-pointedness, which ultimately leads to the experience and realisation of the Formless – The Nirakara, The Allah concept of Islam. He was trying to establish harmony and cordiality in the relationship between the two religious communities. By and large, he was loved equally by both the communities among his subjects.[66]

66 RAO, *Guru Charitra*, *op. cit.*, p. 154. In southern Karṇāṭaka, a paradigm of such eclecticism – which in recent times has generated tensions and violence between the Hindū and Muslim communities – is the mountainous locale (around 2,000 meters high) of Bābā Budhan Gīrī in the Chikmagalur District, venerated as a pilgrimage site by both religious communities. Here, inside a cave, the Muslims honor the tomb of saint Bābā Budhan (also known as Ḥaẓrāt Dāda Ḥayat Mīr Qalandar or Bābā Qalandar Shāh Dattātreya), whereas Hindūs venerate the cave itself as the "seat" (*pīṭha*) of Dattātreya. Indeed, the Hindūs believe that Dattātreya 'disappeared' from human sight precisely by entering the narrow mouth of this cave (such belief may be compared with the narration of the *Śaṅkara-vijaya-vilāsa*, which tells of how Dattātreya appeared in Badarīnātha and, holding Śaṅkara by the hand, took him in a nearby cave from which they were never seen to come out: the motif of the entrance in a cave is often utilized to signify death). The Hindū devotees from Mysore believe that one day Dattātreya will reemerge out from the cave of Bābā Budhan Gīrī: this will be his last manifestation, since they worship Dattātreya as the final *avatāra* of Viṣṇu, the eschatological one. This peculiar theology coexists with the belief, universally held in the *Datta-sampradāya*, that Dattātreya is an immortal and eternal *avatāra*, invisible but just to a few and yet constantly present and operating in the world. On this interesting case, see A. BHARATI, *Great Tradition and Little Traditions*: *Indological Investigations in Cultural Anthropology*, Varanasi, Chowkhamba Sanskrit Series Office, Chowkhamba Sanskrit Studies Vol. XCVI, 1978, pp. 68-71; A. BHARATI, *Hindu Views and Ways and the Hindu-Muslim Interface*: *An Anthropological Assessment*, New Delhi, Mun-

The last *adhyāya* of the *Guru-caritra*, the 51st, describes the circumstances of the "great departure" (*mahā-prasthāna*) or death of Nṛsiṃha Sarasvatī: this would have taken place in the lunar month of *māgha* (January-February) of 1458 (*śaka* 1380). In the imminence of the end he sets out from Gāṇagāpūr leaving there his *nirguṇa-pādukā*-s, having infused into them his eternal presence and power. In the *Guru-caritra*, the reason why Nṛsiṃha Sarasvatī decides to leave Gāṇagāpūr is justified by the fact that after the miracle of curing the *navāb* always more crowds – even of Muslims! – were pouring into the village, thus upsetting (and certainly also 'polluting', from a Hindū point of view) its traditional atmosphere of serenity and silence. As an *avatāra* of Datta, Nṛsiṃha Sarasvatī promises to all devotees that he will eternally reside in his 'invisible form' in Gāṇagāpūr and in its *aṣṭa-tīrtha*-s, and that he will always be present everywhere his name is remembered with faith in prayer (*smaraṇa*) and song (*bhajan*, *kīrtan*). Then, together with his four most intimate disciples – Sāyaṃdev, Kavīśvar Nandi, Narahari Kavi and Siddhamuni – he proceeds on foot towards the Kadalī Van (a banana tree grove) on the banks of the Pātāla Gaṅgā (= the Gaṅgā of the lowest region of the hells, the name by which the river Kṛṣṇā is here popularly known), at the foot of the sacred Śrīśailam mountain in Āndhra Pradeś.[67] That Nṛsiṃha Sarasvatī selected this celebrated locale as his last earthly residence, where Śiva Mallikārjuna is worshipped in the most sacred form of the "*liṅga* of light" (*jyotir-liṅga*), is not without significance. It is meant to once again highlight the *śaiva* affiliation of this Datta *avatāra*. Having reached the Kadalī Van, Nṛsiṃha Sarasvatī has his disciples prepare a small raft made with the trunks and leaves of banana trees. The raft, decorated with flow-

shiram Manoharlal, 1981, pp. 78-79; J. ASSAYAG, *Au confluent de deux rivières. Musulmans et hindous dans le Sud de l'Inde*, Paris, Presses de l'École Française d'Extrême-Orient, Monographies, n. 181, 1995, pp. 115-118.

67 On this locale, see A. V. SHANKARANARAYANA RAO, *Temples of Andhra Pradesh*, Bangalore, Vasan Publications, 2001, pp. 73-77. See also Ch. TALBOT, *Precolonial India in Practice: Society, Region, and Identity in Medieval Andhra*, New Delhi, Oxford University Press, 2001, pp. 107, 109, 133, 271-272 n. 31.

ers, is then launched in the river's waters: on top of it, the master solemnly sits in the lotus yogic posture (*padmāsana*). After magnifying the religious merit which is to be derived from reading the *Guru-caritra* and again reassuring his pupils of his constant, active presence amongst them and in Gāṇagāpūr, Nṛsiṃha Sarasvatī mysteriously vanishes from sight. As a token of his grace and as a sign of his reaching the 'other shore' of the eternal abode, the four disciples, as promised by Guru Nāth, each receive a beautiful fragrant flower (*prasāda-puṣpa*), which comes to them miraculously moving against the current on the water's surface.

Especially revealing is Nṛsiṃha Sarasvatī's underlining of how the importance of his words will be effectively understood only by those spiritual aspirants who are devout to the *guru and to God* in equal measure, that is, who make *no distinction* between the two: precisely this is the spirit of the whole *Guru-caritra* and also the essential reason for its appropriation of the Sanskrit *Guru-gītā*. Coming back to our short poem, and keeping in mind its place and context within the *Guru-caritra*, it can be concluded that only the yogic adept who constantly 'plunges' himself/herself into the sacred waters of the *Guru-gītā* is to be viewed as a true *jñānin* or sage. The *Guru-gītā* is therefore to be understood as highest, spiritual "crossing", a veritable *tīrtha* (with Gāṇagāpūr as its 'material' counterpart) leading to final release (*mokṣa*) by cutting the fetters which enchain one to *saṃsāra*.

These remarks lead me to a consideration of the social as well as political 'weight' of the *guru*. The very concrete, tangible worldly power – primarily understood as the ability to exercise control and authority over people – which the spiritual master, typically male, has widely held at all times in Indian history. Too often these themes have been utterly neglected by indologists. Ideally, to be sure, most *guru*-s and certainly all renunciants are by brāhmaṇical law considered to have entered an *a-varṇa* or "caste-less" state, that is, to have died to the world and its poisonous allurements, living a life of poverty depending on alms, always absorbed in the contemplation of the

Absolute.[68] This ideal of simplicity, selfless dispassion and pure love towards all beings has been upheld and lived out by hosts of solitary *yogin*-s, ascetics, *sādhu*-s, and *guru*-s over the centuries: it is certainly not my intention to deny this. Even in the case of those saintly figures who have renounced the world, nonetheless, the issue of power is always present: most often, as a 'divine' might over nature and things – and people as well! – which takes the form of the miraculous, of the wondrous sign (*camatkāra*) that the holy person operates (for instance, through healing), of which all hagiographies are replete. The theme of power in its vast and diversified potential of expression is constitutive of the *guru* or saint: devotees believe it to be an intrinsic and irreplaceable component of his divine charisma.[69] A *yogin* or *guru* who lacked power (*śakti*) would not be considered a true *yogin* or *guru*. The latter is thus always expected to act powerfully, to use his powers in a performative, often spectacular way. Of course, it is also common opinion that the holy man may misuse his powers if misled by his ego, by the reemergence of his pride and greedy attachments. If this happens (and it does happen!), he is thought to eventually lose his powers and fall back to an ordinary, human condition (one is here reminded of the often-mentioned case of the misuse of *siddhi*-s or supernatural attainments by the immature *yogin*). However, an ethical judgment on how the *guru* utilizes his various powers is obviously not in discussion here: the master being revered as the repository and receptacle of divine power, what *must* interest the scholar is the *guru*'s utilization of power *in se*.

68 On the ideal, normative features of brāhmaṇical asceticism, see P. OLIVELLE, *Rules and Regulations of Brahmanical Asceticism*, Albany, N.Y., State University of New York Press, 1995. By the same author, see also *Saṃnyāsa Upaniṣads. Hindu Scriptures on Asceticism and Renunciation*. Translated and with an Introduction by Patrick Olivelle, New York – Oxford, Oxford University Press, 1992.

69 On the issue of the saint's power and charisma, especially relevant is the discussion in L. A. BABB, *Redemptive Encounters*, *op. cit.* See also V. DALMIA and others (eds.), *Charisma and Canon: Essays on the Religious History of the Indian Subcontinent*, New Delhi, Oxford University Press, 2001.

It would therefore be misleading and naïve not to consider the focal issue of the exercise of the *guru*'s 'potency', especially in its social, even political expressions. First of all, as I have already hinted, the discourse of power is tangibly exercised with respect to the master's disciples, both in the monastic milieu (the *āśrama*) as well as in the secular sphere. As the *Guru-gītā* evidences in its ideal representation, the *guru*'s power over the adepts is constantly celebrated in an overall perspective of devotion, service, and obedience, which amounts to psychological and often even material, economical dependence and subservience. The great majority of devotees remain stuck at this first stage, never being able to transcend their utter dependence upon the *guru*'s personal charisma, who then becomes a veritable 'cult-object'. The following steps leading to an interiorization and universalization of the "*guru* principle", eventually opening up to a condition of autonomy, independence, and freedom – material and psychological as well as spiritual – are restricted to a happy few: the religious *virtuosi*, the great *yogin*-s and *jīvanmukta*-s, who often become *guru*-s in turn. Thus, for the vast majority of the adepts there derives a radical form of personal dependence upon the *guru*'s "name and form" (*nāma-rūpa*). Ideally, the master should guide the disciple to a condition of autonomy and responsibility. Having realized that there is only *brahman*, the *guru* should incarnate the paradigm of perfect detachment and selflessness, being intent on nothing else but the good of his *śiṣya*-s. This notwithstanding, the fact remains that the power of the *guru* over his disciples is truly immense. These latter ones are called to honor and serve him in all possible ways, consecrating their whole lives to him and executing all his commands, even if the master should appear to behave in manners which the disciple does not understand or even approve of. As we have seen, according to brāhmaṇical ideology the *guru* is equal to God and, actually, even superior to Him. His charisma over the people is enormous and, as a consequence, great risks of potential abuses ensue. Indeed, the *guru* or pseudo-*guru*, may be (and often is) tempted to misuse the tremendous power he has over the lives – and material substances – of his disciples. Paradoxical as it may appear for one who is recognized as the incarnation of detachment and selflessness, the subtle link between knowledge, power, and economic interests has been and continues to be inextricably tied to the authority of the 'divine' *guru*, who significantly is venerated – as in the past – as a "great king" (*mahā-rāja*) to whom regal honors are to be paid. As David Smith has noted:

> The Shankaracharya of Kanchi was seated on a throne while he was showered with 200 kilos of gold coins on his hundredth birthday in 1993. On his silver throne, Sathya Sai Baba sits above the prime minister and president of India when they share a platform .... The comparison with 'secular monarchies' is appropriate and significant: gurus do set up spiritual kingdoms.[70]

Historically, the ideal separation between life-in-the-world (established on caste norms of subordination and domination) and the spiritual 'renunciatory' realm (*saṃnyāsa*) – though recognizably maintained by an *élite* of saints and mystics – has been often illusory or at least a blurred one. Contrary to the stereotyped image of the *āśrama* as an oasis of peace and non-violence where *guru*-s and *saṃnyāsin*-s dedicate themselves to meditation in view of *mokṣa*, it is proven that many of these ascetics were at the same time clever dealers and also fierce warriors.[71] The ideal, radical dichotomy between the worldly sphere and the renunciatory realm is, in fact, constantly contradicted, with trespasses in both directions. In modern times, for instance, the *śaiva* Gosain-s and the *vaiṣṇava* Bairāgī-s exercised a relevant economic as well as political influence as merchants (even as bankers) and renunciant-soldiers. The murderous violence of these figures is widely attested to in the chronicles. It was from around the 16th century that the main Hindū sects created within themselves sections of warrior ascetics, often utilized in an anti-Islāmic function but also in inter-sectarian combats (*śaiva*-s against *vaiṣṇava*-s, etc.). In the 18th

70 D. SMITH, *Hinduism and Modernity*, *op. cit.*, p. 169.

71 On the *āśrama* and the *liaison* between religion and politics, see the essay by J. ASSAYAG, *L'Inde. Désir de nation*, Paris, Odile Jacob, 2001, pp. 221-257. On this same subject, see also G. J. LARSON, *India's Agony Over Religion*, Albany, N.Y., State University of New York Press, 1995.

century, these sections came to be organized in well-equipped regiments, such as the army of the Nāga *saṃnyāsin*-s.[72] It will be the troops of the British colonial army which, for the first time, will 'tame' these cohorts of renunciant-soldiers, of politicized *sādhu*-s and wandering ascetics, perceived as a dangerous and seditious element especially given their successful role as catalytic agents of the Hindū masses. The annihilation of these special armies was an essential task of the British in their effort to politically control and administer the country, first of all in order to collect the taxes over land property. The British enterprise was crowned with success. In a sense, the representation of the Indian saint itself came to be modified, since now only the traditional and ideal one was to be confirmed and upheld i.e. that of *guru*-s and ascetics exclusively dedicated to the practice of severe penances and meditation.

The *Pax britannica* will lead many *guru*-s and religious institutions to seek new roles and identities in order to redefine and reaffirm their intellectual, socio-economical, and even political stature. This will be done either by cultivating a reformist attitude open to Western ideology and values, following the moderate stance of the Congress movement (as in the politics of a 'father of the Indian nation' such as G. K. Gokhale; this will also be the typical response of many sects and groups of the so-called neo-Hindūism who honor in Rāmmohan Roy (1772-1833), founder of the *Brāhmo Samāj*, their seminal leader), or else by taking a resolute anti-Western and more aggressive, even violent position, upholding an anachronistic return to the supposed purity and order of ancient, brāhmaṇical India (one is here reminded of the politics of a leader such as B. G. Ṭiḷak, who, as

72 On this often neglected issue, see W. R. PINCH, *Peasants and Monks in British India*, Delhi, Oxford University Press, 1996. By the same author, see "Soldier Monk and Militant Sadhus", in D. LUDDEN (ed.), *Making India Hindu. Religion, Community, and the Politics of Democracy*, Delhi, Oxford University Press, 1996. Especially insightful is the essay by V. BOUILLIER, "La violence des non-violents ou les ascètes au combat", in D. VIDAL – G. TARABOUT – É. MEYER (eds.), *Violences et non-violences en Inde*, Paris, Éditions de l'EHESS (Coll. *Puruṣārtha*, 16), 1994, pp. 213-243 (with excellent bibliography).

one of his models, elected the 17th century saint Rāmdās, *guru* and counselor of the valiant anti-Islāmic hero Śivājī).

Nowadays, *guru*-s are often referred to as 'god-men' and the most famous among them have been transformed by the State itself into icons of national, traditional heritage and culture. Spirituality being typically presented as India's 'trademark' – via the neo-Hindū *sanātana-dharma* 'essentialization' – many contemporary *āśrama*-s, temples, and *guru* dwellings (*sthāna*-s) are openly publicized by the national Departments of Tourism as 'paradises in miniature', thus making the visit/pilgrimage to these sites – by groups of Westerners as well as by the Westernized Indian urban middle-classes – an increasingly lucrative business.[73] 'Spiritual economy' sells extremely well, and thus this kind of consumer outlook and management has become more and more organized and prosperous, being regulated according to market laws. Even the *darśana*, or the "vision" of the deity or divine master – so important in traditional Indian culture – is nowadays more and more spectacularized and eventually 'delocalized' through the utilization of the powerful new media of our 'image society' (via TV, videos, movies, the Internet, etc.).[74]

A fundamental aspect is represented by the network of donations and patronages which constitutes the concrete link between donors/devotees and the *guru* and *āśrama* organization. The properties of the *āśrama*-s are either in the sole name of the *guru* or else controlled by boards of trustees. Depending on the *guru*'s and his entourage's entrepreneurial capacities, the profits gained allow the expanding of such spiritual centers and the re-investment of at least

[73] On the business of spirituality and its link with tourism, see A. G. GOLD, *Fruitful Journeys. The Way of Rajasthani Pilgrims*, Berkeley and Los Angeles, University of California Press, 1988; B. N. RAMUSAK, "The Indian Princes as Fantasy: Palace Hotels, Palace Museums, and Palace on Wheels", in C. A. BECKENRIDGE (ed.), *Consuming Modernity. Public Culture in Contemporary India*, Delhi, Oxford University Press, 1996, pp. 151-179.

[74] On the contemporary religious discourse through the use of media, see L. A. BABB – S. S. WADLEY (eds.), *Media and the Transformation of Religion in South Asia*, Delhi, Motilal Banarsidass, 1997 (1st ed. University of Pennsylvania Press, 1995).

part of these substances in order to enlarge the *āśrama* influence and renown, for instance through the offering of social services (*sevā*) to the local communities, such as through the building of schools, hospitals, temples, etc. Usually, the *guru* promotes his leadership through monthly bulletins, sectarian literature, Internet websites, etc. often in more than one Indian regional language and typically in both Hindī as well as English. Through these and other channels, more branches or centers of the movement affiliated to the sanctuary where the *guru* resides are created, both in India as well as in the Indian diaspora and the Western world. This determines a veritable competition among *āśrama*-s and *guru*-s.

In time, the gathering of more disciples and, consequently, of more economic wealth, determines a network of alliances, of reciprocal favors and honors or 'enhancement of status' between the *guru*-God and regional and sometimes even national businessmen and politicians. It's the 'big man' strategy, as the anthropologist M. Mines has called it (1989), applying this originally Melanesian notion to the context of the Indian subcontinent.[75] Being a generous donor, for instance by patronizing sacrificial rites or festivals, is a powerful way to achieve public recognition as a virtuous religious person and also to demonstrate one's economic power. The donor is said to offer the *guru dakṣiṇā* i.e. the ancient "sacrificial salary" which was due to the priest materially executing the sacrifice (*yajña*). In exchange, the *guru* generously bestows public praises and blessings upon the donor, thus enhancing the latter's status by allowing the person to 'participate' – at least to some extent – in his otherworldly, divine charisma, which is supposed to 'rub off' on him or her.[76] In a spiral of reciprocal favors enhancing each other's power/status and authority (sometimes leading to cases of veritable

75 See M. MINES – V. GOURISHANKAR, "Religion and Big-Man Politics in South India: Towards Re-conceptualizing Indian Society", Santa Barbara, University of California, Santa Barbara, 1989; see also M. MINES, *Public Faces, Private Voices. Community and Individuality in South India.* Berkeley – Los Angeles – London, University of California Press, 1994.

76 On this exchange, see my article "Women and Ritual: The Experience of a Contemporary Marāṭhī *āśram*", *Annali di Napoli* 53, fasc. 3 (1993), pp. 279- 302.

corruption), the *guru* more often than not comes to resemble or even act as a political leader.

The constant reconfiguration and renegotiation of the complex ties between religion and politics which has taken place in Indian history, has seen the *āśrama* and the *guru* as crucial protagonists (in the absence of any institutionalized, centralized Church). In modern times, one is reminded of the peculiar role of a leader such as M. K. Gāndhī (1869-1948), emblematic representative of the reformist, neo-Hindū ideology vouching for the ideals – strongly influenced by Western and Christian values – of non-violence, inclusivistic universalism, and tolerance (along the lines of Svāmin Vivekānanda, the great advocate of neo-Hindū reformism at the *World's Parliament of Religions* held in Chicago in 1893). A politically moderate response, strongly if not decisively influenced by Western values, will for the most part characterize the Congress Party's ideology even during the period of J. Nehru's leadership. Precisely the neo-Vedānta form of spirituality, with an emphasis on devotion (*bhakti*) and social service (*sevā*) as well as on a variety of meditative practices (*sādhana*), will become the typical form of religion i.e. the 'Hindūism' of the Westernized urban Hindū middle-classes. Starting from around the second half of the 19th century, this modernized, 'sanitized' form of Hindū religiosity – with the *guru* as its core figure – will be successfully 'exported' to the Western world, creating a most intriguing and complex 'hermeneutic circle' between India and Europe.[77]

By the same token, one must underline the importance of the Hindū 'religious right' in the Indian modern and contemporary political arena, especially after the traumatic experience of partition (1947): the many ways – often aggressive and militant, for the sake

77 On this crucial relation, see W. HALBFASS, *India and Europe. An Essay in Understanding*, Albany, N.Y., State University of New York Press, 1988; E. FRANCO – K. PREISENDANZ (eds.), *Beyond Orientalism: The Work of Wilhelm Halbfass and Its Impact on Indian and Cross-Cultural Studies*, Amsterdam – Atlanta, Ga, Rodopi, 1997, especially pp. 489-514. By W. Halbfass, see also "La scoperta indiana dell'Europa" in E. FIZZOTTI – F. SQUARCINI, *L'Oriente che non tramonta. Movimenti religiosi di origine orientale in Italia*, Roma, Libreria Ateneo Salesiano, 1999, pp. 19-27.

of an assumed *hindutva* animated by a strong anti-Islāmic (as well as anti-Western) component – in which a variety of renouncers and ascetics belonging to different *śākhā*-s and *akhārā*-s, head of monasteries, etc. have actively *engaged* themselves in the politics of the Indian nationalist movement even prior to the Gāndhī era and then *contra* Gāndhī and the Congress Party (as in the case of the *Ārya Samāj*, founded in 1875 by Svāmin Dayānanda Sarasvatī, up to the contemporary developments with the *Rashtriya Svayamsevak Sangh* – founded in 1925 – the *Vishva Hindu Parishad* – founded in 1964 – and the *Bharatiya Janata Party*[78] – founded in 1980). The emblematic anti-Gāndhī figure who fostered communal hatred in the name of the purity of the Hindū race/caste[79] and who elaborated the very notion of *hindutva*[80] calling for 'the Hindūization of politics and the militarization of Hindūism', is V. D. Savarkār (1883-1966). The violent actions of these fundamentalist Hindū groups especially against the Muslim community – such as in the conflicts in Bombay in 1982, or in the terrible bloodshed which occurred in the supposed capital and 'birth-place' of the *avatāra* Rāma in Ayodhyā, culminating in the destruction of the Babri *masjid* and the slaughters perpetrated in Surat, Gujarāt (December 1992) – are all cases in point: important *guru*-s and brāhmaṇical religious leaders have played a major role in actively instigating the Hindū masses against the Muslim minority. Especially after the 1960es, as Jackie Assayag cogently points out:

78 On India's recent receptivity to the right-wing Hindū nationalist party, see Ch. JAFFRELOT, *The Hindu Nationalist Movement and Indian Politics, 1925 to the 1990s*, London, Hurst, 1996; T. B. HANSEN, *The Saffron Wave. Democracy and Hindu Nationalism in Modern India*, Princeton, Princeton University Press, 1999. See also A. VANAIK, *The Furies of Indian Communalism. Religion, Modernity, and Secularization*, London – New York, Verso, 1997.

79 On the notion of race and the caste system, see Ch. JAFFRELOT, "The Idea of the Human Race in the Writings of Hindu Nationalist Ideologues in the 1920s and 1930s: A Concept Between Two Cultures", in P. ROBB (ed.), *The Concept of Race in South Asia*, Delhi, Oxford University Press, 1997.

80 V. D. SAVARKAR, *Hindutva: Who is Hindu?* Bombay, Veer Savarkar Prakashan, 1969 (1st ed. 1924).

> Un nombre accru de politiciens, de bureaucrates, d'hommes d'affaires et de groupes professionnels ou d'intérêts, qui étaient favorables aux usages politiques de l'idéologie religieuse et au loyalisme subséquent, se sont compromis avec des organisations conduites par toutes les espèces de renonçants et de gourous. Certains, très puissants parce qu'ils descendaient de lignages prestigieux dirigeant des monastères fort anciens; d'autres parce qu'ils régnaient sur des empires de dévotion qui fonctionnaient comme des entreprises de collecte de fonds; quelques-uns enfin parce que, à la pointe du renouveau religieux, ils avaient introduit des idées et des pratiques dans la spiritualité et les relations sociales plus conformes aux aspirations des nouvelles classes moyennes – pensons, par example, au développement de la secte Svaminarayan à partir du Gujarat, ou à celle, internationale, des Hare Krishna.[81]

Moreover:

> Depuis les années 1980, le programme nationaliste hindou domine le débat public. (...) Les profits matériels et économiques obtenus grâce au soutien de gourous et grâce aux réseaux de leurs organisations sont plus importants aujourd'hui qu'ils ne le furent dans le quatre décennies qui suivirent l'indépendance. (...) Les gourous – faux ou authentiques – désormais aussi puissants que des syndicats (de la "délivrance"), sont ainsi devenus des acteurs clés dans le monde des affaires et de la politique de la spiritualité, dans laquelle puise encore volontiers l'idéologie officielle de l'État.[82]

Unfortunately, the overall attention of indologists on these economical and political dimensions has been scant up to very recent times. In the consideration of India's *guru* figures, the field of indology has been dominated by a romantic, essentialist bias (as represented by the ideal, utopian setting of the *āśrama* as depicted in the Hindū brāhmaṇical tradition) and by an almost exclusive attention paid to texts and philological issues or to the more experiential, mystical dimensions of religious life. Only in the last one or two decades the

81 ASSAYAG, *L'Inde. Désir de nation*, *op. cit.*, p. 246.
82 *Ibid.*, pp. 246-247.

awareness and interest of scholars (most notably anthropologists and sociologists) for the *guru*-s' implication in in-worldly, socio-economic and political matters – the so-called 'divine enterprise' – has grown, especially focused on India's modern and contemporary situation.[83] The purported other-worldly domain of the *guru*-God is more often than not a pure illusion, being instead related to very mundane and ego-centered concerns. The ideological ground is that of brāhmaṇical orthodoxy as sanctioned in *dharma-śāstric* codes: the overall religious discourse *is* constitutively a power discourse, as it is evidenced by the dominant hierarchy of the caste system, perpetuating conditions of radical, structural inequality.[84] In this regard, one cannot but recall – on the left-side of the political arena – the figure of B. R. Ambedkār (1891-1956), the famous leader of the 'untouchables' and an 'untouchable' himself, who all his life fought against the caste system.[85] He detested the priestly brāhmaṇical system as well as all things Hindū, considered as the root-cause of evil. Even the moderate, paternalistic 'neo-Hindūism' of Gāndhī was envisioned by him as perpetuating discrimination and the tragedy of inequality. He was indeed one of Gāndhī's major critics. His anti-

83 See L. McKEAN, *Divine Enterprise. Gurus and the Hindu Nationalist Movement*, Chicago - London, University of Chicago Press, 1996. See also the review article to this book by ASSAYAG, "L'économie politique de la spiritualité: renoncement et nationalisme chez les gourous hindous depuis les années 1980", *op. cit.*

84 For an English translation of the *Mānava-dharma-śāstra*, perhaps the most authoritative of brāhmaṇical legal codes, see W. DONIGER – B. K. SMITH (trans.), *The Laws of Manu*, London, Penguin, 1991. On *dharma* literature, see P. OLIVELLE (trans.), *Dharmasūtras. The Law Codes of Ancient India*, Oxford, Oxford University Press, 1999. On the religious discourse as power discourse, see S. POLLOCK, "From Discourse of Ritual to Discourse of Power in Sanskrit Culture", *Journal of Ritual Studies* 2 (1990), pp. 315-345. By the same author, see also "Deep Orientalism? Notes on Sanskrit and Power beyond the Raj". In C. A. BRECKENRIDGE – P. VAN DER VEER (eds.), *Orientalism and the Postcolonial Predicament*, Philadelphia, University of Pennsylvania Press, 1993, pp. 76-133.

85 For an appraisal of Ambedkār's figure, see Ch. JAFFRELOT, *Dr. Ambedkar: Leader intouchable et père de la constitution indienne*, Paris, Presses de Sciences Politiques, 2000.

brāhmaṇism eventually brought him to embrace Buddhism: just before dying, he led a mass conversion to Buddhism of thousands of untouchables in the town of Nāgpur, in Mahārāṣṭra. The social phenomenon of neo-Buddhism, a movement which nowadays counts about six million adherents, owes its existence precisely to Ambedkār's anti-Hindū revolt and protest. Even in such a case, the intersection and different instrumental uses of religion and politics over the issue of power, in a struggle to either perpetuate hierarchical inequality (via brāhmaṇism) or, viceversa, to annihilate it (via Buddhism) is most revealing. What we can derive from all this is that, in order to be adequately sophisticated, the study of the '*guru* institute' – always to be set in its proper historical context – must necessarily take into consideration its ideological construction along with its concrete, dynamic forms of manifestation and change, being part and parcel of the complex socio-political texture.

THE FUNCTION OF THE *GURU* IN TANTRIC TRADITIONS

MONIA MARCHETTO

> There are three things which are indeed rare and due to the grace of God: a human birth, the protecting care of a perfected sage, and the longing for liberation.[1]

In the above-quoted verse, Śaṅkara, the greatest *ācārya* of *Advaita-vedānta*, expresses concepts that are of fundamental importance. Once an individual has obtained a human condition – envied even by gods – he/she must take shelter at a master's feet, if he or she has the desire of achieving freedom from the cycle of births and deaths.

According to Tantric traditions, the master's function is essential for the spiritual evolution of a seeker of deliverance.[2] *Tantra* is often described as a symbolic knowledge (*saṅket-vidyā*), directly communicated through a teacher. It is mainly a transmission of techniques and methods from a master (*guru*) to a qualified disciple, through oral and personal instructions. Its approach to reality is dualistic; it is that of man seeking God whose grace alone can free him from worldly involvement. Hence, in *Tantra*, devotion (*bhakti*) to a deity is a primary requirement in order to attain emancipation. And be-

1 *Viveka-cūḍāmaṇi* 3.

2 *Rudra-yāmala-tantra* 2, 6, 5; *Kulārṇava-tantra* 12, 45; *Śarada-tilakam* 2, 142-144.

cause it is a master who leads a devotee to the Godhead, devotion to him/her, too, is very important.

A renowned hymn in praise of the *guru*, ascribed to the *Viśva-sāra-tantra*, the *Guru-stotra*, states that there is no higher penance (*tapas*) than service to the master. With the collyrium stick of knowledge, the *guru* opens the eyes of the one blinded by the disease of ignorance. A master is believed to be established in knowledge (*jñāna*) and power (*śakti*), and grants to a disciple both worldly prosperity (*bhukti*) as well as liberation (*mukti*).[3]

In particular, the ninth and tenth verses of the above-mentioned hymn state:

> Salutations to the *guru* who, by setting the fire of self-knowledge (*ātma-jñāna*), burns away the fuel of *karman* accumulated through innumerable lives!
>
> Salutations to the *guru*, whose grace dries up the ocean of this relative existence completely and makes one realise the Supreme Wealth!

The *guru*'s influence, then, is thought to dissolve the effects of *karman*, that is to say, of action. The concept of *karman* is vast and subtle. The *karman* which is mentioned in the *Guru-stotra* is the so-called *sañcita-karman*, i.e. the totality of the effects of the actions a person has performed during his/her previous births.

Action has to be understood in the ample meaning of the word, that is to say *whatsoever action*, whether it conforms to *dharma* and bears merits (*puṇya-karman*) or it is incorrect, averse to the necessary order of things and thus productive of faults, sins (*pāpa-karman*).

It is this *sañcita-karman* which is reduced to ashes by the burning fire of knowledge. It is popularly believed that the gods Brahmā, Indra, and so on obtained their subtle body through *puṇya-karman*;

3 SWAMI PAVITRANANDA, *Hymns and Prayers to Gods and Goddesses*, Calcutta, Advaita Ashrama, 1988, pp. 3-5.

pigs, dogs, and other animals got their blameable gross body because of *pāpa-karman*. Nonetheless, the body of the gods and the body of animals will both have to be abandoned at the end of life.[4] All *karman*, whether positive or negative, must be destroyed and annihilated since it yields effects that entail ties (*bandha*), which will inevitably bring about a new birth. The fire of knowledge, burning away the fruits of *karman*, is thought to deliver a man from the source of bondage, namely, action along with its cause.[5]

However, there is a kind of *karman* which is not involved in this process of destruction, i.e. the *prārabdha-karman*. It is made up of the effects of those actions which caused the present bodily existence. Once it has started to reap its fruits, the *prārabdha-karman* will continue till the exhaustion of each and every one of its effects, similar to an arrow which, once it has been shot, will continue its run till it hits the mark.[6] The complete exhaustion of the *prārabdha-karman* coincides with death.

In Tantric schools, the notion which the *Guru-stotra* defines as "self-knowledge" corresponds to complex rituals belonging to different lineages of transmission of teachings (*sampradāya*). In particular, a practice which is known as *bhūta-śuddhi* deals with our topic. It is described in different *paddhati-s*, elaborated manuals that explain the correct succession of actions and invocations to be accomplished during the rituals. It is considered preliminary, together with other practices, to the worship of the gods (*pūjā*). According to the *Mantra-mahodadhi* of Mahidhara, a person who is initiated into a way of

4 K. N. VYĀSA, *Kāśīkhaṇḍokta Pañcakrośātmaka Jyotirliṅga Kāśīmāhātmya*, Vārāṇasī, Jyotiṣa Prakāśa, 1987, p. 309.

5 See *Srīmad Bhagavad Gītā Bhāṣya of Śrī Śaṅkarācārya* 22, 1 (Madras, Sri Ramakrishna Math, 1983, p. 161).

6 On this issue, see L. B. MIŚRA, *Yakṣadūtam*, Vārāṇasī, Sāhitya Prakāśan, 1996, pp. 21-23.

spiritual realization (*sādhana*) should perform *bhūta-śuddhi* in order to qualify himself/herself for the adoration of a deity.[7]

The compound *bhūta-śuddhi* means purification (*śuddhi*) of the gross elements (*bhūta*) i.e. one's physical constituents. It is a ritual process which is thought to dissolve the *kāla-puruṣa* (also called *pāpa-śarīra*), that is to say the body constituted of sin/faults.[8] The spiritual aspirant (*sādhaka*) is called to recite or meditate upon particular letters, upon specific sounds called *bījākṣara*-s which correspond to the five elements of the gross body. The repetition of *bījākṣara*-s follows the practice of inspiration, expiration, and the holding of breath according to particular sequences (*prāṇāyāma*).

During *prāṇāyāma*, the *sādhaka* must visualize a situation in which his/her *pāpa-śarīra* burns, the overall body framework is transmuted into a divine one and, finally, it comes to be substantiated of Śiva and Śakti, that is, of God and his Power. Thus, the purpose of the ritual is to generate a divine body (*divya-śarīra*).

The entire Indian tradition, and especially Tantric schools, maintain that individuality, that is to say the body and mind complex considered as a whole, deserves particular attention since it is one's fundamental tool on the way to spiritual realization; this is why purification rituals play an important role for recovering a condition of perfection that is thought to have been lost.

The *bhūta-śuddhi* process is followed by another basic component of every Tantric ritual: *nyāsa*. The doctrine of the *Tantra-śāstra*-s states that a *sādhaka* must himself/herself *become* a deity before worshipping a deity. The meaning of *nyāsa* is "placing" i.e. "fixing" (*sthāpanā*) powerful syllables or words with a vibrating effect (*mantra*) upon the body. The *sādhaka* touches different parts of his/her body with the hands, making special gestures (*mudrā*) and pronouncing specific sounds: typically, either the names of the selected deity

7 *Mantramahodadhi of Mahidhara* (*With his own 'Nauka' Commentary*). Translated into English by a Board of Scholars. Delhi, Sri Satguru Publications, 1998, Taraṅga I, 8-9.

8 *Ibid.*, Taraṅga I, 24-28.

or the syllables which form the name of the chosen god. Through *nyāsa*, the *sādhaka*'s entire body is thought to turn into the *mantra* (*mantra-maya*) and into the divine principle itself (*deva-maya*). Through different kinds of *nyāsa*-s the 'heavy' features of the body, in other words its inertness or dullness, are believed to decrease, and its qualities, that is to say its divinity, to increase.

This ritual is said to be useful to attain a state in which the *sādhaka* feels that the very nature or disposition (*bhāva*) of the deity has come upon him.

The correct performance of all rituals of a *sādhana*, knowledge of the effects of worshipping a deity (*upāsana*), and so on, descend from the uninterrupted chain of masters (*guru-paramparā*). The fundamental element is the ritual transmission of *mantra* through initiation (*dīkṣā*): without this consecration a person is not qualified for *pūjā*.

The *Kulārṇava-tantra* explains that there can be no liberation without initiation, and there can be no initiation without a teacher.[9] Without *dīkṣā* there is neither progress nor success on the spiritual path. Therefore, an aspirant must by all means be initiated by a teacher. The term *dīkṣā* is understood as the compound of two verbs, "to endow" (*dī*) with divine qualities and "to remove" (*kṣi*) obstructions, thereby freeing an individual from phenomenal fetters.[10]

According to the *Śaiva-siddhānta* school, during initiation Śiva presents himself under the form of the preceptor (*guru*, *deśika*, *ācārya*) and, through the descent of his divine influence (*śakti-pāta*), helps an aspirant enter into a *sādhana* and bestows upon him/her the necessary strength to follow the path.

Given the importance of *mantra*, Tantric *sādhana* is also called *mantra-yoga*. The initiated person must understand the meaning of the *mantra* and be fully conscious of it. This consciousness can descend only from a qualified teacher who has perfected the spiritual path and hence has obtained a complete knowledge of the secret of

9 *Kulārṇava-tantra* 14, 93.

10 *Prapañca-sāra-tantra* 5, 2.

the *mantra* (*mantra-rahasya*). In other words, the secret of a *sādhana* comes from the uninterrupted line of teachers of a *sampradāya*. Masters say that resolute determination and absolute trust (*śraddhā*) in a *sādhana* start rising when the totality of merits of innumerable lives manifests its effects.

Concerning the *mantra*, it is said that as the fire hidden in the fuel is brought out by friction, so by the *mantra*'s power devotion to the deity helps the manifestation of the Godhead. The power of a *mantra* is viewed to be the more efficacious if delivered by a competent teacher. In fact, only what is given by the master becomes a *mantra*.

According to the *Paraśurāma-kalpa-sūtra*, the power of *mantra* is beyond every conjecture: it is simply inconceivable.[11] An authoritative commentary to this text, on the other hand, notes that even the power of cosmic illusion (*māyā*) cannot be inquired and understood. Nonetheless, the difference between these two powers is that the power of *mantra* hinders the power of ignorance (*avidyā-śakti*) at its roots: thus, the power inherent in the *mantra* exceeds even the power of *māyā*.[12]

The classic procedure is to establish an absolute identity between the *guru* and one's individual self (*jīva*), between the *mantra* the master transmits and one's own mind (*manas*), and between the deity inherent in the *mantra* and one's own vital breath (*prāṇa*).[13] Without such identification a master will not be able to help a devotee to find his/her own path towards emancipation. Hence the importance of initiation, which binds the devotee and the master together.

The *mantra*, as the term implies, is essentially a mental process. When charged by the master's will and grace, it is said to be capable of annihilating all discursive thoughts, to the point that the mind

11 *Paraśurāma-kalpa-sūtra* I, 8.

12 V. N. MISHRA – P. H. MISHRA (eds.), *Paraśurāma-kalpa-sūtra*. With the Commentaries 'Vṛtti' by Śrī Rāmeśvara 'Nīrakṣīraviveka', Varanasi, Sampurnanand Sanskrit University, 2000, p. 11.

13 *Paraśurāma-kalpa-sūtra* I, 11.

achieves a state devoid of disturbing activities and expressions. Therefore, the mind itself is transmuted in the *mantra*.

According to a popular conception, if the master who communicates the *mantra* is a *guru* (*mantra-dātā*), the *mantra* that he or she communicates is a "superior *guru*" (*parama-guru*). The power inherent in the *mantra* is the higher element in the hierarchy (*parā-śakti*, *parāpara-guru*), and, of course, the highest power of all is the one embodied in the deity which is visualized and realized through the *mantra* (= Parama Śiva).

In Tantric circles, when a master plays the fundamental role of transmitting a ritual teaching, it is believed that his or her identity as a particular human being is utterly vanquished. At that time, the *guru* is the instrument through which the descent of the spiritual influence takes place. This is why the master is typically identified with the supreme deity itself. As the celebrated first verse of the *Guru-stotra* solemnly declares:

> The *guru* is Brahmā, the *guru* is Viṣṇu, the *guru* is [Śiva] Maheśvara, the *guru* is verily the Supreme *Brahman*! Salutations to that *guru*!

THE TWENTY-FOUR *GURU*-S OF DATTĀTREYA *AVADHŪTA*

CORRADO PUCHETTI

Dattātreya is the Absolute itself in the form of the *guru*. His divine personality made him a *yogin* since the beginning, an *avadhūta*. *Avadhūta* means a liberated soul, one who has "passed through" or is "released from" all the attachments and cares of worldly existence, who has attained the spiritual state and has identified himself with the ultimate Principle. Although this term implies renunciation, it actually defines a higher condition which transcends both attachment and non-attachment. An *avadhūta* doesn't feel the necessity to observe any rule, either secular or religious. He neither looks for anything nor avoids anything. He has neither knowledge nor ignorance. Seeing only the identity with the infinite Self, he abides in this realization.

Dattātreya is a divine descent (*aṁśāvatāra*), who, according to purāṇic lore, manifested himself in the house of the sage Atri and his wife Anasūyā. Anasūyā, because of her infallible devotion to her husband, was renowned throughout the three worlds. Her spiritual powers were so great that even the elements of nature would not dare disturb her.

One day, the *trimūrti* of Brahmā, Viṣṇu and Śiva, praised by all the gods, approached Anasūyā for help. The sage Māṇḍavya had cast a curse on Ugraśravas, the vicious husband of Śīlavatī, who, in turn, had cast a counter-curse to the effect that the sun would not rise the next day. As only an ascetic can face another ascetic, the three gods came to seek the help of Anasūyā asking her to convince Śīlavatī to withdraw her curse. Anasūyā did as the gods wished and was successful in restoring light to the world. Then the *trimūrti*, extremely happy for the success of their mission, granted a boon to Anasūyā.[1] She expressed the desire that the three gods should become her sons and they duly accepted.

The sage Atri named the newborn Śiva as Durvāsas i.e. the gloomy one, since the quality (*guṇa*) of *tamas*[2] prevailed in him. Brahmā, who was charming like the moon, was named Candra[3] as in him the quality of *rajas*[4] abounded. Viṣṇu on his part was named Dattātreya, as in him prevailed the pure, spiritual quality of *sattva*.

The figure of Dattātreya, however, soon came to represent all three qualities. For this reason, he is usually depicted with three heads and six arms. In his arms he holds the disc (*cakra*) and conch (*śaṅkha*), symbols of Viṣṇu; the rosary (*japa-mālā*) and water-pot

1 There are different accounts on how the *trimūrti* approached Anasūyā. The marāṭhī tradition says that the three gods wanted to test the loyalty and virtue of Anasūyā. They thus went to her in disguise as three random guests, asking for alms. Anasūyā welcomed them with all honours and offered them food. On their request that she should serve them food naked, she did accordingly and at once, by virtue of her perfect faith in her husband Atri, the three divine guests were turned into infants, happily lying on Anasūyā's lap. The wives of Brahmā, Viṣṇu, and Śiva then prayed Anasūyā to please restore their husbands to their original form, which she did immediately. Pleased by her purity and devotion, the *trimūrti* decided to grant Anasūyā whatever boon she would ask for.

2 The descending quality, symbolized by the colour black.

3 Also known as Soma, another name of the moon. In *Brahmāṇḍa Purāṇa* 39-43, there is the tale of the curse that Brahmā cast on Kāmadeva who had disturbed him while manifesting the worlds, and how the curse was then transferred to sage Atri and from him to the moon.

4 The expansive quality, symbolized by the colour red.

(*kamaṇḍalu*), symbols of Brahmā; and the trident (*triśūla*) and hour-glass shaped drum (*ḍamaru*), symbols of Śiva.[5]

The white cow at his side represents *dharma* or primordial nature. As a sign of his asceticism, he wears wooden sandals. The garland of beads (*rudrākṣa-mālā*) which he wears around his neck symbolizes the series of universes he emanates. The plaited hair is a symbol of the fire of knowledge and can be compared to 'rescue ropes' for the help of his devotees.

Noble and attractive like the moon, his beauty charmed whomever he met. On the mountains and in lonely forests he used to sit deeply absorbed in contemplation. Without any mental impression (*vāsanā*), perfectly free, Dattātreya blissfully wandered throughout the world.

Once King Yadu saw him and was greatly impressed by his perfect detachment and bliss.[6] The King asked Dattātreya by the grace of which *guru* had he attained to such a state of spiritual completeness. Śrī Dattātreya replied by saying that the real teacher of man is indeed his own Self: having attained to the knowledge of his own Self through direct perception and logic inference,[7] man may easily attain to the highest condition. Dattātreya emphasized how the *guru*

5 Instead of the *ḍamaru* and *japa-mālā*, in some representations Dattātreya holds the *gadā*, the mace, and the *padma*, the lotus.

6 Yadu was son of Yayāti and nephew of Nahuṣa, an important sovereign of the lunar dynasty and an ancestor of Kṛṣṇa. The following dialogue between Yadu and the young *avadhūta* identified as Dattātreya is found in *Bhāgavata Purāṇa* 11, 7, 24 – 11, 9, 33.

7 According to Vedānta the *pramāṇa-s* or means to acquire true knowledge (*pramā*) are six: *pratyakṣa*, perception by the senses; *anumāna*, inference; *upamāna*, analogy or comparison; *śabda* or *āpta-vacana*, verbal authority, revelation (which can be *vaidika*, Vedic, or *āpta-laukika*, oral); *anupalabdhi* or *abhāva-pratyakṣa*, non-perception or negative proof; *arthāpatti*, inference from circumstances. Other schools increase the number of *pramāṇa-s* to nine by adding *sambhava*, equivalence, *aitihya*, tradition or fallible testimony, and *ceṣṭā*, gesture. Dattātreya, however, only speaks of the first two as being at the same time necessary and sufficient in order to realize the Self.

is not to be found among men and that no one ever whispered a *mantra* in his ear.[8]

Dattātreya revealed to King Yadu that he followed twenty-four special *guru*-s or "principles" (*tattva*), through which he attained perfection. He then asked the King to listen to his speech with one-pointed mind (*ekāgra-citta*) and proceeded to tell him the following, solemn words:[9]

> From the earth, *pṛthivī*, I have learned forbearance and benevolence towards all living beings. In the same way, the wise one should dedicate his life for the welfare of the entire cosmos. The earth, with its rivers, stones, mountains and many caves, thus was my first *guru*.
> Water, *jala*, is sweet, pure, gentle by nature and the source of sanctity for man. While it quenches the thirst of every creature and sustains innumerable trees and plants, it is never proud of itself. On the other hand, it humbly seeks the lowliest places. The wise, like water, purifies whoever sees, touches or prays to him. The water can be both the means of purification and the aim of worship, as the saint is.
> My third teacher is the fire element, *agni*. Sometimes it manifests itself as blazing flames, other times as smouldering embers, covered by ash. However, it is always present in all objects as latent heat. In this form it is omnipresent. The god of fire accepts the offerings from everyone, irrespective of his moral worth, and thus burns down his sins. Even so, it still remains the ever pure divinity, the fire-god. So too an *avadhūta* should accept food from everyone, burning down his sins. The digestive fire inside the stomach[10] has indeed the same nature of fire: as all the substances poured into the fire are immediately burned, so all food accumulated in the stomach is assimilated

8 In the *kali-yuga*, because of the increasing of a materialistic tendency, the transmission of spirituality is said to have become hidden, esoteric. During the rite of initiation, the master possessing metaphysical knowledge, covered by a veil, whispers a secret *bīja-mantra* into the disciple's ear. Dattātreya, being the *guru* - both with and without form - is understood to be the embodiment of knowledge.

9 My English translation follows SVĀMĪ PARAMĀNANDAJĪ, *Śrī Dattātreyajī kā vṛttānta*, Kāśī, n.d.

10 See *Bhagavad-gītā* 15, 14.

without leaving any residues. He who knows, with his behaviour concealed just like fire is covered by ashes, eats whatever food is offered to him. In so doing, he burns the past and future miseries of the giver of food.

Air, *vāyu*, is pure and odourless in itself, and blows on both sweet or foul-smelling things without any discrimination or preference. Though it momentarily seems to take on the smell of its surroundings, in a short while it reveals its pristine quality. A spiritual aspirant should live in the world unaffected by the dualities of life, and, as the air becomes the breath in the body, giving energy and happiness to all creatures without request, so he should continue to wander without any attachment.

Stars, wind, clouds, and all creation are contained in space, *ākāśa*, without restricting space itself, which remains absolute and all-pervading. Analogous with respect to the body is the soul, which although being in this world is not conditioned by it. He who has realised his identity with the *ātman* is not touched by what is a mere creation of time. Thus I recognised space as one of my *guru*-s.

Of all things in nature, the moon, *candra*, is unique. It appears to wax and wane during the bright and dark fortnights. In fact, the lunar globe remains ever the same. In this it is like the Self of man. While a man appears to pass through the stages of infancy, youth, maturity, and old age, his real Self remains unchanged. Moreover, the moon only reflects the light of the sun but has no light of its own. So the soul or mind of man is only a reflection of the light of awareness of the real Self.

As the sun, *sūrya*, draws up the water on earth as vapour and again casts it down as rain in the proper season, so the sage gathers wisdom through his senses and imparts it to his worthy disciples at the proper time for the maintenance and balance of the cosmos.

From the pigeon, *kapota*, I have learned to renounce all family ties. Once a pair of pigeons lived together in a tree. They bred their young and were bringing them up with deep affection and love. One day a hunter caught the young fledglings in a snare. The mother bird, wearied by grief, threw herself into the net, and so the pigeon, unable to bear the separation from his sweetheart, also jumped into the snare and met his end. Reflecting on this I realised how, even after being born as an intelligent human being, man is caught up in the coils of possessiveness and brings about his own spiritual destruction. The

Self is originally free, but when associated with bodies and senses gets identified with them, and thus gets caught in the endless cycle of birth and death.

The python, *ajagara*, is a sluggard, unwilling to move out briskly for its prey. Lying in its lurch it devours whichever creature it comes across, be it sufficient or insufficient to appease its hunger. The *avadhūta* accepts with contentment what he gets spontaneously. Like the python, he has shaken off sleep and wakefulness and abides in a state of incessant contemplation of the Self. Though endowed with a sturdy body, the wise refrains from all actions which are characterized by a sense of identification with the body. Unmindful of both purity and impurity, he withdraws the power of perception from his senses and centres it on the Self. Thus, the python was one of my teachers of wisdom.

Imperturbable like the sea, *samudra*, is the wise. Any number of overflowing rivers may join it, yet it maintains its level, remaining stable within its limits, *maryādā*. In the same way, the mind remains stable even whilst absorbing different images. Like the unfathomable sea, the *avadhūta* is unconquerable and cannot be troubled by anything.

The moth, *pataṃga*,[11] is attracted by the fire and jumps into it getting burnt. Similarly, the ordinary man is enticed by the illusory pleasures and gets caught up in the ceaseless cycle of birth and death. On the other hand, the *jīvanmukta* engrosses his mind in *brahman*, having burnt down the illusion of being a limited self.

The bee, *madhukarī*, is lured by the sweet scent of the lotuses, at sunset. It resides in the lotus as the latter closes up for the night, and thus gets imprisoned. In the same way, a wandering monk, if he is not wise and wary enough, is tempted by the same objects and dainty dishes offered to him by householder devotees. Such a one easily yields to their persuasion to linger and finally stays on in their houses, enslaved by the luxuries. Therefore, a monk should be careful to accept from them only what is strictly necessary to keep his body and soul together. Like a bee, he should collect only small

11 See *Bhagavad-gītā* 11, 29.

quantities of food from house to house.[12] The wise extracts the essence from each source, as the bee extracts the honey from the flower.

The elephant, *gaja*, was attracted by a stuffed cow elephant raised by human beings in the forest. The wild elephant mistook it for a mate, approached it, and was then skilfully bound in fetters by the cunning human beings. In the same way, the un-regenerated man is tempted by the opposite sex and gets bound by the fetters of infatuation. The wise man doesn't pursue the company of women, also because he would be defeated by more powerful rivals, as the elephant is defeated by stronger elephants.

The fourteenth *guru* that awakened my spirit is a prostitute named Piṅgalā. One day she eagerly awaited a particular client in the hope that he would pay her amply. She waited and waited until late in the night. When he did not turn up she was at last disillusioned and reflected thus:

How stupid I am! By neglecting the divine spirit within, who is of the nature of bliss eternal, I foolishly waited for a debauchee who inspires my lust and greed and who is most likely to inflict on me the most unbearable torments. I shall expand myself on the Self, unite with It and win eternal joy.

Through such repentance she attained blessedness. From the prostitute, I have learned to renounce all hopes and desires.

The fish, *mīna*, greedily swallows the bait and is at once caught by the hook. From it, I realized how man meets his destruction by craving for delicious food. I learned that the wise one should eat only wholesome food in order to sustain his life and health. As the bait conceals the hook, behind every sensual pleasure a karmic reaction lies in ambush.

In a village an arrow-maker was totally absorbed in moulding a sharp arrow. He grew so oblivious of all else that he didn't even notice a royal pageant passing by. This sight awakened me to the truth that a single minded, all absorbing contemplation of the Self spontaneously eliminates all temptation for trivial, worldly interests. Con-

12 Indeed, there is a method of begging called *mādhūkara*. The renouncer begs from several houses at random, taking a morsel from each so not to become a burden on the householders.

centration on one point is the sole secret of success in any spiritual discipline. Thus the arrow-maker is my sixteenth guru.

It is said that deer, *hariṇa*-s, are very fond of music and that poachers employ it to lure them before hunting them. From this I learned that a spiritual aspirant who has a weakness for merry, secular music will soon get bogged down by passions and sensual desires, to the point that he will ultimately lose whatever spiritual progress he had achieved. Such indeed is the story of the sage Ṛśyaśṛṅga.[13]

A bird of prey, *kurara*, was carrying a piece of meat. Many other birds attacked it so that the poor bird was much pestered. At last, it wisely let its prey fall and all the other birds rushed after it. The acquisition and possession of what is considered dear among men leads to clashes, as I have understood from the bird of prey.

Like the suckling baby, *bālaka*, who after drinking his milk is soothed and carefree, so after eating the food collected through alms I stay serene and content. Only two persons do not care for either honour or dishonour: the suckling baby who doesn't know anything and never works, and the man who has realized the Being beyond all qualities.

As the serpent, *sarpa*, doesn't build any den but eventually comes to inhabit anthills or ready-made shelters, similarly I stay in buildings raised by worldly men, in crumbled temples or caves. The sage shouldn't deceive his own nature with his actions and words, as the mere sight of a serpent doesn't tell us if it is venomous or not.

When the bees have gathered much honey, along comes the honey-collector, *madhuhan*, to rob the store. As the bees gather their honey through much work, so man with strong efforts collects different things throughout his life which must be left at the time when the

13 In the *Mahābhārata*, Ṛśyaśṛṅga is a sage nephew of Kaśyapa and son of Vibhāṇḍaka. The latter had an emission of semen at the sight of Urvāśī. The semen fell into a lake and a doe happened to drink its water. Thus a child with antlers was born, called Ṛśyaśṛṅga. Since his birth he had never seen any other human being but his father. The King of the Aṅga-s, Lomapāda (friend of Daśaratha), was informed by his counselors that, in order to make the rain fall, a sage who had never seen a woman had to break his asceticism (*tapas*). Ṛśyaśṛṅga was then captivated by the songs of a damsel sent by the King. He then married Lomapāda's daughter, Śāntā. Ṛśyaśṛṅga also appears in the *Rāmāyaṇa* (I. 14-16).

yamadūta, the messenger of death, comes. This example shows that the accumulation of things brings about great pain. Like the honey-collector, the *saṃnyāsin* or renunciant is the first to partake in the offerings presented by the householder, who has earned the money to buy them with great exertion.

Once a girl, in the absence of her parents, had to answer to the request of a monk who was begging for alms. She told him:

I am pounding food grains, oh sage. If you wait a while I will give you a part of it.

As she started battering the food grains the bangles on her hand started bouncing one against the other producing a loud noise. The girl considered it inauspicious that the monk should hear that noise. As a hindū maiden, she was not expected to remove all her bangles at any time. She then decided to keep only two on each hand and remove the rest. Even then, however, they were still bouncing one against the other and making noise. Finally, she decided to keep only one bangle on each hand and finished her work. From this episode, I understood that by living in the midst of many people a lot of unwanted gossip ensues, and no spiritual practice can be pursued. Even when two spiritual seekers stay together it is no better: only in solitude can one assiduously carry out his task.

The spider, *aṣṭapāda*, creates the web from the thread which it secretes in the form of a fluid. After some time, it gathers up the web into itself. In a similar way, at the end of a cycle, through the energy of time, Nārāyaṇa withdraws in himself the universe which he had created through *māyā*, his inscrutable power of projection, maintenance, and dissolution. As the spider falls into the web it has made, so men - having built up a 'web of illusions' with their fantasies - fall into it becoming prisoners of themselves.

The caterpillar is also one of my teachers of wisdom. The wasp carries its caterpillar to a safe corner and closes it up in its nest and goes on buzzing about it. The young caterpillar is so frightened by the incessant buzzing that it cannot think of anything else other than the wasp. Through such uninterrupted contemplation of its mother, the caterpillar soon grows into a wasp! Similarly, the true disciple is so charmed and awed by the spiritual eminence of his *guru* that he cannot think of anyone or anything other than him. Through such contemplation, he himself soon blossoms into a great spiritual master.

> On whatever form an individual being - out of love, hatred, or fear - fixes his mind, that very form he achieves.

The aforementioned twenty-four *guru*-s are but twenty-four principles, *tattva*-s, of which the teacher reveals as many qualities. This number is connected with the twenty-four archetypal elements of the Sāṃkhya doctrine as well as with the twenty-four syllables of the *gāyatrī-mantra*. The twenty-fifth teacher is the body itself, on analogy with the *puruṣa* of Sāṃkhya and the sacred syllable *oṃ* which is placed at the beginning of the *gāyatrī-mantra*. Dattātreya concludes:

> Lastly the body is my teacher, being the cause of discrimination and equanimity. Through the body I have adequately reflected on the higher principles, though I have realized it belongs to others.[14] The body - through which one maintains a house and family, gathers a variety of objects, and collects riches with great pain - in the end dries up like a tree, leaving behind the seed for a new body. Hunger attracts it on one side while thirst attracts it on the other. The sexual impulse leads it somewhere, and the skin, the stomach, and the ears lead it in still other directions.
> After many births the sage gets a human body which, though very fragile, can bring one to the supreme goal, that is, the realization of the Self. On the other hand, sensual enjoyments can be experienced with any other body.

The *brahman*, the One without a second, is sung in different ways by the sages. The *guru* who unveils the highest truth is one, but there can be different teachers in helping the disciple to assimilate it. Vasiṣṭha answered the questions of Rāma, dispelled all ignorance, and was considered the *guru* of Rāma. So it happened between Naciketas and Yama, Arjuna and Kṛṣṇa, Yājñavalkya and Sūrya. Yājñavalkya, in turn, taught the liberating knowledge to Janaka, and Janaka taught it to Śukadeva. As is shown in these cases as well as in the story of Dattātreya, the one longing for final liberation (*mumukṣutva*) can

14 Indeed, the body belongs to the animals that will devour it after death.

find access to the Supreme through the "good company" (*satsaṅga*) of authoritative teachers.

ESSENTIAL BIBLIOGRAPHY

Bahadur, Sri Jaya Chamarajendra Wadiyar, *Dattātreya*: *The Way and the Goal*, London, George Allen & Unwin, 1957.

Bharadvaja, A. E. (trans.), *Sree Guru Charitra*, Ongole, Sai Baba Mission, 1985.

Mal, Kanoo (trans.), *Awadhoota Gita*, Madras, S. R. Murthi & Co., 1920.

Pandey, R. (ed.), *Śrīmad Bhāgavatam*, Delhi, Chaukhamba Sanskrit Series Office, 1996.

Paramānandajī, Svāmī, *Śrī Dattātreyajī kā vṛttānta*, Kāśī, n.d.

Rigopoulos, Antonio, *Dattātreya*: *The Immortal Guru, Yogin, and Avatāra*. A Study of the Transformative and Inclusive Character of a Multi-faceted Hindu Deity, Albany, N.Y., State University of New York Press, 1998.

THE JEWEL OF THE SECRET PATH OR THE NEGLECTED *GURU*? SOME REMARKS ON THE *GURUVĀDA* AMONG THE BĀULS OF BENGAL

FABRIZIO FERRARI

The songs of the Bāuls of Bengal are fairly widespread in India and recently in the rest of the world as a world-music phenomenon. Although the term *bāul* is generally used to indicate folk singers belonging to the Bengali rural environment and displaying a lunatic behavior, I will herein refer to 'Bāul-ism' only in its *sampradāya* or *panthā* significance so as to avoid the romantic image of the 'fools of God' brought forth by previous studies. This paper is divided in three parts relative to the teachings and the *guru*'s role in the Bāul tradition. First the different phases of initiation will be examined both in the Hindū and Islāmic context, in order to emphasize the initiatory character of the Bāul path. Following that, I will focus on two kindred misconceptions that degenerated into a sort of annihilation of the figure of the *guru* and moved onto transforming Bāuls from their pre-Tagorian quasi-beggar status into the pretentious role of 'mystic minstrels of Bengal'.

Jay guru: this simple utterance is the salutation formula used by all Bāuls in order to stress their profound devotion to the figure of the spiritual guide, the ferryman that leads to the state of *jyānte marā* ("dead while alive"). The meaning of the word *bāul* has been extensively analysed by many scholars and although no hypothesis can be assumed for certain, it is actually fascinating to inquire into the roots of this still living syncretistic, esoteric tradition of Bengal. The quest for the origin of the name *bāul* can be divided into two mainstreams depending on the predominance of the Hindū or Islāmic element. Dimock (1989: 250) claims that the term is a Bengali corruption of the Sanskrit word *vātula* ("infected with the wind disease", i.e. "mad") or *vyākula* ("confused", "disordered"), but a meaning can be derived also by looking at the esoteric *sādhana* of the sect. Accordingly, *bā* is understood to mean *bāyu*[1] ("wind") and *ul* to mean *ullekh* ("reference", "information") so as to underline the search for God in the wind of divine emotion. Another interesting interpretation looks at the triangular form of the Bengali letter *ba* as resembling the *yoni*, the female genitalia, whilst *ul* is said to stand for *ullās* ("delight", "joy"; "satisfaction"), so that the success of the *sādhaka* who controls his own body during sexual-yogic practices is emphasized (Karim 1971: 24-25; also Das 1992: 393-394, fn. 33).

Where the Islāmic influence grew stronger, Bāuls were regarded as Sufis and their name said to have been originated from Arabic *bāl* ("mind", "heart"). There is also a possible link with the term *buhlūl* ("mad"), an appellative of Abu Walid Ibn Amre Seirafia Khufi (d. 806 CE), the founder of the Buhluliya *ṭarīqa* (Karim 1980: 61). Furthermore, even if "the world 'baul' may also be derived from the name of a Qalander spiritual leader, Bu' Ali" (*ibid.*: 102),[2] one must remember that Muslim Bāuls are often called Āuls: this term seems to be a corruption of the Arabic *auliyā'* ("friend"; "devotee") which in the Islāmic esoteric tradition calls to mind the *wali-Allāh*,[3] the friend of God.

1 Sanskrit: *vāyu*.

2 Unfortunately, Karim does not furnish any proof to validate such an origin.

3 In Arabic, *auliyā'* is the broken plural of the noun *wali*.

The Bāul *sampradāya* (or *bartamān-panthā*, as others prefer)[4] does not stress any mark of distinction: men and women of all castes, religions, and social conditions can be equally initiated into the *mānuṣer dharma*, the "religion of man". The esoteric path followed by Bāuls is fully committed to the search of the *maner mānuṣ*, the "Man of the Heart", understood as the divine essence of man. The *sādhaka* must realize his/her own divine origin by experiencing the state of supreme beatitude (*mahā-ullāsa*; *mahā-sukha*), which is regarded as the time in which the transcendental dimension of the human being coexists with the immanence of God (Ferrari 2002: 22).

For many years all studies on the Bāuls have been carried out 'under the shadow' of Rabīndranāth Ṭhākur (= Tagore). Before him, Bāuls were simply considered as nothing but beggars, "a godless sect" that "[...] makes it a point to appear as dirty as possible" (Bhattacharya 1968: 381). In view of the fact that this issue is still debated, it should be pointed out that Bāuls are deeply rooted into the esoteric traditions of Hinduism, Buddhism,[5] and Islām. The path they follow in order to reach the absolute identity with the divine is subjected to initiation (*prabartanā*) and requires *sādhana*. Although it is definitely not easy – and maybe pretentious – to devise a satisfactory framework of the Bāul *sādhana*, an attempt will be provided on the basis of conversations and interviews carried out during field-work in West Bengal.[6]

4 Openshaw (1995: 110-111) states that "whereas the *barttamān panthī* base themselves on the existent (*barttamān*), by which they mean, among other things, what can be ascertained through the senses, and what is based on one's own judgment, they reject as hearsay or inference (*anumān*) the more orthodox ideology and prescriptions based on authorized scripture, and indeed, as a rule, any other knowledge which is not based on one's own experience." This, however, has not to be interpreted as contradicting their *sādhana*: initiation and the figure of the *guru* are basic and transcend any given tradition.

5 Mainly Sahajayāna Buddhism.

6 Personal enquiries were carried out in the Birbhum, Burdwan, and Bankura districts of West Bengal, and in the cities of Kolkata and Varanasi from 1999 to 2002.

The Bāul *panthī*-s don't follow any tradition and don't consider themselves Hindūs or Muslims. They rather developed their own *dharma*:

> Your path moves through temples and mosques,
> I hear your call, o Lord, still I can't move [...].[7]

The veneration of the *guru*, the observance of his teachings, the learning of an 'intentional language', and the oral transmission of songs are the main features of the cult. The *guruvāda* or doctrine of the preceptor represents the real essence of Bāul *sādhana*. In order to display such a conception, I will present some of the teachings and rituals connected to the *guru-śiṣya* and the *pīr-murīdi*, namely, the relationship between the disciple and his preceptor in the Hindū and Islāmic contexts respectively.

> You [= *guru*] are the charioteer of my heart's desire,
> I go wherever you drive me.
> O *guru*, you are the essence of the Tantra-s,
> o *guru*, you are the essence of the *mantra*-s,
> o *guru*, you are the essence of the *yantra*-s.[8]
> If you don't play the music, who will do it?
> The eye of my mind is blind since birth.
> *Guru*, you are always conscious.

7 '*tomār path ḍhekyāche mandire masjide*', Madan Bāul (Bhattacarya 1408 B.S.: 1043-1044).

8 Datta (1978: 448) prefers to render the verse '*guru tumi tantrer tantrī / guru tumi mantrer mantrī / guru tumi yantrer yantrī*' with a different translation: "*Guru*, you make from me the strings/ *Guru*, you make from me the music / *Guru*, you make from me the instrument." I have chosen not to translate the words *tantra*, *mantra*, and *yantra* due to their high esoteric significance. Furthermore, Datta's translation seems to me not to reflect the exact grammatical meaning of the verse.

Longing to see your feet, Lālan says:
put the collyrium of knowledge into my eyes.[9]

The only liturgy practised by Bāuls is singing. Songs have the power to relieve the spirit of the madcap who is distressed by experiencing God through *bhāva*,[10] the state of supreme bliss that drives practitioners to divine madness (*divyon māda*).

In the course of time, every lineage (*gotra*) transmits and produces a *corpus* of songs. From the beginning of the twentieth century, many scholars offered their own contribution in collecting as many lyrics as possible. Yet, this seems a desperate endeavour since a countless number of songs has been composed over time. Many of these songs, belonging to well-reputed Bāuls[11] or simply considered 'traditional', are constantly rewritten or interpolated. Broadly speaking, Bāul songs might be differentiated into six different typologies according to their subject:

1. *gurubandana* or *murśidā gān*: the holy figure of the preceptor is emphasized as the Holder of Knowledge. He is the only one who can lead his disciples to *samādhi*;

9 '*guru su-bhāb deo āmār mane*', Lālan Phakir (Bhattacarya 1408 B.S.: 588-589).

10 I avoid translating *bhāva* as "ecstasy" for, as it will be argued below, such a term is more fitted for the rapture of mystical experience. For an analysis of the various meanings of *bhāva*, see McDaniel (1989: 20-25): in her enlightening overview, *bhāva* – among other explanations – is likened to a momentary mental alteration depending on "the religious experience of traditional holy men and women performing spiritual practices [seriously taken] if they are part of a lineage" and "a spontaneous response to natural beauty, often when alone, by seriously religious people." In the former instance, *bhāva* is experienced by Bāuls through madness (*pāgalāmi*) and supreme joy (*mahā-ullāsa*, *mahā-sukha*), as the result of the extinction of the self (*samādhi*).

11 Unfortunately, this phenomenon is increasing more and more due to the massive distribution of world music. The most popular Bāul songs are performed by many Bāul and non-Bāul artists to such an extent that the original melody and quite often the words themselves are distorted (Ferrari 2002: 50).

2. *maner mānuṣer gān*: the quest for God is the quest for man. With reference to Tantrism, *bhakti*, and Sufism, the *maner mānuṣ* is celebrated as the divine essence of man;
3. *sādhana gān* or *mārphatī gān*: the esoteric teachings are illustrated through an "intentional language" (*sandhā bhāṣā*), and the main purpose is to transmute the gross body (*sthūla śarīr*) into a subtle one (*sūksma śarīr*);
4. *prem-tattva* or *bhakti-tattva*: through the description of the divine *līlā* between Rādhā and Kṛṣṇa or Muhammad's love relationship with Allāh, the dualism manifested in the Universe is realized together with the natural tendency of man to transcend it by means of pure love;
5. *ulṭā gān*: a strong opposition to both Hindū and Muslim orthodoxy is stressed. Any kind of discrimination is banned and the Holy Scriptures are often ignored because of the deceit resulting from a literal, non-spiritual interpretation of them;
6. *śabda gān*: no particular religious meaning seems to be present here. These songs should be considered as entertainment lyrics, basically of a descriptive kind.

The significance of the *guruvāda* is herein examined through the study of the *gurubandana* songs and the hidden meanings concealed by their *sandhā bhāṣā*, also known as "twilight language" (*sandhyā bhāṣā*) or "upside-down language" (*ulṭa-bhāṣā*).[12]

The initiation (*prabartanā*)[13] among both Hindū and Muslim Bāul communities is generally named *mantra dīkṣā*. During this stage the disciple is expected to receive his own *mantra*[14] and his efforts are

[12] On this issue, see, among others, Bharati 1961: 261-262 and Bharati 1993: 164-173. On *sandhā bhāṣā* among Bāuls, see Openshaw 2002: 62-71.

[13] On account of the fact that Bāuls can be initiated by both *guru*-s and *murśid*-s, the kind of *sādhana* that will be imparted depends on the *gotra* and religious background of the preceptor.

[14] "The praises to Kṛṣṇa and the seed-syllable (*bīja*) are identified with the female and male fluids, respectively, while the tongue of the master and the initiate's ear are likened to the penis and the vagina. While the physical form of such intercourse leads to the birth of the body of flesh and blood, the Sahajiyā initia-

committed to the acknowledgment of the divinity of the human body (*deha-tattva*) through practising yogic postures (*āsana*-s), the retention of breath (*kumbhaka*), and the visualization of the *guru*.

After *mantra-grahaṇa*[15] and in order to make the body fit for the following stage, the initiate is requested to purify himself through the absorption of the four moons (*cāricandra*), a ritual which is believed to lead to the identification of the individual self with the Universal Self. Among Bāuls, the issue of the equivalence between microcosm and macrocosm is especially stressed. As a consequence, the human body is considered as nothing else but a perfect replica of the whole manifestation.

The 'four moons', *biṣṭa* or *māṭhi* ("stool"), *mutra* or *rasa* ("urine"), *rajas* or *rūpa* ("menses") and *śukra* or *rasa* ("semen"), are visualised through four colours (black, yellow, red, and white) and are respectively likened to the four elements (earth, water, fire, and air). When the 'moons' are absorbed by ingestion, the body is thought to be purified and the *sādhaka* is requested to sublimate his subsequent sexual intercourse so as to perceive the 'essence' of the universe itself.[16]

Despite the fact that some discrepancies may be recognised in collecting the 'four moons', according to my informants[17] they are gathered in a ritual pot (*kujā*), blended (milk and sugar is sometimes added to them), and finally consumed by both *sādhaka* and *sādhikā* (Bhattacarya 2001: 424-425). The assembling tools are indicated as "works" (*kāj*): *māṭhir kāj* and *mutrer kāj* are the collection of the

tion leads to the birth of the divine body. Attainment of this divine body means that the couple has realized the all-powerful inner person (*mānuṣa*), who is at the heart of reality" (Hayes 1995: 348-349).

15 The act of giving a personal *mantra* to a disciple.

16 Nabīn Dās Bāul from Tārāpiṭh and Debdās Bāul from Bolpur explained this as the perception of the *maner mānuṣ* who displays his existence through *mahābhāva*; personal interview, Bolpur, January 2001.

17 For reasons of confidentiality, I do not mention the names of those Bāuls who wished to remain anonymous.

second or third daily ejection,[18] the *rūper kāj* is the way the *sādhana saṅginī* filters her own blood to save the part containing ova,[19] and the *raser kāj* is the extraction of semen done by the *sādhaka* through fellatio. However, not all Bāuls perform this practice[20] for some of them purify their body with a mixture of milk (*kṣīr*), water (*nīr*), molasses (*guṛ*), and cardamom (*elāc*), so as to 'synthesise' in a non-bodily way the four elements. They then interpret the sexual intercourse which follows as the union between the individual soul and the Universal Spirit.[21]

18 Das (1992: 418) writes that "in cases in which only menstrual blood and semen are taken in together, urine and stool are usually ingested a fortnight later". However, I have found no confirmation of this during my interviews.

19 Usually the blood is collected on the third day from the appearance of the menstrual blood in the body of the *sādhana saṅginī*, for it is believed that at such time the ova (= the receptacle of life) are present.

20 There is some confusion regarding this topic since in Bāuls' songs there is no evidence of a *sādhana* practiced without a female companion. Nonetheless, I myself met some Bāuls who categorically said to be extraneous to such practices. In this way they possibly expressed their attainment of a higher stage in the initiatory process, when the body reflects the whole macrocosm and the earthly dualism represented by male and female (Capwell 1986: 49). Yet, it is my conviction that most of them refuse to indulge in talking about *sādhana* and other practices (such as smoking hemp) only to fulfil Bengali *bhadralok* ("gentry") romanticism. As a matter of fact, in one of the most important folk festivals of Bengal, the Pous Mela in Shantiniketan, the Vishvabharati Committee has the authority to decide what should be sung by guest Bāuls, so as to satisfy the Tagorian cultural elites. Needless to say, no fee is granted to those Bāuls performing out of the Vishvabharati program.

21 "You must realize, brother, that everything has its uterine blood and semen. Semen and uterine blood will develop when one assumes the condition of Rādhā. The condition of being Rādhā I call the 'law of loving one who belongs to another' (*parakīyādharma*). All of the principles of greed and devotion can be found in that condition;" Ākiñcanadāsa, *Vivarta-vilāsa*, quoted by Hayes (1995: 351).

Four moons	**Corresponding element**	**Colour**	**Work**	**Sublimated element**
māṭhi (stool)	earth	black	*māṭhir kāj*	*kṣīr* (milk)
mutra (urine)	water	yellow	*mutrar kāj*	*nīr* (water)
rūpa (menses)	fire	red	*rūper kāj*	*guṛ* (molasses)
rasa (semen)	air	white	*raser kāj*	*elāc* (cardamom)

The second step of the Bāuls' *sādhana* is called *sikṣā dīkṣā*, a path that aims at sublimating the physical union of man and woman into a transcendental unity.[22]

Tell me: what *guru* are you looking for?
Guru is like mother and father who gave you the body:
do look for him.
Both *sikṣā-guru* and *dīkṣā-guru*
permit the transmission of *mantra* in your ear.
The *guru* of the heart is the Kalpataru,[23]
the *guru* is the hidden root [...].[24]

The knowledge of the *guru* (*gurujñān*) is directed to lead the disciple to an understanding of sexual intercourse as nothing but a ritual act: he must control every impulse in order to experience his own feelings as natural (*sahaja*)[25] and free himself from egotism (*ahaṃkaraṇa*).

22 See the *dehatattva* song translated by Salomon (1979: 67). It concerns the conversation between Bilvamaṅgal and his *guru* on occasion of the river crossing episode. The song is said to be sung by Sanātan Dās Bāul.

23 A mythical wish-fulfilling tree.

24 '*bolo kon gurur kara ambeṣaṇ*', Dinamaṇi (Bhattacarya 1408 B.S.: 866-867).

25 The term *sahaja* has been extensively analysed. Davidson emphasises the importance of the Tibetan translation: "simultaneously born" (*lhan cig skyes pa*; Davidson 2002: 45). See also the report on the discussion between Guenther (who translates "co-emergence"), Shahidullah (who translates "l'Inné") and

Bāuls believe that the divine principle or *maner mānuṣ* dwells in the *ājñā-cakra*, on the top of the head. From there it is supposed to swim as a fish (*mīn rūpa*) following an opposite path that leads to the *mūlādhāra-cakra*, on the perineum, where it is touched by the female energy (*kuṇḍalinī*). Once the feminine element has activated the masculine one, the fish will move from the earthly level (corresponding to the moment of its catch) up to the divine station[26] manifesting the full consciousness of the inner divinity of man.

> [...] Distressed Dinamaṇi says:
> is the *guru* a man or a beautiful woman?
> O sensual six-petal lotus,[27]
> are you *kulakuṇḍalinī*?
> In my lotus-heart is a blue lotus.
> To the blue lotus is tied a golden lotus:
> after blooming, it dwells right there.[28]

Sexual intercourse (*maithuna*) is divided up into four different phases: a) *nihārana* ("inner observation"), in which the Bāul is absorbed in deep meditation by means of the repetition of his own *mantra*; b) *sparśana* ("contact") or the physical union between *sādhaka* and *sādhana saṅginī*; c) *mārjana* or "rubbing"; d) *stambhana* or "retention", in which phase the *sādhaka* must retain his semen. During this last stage (also called *ūrdhbaretāh*), the initiate is expected to absorb the woman's blood through his penis so as to let it be melted with his own semen. Hence, by practising the triple retention of breath, thought, and semen the annihilation of desire is thought to be reached, and the fish (i.e. the *maner mānuṣ*) may reach the *sahasrāra-cakra* (or *sahaja-cakra*) over the top of the head, where *sahaja samādhi* will be finally experienced.

Snellgrove (who translates "the Innate"); *ibid.* p. 50. Kværne's interpretation of *sahaja* brings him to translate it as "simultaneously-arisen" (Kværne 1975: 89).

26 It corresponds to the state of *mahābhāva*, which manifests through *pāgalāmi*.

27 The six-petal lotus corresponds to the *svādhiṣṭhāna-cakra*, located on the genitalia.

28 '*bolo kon gurur kara ambeṣaṇ*', Dinamaṇi (Bhattacarya 1408 B.S.: 866-867).

The whole *cāricandra-sādhana* is basically dependent on the day of the new moon (*amābasyā*),[29] since Bāuls believe that exactly at that time (*mahāyug*) the three streams of blood that constitute woman's menses (*rajo rūp*) i.e. *kāruṇya bāri* ("the water of compassion"), *tāruṇya bāri* ("the young water"), and *lābaṇya bāri* ("the charming water") join together in the female genitalia (*bhaga*). Accordingly, the *sandhā śabda* used by Bāuls to indicate it is *triveṇī*, the confluence of the three holy rivers: Ganges, Yamunā, and the heavenly Sarasvatī.

> [...] Full moon appears in the new moon.
> If anyone wishes to look at this,
> Lālan says, for ever
> be seated on the *triveṇī*.[30]

Besides the process of sublimation of physical love (*kāma*) into pure love (*prema*),[31] one must consider that many Bāuls belong to – or at least refer themselves to – a *vaiṣṇava* background that is deeply rooted both in the teaching of Caitanya and in the *sāhajiyā* philosophy. As a matter of fact, they consider the erotic *sādhana* as a way to experience the five feelings of the religious mood (*sthāyi bhāva*) that a devotee (*bhakta*) should experience in his relationship with God (i.e. Kṛṣṇa).[32] The yogic process followed by Bāuls in this context is

[29] I was recently told by some Bāul *sādhakas* that sexual *sādhana* might also take place when the woman is not menstruating: in such circumstances, it seems that the white female sexual liquid (*strī-bīrya*) is a substitute for blood. However, no Bāul song seems to validate this.

[30] '*sonar mānuṣ bhāsche rase*', Lālan Phakir (Bhattacarya 1408 B.S.: 575).

[31] Such a procedure is generally equated by Bāuls to the separation of milk (*kṣīr*) from water (*nīr*), which leads to 'catching' the *maner mānuṣ* through the thickening of semen in which it is swimming (Bhattacarya 2001: 374).

[32] The *mādhurya* or *śṛṅgāra rasa* (i.e. the state of separation in which the devotee identifies himself with Rādhā) is the most important in *vaiṣṇava-sāhajiyā* thought and poetry. The other four *rasas* are: *śānta* (Kṛṣṇa is the supreme deity and the devotee the lowest creature), *dāsya* (Kṛṣṇa is the *guru* and the *bhakta* a disciple), *sākhya* (Kṛṣṇa and the devotee are mates), *vātsalya* (Kṛṣṇa is a child and the devotee is his parent).

compared to Kāma's skill as an archer, and is known as *pañcabāṇa sādhana*.

The first arrow, *madan*, is the joyful love represented by *rati*, the energy generated by sexual intercourse. To activate it, retention of breath has to be carried out by both practitioners whilst the arrow is visualized between the eyebrows, in the point corresponding to the *ājñā-cakra*.

The second arrow, *mādan*, is the intoxication of love and is identified with *rasa*, the active energy generated through an inverted movement of the breath (*praṇa*). When the sexual energy has developed to its maximum extent, it is sublimated into pure love and both the *sādhaka* and the *sādhikā* focus their faculties upon the *ājñā-cakra* in order to experience *āropa*, the state through which man is able to identify his own nature with God's nature.

> *Rasa* and *rati* are devotion and love.
> In *triveṇī* are the three worlds.
> The *guru* is the lord of ultimate *rati*,
> for surely he is mad (*khepā*).
> Three *rati*-s, three sports of *rasa*.
> Without the lover (*rasika*), passion (*madan*) is a blaze:
> in each arrow is *madan*,
> whilst *mādan* is tied (*uday*) to awakening.[33]
> Caṇḍīdās and Rajakinī
> are joyfully confectioning sweets from *rasa*:
> they have understood its meaning
> by floating inside the sweet *rasa*.
> Three *rati*-s in the sky,
> and three desires of *rasa* on the earth.
> Tṛpti says: The sovereign *guru* is
> shelter, liberation, acquaintance.[34]

33 Many Bāuls say that the word *uday* is a *sandhā śabda* for "sexual intercourse".

34 '*rasarati niṣṭā rati*', Tṛpti Brahmā (Brahma 1994b: 29). Note that the author is an amateur Bāul.

The third arrow is *śoṣaṇa*, the absorption of the couple into *prema*, pure love. The *sādhaka* is required to make use of the yogic tools he learned during *mantra dīkṣā* in order to control his body and particularly to retain his semen. When he has accomplished this, the blood of the woman must be absorbed and 'melted' with the semen, so that the earthen duality represented by *rūpa* and *rasa* may be synthesised in the human body as divine unity.

When the fourth arrow, *stambhana*, is shot, any feeling but love is set aside: the couple becomes completely impermeable to external stimulations and, due to breath retention, the perception of the world is suspended. The lovers are now floating into a state of absolute emptiness (*śūnyatā*) which coincides with the Supreme Principle. Through a process of canalisation of all energies in the *suṣumnā*, they reach a state where everything is natural (*sahaja*) and non-differentiated (*nirguṇa*).

With the last arrow, *mohana*, absolute bliss, the state of being dead while still living (*jyānte marā*) is finally gained and the couple is utterly transmuted. Every egotistic perception is definitely overcome and the concept of duality itself is done away with.

Bāul *panthī*-s are subjected to an initiatory path that leads to the extinction of the ego (*samādhi*): the only distinction mark which might be recognized among them is a different rank within the initiatory process, whose last stage is represented by *sannyāsa dīkṣā*.[35]

The way of the ascetic is regarded as a sort of synthesis of both *mantra dīkṣā* and *sikṣā dīkṣā*, and just like these two phases are looked upon as Kṛṣṇa and Rādhā respectively, the last one finds its correspondence in Caitanya (1486-1534), the Bengali *vaiṣṇava* saint widely reputed to be the incarnated union of the divine lovers.

The *sannyāsa* Bāuls live in asceticism (*bhek*) and sometimes endure penances, albeit they continue to appear during *mahotsab*, the religious gatherings in which Bāuls sing and dance.

35 Openshaw (2002: 142) remarks that "it is appropriate to deal with the *bhek-guru* before the *śikṣā-guru*", though interestingly Bāul *panthī*-s themselves often disagree on such an issue. Most of the ascetic Bāuls I met declared to have reached their condition "after practicing sexual-yogic practices taught by their own *śikṣā-guru*."

> [...] Look for the *guru*
> by means of absorbing devotion.
> Meditation will be successful
> as your prayer and worship [...].[36]

In an attempt to inquire into the practices of *bhek-guru*-s, I found more than one difficulty due to the (respectable) reticence of most ascetics I came in contact with. The fact is that they are basically beyond any classification and do not follow any guide: their own preceptor is the inner *guru* i.e. the Self,[37] also identified as *ālekh sā̃i*, the Invisible Lord.[38]

It is not clear if *sannyāsī* Bāuls avoid to impart knowledge or not (Openshaw 2002: 142), as I noticed that occasionally their abode is the destination of Bāuls who come there to get instruction from them. On the other hand, many Bāuls opt for a complete renunciation of the world, isolating themselves from all communities (Bāul as well) and abandoning both singing and playing music since now "[...] it is the wind of madness that 'plays' their bodies".[39]

To complete this survey on the esoteric teachings taught by Bāul *gurus*, a few notes must be added about the Āul *sādhana*, or the path followed by those initiates who are spiritually trained within a Muslim environment.

Leaving aside all speculations concerning the *maner mānuṣ*, Āuls claim that man has to awake from his unconsciousness and realise Allāh within himself. Once the initiate has acknowledged this, he perceives the enlightened essence of the *Insān al-Kāmil*, the Perfect Man.[40]

36 '*bolo kon gurur kara ambeṣaṇ*', Dinamaṇi (Bhattacarya 1408 B.S.: 866-867).

37 On this same topic, see Guénon 1946: 276.

38 Some Bāul *phakir*-s assert that this term might be considered as a corruption of the Arabic *al-laqaḥ* i.e. "semen".

39 Nityānanda Dās Bāul on *bhek-gurus*, personal conversation, Varanasi, January 2000.

40 The theologies of the *insān al-kāmil* and the *maner mānuṣ* – despite their affinities – have an independent origin: they are the result of an esoteric search for the Absolute which grew up in different environments. "The Perfect Man is he who has realized in himself all the possibilities of being; he is, so to speak, the

> […] Celui qui a Kāmil pour *guru* a bien su saisir cet Homme.
> Sans peine – ayant traversé le fleuve – il est assis sur la berge;
> Gosāicānd se dit: il n'a nulle peur de la Mort et du Temps.[41]

The Universal Man is understood by *murśid*-s as the Prophet of Light, *nur mohāmmad* or *nurer nabi*, and can be virtually equated to the *maner mānuṣ*. As a matter of fact, the disciple (*murīd*) will focus his efforts on the divine presence that dwells in his heart so as to go back to the primordial state represented in the *Quran* (7: 172) by the Day of Alast, when God manifested His own Essence to a not yet generated humanity.

The Āuls seek the realization of the self through the inner quest for God. To fulfil such a task they follow a way that includes sexual-yogic practices:[42] when the physical love (*'ishq-i majāzī*) is sublimated into pure love (*'ishq-i haqiqī*), the divine synthesis (*jugal prem*) occurring between Allāh and Muhammad might be finally experienced.[43]

model for everybody, for, in fact, every being is called to realize his innate possibilities in accordance with the divine name that is his particular *rabb* ('Lord', i.e. divine essence). However only the prophets and the saints reach that level. Iqbal's ideas of the Perfect Man as he who has developed his individual possibilities to the fullest bloom are derived from these theories rather than from the Nietzschean superman" (Schimmel 1975: 273).

41 *'mānuṣ ki kathā yāy dharā'*, Gosāicānd (Mukherjee 1985: 65). Translation by Prithwindra Mukherjee.

42 Marriage is traditionally supposed to be a duty in the exoteric sphere, but in Sufism the love of the Prophet for women is told as a model of perfection for it reflects nothing but the love for God. 'The 'mystery' of women lies in the fact that the sexual act provides the occasion for experiencing what Ibn al-'Arabī calls God's 'greatest self-disclosure'. In his transcendence, God cannot be experienced. But in the perspective of the subtle microcosm/macrocosm correspondences, God shows Himself in all things and can be experienced through all things. The whole cosmos and everything within it is God's self-disclosure. And the most favourable 'locus' for experiencing God's self-disclosure is the sexual act (see Murata 192: 186).

43 In Bengali Sufism and in Āul songs, the analogy between the *Rādhā-Kṛṣṇa-līlā* and the search of the lover (*āshiq*) for his Beloved (*mashuq*) is quite common: the lover is Muhammad and the Beloved is Allāh.

Referring to a song of Lālan Phakir, an old Bāul I met in Ilam Bājār (Birbhum) was repeatedly singing:

> *Lā Ilāhā* is the body, *Illāllāh* is life:
> together they are united in love.[44]

In the course of their esoteric path (that is quite often looked at as the Prophet's *mi'raj*), Muslim Bāuls consider the body as a microcosm (*al-kawn al-saghīr*) embodying the macrocosm (*al-kawn al-kabīr*), a reality that the *murīd* is expected to fully acknowledge by practising the *cāri-makām-bhed* i.e. the "piercing of the four stations".

Here, I present an overview[45] of the Āul *sādhana* according to the teachings of Bāul *phakir*-s (Ar. *faqīr*). It must be underlined that there are many differences among the various *gotra*-s, and that some *murśid*-s seem to ignore basic concepts related to Sufism.

The four stations (Ar. *maqām*; pl. *maqāmāt*) are looked at as the four different stages the initiate must undergo in order to experience the annihilation of one's own self in God (*fanā'*) and the perception of the *nurer nabi*. To every station a state (Ben. *mañjil*; Ar. *manzil*) and a particular work (*kāj*) are connected; furthermore, in many *ṭarīqāt* one finds the presence of a corresponding angel (Ben. *phereśtā*; Pers. *firishta*), a prophet (*nabi*),[46] an animal, and a symbolic colour (Roy 1983: 172-175).

The four stations are *śarīyat*, on the perineum (*mūlādhāra-cakra*), *tarīkat*, on the navel (*maṇipura-cakra*), *hakikat*, on the head (*ājñā-cakra*), and *māraphat*, on the heart (*anāhata-cakra*). These correspond respectively to the stages of *nācut*, *malkut*, *jabrut*, and *lāhut*.

44 The singer was actually unable to quote the whole song, therefore I cannot furnish any valid reference.

45 It is difficult to analyse this kind of *sādhana*. Actually, it is impossible to point out *the* 'one' influence related to their fourfold esoteric path and its implications.

46 "[...] In Bengali Sufism the concept of the *nabi*, 'prophet', was identified with the Hindu notion of *avatār*, 'incarnation'. Thus it is not unusual for Bengali Sufis to describe Muhammad as an incarnation of Allah" (Salomon 1994: 294).

At the first stage (*śarīyat*), the initiate is taught how to practise body postures (*āsana*-s), the retention of breath (*kumbhaka*), the recollection of the names of God (Ben. *dikr*; Ar. *dhikr*) or the repetition of *mantras* and – most of all – the visualisation of his spiritual guide (*murśider mūrti*). The neophyte has thus all the necessary tools to perceive his own essence and confront it with the divine one so as to identify the *jīvātma* with the *paramātma*.[47]

The next station (*tarīkat*) represents a very crucial point in the *sādhana* because now sexual intercourse occurs. The stage is divided into two separate phases i.e. the so-called abode of the sun and abode of the moon, respectively corresponding to the ascendant and descendant breaths. The physical union of the practitioners[48] is held on the day of the new moon and it is symbolized by the equal presence of the moon (semen or masculine element) and the sun (blood or female element). According to Āul phakirs, the *Qur'an* itself bears witness of this practice and many passages are quoted to validate the erotic *sādhana* (Jha 1995: 108).

> Surely We have created man from sperm mixed with ovum, to try him, so We made him hearing and seeing (*Qur'an* 76: 2).
> The hour drew night and the moon was rent asunder (*Qur'an* 54: 1).

On *hakikat*, the six vices (*chay ripu*) that make the human soul impure must be vanquished and – at a physical level – the semen must descend from the cerebral plexus down to the perineum, where it is 'melted' with the woman's blood. The reverse path is thus completed, and the initiate is now able to grasp the *nurer nabi* by means of the synthesis of the earthly dualism within his body.

47 No wonder that Bāul *phakir*-s are familiar with this kind of lexicon. There are many examples of 'Muslim' Bāul songs in which Hindū terminology and conceptions are used.

48 It is noteworthy that "[...] according to a sound hadith [...] the womb is a branch (shajana) of the All-Merciful. The Arabic word for womb (*raḥim*) derives from the same root as the words mercy (*raḥma*) and All-Merciful (*raḥmān*). The mother's womb is the locus of God's life-giving mercy" (Murata 1992: 182).

Immediately after that, once *māraphat* is reached, the *murīd* begins to practise the triple retention of breath, thought, and semen and the recollection of the names of God. The body is purified through the ingestion of the four moons, also called *cārimāṭī* ("the four earths"),[49] and sexual intercourse is sublimated into the divine marriage between the Prophet of Light and Allāh.

In the end, everything is perceived as *nirguṇa* and – following the achievement of the state of *sahaja samādhi* or *śūnya samādhi* – the practitioner is finally absorbed into the One (*fanā'*).

> In that man shines the light of the Prophet:
> if you search for his body, you will get it.
> The seat is enclosed with grey, white, red, and yellow light.
> There are four stations: *nāchut*, *lāhut*, *mālkut*, and *jabrut*.
> On the four stations, at the door-stages, many hidden rays shine.
> The seat of light is in *lā-mokām*: an orchestra plays in the wind.
> The light has no hands, no feet, no nose, no ears:
> without form, it moves strong and fast to *triveṇī*.
> It becomes a bee abiding in the lotus, on the *ghāṭ*, but doesn't eat the honey.
> With big effort the bee gives rise to devotion,
> but what's his effort for? I have been involved in terrible troubles.
> Subdued, Pāñj says: only Fatima knows the labour of light.[50]

The next crucial issue about the teachings of Bāul *guru*-s is represented by *sandhā bhāṣā*, the obscure language used by initiates of the *bartamān-panthā* which is taught as a "specialized extension of the mantric language" (Bharati 1993: 164). It is not my intent to present a detailed outlook of the *sandhā bhāṣā*. However, the importance of this practice must be emphasized given its close relation with *guru*-ship, initiation, and the transmission of knowledge.

[49] Not all Bāul *phakir*-s move onto absorbing the four moons after sexual intercourse. I was told that some of them are permitted by their *gurus* to carry on this practice at prior stages.

[50] '*ei mānuṣe nabīr nure khalak dey*', Phakir Pāñj Śāh (Bhattacarya 1408 B.S.: 750).

Besides the cult of the *guru*, Bāuls fully developed all aspects related to esotericism, e.g. the secrecy of initiation and its ritualism, the symbolism connected with initiation, initiatory death coupled with the 'second birth' (and the adoption of a new name),[51] and the use of intentional language. The aim of the latter is to let the listener "feel like a fool" (Hess 1983: 314) but, at the same time, it is thought as the perfect vehicle through which initiates may realize profound truths.

One moon has touched the body of another moon:
I think about it but what can I do?
From the daughter's womb is the mother's birth:
I think about it but what can I do?
There was a girl of six months,
after nine months she conceived
and eleven months later three children were born:
who will be the *phakir*?
With sixteen arms and thirty-two heads
the child is speaking in the womb.
Who are his mother and father?
This is the question.
There is a room without doors,
there is a man who can't speak.
Who supplies his food?
Who gives him the evening lamp?
Madan Sāi Phakir says:
The son dies touching his mother's body.
The one who will understand these words,
will obtain the condition of *phakir*.[52]

51 Bāuls often add to their new name the word *dās* meaning "servant" e.g. Kartik Dās Bāul, Debdās Bāul, Prabhā Dāsī. Muslim Bāuls use the appellative of *phakir* or *śā*. Some Bāuls use to qualify themselves as *kṣepā* ("mad"), which is a term of great respect.

52 '*cander gāye cand legeche*', Madan Phakir (sung by Debdās Bāul and Kannai Dās Bāul in Kenduli, January 16, 2001). The *maner mānuṣ* (the moon) floats in the seminal liquid which is kept in the *ājñā-cakra*. When the moon is 'melted' with the woman's blood on the day of the new moon (*amābasyā*), the practitio-

In their *sandhā bhāṣā*, Bāuls mix significances belonging to both Hindū and Islāmic esotericism. Since singing is their sole form of cult, they establish a clear distinction between teachings and mes-

ner experiences the Unity of the Self with the Absolute. The sexual energy activated by the female companion is likened to the work of a mother who awakes the Man of the Heart and permits his gradual climb to the cerebral plexus. According to my informants, the months herein refer to particular days of the menstrual cycle of the *sādhikā*, who is called mother (*mā*), daughter (*meye*) or even virgin (*kanyā*). The "girl of six months" (*chay māse ek kanyā chilo*) is the female companion on the sixth day starting from the end of the cycle, when ova are produced in the ovaries. On the fifteenth day i.e. nine days later (*nāy māse tār garba holo*), ova are ready to be fecundated and, eleven days after (*egāra māse tinti santān*), the ejection process begins. This is understood as a delivery in which triplet brothers are born, for ova are carried by the three flows that make up the menstrual flood. When man and woman join together in sexual intercourse, both practitioners are lead to the transcendent state of divine unity: they abandon the realm of form in which humans have 'sixteen arms' (the five *karmendriya*-s, the five *jñānendriya*-s and the six *ṛpu*-s) and 'thirty-two heads' (the main *nāḍī*-s). The body is conceived as a room with nine doors (eyes, ears, nostrils, mouth, anus, and sex organ), where a *sādhaka* must annihilate every external stimulation in order to perceive his own self. The final statement appears to indicate the *rūper kāj*, the "extraction of the ova", one of the four works of the *cāricandra sādhana*. The verb *chulā* – here translated "to touch" – is generally used to indicate "peeling", "scraping", and this is referred to the special procedure used by the *sādhikā* to separate the ova from blood. When the body is finally pure, the initiate is able to defy emotions and abide in pure love, *prema*.

A different interpretation is furnished by Capwell (1986: 185) through the exegesis of Yotin Dās Bāul: "[...] The three months refer to the three residences of man: 1) in our father's head (storage place of immobilized semen); 2) in our mother's womb (after conception); 3) in the material world (after birth). Three months are needed for the distillation of semen in the father's head. Nine plus three make twelve, the years of the girl first menses. The term of pregnancy is supposed to be ten months and ten days. Three offspring are the three attributes we have at birth: 1) *jñān*; 2) *buddhi*; 3) *bal* (consciousness, intellect, physical capacity); or 1) *kṣudhā*; 2) *śabdo*; 3) *bhay* (hunger, vocal sound, fear); or the three deities Vishnu, Shiva, Brahma; of these, Vishnu is a fakir because he is a *sādhok* (ascetic devotee)".

sages which are thought to be worldly or exoteric, and those which are meant for initiates only.

In the following song, special emphasis is given to the esoteric meaning of *abjad*, the Arabic script.[53]

> In *aleph*, *lām*, and *mim* the whole *Qur'an* is summarised.
> *Aleph* for Allāh, *mim* is the Prophet's name,
> in *lām* two significances are concealed:
> one is Muhammad's path (*śarīyat*), the other is knowledge (*māraphat*).
> In the middle stands *lām*, on the right and left side
> are both *aleph* and *mim*.
> How can a tree sprout out from a seed? This very fact
> I cannot understand.
> The meaning of the *Qur'an*
> is manifest in its signs.
> O Lālan, do you understand now the meaning of your quest
> without being lost on a wrong path?[54]

Both *sandhā bhāṣā* and *mantra-grahaṇa* represent in a sense the nucleus of initiation and refer to the irrefutable authority of the *guru* whose power represents the truth itself of the initiatory message (Bharati 1993: 193 ff.). As follows, the esoteric path is considered by Bāuls a secret which by no means should be divulgated to non-initiated ears. The teaching of the *guru* is *āgama* or, in the Muslim

53 Sometimes, aside of the esoteric meaning of the *abjad*, it is interesting to note other interpretations: "The *Quran* begins with the word *bismillah*, meaning 'in the name of Allāh'. For the Muslim Bāul, this word is extended into *bis mi Allāh*, 'Allāh is in the *bis* (sperm)'" (McDaniel 1989: 164). Similarly, Openshaw notes that some Bāuls often say "I am *bij*, I am *rajaḥ*" (*bij halām āmi*, *rajaḥ halām āmi*) or, alternatively, by a process of internalisation, "I am within *bij*" (*āmi bijer bhitar thāki*) (Openshaw 1997: 25). Moreover, some Bāuls refer to God as Bhagabān, a term which is taken to mean the union of male and female (*bhaga* = vagina; *bāṇ* = arrow = penis); *ibid.*, p. 29.

54 '*aleph lām mimete korān tāmām śodha likheche*', Lālan Phakir (Brahma 1987: 144).

tradition, *bāṭin*: in both cases, the secrecy of the initiatory way is stressed.

> [...] Can you get that union[55]
> through incantations and prayers only?
> Why *yogis* and ascetics
> carry on inspiration, expiration, and *kumbhaka*?
> This you have to know from the *guru*:
> respect every single word he says
> and do not permit it to be divulgated.
> Gõsāi Caṇḍī says: when shall I perform *sādhana* again?[56]

Since it is clear that among those who call themselves Bāuls there exists a hierarchy founded on *guru*-ship and initiatory stages, my successive query will move from this very standing point.

Bāul *panthī*-s are initiates: they actually refer to those esoteric movements born from the Hindū, Buddhist, and Islāmic traditions and can basically be viewed as an offspring of Tantrism, Sahajayāna Buddhism, and Sufism. Yet, according to a gross classification, Bāuls are quite often regarded as mystics, a conception that has led to a sort of annihilation of the figure of the *guru* and hence to the loss of the true nature of the sect.

As I have pointed out, the status of Bāul cannot be equated to a condition of the soul: the word *bāul*, which is broadly (and incorrectly) translated as "madman" aims at giving more emphasis on the behaviour of the singer than to the *divyon māda* experienced by the initiate in the course of his esoteric training. The outcome of initiation is opposite to that of any mystical experience. Moreover, mysticism is always related to a specific religious milieu, whilst initiation is beyond religion itself. In other words, Bāuls cannot be looked at as Hindūs, Muslims, Buddhists, etc.: they are initiates into a form of esotericism deeply rooted into the popular traditions of Bengal.

55 The singer refers to the success in linking the *mūlādhāra-cakra* with the *sahasrāra-cakra*.

56 '*harike dharabi yadi, āge śakti sahāy kara*', Gõsāi Caṇḍī (Bhattacarya 1408 B.S.: 712).

The first element denoting Bāuls as non-mystics is their use of an active work in order to achieve the final goal of *sādhana* (i.e. the *jyānte marā* condition). Such a characteristic is quite important since, on the contrary, mysticism is marked by passivity.[57] The mystic is someone who perceives, a sort of sensitive, and since he often does not have the necessary tools to acknowledge such a 'gift', he is possibly unable to control his mind and body.[58]

According to Guénon:

> L'initiation implique trois conditions qui se présentent en mode successif, et qu'on pourrait faire correspondre respectivement aux trois termes de «potentialité», de «virtualité» et d'«actualité»: 1. la «qualification», constituée par certain possibilités inhérentes à la nature propre de l'individu, et qui sont la *materia prima* sur laquelle le travail initiatique devra s'effectuer ; 2. la transmission, par le moyen du rattachement à une organisation traditionelle, d'une influence spirituelle donnant à l'être l'«illumination» qui lui permettra d'ordonner et de développer ces possibilités qu'il porte en lui ; 3. le travail intérieur par lequel, avec le secours d'«adjuvants» ou de «supports» extérieurs s'il y a lieu et surtout dans les premiers stades, ce développement sera réalisé graduellement, faisant passer l'ètre, d'échelon en échelon, à travers les différentes degrés de la hiérarchie initiatique, pour le conduire au but final de la «délivrance» ou de l'«Identité Suprême» (1946: 32-33).

This '*délivrance*' that Bāuls seek through initiation is called *saṃādhi*, a concept that Eliade (1999: 83) translates as "enstasis", a neologism used to stress the character of στάσις despite the frenzy of madness and the immobility of mystic ecstasy.[59]

57 It is therefore necessary to avoid the error of considering the receptivity of the *sādhaka* facing his *guru* as a kind of passive behaviour.

58 Guénon (1946: 14) asserts that mysticism may be viewed as a product of Western tradition, basically Christian.

59 How can you understand the language of madness?
At one moment forgetful, at another moment insane.
Then, at another moment, someone's form is seen.
As I think of it, my mind goes mad,

Once the necessary distinction between the different (but not opposite)[60] natures of mysticism and initiation has been ascertained, it seems to me that the subsequent dangerous ambivalence between religious emotion (*bhāva*) and divine madness (*divyon māda*) should be sorted out (Bhattacharyya 1986: 169).

As it has been stated by many scholars, a very subtle link exists between the so-called ecstatic phenomena (originated by mystical experience) and those related to madness. It is true that at a superficial level not much difference can be recognised. However, the technical vocabulary depends upon the various traditions and demonstrates remarkable variations.

A certain difference due to the external manifestation of these symptoms can be recognised quite easily in Bāul behaviour. As a matter of fact, one may postulate a link between ecstasy and mysticism since the mystical experience manifests itself through immobility, silence, hallucinations, etc.,[61] whilst, on the other hand, initiation aims at achieving *samādhi* and – in the case of Bāuls – it might yield those phenomena that drive the initiates to madness or frenzy. Thus, *divyon māda* is the result of a momentary phase induced by physical and spiritual practices taught by the *guru*, which can subsequently drive an initiate to 'enstatic' *samādhi*.

In the *Bhakti-rasāmṛta-sindhu* (1.2.2-5), Śrī Rūpa Gosvāmi divides devotional emotion in two opposite mainstreams. The first is the result of *sādhana* and he calls it *vaidhi*, the latter is produced

my *bhāva* and mind are the play of madness.
This state stays day and night,
for how can the madman grasp time? [...]

This passage is quoted from McDaniel 1989: 186. Interestingly, *bhāva* (which is not translated!) is herein understood as a *sine qua non*. Without it, madness cannot be experienced.

60 The fact that mysticism and initiation differ to such an extent does not mean that they cannot coexist.

61 The same experiences can be recognised in the hagiographies of the early Church Fathers and in the biographies of Christian Saints (Saint Teresa of Avila, Saint John of the Cross, etc.). For a sound comparative analysis of the various ecstatic phenomena, see Rouget 1985: 14 ff.

through the spontaneous visualization of God and he calls it *rāganuga*. The indicators of the former are referred to as *anubhāva*-s, a category of symptoms that "[...] include dancing, rolling on the ground, stretching, roaring, yawning, drooling, singing, bellowing, panting, indifference toward popular opinion, reeling, hiccoughing, and wild laughter" (McDaniel 1986: 173). All these symptoms are related to a kind of religious experience that is opposite to ecstasy, which – on the contrary – manifests itself through *sattvika-bhāva*-s: "immobility, gooseflesh, trembling, sweating, crying, changing skin and colour, and total loss of consciousness"(*ibid.*).[62]

> O *guru*, you can make me feel *bhāva*.
> I am mean and sinful,
> and I don't know how to worship you.
> Wherever I turn my eyes,
> I see darkness.
> O *guru*, if I pronounce your name
> the stone can float in the water.
> He says: I permitted this floating.
> If I will die by sinking,
> that is your mark.
> Once I've heard you were friend of the means,
> but you have rescued them under general dissension.
> This time I will know your divine grace.
> This is Gaṅgādhar's wish:
> even if I didn't yet come to *bhāva*,
> I cannot endure any more the pain.
> This time I will die saying: *jay guru jay*.
> Still I cannot perceive *bhāva*.[63]

The understanding of the opposition between frenzy (possibly followed by 'enstasis') and ecstasy would seem to solve the problem of

[62] It is thus a contradiction when McDaniel (1986: 183) states that in the phase of feeling *prema* the devotee looses his mind, laughs, weeps, and dances in ecstasy.

[63] '*guru āmāy bhabe kara pāra*', Gaṅgādhar (Bhattacarya 1408 B.S.: 873).

the particular experience of the divine among Bāuls. Yet, as McDaniel remarks, it is undeniable that:

> there is an evident discrepancy between theology and lived experience, seen by comparing ritual text and biography; while the theological texts emphasize development by stages and yogic control, ecstatics in life have chaotic visions and experiences, and alternating experiences of inner destruction and reintegration, [and] this discrepancy is due to different understandings of ritual and spontaneous ecstasy (1989: 280).

Bāuls themselves describe ambiguously their experiences and it seems thus licit to argue for the possibility of the coexistence of ecstatic phenomena (related to mystical perception) in the course of their initiatory path. I myself have interviewed many Bāuls who described to undergo – especially while singing and dancing – a state resembling a sort of mystical perception of God (Ferrari 2002: 42; 56). It is surprising that many scholars cannot accept the idea of a mystical feeling experienced by Bāuls who occasionally undergo ecstatic rapture (Guénon 1990b: 170-171). From the paroxysm of their dance – I was told – suddenly the body stops its movements and everything seems totally steady while *ānanda* is fully detected.

Aside from such a controversial issue, it has to be remembered that the 'responsibility' of such an ambivalence was generated by Tagore's own relationship with Bāuls, his interpretation and – most of all – the subsequent Bengali *bhadralok* idealised image of the 'fools of God'.

When Tagore started to be openly interested in their poetry, Bāuls were not considered very highly for they were basically regarded as wandering mad-caps devoted to an obscene cult. The following acceptance of Bāuls was the reaction of an Indian intelligentsia which at first responded with mute astonishment, and then quickly moved onto justifying Tagore's attraction for Bāul minstrels.[64]

64 I disagree with Roy when he says that it is evident that "[...] Baul songs being properly and ably handled by Rabindranath have been able to cross their narrow circle to occupy a respectable position (*sic*) and in this lies the credit of Rabin-

While I have no intention to provide yet another examination of Tagore's Bāul-ist production, I aim at pointing out those misconceptions that were brought forth by means of tendentious studies, which led to a progressive rebuilding of the image of the Bāul. The so-called mystical aspect of the sect was doubtless emphasised, despite the esoteric teachings and the role of the *guru*. The gap between what a Bāul really is and the fancy image of the ragamuffin mad singer seeking God through his music results quite evident in the end.

Most scholars dedicated their efforts to show how Bāul poetry was fully devoted to stress at the same time the oneness of man and God's presence in man, generating a sort of hysteria for what we may define 'folk universal love'. The first reference work on the Bāuls came out only in 1957, when Prof. Bhattacarya's *Bāṅglār Bāul o Bāul Gān* was published. Before this date, no sound piece of research was produced in order to enlighten the true nature of the Bāuls' *sādhana*.

Tagore's fascination for Bāuls was indeed a breakthrough[65] and possibly Bengali literary elites were not ready for this. But the question is: has Rabindranath Tagore ever rejected the fact that Bāuls were practitioners of a sexual *sādhana*? The answer is: no.

Of course, Tagore had his personal ideas on Bāuls.[66] But what he really appreciated was the simplicity of a poetical message focused on devotion and the equality of men, together with the genuine lyricism of Bengali folk music. He stressed several times all these aspects even though he admitted that Bāuls "[...] have a philosophy, which they call the philosophy of body, but they keep it secret; it is

dranath's genius" (1961: 242). I wonder what exactly is a respectable position in poetry; nevertheless, this statement gives an idea of all misconceptions on Bāuls before and immediately after Tagore's concern.

65 See also Tagore's interpretation of the old blind Bāul in his drama *Phālguṇi*: this character is qualified by paramount wisdom, indifference to the world, and patriotic commitment.

66 Tagore looked at the *Upaniṣad*-s as a source of mystical inspiration, though these texts are based on a transmission of knowledge from *guru* to disciple. He used to compare Bāul 'mysticism' to Upaniṣadic metaphysics (Tagore 1933).

only for initiated (*sic*)" (quoted in Dimock 1959: 86). The fact that Tagore avoided to inquire into Bāul sexual practices is due to his own poetical sensibility and it has to be respected as his personal choice. On the other hand, it's embarrassing that so many scholars and translators have been following in the steps of Tagore's poetical imaginary persisting in such an erroneous evaluation.[67]

Similarly, it is a mistake to believe that Tagore was adverse to esotericism, for he simply was not interested in it (Tagore 1922: 83-85). All in all, he was a poet: one might consider his inspiration as the result of a 'mystical' perception of the soul. As Dimock has noticed:

> [...] One must keep Tantric symbolism clearly in mind when reading and listening to these [Bāuls'] songs. One must realize that the *rasa* so often spoken of is semen; that the river so prominent in many of the songs is not only the river of life, but also the menstrual flux which is important for the esoteric ritual of the Bauls; and that, far from scorning ali ritual activity – as held by Tagore and others – the Bauls have at the very base of their religious way of life the yogic practice of control of breath and sphincters (1987: 376).[68]

67 See Dasgupta's misleading interpretation of the relation between Tagore and the Bāuls. The author celebrates the Nobel Prize poet as "the greatest of the Bāuls of Bengal" (1995: 187); furthermore, he insists on the marginality of sexual *sādhana* thus upholding the Tagorean position.

68 The same subject was previously developed by Dimock in his paper titled "Rabindranath Tagore, the Greatest of the Bāuls of Bengal" (1959: 33-51), in which he wished to prove the link between Tagore and the Bāuls, particularly in the field of Bengali literature. Through a crossed analysis of Tagore's own Bāuls' style compositions and translations of Bāuls' songs, Dimock ascertained a common quest for "the realization of the transcendent". Nonetheless, it is only obvious that Tagore was not a Bāul initiate. It is therefore absurd that Sen (1948: 993) held a certain song by Lālan Phakir ('*khā̃cār bhitar acin pākhī kemne āse yāy*', Bhattacarya 2001: 599-600) as having "the effect of a *dīkṣā mantra*" upon Tagore. As previously noticed, an initiatory *mantra* has no power in a context different from initiation itself: "[...] le *mantra* qui a été appris autrement que de la bouche d'un *guru* autorisé est sans aucun effet, parce qu'il n'est pas «vivifié» par la présence de l'influence spirituelle dont il est unique-

Another opinion is furnished by Zbavitel:

> [Rabindranath Tagore] admitted that not all of them [Bāuls], as a matter of fact only a small number, have a high spiritual or artistic value; but he [Tagore] stressed their immense historical importance, as they throw many interesting side-lights on the development of India's spirit. And Rabindranath appreciated most of all the fact that they spanned the abyss of mutual religious misunderstanding and dustups between the two major communities of the India of that time, Hindus and Muslims (1961: 12-13).

Tagore himself confirms this:

> [Bāuls] are brought together without either hurting the other. This union has not given rise to the calling of meetings or the formation of societies; out of it song has been born. The words of the songs are ripe with the sweetness of an untutored beauty. The voices of Hindus and Muslims mingle in the melodies and the songs; there is no quarrel between the Puran and the Quran in them. Herein lies the truth of the civilization of India: quarrelling and hostility are barbarous. In the songs of the Bauls all antagonisms, all discord, unite in a triumphant chorus of annunciation (quoted in Sen 1952: 122-123).

I have submitted similar questions to Shantiranjan Gangopadhyaya, a reputed Bengali artist and poet now retired in Varanasi. Although he spent several years with Bāuls in the villages of North Bengal,[69] his Tagorian education[70] still drives him to proudly declare the 'pureness' of the Bāul:

ment destiné à être le véhicule" (Guénon 1946: 59). The *guru*'s own *prāṇa* represents the subtle vehicle of the tradition itself, which is nothing but the *paramparā*. Also Bharati (1993: 164) notes how all procedures of initiation must logically follow the *guru*'s gift of the *mantra*.

69 Particularly in the Uttar Dinajpur district, where he held close relationship with Nityānanda Dās Bāul, his wife Prabhā Dāsī, and their Bāul fellows.

70 He was actually trained in Vishvabharati University, Shantiniketan.

> [...] Bāul is pure, he only needs his own music to communicate with God. Some Bāuls do use intoxicants or sex, but the real Bāul follows the wind. He is exactly like the wind: a spiritual flow in which no difference is noticeable. Bāuls stress the human unity in the wind of God and the unity of God in man.[71]

Sexual-yogic practices, smoking hemp,[72] and esoteric teachings among Bāuls are definitely well-known to Gangopadhyaya – and other Bengali educated people as well – but he rather prefers to minimize them. The idealised portrait furnished by Rabindranath Tagore as per his own artistic choice is still influencing the collective imagery of the sect. Coupled with the negation of the *guru* institute, Bāuls are still suffering a misleading reconstruction of their cult.

> If the heart stays firmly embraced to Guru-Nārāyaṇa's feet,
> why should you be scared on the day of death?
> Such a divine man is all around the universe,
> and in the universe abides displaying everywhere sky, fire, water, and earth.
> He embodies the *pañca-tattva*-s, all hermitages, and the abode of death.
> If you offer your mind and body at the *guru*'s feet, what can Yama do when you'll die?
> Even if you go to Gokula, the sweet Vṛndāvana, Ayodhyā, Triveṇī, Kāśī,
> Gayā, the sources of the Gaṅgā, and the seven *āditīrtha*-s,
> nothing is like the smallest particle (*bindu*) at the *guru*'s feet: unknowingly you will know that
> in the universe, nothing is higher than the *guru*, nothing is more important than the *guru*, nothing is more important than the *guru*.

71 Personal conversation with Shantiranjan Gangopadhyaya, Varanasi, October 2002.

72 The most famous Bāul singer, Pūrṇa Dās Bāul, proudly declared the strong opposition of his *gotra* to any intoxicant: "[Mine is] a tradition of *khepa-bauls*. We are the madmen." (Interview by P. Nandy, "No one Respects an Artist. They Think we are Favour Seekers, Parasites", *The Rediff Special*, New Delhi, December 20, 1999).

> *Guru* is the chord of the song, *guru* is the word of knowledge, *guru* is the ultimate shelter.
> Without the *guru*, there are no brothers nor friends. O *guru*, you are the friend, the father, the Lord.
> In the blissful garden of the earth, think to the divine man, radiant in the body.
> There is no inestimable jewel as the *guru*, so please stay in my heart.
> *Āgama*-s and *Purāṇa*-s are the spirit and knowledge of time, just like sacrifices and austerities.
> Devotion, liberation, and the ten *ādyā mahāvidhyā*-s: nothing is like the *guru*.
> Do accomplish with care the devotional service at the *guru*'s lotus feet.
> If Cintamaṇi Dās will dwell in Braj, why should he fear the sound of death?[73]

To sum up, it must be stressed that Bāuls do not resemble that kind of romantic image of the mystic madcap that is so often and enthusiastically spoken of by *bhadralok*-s or simply by fans of 'religious syncretism' and 'minor religious sects'. Indeed, the analysis of the role of the *guru* or *murśid* among Bāuls should permit scholars to move in a less dangerous area in their classifying tendencies. It is my hope that the study of the relationship between Bāuls and their *guru*-s, together with the cult of the teacher as displayed in the *guruvāda*, may enlighten the essence of the Bāul *panthā*. Bāuls are to be looked at as *sādhaka*-s (or *sādhikā*-s). As practitioners of concealed teachings they are initiates. The essence and the entire knowledge of the Bāul *sampradāya* is centred on *guru-śiṣya*, the relationship between teacher and disciple: "I am the sinner, Thou are the Master of the world; there is no other shelter besides your feet!" ('*ami aparādhī tumi he jagatpati, gati nāi tomār caraṇ bine*').[74]

[73] '*yadi man sthir thāke guru-nārāyaṇer yugal-caraṇe*', Cıntāmaṇi Dās (Bhattacarya 1408 B.S.: 725-726).

[74] '*āra āmār keu nāi, āra āmār keu nāi murśid tomā bine*', Anonymous (Bhattacarya 1408 B.S.: 704).

BIBLIOGRAPHY

Bharati, A. 1961, "Intentional Language in the Tantras", *Journal of the American Oriental Society* 81, n. 1: 261-270.

Bharati, A. 1993 (1965), *The Tantric Tradition*, Delhi, Hindustan Publishing Corporation.

Bhattacarya, J. N. 1968 (1896), *Hindu Castes and Sects*, Calcutta, Firma KLM.

Bhattacarya, U. 1408 B.S. (1364 B.S.), *Bāṅglār Bāul o Bāul Gān*, Calcutta , Oriental Book Company.

Bhattacharyya, D. 1986, *Pāgalāmi: Ethnopsychiatric Knowledge in Bengal*, Syracuse, N.Y., Maxwell School of Citizenship and Public Affairs.

Bhattacherjee, B. 1977, "Some Aspects of the Esoteric Cults of Consorts Worship in Bengal: a Field Survey Report", *Folklore* 18, n. 10 (October): 310-324; (December): 385-397.

Brahma, T. 1987, *Lālan parikramā*, Calcutta, Firma KLM.

Brahma, T. 1994a, *Adhīn Lālan bale*, Kushthya, Darbesh Haphij Thanapara Prakashak.

Brahma, T. 1994b, *Bāul padābali*, Daksin Barasat, Kamala Prakashani.

Cakrabarti, R. 1990, "Lālan *tattva*", *Loksaṃskṛti Gobeṣanā Patrikā* 3, n. 3: 219-243.

Cakrabarti, S. 1992, *Brātya lokāyat Lālan*, Calcutta, Pustak Bipani.

Capwell, C. 1974, "The Esoteric Belief of the Bauls of Bengal", *Journal of Asian Studies* 32, n. 2: 255-264.

Capwell, C. 1986, *The Music of the Bauls of Bengal*, Kent, Kent State University.

Das, M. and Piyuskanti M. 1958, *Lālan gitīkā. Lālan śāh phakirer gān*, Calcutta, University of Calcutta.

Das, R. P. 1992, "Problematic Aspects of the Sexual Rituals of the Bauls of Bengal", *Journal of the American Oriental Society* 112, n. 3: 388-432.

Dasgupta, S. 1995 (1946), *Obscure Religious Cults*, Calcutta, Firma KLM.

Datta, G. and Nirmalendu, B. 1966, *Śrīhaṭṭer lok saṅgit*, Calcutta, University of Calcutta.
Datta, R. 1978, "The Religious Aspect of the Bāul Songs of Bengal", *Journal of Asian Studies* 37, n. 3: 445-455.
Davidson, R. M. 2002, "Reframing *sahaja*: Genre, Representation, Ritual and Lineage", *Journal of Indian Philosophy* 30, n. 1: 45-83.
Dimock, E. C. Jr. 1959, "Rabindranath Tagore: The Greatest of the Bāuls of Bengal", *The Journal of Asian Studies* 19, n. 1: 33-51.
Dimock, E. C. Jr. 1967, "The Ideal Man in Society in Vaiṣṇava and Vaiṣṇava-Sahajiyā Literature", in Dimock, E. C. JR. (ed.), *Bengal: Literature and History*, East Lansing, Michigan, Michigan State University, pp. 67-80.
Dimock, E. C. Jr. 1987, "The Bauls and the Islamic Tradition", in Schomer, K. and McLeod, W. H. (eds.), *The Sants. Studies in a Devotional Tradition of India*, Delhi, Motilal Banarsidass, pp. 375-383.
Dimock, E. C. Jr. 1989 (1966), *The Place of the Hidden Moon. Erotic Mysticism in the Vaiṣṇava-sahajiyā Cult of Bengal*, Chicago, The University of Chicago Press.
Eliade, M. 1999 (1954), *Lo Yoga. Immortalità e libertà*, Milano, Rizzoli.
Ferrari, F. 2001, "L'influsso di Jayadeva sulla letteratura bengali dalle origini al XVIII secolo". *Annali di Ca'Foscari* 40, n. 3: 189-211.
Ferrari, F. 2002, *Oltre i campi, dove la terra è rossa. Canti d'amore e d'estasi dei Bāul del Bengala*, Milano, Ariele.
Guénon, R. 1946, *Aperçus sur l'Initiation*, Paris, Les Éditions Traditionelles.
Guénon, R. 1990a (1954), *Aperçus sur l'ésotérisme chretién*, Paris, Ayants-droit René Guénon.
Guénon, R. 1990b (1952), *Initiation et Réalisation spirituelle*, Paris, Ayants-droit René Guénon.
Gupta, A. 1983, *Bāṅglār lokjībane Bāul*, Calcutta, Sambad.

Hayes, G. A. 1995, "The Vaiṣṇava Sahajiyā Tradition of Medieval Bengal", in Lopez, D. S. Jr. (ed.), *Religions of India in Practice*, Princeton, N. J., Princeton University Press, pp. 333-351.

Hess, L. 1983, "The Cow is Sucking at the Calf's Teat: Kabir Upside-down Language", *History of Religions* 22, n. 4: 313-337.

Jha, S. N. 1995a, "Cāri-Candra Bhed: Use of the Four Moons", in Ray, R. K. (ed.), *Mind, Body and Society. Life and Mentality in Colonial Bengal*, Calcutta, Oxford University Press, pp. 65-108.

Jha, S. N. 1995b, *Phakir Lālan Sāin: deś kāl ebaṁ śilpa*, Calcutta, Samvad.

Karim, A. 1971, *Bāul Sāhitya o Bāul Gān*, Kushtia, Lok Sahitya Gabesana.

Karim, A. 1980, *The Bauls of Bangladesh. A Study of an Obscure Religious Cult*, Kushtia, Lalan Academy.

Kinsley, D. 1974, "Through the Looking Glass: Divine Madness in the Hindu Religious Tradition", *History of Religions* 13, n. 4: 270-305.

Kværne, P. 1975, "On the Concept of *sahaja* in Indian Buddhist Tantric Literature", *Temenos* 11: 88-135.

Mansuruddin, M. 1961, *Hārāmaṇi. Lok saṅgīt saṅgraha*, Calcutta, University of Calcutta.

McDaniel, J. 1986, "Ecstasy and Madness among Bengali Vaisnavas", in Thorp, J. P. (ed.), *Women, Development, Devotionalism, Nationalism: Bengal Studies 1985*, East Lansing, Michigan, Michigan State University of Chicago.

McDaniel, J. 1989, *The Madness of the Saints. Ecstatic Religion in Bengal*, Chicago, University of Chicago.

Mishra, V. C. 1987, "Two Truths are Told: Tagore's Kabir", in Schomer, K. and McLeod, W. H. (eds.), *The Sants. Studies in a Devotional Tradition of India*, Delhi, Motilal Banarsidass, pp. 167-180.

Mukherjee, P. 1985, *Les fous de l'absolu. Chant Baul*, Paris, Findakly.

Mukhopadhyay, A. 1988, *Dharma o saṃskṛtir āloke bāul*, Calcutta, Sarat Publishing House.

Murata, S. 1992, *The Tao of Islam. A Sourcebook on Gender Relationship in Islamic Thought,* Albany, N.Y., State University of New York Press.

Nūr korān śarīph. 1421 H./ 2000 A.D., Dhaka, Solemaniya Book House.

Openshaw, J. 1994, *Bauls of West Bengal: With Special Reference to Raj Khyapa and his Followers.* Ph.D. Thesis, University of London, School of Oriental and African Studies.

Openshaw, J. 1995a, "Rāj Kṛṣṇa: Perspectives on the Worlds of a Little-known Bengali Guru", in Ray, R. K. (ed.), *Mind, Body and Society. Life and Mentality in Colonial Bengal*, Calcutta, Oxford University Press, pp. 109-151.

Openshaw, J. 1995b, "The Radicalism of Tagore and the Bāuls of Bengal: An Indigenous Critique?", *South Asia Research* 17, n. 1: 20-36.

Openshaw, J. 1997, "The Web of Deceit: Challenges to Hindu and Muslim Orthodoxies by Bāuls of Bengal", *Religion* 27: 297-309.

Openshaw, J. 1998, "'Killing' the *guru*: Anti-hierarchical Tendencies among the Bāuls of Bengal", *Contributions to Indian Sociology* 32, n. 1: 1-19.

Openshaw, J. 2002, *Seeking Bāuls of Bengal*, Cambridge, Cambridge University Press.

Pal, H. C. 1969, "Bāul-tattber pūrbābhāṣā", *Sāhitya patrikā*, Journal of the Bengali Department, pp. 1-22.

Pal, H. C. 1973, "Bāul Poets on the Mystic Letters", *Journal of the Asiatic Society* 15, n. 1: 81-96.

Ray, M. 1986, "Jaydeb-Keṇḍuli: grām o grāmer melā", *Deś* 53, n. 10: 41-45.

Rouget, G. 1985, *Music and Trance. A Theory of the Relations between Music and Possession*, Chicago and London, University of Chicago Press.

Roy, A. 1983, *The Islamic Syncretistic Tradition in Bengal*, Princeton, N.J., Princeton University Press.

Roy, B. 1961, "Baul Song and Rabindranath", *Folklore* 2, n. 4: 241-243.

Rupa Gosvami (ed.) 1995, *Śrībhakrirasāmṛtasindhu*. With Bengali Translations by H. Das, H. Kutir, Nabadbip.

Salomon, C. 1979, "A Contemporary Sahajiyā Interpretation of the Bilvāmangal-Cintāmaṇi Legend, as Sung by Sanātan Dās Bāul", in Park, R. L. (ed.), *Patterns of Change in Modern Bengal*, East Lansing, Michigan, Michigan State University.

Salomon, C. 1994, "The Cosmogonic Riddles of Lalan Fakir", in Appadurai, A – Korom, F. J. – Mills, M. A. (eds.), *Gender, Genre, and Power in South Asian Expressive Traditions*, Delhi, Motilal Banarsidass.

Salomon, C. 1995, "Bāul Songs", in Lopez, D. S. Jr. (ed.), *Religions of India in Practice*, Princeton, N.J., Princeton University Press, pp. 187-208.

Sannyal, B. J. 1904, *Musalmān baiṣṇab kabi*, Rajshahi, Sanatan Dharma Samiti.

Schimmel, A. 1975, *Mystical Dimensions of Islam*, Chapel Hill, The University of North Carolina Press.

Sen, K. M. 1929, "The Bauls and Their Cult of Man", *Vishvabharati Quarterly* 6, n. 4: 410-431.

Sen, K. M. 1946, *Bāṅglār sādhana*, Calcutta, University of Calcutta.

Sen, K. M. 1951, *Bāṅglār Bāul*, Calcutta, University of Calcutta.

Sen, K. M. 1952-1953, "The Bauls of Bengal", *Vishvabharati Quarterly,* in four parts: vol. 18, n. 2: 123-147; vol. 18, n. 3: 273-282; vol. 18, n. 4: 294-306; vol. 19, n. 1: 57-74 (Rendered into English by Lila Ray).

Sen, K. M. 1974 (1935), *Medieval Mysticism of India*, New Delhi, Oriental Reprint.

Sen, P. K. 1314 B.S., *Bibida-dharma-saṅgīt*, Calcutta, University of Calcutta.

Sengupta, S. 1963, "Rabindranath Tagore's Role in Bengal's Folk Lore Movement", *Folklore* 4, n. 4: 137-152.

Tagore, R. 1922, *Creative Unity*, New York, Macmillan.

Thakur, R. 1290 B.S. "Bāuler gān", *Bharati*, Calcutta, pp. 34-41.

Thakur, R. 1383 B.S., *Gorā*, Calcutta, Vishvabharati Granthana Vibhaga.

Thakur, R. 1386 B.S., *Rabindrā racanābalī: janmaśatabārṣik saṁskaraṇa* (*The Collected Works of Rabindranath: Birth Centenary Edition*), Calcutta, West Bengal Government.

Thakur, R. 1930, *Mānuṣer dharma*, Calcutta, Vishvabharati Granthana Bibhag.

Thakur, R. 1940, *Bāṅglā kābya paricaya*, Calcutta, Vishvabharati University.

Urban, H. B. 1999, "The Politics of Madness: The Construction and Manipulation of the 'Bāul' Image in Modern Bengal", *South Asia* 12, n. 1: 13-46.

Urban, H. B. 2001, "The Market Place and the Temple: Economic Metaphors and Religious Meanings in the Folk Songs of Colonial Bengal", *The Journal of Asian Studies* 60, n. 4: 1085-1114.

Zbavitel, D. 1961, "Rabindranath and the Folk Literature of Bengal", *Folklore* 2, n. 1: 2-14.

THE MASTER ARCHITECT IN THE CORPORATIONS OF INDIA

CLAUDIA RAMASSO

With reference to knowledge
the preceding word is the teacher,
the following word is the pupil,
their union is knowledge,
and their link is instruction.
So it is with reference to knowledge.
Taittirīya Upaniṣad I, 3, 2-3.

In this paper I shall outline the importance and function of the master-builder (*stha-pati*) in the context of the traditional sciences of ancient India as indicated by the term *sthāpatya-veda*, that is, the science of the art of building and fixing in space (*sthāpana*). From a traditional point of view the establishment of a fixed dwelling—for humans as well as for deities—or, in a wider sense, the arrangement of a series of buildings and the conceiving and collocation of an object of veneration in a precisely definite spot, entails the following: the full command of all skills related to the art of building and the awareness of the ultimate aim of its usage, the knowledge of the space upon which one must edify the building and the laws which govern it. Thus, it implies a thorough understanding of the order which is thought to govern the manifested universe. The knowledge of the cosmological principles upon which the science of architecture rests is a fundamental prerequisite for the comprehension of any architectural achievement. At the same time, it constitutes the very basis for an understanding of the essential function of the architect. In this sense, the corporation of artists-artisans might be viewed as an initiatory school. Its discipline of work represents the practical tool through which the transformation of the ordinary individual into the "cosmic man" can ultimately be achieved.

From a technical point of view, the origin of the terms which indicate the architect, the building, and the art of building, is to be traced to the Sanskrit verbal root √*sthā*, meaning "to stay, to remain, to be fixed in a place or in a specific condition". The science of building is also defined as *vāstu-veda* or *vāstu-vijñāna*, that is, the sacred knowledge of the *vāstu*,[1] the place where existence itself (*vastu*) resides.[2] The term *vāstu* means "extension", "vastness". It therefore refers to all those objects which are defined by physical extension, while the word *vastu* refers to everything which is real, existent, the underlying substance of everything which has a shape, the breath that provides life to the flame. These two concepts, alternatively defined as *rūpa*, form, and *nāma*, name or substance, represent the dominion in which the architect defines and displays his field of activity. He avails himself not only of the application of the technique of building but also of a complete understanding of all measures and proportions, and ultimately of the laws that govern universal manifestation. In fact, the science of architecture, contained in the *Atharva-veda-saṃhitā*, is one of the four *upa-veda*-s, that is, the secondary and complementary field of knowledge. Through the act of building, it is understood that the master-architect is able to reproduce the same proportions and symmetries that were established at the time when the primordial unfolding of the universe occurred.

According to the ancient hymns of the *R̥g-veda*, the universe is the work of Viśvakarman, the divine architect and moulder. He is invoked in the tenth *maṇḍala* of the *R̥g-veda* as the one who, by generating the earth, has revealed heaven with his power, he whose manifold eyes, faces, arms, and feet are present everywhere.[3] The name

1 The term *vāstu* is derived from the Sanskrit verbal root √*vās* meaning "to dwell, to live, to reside". See M. MONIER-WILLIAMS, *Sanskrit-English Dictionary*, New Delhi, Marwah Publications, 1986², p. 947.

2 *Maya-mata* II, 1-3.

3 *R̥g-veda* (*R̥V*) X, 81, 2-3.

Viśvakarman is also said to be an attribute of Prajāpati, the lord of manifestation, thus providing explicit evidence of the function that is attributed to him: he represents the active personification of Prajāpati's creative power, a principle with which he will be later identified in the *Brāhmaṇa*-s.[4] According to the *Veda*-s, Viśvakarman forges the world in the fashion of a carpenter who creates the objects of his skill from the wood of a tree.[5] His activities make use of two distinctive features: separating heaven from earth, he establishes the universe (*dhātṛ*); once this is achieved, he then arranges (*vidhātṛ*) within it the multiple components it consists of.[6] Subsequently, Viśvakarman will be identified with the mythical founder of the science of architecture (*vāstu-vidyā*). The first book of the *Mahābhārata* states:

> Indeed, He is the Lord of the arts (*śilpa-prajāpati*), the carpenter of the gods, the most eminent among all artisans, the element or principle that sustains the artisans, venerated by them as great and powerful god.[7]

Moreover, Viśvakarman is depicted as the mythical compiler of the traditional texts concerning the sacred art of architecture.

Those parts of Sanskrit literature concerned with *vāstu* are generally referred to as *śilpa-śāstra*[8] and include numerous technical treatises. Nonetheless, we encounter numerous references to the science of building also in the *Purāṇa*-s and in the *Āgama*-s, as well as in those works dealing with the sciences of astrology, politics, and the

4 *Śatapatha Brāhmaṇa* 8, 2, 1, 10; *Aitareya Brāhmaṇa* 4, 22.

5 *ṚV* X, 81, 4.

6 *ṚV* X, 82, 2.

7 *Mahābhārata* I, 2592.

8 The term *śilpa* indicates the fine arts, sometimes also defined by the term *bāhya-kalā*, that is, the exterior or practical arts. They comprehend sixty-four different categories, including architecture, sculpture, metallurgy, carpentry, and jewellery, but also the art of rehearsal, dancing, music, medicine, and poetry. Cf. MONIER-WILLIAMS, *Sanskrit-English Dictionary*, *op. cit.*, p. 1073.

rules of good government (*artha-śāstra*) and domestic ritual (*gṛha-sūtra*).[9] Technical indications relating to the appropriate choice of the site, the construction of the building, and the rites that accompany the foundation of a new temple are found in many ancient texts, such as the *Matsya Purāṇa*,[10] the *Garuḍa Purāṇa*,[11] the *Bṛhat-saṃhitā* compiled by Varāhamihira (6th century CE),[12] the *Viṣṇu-dharmottara Purāṇa* (7th century CE), the *Kāmikāgama*,[13] the *Suprabhedāgama*,[14] the *Ajitāgama*, and the *Rauravāgama*[15] (these two latter texts being most probably composed between 400 and 800 CE).[16] We also find reference to the art of building in encyclopaedic works such as the *Mānasollāsa* written by the Chalukyan ruler Someśvara in 1129,[17] and in more recent texts such as the *Tantra-samuccaya* compiled by the keralese Nārāyaṇa Nambūdiri in the 15th century.[18] The most appropriate term to designate the treatises of architecture is *vāstu-śāstra*. Among the principal texts pertaining to the vast repertoire of technical treatises, I may mention the *Maya-mata*, compiled in southern India during the reign of the Chola dynasty, probably be-

9 Cf. L. RENOU, "La maison védique", in *Journal Asiatique* CCXXXI (1939): 481-504.

10 Eight chapters of the *Matsya Purāṇa* deal with architecture and sculpture: 252; 255; 257-258; 262-263; 269-270.

11 *Garuḍa Purāṇa* 46; 47.

12 The text is based on the authority of the mythical master-architects Maya, Viśvakarman, Garga, and Manu; cf. *Bṛhat-saṃhitā* LV, 30.

13 The *Kāmikāgama* dedicates altogether sixty chapters to architecture and sculpture; see P. K. ACHARYA, *Hindu Architecture in India and Abroad*, New Delhi, Oriental Books Reprint Corporation, 1979, vol. VI, pp. 85-91.

14 *Suprabhedāgama, kriyā-pāda,* which outlines the guidelines for the erection of temples and various buildings.

15 See B. DAGENS, *Les enseignements architecturaux de l'Ajitāgama et du Rauravāgama*, Pondichéry, Institut Français d'Indologie, 1977.

16 J. GONDA, *Medieval Religious Literature in Sanskrit*, Wiesbaden, Otto Harrassowitz, 1977, p. 164.

17 G. BOCCALI – S. PIANO – S. SANI, *Le letterature dell'India*, Torino, Utet Libreria, 2000, p. 296.

18 S. KRAMRISCH, *The Hindu Temple*, Delhi, Motilal Banarsidass, 1976, chap. I, note 7.

tween the 9th and 12th century, of clear *śaiva* inclination,[19] and the *Māna-sāra*, also a text belonging to the dravidian cultural area, the present compilation of which probably dates back to the same period of the *Maya-mata.*[20]

The ideal thread connecting each of these works since the very first hints we encounter in the *Veda*-s with regard to the construction of the sacrificial altar—even beyond the technical indications they provide—consists in the ritual function inherent to the science of architecture. Its precepts, following the direct transmission from master to disciple and father to son (according to the traditional *paramparā* pattern), has been perpetuated in India till the present day. In order to understand the role played by the *stha-pati* in the context of the various corporations of artisans (*śreni*), it is necessary to familiarize oneself with the traditional mentality as transmitted over innumerable generations by hindū brahmanical orthodoxy (*sanātana-dharma*).

19 Regarding architecture, most texts pertaining to the tradition of *śaiva-siddhānta* follow the indications provided by the *Maya-mata*, as for instance the *Īśāna-śiva-guru-deva-paddhati* and the *Śilpa-ratna*; see B. DAGENS (trans.), *Maya-mata, an Indian Treatise on Housing, Architecture and Iconography*, New Delhi, Sitaram Bhartia Institute of Scientific Research, 1985, p. vi.

20 *Ibid.*, pp. vii-viii. P. K. Acharya, translator and commentator of the *Māna-sāra*, suggests that this work should be assigned to the Gupta period; ACHARYA, *Hindu Architecture in India and Abroad, op. cit.*, vol. VI, pp. 186-209. Nowadays the corporations of builders and constructors (*viśvakarma-śilpi*) of northern India - apart from the above mentioned texts - make additional use of the following manuals of architecture: *Vāstu-rāja-vallabha*, *Sama-rāṅgaṇa-sūtrādhāra*, *Rūpa-maṇḍaṇa*, *Śilpa-prakāśa*, *Pratimā-māna-lakṣaṇa*, *Kṣīrārṇava*, *Śilpa-śāstra*, *Vāstu-vidyā*, *Manuṣyālaya-candrikā*, *Sakalādhikāra*, *Śilpa-ratna*, and *Śilpa-ratnākara;* see GANAPATI STHAPATI, *Sthāpatya Veda*, Chennai, Dakshina Publishing House, 2001, p. 67. All these texts have been published. Ganapati Sthapati is one of the most renowned traditional architects of contemporary India. From 1961 to 1988, he directed the *Government College of Architecture and Sculpture* at Mahabalipuram (Tamil Nadu). At present, he is the director of a research institute founded by him in the same town, the *Vāstu Veda Research Foundation*, which publishes a journal titled *Vāstu Puruṣa.*

The planning task of the architect stems from the precise knowledge of the pattern according to which the physical universe—basis of every human edifice—has come into being. In the beginning, there existed only one primordial being in the shape of the cosmic egg (*puruṣa*). It then expanded into every possible direction. It is through the self-sacrifice of this *puruṣa* that heaven and earth, the sun and the moon, the vital breath as well as all human beings distinguished by the four social categories (*varṇa*) came into being.[21] Thus, the process of differentiation is thought to have been brought about by the dismemberment of the primordial being. From a different point of view, the origin of the universe is explained as due to the fall of the *puruṣa*. According to the *Bṛhat-saṃhitā*, at the beginning there was a being whose body obstructed heaven and earth. Hence, the gods suddenly seized it and threw it to the ground with its face downwards. Each of its parts was firmly held by one god who, in the process, became the tutelary deity of that particular place. On him was bestowed the title *vāstu-nara*, that is, "man representing spatial extension".[22] He is the efficient cause of manifestation: through his ritual self-sacrifice he gives way to the process of becoming, and by precipitating down to earth (*bhūmi*, lit. "the existing") he gives rise to the physical universe.

His shape is represented by the *vāstu-puruṣa-maṇḍala*. He is understood as the metaphysical principle (*puruṣa*) who, by collocating itself within the material cause of the universe (*prakṛti*, but also *vāstu*, "extension"), confers order to it according to a precise scheme. He is the inner regulator, the law that governs the universe, the measure of everything that exists. The terminology used in this context is analogous to the one found in the Indian schools of philosophy. According to the terminology used by the *vāstu-vedin*, this primordial being, defined as *vāstu-puruṣa* representing the substance of the universe, is identical to *nirguṇa-brahman*, the unqualified meta-

21 The sacrifice of the cosmic man, *puruṣa*, is presented in the most ancient Vedic hymns; cf. *ṚV* X, 90, 1-16.

22 *Bṛhat-saṃhitā* LIII, 2-3.

physical Absolute. It brings manifestation into being by becoming *saguṇa-brahman*, the defined, qualified principle.[23] The *vāstu-puruṣa-maṇḍala* is represented by a regular polygon within which is sketched a human figure, with legs folded at the knees at the height of the pelvis so as to form, together with the chest, two angles of ninety degrees. The hands of this figure are joined at the chest, in a position known as *añjali-mudrā*. The spine corresponds to one of the two diagonals, so that the head touches the inner vertex of the polygon, whereas the feet, soles united, are located at the opposite vertex. The polygon's surface is entirely filled by the *puruṣa*'s shape. The whole structure rotates around the navel situated at the square's centre, thus being identified with the uterus, the matrix whence everything has its origin.

The square is the essential and most perfect shape of Indian architecture. It represents the world in its multiform extension, the unfolding of all possibilities comprised in manifestation as depicted in its dynamic aspect inside the circle. On the other hand, the square presupposes the circle whence it is derived. The four sides of the square counteract the centrifugal forces expanding from the centre towards the outer space, thus lending itself to the representation of all that is fixed and stable. The earth, dominated by time, is represented as a square because it is limited by the four horizons. These consist of the two exact points where the sun rises and sets along a horizontal line extending East to West, and by a vertical line or axis linking the celestial vault in the North to its opposite in the South. The intersection of these two lines corresponds to the meridian. The *pṛthvī-maṇḍala* i.e. the diagram representing the earth, coincides with the *vāstu-puruṣa* acting at the same time as its natural abode. In it are contemplated the rhythm of the sun and moon. Hence, it is possible to say that the *vāstu-puruṣa-maṇḍala* comprehends the divisions or rhythms which scan temporal existence. The area of the polygon is subdivided into a series of squares (*pada*), into sixty-four or eighty-one squares, generated by the multiplication of the base of the square by

[23] GANAPATI STHAPATI, *Sthāpatya Veda*, *op. cit.*, p. 267.

either three or four. Within this complex structure are collocated the *puruṣa*'s forty-four tutelary deities. These deities surround the innermost portion of the square (*brahma-sthāna*) made up of five or nine *pada*-s occupied by Brahmā himself. The gods are distributed all along three concentric frames, surrounding the *brahma-sthāna*. These frames represent the "path of gods" (*daivika-pada*), the "path of humans" (*manuṣya-pada*), and the "path of demons" (*paiśacika-pada*) standing for spiritual light, consciousness, and gross matter in accordance to the three levels in which the universe is subdivided (*tri-bhuvana*).[24] This order is also defined as *vāstu-dharma*. Whatever the internal division of the square, the last frame contains thirty-two gods, the *pada-devatā*-s, the most important of which are the deities located at the four cardinal points. The twelve remaining gods occupy the first frame following the innermost *brahma-sthāna*: these are the twelve Āditya-s.

There are altogether thirty-two different types of *vāstu-puruṣa-maṇḍala*-s, the most important of which present a basis side of one, two, three, seven, eight, and nine square units respectively. Each of these *vāstu-puruṣa-maṇḍala*-s serves different purposes. Two of them are considered fundamental. The *maṇḍala* composed of eight squares or *pada*-s, called *maṇḍūka-vāstu-maṇḍala* and depicting the subtle (*sūkṣma*) form of *puruṣa*, represents the ideal measure used for temple constructions, whereas the *parama-śāyika-vāstu-maṇḍala*, comprising nine square units, is used for building royal palaces

24 *Ibid.*, p. 270. A footnote to this text provides a much more detailed explanation of the *maṇḍala*. Beginning from the outer part, the *paiśacika-pada* corresponds to the *anna-maya-kośa*, the *manuṣya-pada* to the *mano-maya-kośa*, the *daivika-pada* to the *jñāna-maya-kośa*, the *brahma-pada* to the *vijñāna-maya-kośa*, and the *brahma-bindu* to the *ānanda-maya-kośa* represented by the *mantra om*. The concept of the five sheaths or *kośa*-s making up the 'geometrical body' of the *puruṣa* is almost identical with that presented in *Taittirīya Upaniṣad* II, 1-6, where the five sheaths containing the soul or *ātman* present in all living creatures are the *anna-maya-kośa*, the *prāṇa-maya-kośa*, the *mano-maya-kośa*, the *vijñāna-maya-kośa*, and the *ānanda-maya-kośa*.

and, by extension, the dwellings of humans as well as entire villages, representing the gross form (*sthūla*) of the cosmic man.[25]

The *vāstu-puruṣa-maṇḍala* thus represents the archetype of every construction, since all buildings are meant to symbolize an exact replica of the universe. Likewise, mankind is identified with the divine citadel (*brahma-pura*).[26] The *maṇḍala* represents the entire range of possibilities in the realm of manifestation. But the diagram of the *vāstu* does not in fact coincide with the building plan: it rather supplies the 'rhythmic scanning' which is at the basis of the building project of the edifice or of the urban design. The concept of *tāla*, the time unit (*kāla-mātra*) used in music as well as in poetical compositions, appears side by side with that of *pada* which represents the space unit. Time is calculated through mathematical formulae. Similarly, space is measured through geometrical formulae. Space and time, rhythm and shape, are the foundation of the science of architecture.[27]

The master-builder called in by the client (*kāraka*) for the task of planning the work, who in the case of a temple construction is referred to as *yajamāna* (lit. "sacrificer"), becomes the doer of the work (*kartṛ*), just as Viśvakarman had been the moulder of the universe. In the case of temple planning, the *stha-pati* is assisted in his task by the priest-architect (*sthāpaka*), who checks his activities and carries out the corresponding rituals.[28] The relationship between *stha-pati* and *sthāpaka* is analogous to that between Viśvakarman and Prajāpati.

The *stha-pati* acts in a ritual manner in all phases of his work and coordinates the realization of the entire project. He is the *guru* of three other figures of *śilpin*-s who assist him in his task: the *sūtra-grāhin,* the *vardhakin*, and the *takṣaka*. Altogether these four masters

25 GANAPATI STHAPATI, *Sthāpatya Veda, op. cit*., p. 269. Cf. *Matsya Purāṇa* CCLIII, 47; *Bhaviṣya Purāṇa* CXXX, 1; *Agni Purāṇa* XCIII, 1.

26 See A. K. COOMARASWAMY, *Selected Papers, 1. Traditional Art and Symbolism*, Princeton, Bollingen Series LXCXXIX, 1977, pp. 4-5.

27 See GANAPATI STHAPATI, *Sthāpatya Veda, op. cit*., pp. 279-298.

28 *Śilpa-ratna* I, 29-42.

supervise all phases of construction, from its planning to the completion of the actual building. They represent a family of artisans, known as *śreni*, and claim divine origin for themselves. In the second chapter of the *Māna-sāra*, called *śilpi-lakṣaṇa* and dealing with the rank and qualification of the different *śilpin*-s, it is said that the four faces of Brahmā were generated by the four celestial architects i.e. Viśvakarman, Maya, Tvaṣṭṛ, and Manu. Their sons are called *stha-pati*, *sūtra-grāhin*, *vardhakin*, and *takṣaka* respectively.[29]

The *stha-pati* is the master-planner and general director of the entire architectural complex. He possesses deep knowledge of the science of architecture (*vāstu-vidyā*) and of the arts (*śilpa*), and he himself is regarded as an artist (*citra-jña*) and an expert scientist in the fields of arithmetic, algebra, and geometry (*gaṇita-jña*). He must also be a man possessing excellent qualities, of perfect physical features, full of compassion, detached, an expert historian and geographer (*Maya-mata* V, 13-18). In sum, he must be a knower of all sciences (*Maya-mata* II, 24). He must especially be well-versed in the knowledge of the *Veda*-s (*Māna-sāra* II, 26) and possess all the qualities of an *ācārya* (*Māna-sāra* II, 31), that is, of a spiritual guide who knows and teaches the *ācāra,* the rules of proper conduct. He is the master of the opening rituals of a new dwelling (*Māna-sāra* II, 14-17; II, 58; II, 73-74; II, 83; II, 85).

The disciple receiving directions from the *stha-pati*, a function often carried out by the son of the architect, is the *sūtra-grāhin* or *sūtra-dhāra*. Being knowledgeable in the *śāstra*-s, he deals with the correct and proportionate measurement of the building and its decorative parts using a thread (*sūtra*) for the purpose.[30] Through his indications and guide, the work comes into being thanks to the *takṣaka*, the engraver, and the *vardhakin*, the carpenter. In fact, the *takṣaka* is the real master-carpenter responsible for engraving the parts in stone

29 *Māna-sāra* II, 11-12; II, 17-20. Viśvakarman originated from Brahmā's Eastern face, Maya from his Southern face, Tvaṣṭṛ from his Northern face, and Manu from his Western face.

30 *Maya-mata* V, 18-19.

and wood as well as for the preparation of the bricks: these will then be assembled by the *vardhakin*. Both of them are said to be strong, pure, and highly capable. They almost always remain faithful to the instructions of the *stha-pati*, who through his plan and action is thought to ultimately reveal the will of Viśvakarman.[31] Each of them belongs to a family of artisans in which the knowledge of the correct working practice is transmitted from father to son.

Assisted in these specific competences by his disciples-collaborators as well as by the *sthāpaka*, the master-architect proceeds in the task assigned to him. First of all, he establishes the site selected for this purpose and then moves on to transform it into a proper receptacle for the dwelling that is to rest on its soil. Although the main phases of the work are the same, the building of a temple, if compared to that of a human dwelling, requires the performance of a higher number of rituals.

The phases which precede the building of a temple are meant to consecrate the chosen site, thus making it pure and stable. After being classified according to the characteristics of taste, smell, colour, and texture, the soil is levelled, ploughed, and cleaned so as to prepare it for a new sowing. The *stha-pati* offers oblations to the gods pronouncing the ritual formulae *svasti* ("hail!") and *jaya* ("victory!"). He claims the actual possession of the territory while pronouncing the formula: "May spirits, gods, and men depart! May they leave this place and go elsewhere since I have taken possession [of it]".[32] The appropriateness of the chosen site is then demonstrated by digging a hole into the ground and lighting a flame in it: if it keeps burning till the following day, it will confirm the favourable choice of the site. After determining the four cardinal directions with the help of a gnomon fixed into the ground, the *stha-pati* traces the *vāstu-puruṣa-maṇḍala* with the help of a golden or silver stylus and using milk curd or rice flour, 'tying' the gods to the earth through the *yantra* thus traced. The extension of the *maṇḍala*-square does not necessar-

31 *Maya-mata* V, 20-25.
32 *Maya-mata* IV, 1-3.

ily correspond to that of the site upon which the main building will be edified: indeed, the *maṇḍala*-square is the very symbol of the universe that is to be generated, and not the plan of the edifice. It provides the proportions and the 'rhythm' of the construction, measured according to precise arithmetic calculations based on the *pada*'s typology. Moreover, this process establishes the location of the temple's main entry as well as the four "vital points" (*marman*) of the edifice that are not to be hindered through the building of doors, columns, or walls. The placing of the *garbha-gṛha*—the innermost cell housing the deity to which the temple is consecrated—is determined according to the *brahma-sthāna*. Having 'linked' heaven and earth through the *vāstu-puruṣa-maṇḍala*, the *stha-pati* then calculates the dimensions of the temple in accordance with a peculiar unit of measurement: the first phalanx of the donor's thumb, which takes the name of *aṅgula*.[33] He thereby determines a special link between the sacrificer (*yajamāna*) and the temple. The master-architect thus proceeds from the macrocosm to the microcosm setting order into gross matter, since measuring means setting in order. Indeed, one of the names by which the temple is known is *vimāna* i.e. "the measured one".

The next step consists in digging a hole into the ground in correspondence with the central spot known as *brahma-bindu*, the navel of the *puruṣa*, the temple's most sacred place: here, the image of a coiled snake is traced. This snake represents the primordial serpent Śeṣa, the basis of the entire cosmos. Then the hole is filled up to three quarters with sand and earth, soaked with ritually pure water and cow's urine.[34] Subsequently, the first five of the nine bricks which constitute the symbolic foundations of the building are put in place. Finally, the architect places in the pit a miniature model of the sacred building containing different types of seeds, pebbles, and small conches as well as a golden image of the god to which the

33 See P. C. BAGCHI, "Piṅgalāmata", *Journal of the Indian Society of Oriental Art*, vol. XI, p. 157.

34 *Maya-mata* IV, 4-10.

temple is dedicated. In this way, the soil—understood as a divine uterus—is believed to be fertilized by the golden semen of the god safeguarded within the miniature model of the planned building, the dimensions of which are intimately linked to the *yajamāna*. This rite is called *garbhādhāna*, the offering of the semen,[35] and follows the laying of the first bricks, the *iṣṭaka-nyāsa*. Each of these phases is accompanied by the recitation of a *mantra* and invocations to the gods.

From this moment onwards, the temple will expand in both length and breadth. The first cell to be built is the *garbha-gṛha,* a simple cubicle with no openings except for its entrance door, which will house the image of the main deity. This image represents the womb from which the new building will be born, a three-dimensional symbol of the cosmic mountain. At this stage, the master-architect chooses the building materials and organizes their purchase. He invokes the spirits that dwell in trees so as to induce them to leave their abode, selects the 'male' and 'female' stones, and ritually follows the preparation of the bricks, the plaster, and the cement to be used in the building.[36] His assistants are at his side ready to advise him. Their activity also follows a ritual pattern: all their operations are accompanied by the recitation of sacred spells. The materials used in the construction of the temple are assimilated to the different parts of the dismembered *puruṣa*. While assembling the different parts of the edifice, the master-builders are thought to reiterate the different stages in the process of manifestation. The *puruṣa* crushed to the ground is once again projected towards the celestial vault and beyond it through the vertical dimension of the temple. This latter one coincides with the tapered pinnacle (*śikhara*) which rises above the *garbha-gṛha* and which represents the threefold world of manifestation. The top or upper point of the *vimāna* culminates with a circular stone

35 The ritual of the *garbhādhāna* is of very ancient origin and also takes place at the time of conception; see *ṚV* X, 184; *Atharva Veda* V, 25, 5.

36 *Maya-mata* XV, 81-121.

(*āmalaka*) surmounted by a pole, symbolizing the sun and the transcendent domain which lies beyond the manifested world.

The temple thus conceived is not just a place consecrated to the cult of the gods but represents the very shape of *puruṣa*, the shape he has assumed when he 'poured' himself into the manifest world.[37] Similarly, the figures of the gods shaped by the marble-cutters are not to be conceived as mere idols (*pratimā*) but rather as the 'coagulation' of the divine essence (*mūrti*). The temple is not a place destined to a congregational cult. No collective rites will be celebrated in it. Born out of the initial donation made by the *yajamāna*—who from the knowledge held by both the priest and the artisan reaps merits in this world and the hereafter—the temple offers to all pilgrims the possibility of delving into the divine principle. Glancing at the divine image (*darśana*) and venerating it (*pūjā*) are the ultimate aims of a visit to a temple. The architectural accomplishment is not only aesthetically balanced and pleasant to the eye, but corresponds to the level of consciousness or insight which the master-builder has reached through his spiritual training. The technician and planner is thus thought to attain a mystical knowledge of the cosmos.

A last but crucial point concerns the collocation assigned to the families of architects in the context of the traditional *varṇa*-s or social categories, also in relation to the ritual position held by the *śreni* of builders and claimed by its members. According to brahmanical sources,[38] the *stha-pati* belongs to the *śūdra* caste i.e. the servant class, and is excluded from the rituals of the priestly class of *brāhmaṇa*-s, who alone have access to the *Veda*-s. Although possessing a knowledge pertaining to the realm of cosmology, all builders are called upon to produce articles made up of earth, wood, or stone, in a fashion similar to that of other low castes such as blacksmiths,

37 GANAPATI STHAPATI, *What is a Temple?*, Chennai, Dakshina Publishing House, n. d., p. 2.

38 *Manu-smṛti* III, 163.

jewellers, and potters. Therefore, they are understood to be impure from a ritual point of view.

As we have seen, the *stha-pati* is admitted to the different ritual phases that accompany the construction of a temple or any other edifice. In certain cases, *stha-pati*-s play an important role as chief architects. However, it is the *sthāpaka*, a brahmin, who carries out all the rituals necessary for the correct execution of the work. The *Śilpa-ratna* states:

> He who intends to build villages, royal palaces, water cisterns or temples must choose a *guru* or a *śilpin* for that purpose. The *guru* should be a brahmin of elevated lineage... possessing a sound knowledge of the sacred texts, the *Veda*-s and the *Āgama*-s, observing the norms of conduct inherent to his caste (*varṇa*) and stage of life (*āśrama*)... One should select a *stha-pati* well-versed in the *Śilpa-śāstra*-s and a *sthāpaka*... who should have all the prerequisites of an *ācārya* and... who must carry out the architectural rites (*vāstu-karman*). The temple, or any other building begun by these two, must be brought to completion by these two alone and by nobody else.[39]

The division of roles, however, is not always evident, especially in those texts where the term *sthāpaka* is omitted. In some treatises of architecture, the rites which accompany the construction of buildings are an exclusive prerogative of the chief-architect (*stha-pati*). The position of the *stha-pati* is thus often equivalent to that of the *sthāpaka*. Indeed, though formally belonging to a caste which is excluded from the performance of rites, he combines due to his theoretical and technical skills a ritual as well as a priestly function.

As underlined, the corporations of artisans claim divine descent. They define the social group they belong to as *viśva-karman*, claiming that their families descend from the five faces of the divine architect, Viśvakarman. The five faces or sons of Viśvakarman are named Manu, Maya, Tvaṣṭṛ, Śilpa, and Viśvājña. They are said to be the an-

[39] *Śilpa-ratna* I, 29-42.

cestors of blacksmiths and carpenters, of all those who produce brassware and bronze statues, and of all sculptors, architects, and goldsmiths. The supreme position that the corporations of artisans attribute to this deity and to the art of building (= the transformation of gross matter into a microcosm set in a precise order and following precise rules) allows them to claim for themselves a ritual position that is far superior to the social status they hold within the caste system. The ritual function in which they participate corresponds to the sacred sphere, for they call themselves *viśva-brāhmaṇa*-s, the priests detaining the knowledge of the *viśva*, that is, of the entire universe. This is of course in contrast with the exclusive ideology of the brahmanical caste.[40]

The various families which constitute the corporations of artisans in southern India are known by the name of *pāñcalā* i.e. the "five components", or by the even more revealing term of *kammālan*.[41] The Tamil word *kammālan* bears the meaning of "directing the eyes" and "providing the sight of something". The double meaning is extremely significant: the *kammālan* not only produces objects which can be appreciated through the eye, as the artisan does, but is also he who 'opens the eyes', thus showing a person the truth. In particular, the *kammālan*-s are the sculptors who perform the ritual of the 'opening of the eyes' of the *mūrti*-s installed within temples, precisely by painting their eyes.[42] They claim the status of *brāhmaṇa*-s and practice the prescriptions and ceremonies of the priestly caste, calling themselves *ācāri*-s and *patthar*-s, that is, *ācārya*-s and *bhaṭṭa*-s. Within this closed social group, the *stha-pati*-s claim an elevated position, since they study Sanskrit and the sacred texts of the *Veda*-s, and wear the sacred thread, an exclusive prerogative of

40 J. BROUWER, *The Makers of the World*, New Delhi, Oxford University Press, 1995, pp. 40-48; A. K. COOMARASWAMY, *The Indian Craftsman*, New Delhi, Munshiram Manoharlal, 1989^2, p. 33.

41 The *kammālan*-s define themselves as *deva-brāhmaṇa*-s or *deva-kammālan*-s; *ibid.*, p. 35.

42 E. THURSTON, *Castes and Tribes of Southern India*, Madras, 1909, p. 106.

brahmins.[43] In other words, the artisans claim for themselves the role of a separate clan, different from all the rest, singling out within the social subdivision they belong to different specific obligations which culminate in the function of the *ācārya* in his role as master-builder, the *stha-pati*. Furthermore, the corporations of artisans in charge of the construction of hindū temple-complexes as well as of buddhist sanctuaries in various parts of the subcontinent, have been and continue to be constantly on the move throughout India. This peculiar mobility of the corporations of artisans, documented since the 2nd century BCE in the buddhist sanctuary of Sāñcī, in what is today Madhya Pradesh, continues till the present day: for instance, the *śreni* of Tanjavur, in Tamil Nadu, offers a striking example of such mobility. For this reason and because of the initiatory characteristics in the transmission of their working practice, the *pāñcalā*-s present themselves as a unique social group within the hindū caste system.

BIBLIOGRAPHY

PRIMARY SOURCES

Agni Mahāpurāṇa, Delhi, Nag Publishers, 1996.
Aitareya Brāhmaṇa. With the vṛtti Sukhapradā, New Delhi, Rashtriya Sanskrit Sansthan, 2002.
Ajitāgama. Édition critique par N. R. Bhatt, Pondhichéry, Institut Français d'Indologie, 3 vols., 1964, 1967, 1991.
Atharva Veda Saṃhitā, Varanasi, Chaukhamba Sanskrit Prakashan, 2002.
Bhaviṣya Mahāpurāṇa, Delhi, Nag Publishers, 1995.
Bṛhat Saṃhitā, Nayī Dilli, Rañjana Publications, 1997.

43 *Ibid.*, pp. 106-108, 118-120; GANAPATI STHAPATI, *Contribution of the Visvakarmas to the Science, Technology & Culture of Indian Origin*, Chennai, Dakshina Publishing House, 2000, chap. VIII, pp. 1-2.

Devatāmūrtiprakaraṇam and Rūpamaṇḍaṇam. Sanskrit with notes and commentary by Upendra Mohan Sankhyatirtha, Calcutta, Metropolitan Printing and Publishing House, 1936.

Garuḍa Mahāpurāṇa, Delhi, Nag Publishers, 1996.

Hymns of the Ṛg Veda in the Saṃhitā and Pada Texts. Reprinted from the *Editio Princeps* by F. Max Müller, Varanasi, 1965 (3rd ed.).

Īśānaśivagurudevapaddhati, New Delhi, Rashtriya Sanskrit Sansthan, 2002.

Kṣīrārṇava. Sanskrit, Gujarati and Hindi, Ahmadābād, Balavantarāya Somapūra, 1967.

Mahābhārata, Bombay, Nirṇayasagar Press, 1909-1919.

Mānasāra, New Delhi, Oriental Books Reprint Corporation - Munshiram Manoharlal, 1979.

Manasollāsa, Baroda, Central Library, 1925-1961.

Manuṣyālaya Candrikā, 1964.

Matsya Purāṇa. Text with English Translation and Notes, Delhi, Nag Publishers, 1997.

Mayamata. Édition critique, traduction et notes par B. Dagens, Pondichéry, Institut Français d'Indologie, 1970.

Pratimā Māna Lakṣaṇa. Sanskrit, English and Tibetan, Delhi, Bharatiya Publishing House, 1978.

Pūrvakāmikāgama. Edited by C. Svāmināthaśivācārya, Madras, 1975.

Rājavallabha, Amadāvāda, Mahādeva Rāmacandra Jaguṣṭe, 1965.

Rauravāgama. Édition critique par N. R. Bhatt, Pondichéry, Institut Français d'Indologie, 3 vols., 1961, 1972, 1988.

Samarāṅgaṇa Sūtradhāram, Delhi, New Bharatiya Books, Kāraporeśana, 1998.

Śatapatha Brāhmaṇa, Bombay, Śrī Venkaṭeśvara Press, 1942.

Śilpa Prakāśa. Sanskrit with Translation by Alice Boner, Leiden, E. J. Brill, 1966.

Śilpa Śāstra. With Introduction, Notes, and English Translation by P. N. Bose, Delhi, Motilalal Banarsidass, 1928.

Śilparatna, Tañjāvūr, Tañjai Manonar Carapōji Caracuvati Makāl Nulakaccaṅkam, 1989.

Suprabhedāgama, Madras, 1928.
Taittirīyopaniṣad, Varanasi, Chowkhamba Sanskrit Series Office, 2002.
Tantrasamuccaya, Lakhnau, Uttar Pradesh Saṃskṛta Saṃsthāna, 1997.
Uttarakāmikāgama. Edited by C. Svāmināthaśivācārya, Madras, 1988.
Vāstu Vidyā. Notes by K. Mahādeva Śāstrī, Trivandrum, T.S.S., 1940.

MODERN WORKS

Acharya, P. K. (trans.), *Architecture of Mānasāra*, London, Oxford University Press, 1934.

Acharya, P. K., *Hindu Architecture in India and Abroad*, New Delhi, Oriental Books Reprint Corporation, 1979 (2nd ed.).

Bagchi, P.C., "Piṅgalāmata", *Journal of the Indian Society of Oriental Art*, vol. XI.

Boccali, G. - Piano, S. - Sani, S., *Le letterature dell'India*, Torino, Utet Libreria, 2000.

Brouwer, J., *The Makers of the World*, New Delhi, Oxford University Press, 1995.

Coomaraswamy, A. K., *Selected Papers, 1. Traditional Art and Symbolism*, Princenton, Bollingen Series LXXXIX, 1977.

Coomaraswamy, A. K., *The Indian Craftsman*, New Delhi, Munshiram Manoharlal, 1989 (2nd ed.).

Dagens, B., *Les enseignements architecturaux de l'Ajitāgama et du Rauravāgama*, Pondichéry, Institut Français d'Indologie, 1977.

Dagens, B. (trans.), *Mayamata, an Indian Treatise on Housing, Architecture and Iconography*, New Delhi, Sitaram Bhartia Institute of Scientific Research, 1985.

Ganapati Sthapati, *What is a Temple?*, Chennai, Dakshina Publishing House, n. d.

Ganapati Sthapati, *Contribution of the Visvakarmas to the Science, Technology & Culture of Indian Origin*, Chennai, Dakshina Publishing House, 2000.

Ganapati Sthapati, *Sthāpatya Veda*, Chennai, Dakshina Publishing House, 2001.

Gonda, J., *Medieval Religious Literature in Sanskrit*, Wiesbaden, Otto Harrassowitz, 1977.
Kramrisch, S., *The Hindu Temple*, Delhi, Motilal Banarsidass, 1976.
Monier-Williams, M., *Sanskrit-English Dictionary*, New Delhi, Marwah Publications, 1986 (2nd ed.).
Renou, L., "La maison védique", *Journal Asiatique*, CCXXXI, 1939.
Thurston, E., *Castes and Tribes of Southern India*, Madras, 1909.

THE FIGURE OF THE *PAṆḌITA* AS *GURU*

GIANNI PELLEGRINI

This paper aims at explaining some of the main terms and figures related to the transmission of knowledge in the brāhmaṇical tradition. I will make some observations on the path leading a student of Sanskrit to acquire titles such as *śāstrī, ācārya*, and *paṇḍita*. Their function as means of knowledge, *guru*, both of a worldly (*laukika-vyāvahārika*) and spiritual (*adhyātmika-paramārthika*) nature will be highlighted. The individual characteristic of each term will be delineated in reference to the texts.

Once Śukadeva[1] thus spoke to his venerable father Vyāsa:

> There is no trace of happiness in this *saṃsāra*. As worms enjoy pleasures in the midst of excrements, so ignorant persons find pleasures in *saṃsāra*. Those who have studied the *Veda* and the other *śāstras* and yet are attached to the world, are certainly deluded and blind like horses, pigs, and dogs; no one is more stupid and ignorant than those persons. Getting this extremely rare human birth and

1 Śukadeva, son and pupil of Vyāsa, is the narrator of the majority of Purāṇic texts set in the Naimiṣa forest.

> studying the *Vedānta* and other *śāstras,* if people are nonetheless still attached to this world then who may ever attain liberation? What more wonder can you find in this world than the fact that persons attached to wives, sons, and houses are called *paṇḍita*-s? That man who is not bound by this *saṃsāra*, made up of the three *guṇa*-s of *māyā*[2], is a *paṇḍita*: only such a man is intelligent and has understood the real import of the *śāstras*.[3]

But what does this term *paṇḍita* mean? And what are the 'stages' leading to such a condition?

In India traditional doctrines were always transmitted orally, even if these doctrines were fixed in written texts. This is due to profound reasons: since not only words need to be passed on, it is above all necessary to ensure the actual participation in the tradition. This participation is a transmission of knowledge from master to pupil (*paramparā*), the origin of which is lost in time (*anādi*). This passage is present at each level of teaching, even in those disciplines known as sciences (*apara-vidyā, vijñāna*): these could not exist if not through a participation, although indirect, in the essence of what is understood to be supreme knowledge (*para-vidyā, jñāna*).

In the *Bṛhadāraṇyaka Upaniṣad* (II. 4. 5), Yājñavalkya explains to his wife Maitreyī:

आत्मा वा आरे द्रष्टव्यः श्रोतव्यो मन्तव्यो निधिध्यासितव्यः

> My dear, the *ātman* should be realized, should be heard of, reflected and meditated upon!

From these words, we can discern four different steps in the path leading to knowledge, in which the need to see concerns the laws of the world and their relation to the *ātman*. These are: to listen to the

2 The three *guṇa*-s are the qualities which characterize all materiality. They are: *sattva* which is bright, ascending, white; *rajas*, which is expansive, active, red; and *tamas*, which is descending, obtuse, dark. Before manifestation they are perfectly balanced (*sāmyāvasthā*).

3 *Devī-bhāgavata Purāṇa* I. 14. 1-70.

truth about the *ātman*; to ponder over what has been heard; and lastly to meditate upon and realize what has been pondered over. If this four-fold path is to be followed in order to attain supreme knowledge (*para-vidyā*), then, in virtue of the profound equivalences linking all levels of existence, even its secondary, inferior forms (*apara-vidyā*) are to approached and achieved in a similar way. Here too we can identify four stages: the studying or listening to the words of the master (*adhīti, adhyayana*); the comprehension and reflection upon what has been studied (*bodhana*); experimenting upon oneself what has been learned and understood so as to lead a life according to these principles (*ācaraṇa, śiṣṭācāra-sadācāra*); and, finally, spreading what has been understood and experimented (*prācaraṇa*), since the world too must partake of this knowledge:

सर्वद्रव्येषु विद्यैव द्रव्यमाहुरनुत्तमम्।
अहार्यत्वादनर्घत्वादक्षयत्वाच्च सर्वदा ॥

> Learning, of all things, [the wise] declare to be without a superior, since [learning] cannot be taken away, valued or exhausted.[4]

The diverse cosmological and metaphysical/philosophical frameworks present in India are not thought to be mutually exclusive. This is claimed to be supported by the etymology of the term with which they are referred to: *darśana* comes from the root √*dṛś* "to see", and means "point of view".[5] This vision is said to be founded on the eternal, transcendent *Veda* (*apauruṣeya*).[6]

4 *Hitopadeśa Prastāvikā* 4.

5 *dṛśyate, jñāyate, vicāryate tattvam aneneti darśanam*: "*Darśana* is the means through which reality is seen, known, and reflected upon." To study a *darśana* one must have certain qualifications (*adhikāra*), a searching intellect capable of enquiring into the essence of things. Here too four elements (*anubandha-catuṣṭayam*) are mentioned: *adhikārī*, the one qualified to study the *śāstra*; *prayojanam*, the aim of any particular *śāstra*; *viṣaya*, the subject of it; *sambandha*, the tie between the aim and the subject of the *śāstra*.

6 *Veda*, √*vid*, from which *vidyā*, "knowledge". Sight symbolizes knowledge, and visual perception is the main instrument of knowledge (*pratyakṣa pramāṇa*). Knowledge is understood as an inner vision, an intuition.

Having a common origin in the *Veda*-s, the various *darśana*-s are thought to be in fundamental agreement, not contradicting each other. They are believed to be complementary. If their expositions can be modified in order to adapt them to the changing ages and circumstances, the essence of their doctrines remains unchanged.[7]

The *śruti* is understood as the origin of every concept. In it, six auxiliary limbs (*aṅga*) are said to be implicitly contained. Without their knowledge, the understanding of the *śruti* is impossible.[8] One of these *aṅgas* is known as *śikṣā*, that is, the science of the correct pronunciation and articulation of Vedic texts, necessitating the knowledge of all euphonic laws and of the symbolic value of each syllable. Besides this, *śikṣā* also means "education", "learning", "comprehension", "teaching". This feminine noun is derived from root √*śikṣ*, the traditional explanation of which is "to give knowledge to a pupil" (*vidyopādāna*), "to teach a pupil science", so as to make him/her a *śikṣita*, a "learned person".[9]

7 The Vedic corpus is believed to be a coherent whole, in which all point of views can be appreciated both in an analytical sense – a logical sequence – as well as in a synthetic sense, that is, simultaneously. Therefore, the historical phases in which the Vedic tradition developed is thought to be of no special relevance.

8 The six *vedāṅgas* are: *śikṣā, vyākaraṇa, kalpa, nirukta, chanda, and jyotiṣa*: *śabdaśāstraṃ mukhaṃ jyotiṣaṃ cakṣuṣī śrotramuktaṃ niruktaṃ ca kalpa / yā tu śikṣāsya vedasya sā nāsikā pādapadmadvayaṃ chanda ādyairbudhaiḥ //*: "The ancient sages proclaimed that grammar is the face of the *Veda*, astronomy-astrology the two eyes, the science of etymology the ears, the science of ritual the hands, the science of pronunciation the nose, and prosody the lotus-feet".

9 Some interesting observations have been suggested on the use of *upādāna* instead of the simpler *dāna*. The key is in the prefix *upa*, indicating closeness, equality, subordination. *Vedānta* accepts the presence of two causes. The essential cause (*nimitta-kāraṇa*, the efficient cause for Aristotle) and the *upadānā-kāraṇa*, the substantial, material cause. Anything useful to the essential cause to produce an effect (*kārya*) is *upādāna*. For example, the potter is *nimitta-kāraṇa*, while the lathe, the clay, the stick to turn the wheel, etc. are all *upādāna*. According to the *Vaiśeṣika* system, *upādāna* is divisible into two groups: *samāvayī*, "inherent", the substance from which an object is produced (in the

Let's now see those who have the ability and authority to teach. The qualifying adjective *paṇḍita* is referred to people whose profession is teaching or who have acquired a great intellectual mastery through Sanskrit. First of all, I would like to underline that the equation between *brāhmaṇa* and *paṇḍita* is not an implicit one. For the first one is defined by birth (*jāti*) and dharmic duties (*adhikāra*), while a *paṇḍita* is characterized by one's own intellectual path. Patañjali confirms this in his *Vyākaraṇa-mahābhāṣya*, where he distinguishes between *paṇḍita* (*śiṣṭa*) and *brāhmaṇa*.

The qualification and authority of the *paṇḍita* indicates that his culture is not merely grounded in books but is the outcome of a continuous transmission of knowledge from master to pupil. Indeed, the importance of his function lies in preserving and transmitting the heritage received from his predecessors.[10]

The *paṇḍita* is not only a scholar (*vidvān*) but is often a sage. A person with a great ability to memorize, an oral knowledge of the *Veda*-s, of one or more *śāstra*-s, of the methods of editing and copying texts, and a special relationship with his pupils (*guru-śiṣya-sambandha, saṃvāda*). The *paṇḍita* doesn't prevent the use of books, although he does not believe in written texts as a source of knowledge since he privileges oral communication and transmission. The *paṇḍita* must safeguard the mnemonic study as a method of education. When this is combined with a strong *guru-śiṣya* relation, the continuity of the doctrinal school is guaranteed. The *paṇḍita* is open to all fields of learning, even if he is a specialist of traditional knowl-

example, the clay), and *asamāvayī*, "non-inherent", all other things. In our context, *śikṣā* is the substantial cause (*upādāna*) in the acquisition of *vidyā*; see "Hindu Education", *Kalyāṇ Kalpataru* 46, 1, Gorakhpur, Gītā Press, 2000, pp. 322-328.

10 Among several functions, the three main ones are: the acquisition of knowledge (*grahaṇa*); *svādhyaya*, the daily recitation of the *Veda*-s; the teaching and transmission of knowledge to others (*adhyāpana*). Whoever goes against these rules is said to become a demon, a *brahma-rākṣasa*. Therefore, the responsibility of the *paṇḍita* is that of safeguarding Sanskrit culture as a vehicle of knowledge and as an instrument for upholding *sanātana-dharma*.

edge, since everything which is of quality is worth learning, without pride or jealousy. Indeed, the whole universe is one's master for a person capable of discernment.

The *paṇḍita* is a master, an adviser, a spiritual *guru*, a legal consultant and a model of purity.[11] In 1959, the Indian Commission for the Sanskrit Language published the following statement:

> A *paṇḍita*, who devotes 15 or 20 years to the study of a particular *śāstra* or a group of allied subjects, generally becomes a master of his subjects. His knowledge is precise and ready; there is no fumbling or hesitancy about him. He does not need notes, not even books, for expounding the text.[12]

Let us consider the path leading a student (*vidyārthin, chāttra*) to acquire the titles of *śāstrī, ācārya,* and *paṇḍita guru*. Nowadays, Sanskrit is taught in thousands of private institutions known as *vidyālaya*-s or *pāṭha-śālā*-s. The course of study is carried out in the following way:

a) The pupil receives his first education from the family, local teachers, or privately in the *pāṭha-śālā* or *guru-kula*. This lasts four

11 The *paṇḍita*, both in school and in society, held and still holds various positions: reciter (*pāṭhaka, purohita*) in rituals related to the *saṃskāra*-s; court-poet (*kavi*; as, for instance, the *paṇḍita-rāja* Jagannātha); legal advisor (*dharmādhikārin*); minister (*mantrin*); teacher (*ācārya, upādhyāya, adhyāpaka*). In university (*viśva-vidyālaya, vidyā-pīṭha*) he holds several other positions: head-master (*prācārya*), professor (*ācārya*), reader (*pravācaka*), chancellor (*kulādhipati*), and vice-chancellor (*kula-pati, kula-guru*).

12 Education in India is influenced by two main factors: the implementation of the English system of education in colleges and universities, and the use of regional languages through the so-called *Three Language Formula*. Besides his or her mother-tongue, each student is required to study English and Hindī. These developments have considerably weakened the traditional learning system. On this issue, see A. MICHAELS (ed.), *The Pandit. Traditional Scholarship in India*, New Delhi, Manohar, 2001, pp. 4-15.

years, during which the fundamental elements of the language are learned;

b) The second stage is called *prathamā* or *praveśikā*.[13] It lasts two years and is always taught in the *vidyālaya*;
c) The next stage, *pūrva-madhyamā*, lasts two years and takes place in the *vidyālaya* or *mahā-vidyālaya*;
d) With the next two years, one arrives at the *uttara-madhyamā* exam. When this is passed successfully, the *viśarada* or "mature" level is reached, and the title of *upa-* or *prāk-śāstrī* is awarded;
e) With the following step the pupil starts a three-year course called *śāstrī*, in the *mahā-vidyālaya* or *viśva-vidyālaya*;
f) The next two years allow the student to achieve the status of an *ācārya*;[14]
g) The Ph.D. requires two or more years and is granted at *viśva-vidyālaya*-s, such as the Sampūrṇānanda Saṃskṛta Viśva-vidyālaya of Vārāṇasī, the Bhandarkar Oriental Research Institute in Poona, or the Gaṅgānāth Jhā Kendrīya Saṃskṛta Vidyāpīṭha in Allāhābād. Then, the pupil receives the title of *vidyā-vāridhi*;
h) Lastly, there is the D.Litt. with which one becomes a *vidyā-vacaspati* or *cakravartin*.

The study of the language is paramount along with the memorization of texts which the pupil must know word by word and fully understand in their contents and in the exact order of their exposition.[15]

13 All levels in which the course of traditional studies is subdivided, are referred to by feminine adjectives, which agree with the feminine noun *parīkṣā* i.e. "exam".

14 The title *śāstrī* in Vārāṇasī corresponds to the title *vidvān* or *kovida* awarded in Calcutta and other places. Besides this, other titles corresponding to that of *ācārya* are *śiromaṇi, tilaka, mahopādhyāya.*

15 For *paṇḍita*-s there exists an exam known as *aṣṭāvādhāna*, "paying attention to eight simultaneous events", testing one's ability to memorize and concentrate; see P. S. FILLIOZAT, *The Sanskrit Language: An Overview*, Vārāṇasī, Indica, 2000.

Besides this, the techniques of exegesis (*mīmāṃsā*) and logic (*tarka, nyāya*) are taught.

Generally, in a complete course the pupil must memorize some sections of the *Amarakośa*, a dictionary of synonyms in verses, the *sūtra*-s of Pāṇini with the *vārttika*-s of Kātyāyana, the declensions of nouns and conjugations of verbs, and the *nīti-śāstra*, that is, the science of ethics and diplomacy. This is complemented with the study of portions of the *Hitopadeśa* or *Pañca-tantra*, the *Mūla-rāmāyaṇa*, sections of the *Purāṇa*-s, *sarga*-s of the *Raghuvaṃśa-mahā-kāvya*, and the *Kumāra-sambhava*, *Megha-dūta* and *Abhijñāna-śakuntalā* of Kālidāsa. Furthermore, one must study prosody, the *Bhagavad-gītā*, and Vedic texts such as *Brāhmaṇa*-s, *Sūkta*-s, and *Upaniṣad*-s coupled with the *Dharma-śāstra*-s and the foundational *sūtra*-s and most important commentaries of *Nyāya, Sāṃkhya*, and *Vedānta*.

The method of education is analytical. First, the *ācārya* reads or recites the verses. He then reads them again breaking down the rules of euphonic combination and creating a syntactic construction in prose (*anvaya*). Next he explains the various compounds and the meaning of each word through their roots (*dhātu, prakṛti*) and suffixes (*pratyaya*). The *ācārya* then proceeds to offer the meaning of the whole passage, and, finally, the translation. In this way, the student is given a full, in-depth understanding which will facilitate the process of memorization.[16]

[16] Kauṭilya tells us of a method in eight stages through which the pupil acquires the transmission: 1) *śuṣruṣa*, the desire to hear the words from the mouth of the *ācārya*; 2) *śravaṇa*, listening; 3) *grahaṇa*, learning; 4) *dhāraṇa*, memorizing; 5) and 6) *ūha-apoha*, reflection, consisting in searching where to apply the teaching; 7) *artha-vijñāna*, the refined understanding of the contents of education, of all its subtleties; 8) *tattvābhiniveśa*, going deeply into the real meaning of what has been received; *ibid.*, pp. 77-78.

The position of the *guru*, or *ācārya*, is beyond question.[17] The pupil does not even dare to question his orders or corrections. Each time the student meets the master, he or she touches his feet with the right hand and then places it on his/her eyes or forehead.[18] The *guru* is thought to be perfect under every aspect, and is always sincerely devoted to the good and the instruction of his pupils. This kind of very disciplined and often strict education, is followed with great efforts so as to make the student a *jītendriya*. That is, the pupil must become capable of controlling the senses, his/her body and mind.[19]

I now come to an analysis of each of the previously mentioned titles. As seen, I have often used interchangeably the terms *śāstrī*, *ācārya, paṇḍita,* and *guru*. All, these, in truth, are related to teaching

17 One is reminded of the following verses from the *Guru-gītā*: *na guroradhikaṃ tattvaṃ na guroradhikaṃ tapaḥ / tattvaṃ jñānātparam nāsti tasmai śrīgurave namaḥ //* 74 *// gururādiranādiśca guruḥ paramadaivatam / guroḥ parataraṃ nāsti tasmai śrīgurave namaḥ //* 77 *// yasmātparataram nāsti neti netīti vai śruti / manasā vacasā caiva nityamārādhayed gurum //* 82 *// śrīgurugītā //*:
[74] "Salutations to Śrī Guru! There is no truth higher than the Guru, no austerity greater than [service to] the Guru, no truth greater than knowledge."
[77] "Salutation to Śrī Guru! The Guru is the origin, he who is without origin. The Guru is the Supreme Deity. There is nothing higher than the Guru."
[82] "Nothing exists which is higher than he. The *Veda*-s describe him as 'not this, not that'. Therefore, always worship the Guru with mind and speech!"

18 *dhyānamūlaṃ gurormūrtiṃ pūjāmūlaṃ gurorpadaṃ / mantramūlaṃ gurorvākyaṃ mokṣamūlaṃ gurorkṛpā //* 76 *// śrīgurugītā //*:
[76] "The root of contemplation is the Guru's form, the root of worship is the Guru's feet; the root of the *mantra* is the Guru's word, the root of liberation is the Guru's grace!"

19 A popular saying runs as follows: *kākaceṣṭaḥ bakadhyānaḥ śvānanidrastathaiva ca / alpāhārī gṛhatyāgī vidyārthipañcalakṣaṇāni //*:
"These are the five characteristics of the student: he acts like a raven, he is careful like a heron, he sleeps like a dog, he eats little, and he lives far from home".
Moreover: *guroḥ kṛpāprasādena ātmārāmaṃ nirīkṣayet / anena gurumārgeṇa svātmajñānam pravartate //* 83 *// śrīgurugītā //*:
[83] "It is by the grace of the Guru that it is possible to attain the bliss of the Self! It is through the way showed by the Guru that the knowledge of one's own Self is disclosed!".

and education. Yet we will see that the term *paṇḍita* as explained by the texts is most strongly identified with the figure of the *guru*.

Śāstrī is one of the most elevated titles in the traditional hierarchy of Sanskrit transmission. The *śāstrī* course lasts three years, each year ending with an exam, thus dividing a *śāstrī* curricula into three sessions (*khaṇḍa*). A *śāstrī* is one who knows the contents of the *śāstra*-s in depth, understands and discusses them. One of his fundamental functions is to defend the point of view of his school, the *Veda*-s, and the *sanātana-dharma* in the dialectic disputes (*śāstrārtha*) against *Veda* opponents (*nāstika*).[20] Typically a *śāstrī* has a general education covering diverse subjects (*Veda, Kāvya, Vedānta, Jyotiṣa, Dharma-śāstra, Vyākaraṇa, Itihāsa, Purāṇa*), though he is especially learned in one specific branch of knowledge.

In order to offer the most subtle and convincing proof without error or contradiction, the *śāstrī* especially nurtures the *tarka* or *nyāya-śāstra*, the science of logic. Preliminary to the study of *Nyāya, Mīmāṃsā, Vedānta*, and all other *śāstra*-s is the study of grammar (*vyākaraṇa*), which allows the understanding and interpretation of even the most complex and cryptic texts such as the *Brahma-sūtra* and *Upaniṣad*-s. It is, however, paramount to confront and discuss each matter with experts of one's chosen subject. In this regard, Caraka said:

> A physician should debate with a physician. For a debate with an expert gives rise to that pleasure which comes from being intent upon

[20] There are several dialectic competitions (*pratiyogitā*) organized by the *Saṃskṛta-sabhā*-s and *Pariṣad*-s: of poetry, recitation, reading, and composition. There are competitions in which one recites a verse and another contestant must instantly compose a stanza beginning with the last syllable of the recited verse (*ślokāntyākṣarī*). In other cases, one must compose verses ending with a given hemistich (*pada*). Winners receive special recognitions (*vāktṛktva-padaka*). These institutions also organize meetings among *paṇḍita*-s, in which they compete and test their doctrine and poetic ability (*śāstrārtha, vivāda, vākyārthagoṣṭi, vigṛhya, sambhāṣya*).

> knowledge. It reinforces cleverness, it creates strength of expression, and it makes one's reputation shine.[21]

Climbing the hierarchy, we find the figure of the *ācārya*. This title can be acquired after three years of *śāstrī* followed by two years of further, intense study in which a chosen subject is mastered. Then the title *ācārya* is preceded by the subject-matter in which one has specialized: *Vedānta-ācārya, Vyākaraṇa-ācārya, Veda-ācārya, Tantra-ācārya*, and so on. The *Manu-smṛti* (II. 144) gives the following definition of *ācārya*:[22]

उपनीय तुयः शिष्यंवेदमध्यापयेद् द्विजः ।
संकल्पंरहस्यं च तमाचार्यंप्रचक्षते ॥

> That twice-born who, having initiated the pupil, teaches him the *Veda*-s, the ritual science, and the secret doctrines [= the *Upaniṣad*-s], is called an *ācārya.*[23]

21 Quoted in FILLIOZAT, *The Sanskrit Language*, *op. cit.*, pp. 93-94.

22 The following verse from the *Manu-smṛti* (II. 141) thus defines the *upādhyāya*: *ekadeśaṃ tu vedasya vedāṅgānyapi vā punaḥ / yo'dhyāpayati vṛttyartham upādhyāyaḥ sa ucyate //*:
"He who gets paid for teaching the *Veda*-s and a *Vedāṅga* is called an *upādhyāya*." Moreover, the *Manu-smṛti* (II. 142, 145, 171) states: "He who performs rituals such as the *Niṣeka*, etc..., according to scriptural injunctions, and feeds the disciple, that *brāhmaṇa* is called a *guru* ... An *ācārya* excels ten *upādhyāya*-s, a father excels a hundred *ācārya*-s, and a mother excels one thousand fathers in respect and veneration ... Before initiation with the sacred thread, a *brāhmaṇa* is not competent for any ritual. It is the *ācārya* who bestows upon him the knowledge of the *Veda*-s. This is why the *ācārya* is called his father."

23 See, for example, the great *guru*-s of the past such as *Śaṅkarācārya, Rāmānujācārya, Madhvācārya, Vallabhācārya, Rāmānandācārya*. Besides the initiation name they bear the term *ācārya* as their title, to signify doctrinal excellence and spiritual authority. In the *Bhagavad-gītā* (I. 2-3) Droṇa alone is called an *ācārya*. Several times he is said to be the *guru* of both the *Pāṇḍava*-s and *Kaurava*-s, teaching them the science of *dhanur-veda*.

Ācārya is constituted by the prefix *āṅ*, here meaning direction towards something, and the root √*car* "to go", "to proceed". The noun *ācāra* refers to one's behavior: the *ācārya* is he who reveals supreme knowledge and behaves accordingly. In this case, even the titles *paṇḍita* (scholar, sage) and *guru* (spiritual master) are appropriate.

The *Kulārṇava Tantra* (XVII. 11-12) declares:

स्वयमाचरतेशिष्यानाचारेस्थापयत्यपि ।
आचिनोतीह शास्त्रार्थानाचर्यस्तेन कथ्यते ॥
चराचरसमा सन्नमध्यापयति यः स्वयम् ।
यः आदियोगसिद्धत्वादाचार्य इति कथ्यते ॥

He (the *ācārya*) conducts himself (*ācarate*) according to *dharma* and establishes his disciples in the *ācāra*; he incorporates the various qualities referred to in the *śāstra*-s: therefore he is called an *ācārya*. He who teaches to all that come to him, both moving and unmoving (*carācara*) creatures, and who is perfect in the practice of *yama*, etc. is called an *ācārya*.[24]

The *ācārya* is one who is entitled to offer his teaching (*upadeśa*) in any field of knowledge, destroying ignorance. It is thus appropriate to compare him to the *guru*, the traditional definition of whom is to be found in the *Guru-gītā*:

गुकारस्त्वन्धकारश्च रुकारस्तेज उच्यते।
अज्ञानग्रासकं ब्रह्म गुरुरेव न संशयः ॥ २३ ॥
गुकारो प्रथमो वर्गोमायादिगुणभासकः।
रुकारो द्वितीयो ब्रह्म मायाभ्रान्तिविनाशनम् ॥ २४ ॥

24 S. MALVĪYA (ed.), *Kulārṇavatantram*, Vārāṇasī, Śrīkṛṣṇadās Academy, 2000. See also *Hitopadeśa* I. 103: "To be wise in giving advice to others is very easy; but to be true in discharging one's duties is the special prerogative of rare souls."

(23) The syllable *gu* is darkness, and the syllable *ru* is said to be light. There is no doubt that the *Guru* is indeed the Supreme Knowledge which swallows up [the darkness of] ignorance.
(24) The first syllable *gu* represents *māyā* whereas the second syllable *ru* represents the Supreme Knowledge which destroys the illusion of *māyā*.[25]

Finally, some considerations on the figure of the *paṇḍita*. The adjective *paṇḍita* seems to be derived from root √*paṇḍ*, which means "to pile up", "put together", "aggregate". According to Bhaṭṭojī Dīkṣita,[26] the feminine noun *paṇḍā* would mean *buddhi*, that is, "pure intellect", "awakening", "realization", "intelligence", "wisdom", "knowledge". In short, "knowing something as it is", "the discerning faculty allowing the knowledge of reality". Traditional etymological dictionaries such as the *Śabdārtha-cintamaṇi*, the *Śabda-kalpa-druma*, and the *Vācaspatīya* give a more specific meaning of the term: *paṇḍā tattva-viṣayinī buddhiḥ* i.e. "cognition concerning reality", "knowledge pertaining to what is real"; *nirṇayātjñānam* i.e. "cognition in which a determination [having as its subject the real nature of an object] is produced"; *vedojjvalā buddhiḥ* i.e. "enlightened understanding of the *Veda*-s."[27]

25 *Kulārṇava Tantra* XVII. 7-10 adds: "The syllable *gu* indicates darkness and the syllable *ru* what annihilates it; thus the person who destroys the darkness of ignorance is called *Guru*. The *ga* syllable is understood as the giver of perfection and the syllable *ra* what annihilates all stains. The *u* vowel is Viṣṇu himself. The three together form the word *Guru*, the Supreme *ātman*. The syllable *ga* is the richness of wisdom and the syllable *ra* what enlightens such richness. The *u* vowel is one's identity with Śiva: this is why he is called *Guru*. Because through secret knowledge he leads to the knowledge of the *ātman* and permits one to attain union with It, and [because] his aspect is that of Rudra and the other deities, he is called *Guru*." *Guru-gītā* 46 adds: "The syllable *gu* is that which transcends all attributes and the syllable *ru* is that which is without form. The *Guru* is he who leads to that state which is beyond attributes."

26 *Siddhānta Kaumudī, Uṇādi-sūtra* I. 111. See A. AKLUJKAR, "Paṇḍit and Paṇḍits in History", in MICHAELS, *The Pandit*, *op. cit.*, pp. 17-19.

27 Jainas paraphrase the term *paṇḍā* thus: *ratna-traya-pariṇatā buddhiḥ*: "a mature intellect as far as the three jewels are concerned [= *jñāna*, "knowledge";

In any case, the authoritative source for the derivation of the term *paṇḍita* – "he who possesses intelligence" – from *paṇḍā* is *Aṣṭādhyāyī* V. 2. 36 (see also *Laghu-siddhānta-kaumudī*, *Bhavanādyarthaka* 55. 4):

तदस्य संजातंतारकदिभ्य इतच्।

The suffix *itac* is attached to the terms of the *tāraka* class when the meaning is related to something we are observing.

The explication (*vṛtti*) of this passage is as follows:

तारकसंजाता अस्य तारकितं नभः । पण्डितः । आकृतिगणोऽयम् ।

This is what is found in the *tāraka* class, as [in the sentence] "the sky in which stars have come about". The term *paṇḍita* is also formed thus [when there is the suffix *itac*]. This is a class of terms which are gathered together according to their form.[28]

On the basis of the above-mentioned *sūtra*, Indian grammarians include *paṇḍā* in a class of fifty-three terms called *tārakādi* ("beginning with *tāraka*"). According to Pāṇini, the adjectives *tārakita* ("starry"), *puṣpita* ("blossoming"), and *paṇḍita* ("wise") derive from the nouns *tāraka* ("star"), *puṣpa* ("flower"), and *paṇḍā* ("wisdom"). To these, he adds a suffix (*pratyaya*) *itac* – which results in *ita*, dropping the final *c* – which is distinct from the suffix *kta* (*ta, ita* of

darśana, "correct vision"; *caritra*, "appropriate moral conduct"]. They also use the compound *paṇḍita-maraṇa*, "death of a *paṇḍita*", when they refer to the voluntary, non-violent death of a person of exceptional spiritual qualities. Therefore, a *paṇḍita* is he who possesses the 'three jewels' within himself.

28 VARADARĀJĀCĀRYA, *Laghusiddhāntakaumudī*. Edited by M. S. Kuśvaha. Vārāṇasī, Chaukhāmbā Vidyābhavan, 1999. Modern philologists suggest linking *paṇḍita* with *prajñita* and *prajñā* ("knowledge", "wisdom") with *paṇḍā* hypothesizing that *paṇḍā* might be taken as a prakritization of *prajñā*. An analogy is also suggested between *prajñita* and *saṃjñita*; see AKLUJKAR, *Paṇḍit and Paṇḍits in History*, *op. cit.*, p. 18.

the passive perfect participle). He then specifies that this *itac* must be added only to the *tārakādi* class, when the terms of this class relate to or qualify a noun. For instance, *tārakitaṃ nabhaḥ* means "the sky where stars have arrived", thus "starry sky".

The *paṇḍita* is one "endowed with discerning ability" (*paṇḍā*). The *Śabda-kalpa-druma* states that a *paṇḍita* is he who "possesses that kind of intelligence capable of discriminating the truth from the untruth":

यस्य सदसद् विवेचनी बुद्धिरस्ति इति स पण्डितः ।[29]

The term *paṇḍita* has several synonyms, all implying the meaning of "research", "analysis", "reflection": *śāstra-jña*, *vidvān*, *vacaspati*, *kovida*, *budha*, *maniṣin*, *prājña*, *kavi*, *dhīra*, *vicakṣaṇa*, *dūra-darśin*, *viśarada*, *vidagdha*. The *Śabda-kalpa-druma* quotes a text known as *Cintāmaṇi*, perhaps the *Abhidharma-cintāmaṇi* of Hemacandra:

निषेवते प्रशस्तानि निन्दितानि न सेवते । अनास्तिकः श्रद्धवानेतत् पण्डितलक्षणम् ॥

> He dedicates himself to recommended activities and avoids prohibited actions. He is not a non-believer [in the Supreme Reality and the *Veda*-s] and he trusts the teaching which he received: this is the peculiarity of the *paṇḍita*.

Moreover, *Hitopadeśa* I. 14 states:

मातृवत्परदरेषु परद्रव्येषु लोष्टवत् ।
आत्मवत्सर्वभूतेषु यः पश्यति स पण्डितः ॥

[29] The *Śabda-kalpa-druma* further states that a *paṇḍita* is he "who is endowed with *paṇḍā*" (*paṇḍayā anugataḥ*), "who has quickly distanced himself from guilt" (*pāpād ḍinaḥ*), and "from whom the knowledge of Reality is to be acquired" (*paṇḍyate tattvajñānaṃ prāpyate smāt*).

He who looks upon another's wife as a mother, another's wealth as a clod of earth, and upon all creatures as his own self, is truly a wise man.

And the *Daśa-rūpakam* of Dhanaṃjaya proclaims (IV. 26):

न पण्डिताः साहसिका भवन्ति श्रुत्वापि ते संतुलयन्ति तत्त्वम्।
तत्त्वंसमादय समाचरन्ति सर्थप्रकुर्वन्ति परस्य चार्थम् ॥

Paṇḍita-s do not act rashly. Even after hearing something, they ponder over it and determine the truth. Having accepted the truth, they act and accomplish their own interest as well as that of others.[30]

From these lines we understand that a *paṇḍita* can be recognized as such from his actions and well-thought decisions. As noted, the adjective *paṇḍita* can be combined with *prājñita*, "endowed with intellect/knowledge/wisdom". A *paṇḍita* is entitled to offer spiritual teachings, being completely dedicated to the search of truth. *Bṛhadāraṇyaka Upaniṣad* III. 5. 1 states:

तस्माद् ब्राह्मणः पाण्डित्यं निर्विद्य बाल्येन तिष्ठसेत् ।
बाल्यं च पाण्डित्यं च निर्विद्याथ मुनिः ।
अमौनं मौनं निर्विद्याथ ब्राह्मणः ॥[31]

Therefore, a *brāhmaṇa* becoming uninterested in the state of a *paṇḍita* should aspire to abide in the state of a child. Furthermore,

30 DHANAMJAYA, *Hindī Daśarūpakam*. Edited by B. VYĀS. Vārāṇasī, Chaukhāmbā Vidyābhavan, 2000.

31 The variant *paṇḍitaḥ* instead of *brāhmaṇaḥ* is found in the *Mādhyandinā śakhā*, favored by Śaṅkarācārya. For Śaṅkarācārya, *brāhmaṇaḥ* means "one who knows *Brahman*" (*brahma-vit*) and he interprets *pāṇḍitya* as *ātma-vijñāna*, "knowledge of the Self". He understands *bālyena* as *jñāna-bala-bhāvena*, "with the strength of the knowledge of the real Self", and *mauna* as *anātma-pratyaya-tiraskāraṇasya paryavasānaṃ phalam*, "the culmination resulting from excluding the experience of things that are not the true Self"; ŚAṄKARA, *Bṛhadāraṇyakopaniṣad Śaṅkarācāryabhāṣyopeta*, Gorakhpur, Gītā Press, 1994.

> having become uninterested in both the state of a child and the state of a *paṇḍita*, he should become a person given to silence. Then, becoming uninterested in both silence and its opposite he becomes a veritable *brāhmaṇa*.

These three stages are in fact the intrinsic attributes of the *jñānin*, "the one who knows". The first stage is that of knowledge, represented by the function of teaching: he who has knowledge is qualified to communicate it to others or, to be more precise, to awaken in them the corresponding possibilities since knowledge is rigorously personal. The *paṇḍita* is therefore a *guru*, a spiritual master. The second stage is that of *bālya* i.e. "childhood", a germinal, non-expansive state in which all powers are concentrated in one single point, producing a spontaneous and undifferentiated simplicity (*sama-rasa*), beyond individual characteristics. Finally, there is the state of *mauna*, a silent condition in which one attains supreme union or *kaivalya*, "isolation", which expresses a state of perfection and totality at the same time.

The *Chāndogya Upaniṣad* (VI. 14. 2) further contributes to penetrate the meaning of the term *paṇḍita*, also connecting it with *ācārya*:

> स ग्रामाद् ग्रामं पृच्छन् पण्डितो मेधावी गन्धारानेवोपसम्पद्येत ।
> एवेवेहाचार्यवान्पुरुषो वेद ॥

> One [who has been taken away from Gāndhara, his home-town], being a *paṇḍita* retentive [of all information given to him], will find his way back to Gāndhara by inquiring [about his home-town] in all villages. In this world, exactly in such a way a person having [the benefit of] a teacher is brought to knowledge.[32]

32 Here Śaṅkarācārya glosses *paṇḍitaḥ* with *upadeśavān*, "having the instructions/teaching", and the adjective *medhāvī* as *paropadiṣṭa-grāma-praveśa-mārgāvadhāraṇa-samarthaḥ* i.e. "capable of understanding the way back to the village from the indications given by others". Moreover, *medhāvī* is "one who has the mind capable of retaining/holding": a person who, having investigated reality through the right means (*pramāṇa*), can find his way back with the help of some advice.

The *paṇḍita* is here seen as someone who, making a strenuous effort and asking everyone about the way back home – his true abode, the Self – is able to succeed and to actually find it, thus reaching his destination.

The *Hitopadeśa* (I. 3) proclaims:

शोकस्थानसहस्राणि भयस्थानशतानि च ।
दिवसे दिवसे मूढमविशन्ति न पण्डितम् ॥

Day by day, thousands occasions for sorrow and hundreds [occasions] for fear overtake the fool but not the *paṇḍita*.

And the *Bhagavad-gītā* (II. 11) adds:

गतासूनागतासूंच नानुशोचन्ति पण्डिताः ॥

Paṇḍita-s do not mourn either the dead or the living.

Moreover, *Bhagavad-gītā* IV. 19 reads:

यस्य सर्वे समारम्भाः कामंकल्पवर्जिताः ।
ज्ञानाग्निदग्धकर्माणि तमाहुः पण्डितं बुधाः ॥

The wise man calls him a *paṇḍita* whose undertakings are in their entirety free from desire and attachment, and whose actions have been burnt up by the fire of knowledge.

And *Bhagavad-gītā* V. 18:

विद्यावनयसम्पन्ने ब्राह्मणे गवि हस्तिनि ।
शुनि चैव श्वपके च पण्डिताः समदर्शिनः ॥

> *Paṇḍita*-s see the same thing in a *brāhmaṇa* endowed with wisdom and education, in a cow, in an elephant, in a dog and in a *caṇḍāla*.[33]

To sum up, we have seen the steps a student must take in order to acquire the titles of *śāstrī* and *ācārya*[34] and have noticed the various applications of the term *paṇḍita*. Both the *ācārya* and the *paṇḍita*, when worthy of these titles, are rightly identifiable with the *guru* – whose example and teaching is viewed as a proof of the eternal immutability of Being, as opposed to the unending becoming of the world. *Guru-gītā* 89 solemnly declares:

ब्रह्मानन्दं परमसुखदं केवलं ज्ञानमूर्तिं
द्वन्द्वातीतंगगनसदृशं तत्त्वमस्यादिलक्ष्यम् ।
एकं नित्यं विमलमचलं सर्वधी साक्षीभूतं
भावातीतं त्रिगुणरहितं सद्गुरुं तं नमामि ॥

> I bow to the *Sad-guru*, who is the bliss of *Brahman* and the giver of the highest joy. He is absolute. He is knowledge personified. He is beyond duality; all-pervasive like the sky and object of the great Upaniṣadic statement "Thou are That". He is one, he is eternal, he is pure, he is steady, he is the witness of all thoughts; he is beyond the phenomenal realm of existence and free from the three *guṇa*-s.

33 See also *Bhagavad-gītā* V. 14; *Apastambha Dharma-sūtra* I. 23. 3; *Māṇḍukī-śikṣā* 16. 13; *Nāradīya-śikṣā* I. 3. 13, II. 3. 11; *Hiraṇyakeśin Dharma-sūtra* I. 6. 11; *Yājñavalkya-śikṣā* II. 84; *Śamkhalita Dharma-sūtra* II. 19.

34 *Mahā-mahopādhyāya* is the highest title which the State awards.

BIBLIOGRAPHY

PRIMARY SOURCES

Dhanaṃjaya, *Hindī Daśarūpakam*. Edited by B. Vyās. Vārāṇasī, Chaukhāmbā Vidyābhavan, 2000.

Guru Gītā, Gaṇeśpuri, Gurudeva Siddhapīṭha, 1996.

Kulārṇavatantra. Edited by S. Malvīya. Vārāṇasī, Śrīkṛṣṇadās Academy, 2000.

Manusmṛti. Edited by R. N. Śarmā. Delhi, Chaukhāmbā Saṃskṛta Pratiṣṭhān, 1998.

Nārāyaṇa, *Hitopadeśa*. Edited by N. Rāmācārya. Vārāṇasī, Chaukhāmbā Saṃskṛta Bhavan, 1998.

Śabdakalpadruma. Edited by R. R. Bahādur. 5 vols. Delhi, Nag Publishers, 1988.

Śaṅkara, *Bṛhadāraṇyakopaniṣad Śaṅkarācāryabhāṣyopeta*, Gorakhpur, Gītā Press, 1994.

Varadarājācārya, *Laghusiddhāntakaumudī*. Edited by M. S. Kuśvaha. Vārāṇasī, Chaukhāmbā Vidyābhavan, 1999.

SECONDARY SOURCES

Adhikārī, H. P., *Saralam Saṃskṛtam*, Vārāṇasī, Sampūrṇānanda Saṃskṛta Viśvavidyālaya, 2001.

Cenkner, W., *The Tradition of Teachers: Śaṅkara and the Jagadgurus Today*, Delhi, Motilal Banarsidass, 1983.

Filliozat, P. S., *The Sanskrit Language: An Overview*, Vārāṇasī, Indica, 2000.

Guénon, R., *L'uomo e il suo divenire secondo il Vedānta*, Milano, Adelphi, 1992.

Kalyāṇ Kalpataru 46, 1, Gorakhpur, Gītā Press, 2000.

Malvīya, R., *Saṃskṛt ke vidvān aur paṇḍit*, Vārāṇasī, Chaukhāmbā Vidyābhavan, 1972.

Michaels, A. (ed.), *The Pandit. Traditional Scholarship in India*, New Delhi, Manohar, 2001.

Mookerji, K. K., *Ancient Indian Education*, Delhi, Motilal Banarsidass, 1989.
Nigamānanda Sarasvatī, Svāmī, *Jñānī Guru*, Hāliśahar, Āsāmabaṅgīya Sārasvata Māṭha, 1986.
Upadhyāya, B. D., *Kāśī kī pāṇḍitya paramparā*, Vārāṇasī, Viśvavidyālaya Prākāśan, 1983.

THE SUBTLE TEACHER. TYPOLOGIES OF SHAMANIC INITIATION: TRANCE AND DREAM AMONG THE LANJIA SAORAS OF ORISSA

STEFANO BEGGIORA

The region inhabited by the Lanjia Saoras, one of the most consistent tribal groups in Orissa, India, spreads in the jungles, on the table-lands situated South of the Rayagada district, in an area comprised between Udayagiri in the North, Gunupur in the West, and Parlakhemundi in the South, very close to Andhra Pradesh. The easiest and most direct access to it is certainly through the road that connects the village of Gunupur—a hamlet at the cross-roads of the agricultural centres of the area—to the village of Pottasing, some twenty miles away on the table-land situated in the middle of the Saoran territory. Actually, there are no other roads and, though things have improved in these last few years, the villages can be reached walking along pathways and climbing on the hills. Because of the difficulty of penetrating in a hard, often harsh and unhealthy region with no link-roads, the tribes of these villages have lived untouched for centuries, keeping their own culture and traditions unspoiled. True, nowadays the ceaseless work of the Roman Catholic missionaries has managed to convert a good part of the population and to impose the dismissal of everything belonging to the past. At the same time, however, many communities in the region still maintain their beliefs and magic-religious understanding of the universe, of a shamanic kind. For this reason, this area has been chosen as a study-field.

When this year I came back to Pottasing—a Dom village situated approximately at the centre of the Saoran territory—some local friends of tribal origin[1] were kind enough to prepare a hut for me in the village below, Regingtal. My lodging was adjacent to the hut of young Lokino, the latest born in the community of Regingtal, who every night made himself heard, calling for his milk at regular intervals of time.

On the other side of the road, at the foot of a thicket of huge palm trees, was another group of mud-huts built on a straight line. There was the hut of a woman who I had tried to meet for two years. In the discussions at the village, later on, she was facetiously called *Madam* Gajino.[2]

During recent years, I often chanced to pass through the village of Regingtal but one particular occasion comes to my mind: in February 1999, I stopped there for a couple of days to see the celebration of the Guar, which in anthropology is defined as a second funeral. Twelve days after cremation, the ashes of the dead are buried in the *ganuar*, that is, the "place of the erection of the stones", and then what we might call the real funeral begins. A stone, the size of which is proportionate to the importance that the dead had in the community, is erected and a buffalo is sacrificed, to serve as guide along the difficult trip to the world of the dead.[3]

1 The whole area is inhabited by the Lanjia Saoras with the exception of Pottasing, a Dom village. The Doms living in this area are a group of Christian outcastes, probably of nomadic origin, who for many years have found integration in the various tribal groups. They speak the Oriya language and generally have a superior instruction compared to those living in the surrounding communities. Therefore, they act as mediators in bureaucratic issues between the police and tribal people. But they work in their own, exclusive interest: as money-lenders, they often determine the ruin of entire family groups.

2 *Madam* Gajino. Bhambro Gajino is the woman-shaman from Regingtal.

3 As far as the definition "second funeral" is concerned, see C. von FÜRER-HAIMENDORF, "Megalithic Ritual among the Gadabas and Bondos of Orissa", *Journal of the Asiatic Society of Bengal, Letters*, vol. IX, 1943, pp.

On that occasion, I noticed that the ritual was officiated by a girl, the *kuramboi*, that is, the shaman in the Saoran language, who had induced herself into a state of *trance* and was possessed by the spirit of the dead. My Dom guides and interpreters had to leave and I remember that a Saoran man remained with me. He spoke Hindi which he had learned when he was working "abroad", in the plantations of Assam.[4] I had the occasion to exchange a few words with this girl, who was young but authoritative. When, later on, I asked the name of the girl-shaman from Regingtal, I was told that she was Bhambro Gajino. It actually was a mistake, because the girl was a powerful *kuramboi* from a far away village who had been invited there for the important occasion: she officiated the whole ritual of the Guar under the supervision of an old woman, the guide of the Regingtal tribe itself.

I was amazed when, having climbed to the road-bed, I saw that an old woman was waiting for me on the porch which is usually built on the front of the hut, together with her husband and other members of the same *birinda*.[5] I was told that she, obviously Bhambro Gajino, and her husband, Tordae Ajari, were both shamans and for many years had been the defenders and spiritual guides not only of those

149-178. Concerning the Guar of Regingtal and other funeral ceremonies among the Saoras, see S. BEGGIORA, "Buffalo Sacrifice and Megalithic Cults in the Shamanism of the Orissan Tribes. A Central-Asiatic Model", *Central Asiatic Journal*, vol. 47, 2003, pp. 3-14; S. BEGGIORA, "Il sacrificio del bufalo nei rituali funebri e di fertilità presso alcuni gruppi tribali dell'Orissa", in A. AMADI (ed.), *Il sangue nel mito. Il sangue purificatore nel sacrificio del bufalo nell'Asia meridionale*, Venezia, Grafica L'Artigiana, 2002, pp. 125-138.

4 Among the Doms I found some people who could speak English and who accepted to translate for me. But, being Christians, they could not take part in or go near to any ceremonies of this kind. A few Saoras, on the other hand, have learned Hindi. With the recruiting campaigns for going to work in the Assam plantations, many tribal people have accepted to leave their villages for some years. Since they all speak different languages, Hindi has become their shared language; see E. CHAUSSIN, "Aspect de la migration des Saora de l'Orissa en Assam", *L'Ethnographie*, Paris, CNRS - Gabalda, 1978, pp. 74-91.

5 The word *birinda* indicates the clan in the Saoran language.

living in the village but also of the people living in the neighbourhood. The accent was immediately put on the fact that they were both healers but that "the man, Ajari, heals by using plants; whereas the woman, Gajino, heals by using *trance*".

I believe that this distinction is of extreme importance, in that it takes us back to the nowadays almost forgotten, ancient classification of the Saoran shamans. The word *kuran*, in the Saoran language, is generic and might be translated as "shaman". The *-maran* and *-boi* suffixes mark the masculine and feminine gender respectively. In ancient times, they were classified into *guarkumbmaran* / *raudakumbmaran* and *regamaran* / *tedungmaran* (or with the feminine suffix in case of women). The difference between the two groups is essentially of an initiatory kind. It consists in the capacity or incapacity of inducing oneself into a *trance*, so as to communicate with the supernatural spheres and re-establish the balance between the two worlds. Those having this faculty, as we will see, are directly initiated by the spirits of the other-world, while the ones belonging to the lower class, though receiving a sort of call, get their knowledge from the older teachers of their own community.

Guarkumbmaran and *raudakumbmaran* are therefore the most powerful shamans, like Bhambro Gajino, who can directly communicate with the spirits through *trance*. The *guar-* suffix indicates those who are authorized to participate in the Guar ceremony, while the *rauda-* suffix indicates generic spirits of the dead who are believed to abide in the other-world.

On the other hand, the term *rega* or *regan* means medicine in the Saoran language. Thus, we can literally translate *regamaran* as "medicine-man". They are people of deep knowledge who know the various herbs and medicinal plants and prepare remedies for various diseases. People say that the Saoran *regamaran* can distinguish more than two-hundred different medicinal plants and mix their components as remedy for any kind of illness. *Tedung* means the faculty to divine: not, however, by means of the possession of superior spirits—who tell the future through the shaman's words of mouth, as an oracle—but via the performance of simple ritual acts thought to throw light on the immediate future.[6]

Coming back to Tordae Ajari and the medicine-men, the focal issue concerns the implied cause-effect relationship of the disease itself. As in other tribal shamanic communities, the Saoras believe that all accidents that happen during a trip or during hard work in the forest, as well as all kinds of illnesses, death itself, are not at all casual or due to simply 'natural' causes. The Saoras understand all these calamities as being attacks from one or more spirits coming from the world of the dead or from ancestral entities who happen to be in the sacred places in the forest. There can be various reasons for these evil attacks: from the unconscious crossing of some 'prohibited' place, to the breaking of taboos or the non performance of the burial duties due to ancestors.

These people believe that all victims become possessed and that their houses are probably haunted by a spirit.[7] The empiric manifestation of such possession typically arises with the emergence of diseases of various kinds, all of which are linked to the peculiar nature of the haunting spirit.[8] In such cases medicine-men, with their natural remedies, are thought to be able to intervene only upon the negative effects of the disease: thus, they can soothe a wound or turn down one's fever. But for a true exorcism, that is to say for a cure that extirpates the real cause of the disease at its root, the presence of an upper class shaman is said to be needed. Through *trance* he will be

6 Some people use the technique of throwing stones of a particular shape on the winnowing fan. After ritual invocations, they get their auspices by interpreting the position of the stones. Regarding the shamanic priestly function, Elwin made a similar classification; see V. ELWIN, *The Religion of an Indian Tribe*, London, Oxford University Press, 1955, p.128 ff.

7 In this second case, inexplicable breaking of objects, night visits of wild animals, death of cattle and so on might happen.

8 Spirits connected with the sun are believed to cause illnesses producing heat, such as high fevers, burnings, etc. Spirits connected with night and darkness are linked to temporary blindness and may cause accidents of various kinds, such as falls, collapses, and fainting.

able to discern the haunting spirit, and then to tell the cause of the break that led to such consequences. In the end, in most cases, the spirit itself will indicate a substitute victim, such as, for instance, an animal, the sacrifice of which will be necessary for the healing of the patient.

For these reasons, authentic shamans are only those who are endowed with both types of knowledge and power; all others are classed as generic healers. Nowadays, however, the old classifications are disappearing among the Saoras and a *kuran* is held as an upper class shaman, who, by his own will, can induce himself into a *trance* and communicate with the supernatural, and who, at the same time, is a knower of all rituals and of the secrets of the forest, of its products and their usages.

The case of Bhambro Gajino and Tordae Ajari gives us a useful illustration. It is even possible that the latter was initiated and trained elsewhere, but that, after his union with Bhambro Gajino, he improved his own knowledge, acting as an assistant to his wife. Indeed, among the Saoras the *kuramboi*, the women-shamans, are in most cases thought to be more powerful than their male counterparts.

In these years, I have witnessed a variety of healing rituals and exorcisms carried out by shamans, both in *trance* and not, but I was particularly struck by the facts that recently took place in the village of Tolna. Here, I was often a guest of Darsana Soboro, a *kuranmaran* to all effects who took the place, and the name, of the old shaman woman of the village, still living but too old to officiate.[9] Darsana Soboro was very kind and open-hearted and gave me many explanations concerning the information I had collected during the last few years. One day, during one of the interviews, an old woman with a child came to his hut. The child had a big cyst on his neck and various purulent excoriations on his neck and head. Darsana Soboro im-

9 One day I was introduced to this old woman and I was told that her name is Darsana. I don't know why, but the man-shaman from the same village bears the same name (it is a masculine name, anyway). However, I don't think the two are in any way related to each other. The family name Soboro is a common name simply meaning Savara i.e. Saora.

mediately detected the presence of a particularly dangerous *sonum*, a spirit in the Saora language. It should be noted that all diseases of the lymphatic system, and therefore of balance or inner "energy", are considered a direct symptom of the presence of negative influences. Darsana Soboro said that it was absolutely necessary to organize a ritual, during which he would fall into a *trance* in order to chase the spirit away.

Reluctantly, the woman revealed herself to be the grandmother of the child and said she had secretly taken him from his home, because his father had become a Christian. The father would certainly know of a ritual of exorcism performed on his child and the missionary enclave would not approve of it. What's more, the Catholic doctors had already ordered that the child should take a medicine to be bought in the nearest village chemist's shop (many miles away), but it was too expensive and the results had been unsatisfying. The woman hoped that she could solve the problem with a *regan*,[10] prepared by Darsana Soboro himself with some herbs. However, the shaman turned the woman away telling her that if they did not cool that particular spirit down and in a hurry, the child would certainly die.

A similar case happened a few days later. A mother, accompanied by her sister, took her new-born child to Darsana Soboro's house. The child was shaken by a very high fever. The shaman interpreted the disease as an attack by a snake-spirit, emanated by Uyungsim, who had been sent to seize the child. Uyungsim is the *sonum* of the sun. It is not a real deity but a superior spirit, with creating potentialities. Androgynous, Uyungsim is known as the Great Mother[11] and as the Smith Sun. It is believed that Uyungsim himself 'moulds' new human beings in an ancestral pot and then 'sends' them to be incarnated in the womb of the mothers-to-be. His emissaries are the sun-rays, imagined as snake-spirits. It is often believed that, in case of premature death, the snakes themselves come back to take the child. For this reason, the newborn children are ritually washed, so as to

10 Any medicine extracted from plants.

11 Also called Yuyungsim. *Yayangma* means mother and *yuyung* grandmother.

'cool' them, as if through this act performed by the shaman they could be withdrawn from the fiery element.

The mother spoke clearly right from the beginning: in case the spirit asked to sacrifice a buffalo as a substitute victim for the child, then the family, which was very poor, could not afford it.[12] She asked Darsana Soboro to perform a ritual instead, offering food and palm wine to Uyungsim and to his emissaries and preparing protective amulets for her and her child, but without falling into a *trance* since then the situation could become extremely dangerous and with no way out. The shaman did all that was possible. The people that were there, including myself, took part in the ritual. During the very long invocation, I noticed that Darsana Soboro was on the verge of falling into a *trance*, but he controlled himself and brought the ritual to its end. When he finished, he harshly warned the mother: the shaman could not guarantee the success of the ritual, so simple and ordinary compared to such a violent attack, coming from one of the most powerful spirits.

A third case that came up during my stay had an immediate positive ending: Darsana Soboro recognized the disease as being caused by a benevolent spirit, belonging to the clan, who only needed to be 'cooled down' because of some minor fault. The shaman from Tolna, though a *kuran* to all effects, was asked to act as a simple *regamaran*, something which was surely in his capacities but which would not always guarantee positive results.

What are, then, among the Saoras, the requisites that determine the function, power, and 'level' of any given shaman? Once again, as I had frequently done in the previous months, that day on the roadbed of Regingtal I asked this question to Bhambro Gajino and Tordae Ajari. The woman took the word. Here, I report a translation of what she said:

12 Besides the peculiar characteristics of each patient, the more powerful the spirit is thought to be, the more 'precious' the chosen substitute victim must be.

> You are asking how people begin [she looks at others for their assent], how I began. Well! I was more or less this size [she makes a sign with her hand], say, I was twelve, fifteen years old. I happened to fall into a trance for the first time. I actually had a teacher, my grandmother; she was the *kuramboi* of Regingtal before me. She was the most powerful of all! She taught me everything, nobody else did. So it happened the first time: she was near me and she taught me how to perform the *pūjā*. So I learned how to do the *pūjā* and all the rest. She sat beside me, yes, in that position, with her legs stretched out and the sieve in her hand... as they always do nowadays.[13]

I asked her how old her grandmother was, and Bhambro Gajino frankly answered that she had died when she was still very young, years before she became a *kuramboi*.

To be sure, these words might sound strange. However, having accumulated some experience, I can say that this way of expressing oneself is typical among Saoras. They don't feel the need to make any distinction between natural and supernatural spheres or levels. To them, it is superfluous. All the people gathered there—except me—knew in fact that Bhambro Gajino's grandmother, who was probably a great personality in the village, had died many years before and that young Bhambro had been initiated *by her spirit*.

This point is of great interest since it casts light on the *forma mentis* of the entire tribal community (and not only on the shaman's self-understanding): the natural and the supernatural are thought of as a *continuum*. Once I understood this, I asked the *kuramboi* if her grandmother was a *sonum*, that is, a spirit, and if she appeared to her in her dreams. She lively answered:

13 The interview took place in Regingtal on March 3, 2001. The Saoran language uses the Hindī word *pūjā* to indicate any kind of ritual. The hint to the position taken by the shaman indicates the classic *trance* posture, with legs stretched out and the winnowing fan in one's hand. The latter is used as a sort of percussion instrument to accompany the invocation.

> Not a *sonum*! *Ilda*... *ildasim* [she repeats]! She talked to me in my dreams, yes, sometimes she came. That's the reason why I fell into a trance![14]

Usually, among the Saoras, during the initiation of a to-be-shaman—which takes place in pre- or post-puberty age—a particular class of spirits, the *ilda*, appears to him/her in dreams. This happens because the person has not yet acquired the faculty of falling into a *trance*.

One spirit stands out among others, whose gender is opposite to that of the to-be-shaman: the spirit insists on having sexual intercourse with him/her. The young man or woman experiences fear but also a sort of spiritual ecstasy. While sleeping, this 'guiding-spirit' takes the initiate away from his/her world bringing him/her to face a series of tests and terrible visions which will constitute the essence of shamanic initiation. A state of temporary 'madness' often follows this period of ecstatic dreaming. This may lead the initiate to wander in the forest for days, with no memory and in a state of confusion. In the tradition of many tribal groups of Central Asia, these experiences typically occur prior to one's initiation.[15]

14 The *sonums* are superior, ancestral entities or their sub-emanation or even the spirits of the dead (who are also called *raudas*). The *sonum* is a potentially haunting spirit. The *ilda*, or *ildasim*, on the other hand, is an entity which belongs to an upper class than the ordinary dead, and protects its own followers, thus bearing a fundamental role in the initiatory phase; see ELWIN, *The Religion of an Indian Tribet*, *op. cit.*, p. 68 ff. By the same author, see "The Saora Priestess", *Bulletin of the Department of Anthropology* I, I, Bombay, 1952, pp. 59-85.

15 Sometimes it is a wild spirit of the forest, occasionally related, for instance, to the Tibetan legends concerning the *yeti*; see N. WOJKOWITZ, *Oracles and Demons of Tibet*: *The Cult and Iconography of the Tibetan Protective Deities*, Leiden, E. J. Brill, 1956, pp. 538-554. In the Himalayas, the Chepang from Nepāl show a similar initiatic case as far as the *banjankhri* (*van-jhankri*, "spirit of the *jhankri* of the forest") is concerned; see D. RIBOLI, *Tunsuriban*: *Shamanism in the Chepang of Southern and Central Nepal*, Kathmandu, Mandala B. P., 2000, pp. 81-82. For similar cases in the initiatic phase among the Buriats, see the essays in the collective volume titled *Shamanism*: *Soviet Studies of Traditional Religion in Siberia and Central Asia*, Moscow, Polizdat, 1984.

Among the Saoras, the initiate, in time, accepts to marry this 'kidnapping' spirit. In quality of heavenly husband or wife, this spirit will be the guiding spirit of the shaman for the rest of his/her life.

In this phase, the sexual element is of primary importance. It is easy to guess that, since these are boys and girls in their teens, the sexual 'experience' very often occurs in dreams. I believe that the fear and shyness that these adepts exhibit is not to be identified with the fear of sexual maturity in and of itself. I had the feeling that, in a way, the initiates themselves understand what is going to happen to them. Here, the initiatic trial is not simply a ritual passage to the adult age but is the acceptance of a great burden: the weight of carrying upon their young shoulders the responsibility for the safety of the whole community, be it alive or dead. That's why nowhere in the world people become shamans out of passion or predisposition. The initiate is believed to receive a real supernatural call, to which he/she is obliged to answer. If a person refuses to positively answer such call, he/she will experience a condition of 'initiatic madness' for the rest of his/her life.

At a second stage, union with the guiding spirit, contrary to what one might suppose, has nothing to do with sex. The spiritual marriage symbolizes, in front of the whole community, that the initiate has accepted his/her 'profession' and its duties, faithfully abandoning himself/herself to the guiding spirit.

This is what I was able to reconstruct during these years of field-research. I report the case of Bhambro Gajino because it exhibits some interesting variants. She is not tormented by the *ilda* spirits. If, on the one hand, the *ildas* are superior, otherworldly eternal spirits (not the ghosts of ordinary dead people), the shaman from Regingtal receives the visit of her grandmother—and not of a male partner—at night. Here, the sexual element is completely lacking. Nonetheless, Bhambro Gajino very much insists on the power that her grandmother had and still has (both before and after her death). It is not to be excluded that, precisely for this reason, her spirit is considered to be superior. At the same time, the shamans themselves, when ordained, are thought to be part of a self-standing caste: as in other Indian traditions, being married to an *ilda* means to become one of them.

According to tradition, in the *trance* and dreaming *continuum*, the couple, that is, the shaman and the guiding spirit, have children. These will be born in the other-world as *ildas* and will become the guiding spirits of future shamans.[16] Besides the obvious problems involved in communicating with the local people, it is not easy to discuss these issues with the *kuran* themselves, since it often means talking about painful and very personal, intimate experiences related to their youth.

Anyway, Bhambro Gajino used to contact her spirits in her sleep, since she was still not able to control the ecstatic experience. Twice she insisted on the fact that she happened to fall into *trance* after a dream. Therefore, the experience would not be intentional but casual and due to the contingent psychic situation. Only later on did the guiding spirit teach her how to control the *trance* and do the *pūjā*, that is, the rituals. What's more, Bhambro's idea that nobody else intervened in her training, would endorse the idea of the existence, up to this day, of shamans belonging to the ancient *raudakumbmaran* tradition in the Saoran territory.

These are shamans who are believed to be able to acquire their knowledge on their own, without teachers, directly communicating with the world of spirits through *trance* or, at night, through their dreams. Last year I wrote that this supposition is probably strained or, if this tradition has ever really existed it is nowadays lost. But in the village of Pattili, after the old *kuramboi* Ilda Gomango—who so kindly hosted me when I arrived in the region for the first time—had recently converted to Christianity, a charming and very young *kuramboi* took her place, Mirmil Soboro, bearing the characteristic Saoran tattoos on her face. The Saoras had the habit of tattooing the young girls with natural colours, tracing geometric figures on their

16 It is a kind of 'spiral' transmission, in which shamans 'marry' their own cousins from the other-world, handing down a tradition which is half-way between the natural and the supernatural. On this issue, see my unpublished BA thesis: *Culti sciamanici presso i Lanjia Saora dell'Orissa*, Venice, Ca' Foscari University, 1999, chap. 3. See also P. VITEBSKY, *Dialogues with the Dead*, New Delhi, Cambridge University Press, 1993, pp. 58-59.

faces (usually two wide circles on the cheeks and a black line from the forehead down to the chin). These tattoos marked the girls' passage to adulthood, meaning the wedding-age. Nowadays, though still in use, tattoos are disappearing because the missionaries say they are a sin against the Church: exhibiting tattoos reinforces one's belonging to the tribal group and thus one's exclusion from the community of converted Christians.

The experience of Mirmil Soboro is, therefore, very similar to the experience of Bhambro Gajino: her force and her knowledge come exclusively from her personal guiding spirit and from Lele Soboro, an initiate member of the clan who died recently and started appearing to her soon after his death, during her ecstatic moods. In spite of her young age, the neo-shaman from Pattili has acquired a certain fame and is loved by all.

On the other hand Darsana Soboro told me, in Tolna, that he had had various teachers, both human and from the other-world. One day, he said something which I consider of extreme importance. I report it word by word:

> You see, I actually learned a lot from my teacher, but all this has little importance and I could even forget it... instead what I learned in my dreams [touching his forehead] is forever fixed in my memory![17]

The faculty of falling into a *trance*, then, is even among Saoras the main characteristic of shamans. In this case, it doesn't seem finalized to collective rituals and religious functions, since it can be self-induced for any purpose. Prior to the ecstatic experience there is a dream experience. The visions acquired in both states seem to have equal importance and will accompany a shaman for the rest of his/her life. These experiences also come to be shared by the entire group. From time to time, the members of the different clans gather around their shamans in order to listen to the story-telling of these visions. They also ask for explanations about what the shamans actu-

17 This interview took place in Tolna on March 7, 2001.

ally saw, thus creating a 'bridge' between this world and the other-world. Indeed these experiences bear a social dimension, being shared by all. This is precisely the key through which the Saoras interpret their lives in this world.

Saoras maintain very strong ties with the supernatural or the other-world, as one may wish to call it. As I witnessed on various occasions, the daily actions and *forma mentis* of the people take into account both the world of spirits as well as the real world. Since early morning and all through the day, every action is interpreted as referring to one's routine life *and by the same token* to be related to an other-worldly dimension. Similarly, at night, dreaming is understood as the open expression of this parallel dimension. During sleep the soul is said to leave the body and to 'float' in the world of spirits, meeting with other souls belonging both to the dead and to the living, interacting with them. Saoras do not consider these dream visions as fictitious or unreal. They place them on the same level as the experiences one has in the waking state: though easy to be distinguished one from the other, they are believed to have the same importance. This might explain their tendency, during conversations, to 'jump' from one level to the other. With no notice, they 'cross' and 'move' from one context to the other, following their train of thought. During any discussion these two levels—the worldly and the other-worldly—are strung together by the thread of speech itself. A 'thread' which, at least according to our own rational standards, is totally illogical.

Let me stress that this is not a prerogative of the shamans alone but a characteristic of the whole community. If the dreams of ordinary people are confused or disconnected, shamans are able to voluntarily control their own dream activity creating a sort of *continuum* among dreams: the waking state and the dream state thus become an integrated whole, one simply being the interface of the other. During a *trance*, the mechanism is the same. The shaman can induce himself/herself into an altered state of consciousness during the waking hours, entering the world of spirits as he/she can do while asleep. The tight link between what happens in dreams and what happens during *trance* finds its codification in the shaman's voluntary control of both.[18]

Anyone can sometimes have recurring dreams i.e. dreams in which the same situations recur over and over. It is rarer to continue a dream, that is, to resume 'the story' from where we left it once we wake up. This phenomenon appears to be common among the Saoran shamans who develop a life full of memories, emotions, and happenings from the other-world. It is never clear if something they tell you has actually happened in the real world or in a state of *trance*-dream, and nobody feels the need to specify it.

For instance, I remember that a few years ago I asked a shaman about his initiation. He answered by saying that he had started "precipitating in space". Obviously, this had not really happened but it was a way for the shaman to make me realize that, during an altered state of consciousness i.e. sleep or *trance*, he had been 'seized' by a flying spirit who, in order to frighten him, had precipitated him in the chasm of the world of the dead.

The hypothesis of a sort of 'parallel life' would even justify the above-mentioned idea that, once 'married', the shaman and the guiding spirit have children, who are born and live in another dimension. I remember a dialogue I had with a shaman who was married to a woman of the village and who claimed to have a certain number of children. This number, however, did not balance in my mind: the

18 This is my interpretation though it is not an easy subject. And it could not be otherwise since then the very premises of a shaman's function would be missing. I think it is my duty to recall what Mirmil from Pattili told me. She thought that it was not possible to talk of an absolute control, in the end. When she got in a state of *trance*, she sometimes would not be able to voluntarily get out of it. She added that she suspected many other shamans lived similar experiences. This statement, though fascinating, clashes with what I have written here and would turn the powerful Saoran *kuran* into a kind of sorcerer who cannot always control the energies he/she stirs up. I like to think that what Mirmil told me was due to her youth and maybe to her little experience, but I have no other clues in this regard. On these issues, see my recent monograph *Sonum: spiriti della giungla. Lo sciamanismo delle tribù Saora dell'Orissa*, Milano, Franco Angeli, 2003, pp. 66-107.

children in the house were less than what he told me. He actually spoke of the *total* number of children he had had from both his earthly wife and his guiding spirit, but felt no need to distinguish among them.[19]

If what I have presented so far portrays the fervent visionary world of Saoran religion, at the same time I understand that these conceptions may sound odd or difficult to accept. It is not easy to convey the freshness, spontaneity, innocence and, sometimes, ingenuity with which the Saoras themselves talk about these subjects.

Another striking example is offered by the magnificent *anital*.[20] In Orissa, the Saoras are famous for their characteristic wall-paintings, erroneously defined as tribal art. The *anitals*, in fact, are not figurative representations (they are painted inside the huts and not outside as among other tribes), but pictures having an exorcising purpose often utilized in initiation. Every *anital*, through a complex combination of figures and symbols, tells a story, the protagonists of which are, once again, at the same time human and other-worldly beings. In order to make a perfect job—and it could not be otherwise since it is a ritual work—the painter must 'see' all the minimal details of the scene he is going to depict. Therefore, tradition says that the night before the wall is to be decorated, the shaman or one of his followers must sleep at the foot of the wall. The dreams dreamed that night, mixed to the events of those days, will inspire the painter's hand in his work. The joyous enthusiasm with which the inhabitants of the village notice a detail or remember an event, is similar to the enthusiasm of a group of friends looking together at old photographs.

But the influence of missionaries is becoming heavier and heavier, even in the case of these unique examples of tribal religious identity: the *anital*, as any other expression of tribal lore, must be wiped

19 The presence of a 'subtle' master and having sex with him/her is a common pattern also in the shamanism of the Monpa tribes of Arunachal Pradesh. I have documented many cases of it in a recent survey in November 2002.

20 Or *ittal* i.e. "wall-painting". The term comes from the verbal root *id*, "to write", and *talan*, a contraction of *kittalan*, "wall"; see V. ELWIN, *Tribal Art of Middle India*, London, Oxford University Press, 1951, pp. 183-214.

out. How difficult it must be for the people of the various tribes to understand this intolerant attitude towards an important element of their tradition and of their daily life. Typical of the Indian mentality, they are open to different religious ideas though they cannot easily accept that one religion should prevail over all others, to the point of causing their annihilation. The *anitals* are thus being progressively eliminated, though some are hidden by the local people. At the same time, many sacred places such as the tribal graveyards are being destroyed and violated. Village families are split and sometimes violent disorders erupt among different religious factions. The Doms lead the converts. And the people who refuse conversion are often victims of injustice and abuses from the local army, which is strongly present here in order to contrast the infiltration of Naxalite Maoist terrorists[21] among the tribes. Young people want no part of this. Thus, many convert to Christianity in hopes of an improbable better future and of a still more improbable modernization.

The shaman cults and related initiations, of which I write about in this paper, are susceptible to countless variants, depending upon the different local traditions. However, in this context, it is difficult to imagine shamans carrying out their rituals in harmony with their own traditions and the surrounding environment. If, until some decades ago, they could gradually change with the changing of tribal society, nowadays, in the context of national modernization, they may easily disappear forever. I can neither say how long the *ilda* will continue to come in people's dreams in order to get married with the *kuran-maran* or *kuramboi*, nor if it is possible to foresee how long the *sonum* and the ancestors' spirits will manifest to their descendents in this ancient land. However, if the contemporary exploitation doesn't end the ancient culture of a population which emerged from the mists

21 These are Communists, followers of the Bengali Naksalbari movement. Nowadays, they fight for the rights of the tribal people and of the poorest farmers in Orissa. Their original program was to "turn India into Mao's China".

of legend[22] is certainly destined to disappear into oblivion in a few generations' time.

[22] The origins of the Saoras are not yet clear. They are traditionally said to descend from the mythic Savaras who, in Orissa, are linked to the origins of the cult of Jagannāth. The issue is discussed in Elwin's introduction to *The Religion of an Indian Tribe*, *op. cit.*, as well as in my thesis, *op. cit.*, pp. 18-29.

TEACHING AND SPIRITUAL COUNSELLING IN INDIAN BUDDHIST TRADITIONS. SOME CONSIDERATIONS ON THE ROLE OF THE *KALYĀṆAMITRA**

FRANCESCO SFERRA

That self-experience is beyond thought, that essence is beyond mind's reach; it is incomprehensible to the learned. But can that essence remain un-comprehended by him who is graced by the feet of the Guru?

(Tillopāda, *Dohākośagīti*, st. 5, transl. H.C. Bhayani)

1. The emphasis generally placed by Buddhism, and some of its traditions in particular, on the role of personal effort, the conception of individual karmic responsibility, and the fact that the obedience to a superior (teacher, preceptor, etc.) is not a value in itself, may lead us to think that what the individual can offer to and/or receive from another concerning a spiritual path is – according to the main Buddhist traditions – something secondary, although not negligible, and that, more generally, the link between persons following the spiritual path is not as strong and important in Buddhist communities.

* I would like to thank Susan Ann White for her help with the English text.

However, we can arrive at a better understanding simply by reading some passages from classical Buddhist texts or from the writings of contemporary authors, or by listening to a Dharma talk by a Buddhist teacher. As early as the Pāli Canon, teachings are ascribed to the Buddha himself that emphasise the importance of and the need for 'others' in developing our spiritual training. Of course, by others are not meant "ordinary people" (*puthujjana*), but first and foremost members of the Saṅgha, the Buddhist community of monks, and also people endowed with qualities that make them "good friend(s)" (*kalyāṇamitta*), who may be monks but, sometimes, even laymen.

The role of the *kalyāṇamitta*s (Sanskrit: *kalyāṇamitra*[s]) is of crucial importance to the community, so crucial that we may say that a community – whether monastic or composed of lay practitioners and followers – is truly religious *only* if it offers hospitality to *kalyāṇamitta*s and encourages the 'birth' and existence of others. In the light of Buddhist teachings we may also say that the community and more generally the *ariyasaṅgha* (Skt: *āryasaṅgha*), the Noble Community or the Community of the Nobles (which also includes some lay people),[1] is not the Third Refuge (*saraṇa*) or the Third Jewel (*ratana*) because it celebrates rites, such as the *uposatha*, or transmits the words of the Buddha, but essentially because it is a community of *kalyāṇamitta*s, i.e. "good friends" or people "who have good friends", where the compound is interpreted respectively as *kammadhāraya* or *bahubbīhi*.[2]

In fact, in traditional definitions of the terms *saṅgha* and *ariyasaṅgha* in both ancient and modern texts, we do not usually find references to rituals or to the transmission of the Buddha's teaching

1 The compound *ariyasaṅgha* recurs mainly in commentarial literature. It is interpreted in two ways (as a *kammadhāraya* or as a *tappurisa*), as we can see, for instance, from a sentence in the *Visuddhimaggamahāṭīkā*: *ariyo ca so saṅgho ca, ariyānaṃ vā saṅgho ariyasaṅgho* (*ad* 7.89).

2 Some scholars have pointed out that the interpretation of the compound as a *tappurisa* (which frequently occurs in early translations) is not confirmed by the texts (see Alsdorf 1961: 13-17, Collins 1987: 55, Bodhi 2000: II, 1890-1891, note 6).

(*dhamma*), even though these are fundamental aspects of Buddhist (monastic) life, and, as Richard Gombrich has pointed out, it is the Saṅgha's duty to preserve the scriptures (1988: 152-153). Instead we notice the emphasis on the spiritual qualities of the community, on its behaviour conforming with the Dhamma (Skt: Dharma) and the Vinaya, and on its taking the irreversible path that will lead to the realisation of *nibbāna*.[3] Regarding this, it is no coincidence that the recollection (*anussati*) of the qualities and the peculiar characteristics of the Saṅgha – its being fit for gifts, fit for hospitality, etc. – is, according to some texts, a specific subject of meditation (cf., for example, *Visuddhimagga* 7.89-100). The traditional explanation of the compound *ariyasaṅgha* makes reference to those individuals who are "Noble" because they have attained a condition of pureness, that is, a condition devoid of afflictions and impurities, and hence they have achieved both right view and moral sensitivity.[4] In other cases, the word "Noble" alludes to the *mahāpuruṣapudgala*s, those who belong to one of the eight categories of beings that have reached, or are in the process of reaching, one of the four stages on the path to *nibbāna*, that is, the stages of Stream-enterer (*sotāpanna*), Once-returner

3 In several texts we read these words, which are still part of the daily chants of many Theravāda communities: *supaṭipanno bhagavato sāvakasaṅgho, ujuppaṭipanno bhagavato sāvakasaṅgho, ñāyappaṭipanno bhagavato sāvakasaṅgho, sāmīcippaṭipanno bhagavato sāvakasaṅgho, yad idaṃ cattāri purisayugāni aṭṭha purisapuggalā, esa bhagavato sāvakasaṅgho āhuneyyo pāhuneyyo dakkhiṇeyyo añjalikaraṇīyo anuttaraṃ puññakkhettaṃ lokassa* (cf., for instance, *Aṅguttara Nikāya*, ed. vol. 3, p. 286, *Dīgha Nikāya* 16.2.9, *Majjhima Nikāya* 7, ed. vol. 1, p. 37, *Visuddhimagga* 7.89).

4 Vajirabuddhi (VI cent.) is very clear in this regard: ***ariyasaṅghan*** *ti vigatakilesattā ariyaṃ parisuddhaṃ ariyānaṃ ariyabhāvaṃ vā pattaṃ sīladiṭṭhisāmaññena saṅghatattā saṅghaṃ* (*Vajirabuddhiṭīkā ad Vinayapiṭaka Aṭṭhakathā*, Pārājikakaṇḍavaṇṇanā, st. 3: *guṇehi yo sīlasamādhipaññāvimuttiñāṇappabhutīhi yutto | khettaṃ janānaṃ kusalatthikānaṃ tam* ***ariyasaṅghaṃ*** *namāmi*; the first two stanzas are devoted respectively to the Buddha and to the Dhamma). The sentence *sīladiṭṭhisāmaññena saṅghatattā saṅghaṃ* recurs in this or similar forms in other texts (cf., for instance, *Visuddhimagga* 7.90; *Udāna Aṭṭhakathā ad* 2.8; *Theragāthā Aṭṭhakathā ad* Dukanipāta 9).

(*sakadāgāmi*), Non-returner (*anāgāmi*) and Venerable (*arahat*) (cf. Harvey 2000: 39-40).

In other words, the community is founded on a moral value rather than shaped by external events, although the latter are not rejected and maintain their proper importance. However, precedence is always given to moral virtues and to the various levels of spiritual realisation and wisdom, primarily inner qualities that are then expressed in everyday behaviour, as some contemporary authors have insightfully pointed out.

Buddhadāsa Bhikkhu writes:

> In everyday language, the word 'Sangha' refers to the community of monks who wear the yellow robe and wander from place to place. This is the Sangha as it is understood in everyday language, the language of the unenlightened person who has not yet seen the Truth. In Dhamma language, the word 'Sangha' refers once again to the Truth, to the Dhamma itself. It refers to the high qualities, of whatever kind and degree, that exist in the mind of the monk, the man of virtue. There are certain high mental qualities that make a man a monk. The totality of these high qualities existing in the mind of the monk is what is called the Sangha. The Sangha of everyday language is the assembly of monks themselves. The Sangha of Dhamma language are those high qualities in the minds of the monks (1988: 21).

These are interesting comments for several reasons, and in our case also because the author provides, deliberately perhaps, a vague definition of a "monk" ("a man of virtue"), which, in theory, could also fit someone who does not wear the monastic robe. Buddhadāsa Bhikkhu expresses very well the possibility of interpreting Buddhist words on two levels, which we could describe as a 'simple level' and a 'profound level'. On a profound level, the Saṅgha is defined on the basis of moral value, that is, as synonymous with the sum of the wholesome qualities of the mind, which Buddhadāsa Bhikkhu associates with Truth, the Dhamma itself.

In his definition of Saṅgha, Suvaḍḍhano Bhikkhu, on the other hand, makes no reference to monks but he too explains its meaning in relation to Dhamma:

> [T]he Dhamma is truly the Way of practice to the end of all defilements and suffering; and the Sangha are those who are truly following the Dhamma Way to its fruition (p. 2).

Ajahn Sumedho is even clearer:

> The Third refuge is Sangha, which means a group. 'Sangha' may be the *Bhikkhu-Sangha* [the order of monks] – or the *Ariya-Sangha*, the group of the Noble Beings, all those who live virtuously, doing good and refraining from evil with bodily action and speech. Here, taking refuge in the Sangha with '*Sangham saranam gacchami*' means we take refuge in virtue, in that which is good, virtuous, kind, compassionate and generous. [...] Taking refuge in the Sangha means, on the conventional level, doing good and refraining from evil with bodily action and speech (1989: 16).

From the above we understand the prime importance of the elements that permit the Saṅgha to be equal to its goal: a) external elements, such as monasteries, the concrete support of lay followers – who, by the way, are members, in their turn, of the Saṅgha if we interpret the term in a wider sense (cf. Lamotte 1958: 59, 92) –, centres for the practice of Dharma; b) internal elements, such as the spiritual practice of every member, the rules of discipline, *pāṭimokkha* (Skt: *prātimokṣa*), the masters, the preceptors and the *kalyāṇamitta*s.

In considering some of the written sources that have come down to us, we shall attempt to underline the main nuances in the interpretation of the figure of the "good (or spiritual) friend" in the principal Indian Buddhist traditions from around the IV cent. BCE to the XII-XIII centuries CE. We shall examine briefly some qualities that make him recognisable, his function within the Saṅgha, in the transmission of spiritual teaching, and his increasingly important role in the acquisition of the fruits of the inner path.

On this subject there are specific writings to which I refer the reader for further details. For the ancient phase of Theravāda Buddhism, in particular, see the interesting article by Steven Collins (1987) which clarifies the role of the *kalyāṇamitta* in the early Buddhist community, the context in which we find the term and its meaning in the main texts of the Pāli canon. See also the paper by James W. Boyd (1972), which is rich in textual references on our subject. As regards the Mahāyāna, we could start with a classic text, the *Śikṣāsamuccaya* by Śāntideva (VII-VIII cent.) who gathered numerous quotations from Mahāyānic *sūtra*s, an English translation of which is available (Bendall and Rouse 1971[2]). The works of Har Dayal (1932: 63), Nalinaksha Dutt (1930: 312-313) and Karunesh Shukla (1991: cxxxv-cxxxvii) offer numerous references to texts, as well as food for thought. For the Vajrayāna I refer the reader to the recent book by Alexander Berzin (2000). This is a useful contribution, especially where related practical issues are concerned; the author analyses the delicate problem of the relationship between the master and the disciple in Tibetan Buddhist traditions, and also quotes and comments on several Indian sources and Tibetan translations of Sanskrit texts now lost. Some general reflections on the role of the *guru* in Buddhism are found in a paper by Alex Wayman (1987) and, concerning Tibetan traditions, in another paper by Herbert V. Guenther (1966-67), published in the fourth volume of the journal *Hermes*, dedicated to spiritual guidance in the East and West.

1.1 The term *kalyāṇamitta* is used both generically and technically in Buddhist texts. In Pāli works the term is used in at least three ways that sometimes overlap: on a 'basic level', in which the word is synonymous with *sappurisa* ("good man"), and on two different 'Buddhist levels', where it alludes to a particular figure on the Buddhist Path. Here, the first meaning is still general: the good friend is a "helper" (which we shall elaborate on below); the second is more specific: he is the "giver of a meditation subject" (*kammaṭṭhāna-dāyaka*).

1) *Basic level*: at this level the general context is Buddhist, but no explicit reference to a Buddhist Path is made although it may be implicit; and the term "good friend" (compounded [*kalyāṇamitta*] or un-compounded [*kalyāṇa/mitta*]) is sometimes 'Buddhicised' in later commentaries. We know from the *Dhammapada*, for instance, that

we have to follow good friends (cf. 6.3 [78], 25.16 [375]), or that he who has a good friend develops what is wholesome and abandons what is unwholesome (*Itivuttaka* 17 [1.2.7]). From *Theragāthā* 682 we know that "he who is calm, steady, intelligent, with his senses under control, he who has good friends, who is wise, can overcome suffering" (*anuddhato acapalo nipako saṃvutindriyo | kalyāṇamitto medhāvī dukkhassantakaro siyā ||*). At this level there are naturally instances in which the term *pāpamitta* ("bad friend") is used in a generic sense: he is described as someone who makes the monk reject wholesome things but no clear reference is made to abandoning the Buddhist Path.

It is worth noting that we find also passages that speak of overcoming suffering, developing what is wholesome, etc., but make no reference whatsoever to the *kalyāṇamitta*s; nevertheless, these passages pivot on spiritual friendship. Regarding this, there are two almost identical *sutta*s in the *Saṃyutta Nikāya* that are worth mentioning (1.4.1, 2.3.1). Both *sutta*s are divided into two parts, the difference between them being that in the first part the former relates that eight deities (*devatā*) approach the Blessed One, and the latter that the young *deva* Siva approaches the Blessed One. Both the eight deities and Siva speak of the advantages to be gained by associating only (*yeva*)[5] with good men (*saddhi*), creating a close relationship with them and assimilating their teaching (*dhamma*):

> One becomes better, never worse; [...] wisdom is gained, but not from another; [...] one does not sorrow in the midst of sorrow; [...] one shines amidst one's relations; [...] beings fare on to a good destination; [...] beings abide comfortably (transl. Bodhi).

The second part of both *sutta*s contains the words of the Blessed One. In the first *sutta*, the Blessed One, when asked to judge who has spoken well, replies:

5 The use of *yeva* with a restrictive meaning is in keeping with the interpretation by Bhikkhu Bodhi (2000: I, 105-106, 152-153) and by M.A. Rhys Davids (1917: 26-27, 81), but other interpretations are also possible.

> You have all spoken well in a way. But listen to me too: [...] Only by associating with good men, is one released from all suffering of transmigration.

In the second *sutta*, the Blessed One addresses Siva directly without his having asked any question, repeating the concluding stanza.

Here, the Buddha's words tell us that one can reach the highest possible goal by associating with good men,[6] but this goal is not explicitly described as *nibbāna*, even though it is common knowledge – and many texts confirm this – that liberation from (or the end of) every kind of suffering corresponds to *nibbāna*, as we read in the first of the two closing stanzas of *Saṃyutta Nikāya* 21.4: *nibbānaṃ adhigantabbaṃ sabbadukkhappamocanaṃ.*[7] It should also be noted that in the above *sutta*s good men are never actually referred to as *kalyāṇamitta*s, either in the text or in the commentaries: *saddhi*, good man, is glossed with *paṇḍita* and *sappurisa* in the *Aṭṭhakathā*, and with *sādhu* in the *Ṭīkā*.

2) *First Buddhist level*: The essential qualities of the *kalyāṇamitta* are the same as those of a good man (*sappurisa*) and a wise man (*paṇḍita*). These qualities are commonly and universally attributed

6 The commentary (*aṭṭhakathā*) summarises this concept: "Not only does one become better; not only does one gain wisdom", etc., "but one is also freed from all suffering of transmigration": ***sabbadukkhā pamuccatīti*** *na kevalaṃ seyyova hoti* (st. 3), *na ca kevalaṃ paññaṃ labhati* (st. 4), *sokamajjhe na socati* (st. 5), *ñātimajjhe virocati* (st. 6), *sugatiyaṃ nibbattati* (st. 7), *ciraṃ sukhaṃ tiṭṭhati* (st. 8), *sakalasmā pana vaṭṭadukkhāpi muccatīti.*

7 The verse recurs in *Nettipakaraṇa* (ed. p. 151). The concept appears again and again. We quote only a few examples: 1) [...] *nibbānaṃ patvā sattānaṃ sabbadukkhaṃ viviccati | tasmā nibbānaṃ* ***viveko*** *ti vuttaṃ | sabbāni vā etāni nibbānasseva nāmāni* [= *nimokkho, pamokkho, viveko*] | *nibbānañ hi patvā sattā sabbadukkhato nimuccanti pamuccanti viviccanti* (*Saṃyutta Nikāya Aṭṭhakathā ad* 1.2); 2) ***nirodho cā*** *ti sabbadukkhanirodhaṃ nibbānañ ca* (*Therāpadāna Aṭṭhakathā ad* 1.538); 3) *duḥkhasya nirodho duḥkhanirodhaḥ – nirvāṇam* (*Arthaviniścayasūtranibandhana*, ed. p. 169).

also to a person who is following a spiritual path,[8] and are fully developed in a Buddha or a Tathāgata (*sammāsambuddho yeva sabbākārasampanno kalyāṇamitto*: *Visuddhimagga* 3.62, ed. H. C. Warren and Dh. Kosambi, p. 80). Therefore, the difference, as we shall see, between the *kalyāṇamitta* and the good man is not so much a question of qualities but rather of the function and the role that he performs in relation to the Buddhist spiritual path followed by others. In a technical and strictly Buddhist sense, as S. Collins has stressed, he is "someone who helps another on the Buddhist Path" (1987: 53). This function, whose essential aspects remain constant, became more clearly defined through the centuries. At this level, the *pāpamitta*, "bad friend", is the one who induces others to stray from the Buddhist Path.

To grasp the complexity of the *kalyāṇamitta*'s function, as understood in the present Theravāda tradition, it is worth quoting the definition given by the well-known scholar and monk Phra Prayudh Payutto, who writes:

> *Kalyāṇamitta* does not mean 'good friend' in the usual sense, rather it refers to a person who is well prepared with the proper qualities to teach, suggest, point out, encourage, assist, and give *guidance* for getting started *on the Path of Buddhist training*. [...] In the process of the development of wisdom, having a spiritual friend is an important part of the stage related to confidence. In the Buddhist system of learning and training, the meaning of spiritual friend extends to teachers, advisors, and so on; this also encompasses the qualities of the teacher, his methodology, various strategies, and all of the things a person can do to achieve success in teaching and training. All of these things, which are considered external factors in the process of the development of wisdom, make for a major subject that could easily become a separate volume (1995: 224-225, my italics).

8 According to *Puggalapaññatti* 24, he has faith, he is virtuous, learned, generous and wise. See also *Aṅguttara Nikāya*, ed. vol. 4, p. 32: *piyo garu bhāvanīyo vattā ca vacanakkhamo | gambhīrañ ca kathaṃ kattā no caṭṭhāne niyojaye* || (quoted also in *Visuddhimagga* 3.61).

This quotation clearly shows that the term *kalyāṇamitta*, although 'Buddhicised', is still generic; in fact, it can be applied equally to a friend, a teacher (*ācariya*), a preceptor (*upajjhāya*), etc. Elsewhere in his text, Payutto states:

> The term *kalyāṇamitto* does not simply mean friend. Rather it refers to someone—be it a monk, guru, teacher, friend, or helper—who makes valuable suggestions and provides direction and spiritual support (1995: 280, note 22).

What is important to note is that, at this Buddhist level, the *kalyāṇamitta* is not a specific figure, but signifies the function, or better still the qualification – we would say the most important – that makes a master a spiritual master, a friend a spiritual friend, and so forth. All members of the Saṅgha are required to become a *kalyāṇamitta*; it is not a title that is conferred on someone upon completing a particular course of study, nor an attribute solely of masters or preceptors, even if the term is sometimes used to describe the *upajjhāya* (lit. "preceptor") or the *ācariya* (lit. "teacher"),[9] and, in other contexts, the *kalyāṇamitra* is presented as a separate figure, for example when the word appears in *dvandva* compounds in the *Arthaviniścayasūtra*, where, in the explanation of the twenty-eighth of the thirty-two principal signs denoting a *mahāpuruṣa* (the fact that his hair rises up and curls to the right), it is stated that this depends on his having well grasped the instructions of his masters, preceptors and spiritual friends in previous lives.[10]

9 Cf. Collins 1987: 60. There are also instances of this in Sanskrit texts: in *Divyāvadāna* 25 some monks wish to become Venerable because of a *kalyāṇamitra*, that is, a preceptor ([…] *vayam apy upādhyāyam eva kalyāṇamitram āgamya tasyaiva bhagavato 'ntike sarvakleśaprahāṇād arhattvaṃ sākṣātkuryuḥ*, ed. p. 347, lines 16-18). On the difference between *upajjhāya* and *ācariya* in the Pāli Canon, see Hara 1980: 93-118.

10 *ūrdhvāgrapradakṣiṇāvartaromatā – tathāgatasyedaṃ mahāpuruṣasya mahāpuruṣalakṣaṇaṃ pūrve ācāryopādhyāyakalyāṇamitrānuśāsanīpradakṣiṇagrāhitayā nivṛttam* (ed. pp. 60-61). The explanation of this sign is based on the double interpretation of the word *pradakṣiṇa*, which in Classical Sanskrit denotes primar-

3) *Second Buddhist level:* The third meaning of the term *kalyāṇamitta*, "giver of a subject of meditation", is very precise and technical. As Collins duly observes, this role has been overemphasised in secondary literature (1987: 63). It should be noted that "giver of a subject of meditation" is actually one of the functions of the teacher (*ācariya*) and, as far as we know, it is not used in later Buddhist literature to denote an exclusive function of the *kalyāṇamitra*. In fact, in Chapter III of the *Visuddhimagga*, where Buddhaghosa lists and subsequently describes the factors that foster the development of mundane concentration (*lokiyo samādhi*), he says that immediately after the severing of the ten impediments (dwelling, family, gain, class, building, travel, kin, affliction, books, supernormal powers), the practitioner must approach a good friend, who, later in the text, is defined as "the giver of a meditation subject" (*kammaṭṭhānadāyaka*) (3.28). In the passage where the author goes into more detail and explains who a *kalyāṇamitta* is, where he should be sought and how one should behave towards him, the term is often substituted with the word *ācariya* (3.61-73).

1.2 The term *kalyāṇamitta* is perhaps most frequently used as a *bahubbīhi* compound. It would be useful to examine more closely some aspects of this usage.

According to *Itivuttaka* (16-17 [1.2.6-7]) having good friends (*kalyāṇamittatā*) is the most useful external factor (*bāhiraṃ aṅgaṃ*) for attaining the supreme rest (*anuttarayogakkhema*), whereas "right attention" (*yonisomanasikāra*) is the main internal factor (*ajjhattikaṃ aṅgaṃ*).[11] But what does "external factor" mean exactly? There are

ily something or someone that moves in a clockwise direction around a person or object as a token of respect, but in Buddhist texts also has the specific meaning of "skilful, clever, successful". *Pradakṣiṇagrāhitā* is the "state of grasping (that is, learning) well" (cf. Edgerton 1953: 379). See also Samtani 2002: 208, 254.

11 In the *Aṭṭhakathā* we find the explanation of the compound *kalyāṇamittatā* (*ad* 17): ***kalyāṇamittatā*** *ti yassa sīlādiguṇasampanno aghassa ghātā hitassa vid-*

two passages, which we shall examine briefly here, that shed light on this.

In *Udāna* 4.1 (31) [= *Aṅguttara Nikāya* 9.3] having a *kalyāṇamitta* is presented as the first of five factors (ed. p. 36) for liberating the mind (*cetovimutti*) completely. The other four factors are: 1) *sīla* ("morality", "moral sensibility"), understood here as observance of monastic precepts; 2) *sammāvācā* ("right speech"); 3) *viriya* ("effort", "energy"), which is defined on the basis of three of the four modalities normally used to describe right effort (*sammappadhāna*); and 4) *paññā* ("wisdom"), referred to here as "knowledge of becoming and disappearing". What is interesting is that, in relation to the four factors, the *kalyāṇamitta* is the one constant element while the others change ("One would expect a monk who has a good friend to develop morality; one would expect a monk who has a good friend to develop right speech", etc.). We are all familiar with this compositional strategy in Buddhist literature and it is worthy of consideration. The repetition alone is enough to show that a central role is accorded to the *kalyāṇamitta* in the text we are examining. But the teaching goes further. The *sutta* states that he who possesses these five factors has to practice four other things: a) contemplation of what is impure to overcome attachment; b) loving kindness (*mettā*) to overcome aversion; c) mindfulness of inspiration and expiration (*ānāpānasati*) to still the mind; d) perception of impermanence (*aniccasaññā*) to uproot the concept "I am" through the perception of non-self (*anattasaññā*). He who accomplishes these last four steps attains *nibbāna* in this very life.

To conclude, the *sutta* describes a path for attaining *nibbāna*, and in doing this attributes a crucial role to the *kalyāṇamitta*. He is seen as the indispensable (external) condition for developing basic morality (*sīla*, *sammāvācā*), for cultivating right effort (*viriya*) and for developing wisdom (*paññā*). The *sutta* does not state that the *kalyāṇamitta* leads us directly to *nibbāna* (which is mentioned only in

hātā sabbākāreṇa upakārako mitto hoti, so puggalo kalyāṇamitto, tassa bhāvo kalyāṇamittatā.

the second part) nor does it specify what he actually does to this end; the *sutta* simply associates him with the beginning of a process divisible in two stages. The first stage, for which the presence of the *kalyāṇamitta* is the *sine qua non*, is propaedeutic.

It is interesting to note that the names of the other four factors listed in the first part of the *sutta* are in some way related to the Eightfold Path: two of them (*sīla* and *paññā*) pertain to two of the three sections of the Path, while the other two refer to two of the eight elements that compose the Path (*sammāvācā* and *viriya*). *Viriya* is the one linked to the third section of the Path, that is, *samādhi*. In essence it would appear that the *kalyāṇamitta* is presented as a prerequisite for practicing the Eightfold Path, and some aspects in particular. This will become more evident from the following.

In two important passages in the *Saṃyutta Nikāya* (3.18, ed. vol. 1, pp. 87-89; 45.2 ff., vol. 5, p. 2 ff.) the *kalyāṇamitta* is directly associated with the Eightfold Path.[12] The core of the teaching remains the same; what changes is the context. In the first part of the teaching there is a dialogue between Ānanda and the Buddha. The former states that the importance of a good friend is equal to half of religious life; the Buddha replies that having a *kalyāṇamitta* is the whole spiritual life. The Buddha does not make an abstract statement; he says that the *kalyāṇamitta* is the whole spiritual life in the sense that he is connected with the Fourth Noble Truth, that is, the Eightfold Path: in order to develop our spiritual life along the Buddhist Path (*magga*), we need a *kalyāṇamitta*. It is interesting that also here the same strategy of repetition is adopted:

> When a bhikkhu has a good friend, a good companion, a good comrade, it is to be expected that he will develop and cultivate the Noble Eightfold Path. [...] He develops right view... right intention... right speech... right action... right livelihood... right effort... right mindfulness... right concentration" (transl. Bodhi 2000: II, 1524).

12 See also Feer 1866: 316-321, 329, and Feer 1873.

These words are repeated several times (cf. *ibidem*, *suttas* 49-90).[13]

The text continues with other important considerations on the role of other factors, such as the accomplishment in virtue (*sīlasampadā*), the wish to accomplish the wholesome (*chandasampadā*), etc., through which the Eightfold Path can be developed and cultivated.

In each of the above cases it is clearly evident that the perfection of *sīla*, *samādhi* and *paññā*, without which we cannot reach the ultimate goal, is linked to the presence of a *kalyāṇamitta*. He cannot do the practitioner's work for him, but can help him with practical suggestions, by setting an example (the Buddha is the first of the *kalyāṇamitta*s, followed by other celebrated monks)[14] and, eventually, by giving him specific subjects to meditate on, which are strictly related to *samādhi*. In the latter case the *kalyāṇamitta* is an *ācariya*.

2. In Mahāyāna scriptures the description of the basic qualities of the *kalyāṇamitra* does not diverge greatly from the one we find in the texts of the Pāli Canon. In some passages of the *Śrāvakabhūmi* (cf. ed. pp. 127-135) and the *Bodhisattvabhūmi* (cf. ed. pp. 10, 163-164), for instance, Asaṅga (IV cent. CE) analyses in detail *kalyāṇamitratā* and outlines the specific duties and qualities of the *kalyāṇamitra*. He possesses: 1) moral sensitivity (*śīla*); 2) knowledge of the doctrine (*bahuśruta*); 3) spiritual realization (*adhigama*); 4) compassion (*anukampaka*); 5) unwearied mind (*aparikhinnamānas*); 6) forbearance (*kṣamā*); 7) fearlessness (*vaiśāradya*); 8) an eloquent way of speaking (*kalyāṇavākya*).

Unlike the Pāli texts, the *Bodhisattvabhūmi* and the *Śrāvakabhūmi* classify the *kalyāṇamitra*s in five basic types: 1) impeller (*codaka*) towards supreme morality and good behaviour; 2) reminder (*smāraka*) of sins, of teachings and of what is wholesome; 3) instructor (*avavādaka*) through talks on morality, wisdom, liberation, etc.; 4) giver of precepts (*anuśāsaka*) (he can be an *ācārya*, an

[13] Cf. also Bodhi 2000: I, 406, note 234; II, 1890-91, notes 5-6.

[14] Cf. Collins 1987: 57-59.

upādhyāya, a *sahadhārmika*, a *guru* and a *gurusthānīya*); 5) teacher (*dharmadeśaka*) who gives talks on several topics, such as generosity, morality, the Four Noble Truths. Here too, a technical definition of the term is introduced, which does not seem to reflect a conception based mainly on a specific figure rather than a function (or a group of functions) that can be attributed to different individuals.

If we compare the way in which the characteristics and functions of the *kalyāṇamitta/°mitra* are treated in the Pāli Canon and in Mahāyāna texts, certain differences emerge that are worth analysing in brief. There are at least three, two of which are related to typical aspects of the Great Vehicle.

2.1 The first difference concerns the emphasis on the rarity of the *kalyāṇamitra*. In a passage of the *Gaṇḍavyūha* (quoted in *Śikṣāsamuccaya*, ed. p. 2) the *kalyāṇamitras* are listed among the things that are difficult to obtain (*durlabha*), such as a human birth, the birth of a Buddha, etc. It is not surprising that some works state that the disciple must propitiate and venerate the *kalyāṇamitra* and must not abandon him even if it costs him his life, as we read in the *Bodhicaryāvatāra* (5.102-103ab):

> Never, even at the cost of one's life, should one forsake a spiritual friend who observes the vows of a Bodhisattva and who is well versed in the matters of the Mahāyāna. One should learn from the *Śrīsambhavavimokṣa* respectful behaviour toward spiritual mentors (transl. V.A. Wallace and B.A. Wallace, p. 59).

And in a passage of the *Caturdharmakasūtra* quoted in the commentary by Prajñākaramati on these verses it is said: *kalyāṇamitraṃ bhikṣavo bodhisattvena mahāsattvena yāvaj jīvaṃ na tyaktavyam api jīvitahetor.*[15] Caring for the *kalyāṇamitra* is the first step in caring for

[15] Ed. P.L. Vaidya, p. 80 (quoted also in the *Śikṣāsamuccaya*, ed. p. 41, where we read *parityaktavyam* instead of *tyaktavyam*). On the veneration (*sevā*) of the *ka-*

ourselves, as we gather from a passage of the *Śikṣāsamuccaya* (ed. p. 34, transl. p. 37): [...] *tac cātmabhāvādikaṃ kathaṃ pālayet | kalyāṇamitrānutsarjanāt |*.

The advantages to be gained from the *kalyāṇamitra* are described by Śāntideva in the *Śikṣāsamuccaya* through the quotation of passages of the *Gaṇḍavyūha* (ed. pp. 34-36):

> Śrīsambhava says: 'Restrained by trusty friends, O noble youth, Bodhisatvas fall not into evil destinies; taken into guidance by them they transgress not the doctrine of the true Bodhisatvas; shielded by them they become recluses from the world; with their respect Bodhisatvas become men whose acts are free from violent transport in all the actions of the Bodhisatva; through their favour Bodhisatvas become unassailable by the depravities of action. It is our trusty friends that inform us of what should not be done; they it is who keep us from each temptation to indifference; and drive us forth from the City of Re-birth. Accordingly, fair sir, ceasing from such thoughts we must have recourse to our trusty friends. [...] [L]ike a good son, in ever watching the face of the true friend, thou, my son, must give thine own self the name of the sick man: thy Friend, the name of the physician: his precepts the name of the medicine [...].[16] The Bodhisatva who is possessed of the precepts of the Good Friend propitiates the venerable Buddhas. The Bodhisatva who remains in harmony with the words of the Friend, comes near to the omniscience of a Buddha, and when he never doubts one true Friend's words, all true friends draw near him. And he who never lacks the Friend's regard, has every object realised'. (transl. Bendall and Rouse: 1971^2: 37-39).[17]

lyāṇamitra see also the *Mahāyānasūtrālaṃkāra* (and the *Bhāṣya*) 15.9-15 (ed. C. Bagchi, pp. 116-117).

16 Up to this point, the passage of the *Gaṇḍavyūha* is also quoted by Prajñākaramati in his *Bodhicaryāvatārapañjikā*, ed. P.L. Vaidya, p. 80.

17 In the *Aṣṭādaśasāhasrikāprajñāpāramitā* we read: "[A Bodhisattva] cannot reach the knowledge of all modes without having honoured the Buddhas, the Lords, having fulfilled the wholesome roots, or having gained good spiritual friends" (transl. Conze 1962: 365).

2.2 The second difference lies in the association of the *kalyāṇamitra* with the teaching of voidness, the absence of one's own nature in *dharma*s and *pudgala*.[18] Regarding this, there is an explicit passage of the *Aṣṭasāhasrikāprajñāpāramitā* (ed. P.L. Vaidya, p. 238), which I quote here from the translation by David Snellgrove (1987: 177):

> Son of good family, you should strive for the Perfection of Wisdom by developing the conviction that all *dharmas* (elements) are void, signless and effortless. You must practice abandoning signs, existence and the false view of any being. You must avoid bad friends. You must honour, love and stay close to good friends. These are they who teach the Dharma saying: 'All *dharmas* are void, signless, effortless, non-arisen, unborn, unobstructed, nonexistent.' Progressing thus, my son, you will before long be able to study the Perfection of Wisdom either as found in a book or in the person of a monk who preaches the Dharma. You should invest with the name of Teacher (*śāstṛ*) the one from whom you learn about the Perfection of Wisdom. You should be grateful and appreciative, thinking: 'This is my good friend from whom I am learning the Perfection of Wisdom, and learning this I shall become irreversible in regard to supreme and perfect enlightenment. I shall be near to those Tathāgatas, Arhats, Fully Enlightened Buddhas, I shall find myself in Buddha-paradises where there is no lack of Tathāgatas, I shall avoid unfortunate conditions and enjoy propitious conditions.' Weighing up these advantages, you should invest this monk who preaches thus the Dharma with the name of Teacher. You should not be attached to this monk who preaches the Dharma with thoughts that are affected by ideas of worldly gain. You should be attached to him in your quest for the Dharma because of your respect for the Dharma.

In this context the *kalyāṇamitra* is the one who leads to the supreme awakening;[19] whereas the *pāpamitra* is the person who turns one

18 *samastavastunairātmyādideśakaḥ kalyāṇamitram* (Haribhadra's commentary on *Abhisāmayālaṃkāra* 1.37).

19 *satataṃ kalyāṇamitrāvirahito na cireṇa yathābhiprāyeṣu buddhakṣetreṣv anuttarāṃ samyaksambodhim abhisaṃbhotsyate* (from a passage of the *Kṣitigarbhasūtra* quoted in the *Śikṣāsamuccaya*, ed. p. 89, lines 4-6).

away from the Great Vehicle and leads one to the view-points of the so-called Lesser Vehicle.

2.3 The third difference, perhaps the most important, concerns the association of the *kalyāṇamitra* with the "thought of awakening" (*bodhicitta*), which on the one hand represents the perfection of *śīla*, *samādhi* and *prajñā*, and on the other the ultimate goal itself, the indissoluble union of voidness and compassion.

The evolution of the concept of *bodhicitta*, which accompanies the development of the Mahāyāna up to and including the Tantric systems, is reflected – and this could not be otherwise – in the evolution of the figure of the spiritual guide.

The presence of the *kalyāṇamitra* is indispensable for attaining the *bodhicitta* and progressing further along the path.[20] This can be seen from many Mahāyāna works. Just to quote two examples, in the *Bodhisattvabhūmi* it is considered as the second of the four main causes (*hetu*) of the development of the *bodhicitta*,[21] and in the *Abhisāmayālaṃkāravṛtti* (*ad* 1.49-51) the propitiation of the *kalyāṇamitra* (*kalyāṇamitrārāgaṇa*) is the fifth of ten factors that permit the attainment of Pramuditā, the First Earth (*bhūmi*) of the Bodhisattvas. It should be noted that this propitiation or service (*sevā*), on which Mahāyāna texts place more and more emphasis, is a fundamental aspect of the relationship between master and disciple in Buddhist Tantric traditions, as we shall now see.

20 Cf. Haribhadra's *vṛtti ad Abhisāmayālaṃkāra* 5.27cd-29, ed. p. 74: *kalyāṇamitrādivaikalyād bodhicittānutpāde* [...].

21 These causes are: 1) inclusion in a Bodhisattva family (*gotrasampat*); 2) *kalyāṇamitra*; 3) compassion (*kāruṇya*); 4) courage in helping beings (*abhīrutā*). Another four main causes result in the abandonment of the *bodhicitta*: 1) *pāpamitra*; 2) lack of compassion; 3) fear and reluctance to help beings; 4) lack of the four main causes for the development of the *bodhicitta* (cf. ed. pp. 10-12). Cf. also *Śikṣāsamuccaya*, ed. p. 52, transl. p. 53.

3. In the Sanskrit texts of the Buddhist Tantric systems, the term *kalyāṇamitra* is found less frequently. The more popular word for indicating the guide for the inner path, he who has the function of spiritual advisor, is *guru* (perhaps due to the growing influence of Hindū Tantric traditions). Often the terms *guru* and *ācārya* are used in the same context: the two terms do not appear to differ in meaning. In Tantric systems *guru* and *ācārya* embrace most of the figures who act as spiritual guides.

Even when the term *kalyāṇamitra* is used it seems to have a generic meaning and stands for *guru*; what is valid for the *kalyāṇamitra* is also valid for the *guru*. The first thing to note is the necessity for the propitiation or service mentioned earlier. Honouring and venerating the *kalyāṇamitra*, as well as the *guru*, is sometimes presented as an indispensable condition for embarking on the inner path. When this honouring and venerating is done in the correct way – without holding anything back, and as the expression of a true aspiration to follow the spiritual path – it becomes the first step towards increasing spiritual maturity, which gives birth to a growing understanding of truth and results in the attainment of ever greater degrees of liberation. We will limit ourselves to quoting a few examples. At the close of the third *pariccheda* of the *Caryāmelāpakapradīpa* it is said that he who wishes to attain the *cittaviveka* must worship the good friend (*cittavivekam anveṣayitukāmaḥ kalyāṇamitraṃ paryupāste*, ed. p. 37). Later the author, Āryadeva, goes as far as saying that he who desires Buddhahood must examine the nature of his own mind after having recourse to the Vajrayāna and after venerating the *kalyāṇamitra*[22] (*vajrayānam āśritya buddhatvakāmena kalyāṇamitram ārādhya svacittasvabhāvo 'nveṣṭavyaḥ*, ed. p. 38). Further on the author stresses the importance of the *kalyāṇamitra* in knowing the true

[22] The good friend must be worshipped until *niṣpannakrama* is reached: *atra vajrayāne utpattikramābhyāsād aṣṭamīṃ bhūmiṃ prāpya punaḥ punaḥ sugatād upapadya yāvan niṣpannakramaṃ na labhate tāvat kalyāṇamitram ārādhayate* (*Caryāmelāpakapradīpa*, ed. p. 68).

nature of one's own mind.[23] According to the *Guhyasiddhi* (6.52-55), the union (*saṃparka*) with the *kalyāṇamitra* is one of the factors that are instrumental in reaching the state of Vajrasattva.

Similar concepts concerning the *guru* ("master") are expressed elsewhere. Here we shall simply make reference to a few passages. The master must be praised and venerated since without him it is impossible to attain anything, neither perfection nor liberation, as we read in several stanzas in Chapter IX of the *Guhyasiddhi*, dedicated entirely to the subject of relating to the *guru*: "The supreme pledge (*samaya*) is the adoration (*pūjana*) of the *guru*" (st. 8ab: *samayānāṃ ca sarveṣām uttamaṃ gurupūjanam*); the best way to honour the master is to offer him one's own *mudrā* (cf. stt. 12-16, 20). It is necessary to give everything to the master, from jewels to houses, from cattle to one's wife and children, and even oneself (cf. *Abhisambodhikrama* 36-37 and *Cakrasaṃvaratantra* 3.10-14). According to the *Svādhiṣṭhānakrama*, the master eliminates sin and fear, leads the disciple to the other shore, to the other side of the ocean of pain (st. 48: *ācāryo harate pāpam ācāryo harate bhayam | ācāryas tārayet pāraṃ duḥkhārṇavamahābhayāt ||*). If the master is satisfied with the praise accorded to him, he enables the disciple to attain the supreme knowledge of the Omniscient One (cf. st. 45). The vision of relative truth (*saṃvṛtisatya*) – which corresponds to the *svādhiṣṭhānakrama* – can only be had with the master's help (st. 10: *svādhiṣṭhānakramo nāma saṃvṛteḥ satyadarśanam | gurupādaprasādena labhyate tac ca nānyathā ||*). The *Caryāmelāpakapradīpa* states that the incorporeal absolute truth can only be known through the words from the master's mouth (ed. p. 61: *paramārthasatyaṃ punar amūrtikaṃ niraupamyaṃ sarvārambhaṇāpagataṃ pratyātmavedyam | tena guruvaktreṇa vinā na jñāyate*). He who receives the master's blessing can meditate upon the supreme reality with pure and firm mind and become the Adamantine Being (cf. *Abhisambodhikrama* 38). This is

[23] *kalyāṇamitravirahāt svacittasya yathābhūtaparijñānam anadhigamya* [...] *duḥkham anubhavanti* (p. 52).

echoed by many passages of Chapter II of the *Prajñopāya-viniścayasiddhi*:

> Not even the Victorious are able to express [the truth] in words by saying 'it is this'; it cannot be perceived in external realities, since it can only be known within ourselves [...]. It is never attained through the knowledge deriving from listening or reflection, since it is not related to words or their meanings [...]. Thus, it is right to worship a good master without attachment; without him truth (*tattva*) can never be attained, not even in tens of millions of *kalpas*. If the jewel of truth is not attained, there is no perfection (*siddhi*), in the same way that a shoot cannot appear without a seed even when a field has been prepared to receive it .[24]

A typically Tantric concept is formulated, for example, in the *Guhyasiddhi*: worshipping the master ensures also the attainment of perfections (*siddhi*): "In the three worlds there is nothing more precious than the master. By making offerings to him, wise men reach perfections in many ways" (9.11: *ācāryāt paramaṃ nāsti ratnabhūtaṃ tridhātuke | asya prasādāt prāpyante siddhayo 'nekadhā budhaiḥ* ||);[25] "Here beings obtain the secret doctrine (*sampradāya*) – well hidden, which confers all perfections, divine – when the adamantine master is satisfied" (9.22: *prāpnuvanty atra te sattvāḥ sampradāyaṃ sugopitam | sarvasiddhipradaṃ divyaṃ saṃtuṣṭe guruvajriṇi* ||).

3.1 In Tantric systems the master is not just the main external condition for spiritual development (as in Pāli texts), nor is he simply associated with the transmission and attainment of the *bodhicitta* (as in

[24] Stt. 3, 5-7: *idaṃ tad iti tadvaktuṃ naiva śakyaṃ jinair api | pratyātmavedyarūpatvād bāhyārthe na ca gṛhyate* || (3) [...] *śrutādijñānagamyaṃ tan na bhaved vai kadācana | śabdārthayor asaṃbandhāt* [...] || (5) *ata eva sadāsaktyā yuktaṃ sadgurusevanam | na ca tena vinā tattvaṃ prāpyate kalpakoṭibhiḥ* || (6) *aprāpyate tattvaratne tu siddhir naiva kadācana | suviśuddhe 'pi satkṣetre bījābhāvād yathāṅkuraḥ* || (7).

[25] Cf. also *Advayasiddhi*, st. 33: *ācāryāt parataraṃ nāsti trailokye sacarācare | yasya prasādāt prāpyante siddhayo 'nekadhā budhaiḥ* ||.

Mahāyāna texts). To be sure, Tantric texts sometimes stress that the *bodhicitta* – understood to embrace various meanings, since it is a) aspiration; b) one of the elements upon which the daily meditation is centred; c) the final goal of the spiritual path; and d) the expression of the mystery of the ultimate reality – can only be attained through the master.[26] But here the master is even identified with the actual foundations of the Buddhist spiritual path.

The *guru* is, in fact, the embodiment of the Three Jewels. He is identified with all the Buddhas[27] and with the Supreme God who should be venerated (cf. *Advayasiddhi* 34cd: *ācāryaḥ paramo devaḥ pūjanīyaḥ prayatnataḥ*). In the *Gururatnatrayastotra*, after the praising of the Buddha, the Dharma and the Saṅgha, there is a final stanza (st. 7) in which the *guru* is identified with the Three Jewels: praising the *guru* is praising the Three Jewels (*gurur buddho gurur dharmo guruḥ saṅghas tathaiva ca | gurur vajradharaḥ śrīmān tasmai śrīgurave namaḥ ||*). This stanza appears in many other texts.[28] In the *Tattvajñānasaṃsiddhi* it is stated that the virtuous one shows the same devotion to the *guru* and to the Buddha ([...] *guṇino guru-buddhābhinnasadbhakteḥ*: st. 3.6).[29] Whereas in the *Paramārthasevā*, it is stated that the Buddhas venerate the master, the Bodhisattvas honour him and the Siddhas celebrate him with songs: *saṃpūjito nityam anantabuddhaiḥ sa vandito diggatabodhisattvaiḥ | gītaḥ sa*

26 In the *Guhyasiddhi* (9.10) we read that the *bodhicitta* can be attained swiftly through an offering laid at the master's feet (*niḥsvabhāvātmakaṃ śuddhaṃ bodhicittam iti smṛtam | tasya prāptir bhavaty āśu gurupādaprasādataḥ ||*).

27 In a stanza of the *Māyājālamahātantrarāja* quoted in the *Guhyasamājapradīpoddyotana* (ed. p. 216) we read: *ācāryaḥ kathaṃ draṣṭavyaḥ sarvabuddhasamo guruḥ | sarvavajradharo rājā ratnaketus tathāgataḥ ||*.

28 It is quoted, for instance, in the *Abhisamayamañjarī* of Śubhākaragupta which dates to the 12th century (ed. p. 30). For further references see Sferra (2003), note 12.

29 In the commentary we read: ***gurubuddhābhinnasadbhakter*** *iti | guruś ca buddhaś ca gurubuddhau, tayor abhinnā samyag bhaktir yasyo sa tathā* (*Marmakalikā*, ed. p. 53).

siddhair bahuvajragṇair (st. 24ac).[30] A similar concept can be found in many works, such as the celebrated *Gurupañcāśikā* attributed to Āryadeva (st. 2: *abhiṣekāgralabdho hi vajrācāryas tathāgataiḥ* | *daśadiglokadhātusthais trikālam etya vandyate* ||).[31]

Of course, many historical and doctrinal elements that have determined the evolution of the conception of spiritual guidance in Indian Buddhist traditions are still unknown and further in-depth research would be necessary to bring them to light. Here, we will limit ourselves to note that in the Mahāyāna the evolution of the actual figure of the spiritual guide mirrors the development of the notion of *bodhicitta*. The *Guhyasamājatantra* goes so far as saying that there is no difference between the *guru* and the *bodhicitta*. Thus, we would like to conclude by quoting a passage from Chapter XVII of this text:

> Then Maitreya the Bodhisattva, the Great Being, bowed before all the Buddhas and said: "How should the Lord the Vajra-Teacher consecrated in the hidden Secret Union of the Vajra of the Body, Speech and Mind of all the Tathāgatas be regarded by all Buddhas and all Bodhisattvas?" All the Buddhas replied: "Son of good family, he is to be regarded by all Buddhas and all Bodhisattvas as the Vajra of the Thought of Enlightenment. And why so? *The Teacher and the Thought of Enlightenment are the same and inseparable.* We will just explain briefly. All the Buddhas and Bodhisattvas who dwell, who hold and maintain places in all the ten directions throughout the past, present and future, worship the Teacher with the worship of All Buddhas, and then returning to their Buddha-paradises make this pronouncement of vajra-words: 'He is the father of all us Buddhas,

30 National Archives Kathmandu, MS 5.7235 [Nepal-German Manuscript Preservation Project, Mf. B30/31], fol. 4 *recto*, lines 3-4. Fragments of and quotations from the Sanskrit text of this important work by Puṇḍarīka have been found in MSS and printed sources. I am working on a critical edition of the extant Sanskrit portion of the text.

31 This stanza is also quoted in the *Kriyāsamuccaya* (facsimile ed. by L. Chandra, fol. 2*r*, lines 7-8) and briefly commented on in the *Hevajratantrapiṇḍārthaṭīkā* by Vajragarbha (chapter 1, stanzas 19, 21-23) and in the *Vimalaprabhā* by Puṇḍarīka (ed., vol. 2, p. 4).

the mother of all us Buddhas, in that he is the Teacher of all us Buddhas.' Furthermore, O son of good family, the merit of a single pore of the Teacher is worth more than the heap of merit of the Vajra Body, Speech and Mind of all the Lords the Buddhas of the ten directions. And why so? The Thought of Enlightenment is the very essence of All Buddha-Wisdoms, and being the source it is the repository of omniscient wisdom" (transl. Snellgrove 1987: 177-178, my italics).[32]

REFERENCES

(Bibliography is limited to the secondary sources quoted in the text. For primary sources, I would refer the reader to the *editio princeps* of the quoted texts or to the work of the editor mentioned in the text or in the notes)

Alsdorf, Ludwig (1961) "*Sasajātaka* und *Śaśa-avadāna*", *Wiener Zeitschrift für die Kunde Süd-Asiens* 6: 1-17.

[32] *atha khalu maitreyo bodhisattvo mahāsattvaḥ sarvatathāgatān praṇipatyaivam āha | sarvatathāgatakāyavākcittavajraguhyasamājābhiṣikto bhagavān vajrācāryaḥ sarvatathāgataiḥ sarvabodhisattvaiś ca kathaṃ draṣṭavyaḥ | sarvatathāgatāḥ prāhuḥ | bodhicitto vajra iva kulaputra sarvatathāgataiḥ sarvabodhisattvaiś ca draṣṭavyaḥ | tat kasmād dhetoḥ | bodhicittaś cācāryaś cādvayam etad advaidhīkāram | yāvat kulaputra saṃkṣepeṇa kathayāmaḥ | yāvanto daśadiglokadhātuṣu buddhaś ca bodhisattvāś ca tiṣṭhanti dhriyanti yāpayanti ca | sarve te triṣkālam āgatya tam ācāryaṃ sarvatathāgatapūjābhiḥ sampūjya svabuddhakṣetraṃ punar api prakrāmanty evaṃ ca vāgvajrākṣarapadaṃ niścārayanti | pitāsmākaṃ sarvatathāgatānāṃ mātāsmākaṃ sarvatathāgatānām | tad yathāpi nāma kulaputra yāvanto buddhā bhagavanto daśasu dikṣu viharanti teṣāṃ ca buddhānāṃ bhagavatāṃ yāvat kāyavākcittavajrajaḥ puṇyaskandhaḥ sa ca puṇyaskandha ācāryasyaiva romakūpāgravivare viśiṣyate | tat kasmād dhetoḥ | bodhicittaṃ kulaputra sarvabuddhajñānānāṃ sārabhūtam utpattibhūtaṃ yāvat sarvajñajñānākaram iti* (ed. Y. Matsunaga, pp. 104-105); the same passage is quoted by Indrabhūti in his *Jñānasiddhi* (chapter 17, ed. p. 151).

Bendall, Cecil and W.H.D. Rouse (1971²) *Śikṣā Samuccaya. A Compendium of Buddhist Doctrine Compiled by Śāntideva*, translated by..., Delhi (London 1922¹).

Berzin, Alexander (2000) *Relating to a Spiritual Teacher. Building a Healthy Relationship*, Snow Lion Publications, Ithaca (NY).

Bhayani, Harivallabh C. (1998) *Dohākośagīti of Kṛṣṇapāda, Tellopāda along with Songs of Vinayaśrīpāda, Śāntipāda and Stray Lyrics and Citations from Some Other Siddhas*, Restored Text, Sanskrit Chāyā and Translation, Central Institute of Higher Tibetan Studies, Sarnath, *Bibliotheca Indo-Tibetica Series* 42, Varanasi.

Bodhi, Bhikkhu (2000) *The Connected Discourses of the Buddha. A New Translation of the Saṃyutta Nikāya*, 2 vols., Wisdom Publications, Somerville (MA).

Boyd, James W. (1972) "Buddhas and the *kalyāṇamitta*", *Studia Missionalia* 21: 57-76.

Buddhadāsa, Bhikkhu (1988) *Key to Natural Truth*, Bangkok.

Collins, Steven (1987) "*Kalyāṇamitta* and *Kalyāṇamittatā*", *Journal of the Pali Text Society* 11: 51-72.

Conze, Edward (1962) *The Gilgit Manuscript of the Aṣṭādaśasāhasrikāprajñāpāramitā. Chapters 55 to 70 corresponding to the 5th Abhisamaya*, edited and translated by..., Istituto Italiano per il Medio ed Estremo Oriente, *Serie Orientale Roma* 26, Roma.

Dayal, Har (1932) *The Bodhisattva Doctrine in Buddhist Sanskrit Literature*, London.

Dutt, Nalinaksha (1930) *Aspects of Mahāyāna Buddhism and Its Relation to Hīnayāna*, London.

Edgerton, Franklin (1953) *Buddhist Hybrid Sanskrit Grammar and Dictionary. Volume II: Dictionary*, New Haven.

Feer, Léon M. (1866) "Études bouddhiques. Le sûtra. Les quatre préceptes", *Journal Asiatique*, sixième série, tome VIII (octobre-novembre): 269-357.

Feer, Léon M. (1873) "Études bouddhiques. L'ami de la vertu et l'amitié de la vertu (*kalyāṇamitra-kalyāṇamitratā*)", *Journal Asiatique*, septième série, tome I (janvier): 5-66.

Gombrich, Richard F. (1988) *Theravāda Buddhism. A Social History from Ancient Benares to Modern Colombo*, London and New York.

Guenther, Herbert V. (1966-1967) "The Spiritual Teacher in Tibet", *Hermes. Recherches sur l'expérience spirituelle 4. Le Maître spirituel dans les grandes traditions d'Occident et d'Orient*, pp. 226-240.

Hara, Minoru (1980) "Hindu Concepts of Teacher: Sanskrit *guru* and *ācārya*", in M. Nagatomi *et al.* (eds.), *Sanskrit and Indian Studies: Essays in Honor of Daniel H. H. Ingalls*, Reidel, Dordrecht, pp. 93-118.

Harvey, Peter (2000) *An Introduction to Buddhist Ethics*, Cambridge.

Lal, B. (2004) "*Mahāyāna evaṃ Tantrayāna meṃ guru-pratyaya vimarśa*", *Dhīḥ. Journal of Rare Buddhist Texts Research Project* 37: 33-50.

Lamotte, Étienne (1958) *Histoire du Bouddhisme Indien, des origines à l'ère Śaka*, Louvain.

Payutto, Prayudh Phra (1995) *Buddhadhamma. Natural Laws and Values for Life*, Albany (NY).

Prasad, Maulichand (1984) *A Comparative Study of Abhisamācārikā*, K.P. Jayaswal Research Institute, Patna.

Rhys Davids, M.A. (1917) *The Book of the Kindred Sayings (Saṃyutta-Nikāya) or Grouped Suttas. Part I. Kindred Sayings with Verses (Sagāthā-vagga)*, translated by…, London.

Samtani, Narayan Hemandas (2002) *Gathering the Meanings. Essential Teachings of the Buddha. The Arthaviniścaya Sūtra and Its Commentary Nibandhana*, Translated with an Introduction and Notes by…, Berkeley (CA).

Sferra, Francesco (2003) "Some Considerations on the Relationship Between Hindu and Buddhist Tantras", in G. Verardi and S. Vita (eds.), *Buddhist Asia 1*, Italian School of East Asian Studies, Kyoto, pp. 57-84.

Shukla, Karunesh (1991) *Śrāvakabhūmi of Ācārya Asaṅga. Part II*, *Tibetan Sanskrit Works Series* 28, K.P. Jayaswal Research Institute, Patna.

Snellgrove, David (1987) *Indo-Tibetan Buddhism*, 2 vols., Boston.

Sumedho, Ajahn (1989) *Now is the Knowing*, Amaravati Buddhist Centre (Hertfordshire).

Suvaḍḍhano, Bhikkhu (no date) *A Guide to Awareness. Dhamma Talks on the Foundations of Mindfulness*, Bangkok.

Wallace, Vesna A. and B. Allan Wallace (1997) *A Guide to the Bodhisattva Way of Life (Bodhicaryāvatāra) by Śāntideva*, translated from the Sanskrit and Tibetan by..., Ithaca (NY).

Wayman, Alex (1987) "The Guru in Buddhism", *Studia Missionalia* 36: 195-213.

THE SPIRITUAL TEACHER IN THERAVĀDA BUDDHISM: INNER MOTIVATIONS AND FOUNDATIONS OF MINDFULNESS*

CLAUDIO CICUZZA

In the Pāli Buddhist canon various distinctions are made in presenting the teacher figure, due to the different roles that the spiritual guide fulfilled within the monastic community: he could be a teacher

* Abbreviations: AA: *Abhisamayālaṅkāra*; AN: *Aṅguttara Nikāya*; As: *Atthasālinī* (*Dhammasaṅgaṇi-aṭṭhakathā*); Bv: *Buddhavaṃsa*; Dhp: *Dhammapada*; Dhp-a: *Dhammapada-aṭṭhakathā*; Dhs: *Dhammasaṅgaṇī*; DN: *Dīgha Nikāya*; It: *Itivuttaka*; It-a: *Itivuttaka-aṭṭhakathā*; Nidd I: *Mahāniddesa*; Nidd-II: *Cūḷaniddesa*; Nidd-a: *Mahāniddesa-aṭṭhakathā* (*Saddhammapajjotikā*); MN: *Majjhima Nikāya*; Mp: *Manorathapūraṇī*; Mvy: *Mahāvyutpatti*; Paṭis: *Paṭisambhidāmagga*; Paṭis-a: *Paṭisambhidāmagga-aṭṭhakathā* (*Saddhammapakāsinī*); Ps: *Papañcasūdanī*; Sn: *Suttanipāta*; SN: *Saṃyutta Nikāya*; Spk: *Sāratthappakāsinī*; Sv: *Sumaṅgalavilāsinī*; Sv-pṭ: *Linatthappakāsinī*; Ud: *Udāna*; Ud-a: *Udāna-aṭṭhakathā*; Vibh: *Vibhaṅga*; Vibh-a: *Vibhaṅga-aṭṭhakathā* (*Sammohavinodanī*); Vin: *Vinaya*; Vism: *Visuddhimagga*. All Pāli texts are quoted in the Pali Text Society Edition (PTS) except *Visuddhimagga* (ed. H. C. WARREN). I have also taken into account the E-book edition *Chaṭṭha Saṅgāyana* (version 3) of the Vipassana Research Institute (CSCD). I should like to thank Raniero Gnoli, Mauro Maggi and Peter Skilling, for their willingness in talking over some parts of the article with me, and Barbara Goss for her English translation.

(*ācariya*),[1] a preceptor (*upajjhāya*), an instructor (*ovādaka*),[2] etc.[3] Other subdivisions are based on the specific characteristics of the teacher. For instance, a distinction may be made according to the teaching method used: there are some teachers who explain a subject concisely and others extensively, but both of them lack coherence; then there are teachers who explain a subject either concisely or extensively, and are coherent.[4] The *Sermon on the Five Teachers*[5] gives the example of five types of teacher, each of whom is impure in a different way: one in his morals (*sīla*), another in his way of life (*ājiva*), a third in his teaching of the Dhamma, a fourth in the explanation of his teaching (*veyyākarana*), and a fifth in his knowledge and deep insight (*ñāṇadassana*). The list comes to an end with a last teacher, pure in all the aforesaid matters, who is the Buddha himself. A further subdivision can be deduced from the mention that the Bud-

1 There are four or five different functions of *ācariya*: initiation-teacher (*pabbajā-ācariya*), ordination-teacher (*upasampadā-ācariya*), tutelar teacher (*nissaya-ācariya*), teacher of textual study (*uddesa-ācariya*), and teacher who gives admonitions (*ovāda-ācariya*). See *Mahāvagga Aṭṭhakathā* (PTS V, 1085) *ad* Vin 1.5.5 (PTS I, 187) and *Parivāra Aṭṭhakathā* (PTS VII, 1379) *ad* Vin 5.14.14.4 (PTS V, 206).

2 Or "he who gives admonitions", with the frequent synonym *anusāsaka*. See for instance Dhp-a (PTS II, 110) *ad* Dhp 77 (PTS 11).

3 There is a fair amount of literature on this subject. For an overall view of the matter, as well as a good bibliography, see the recent English translation of M. WIJAYARATNA, *Buddhist Monastic Life According to the Texts of Theravāda Tradition*, New York 1990.

4 See AN 4.14.9 (PTS II, 138): the *sutta* makes special reference to the *dhammakathikās*, "those who explain the Dhamma". Just before this, in the same *vagga*, there is a list of persons who are classified according to their ability to understand the Dhamma: those who realize it as soon as it is told to them (*ugghaṭitaññū*); those who only realize it after being given a detailed explanation (*vipañcitaññū*); those who need guidance (*neyya*); and those for whom the utmost that can be attained is in the words (*padaparama*), that is, they are incapable of attaining awakening and at the very most are able to achieve a verbal comprehension of the Dhamma (AN 4.14.3, PTS II, 135).

5 See Vin 2.7.1 (PTS II, 186-187) and AN 5.10.10 (PTS III, 122-126). Cf. also a similar version, in Sanskrit, in R. GNOLI (ed.), *The Gilgit Manuscript of the Saṅghabhedavastu*, vol. II, Rome 1978, pp. 75-78.

dha makes of some particular persons amongst all those who had the possibility of frequenting him during his lifetime. He considers them his "foremost" (*agga*) pupils and many of them were probably the first ones to spread the Buddha's teachings.[6] For example, Aññā-koṇḍañña was outstanding amongst the most learned elders (*rat-taññū*), Sāriputta was eminent amongst those possessing great wisdom (*mahāpañña*), Mahāmoggallāna distinguished himself amongst those who developed supernatural powers (*iddhimant*), Mahākassapa was foremost amongst those who were greatly skilled in the practice of austerity (*dhutavāda*),[7] Anuruddha was pre-eminent amongst those who developed supernatural vision (*dibbacakkhu*), etc.[8] We may also add Upāli, outstanding amongst those versed in the Vinaya (*vinayadhara)*,[9] and Ānanda, excellent amongst those who have heard much, amongst those who are learned (*bahussuta*), amongst those who have a strong memory (*satimant*), amongst those who know all the phases of the Buddha's teachings (*gatimant*),[10] amongst those who apply great energy and resolution to their study and to learning from the Buddha's teaching (*dhitimant*) and, lastly, amongst all the Buddha's attendants (*upaṭṭhāka*).[11]

Apart from the distinctions that are made according to different roles or personal aptitudes, the purpose of this paper is to study the very concept of "teacher", to understand what deep-seated motives led the Buddha, the supreme teacher, to teach the Dhamma and in what way a teacher, who is good and capable in that he possesses

6 See AN 1.14.1 (PTS I, 23) and the lengthy commentary in Mp (PTS I, 124-209).

7 In the commentary (Mp, PTS I, 161-163) there is a particularly interesting explanation of the term *dhuta*. See also NYANAPONIKA THERA and H. HECKER, *Great Disciples of the Buddha*, Somerville 1997, pp. 118-119, 122.

8 Cf. DN 16.6.8 and ff. (PTS II, 156-168). For the whole matter see also S. BUTR-INDR, *The Social Philosophy of Buddhism*, Bangkok 1995, pp. 108-113, 175-205.

9 AN 1.14.4 (PTS I, 25).

10 Cf. Mp (PTS I, 286) *ad* AN 1.14.4 (PTS I, 25).

11 AN 1.14.4 (PTS I, 24-25).

some well-defined qualities, should behave towards his pupils. Of all the terms that are used in the canon to point to the figure of the spiritual guide, the one which seems to distinguish most clearly the teacher, in a sense that goes beyond any definition based on his role in the community, is *satthar*, a term which is also an epithet of the Buddha himself.[12] A classical explanation of *satthar* expresses the idea of a teacher who saves beings from *saṃsāra*, who is a guide, a leader, a conciliator, who nurtures wisdom, concentration, examination, purity, and serenity.[13]

In close connection with the Buddha, taken in the sense of *satthar*, there are two more teacher figures that, out of compassion, have come into the world for the welfare and happiness of living beings.[14] They are two different types of disciples (*sāvaka*) of the teacher (*satthar*), who have reached a different degree of spiritual evolution but are both capable of guiding human beings along the difficult path of spiritual apprenticeship. The first is the disciple who has reached the state of Arahant and the second is the disciple who is still a student (*sekha*). These figures are closely connected with the Buddha and personify the task and the mission of spreading Buddhist teaching. Compassion is definitely one of their main characteristics, together with a set of prerogatives that belong to the good teacher and that, as we shall see in the following examples, represent the chief distinctive elements of the spiritual guide.

This study is divided into three parts: a) first of all I shall consider, with particular reference to the *Lohiccasutta*, some of the psychological aspects that distinguish the "blameworthy teacher" and, as a result, obtain some criteria of the qualities of the proper teacher; b) I shall then turn my attention to the time when the Buddha decides to reveal his message, to the time when, to all intents and purposes, he

[12] As a matter of fact, it is one of the nine attributes of the Buddha which appear in various parts of the canon, for example in DN 2.40 (PTS I, 62).

[13] See Nidd I 190 (PTS II, 246) *ad* Sn 955 (= Nidd II 119 *ad* Sn 1148).

[14] See It 84 (PTS 78-80).

becomes a teacher;[15] c) I shall conclude with a careful examination of the ways in which the teacher must carry out his duties, paying particular attention to the *Saḷāyatanavibhaṅgasutta*, in which we come across a threefold *satipaṭṭhāna* that seems to be especially meant for the teacher. The practice expressed in the threefold *satipaṭṭhāna* is, together with the qualities that characterize the proper spiritual guide, the very core of the relationship between teacher and disciple.

The three parts of the study are decidedly interconnected, since the description of the blameworthy teacher contains the coordinate terms to describe the figure of the good teacher and vice versa.

1. Characteristics of a Teacher

1.1. *Three Blameworthy Teachers*

The *Lohiccasutta*[16] is one of the most important texts for understanding the concept of "teacher". The *sutta* begins by stating the opinion of a *brāhmaṇa*, Lohicca, who thinks that the mere fact of teaching is negative and that it actually conceals a search for personal satisfaction. The Buddha, taking his cue from this statement, begins by criticizing it and pointing out what sorry consequences it would have.[17] He then goes on to describe three types of teacher who deserve criticism and reproach: they are victims of desire and are guilty of negative behaviour which – where the third blameworthy teacher is concerned – includes giving people the idea of inactivity and indiffer-

[15] There is no space here to dwell on the concept of *paccekabuddha*, "the solitary awakened one", although it is connected with the subject of this paper. I intend to go into this problem in greater depth in a future study. On this issue, I can certainly mention R. KLOPPENBORG, *The* paccekabuddha: *A Buddhist Ascetic. A Study of the* paccekabuddha *in Pāli Canonical and Commentarial Literature*, Leiden 1974.

[16] DN 12 (PTS I, 223-234).

[17] DN 12.13-15 (PTS I, 228-230).

ence.[18] This explanation ends with a description of the teacher who is not blameworthy and this coincides with the Buddha himself.

Lohicca's opinion is stated in the first part of the *sutta*:[19]

> At that time a wicked idea such as this dawned upon the bráhmaãa Lohicca: «In this world an ascetic (*samaãa*) or a bráhmaãa who has obtained some wholesome doctrine (*dhamma*), after he has obtained it, should not impart it to others: because, what will one be able to do for another (*paro parassa*)? I maintain that such an attitude is wicked and is rooted in desire, as if a person, after having severed an old bond, were to form a new one: because, what will one be able to do for another?»

The commentary specifies:[20]

> [This idea] is «wicked» (*pápaka*), miserable, as it is lacking in [true] compassion for others;[21] moreover, it is no different from nihilism or eternalism. [This wicked idea] «dawned», that is to say it occurred, not only at a mental level: as a matter of fact, according to this [point of view], he also speaks in a similar fashion in the middle of the assembly. He declares: «Whatever will one be able to do for another?», that is to say «He who receives the teaching what will he ever be able to do for the teacher?».[22] And he continues: «This wholesome doctrine (*dhamma*) was obtained by him alone and he alone must put it into practice, revering and respecting it».

Lohicca – as it is explained in the *Sumaṅgalavilāsinī* – maintains that a man who has discovered some wholesome doctrine and wants to teach it to others is, in actual fact, moved by desire and a quest for personal satisfaction and only wants to obtain, through his teaching, gratitude from his pupils. This is the only real reason that makes a

[18] See Sv-pṭ (PTS I, 517) *ad* Sv *ad* DN 12.18 (PTS I, 231-232).
[19] DN 12.2 (PTS I, 224).
[20] See Sv (PTS II, 395) *ad* DN 12.2 (PTS I, 224).
[21] I read *parānukampāvirahitattā* instead of *parānukampā virahitattā*.
[22] Here is how the commentary interprets the deliberately indefinite *paro parassa*.

person assume the role of teacher: thus the desire to teach is, in Lohicca's opinion, not *kusala* at all but, on the contrary, absolutely negative in that it arises out of cupidity. Therefore he goes so far as to think that nobody can really do anything for anyone else because the mere desire to impart a beneficial teaching to others conceals a form of attachment.

This attitude meets with the Buddha's disapproval insofar as it becomes an obstacle for those who follow the Buddhist Dhamma, spreading a false and harmful idea of the relationship between teacher and disciple. Moreover, since this attitude is completely lacking in genuine concern for the welfare of other beings, it has negative consequences for the person who upholds it, condemning him to rebirths in the purgatories or as an animal.

Then, taking his cue from Lohicca's statement, the Buddha speaks of the three types of blameworthy teacher:[23]

> Lohicca, in the world there are three teachers (*satthar*) who deserve rebuke. The criticism that a person may express about them is real, true, just, and not deplorable. Who are these three teachers? Here, o Lohicca, there is a teacher who has not managed to achieve the aim of samaṇaship, for which he left his home and espoused asceticism.
> Without having achieved it, he teaches a doctrine (*dhamma*) to his pupils, saying to them: «This is for your welfare, this is for your happiness!». His disciples do not desire to hear his teaching, do not make any effort to hear, do not pay attention to understand, and err, deviating from the teaching of the teacher.
> For this reason he ought to be rebuked in the following manner: «Venerable One, you have not managed to achieve samaṇaship, for which you left your home and espoused asceticism. Without having achieved it, you teach a doctrine to your pupils, saying to them: "This is for your welfare, this is for your happiness!". But the pupils do not desire to hear you, do not make any effort to hear you, do not pay attention in order to understand, and err, deviating from the teaching of the teacher. I say that such an attitude is wicked and has its roots in desire, like a person making advances to a woman who

DN 12.16 (PTS I, 230).

> recoils, or trying to embrace her although she turns her back on him: because, what will one ever be able to do for another?» This, Lohicca, is the first teacher in the world who deserves rebuke. The criticism that a person may express about him is real, true, just, and not deplorable.

In the case of the first blameworthy teacher, it is clear that he not only attempts to offer something that he does not possess, but he is also completely unaware of the fact that his teaching is not accepted by his pupils. He is like someone trying to love a woman who rejects him. The real reason for this attitude and for the desire to teach is thought to arise out of craving (*lobha*). In the sub-commentary it is specified that cupidity, that is to say, the desire for achievement and honours, arises all of a sudden, owing to the fact that one has a following of persons.[24] In the commentary we read:[25]

> «I say that this attitude [has its roots] in desire. It also belongs to this teacher who, thinking, "These are my pupils", is teaching with cupidity[26] to some [persons], although they lead their lives deviating from [his] teaching». He, too, deserves this criticism: «This attitude of yours, rooted in desire, is the reason why you have become like one who makes advances to a woman who recoils, or like one who tries to embrace her although she turns her back on him». [The phrase] «What will one ever be able to do for another?» [means]: «Begin by perfecting and correcting yourself in the doctrine in which you have instructed others! Because, what will one ever be able to do for another?» In this way [the teacher] deserves criticism [because he did not develop first of all in himself the doctrine which he claimed to teach].[27]

24 See Sv-pṭ (PTS I, 517) *ad* Sv *ad* DN 12.16 (PTS I, 230).

25 Sv (PTS II, 397) *ad* DN 12.16 (PTS I, 230).

26 See above, note 24.

27 It is interesting to note that the sub-commentary interprets the explanation in the *Sumaṅgalavilāsinī* concerning this first example of a blameworthy teacher as being relevant in part to the second blameworthy teacher as well (Sv-pṭ [PTS I, 517] *ad* DN 12.18 [PTS I, 231-232]). As a matter of fact, the phrase *«This attitude of yours, rooted in desire»* is, according to the *Līnatthappakāsinī*, the way

The idea that one needs to have direct knowledge of something before teaching it to one's pupils is expressed in the description that the Buddha gives Lohicca of the second blameworthy teacher:[28]

> Here, o Lohicca, is another teacher who has not been able to achieve the aim of samaṇaship, for which he left his home and espoused asceticism.
> Without having achieved it, he teaches a doctrine to his pupils, saying to them: «This is for your welfare, this is for your happiness!». His disciples want to listen to him, make an effort to listen to him, pay attention so as to understand and lead their lives without deviating from their teacher's teaching.
> For this he should be criticized as follows: «Venerable One, you have not succeeded in achieving the aim of samaṇaship, for which you left your home and espoused asceticism. Without having achieved it, you teach a doctrine to your pupils, saying: "This is for your welfare, this is for your happiness!". Your disciples want to listen to you, make an effort to listen to you, pay attention so as to understand you and lead their lives without deviating from their teacher's teaching. I say that such an attitude is wicked and has its roots in desire, as if a person, having abandoned his own field, were to start thinking about weeding another field: because, what will one ever be able to do for another?». This, Lohicca, is the second teacher in the world who deserves rebuke. The criticism that a person expresses about him will be real, true, just, and not deplorable.

in which the rebuke of the first teacher is worded; the phrase *«Begin by perfecting* [*and correcting*] *yourself in the doctrine* [*in which you have instructed others!*]*»* expresses, on the contrary, the rebuke of the second teacher. In short, the sub-commentary splits the comment on the first blameworthy teacher into two parts and takes the idea of it being necessary to try out upon oneself the teaching one intends to impart as being relevant to the second blameworthy teacher. The concept can be taken as applying just as well to both teachers. In the second example, the fact that a person must first find his own fulfilment in the spiritual path that he teaches to others is possibly emphasized because, in this case, the teacher manages to convince his pupils to follow him (see Sv-pṭ [PTS I, 517] *ad* Sv *ad* DN 12.18 [PTS I, 231-232]).

28 DN 12.17 (PTS I, 230-231).

Here the profound meaning of this rebuke becomes clear: one cannot teach another to tread a spiritual path if he has not trodden it himself beforehand. Therefore, the teacher who is not blameworthy is the one who possesses first-hand experience of the spiritual path along which he guides his disciples[29] the Buddha, as we are told in the *Gotamakacetiyāsutta*,[30] teaches the Dhamma in a logical manner (*sanidāna*),[31] in a convincing and liberating manner (*sappāṭihāriya*),[32] and, above all, as a result of real, direct knowledge (*abhiññā*) [of it].[33] We also come across this need for direct knowledge of what one teaches in a well-known passage of the *Dhammapada*, where we read:[34]

> First one must settle oneself in what is positive, then one can instruct another person: the wise man who acts in this way will not be dis-

29 «*The Blessed* [*teacher* (satthar)] *brings into being the path that has never been, creates the path that has never been created, discloses the path that has never been disclosed, knows the path, is an expert on the path, is skilled in the path*»; see Nidd I 190 (PTS II, 246) *ad* Sn 955 (= Nidd II 119 *ad* Sn 1148).

30 AN 3.13.3 (PTS I 276).

31 For the translation of *sanidāna*, see P. A. PAYUTTO, *A Constitution for Living Buddhist Principles for a Fruitful and Harmonious Life*, Bangkok 1998, p. 69. Another possible translation is "on good grounds" or "with a sound basis"; see NYANAPONIKA THERA and BHIKKHU BODHI, *Numerical Discourses of the Buddha*, Oxford 1999, p. 77, and BHIKKHU NYANAMOLI and BHIKKHU BODHI, *The Middle Length Discourses of the Buddha. A New Translation of the Majjhima Nikāya*, Boston and Kandy 1995, p. 635.

32 For the translation of *sappāṭihāriya*, see SISTER VAJIRA and F. STORY, *Last Days of the Buddha. The Mahā-parinibbāna Sutta*, Kandy 1998^2 [1964^1], note 23. For an ample explanation of the term *pāṭihāriya*, see Ud-a (PTS 9-11) *ad* Ud 1.1 (PTS 10-11). Cf. also *Abhidharmakośa* 7.47 and the relevant commentary (D. ŚĀSTRI, *Abhidharmakośa & Bhāṣya of Ācārya Vasubandhu with Sphuṭārthā Commentary of Ācārya Yaśomitra*, Patna 1987^3, p. 1114).

33 In this case, the interpretation of *abhiññā* as "direct knowledge" is borne out by the commentary on the passage in question, in which "direct perception" (*paccakkha*) is mentioned. See Mp 3.13.3 (PTS II, 373) *ad* AN 3.13.3 (PTS I, 276); see also MN 77.12 (PTS II, 9).

34 Dhp 158-159 (PTS 23-24).

> tressed. He should treat himself according to the principles that he teaches to others. Only the person who is well controlled can control others: the difficult thing, indeed, is self-control.

Then the Buddha concludes his description of the blameworthy teachers by illustrating a third figure:[35]

> Then there is another teacher, o Lohicca, who has succeeded in achieving the aim of samaṇaship, for which he left his home and espoused asceticism.
> Having achieved it, he teaches a doctrine to his pupils, saying to them: «This is for your welfare, this is for your happiness!». But his pupils do not wish to hear him, do not make any effort to hear, do not pay attention in order to understand, and err, deviating from the teaching of the teacher.
> For this reason he ought to be rebuked in the following manner: «Venerable One, you have succeeded in achieving samaṇaship, for which you left your home and espoused asceticism. Having achieved it, you teach a doctrine to your pupils, saying to them: "This is for your welfare, this is for your happiness!". But your pupils do not wish to hear you, do not make any effort to hear you, do not pay attention in order to understand, and err, deviating from the teaching of the teacher. I say that such an attitude is wicked and has its roots in desire, as if a person, after having severed an old bond, were to form a new one: because, what will one ever be able to do for another?»
> This, Lohicca, is the third teacher in the world who deserves rebuke. The criticism that a person may express about him is real, true, just, and not deplorable.

The commentary specifies:[36]

35 DN 12.18 (PTS I, 231-232).

36 Sv (PTS II, 397-398 *ad* DN 12.18 (PTS I, 231-232). This passage and the relevant commentary (see note 38) are both crucially important and difficult to interpret: the following is a tentative reading. The teacher's attitude, as the subcommentary seems to suggest, is blameworthy because it leads other people to think that he is by now a victim of deep distrust and that no other pupil, by approaching him, can convince him to change his position.

> [The phrase] «What [will] one ever [be able to do] for another?» in connection with the third criticism [means]: «What will a pupil ever be able to do for the one who teaches, after there has been a rejection of the teaching?[37] Without a doubt the [teacher], in such circumstances, falls into a state of inactivity and indifference (*appossukkatā*) and thinks that the doctrine, that has been understood by him alone, must be lived by him alone, revering and respecting it». In this way [such a teacher] deserves criticism.[38] This is the meaning.

The teacher, then, falls prey to discontent due to the fact that none of his pupils follow him: this leads to a state of inactivity and indifference which, spreading to other people, causes serious harm to them as well.

It is worth noticing that the phrase *«what will one ever be able to do for another?»* is pronounced not only by the *brāhmaṇa* Lohicca but also with reference to the three blameworthy teachers.[39] Apart from the overall lack of confidence in there being any possibility of doing something for someone else that this phrase expresses, the commentary on Lohicca's words states that, in this particular case, it is the pupil who cannot give anything to the teacher, thus belittling the ideal of teaching as a selfless, gratuitous task and leading to a relation which is not beneficial. In the case of the three blameworthy

[37] I read *anusāsana-m-asampaṭicchanakālato* instead of *anusāsanaṃ asampaṭicchanakālato*.

[38] *«"In this way* [*such a teacher*] *deserves criticism" means that he deserves criticism on the grounds of what has been said above, namely on account of the fact that he favours the development of a state of inactivity and indifference in his pupils»*; Sv-pṭ (PTS I, 517) *ad* Sv *ad* DN 12.18 (PTS I, 231-232). Here, I take *niyojana* as meaning "urging to", "inciting to".

[39] The phrase *«what will one ever be able to do for another?»* is taken into account in the commentary on the first blameworthy teacher but not in the commentary on the second one; see Sv (PTS II, 395) *ad* DN 12.16-17 (PTS I, 230). In the first two cases, it could represent the criticism which is directed against the first two teachers, both of whom have failed to achieve the aim of *samaṇa*-ship. Thus, it could be meant to point out that these two types of teachers have nothing to offer to their pupils since they have not achieved the spiritual progress which they claim to have reached.

teachers, the words seem to indicate that they themselves, through their attitude, make it impossible for anyone to do anything for others. The first two cannot really help others because they themselves have not fulfilled the aim of asceticism, whereas the third teacher, although he has fulfilled this aim, is not capable of overcoming the disappointment caused by his students' negative reaction and therefore makes it impossible for other students to do anything for him as he has now chosen to lead a life that denies any sort of relationship with his disciples. These few words, especially as pronounced by Lohicca, sum up what is perhaps the most negative and harmful idea and type of behaviour that a person can have or provoke in others: namely, the belief that any sort of interaction with other people is impossible and the consequent acceptance of an extreme individualism which leads to moral isolation and a lack of any fraternal relations. When this phrase is pronounced with reference to a teacher who acts wrongly, it is legitimate and expresses a definite criticism about him: he is blameworthy because, on account of his negative qualities, he has not been capable of doing anything for his disciples, or because he makes other people think he has given up all relationships with others. The crux of the matter is the capacity to interact with others, a quality which should never be lacking. Therefore, the teacher's behaviour is faulty because its chief result is to deprive him of contact with his disciples and, what is perhaps even worse, it makes this tendency towards isolation spread to other people as well.[40]

A clear distinction is drawn between the first and the third teacher, that is, between the two teachers who are rejected by their pupils. While the first one is dissatisfied because he has not fulfilled his purpose and frantically tries to attract a following of pupils so as to demonstrate, through them, a state of knowledge and authority that he does not really possess, the third one, although he has achieved

40 In this respect the *Sedakasutta* (SN 5.3.2.9 [PTS V, 168-169]) is highly significant when it points out that, contrary to all individualistic attitudes, contact with others is important and necessary.

his aim, cannot cope with the negative reaction of his pupils: he is not able to keep a firm mind, to stay mindful and totally aware, as the good teacher does.

In his explanation, then, the Buddha singles out three types of blameworthy teachers, whose attempts to teach obtain poor results: the first two have not achieved the aim that the ascetic sets himself, while the third one has achieved it. Each of these three teachers arouse feelings of reproach in other people. This is due to their incorrect behaviour, which, in turn, is the consequence of faulty reasoning: the first is moved solely by the desire for honours and recognition, the second claims to teach a doctrine without having gone into it personally, and the third, after his failure with his students who are reluctant to follow him, causes an attitude of isolation and inaction to arise in others as well as in himself. In all three cases, desire (*lobha*) is at the heart of the matter, as it stops each one of the three blameworthy teachers from doing something for others.

1.2. *The Good Teacher*

In the next part, which brings the *Lohiccasutta* to an end, the Buddha points to himself as being the fourth teacher, the one who is free from blame. In order to bear out this claim, a description of the various stages of the Buddha's spiritual evolution is inserted. The description can also be found, with some variants, in the first *sutta*s of the *Dīgha Nikāya*.[41] The proof of the good teaching and hence of the

[41] The spiritual path followed by the Buddha is given in the first thirteen *sutta*s of the DN (though each time in slightly different terms), and, more concisely, in other parts of the canon too (see, for instance, MN 77.14-38 [PTS II, 10-22]). Each time its purpose is to indicate the way to obtain the fruit of *samaṇa*ship (DN 2 and 10), the right conduct (*caraṇa*) and the right knowledge (*vijjā*) (DN 3), morality (*sīla*) and wisdom (*paññā*) as characteristics of the true *brāhmaṇa* (DN 4), to show which is the most profitable sacrifice (*yañña*) (DN 5), to understand and overcome such problems as *"Is the soul the same as the body or different?"* (DN 6 and 7), to show the accomplishment of morality, mind, and

irreproachability of the teacher lies in the fact that the pupil follows the same spiritual process as the Buddha and, by so doing, attains awakening just as the teacher attained it. I shall come back to this point in my conclusions.

The characteristics of the three blameworthy teachers – by contrast – tell us something about the requirements of the good, proper spiritual guide. He must not desire any sort of recognition from his pupils, nor must he seek fame.[42] In his search for spiritual welfare he must delve deeply and only teach others what he himself has already put into practice. Lastly, he must not give way to discouragement if he is rejected by his pupils but maintain equanimity and presence of mind. The correct way to react to the pupils' rejection of one's teaching is clearly set out in the *Saḷāyatanavibhaṅgasutta* and we shall pay closer attention to it later on.

Another extremely important quality that distinguishes the good teacher, which shows a psychological understanding of great subtlety, can be derived from reading the list of the five types of avarice (*macchariya*).[43] Indeed, the last type of avarice concerns the Dhamma and consists in a refusal to teach the doctrine for fear that one may be surpassed by one's pupil.

higher wisdom (DN 8), to show that perceptions (*saññā*) come and go because of causes and conditions, and that some of these can be made to appear and/or vanish through training (*sikkhā*) (DN 9), to show the miraculous results of the teaching (*anusāsanipāṭihāriya*) (DN 11), and to show the way leading to Brahmā (DN 13).

42 See above, note 24.

43 Namely, avarice and attachment concerning: (*a*) a particular place or one's homeland (*āvāsa*); (*b*) one's own family or social group (*kula*); (*c*) property (*lābha*); (*d*) outward appearances and lofty inner feelings (*vaṇṇa*); (*e*) knowledge of the Dhamma. See Sv (PTS III, 1026-1027) *ad* DN 33.2.1 (PTS III, 234); see also AN 5.26.4 (PTS III, 272) and As (PTS 373-377) *ad* Dhs 3.5.10 (PTS 199).

> The monk who possesses avarice of the Dhamma (*dhammamacchariya*) will not give to others as he thinks: «If he gains a deep knowledge of this Dhamma he will surpass me!».[44]

Thus the qualities that distinguish the good teacher also include a capacity to open up oneself completely to the pupil, coupled with a complete lack of fear concerning the possibility that he may lose his position of superiority.

To be attached to the fact that one possesses greater knowledge and to try to maintain this difference by preventing the pupil from learning and making progress and catching up with his teacher (and possibly even surpassing him), reveals a profound sense of insecurity that a spiritual guide should not have and shows his lack of understanding and incorrect application of the *magga*. This weakness, often skilfully disguised, will continue to be present until it begins to give way to deep calmness and a lasting sense of compassion for the pupil.

In the light of these remarks and on the grounds of the evidence we get from the examples given in the *Lohiccasutta*, we can see that the bond between teacher and pupil is based on a one-to-one relationship, with mutual understanding and reciprocal dependence. This relationship goes beyond any hierarchical difference in rank and, even if such a difference does exist, one must never become attached to it. In the *Lohiccasutta* the moral judgement that is expressed about the teacher is formulated after taking into account the pupil's reaction to his teaching. The role played by the pupils is anything but passive and they are just as important as the teacher, even though their position is different. The teacher would not be a teacher without his pupils and vice versa. Emphasis is placed not only on the

44 And the text goes on to say: «*But if, on the other hand, one does not offer* [*the teaching*] *through love of the Dhamma* [*because the person he intends teaching it to is changeable and unfit and could be harmful to the Dhamma*] *or through love of men* [*because the Dhamma is too subtle and difficult and could be misunderstood, causing problems to the person*], *then this is not* dhammamacchariya»; see Sv (PTS III, 1027) *ad* DN 33.2.1 (PTS III, 234).

teacher's learning and authority but most of all on the fact that his relationship with the pupil is, in and of itself, a means of spiritual practice, which makes it evident that the true aim must always be final liberation. In this connection, in the Vinaya there is a rule, or protocol (*vatta*), which is highly significant: it concerns pupils (*antevāsika*) and teachers (*ācariya*) in practically the same manner for both categories. According to this rule, if either the pupil or – and this is important – the teacher feels dissatisfaction (*anabhirati*) for the Doctrine, or has anxiety (*kukkucca*) or a wrong viewpoint (*diṭṭhigata*), then it is the teacher's duty towards the pupil and the pupil's towards the teacher to put matters right, either personally or by asking someone else's help or by giving a Dhamma-talk.[45] This seems to suggest that the Dhamma prevails over conventional roles and that these, albeit formally well established, cannot become cold and restrictive: the Buddha himself ruled that the bond between teacher and pupil should be thought of as being similar to a father-son relationship.[46]

P. A. Payutto has set out very clearly the specific qualities of the good teacher.[47] Of these, besides the seven characteristics of the *kalyāṇamitta*, the "good friend",[48] I would also like to mention some

[45] See Vin 1.1.18-19 (PTS I, 58-61) (= Vin 2.8.13-14 [PTS II, 231]). The same rules also apply to the preceptor (*upajjhāya*) and the pupil (*saddhivihārika*).

[46] See Vin 1.1.15, 18 (PTS I, 45, 60).

[47] PAYUTTO, *A Constitution for Living Buddhist Principles for a Fruitful and Harmonious Life*, *op. cit.*, pp. 67-69.

[48] On these characteristics, see S. COLLINS, "Kalyāṇamitta and Kalyāṇamittatā", *Journal of the Pali Text Society* XI, 1987, pp. 51-52. The teacher must be: 1) *Piyo*: "affectionate", kind and compassionate: he shows interest in his pupils and creates a friendly atmosphere; 2) *Garu*: worthy of respect, firm: he inspires confidence; 3) *Bhāvanīyo*: educated and competent: he practises constantly and makes progress; 4) *Vattā*: capable of speaking, of making himself understood and able to give suitable advice; 5) *Vacanakkhamo*: patient in discussion: he does not get angry and is not offended; 6) *Gambhīrañca kathaṃ kattā*: he is capable of explaining the most profound and difficult matters; 7) *No caṭṭhāne niyojako*: he does not lead his pupils along unsuitable and useless paths. See AN

prerogatives of the teaching method that reveal the good teacher's motivations and ambitions and his way of presenting what he has to teach. The five "qualities of the person who teaches the Dhamma" (*dhammadesakadhamma*) consist in his capacity to teach gradually, knowledge of the method, being guided by compassion, not desiring payment, and not belittling himself or others.[49] Another set of qualities that a teacher should have can be traced in many of the *sutta*s, as Payutto has pointed out. They draw attention to the Buddha's desire to show the innermost meaning of the Dhamma, to encourage its practice, to make the pupils enthusiastic, and to inspire them with joy.[50]

The *Candūpamasutta*[51] is a particularly important *sutta* that gives us a clear idea of what the concept of a correct, pure teaching method is. The teacher who says to his pupils: *«Listen to my doctrine, believe in it and devoutly make your faith manifest!»* is thought to impart an impure teaching. The teacher who, on the other hand, imparts the pure teaching, is the one who says to his pupils:

> «May they hear my doctrine! This doctrine has been well announced by the Blessed One, visible here and now, incessantly effective, inviting inspection, leading to Nibbāna, to be experienced by the wise for themselves. After hearing the doctrine they must understand it and only after they have understood will they be able to follow it according to reality».

He teaches the doctrine on the grounds of its intrinsic goodness, motivated by compassion, understanding, and shared emotion. This shows us how the good teacher is moved by a strong feeling of com-

7.4.6 (PTS IV, 32) and PAYUTTO, *A Constitution for Living Buddhist Principles for a Fruitful and Harmonious Life*, *op. cit.*, pp. 67-68.

49 See AN 5.16.9 (PTS III, 184).

50 For instance, we also find the terms *sandassetvā*, *samuttejetvā*, and *sampahaṃsetvā* in the *Soṇadaṇḍasutta* (DN 4.27, PTS I, 126). The same idea is clearly expressed in It 104 (PTS 107).

51 SN 2.5.3 (PTS II, 198-200).

passion towards human beings. His teaching is not dogmatic but clear and subject to enquiry by the pupils: it must not be accepted uncritically but constantly tested through direct experience. The description of the Buddha's teaching of the Dhamma and the discipline is particularly eloquent: it is defined as luminous and clear as only the light of the sun and the moon can be.[52]

A further important aspect of the good teacher's method of teaching is mentioned in the concluding part of the *Mahāsuññatasutta*.[53] Here, the Buddha declares that he will not educate his disciples in the same way as the potter moulds his pots: for the potter examines each pot just once, while the clay is still fresh, and then, voicing the hope that it will not break into pieces, he does not check it any more except for going over the finished pots once they have been fired, to pick out the broken or faulty ones. The Buddha, on the other hand, tests the pupil step by step and does not keep silent[54] but guides him all the time and removes any possible faults as they crop up, right from the beginning. Thanks to this attitude the teaching will certainly bear fine results and the essence of the whole message will take root. Such positive result is due entirely to the teacher's constant and unflagging commitment.

> I shall speak to you, Ānanda, incessantly correcting you; I shall speak to you, Ānanda, incessantly cleansing you. [For you, who are receiving the teaching from me,] the essence [of the paths and the fruits] will take root.[55]

52 AN 3.13.9 (PTS I, 282-283).

53 MN 122.27 (PTS III, 118).

54 Cf. Dhp-a (PTS II, 108) *ad* Dhp 76 (PTS 11).

55 The interpretation of this passage – translated here on the basis of the commentary (Ps [PTS IV, 166-167] *ad* MN 122.27 [PTS III, 118]) – certainly benefits from the reading of the *Mahāsāropamasutta* and the relevant commentary and sub-commentary (cf. MN 29.2, 7 [PTS I, 192-193, 197], Ps [PTS II, 231-232] and Ps-pṭ [CSCD 307, 311]). On the grounds of these texts, I think it plausible that "essence" (*sāra*) denotes liberation (*vimutti*). Cf. also ÑĀṆAMOLI THERA, *The Greater Discourse on Voidness. Mahāsuññatā sutta* (*Majjhima Nikāya 122*), Kandy 1965, p. 33.

Teaching must therefore be continuous and it must guide the pupil in every phase of his growth, from his very first steps. This is the only way the teacher can be sure of offering his disciples an understanding of the essence of the doctrine which he has taught them. As we shall see when we come to analyse the *Saḷāyatanavibhaṅgasutta*, the teacher must put forward his teaching with patience, equanimity, and compassion. He must not counter the pupils' reactions but keep them in mind and go on with his teaching.

2. The Birth of a Teacher

Historically speaking, the Buddha's decision to tell the world about the path to Nibbāna that he himself had taken, marks the exact moment in which the figure of the Buddhist teacher (*satthar*) makes its first appearance.[56] This is one of the finest representations we have of the Buddha's earthly existence and it is of the utmost importance if we think that the whole Buddhist message comes into being with that gesture of goodwill. It is in that very moment that Siddhārtha, now fully awakened and in a state of absolute freedom from all impurity, both physically and mentally, makes the difficult decision to operate in a world where mankind is full of suffering and incapable of awareness. At that time, he makes the choice between keeping silent

[56] See, for example, MN 26.19-24 (PTS I, 167-179), SN 1.6.1.1 (PTS I, 136-138) and Vin (PTS I, 4-7). See, in addition, the same event concerning the Buddha Vipassī in DN 14.3.1-7 (PTS II, 35-40). Cf. the different plot of the story in chapter 25 of the *Lalitavistara* and in *Buddhacarita* 14.96-103; cf. also GNOLI, *The Gilgit Manuscript of the Saṅghabhedavastu*, *op. cit.*, vol. I, Rome 1978, pp. 127-130. On this topic see P. SKILLING, "Ārādhanā Tham: Invitation to Teach the Dhamma", in *Manusaya. Journal of Humanities*, Special Issue No 4, Bangkok 2002: 84-92. I shall deal elsewhere with the problem of the episode concerning Tapussa and Bhallika which, it seems, anticipates the first *dhammadesanā*; see Mp (PTS I, 382-384) *ad* AN 1.14.6 (PTS I, 25-26), but also Vin 1.1.6 (PTS I, 3-4) where the story is told differently.

– not a blameworthy silence, being rooted in the awareness of the human condition and the complexity of the Buddhist Dhamma, which is difficult, profound, and extremely hard to follow since it goes against the tide[57] – and attempting to find a remedy for the suffering of mankind: an attempt that can be made confidently, as he is sure of the possibility of obtaining positive results.

To begin with, the Buddha ponders over the sorry situation of human beings, victims of worldliness (*ālaya*)[58] from which they cannot escape. Then he turns his attention to the extreme difficulty of understanding the Dhamma[59] and the difficulty of realizing the condition of pacification of all formations, the relinquishing of all attachments, the destruction of craving, dispassion, cessation, and Nibbāna.

> Can there be any sense in teaching what I have attained with such difficulty? This Dhamma is not easy to understand for those who are ruled by lust and aversion!
> The persons who are driven by lust and shrouded in darkness are not able to perceive what goes against the world's normal course, namely what is subtle, profound, hard to understand, imperceptible.
> Thinking these thoughts, monks, my mind yielded to inactivity (*appossukkatā*) rather than to the teaching of the Dhamma.[60]

57 See Ps (PTS II, 176) *ad* MN 26.19 (PTS I, 168).

58 I here follow the translation of the term *ālaya* which is given in BHIKKHU NYANAMOLI and BHIKKHU BODHI, *The Middle Length Discourses of the Buddha*, *op. cit.*, pp. 261, 1216-1217, note 306.

59 On the concept of specific conditionality (*idappaccayatā*) i.e. dependent origination (*paṭiccasamuppāda*), see also Vism 17.5-7 (ed. P. 440-441) and C. CICUZZA, "Osservazioni sul concetto di *natura* nel Buddhismo antico. Causalità ed equanimità", in G. BOCCALI – P. M. ROSSI (a cura di) *Atti del Seminario "La natura nel Pensiero, nella Letteratura e nelle Arti dell'India" in occasione dell'Undicesimo Convegno Nazionale di Studi Sanscriti (Milano 23 novembre 2002)*, Torino 2004, pp. 1-19.

60 MN 26.19 (PTS I, 167-168).

This, as the commentary points out,[61] seems to contradict what the Buddha had said in his previous life about his intention (*patthanā*) of saving all human beings from suffering.[62] The reason for this unexpected surrender to inactivity probably lies in the fact that it was only after he had attained his spiritual fulfilment that the Buddha actually realized the immense difficulty of the process of liberation. This definitely confirms that one of the essential requirements of the teacher is that he must first of all be deeply versed in the spiritual path that he wants to teach. The decision that leads the Buddha to teach belongs only to his last life: it is only after he has attained awakening that he can consciously and authoritatively teach others how to attain it, since he now has direct knowledge of it.

Apart from the difficulty of the Dhamma, another reason for the Buddha's silence is, as I have mentioned, the awareness that human beings are victims of defilements (*kilesa*), driven by lust, prey to hatred (*dosa*), and confused by ignorance (*moha*). Thus, they would find it hard to understand a message which is so profound and difficult to follow.

At this point, the god Brahmā Sahampati intervenes and asks the Buddha to reveal the Dhamma he has discovered:

> Open wide the door of the Deathless One! Let them hear the Dhamma that has been understood by the Unblemished One!
> As one who, having climbed to the top of the mountain, stands upon a rock and can see all the people below,
> Likewise, o Wise One, All-Seeing, ascend into the palace which is the Dhamma!
> Let He who is without suffering look at the people who are sunken in woe and overwhelmed by birth and old age!
> Arise, o Victorious Hero, Caravan-leader, free of deprivations, and walk in the world!

[61] See Ps (PTS II, 176-177) *ad* MN 26.19 (PTS I, 167-168). The text also appears in Sv (PTS II, 466-467) *ad* DN 14.3.2 (PTS II, 36).

[62] See Bv 2.55-59 (PTS 9). Cf. also Ud-a (PTS 133) *ad* UD 2.8 (PTS 15-18), It-a (PTS I, 121-122) *ad* It 2.1.1 (PTS 31-33).

> O Blessed One, teach the Dhamma because there will be people capable of understanding!

The purpose of Brahmā's intervention is, according to the commentary, to induce even those who worship the Hindū god to think of the Buddha's Dhamma as a good teaching that is worth following. But, apart from the exegesis given in the commentary, Brahmā's sole purpose in the *sutta* is to give the Buddha the opportunity (*avakāsa*) of teaching the Dhamma.[63]

The words of the last verse are particularly important as they give the assurance that in the future there will be someone who is capable of understanding the Dhamma. This reveals an implicit trust in man and in the possibility of finding a solution to the problem of suffering, and it seems to shift the emphasis from the teacher to the message. No importance is given to the satisfaction or dissatisfaction that a teacher may feel when confronted with the reaction of his pupils: what matters is that the message should get through and reach someone who is capable of understanding it. And his or her presence is certain.

The moment in which the Buddha decides to teach is marked by his decision to look at living beings in a different light, understanding their faculties, their different states of mind, and their inclinations.[64] He is moved by a heartfelt compassion for their condition and it is this factor, as we have just seen, which makes the Buddha overcome any hesitation about the possibility or need of explaining the Dhamma.[65]

Another condition which is essential for teaching is equanimity: only if one has a profound inner equilibrium can the various reac-

[63] MN 26.21 (PTS I, 169).

[64] Cf. MN 26.21 (PTS I, 169) and the relevant commentary in Ps (PTS II, 179). In the *sutta*, mention is made of the "Buddha's eye" (*buddhacakkhu*), which is qualified as *indriyaparopariattañāṇa* and *āsayānusayañāṇa*.

[65] On this last characteristic, see L. SCHMITHAUSEN, "The Early Buddhist Tradition and Ecological Ethics", *Journal of Buddhist Ethics* 4, 1997, pp. 11-12, 46-50, note 53.

tions of the pupils (or of just one pupil in the different phases of his progress) become a basis for awareness, and this awareness can then become an essential condition for a correct teacher-pupil relationship. This factor will be made clearer from the reading of the *Saḷāyatanavibhaṅgasutta*.

One concept which is important to emphasize is that the Buddha is not a victim of the same type of inactivity that, according to the commentary, is typical of the third blameworthy teacher in the *Lohiccasutta*. The latter, after he has tried to teach and has realized that nobody can understand or follow his message, gives others the impression of surrendering to the situation, giving up teaching and withdrawing into himself. In this case, the meaning of *appossukkatā* might come close to the idea of indifference and neglect, though I think it would be more correct to interpret it as a significant lack of confidence and energy. Therefore, as we saw above, this attitude is blameworthy because it has the side effect that it spreads to others and nullifies their efforts and confidence.

The situation of the Buddha – and presumably of any other good teacher who keeps silent – is different for the very reason that he has not yet decided to teach. His *appossukkatā*, his momentary inactivity, is due entirely to his awareness of the difficulty of the doctrine he has discovered and the extremely negative situation of mankind. Thus, the Buddha's attitude before the *dhammadesanā* is opposite to the attitude held by the blameworthy teachers.[66] It might be said that the Buddha depicted in the texts emerges as a teacher after an intense inner conflict, which is one of the greatest moments in Indian religious literature.

66 Perhaps this attitude can be compared to the one which inspires the solitary Buddhas. On this issue, see KLOPPENBORG, *The* paccekabuddha: *A Buddhist Ascetic*, *op. cit.*, pp. 76-78.

3. The Teacher's Way

The last part of the *Saḷāyatanavibhaṅgasutta*[67] tells us how the noble teacher,[68] the supreme leader of men who are to be tamed (*anuttaro purisadammasārathi*), goes about his teaching.[69] This way of interacting with the pupil is the result of an extremely long and difficult process of evolution, which finds its fulfilment with the acquisition of a profound compassion towards living beings, an intense desire for their welfare, and a particularly lofty form of equanimity. We shall shortly see the differences between the teacher described in this text and the third blameworthy teacher as portrayed in the *Lohiccasutta*.

The practice which goes hand in hand with the work of the teacher is called "threefold *satipaṭṭhāna*": it is mentioned only in the *Saḷāyatanavibhaṅgasutta* and it is one of the three types of *satipaṭṭhāna*.[70] Also Mahāyānic texts accept the threefold foundation of mindfulness: for example, in the *Abhisamayālaṅkāra*, the threefold *satipaṭṭhāna* (here *smṛtyupasthāna*) is seen as one of the extraordinary characteristics (*āveṇikadharma*) of the Buddha, typical of the Dharmakāya.[71] The equanimity that this form of *satipaṭṭhāna* pre-

67 MN 137 (PTS III, 215-222).

68 In the *Papañcasūdanī* the term *ariya*, "noble", is qualified as *sammāsaṃbuddha*, "fully awakened"; see Ps (PTS V, 27) *ad* MN 137.21 (PTS III, 221).

69 See MN 137.3, 21-25 (PTS III, 216, 221-222).

70 See Sv (PTS III, 752-755) *ad* DN 22.1 (PTS II, 290). Cf. Ps (PTS I, 237-240) *ad* MN 10.2 (PTS I, 56), Spk (PTS III, 178-179) *ad* SN 5.3.1.1 (PTS V, 141), Nidd-a (PTS I, 47-51) *ad* Nidd I 3 (PTS I, 9), Paṭis-a (PTS III, 695-696) *ad* Paṭis 3.4.8.1 (PTS II, 232), Vibh-a (PTS 214-215) *ad* Vibh 7.1.1 (PTS 193).

71 See AA 8.5 and Haribhadra's commentary (K. H. AMANO, *Abhisamayālaṃkāra-kārikā-śāstra Edited for the First Time from a Sanskrit Manuscript*, Kyoto 2000, p. 105; U. WOGIHARA, *Abhisamayālaṃkārālokā Prajñāpāramitāvyākhyā*, Tokyo 1932-1935, p. 915[14-16], 916[2]). See also E. CONZE, *Abhisamayālaṃkāra*, Rome 1954, p. 97, who translates *trividhā smṛtyupasthāna* as "the threefold mindful equanimity", and J. J. MAKRANSKY, *Buddhahood Embodied*, New York 1997, pp. 170-175, 234. In the *Mahāvyut-*

supposes and which is the result of the entire process set out in the *Saḷāyatanavibhaṅgasutta*, is clearly referred to in Haribhadra's commentary:[72]

> The threefold foundation of mindfulness means that He is free from attachment, aversion, and both – respectively towards those who desire listening to his teaching, those who do not desire listening to his teaching, and towards people who desire and do not desire listening to his teaching – because He abides equanimous (*upekṣaka*) and mindful.

In the *Saḷāyatanavibhaṅgasutta* this threefold *satipaṭṭhāna* is placed at the end of a process of evolution that comes about in various phases, which are summed up in the appendix to this article. Such an inward development takes one's equanimity to its highest perfection.

First of all, the text points out that there are three different types of reaction to contact with internal bases, external bases, and consciousness: a reaction of joy, of sorrow, and of equanimity. These reactions refer to two groups of persons, those who lead the life of a householder and those who practise renunciation. In the case of the first group, joy is associated with what has been achieved, grief is associated with what has not been achieved, and equanimity is necessarily superficial as the people in this group have not practised the doctrine thoroughly. In the case of the second group, joy and equanimity come from seeing things as they really are, namely impermanent, sorrowful, and subject to change, whereas grief arises when, having become aware of how the world really functions, they long for supreme liberation.

In the next phase, these states are overcome by means of one another: first, only the joy, grief, and equanimity of the ones who prac-

patti, too, the threefold *smṛtyupasthāna* is taken as one of the *āveṇikadharmas*; see Mvy 187-190.

72 See K. H. AMANO, *Abhisamayālaṃkāra-kārikā-śāstra-vivṛti. Haribhadra's Commentary on the Abhisamayālaṃkāra-kārikā-śāstra Edited for the First Time from a Sanskrit Manuscript*, Kyoto 2000, p. 105.

tise renunciation are left; then, only the equanimity based upon unity;[73] lastly, the condition of non-identification (*atammayatā*), which makes it possible for the person practising meditation not to identify himself even with the highest forms of this practice.[74] According to the commentary,[75] this state of non-identification (*atammayatā*) coincides with a total absence of longing (*nittaṇhā*) and with the insight leading to emergence i.e. spiritual awakening.[76]

The *sutta* continues with the description of the threefold *satipaṭṭhāna*, along the pattern that was previously used in the *Lohiccasutta* to describe the three blameworthy teachers, with the fundamental addition of *anukampako hitesī anukampaṃ upādāya*, "compassionate and seeking their welfare, out of compassion", a phrase which to all intents and purposes portrays the good teacher. The first of the three cases which are taken into account is the following:

> Here, monks, the Teacher (*satthar*) teaches the Dhamma to the disciples out of compassion, compassionate and seeking their welfare: «This is for your welfare, this is for your happiness!». His disciples do not desire to hear his teaching, do not make any effort to hear, do not pay attention in order to understand, and err deviating from the

73 The equanimity which is "unified and based upon unity" (*ekattā ekattasitā*) concerns immaterial attainments. Depending and relying upon it, the adept abandons and transcends that equanimity which is "diversified and based upon diversity" (*nānattā nānattasitā*), which concerns forms, sounds, etc.; see MN 137.18-19 (PTS III, 220).

74 See MN 137.20 (PTS III, 220). On this function of non-identification, see also MN 113.21-28 (PTS III, 42-44). *Jhānupekkhā*, "equanimity of *jhāna*", which is mentioned in the commentary with regard to this last phase of the process (Ps [PTS V, 27] *ad* MN 137.20 [PTS III, 220]), also appears in the classification of the various forms of *upekkhā* proposed by Buddhaghosa in the *Visuddhimagga* (Vism 4.163 [ed. p. 130]).

75 Ps (PTS V, 27) *ad* MN 137.20 (PTS III, 220).

76 See PS (PTS IV, 99) *ad* MN 113.21-28 (PTS III, 42-44) on *nittaṇhā* and Vism 21.83-110 (ed. pp. 567-572) on *vuṭṭhānagāminivipassanā*, "insight leading to emergence". See also BHIKKHU BODHI (ed.), *A Comprehensive Manual of Abhidhamma. The Abhidhammattha Sangaha of Ācariya Anuruddha*, Kandy 1999, p. 355.

> teaching of the Teacher. With that, monks, the Tathāgata is not delighted and feels no delight,[77] yet he dwells, not overflowing with defilement,[78] mindful and fully aware.

The second case that is analysed is the one in which some disciples do not follow the Tathāgata's teachings while others do. In this instance, he is not delighted with those who do not follow and is delighted with those who do follow. Although he experiences these natural feelings, by remaining constantly mindful and fully aware as the teacher in the first example, he overcomes the two extremes of delight and displeasure, "dwelling in equanimity". And it is precisely in this second case that the value of equanimity – which has developed as a result of the aforesaid practices – and its importance in the work of the spiritual leader is especially evident. Lastly, in the third case, the disciples follow the master and, although he is delighted about this, he stays mindful and fully aware, not overflowing with defilement.

It should be borne in mind that the Pāli version shows some differences compared with Haribhadra's interpretation. In the commentary on the *Abhisamayālaṅkāra*, the Tathāgata, facing his pupils' refusal to listen (*aśrotukāma*) to his teaching, is free from aversion (*pratigha*) while, in face of their acceptance (*śrotukāma*), he is free from attachment (*anunaya*). In the Pāli version,[79] the concept expressed in the text is that the Tathāgata, although obviously not de-

77 The commentary specifies that this dissatisfaction is not the sort of dissatisfaction which is based upon the life of a householder, but it is entirely due to the awareness of the situation in which those who have not entered upon the Path continue to live, since they do not follow his message; see Ps (PTS V, 27) *ad* MN 137.22 (PTS III, 221).

78 Cf. K. R. NORMAN, *The Group of Discourses*, Oxford 1992, p. 7 (translation of Sn 63). The term *anavassuto* is here qualified as *rāgāvassavena* and thus could also be translated as "free from lust".

79 Both in the PTS edition and in the Thai version (ed. by MAHĀMAKUṬARĀJAVIDYĀLAYA, Bangkok 1927, vol. 14, p. 408).

lighted (*na c'eva attamano*)[80] when his pupils refuse to listen to his teaching, nevertheless remains mentally pure and aware. At the same time, although he is – just as obviously – delighted (*attamano c'eva*) when they do accept it, he still remains mentally pure and aware.[81] It is, I think, worth pointing out that not only do the terms used by Haribhadra – aversion (*pratigha*) and attachment (*anunaya*) – not tally with the ones used in the Pāli version (*na attamana* and *attamana*), but the mental states described are also fundamentally different. In the Pāli version that is here accepted, it is admitted that the teacher feels a natural lack of delight when he sees that his pupils are not following him, but in spite of this he is still mindful and fully aware, not overflowing with defilement. In the Sanskrit version, he is free from any aversion towards them. Although both versions are valid, they express two slightly different concepts: the Pāli version focuses on the moment of discouragement which is quick to arise when the teacher notices the unsuccessful outcome of his teaching, whereas the Sanskrit version analyses the subsequent reaction, namely the aversion felt towards the pupils. The discouragement and delight in the first case, as well as the aversion and attachment in the second case, are overcome thanks to the virtue of equanimity which has been developed by spiritual practice.

In sum, it can be said that in comparison with the description of the third blameworthy teacher in the *Lohiccasutta*, in the above explanation of the good teacher's practice of awareness the following factors are highlighted: freedom from defilements such as longing, etc., compassion, equanimity, awareness, and mindfulness. These factors determine the chief qualities of an outstanding teacher, who can rightly be said to be "an incomparable leader of persons to be tamed": these qualities are his capacity of maintaining equanimity,

80 According to the commentary, the disappointment is due to the awareness of the objective difficulty of the human condition; see note 77 above.

81 In CSCD a different reading is proposed: *na ceva anattamano* instead of *na c'eva attamano* and *na ca attamano* instead of *attamano c'eva*. Here, I have opted for the reading of the PTS since it is confirmed by the commentary (Ps [PTS V, 27-28] *ad* MN 137.22-24 [PTS III, 221]).

mindfulness, and full awareness in all his reactions to the attitudes expressed by his pupils, coupled with a strong feeling of compassion towards all beings.[82] Thanks to these qualities, the teacher is able to carry on with his teaching constantly and uninterruptedly, his sole aim being the spiritual education of his pupil. He maintains a lasting state of mindfulness that constantly reminds him of his task as an educator and does not let him become distracted by his pupils' positive or negative reactions. At the core of this attitude there lies, I think, the practice of meditation, in which the mind is constantly brought back to the subject of meditation with repeated exercises of concentration, so as to overcome its natural tendency to wander. This is probably the true sense of the *satipaṭṭhāna* with regard to teaching: the relation between the teacher and his pupil must be thought of as a base for mindfulness, a real meditative practice. The ongoing, close interaction between teacher and pupil is evident, as is the fact that this relationship is vital for both of them.

4. The Miracle of Teaching

The fact that the Buddha's words are able to bring about a profound change in the disciple and persuade him to follow the Dhamma, setting in motion the beneficial process that will lead him to awakening, was believed to be of such extraordinary importance that the teaching of the Dhamma was considered one of the three wondrous methods of conviction, or miracles (*pāṭihāriya*).[83] The other two miracles are the miracle of supernormal powers and the miracle of thought reading.

82 On this point, see also SCHMITHAUSEN, *The Early Buddhist Tradition and Ecological Ethics*, *op. cit.*, pp. 11-12, 50-51, notes 54-56.

83 See, for instance, DN 11 (PTS I, 211-223) and AN 3.6.10 (PTS I, 168-173). Cf. also *Abhidharmakośa* 7.47 and the relevant commentary (D. ŚĀSTRI, *Abhidharmakośa & Bhāṣya of Ācārya Vasubandhu with Sphuṭārthā Commentary of Ācārya Yaśomitra*, Patna 1987^3, pp. 1114-1115).

The miracle of teaching (*anusāsanīpāṭihāriya*) formally consists in giving the following instructions:[84]

> You should direct your thought in this way, you should not direct it that way. You should attend [to things] in this way, you should not attend [to them] that way. You should abandon this, and, after the attainment of that, you should dwell in it.

The commentary specifies that one's thoughts should go in the direction of renunciation and not of desire; that one must develop the idea of impermanence, suffering, etc. and not the idea of permanence; that what must be abandoned is attachment to the five objects of desire; finally, that once the supra-mundane Dhamma of the four paths and fruits has been attained, one must dwell in it.[85]

The other two miracles are, so to speak, preparatory to teaching, in the sense that they make the disciple ready to listen to the Dhamma but they must not be taken as the main ones. The commentary gives the example of Sāriputta (Dhammasenāpati) who, in teaching, utilizes his capacity for thought reading, while Mahāmoggallāna exercises his various supernormal powers. But the Buddha maintains that these two methods are imperfect (*sadosa*) and, as such, he disapproves of them, solely upholding the miracle of teaching. The first two can only attract people for a short time and thus cannot lead one out of *saṃsāra*. Indeed, teaching is the only method which can truly help living beings.[86]

What is meant is that the Buddha's teaching is able to bring about a miraculous transformation in human beings: it can change negative mental attitudes (such as attachment to worldliness and its enjoyments; attachment to pride and its enjoyments; attachment to what is not peaceful and its enjoyments; abiding in a state of ignorance),[87] all of which cause suffering and are deeply ingrained in human beings

[84] DN 11.8 (PTS I, 214).
[85] See Sv (PTS II, 389-390) *ad* DN 11.8 (PTS I, 214).
[86] *Ibid.*
[87] See AN 4.13.8 (PTS II, 131-132).

from countless lives. Whatever is capable of freeing people from these powerful bonds cannot but be considered miraculous.

The miracle of teaching is illustrated by the exposition of the various stages in the Buddha's spiritual evolution, as they emerge in the pattern set out in the first thirteen *sutta*s of the Dīgha Nikāya.[88] The earthly existence of Siddhārtha until he attained the Bodhi, that is, the entire spiritual progress of the Buddha, gives disciples an example as to how to carry out their search for liberation from suffering. It can be said that what marks the miraculous aspect of teaching – namely its capacity to lead living beings to change inwardly – is precisely the paradigmatic, ideal life of the Buddha in his search for truth. His life experience bears a saving power which brings about a veritable transformation in people: it is the example set out by his life that suggests, more effectively than anything else, the best and most advantageous way to achieve salvation from *saṃsāra*, as though the Buddha's own life was the one and only real teacher.

[88] See above, note 39.

APPENDIX
(Scheme of MN 137)[89]

A) Summary

1) Six internal bases (*ajjhattika āyatana*); 2) Six external bases (*bāhira āyatana*); 3) Six classes of consciousness (*viññāṇakāya*); 4) Six classes of contact (*phassakāya*); 5) Eighteen kinds of mental exploration (*manopavicāra*); 6) Thirty-six positions of beings (*sattapadā*); 7) By depending upon this, abandon that; 8) Three foundations of mindfulness which the Noble One cultivates; 9) By cultivating the three foundations of mindfulness, the Noble One is a teacher fit to instruct a group; 10) Among training teachers, it is He who is called the incomparable leader of persons to be tamed.

B) Base Situation

SIX INTERNAL BASES	SIX CLASSES OF CONSCIOUSNESS	SIX EXTERNAL BASES
	↓	
	SIX CLASSES OF CONTACT	
	↓	
	EIGHTEEN KINDS OF MENTAL EXPLORATION	

For each of the six classes of contact among internal bases, external bases, and consciousness, there are three *manopavicāra*, by means of which the person concentrates upon the form, etc. as a cause of joy, grief, and equanimity.

↓

THIRTY-SIX POSITIONS OF BEINGS

The various types of joy, grief, and equanimity are divided up into two distinct groups: the ones based upon the life of a householder and the ones

89 The following scheme is based upon Ps (PTS V, 21-28) *ad* MN 137 (PTS III, 215-222), and the translation of the passages follows the version given by Bhikkhu Bodhi in BHIKKHU NYANAMOLI and BHIKKHU BODHI, *The Middle Length Discourses of the Buddha*, *op. cit.*, pp. 1066-1073.

based upon renunciation. The former result from desire (*kāma*), the latter result from insight (*vipassanā*).

GEHASITA

1. *Joy*. It arises when one regards as an acquisition the acquisition of forms, etc., cognisable by the eye, etc., that are wished for, desired, agreeable, gratifying, and associated with worldliness – or when one recalls what was formerly acquired and which has passed, ceased, and changed.

2. *Grief*. It arises when one regards as a non-acquisition the non-acquisition of forms, etc., cognisable by the eye, etc., that are wished for, desired, agreeable, gratifying, and associated with worldliness – or when one recalls what was formerly not acquired and which has passed, ceased, and changed.

3. *Equanimity*. On seeing a form, etc., with the eye, etc., equanimity arises in a foolish infatuated ordinary person, in an untaught ordinary person who has not conquered his limitations or conquered the results [of action] and who is blind to danger. Such an equanimity does not transcend the form, etc.

NEKKHAMMASITA

1. *Joy*. It arises when, by knowing the impermanence, change, fading away, and cessation of forms, etc., one sees as it actually is with proper wisdom that forms, etc., both formerly and now are all impermanent, suffering, and subject to change.

2. *Grief*. When, by knowing the impermanence, change, fading away, and cessation of forms, etc., one sees as it actually is with proper wisdom that forms, etc., both formerly and now are all impermanent, suffering, and subject to change, one generates a longing for the supreme liberations thus: *"When shall I enter upon and abide in that base that the Noble Ones now enter upon and abide in?"* In one who generates such longing for the supreme liberations, grief arises with that longing as condition.

3. *Equanimity*. When, by knowing the impermanence, change, fading away, and cessation of forms, etc., one sees as it actually is with proper wisdom that forms, etc., both formerly and now are all impermanent, suffering, and subject to change, equanimity arises. Such an equanimity transcends the form, etc.

C) Process: "By Depending Upon This, Abandon That"[90]

Six joys based upon renunciation	>	Six joys based upon the life of a householder
Six sorrows based upon renunciation	>	Six sorrows based upon the life of a householder
Six equanimities based upon renunciation	>	Six equanimities based upon the life of a householder
Six joys based upon renunciation	>	Six sorrows based upon renunciation
Six equanimities based upon renunciation	>	Six joys based upon renunciation
Equanimity unified based upon unity	>	Equanimity diversified based upon diversity
Atammayatā	>	Equanimity unified based upon unity

90 *tatra idaṃ nissāya idaṃ pajahatha*. The sign > in the following paragraph means that, depending and relying (*nissāya* ... *āgamma*) upon the first one, they have to abandon and transcend (*pajahatha* ... *samatikkamatha*) the second one.

TULKU, THE *GURU* BY BIRTH

FABIAN SANDERS

In the tradition of Himalayan Buddhism, known as Vajrayāna or Tantrayāna, the spiritual master is of central importance. The function of the master and his figure have an unprecedented role when compared to the other non tantric schools of Buddhism, and, indeed, it appears closer to conceptions which are more familiar to the Hindu tradition. The main reason is that Tibetan Buddhism is an esoteric and initiate tradition in which the ordinary man, the profane, undergoes a process of radical transformation: in other words one is believed to die to his/her previous life and to enter a new condition by virtue of the power of initiation. The *lama* (tib. *bla ma*), a term meaning "unsurpassed" or "supreme", confers initiation after having tested the disciple and having found him or her worthy to receive it.

In order to better clarify the significance of this event, a brief explanation of the concept of initiation among Himalayan Buddhists is in order. By the act of initiation, which may take the form of a highly elaborated ritual or be completely informal, the *lama* or *guru* is said to transmit to the disciple a divine spiritual "seed" or principle. This is believed to cause an extremely subtle yet absolutely real transformation in the adept. The transmitted principle establishes a 'spiritual

INDOASIATICA 2/2004, [409-417]

continuity' between the initiate and his final goal, just like a ray of light with its source. Through this continuity, the spiritual aspirant (*sādhaka*) may identify himself/herself with the deity involved in the initiation, which is a symbol or aspect of the supreme condition i.e. enlightenment. The innumerable deities of the Tibetan pantheon, particularly the ones who are said to be beyond the domain of cyclic existence (*saṃsāra*), are to be viewed as symbolic complexes, pure manifestations of the enlightened mind. The adept must train himself/herself in order to mentally visualize the deity during meditative sessions, gradually coming closer to it and finally merging with the deity, giving up his individuality. This self-identification with the deity is realized through the careful pursuance of a very precise method, specific to that deity, which the master explains in detail after the initiation has been granted.

The *lama* is a man, who, having received initiation, carefully applies and practices the related method with success. He is thus fit to transmit his knowledge and power to his disciples, so that they may experience for themselves the spiritual realization which he has achieved. This experience is essentially incommunicable by any ordinary means, since it does not pertain to the functions of the conceptual mind. The *lama* is a ring in the uninterrupted chain of the transmission of knowledge, the beginning of which resides in the enlightened condition itself, symbolized by the deity giving the name to the initiation rite. In the newly initiated a new life begins, as if he/she had passed through a process of death and rebirth. The adept is given a new name and the main purpose in his/her life becomes to journey to the very end of the path which the master has shown. All this is believed to be possible through the help of the *guru*, which is, ultimately, divine grace itself.

In the light of all this, one can understand why there is no text, *Tantra* or commentary that does not begin with a few verses of homage to the Buddha-s, the Bodhisattva-s, and the deities, celebrating their omniscience and their being at the root of what the human *guru* transmits. In this sense, the *lama* represents nothing else than the condition of the Buddha himself and the concrete possibility to realize it. The same can be said for the rituals which are performed in the monasteries, which invariably begin with an invocation to all the masters belonging to the spiritual lineage.

One of the most fundamental practices of any practitioner of Tibetan Buddhism, whatever be his/her level of accomplishment or the school he/she belongs to, is that of *guru-yoga* (tib. *bla ma'i rnal 'byor*) i.e. "union with the master". This practice varies according to the different schools and also the levels of insight of individual practitioners, but the central concept always remains the same. By a meditative process of visualization, the adept brings his/her body, speech, and mind to an actual identification, a state of non-duality with the *lama* which is inseparable from Buddhahood. To help in this process, great emphasis is placed on the personal representation the practitioner has of his/her master: the adept should visualize him as identical with the Buddha or his Yidam i.e. his personal tantric deity. This is well explained by a quote attributed to *guru* Padmasambhava, the great tantric master, often called "the second Buddha", which goes like this:[1]

> He who considers his *guru* to be a Buddha will realize the condition of a Buddha, he who sees him as an ordinary man will remain an ordinary man, and he who looks upon him as if he was a dog will realize the condition of a dog.

Another example sometimes mentioned by Tibetans is that of the sun, which radiates its light in all directions without distinction. However, in order to light a fire one will require a lens, so as to concentrate the light on some ignitable matter. In the same way, the teaching or truth of all the Buddha-s (*buddha-dharma*) shines in every corner of the universe but in order to acknowledge and take advantage of it the disciple needs to rely upon a qualified master who will 'concentrate' the *dharma* upon him and kindle the 'fire of knowledge'. Because of the centrality of the master or *guru*, Tibetan Buddhism is sometimes called Lamaism, a definition which is not

1 I here report a quote I've heard from Chögyal Namkhai Norbu Rinpoche.

quite correct and which is also not liked by Tibetan Buddhists. Indeed, this definition may suggest that the beneficiary of worship and devotion is the person of the *lama*, considered as a mere human individual. On the contrary, the *lama* is to be understood as he who makes the condition of Buddhahood accessible.

In view of these conceptions, the need for a divine presence within the human domain has been somehow institutionalized in tantric Buddhism through the doctrine and practice of the *tulku* (tib. *sprul sku*). The theory and application of this doctrine, even though it may have similar or comparable aspects in other traditions, is unique to Himalayan Buddhism. In order to better explain the nature of this conception, I will briefly mention the Vajrayāna doctrine of the *buddha-kāya*-s, the three "bodies of the Buddha".[2] These are the three levels of manifestation of the Buddha, from the more subtle one down to the grosser. They are generally known as the *tri-kāya* (tib. *sku gsum*): the *dharma-kāya* (tib. *chos sku*), the intellectual or spiritual body; the *sambhoga-kāya* (tib. *longs sku*), the fruition or enjoyment body; and the *nirmāṇa-kāya* (tib. *sprul sku*), the body of emanation or apparition. This last term generally refers to the manifestation in the human world of Buddha-s and Bodhisattva-s, but in addition to this meaning in the Vajrayāna it has come to designate a particular kind of person. These macrocosmic dimensions of the Buddha have their microcosmic correspondence in the three levels of experience, or instruments of action, of man: body, speech, and mind. Between the three macrocosmic *kāya*-s and the microcosmic body, speech, and mind, a kind of correspondence or homogeneity is thought to exist, which is the very characteristic that makes it possible for the individual to 'universalize' them through meditative practice. The fruit of this practice is the loosening up of all the implicit limitations of the individual condition, with the final annihilation of any distinction between the individual and universal state.

2 To be sure, the term "body", used as a standard translation for Sanskrit *kāya* and Tibetan *sku*, may sometimes cause confusion to those who are not familiar with Buddhist doctrines.

Through the practice of meditation the *sādhaka* must bring to the surface of his/her own awareness these ever more subtle yet less and less illusory dimensions and engross himself/herself into them, to the point of becoming part of them. In common parlance, it is said that he/she must replace the "impure vision" deluded by judgment and desire, with the "pure vision" or the fundamental illusory nature of all phenomena as well as their intrinsic emptiness. Thus, in the land of Tibet a particular interpretation of the concept of *nirmāṇa-kāya* or *tulku* took shape. As was mentioned before, this "emanation body" is one of the ways through which the perfect condition of the Buddha-s may become accessible to beings entangled in the realms of transmigration. In essence, it is a means of teaching. In the Tibetan view this can be achieved by a number of ways, one of which being the manifestation of individuals endowed with peculiar characteristics: the so-called incarnated *lama*-s, the *guru*-s by birth.

In obeisance to a karmic predisposition, the *tulku* – though appearing as an ordinary man – is the receptacle of a divine or spiritual principle which becomes an integral component of his being: an emanation, in this material world, of one or more aspects of Buddhahood. A typical example of this is offered by the Bodhisattva Avalokiteśvara, who is the veritable source of the Dalai Lamas' lineage. One could go further, and point out that this deity is thought to influence the body, speech, and mind of man. Some *tulku*-s are even said to be emanations of a certain deity at the level of the mind, of another one at the level of speech, and so on: the range of possibilities is vast. All these beliefs provide a wealth of precious information on the supposed nature and function of any particular *tulku*.

An interpretation popular in recent times refers to *tulku*-s as great masters of the past who have voluntarily decided to remain in this world in order to help other beings find their path to realization. This explanation, though in some sense correct, appears reductive. The Tibetan idea is that the element qualifying *tulku*-s and which allows the continuity of their lineages is not something purely human in origin and nature. Indeed, this element is said to be constituted by a divine principle which is imbibed by the *tulku*. To be sure, this interpretation might give rise to the cult of some individual, which is not acceptable in the Buddhist *dharma*. In the orthodox view, the great *lama*-s which are at the origin of some *tulku* lineage are those who have realized the "condition of a deity" and, as such, have exceeded their individuality.

But what is the reason for the presence of *tulku*-s in the manifest world? The first and foremost reason is compassion. The enlightened condition of a Bodhisattva enables him to witness the condition of suffering in which all beings entangled in the cycle of births and deaths find themselves. He thus takes action in order to help all creatures utilize and fulfill their dormant "seed of enlightenment". From his supreme condition the Bodhisattva "descends" to the various manifested worlds in order to inspire all beings. By so doing, he accepts the natural limitations of any particular realm in which he descends: therefore, he typically abides according to the laws of dependent origination (*pratītya-samutpāda*). As mentioned, the *tulku* expresses the continuity in the awareness of Buddhahood all across the diverse dimensions or states of conditioned existence, without which the attainment of liberation would be impossible. In this respect, the function of *tulku*-s is analogous to that of potent, reminding symbols: all *tulku*-s are thus viewed as 'translators' or intermediaries between the condition of Buddhahood and the world of ordinary beings. The special function of the *tulku* is to reveal to all deluded beings – according to their individual characteristics and ability to understand – the divine oneness of reality which is free from any illusory duality.

The main activity of *tulku*-s is teaching. Above all, their exemplary life and their 'revelation' of various ritual practices is believed to lead creatures on the *dharma* path towards enlightenment. It should be noted that *tulku*-s can also get legitimately involved in worldly life, in an effort to direct history towards the *buddhadharma*. Indeed, this latter function is said to be achieved in two ways: by means of a ritual act, since the local deities and all psychic forces in general are believed to be influenced and controlled through the compelling power of ritual; and by means of a direct, personal involvement in political events. In Tibet, the Dalai Lama is an example of both these modes of intervention, as the Khalkha Jetsun

Dampa has been in Mongolia. These figures unite in their very *persona* the function of supreme spiritual authorities as well as that of temporal rulers of their people.

At the time of death, the *tulku* is subject to the law of *karman* as anybody else: through all the *post-mortem* phases which will eventually lead him to a new birth, his fate or karmic trajectory will be coherent with the actions he performed during his lifetime. The divine principle which inspired him – now free from the binding force of *karman* – is believed to remain in this world and influence a newborn child. Besides being endowed with such divine principle, this special child is also believed to be endowed with memories relative to the past experiences of the deceased *tulku*. These memories are of fundamental importance for all the *lama*-s who must search for the new lineage holder, and are also thought to be very useful aids in the practice of *dharma*. When a *tulku* feels that the time has come for him to follow the messengers of Death, he is thought to 'empower' one or more objects – for instance a bowl, a robe, a ritual implement – with some kind of psychic influence. The child who is to be accepted as the new *tulku* must feel a natural affinity with these objects: during all the recognition tests, he must be able to recognize them among the many similar items which are presented to him.

All major Buddhist schools of Tibet i.e. Nyingma, Kagyu, Sakya, and Gelugpa revere a *tulku* as their highest authority. *Tulku*-s are identified in the first years of their lives by a group of *lama*-s selected for this purpose among those who had a close personal relationship with the deceased predecessor. The identification of the presence of the divine principle in a child follows a definite procedure and sets out from some indications, generally symbolic, left behind by the deceased *tulku*. It may be an indication of the direction where to begin the quest, an area, the name of the child, whether the search is to be conducted among the nomad or sedentary tribes, and so on. After selecting a few possible candidates, they are all duly examined. They undergo a number of tests such as the abovementioned recognition of objects, the ascertainment of memories which are not possibly their own, etc. Finally, one or more oracles are questioned to confirm and guarantee the correctness of the choice.

Once he is recognized the young *tulku* must undergo complex training, taking on the heavy responsibilities of his rank as well as its advantages. Thus, the boy will study for many years the sacred *sūtra*-s and the fundamental texts of the Mahāyāna tradition. He will receive various tantric initiations and will be trained in the most significant meditative practices (*sādhana*-s). He will need to complete a number of strenuous retreats, and undergo many other tests and trials before he is finally ready to take up his role as *guru*.

It should be noted that the 'recognition practice' has some exceptions, the best known of which is certainly that of the *sakya trizin* (tib. *sa skya khri 'dzin*), "the holder of the throne of the Sakya", whose office is hereditary within the Khon Family.

The reason behind the strenuous training imparted to the young *tulku*-s is that their human component needs to be elevated up to a degree of complete harmony with the divine principle. In other words, the ego is to be tamed and transcended. The young *tulku* must always be perfectly aware of his function. This means that the actions, or *karman*, of *tulku*-s can be seen and interpreted in two different ways. On the one hand, the actions done in a fully aware and mindful way can be considered as inspired by divine influence. The consequences of these actions are desirable and their effects will be positive for all. On the contrary, the actions done in a state of confusion, unconsciously, in states of intoxication, etc. should be ascribed to the individual. Ideally, the *tulku* should realize a condition of constant contemplation and mindful presence,[3] so as to master every component of his being and conform himself to the inspiring, divine principle.

For a common man it is impossible to clearly distinguish the ordinary actions of a *tulku* from the ones which are divinely 'inspired'. Spiritual realization alone enables one to discern more clearly the hidden plays of causes and effects, the nature of events. The biogra-

3 The technical term generally used in Tibetan to define this condition is *rig pa*.

phies of the great masters and practitioners are full of strange episodes in which the actions of saints bluntly contradict even the most basic doctrines of Buddhism. History in general, which is typically understood as the very history of *dharma* itself, is interpreted as a dramatic play or game, in which human actors perform all possible roles.

In conclusion, it must be remembered that the doctrine of *tulku*-s lacks a systematical theorization in the *sūtra*-s, *Tantra*-s and commentarial literature of Tibetan Buddhism, though allusions and hints are scattered all over the enormous wealth of texts which this tradition has produced. Furthermore, the interpretation of these texts may differ greatly depending upon the attitude or context of the author. A class of texts that offers many interesting indications on the nature of *tulku*-s is that of the hagiographies of masters and saints, in Tibetan called *rnam thar*. These stories are designed to allow interpretations on many different levels, according to the knowledge and interest of the reader. They can be understood as didactical or allegorical accounts as well as manuals for meditation containing sacred revelations and visions. They may be utilized as literary works, historical accounts, technical manuals, and even initiation treatises.

The relative lack of clarity and doctrinal definition concerning the *tulku* institute has given rise, in recent times, to a great proliferation of *tulku*-s and lineages, often due to worldly interests and concerns. Indeed, the presence of a resident *tulku* can greatly enhance the importance of a monastery, since this attracts flocks of pilgrims to the place. Even if the *tulku* is not linked to any significant spiritual lineage, he may increase his status and position by inducing the sponsorship of wealthy families to the monastery. The great difficulties and hardships of the Tibetan community in exile has favored this harmful practice, even if the Dalai Lama himself has repeatedly called for more caution in this respect. To be sure, the undue proliferation of *tulku*-s of lesser 'spiritual quality' can also generate turmoil and sectarian disputes, to the detriment of the genuine practice of the *buddha-dharma*. In the end, even these decadent aspects are perceived as nothing but negligible episodes in the multicoloured representation of history.

DŌGEN ZENJI, A BUDDHIST MASTER IN 13TH CENTURY JAPAN

ALDO TOLLINI

The Reformers of the Japanese Buddhist Tradition

Two events mark the religious history, and more generally the cultural history of Japan in the 12th and 13th centuries. The first is its resumption of contact with China, after a long period of interruption which meant that Japanese Buddhist monks could travel to the continent with the purpose of studying Buddhism. The second, which was closely related to the first, was a wide-spread religious awakening which influenced the history of Japanese Buddhism in the centuries to come. Buddhism had already been practiced in Japan for seven or eight centuries but had entered a period of decline and stagnation. However, at that point a veritable spiritual rebirth took place bringing fresh impetus and vitality to Buddhism. This renaissance was fostered by a few great religious reformers, charismatic leaders who were able to transform Buddhism into a Japanese form of religion.

The revival of Buddhism in the Kamakura period (1185-1333) was characterized by two main currents, both concerned with overcoming the prevailing situation of decline and conventionalism. The first was that of religious leaders who persisted in the traditional approach of importing Buddhist teachings from China, as had always been the case in the past. They sought new spiritual experience in China which at that time was considered to be the homeland of Buddhism, and therefore followed in the wake of a well-established tradition. They justified their position as religious leaders on the strength of having been authorized by Chinese masters whose teachings they could then transmit. They considered themselves to be the heirs to an uninterrupted lineage starting with the historical Buddha, of whom they believed they were the descendants, along the line of Dharma transmission which passed from India to China and from there to Japan. The main representatives of this current were Eisai (1141-1215) and Dōgen (1200-1253).

Another current is represented by those masters and traditions which had little or nothing to do with Chinese schools, which was generated by the personal experience and original conception of representatives of the Japanese Buddhist world. Their legitimacy was not based on the authority of any particular tradition or master, but rather on the power of their own intuition and charisma. In fact, they were all endowed with strong personalities and with special charisma, as in the case of Hōnen (1133-1212), and especially Shinran (1173-1262) and Nichiren (1222-1282).

Without exception all of them considered their teaching to be that of true Buddhism, at times assuming a critical attitude towards other forms of Buddhism. The former current upheld the purity of the doctrine on the basis of uninterrupted transmission from master to disciple, from enlightened person to enlightened person, and claiming that the understanding had been genuinely preserved and had remained unchanged over the centuries and throughout the transmission. The latter, on the other hand, affirmed the validity and efficacy of its own teaching on the basis of its ability to influence the masses through the personality of its own leaders: their strength did not lie in being descendants of a long and prestigious tradition, but rather of convincingly representing the ideal revival of a decaying tradition.

The need for this revival and for a genuine and innovative impetus was strongly felt, mirroring the demand for true spirituality which characterized Japanese culture. The traditional schools were perceived as alien, or as a foreign product that affected the innermost spirit of the Japanese only in a superficial manner. This was why these masters assumed that they were responding to a deeply felt need.

While the representatives of the first current made a case for the soundness and authority of tradition, the others made the expectations of the masses their own, giving birth to more approachable forms of religiosity.

It is most interesting to observe how different ways of personifying the role of the Buddhist master clearly emerged in this situation. Different approaches to teaching, transmission and spiritual authority, in other words different ways of embodying the function of a master appeared and took firm roots among the great religious reformers of this period, i.e. the above mentioned Hōnen, Shinran, Nichiren, Eisai and Dōgen.

As noted, an initial approach to the definition of categories of Buddhist masters is the result of different attitudes towards tradition. Some perpetuate it, holding it in high esteem, for example the masters of the *Zen* tradition, while others reject it proposing original teachings, as, for instance, the Pure Land[1] masters. However, one can outline another category of Buddhist masters, bearing in mind that the above categorization evidently influences that which follows. Thus, we can distinguish three kinds of Japanese Buddhist masters in the Kamakura period:

1. A master who transmits a consolidated tradition without making any personal contributions;
2. A master who transmits a teaching which is the result of personal elaboration;
3. A master who transmits a consolidated tradition as the fruit of personal experience.

Pure Land or Amidism is a Buddhist school that flourished in China and then in Japan, where it developed into two schools: Jōdoshū (School of the Pure land) and Jōdo Shinshū (School of the True Pure Land).

In the first case, the master is convinced of the validity of a consolidated tradition and considers it worthy of transmission. The authority of his teaching is grounded on this tradition and his purpose is that of succeeding in transplanting an alien doctrine into a new environment. In the Kamakura period, Eisai is a typical representative of this kind of master and in fact he does not teach a personal doctrine but transmits the teachings of the Chinese *Linji chan* school. He achieved transmission in Japan by means of doctrinal compromise and political sponsorship, and thought that the *Linji chan* school could become acceptable in Japan only through adaptation. The most important aspect for him was to be successful in his transmission.

Shinran and Nichiren are typical exponents of the second kind of master. For them tradition, that is to say the *Tendai* school, remains in the background and plays an altogether minor role. What counts is the ability to convince and convert. This is the reason why their message is often geared to answering the demands of the people by giving concrete responses. Their strength lies in the popular support they receive and in their fundamental communicative tool, i.e. persuasive ability.

The third kind of master, unlike the first, considers tradition to be a personal experience, and, in a sense, incorporates the other two types of master. On the one hand he strives to transmit a tradition, but at the same time, as in the second case, his teaching is also derived from personal experience and any achievement is the result of original elaboration. In other words, personal contribution becomes encompassed into tradition, or even can coincide with it. This is the case of Dōgen, of whom I will discuss in greater detail below. The principal aim for this kind of master is the transmission of his personal interpretation of the doctrine, and consequently the contents of the doctrine is crucial.

Another distinction between the three kinds of masters can be observed from their attitude towards monastic rules. While the first kind of master, for example Eisai, strictly observes precepts and rules considering compliance with them to be of the utmost importance, for the second kind, for example for Shinran e Nichiren, precepts and rules are not considered to be important, and this is why they were often criticized and misunderstood. Lastly, for Dōgen, discipline and rules are important and in fact he devoted considerable time and energy to describing them accurately and to explaining the importance of observing them. However, for him they are not a central factor in monastic training.

In the *Zuimonki*, he says:

> You should follow the precepts and rules for eating. However, it is wrong to insist on them considering that they are essential, making them into the practice itself and expecting to be able to obtain the Way by adhering to them. We follow them simply because they are the activity of Zen monks and the life style of the children of the Buddha. Even if observing them is good, we must not consider them to be our main practice. However, I do not mean to say that you should neglect the precepts and become indulgent with yourself. Such an attitude would be a distortion and not that of a Buddhist practitioner. We follow the precepts and the rules just because they are normal practice for a Buddhist and are the tradition in a Zen temple. When I was in the monastery in China, I never met anyone who considered them to be the main commitment.[2]

In this regard, it must be remembered that for Dōgen practice does not consist as much in action as in how action is carried out.[3] Since at every moment the reality which surrounds us is that of Buddha-Dharma, we should behave so as to become an integral part of it in an ethically impeccable manner, so that we become consciously part of the world of Buddha-Dharma. Dōgen's insistence on rules is the way in which he transmits the profound meaning with which every single act of our daily life is endowed, since this is in itself practice of the Way. Dōgen thus responds to the superficial attitude we tend to have towards our daily actions: in fact, these actions should be the

2 Furuta SHŌKIN (ed.), *Shōbōgenzō Zuimonki*, Tokyo, Kadokawa shoten, 1989, pp. 17-18. The translations from Japanese of the quoted passages are mine.

3 A remarkable example is found in the *Tenzō kyōkun* (*Instructions to the Cook*), a text in which Dōgen deals with every-day behaviour, using the activity of the monastery cook as an example.

expression of the sacred nature of our existence. Then, when everything we do is considered and experienced as sacred, our life becomes a sacred life and shows how we live out the Way in every aspect of our everyday life.

Dōgen wrote a large number of texts describing in great details the rules for daily monastic life: these are collected in the *Eihei shingi* (*The Pure Dispositions for the Monastery of Eiheiji*).[4] Rather than as a list of prohibitions and obligations, his description of rules and precepts is used to explain how every action in daily life has a deep meaning as practice of the Way and as the expression of a realized Buddha.

Also, the way in which the above mentioned three types of master disseminated their teachings shows marked differences. Eisai had large and important monasteries built, especially in Kamakura, the seat of the Shogun government,[5] and attracted the ruling classes and the wealthier strata of the population. Dōgen, instead, addressed himself to a small group of disciples with whom he retired to the mountains, teaching a highly elitist and demanding doctrine, directed exclusively to monks. Lastly, Shinran and Nichiren, by teaching an "easy practice" accessible to all, were successful among both the rural population and city dwellers, in other words, the lower classes. The *Tannishō*, Shinran's basic text, states:

> We call it "easy practice" just because the invocation of the name has been made easy for uneducated people who have no knowledge of the path of the sutras and of the commandments. On the other hand, the Path of the Saints requires study, and therefore is called "difficult practice".

4 English translation by Daniel LEIGHTON TAIGEN & Shohaku OKUMURA, *Dogen's Pure Standards for the Zen Community: A Translation of Eihei Shingi*, Albany, N.Y., State University of New York Press, 1996.

5 Japan in the Kamakura period was governed by the warrior class, headed by the *Shōgun* who resided in Kamakura.

> […] Even if other teachings may be superior, we cannot follow them, because they are beyond our ability.

Master Dōgen

Let us take a closer look at master Dōgen and how he embodies the role of the master.

For Dōgen true Buddhism is the Buddha-Dharma correctly transmitted from generation to generation, from Buddha to Buddha, from Patriarch to Patriarch, from master to master, and the criteria for the correct transmission of the Dharma is the master's acknowledgement that his disciple has obtained enlightenment. Therefore, true Buddhism is based on the transmission of the experience of enlightenment. In his teaching, true legitimacy consists in having had this experience. In the *Bendōwa* chapter of his *Shōbōgenzō*, Dōgen says:

> Besides, in order to receive and transmit Buddhism, we must be sure to choose a master who has experienced enlightenment and a scholar who knows how to line up words as one's master will not suffice. This would be like a blind man leading a group of blind men. In our line of direct transmission from Buddha to master, we honour those masters who have all experienced enlightenment and who abide firmly in the law of the Buddha.[6]

In the process that leads to enlightenment, it is indispensable to be guided by a master, without whom no true practice is possible. Since the object of transmission is the experience of enlightenment, transmission to another person, in this case the disciple, can only take place through an enlightened person, i.e. a master. Outside of these established roles, there can be no transmission. The relationship between master and disciple serves the purpose of facilitating the passage of a meaningful experience, the ultimate role of the master be-

[6] Etō SOKUŌ (ed.), *Shōbōgenzō*, Tokyo, Iwanami shoten, 1986, vol. 1, p. 63.

ing that of transmitting enlightenment. In the *Mitsugo* chapter of the *Shōbōgenzō*, Dōgen observes:

> However, those who have not heard the teaching of a good master, even though they are seated on the lion's seat (from where the Buddha preaches), have never even seen the truth in a dream.[7]

And, in the *Zuimonki*, he says:

> (You should) gradually change your thought in order to follow your master's instructions.
> [...] You should believe your master if he says that the Buddha is nothing but a toad or a worm, and put aside your previous ideas.
> [...] Suppose you are on the top of a one hundred foot pole and you are told to let go and climb a step further without fearing for your life. In such a situation, if you say that you can practice the Buddha Way only if you are alive, you are not following your master's teachings. Consider this carefully![8]

Dōgen's legitimacy is based on the certification of his lineage from a Chinese master and on the transmission of enlightenment from mind to mind. The authority of his teaching springs from his experience of enlightenment. According to Dōgen, Buddhism does not consist in the canonical texts, nor in the rituals and all the various aspects of monastic life. It is not even doctrine, but rather the experience of enlightenment. This is, after all, the real essence of the Buddha-Dharma. Were it not for enlightenment, what would the Buddha's teaching be? The true value of Buddhism does not lie in the superiority of its doctrine or in its preaching the truth, but in the fact that this Way can lead to enlightenment. This is why Dōgen does not teach Buddhism by preaching and spreading the Buddha's doctrine, but he rather teaches enlightenment, namely, the Path that leads to it. Therefore, for Dōgen the legitimacy of his role as a master comes from

7 *Ibid.*, vol. 2, p. 249.
8 SHŌKIN, *op. cit.*, p. 43.

having obtained enlightenment in the framework of a consolidated tradition.

In the *Shisho* chapter of the *Shōbōgenzō*, he writes:

> Buddhas without fail transmit the Dharma to Buddhas, and Patriarchs transmit the Dharma to Patriarchs, and this ensures the certainty of realization. This is direct transmission. Therefore it is Supreme Enlightenment. Those who are not Buddhas cannot confirm another Buddha and those who do not obtain the confirmation of being a Buddha, cannot be a Buddha.[9]

Dōgen's Buddhism is characterized by a keen sense of spiritual tradition and by the importance attributed to orthodox transmission. This latter one is known as *shōden, jun'ichi no buppō*, or "the unique Buddha-Dharma correctly transmitted".

In the field of *Zen*, transmission took place "from mind to mind" (*ishin denshin*), from master to disciple. The master would find "the right vein" (*shōmyaku*) in the disciple, just as a blood transfusion makes the donor and the recipient identical. Transmission from mind to mind is like a torch-bearer's flame that is always the same, transmitted from one torch to another. The vehicle changes but the flame does not. In the same manner, though transmitted from one man to another, the nature of the teaching and of enlightenment remain unchanged.

In the *Butsudō*, he says:

> This is the correct and traditional teaching of the Buddha. Only the rightful successors of authentic transmission have received the authentic transmission of this Dharma.

Dōgen then continues by saying:

9 SOKUŌ, *op. cit.*, vol. 1, p. 237.

> The true life of this Buddha-Dharma is simply this correct transmission. Since Buddha-Dharma has been correctly transmitted in this way, it has continued in a legitimate manner.
> If the principle of establishing independent schools were correct, the Buddha-Dharma would have declined since its very beginnings in India. Who could ever respect the various schools established independently? Who could ever choose what is right and what is wrong among the various schools established independently? Not being able to choose between what is right and what is wrong, who ever could decide what is the Buddha-Dharma and what is not? If we do not clarify this, how can we speak of Buddhism? [...]
> The Dharma of the Buddhas and the Patriarchs has been completely handed down and there is no need for innovation. This truth is the bones and the marrow of the Way.[10]

Thus the Buddha-Dharma can only be experienced through ceaseless and traditional transmission. The new schools that endeavour to introduce changes in the Buddhist doctrine place themselves outside the true teaching.

It is particularly interesting to note that Dōgen attaches great importance to the issue of orthodoxy. Within an uninterrupted lineage tradition is legitimated, but outside of it who can establish which teaching is the true teaching? On various occasions in his principle work, the *Shōbōgenzō*, Dōgen complains about the new schools which call themselves Buddhist, but that according to him give an erroneous interpretation of the doctrine. At the time, this tendency of accusing other schools of misinterpreting the original teachings was very widespread. Dōgen's stand with regard to the new schools is that of a protector of tradition and orthodoxy.

In the same *Butsudō* text he vehemently opposes the definition of *zenshū* (*Zen* school) which was applied to his teachings. He strongly rejects this definition maintaining that such a school never existed, neither in India nor in China, and consequently there is no reason why it should exist in Japan. In other words, he denies the existence

10 *Ibid.*, vol. 2, pp. 223-224.

of such a school not just concerning his own teaching but in general! A *Zen* school does not exist, because only the correct teaching of Buddhism exists and not schools with different teachings and interpretations.[11] There is only one Buddhism for Dōgen, and this is in the form of a well-defined tradition of correct transmission. For him, the various schools are nothing more than diversions and corruptions and, as such, should be rejected. Buddhism acknowledges no deviation, innovation or interpretation and he considers that only his teaching corresponds to the true, original message of the Buddha. It must be underlined that he was not alone in upholding this opinion: the practice of discrediting other masters was common at the time.

According to Dōgen - who as we have seen was a strong supporter of tradition and lineage - the source of doctrinal authority lies in the teachings of the Buddha himself as well as in those of the masters and Patriarchs of the past. It is from their exclusive example that we must learn what is to be learnt, since they alone had attained the highest peak of wisdom and knowledge. By holding to this attitude, Dōgen strays from the general tendency of the *Chan* and *Zen* schools which consider scriptures, texts, and language in general to be unreliable and not capable of conveying the true teaching. This explains Dōgen's constant quotation of the Chinese Buddhist texts, the *sūtra-s*, and the sayings of the Patriarchs. This insistence on the traditional texts, quoted as the source of the correct teaching, demonstrates that they were particularly important for him.

Although he never questions their contents, his interpretation of the doctrine is certainly original and does not always coincide with that of the texts of the past. Dōgen does not consider himself an innovator (despite the fact that he was one). He sees himself simply as a link in the chain of transmission of the true teaching from mind to mind, believing the *sūtra-s* to be the repository of true teaching as long as they are interpreted correctly. Indeed, truth is lost when the texts are misinterpreted. His originality consists in interpreting the

[11] His descendants, on the basis of his teaching, established the *Sōtō Zen* school, which at present is one of the main Buddhist schools in Japan.

texts creatively and in giving them a personal reading, sometimes utilizing very particular linguistic techniques in his interpretation of the *sūtra-s*. In other words, he maintains that more often than not the texts are not self-evident and that even the parts of them which appear to be merely discursive have profound implications. Thus, texts should be interpreted correctly and adequately "disclosed". Nonetheless, Dōgen stresses that the orthodox doctrine is to be found in the texts and that practitioners should adhere to what is written in them: not however by passively accepting the superficial meaning of words, but rather by searching deeply into their structure, also questioning the inner meaning of each single sentence. The quest for meaning, both in the texts and in daily life, is the means which leads to understanding and enlightenment. The effort the practitioner must make is the quest for the meaning of reality, that is, the understanding of its true nature, which is no different from enlightenment. If correctly used, texts and language are believed to further understanding.

One of the most striking examples of this approach, and also perhaps the most relevant from the point of view of Dōgen's thought, is contained in the *Busshō* ("Buddha-nature") chapter of the *Shōbōgenzō*. Commenting on the famous sentence *yi qie zhong sheng xi you fu xing* (in Japanese: *issai shūjō kotogotoku busshō ari*) of the *Mahā-parinirvāṇa-sūtra*, of which the current meaning is: "All living beings have Buddha-nature", Dōgen interprets it as: "All living beings *are* Buddha-nature". From a linguistic point of view, Dōgen arbitrarily re-groups the words *xi you* (in Japanese: *kotogotoku... ari*) reading them as a single Japanese word *shitsuu*, which is a daring yet not impossible interpretation. The term *you* may mean both "have" and "be", and Dōgen avails himself of this ambiguity to reformulate the meaning of the sentence.

From a doctrinal point of view, the identification of all living beings with Buddha-nature has radical consequences for Dōgen's thought. In other words, since he refuses to consider Buddha-nature as a latent potentiality to be developed through practice, and since he identifies it with sentient beings, Dōgen offers an original interpretation both of practice as well as of realized Buddha nature.

According to tradition, Dōgen is the ideal embodiment of the figure of the master: he renounced political support and sponsorship, refused compromises and half-measures, and chose to base his own prestige on spiritual experience, the only guide he would recognise as valid. For this very reason, he took refuge far from the centres of power and devoted himself to a few but highly motivated disciples, who followed him away from the distractions of worldly society.

After his return to Japan in 1227, Dōgen perceived the difficulty of disseminating his teaching in an environment where rivalry and the need for high-ranking support prevailed. Realizing that he could in no way divulge the teachings he had acquired in China without making compromises, he opted to leave the bustle of the world of politics and went as far away as possible from the predominant Buddhist schools of his times. Having retreated from the world with a small group of followers, he devoted the rest of his life to teaching and writing.

This choice can partly be attributed to his personality, but it also reflects his determination to keep his teaching pure. He stuck to this ideal despite his awareness of the fact that a more compromising attitude would have endowed him with greater prestige and, possibly, more followers.

While in his retreat, Dōgen did not try to attract more disciples, maintaining that those who really wanted to learn Buddhism would leave everything behind them and take refuge in his temple. His attitude was very different from that of Shinran and Nichiren who had developed an independent school. Not being supported by the legitimating force of tradition, and lacking a Chinese background, they entrusted the success of their teaching to their ability to convert the masses: their legitimacy was represented by their popular following. The more followers they had—so they thought—the more their teaching would be acknowledged also by other schools.

Dōgen believed that the malaise of the time was due both to the degeneration of the Buddhist schools and to the widespread instability and decline of social values. His answer lay in his quest for a new spiritual dimension. He thought that the only possible contribution to the foundation of a new spirituality had to spring from within the long-established tradition, not from a deviation from it. He believed that the solution could be found in the regenerative essence of Buddhism. The only possible path was that of returning to the authentic and original Buddhist teachings, which had existed prior to the founding of the different schools: the teachings of the Buddha Śākyamuni. Purity and dedication were the tenets to which he always stuck. He thought that degeneration was not inherent to Buddhism but rather the consequence of the manipulation of the original doctrine, and believed that subjective interpretation led to deviation. The Buddha-Dharma could never be taken as the result of human fabrication, but as a gift, a revelation offered by the Buddhas and Patriarchs to human beings. This is why Dōgen did not consider his teaching to be a personal contribution to Buddhism (as it actually is) but thought of himself as the follower of an uninterrupted tradition dating back to the Buddha Śākyamuni. All masters and Patriarchs are thought to be on the same level, who understand the doctrine in the same way, though couching it in different linguistic expressions. The idea is that the whole of his teaching was transmitted to him by his master, who, in his turn, had inherited the same teaching from his master, and so on.

Devoted to uncompromising practice and untiring teaching activity, committed to the transmission of his own profound experience and indifferent to praise and criticism, Dōgen unequivocally embodies the ideal spiritual master. To be sure, he is considered to have been one of the greatest masters of the Buddhist tradition in Japan. Over and beyond the limited scope of his environment, I think that we can find the more general traits of the spiritual master or *guru* in him. Other great figures of his times, such as Shinran and Nichiren, can also be considered in the same way, though it should be remembered that their experiences were profoundly different. Their almost opposite personalities show in how many diversified ways the paradigm of the *guru* could take form in 13th century Japan. One might ask what Dōgen, Shinran and Nichiren had in common, what made each one of them a *guru*, beyond doctrinal differences, different attitudes and personal charisma? Perhaps it was their commitment to the transmission of their genuine spiritual experience. In other words, their awareness that personal experience is the essence of spirituality and worthy of being passed on to others.

The above description of Dōgen as a spiritual master has become part of an established tradition and is firmly rooted on a popular level. However, Dōgen's successors put a completely different accent on his teaching, starting with Keizan Jōkin (1268-1325) who transformed the *Sōtō* school into a mass movement. When directed to the masses, the uncompromising teachings of Dōgen and their strongly elitist nature came to absorb esoteric rites and popular cults. In everyday life, *Sōtō* monks gave their support to the lay community and, during difficult times such as famines, became the leaders of popular causes thus gaining the trust of the people.

Nevertheless, Buddhism during Dōgen's time should be considered from a more critical perspective since the historical events surrounding the *Zen* school were probably more complex than they appear, although we do not have a detailed picture. It is certain that during Dōgen's and Eisai's times, other *Zen* schools flourished and had an extensive following. Besides, many Chinese masters of the *Chan* tradition came to Japan to teach. No doubt this situation influenced Dōgen. His attitude towards the governing power as well as some aspects of his teaching were conditioned by these competitive movements. For instance, we know that many of his disciples came from the so-called *Darumashū* movement, founded by a certain Nōnin. Certainly the deviation from Dōgen's original teaching, which took place soon after his death, is to be ascribed to the influence that Nōnin's teaching exerted among Dōgen's followers. Besides, Dōgen's insistence on the authority of tradition and the importance of transmission from a Chinese master, may be interpreted as a means for discrediting his rivals, who, like Nōnin, did not have a prestigious background. His persistent affirmation of the purity of tradition and the formal aspects of transmission may be seen as a claim for superiority and a means of criticizing popular self-proclaimed *Zen* masters.

These considerations, however, should not overshadow Dōgen's greatness as he not only convincingly embodied the highly idealized figure of the master, but, above all, was an extremely original and creative *maître-à-penser*. Even nowadays in Japan Dōgen is viewed as one of the greatest thinkers of all times and indeed his teaching has a great deal to offer us.

Dōgen's heritage is both rich and varied. If I were to pin-point the essence of his teaching, I think it might be summed up as his will to bring about the recognition that the self is an intrinsic part of the Buddha-Dharma which constitutes the reality of our lives. While the current image of Buddhism is that of a doctrine that leads to liberation from mundane conditioning, bringing about a state of independence and non-involvement, Dōgen's teaching, on the contrary, seems to lead us in the opposite direction, i.e. to a state in which men and women come to realize that they are part and parcel of the enlightened reality which surrounds them.

BIBLIOGRAPHY

Abe Masao, Heine Steven (eds.), *A Study of Dogen: His Philosophy and Religion*, Albany, N. Y., State University of New York Press, 1992.

Bielefeldt Carl, *Dogen's Manuals of Zen Meditation*, Berkeley, University of California Press, 1988.

Bodiford W. M., *Soto Zen in Medieval Japan*, Honolulu, University of Hawaii Press, 1993.

Cleary Thomas (trans.), *Rational Zen: The Mind of Dogen Zenji*, Boston & London, Shambhala, 1993.

Collcutt M., *Five Mountains. The Rinzai Zen Monastic Institution in Medieval Japan*, Cambridge, Harvard University Press, 1981.

Faure Bernard, "The Daruma-shū, Dōgen, and Sōtō Zen". In *Monumenta Nipponica*, vol. 42, n.1 (Spring 1987): 25-55.

Heine Steven, *A Dream Within a Dream: Studies in Japanese Thought*, New York, Peter Lang Publishing, 1991.

Kim Hee-Jin, *Dogen Kigen: Mystical Realist*, Tucson, The University of Arizona Press, 1987.

Lafleur William R. (ed.), *Dogen Studies*, Honolulu, University of Hawaii Press, 1985.

Leighton Taigen Daniel, Okumura Shohaku (trans.), *Dogen's Pure Standards for the Zen Community: A Translation of Eihei Shingi*, Albany, N. Y., State University of New York Press, 1996.

Merzel Dennis Genpo, *Beyond Sanity and Madness: The Way of Zen Master Dogen*, Charles E. Tuttle Co., 1994.

Otake Akihiko (ed.), *International Symposium. Dogen Zen and its Relevance for our Time* (Stanford University, 23-24 October, 1999), Tokyo, Sotoshu Shumucho, 2000.

Stambaugh Joan, *Impermanence is Buddha-nature: Dogen's Understanding of Temporality*, Honolulu, University of Hawaii Press, 1990.

Takahashi Masanobu, *Essence of Dogen*, London, Kegan Paul International, 1983.

Tanahashi Kazuaki (ed.), *Enlightenment Unfolds: The Essential Teachings of Zen Master Dogen*, Boston & London, Shambhala Publications, 1999.

Tollini Aldo, *Pratica e illuminazione nello Shobogenzo. Testi scelti di Eihei Dōgen Zenji*, Roma, Ubaldini Editore, 2001.

Uchiyama Kosho, *Refining your Life: From the Zen Kitchen to Enlightenment*, New York, Weatherhill, 1983.

Yokoi Yuho, Daizen Victoria (eds.), *Zen Master Dogen: An Introduction with Selected Writings*, New York, Weatherhill, 1976.

Zi yue, "The Master said...", or Didn't He?

Maurizio Scarpari

Mais, pour nous autres qui ne sommes pas à la recherche d'une orthodoxie, la possibilité n'est pas exclue de plusieurs transmissions, toute authentiques, d'un enseignement qui se serait formé et déformé en passant de bouche en bouche, sans cesser d'être attribué à Confucius, et nous ne voyons aucune nécessité de considérer comme faux ce qui n'est qu'une version différente; même quand il y a contradiction, cela prouve seulement que les traditions se sont constituées sur certains points de façon indépendante dans les diverses écoles dont dérivent nos textes, sans qu'il y ait même à proprement parler erreur, puisque l'attribution de tous ces détails d'explication à Confucius ne nous apparaît pas comme nécessaire.

Henri Maspero[1]

In Chinese literature, *zi yue* "The Master said..." refers to Confucius, the supreme master of the tradition and "probably the most influential thinker in human history", according to Roger Ames and

[1] H. MASPERO, "La composition et la date du Tso tchouan", *Mélanges chinois et bouddhiques*, Bruxelles, Marcel Istas (Louvain), 1932, pp. 137-215: 140-141.

Henry Rosemont.[2] The expression *zi yue* is the *incipit* of hundreds of aphorisms quoted in the *Lunyu* (*Selected Sayings* [*of Confucius*] or, in their more frequently translated form, *Analects*),[3] our main source for understanding Confucius' thought. The *textus receptus*, posthumously put together by disciples and followers, is so inorganically structured that it appears to be an unsystematic series of maxims, conversations, and anecdotes often lacking in context and expressed so laconically and in such a minimalist style that very different readings seem possible. The fragmentary and unmethodical nature of the collection has brought about the proliferation of an imposing amount of exegetical criticism as well as the formation of distinct currents among the disciples, the latter being in constant competition with one another. Precepts and doctrines are presented in such a sober manner as to sometimes disconcert the reader. Herbert Fingarette initially described them as "an archaic irrelevance" in a slim volume on Confucius which, thirty years ago, "revitalised all our thinking about the sage".[4] He was subsequently overwhelmed by them and noted: "There are distinctive insights in the *Analects*, which are close in substance and spirit to some of the most characteristic of the very recent philosophical developments".[5] Others recognize the enormous influence of Confucius on the Chinese tradition, going so far as to draw a comparison with "the *combined* influence of Jesus and Socrates in the Western tradition",[6] yet do not hesitate to underline the lim-

2 *The Analects of Confucius: A Philosophical Translation*. Translated, with an Introduction, by R. T. AMES and H. ROSEMONT, Jr., New York, Ballantine, 1998, p. 1.

3 In the *Lunyu*, when Confucius converses with a ruler or a high-ranking official, his surname, Kong, followed by the epithet *zi*, "Master", is used as a form of respect. Where Confucius speaks about himself, he generally uses his personal name Qiu or Kong Qiu. In chapter 19, his courtesy name, Zhongni, is also used.

4 A. C. GRAHAM, *Disputers of the Tao: Philosophical Argument in Ancient China*, La Salle, Ill., Open Court, 1989, p. 23.

5 H. FINGARETTE, *Confucius: The Secular as Sacred*, New York, Harper and Row, 1972, p. vii.

6 B. W. VAN NORDEN, "Introduction", in ID. (ed.), *Confucius and the* Analects: *New Essays*, Oxford, Oxford University Press, 2002, pp. 3-36: 3.

ited philosophical importance of the work.[7] Bryan Van Norden, for example, holds that "the *Analects* is like the *Dhammapada* or the *Gospel* of Matthew. All of these are works of great beauty and ethical insight, and all have helped inspire great philosophy, but none is itself a philosophical work."[8] How, then, can we account for the fact that "no book, in the entire history of the world, has exerted, over a longer period of time, a greater influence on a larger number of people, than this slim little volume?"[9]

Indeed, Confucius and the *Lunyu* have for centuries been considered enormously authoritative and prestigious, and continue to be considered so in China, East Asia, and to a certain extent in the West. What then is the real value of the *Lunyu*, and to what extent can the received text be considered representative of Confucius' thought?

Arguments concerning the attribution, composition, and authenticity of the *Lunyu* have been ongoing for at least the last two millennia. In the opinion of most specialists, the *textus receptus*, in twenty *pian* (books or chapters, see *infra*), is the result of a complex editorial undertaking involving the selection and synthesis of varied mate-

7 One of the first scholars to highlight the limited philosophical importance of the *Lunyu* was Zheng Xuan (127 – 200), the author of the earliest substantially extant *Lunyu* commentary, the *Lunyu Zheng shi zhu* (*Zheng's Commentary on* Selected Sayings [of Confucius]). According to John Makeham, Zheng Xuan, "the single most influential *Lunyu* commentator between Han (206 BCE – CE 220) and Tang (618 – 907) [...] had little to say about the 'philosophical' (*yi li*) dimensions of Confucius' thought, even this lack of interest in treating *Lunyu* as a foundational philosophical source distinguishes his commentary from generations of later commentators who did treat it as a writing which could shed authoritative light on the nature of core Confucian philosophical values. Perhaps it was this reticence in regard to 'philosophical' matters that precipitated the commentary's sudden demise by the early Song (960 – 1279)." J. MAKEHAM, "The Earliest Extant Commentary on *Lunyu: Lunyu Zheng shi zhu*", *T'oung Pao*, 1997, 83, pp. 260-299: 261 and 299.

8 B. W. VAN NORDEN, "Unweaving the 'One Thread' of *Analects* 4.15", in VAN NORDEN, *Confucius and the* Analects, *op. cit.*, pp. 216-236: 230-231.

9 P. RYCKMANS, "An Introduction to Confucius", *Quadrant*, March 1995, p. 18.

rial compiled at different times by Confucius' followers.[10] Scholars cannot agree on a date for the arrangement of the material, but the most credit-worthy of them suggest that it probably took place roughly between the mid-third to the end of the first century BCE.[11] This implies an interval of several centuries between the death of Confucius, which, according to tradition, occurred in 479 BCE and the actual arrangement of the material.[12]

10 On the complex subject of the editing of the *Lunyu*, see J. MAKEHAM, "The Formation of *Lunyu* as a Book", *Monumenta Serica*, 1996, 44, pp. 1-24.

11 As regards the textual history, authorship, authenticity, and date of composition of the *Lunyu* see the general treatment of A. CHENG, "*Lun yü*", in M. LOEWE (ed.), *Early Chinese Texts: A Bibliographical Guide*, Berkeley, The Society for the Study of Early China and The Institute of East Asian Studies, University of California, 1993, pp. 313-323. Anne Cheng does not develop a personal hypothesis, preferring to present those of other scholars, in particular those of Qian Mu (i.e., between the end of the Zhou dynasty [1045 – 221 BCE] and the beginning of the Qin [221 – 207 BCE], owing to traces of interpolations of the Warring States period [475 – 221 BCE]) and Zhu Weizheng (i.e., between 157 and 87 BCE). John Makeham has recently proposed the period 150–140 BCE (see MAKEHAM, "The Formation of *Lunyu*", *op. cit.*, p. 1 *passim*). According to Bruce and Takeo Brooks, on the other hand, the texts collected in the *Lunyu* were compiled during a period stretching between 479 and 249 BCE (see E. B. BROOKS and A. T. BROOKS, *The Original Analects: Sayings of Confucius and His Successors*, New York, 1998, p. 248 *passim*; ID., "Word Philology and Text Philology in *Analects* 9:1", in VAN NORDEN, *Confucius and the* Analects, *op. cit.*, pp. 163-215: 186). This opinion is shared by other authoritative scholars, including D. NIVISON ("The Classical Philosophical Writings", in M. LOEWE and E. L. SHAUGHNESSY (eds.), *The Cambridge History of Ancient China: From the Origins of Civilization to 221 B.C.*, Cambridge, 1999, pp. 745-812: 746).

12 The period during which the *Lunyu* is considered to have been compiled and edited thus falls between the fifth and the first century BCE, covering a significant part of the second phase of the Zhou dynasty, known as the Eastern Zhou (770 – 221 BCE), and the Western Han dynasty (206 BCE – 9 CE). It was during the Eastern Zhou period that, according to tradition, Confucius, Laozi, and a large group of philosophers lived, figures who were to leave their mark on the history of this extraordinary civilization. According to tradition, it was during this golden age of classical Chinese literature and philosophy that most of the revered works of early Chinese thought took form, from the *Lunyu* to the *Laozi*

We are therefore faced with a complex situation which leaves a good many questions unanswered. The most significant of these focuses on the way in which the work gradually took shape and was organized around the charismatic figure of the Master. How was it then, that those apparently banal conversations which took place between the Master and his disciples became the principle source of legitimisation both of classical Confucianism and of Confucius' masterly authority even before the *Lunyu* had assumed a definitive form? And how authoritative can we consider classical Chinese works to be—works that, for the most part, have been handed down to us by thinkers who lived centuries after the period in which such works are said to have been compiled? Moreover, what criteria and motives governed the delicate arranging of the material undertaken by intellectuals from different backgrounds, with such different cultural outlooks, social positions, and ambitions?

It is by no means easy to supply answers to these questions. It is like finding oneself in front of a damaged mosaic the overall design of which we can imagine despite its missing parts. Unfortunately, we do not yet have all the pieces needed to restore it to its original splendour, and the pieces we *do* have might not all be in the right place. However, thanks to a series of fortunate archaeological discoveries, we are currently in a better position than we were in the past to comprehend more fully a world which up to only a few decades ago could be accessed almost exclusively through literary works belonging to the tradition. This world now appears richer and more varied than we could have imagined, and the processes of compilation, editing, and transmission of the written texts during the classical period can be seen more clearly.

Literary sources tell us that as early as the first century BCE various collections of anecdotes concerning Confucius or maxims attributed to him or to his disciples were in circulation, the majority of

Daodejing (*Classic of the Way and the Virtue attributed to Laozi*), and from the *Yijing* (*Classic of Changes*) to the *Zhuangzi* (*Master Zhuang*) to name but a few of the most important texts.

which have since been lost. Such collections represent the different lines of transmission of Confucius' thought, and maybe correspond to the subdivision of the Confucian school into eight factions, as mentioned by Han Feizi (280 – 233 BCE) in the middle of the third century BCE.[13] According to tradition, Zhang Yu (d. 5 BCE), a scholar ennobled as Marquis of Anchang in 25 BCE, was charged to teach the *Lunyu* to the Heir Apparent Liu Ao, son of the Emperor Yuan (r. 49 – 33 BCE), who subsequently rose to the throne (r. 33 – 7 BCE, temple name: Chengdi). Zhang Yu is held to be the author of the *Lunyu zhangju* (*Sections and Sentences of the* Selected Sayings [of Confucius]), which is probably better known as the *Zhang Hou Lun* after the name of its author (*Marquis Zhang's* Selected Sayings [of Confucius]). This is an organic work in twenty *pian* (the same number as that contained in the *Lunyu receptus*) and is considered by many to be the basic collation of the *Lunyu receptus*. This work attempted to reconcile three conflicting versions circulating during the Western Han dynasty: two in *jinwen* (modern style), i.e. the *Lu Lun* (Selected Sayings [of Confucius] *of the State of Lu*) in twenty *pian* and the *Qi Lun* (Selected Sayings [of Confucius] *of the State of Qi*) in twenty-two *pian*, resulting from two different lines of transmission, and one in *guwen* (ancient style), i.e. the *Gu Lun* (Selected Sayings [of Confucius] *in Ancient Style*) in twenty-one *pian*, a version which according to tradition was found in the wall of Confucius' house in 155 BCE. Despite the fact that the authoritativeness of this work was later disputed, it was considered highly prestigious throughout the Eastern Han dynasty (25 – 220 CE) and beyond, and became the standard text. It is highly probable that the *Zhang Hou Lun* was the version chosen along with other classics to be cut 'for eternity' on stone steles in around 178 CE (actually, the texts were cut over the period 175 to 183). Zhang Yu was one of the several court teachers who dedicated themselves to the *Lunyu* during the first century BCE. The first was perhaps the Marquis Sheng of Xia, grand tutor to the Heir Apparent around 73 BCE and author of the *Lunyu*

[13] *Han Feizi* (*Master Han Fei*), 50.

shuo (*Explanations of the* Selected Sayings [of Confucius]). Unfortunately, all that remains of these works is the title. The earliest extant commentary on the *Lunyu* is the already mentioned *Lunyu Zheng shi zhu* by Zheng Xuan.[14]

From the compilation of the *Zhang Hou Lun* onwards, the *Lunyu* took on a substantially definitive form, which is the one we are familiar with today. For centuries it influenced generations of Chinese, becoming a sort of joint inheritance for the whole of humanity. This paper will not trace the developments that took place after the Han period, which raise some interesting philological and exegetic questions. Rather, it will focus on an earlier period in order to analyse the processes of compilation and formation before any definitive editing work was undertaken. In this regard, the following points will be considered:

1) The title *Lunyu* does not appear in any text prior to the second century BCE, even though several passages and many paraphrases of passages present in the *Lunyu receptus* can be found in diverse works dated prior to the second century BCE;[15]

2) In the *Mengzi* (*Master Meng*), the work attributed to Mencius (Meng Ke, c. 390 – 305 BCE) who was the main supporter of the

14 See note 7.

15 The earliest reference to the name *Lunyu* can be found in a passage from the "Fangji" *pian* of the *Liji* (*Record of Ritual*), by many dated to the Han era (for example, in his *The Four 'Tzu Ssu' Chapters of 'Li Chi': An Analysis and Translation of the 'Fang Chi', 'Chung yung', 'Piao chi', and 'Tzu I'*, Ph.D. dissertation, Stanford University, 1978, pp. 112-115, J. RIEGEL dates it to approximately the mid-first century BCE), and by others held to be a case of a marginal annotation being copied into the text (see MAKEHAM, "The Formation of *Lunyu*", *op. cit.*, p. 11, note 39). References to the name *Lunyu* in texts of the second century BCE are found in a memorial by Dong Zhongshu dated 130 BCE included in the *Hanshi waizhuan* (*Han Ying's Illustrations of the Didactic Application of the* Classic of Odes), a text completed approximately in the same period. This whole argument is discussed in detail by MAKEHAM in "The Formation of *Lunyu*", *op. cit.*, pp. 10-13.

Confucian doctrine during the fourth century BCE, Confucius is explicitly quoted twenty-eight times, generally using the formula *Kongzi yue* or *Zhongni yue* "Confucius said...". However, only eight quotations (about a quarter of the total number) can be traced to the *Lunyu receptus*. Of these, only one quotation corresponds entirely, whilst the remainder display some rather significant stylistic differences. John Makeham, commenting on these differences, suggests that

> the wording is so different that even if it were granted that they were quotations from a proto-*Lunyu* corpus that was then in existence, clearly between then and the end of the Western Han the contents of this corpus underwent significant editing. Yet rather than postulating a proto-*Lunyu* corpus that underwent significant editing, it is more reasonable to attribute all twenty-eight passages to a collection or, more probably, a number of collections of Confucius' sayings that were already in existence when *Mencius* was written.[16]

Nevertheless, in four other passages, not explicitly attributed to Confucius, we find recognizable similarities with passages from the *Lunyu receptus*. This would suggest that a number of collections of Confucius' sayings were circulating when Mencius was active or, as argued by Makeham, when the *Mengzi* was written. It would also point to the existence of analogous collections which were not explicitly or directly connected, or not necessarily connectable, to Confucius, which were freely circulating in those intellectual circles linked to the groups frequented by the *Ru*, the Classicists, with whom, rightly or wrongly, the Confucians identified themselves and became identified. The *Ru* were experts in ancient rituals and texts, such as the *Odes* (the *Shi*, which later was canonized as *Shijing*, or

16 MAKEHAM, "The Formation of *Lunyu*", *op. cit.*, p. 16.

Classic of Odes) and the *Documents* (the *Shu* or *Shangshu*, which was later canonized as *Shujing*, or *Classic of Documents*);[17]

17 On the various theories concerning the definition of the *Ru*, see ZHANG BINGLIN, "Yuan ru" (*The Etiology of* Ru), in *Guogu lunheng* (*Critical Evaluation of National Heritage*), Taibei, Guangwen shudian, 1967 (1st ed. 1910), pp. 151-155; HU SHI, "Shuo ru" (*An Explanation of* Ru), in *Hu Shi wencun* (*The Literacy Preserve of Hu Shi*), Taibei, Yuandong, 1953, vol. 1, pp. 1-82 (original ed.: 1934); R. ENO, *The Confucian Creation of Heaven: Philosophy and the Defense of Ritual Mastery*, Albany, State University of New York Press, 1991, especially pp. 6-15 and 190-197; M. NYLAN, "A Problematic Model: The Han 'Orthodox Synthesis,' Then and Now", in KAI-WING CHOW, ON-CHO NG, and J. B. HENDERSON, *Changing Confucian Doctrines, Texts, and Hermeneutics*, Albany, State University of New York Press, 1999, pp. 17-56; L. M. JENSEN, *Manufacturing Confucianism*, Durham and London, Duke University Press, 1997, pp. 153-215, and, for an analysis of the roles occupied by Hu Shi and Zhang Binglin, pp. 219-264; N. ZUFFEREY, *The Origins of Confucianism: The* Ru *in Pre-Qin Times and during the Early Han Dynasty*, Bern, Peter Lang, 2004. With regard to the *Odes* and the *Documents* which are often quoted in pre-Han texts, the accepted opinion, brilliantly illustrated by Martin Kern, is that "nothing suggests that these are the particular books *Shijing* and *Shangshu* in their received versions. On the contrary, just because the received texts very likely went through the editorial hands of the Qin imperial scholars, the 'songs' and 'documents' circulating outside the imperial court, while belonging to the same generic categories of writings, might have included different texts or versions particularly suitable for criticizing the new rule and challenging its official representation with their own versions of 'songs' and 'documents'." See M. KERN's feature article on M. LEWIS' *Writing and Authority in Early China* in *China Review International*, Fall 2000, 7, 2, pp. 336-376: 373, note 35 (bibliographical references appear in note 25). In his *The Stele Inscriptions of Ch'in Shih-huang: Text and Ritual in Early Chinese Imperial Representation* (New Haven, American Oriental Society, 2000) M. KERN argues in favour of a Qin redaction of the *Shi* and the *Shu* (see sections 3.3, 4.2, and 5.3). David Schaberg has collected roughly 250 non-canonical songs and verse fragments from the writings of Warring States and Han periods, which can be added to all received versions of *Shijing* and *Chuci* (*Songs of Chu*). On the many implications that songs' long memory has for the study of historical thought as well as on the relation of poetry and history in early China, see D. SCHABERG, "Song and the Historical Imagination in Early China", *Harvard Journal of Asiatic Studies*, 1999, 59, 2, pp. 305-361. On the nature and function of the *Shijing* S. VAN ZOEREN's volume is particularly interesting: *Poetry and Personality: Reading,*

3) None of the numerous quotations attributed to Confucius present in the *Xunzi* (*Master Xun*) can be found in the *Lunyu receptus*. The *Xunzi* is attributed to Xunzi (Xun Kuang, c. 310 – 215 BCE), who was the main supporter of Confucianism in the third century BCE.

Why is this? One would have expected to find substantial similarities between the Master's maxims, reported in the 'official collection'—that is, the *Lunyu receptus*—and those used by his most stalwart supporters. However, this is not the case. Nor does the situation alter if we change text. One might consider, for example, the *Zuozhuan* (*Zuo's Tradition*), a real mine of historical material from the fifth and fourth centuries BCE. The material for this work was probably gathered and arranged at the end of the fourth century BCE by intellectuals who were in some way connected to the circles responsible for the transmission of the material which was later to be found in the *Lunyu*. The *Zuozhuan* is rich in comment and judgments regarding characters or events from the past. Some of these are introduced by the expression *Zhongni yue* "Confucius said...". Yet, despite there being similarities with the *Lunyu* in terms of style and psychological content, none of this material is present in the *textus receptus*. Eric Henry has suggested that

> the *Zuozhuan* compilers of c. 300 B.C. were functioning more as editors than as creators—they were putting large chunks of pre-existing material into a single text. They did their best to put a Confucian spin on the whole, and to invest it with contemporary relevance, but time was limited, and the material recalcitrant, so much remained in the text that was not *particularly* Confucian in spirit.[18]

Exegesis, and Hermeneutics in Traditional China, Stanford, Stanford University Press, 1991.

18 See E. HENRY, "'Junzi Yue' Versus 'Zhongni Yue' in *Zuozhuan*", *Harvard Journal of Asiatic Studies*, June 1999, 59, 1, pp. 125-161: 149.

How, then, can this be explained? The solution may be found among the new data resulting from archaeological discoveries which necessitate a reanalysis, and, in some cases, a reformulation in more appropriate terms of many aspects of ancient Chinese civilization. These new findings can be only very partially decoded using the received literature. They are complemented by valuable funerary sets discovered over the last few decades, and more importantly in the inscriptions on ritual bronzes (*jinwen*) and in the manuscripts written on bamboo strips (*zhujian*), wooden strips or tablets (*mujian* or *mudu* or *bandu*) and silk (*bo*), which continue to be found in abundance by Chinese archaeologists.[19]

The nature of these manuscripts and their very materiality present us with a more complete picture of the intellectual life and editorial activity that characterized the Eastern Zhou period. When identifying the various phases in the long process of compilation, editing, and transmission of the texts prior to their eventual canonization during the imperial era, and before they were attributed to the traditions for which they became the expression, three main points should be considered: a) the close ties linking text, Master, and disciple, and consequently their reciprocal dependence as far as issues of legitimacy and authority are concerned; b) the complex relationship between the oral and written tradition in the classical period; c) the role of scribes and copyists and their influence on the transmission of the original that they read (if copying) or heard (if writing under dictation) or transcribed from memory.[20]

19 Concerning the pressing need to rethink what we already know about many aspects of ancient Chinese civilization, see my essay "Riscrivere la storia e la cultura della Cina antica: credenze religiose, correnti di pensiero e società alla luce delle recenti scoperte archeologiche", in L. LANCIOTTI (ed.), *Conoscere la Cina*, Torino, Edizioni della Fondazione Giovanni Agnelli, 2000, pp. 113-126, and A. ANDREINI, "Nuove prospettive di studio del pensiero cinese antico alla luce dei codici manoscritti", *Litterae Caelestes*, 2004, 1, pp. 129-155.

20 The last point will not be examined in this article. The methodological aspects of the problem have been treated with great expertise by H. D. ROTH, "Text and Edition in Early Chinese Philosophical Literature", *Journal of the American*

In a very real sense, the transmitted texts are 'books' according to the modern understanding of the word, complete with author, title, and internal divisions. In the Zhou period, however, things were somewhat different; the book as an object did not materially exist, nor did the concept of book exist. The texts paralleled a rich oral tradition and consisted of a variable but limited number of bamboo strips, the main material used in writing before the invention and diffusion of paper. A variable number of characters were written with a brush vertically, from top to bottom, on each strip (*jian*).[21] The written strips were then fastened together to form units of different size, from *ce* (small sets of bamboo strips bound together) to the more authoritative and partially 'definitive' *pian* or *juan*.[22] Short, usually un-

Oriental Society, 1993, 113, 2, pp. 214-227, by W. G. BOLTZ, "The Study of Early Chinese Manuscripts: Methodological Preliminaries", in S. ALLAN and C. WILLIAMS (eds.), *The Guodian* Laozi: *Proceedings of the International Conference, Dartmouth College, May 1993*, Berkeley, The Society for the Study of Early China and The Institute of East Asian Studies, University of California, 2000, pp. 39-69, and by A. ANDREINI, "Scrivere, copiare, inventare: la trasmissione testuale nella Cina antica", *Annali di Ca' Foscari*, 2004, 43, 3, pp. 271-292. See also XU ZHAOCHANG, "Shiguan yuanliu kao" (*An Inquiry into the Origins of the Scribe-Officials*), *Jilin daxue shehui hexue xuebao*, 1997, 1, pp. 64-70.

21 The length of the strips and the number of characters written on each strip were not codified before the imperial age. By the Han the standard length of a strip was between 0.8 and 2.4 Han *chi*, feet (one Han *chi* equals about 23 cm), with a variable number of characters, but usually a multiple of twenty-two or twenty-four. The only exceptions were the government laws that shouid be written on 3 *chi* strips. The use of bamboo, wood, and silk as mediums for writing lasted well after paper was discovered—a discovery which took place in China in about the second century BCE or even earlier.

22 The difference between *pian* and *juan* is not entirely clear. *Ce* refers to a smaller, physical unit of a document, whereas *pian* refers to a larger, literary unit which might include several *ce*. According to some scholars, one or several *pian* could be rolled up into one *juan*, but others believe that the term *juan* simply refers to the different medium used for writing, which could be on silk or paper (whereas in the compilation of a *pian* bamboo or wood seems to have been in use). In the Han period, *pian* possibly referred to the original and most commonly available edition of a literary text (written on the cheapest mate-

titled, and with no indication of their author or authors: these were the features of the ancient Chinese texts, and the newly excavated materials which the earth has jealously guarded for so many centuries confirm our suppositions.[23]

rial—bamboo or wood), whilst *juan* referred to one text or several texts copied onto a more sophisticated and expensive material i.e. silk. The main recipients of these 'luxury editions' were obviously the wealthiest members of the aristocracy, their libraries, and most importantly the imperial library. See TSUEN-HSUIN TSIEN, *Written on Bamboo and Silk. The Beginnings of Chinese Books and Inscriptions*, With an Afterword by Edward Shaughnessy, Chicago and London, The University of Chicago Press, Second Edition, 2004, pp. 96-125, especially pp. 120-122. According to Endymion Wilkinson, the main difference between *pian* and *juan* consists in the fact that the different *ce* "were either fastened together with a single thread at the head of the strips (*pian*) or bound together in a bundle (*juan*), usually with two, or for longer strips, three threads." See E. WILKINSON, *Chinese History: A Manual*, Cambridge, Mass., and London, Harvard University Asia Center, 2000, p. 445. For a full discussion on early written documents, see also E. L. SHAUGHNESSY (ed.), *New Sources of Early Chinese History: An Introduction to Readings Inscriptions and Manuscripts*, Berkeley, The Society for the Study of Early China and The Institute for East Asian Studies, University of California, 1997; E. GIELE, "Using Early Chinese Manuscripts as Historical Source Materials", *Monumenta Serica*, 2003, 51, pp. 409-438; M. KERN, "Methodological Reflections on the Analysis of Textual Variants and the Modes of Manuscript Production in Early China", *Journal of East Asian Archaeology*, 2003, 4, 1-4, pp. 143-181; M. SCARPARI, "Aspetti formali e tecniche di recupero dei codici manoscritti cinesi antichi", *Litterae Caelestes*, 2004, 1, pp. 103-128.

23 See LI LING, "Chutu faxian yu gushu niandai di zai renshi" (*Archaeological Discoveries and a Reconsideration of the Dating of Ancient Texts*), *Jiuzhou xuekan*, 1988, 3, 1, pp. 105-136. With a few rare exceptions, the pre-Han bamboo manuscripts are generally without title. One of these exceptions, however, can be found among the Shanghai manuscripts (see *infra*). One of them, which consists of 13 strips containing 497 characters, has been identified with the *Heng xian* (The Eternal Original Principle) because on the back of the third strip these two characters appear. See MA CHENGYUAN (ed.), *Shanghai bowuguan zang Zhanguo Chu zhushu* (*The Shanghai Museum Warring States Chu Bamboo Texts*), Shanghai, Shanghai guji, 2003, Vol. 3, pp. 103-118, and pp. 285-299 for the annotated transcription by Li Ling. The presence of a title on silk manuscripts belonging to the Han period is more frequent.

This way of compiling the written text allowed for the strips, the sets of strips, and the bundles to be assembled and reassembled in different ways, explaining why the various received versions sometimes display differences in the order of the *pian* and of the work as a whole, with "books" downgraded as "chapters" and in turn "chapters" downgraded as "sections", or "paragraphs", or "sentences", or "passages" within a received text. Erik Maeder draws a very fitting comparison with the modern-day

> looseleaf ring binder into which miscellaneous material, including both class notes by different hands and documentary handouts, can be entered, only later to be rearranged, shortened or expanded as new material is found which is deemed pertinent, and as the compilers' concerns change.[24]

Whoever was in possession of the text could make direct changes, if they so desired or considered it necessary, personally inserting their own observations and annotations. The strips could be removed (even if only as a result of damage or loss), added or moved according to personal conviction and present necessity, creating a sense of permanent textual fluidity. The very concept of original text, or *Urtext*, is thus a highly questionable issue.

Focusing on the problems connected with the creation and transmission of classical Chinese works, Attilio Andreini has completed an excellent study which draws substantially on the enormous experience of textual criticism in the West. He suggests that we might view the original

> as if it were a 'catch basin' in arrangement, possessing a relatively 'open' form that was characterized by a high degree of fluidity. In this sense, the different editions represent intermediary phases which attest to levels of instability compatible with the variants of the tradition and the evolutionary variants of the author, where the term au-

[24] E. W. MAEDER, "Some Observations on the Composition of the 'Core Chapters' of the *Mozi*", *Early China*, 1992, 17, pp. 27-82: 28.

> thor in fact refers to a cultural fulcrum, which might be compared to the medieval *scriptoria* of the Western tradition, where texts in fact were edited, altered, and 'reinvented'.[25]

Mark Lewis has brilliantly observed that the malleability of the text is characterized by a good degree of "fluidity and openness", both on a material and conceptual level, and "sharply contrasts with the fixity and clear limits"[26] of the received 'closed' texts:

> This openness and their evolution over time allowed the texts of the philosophical traditions to become fields in which the factional tensions or splits within a tradition were inscribed, and basic doctrines were adapted to new circumstances. Within the format of the text described above, the notion of authorship was weak. The writers of the early texts would seldom, and the editors and transmitters never, have been the master himself. Consequently, the master was always to some degree an invention of the text. This made possible the later development of traditions in which the master was entirely fictional, or an ancient historical figure who had no relation to the formation of the text. Authority was imputed to a voice, which in the early texts was actually written into the 'enunciatory scene'. Writing was treated as a form of transcription, like that performed by the mythical historians of the right and left who recorded every word and deed of the king. Thus from the very beginning authority appeared in the guise of quotation, with the quoted words rendered authoritative by the implicit presence of disciples as audience and scribes.[27]

25 ANDREINI, "Scrivere, copiare, inventare", *op. cit.*, p. 291 (translated from the Italian).

26 M. E. LEWIS, *Writing and Authority in Early China*, Albany, State University of New York Press, 1999, p. 54.

27 *Ibid.*, p. 95. This is how Lewis sees the role of the 'enunciatory scene' in the *Lunyu*: "As for the *Lun yu*, the most important single feature is that the 'enunciatory scene' portrayed in the text, which may or may not correspond to the actual 'communication situation' in which the recorded phrases were produced, is one in which the author is a recorder of words attributed to an authoritative figure, either Confucius or a leading disciple. As a consequence 'authorship' and 'authority' are separated, and the writer casts himself in the role of a secretary

A clear example of this practice is present in *Lunyu* 15.6, where the disciple Zi Zhang asks Confucius about going forward without obstruction. Confucius provides his disciple with an exhaustive response. The text concludes with the following words, *Zi Zhang shu zhu shen* "Zi Zhang wrote this down on his sash."[28]

Only later were the various bundles assembled in larger collections, thus becoming the texts we are familiar with today. This editorial work was mainly undertaken during the Han period, and more specifically between the second century BCE and the first century CE, and engendered a high degree of exegetic activity. The situation which this, in turn, created, enlivened the debates of the intellectuals of the time in a manner never before seen. Many of these intellectuals were involved in what history has come to know as the "Old

transcribing the speech of another. The communication situation that this mode of enunciation mimics is the act of teaching in which the master, whose words are quoted, addresses an implicit audience of one or more students. As narrative settings are added, this implicit audience can be specified as a disciple, disciples, or a political figure. Other passages assume dialogue form in which a question is asked and answered, and sometimes a longer exchange takes place. However, the writer always remains in the background and speaks only to name the participants and, sometimes, the place." (*Ibid.*, p. 57).

28 *Lunyu* 15.6. *Confucius: The Analects* (Lun yü), Translated with an Introduction by D. C. LAU, Harmondsworth, Penguin Books, 1979, p. 133. The expression "wrote this down on his sash" might refer to the custom dating back to the earliest times of suspending a bamboo strip document from the sash securing one's own robe, which is referred to by several Western Zhou (1046 – 771 BCE) bronze inscriptions. Examples are the inscriptions on a set of bronze vessels, of which at least ten still survive, cast for a man named Song on the occasion of an audience at the royal court he had for his appointment to command various warehouses, in 825 BCE. For a translation and comment of one of these, the Song *gui* inscription, see E. L. SHAUGHNESSY, *Before Confucius: Studies in the Creation of the Chinese Classics*, Albany, State University of New York Press, 1997, pp. 3-4, and his "Western Zhou History", in LOEWE and SHAUGHNESSY, *The Cambridge History of Ancient China*, *op. cit.*, pp. 292-351: 298-299.

Text / New Text (*guwen / jinwen*) controversy", which was a necessary phase in the construction of the canonical Confucian *corpus*.[29]

It was in this way that the works pertaining to the golden period of Chinese philosophy took on a definitive form. Works other than the Confucian texts that can be cited in this regard include the *Zhuangzi* (*Master Zhuang*) and the issue of its complex stratification,[30] or the *Laozi* (*Old Master*) in its different editions (*Classic of the Way and the Virtue* vs. *Classic of the Virtue and the Way*),[31] but

29 One of the main distinctions between the Old and New Text Schools was that the New Text interpretation tended to assign a major role to Confucius himself in the composition of the Classics, whereas Old Text scholars tended to recognize in him the task of transmitting the texts, according to the well-known principle attributed to him in *Lunyu* 7.1: "I transmit but do not innovate; I am truthful in what I say and devoted to antiquity" (*Confucius. The Analects*, *op. cit.*, p. 86). On the controversy between Old Text and New Text Schools, see TJAN TJOE SOM, *Po Hu T'ung: The Comprehensive Discussions in the White Tiger Hall*, Westport, Conn., Hyperion Press, 1973 (1st ed. 1949), pp. 137-145; M. NYLAN, "The *Chin wen/Ku wen* Controversy in Han Times", *T'oung Pao*, 1994, 80, pp. 83-145; H. VAN ESS, "The Old Text/New Text Controversy: Has the 20th Century Got It Wrong?", *T'oung Pao*, 1994, 80, pp. 146-170, ID., "The Apocryphal Texts of the Han Dynasty and the Old Text/New Text Controversy", *T'oung Pao*, 1999, 85, pp. 29-64, M. KERN, "Ritual, Text, and the Formation of the Canon: Historical Transitions of *Wen* in Early China", *T'oung Pao*, 2001, 87, pp. 43-91.

30 On the complex stratification of the *Zhuangzi* see the seminal essay by A. C. GRAHAM, "How Much of *Chuang-tzu* Did Chuang-tzu Write?", in his *Studies in Chinese Philosophy & Philosophical Literature*, Singapore, The Institute of East Asian Philosophies, 1986 (1st ed. 1979), pp. 283-321. See also H. ROTH, "Who Compiled the *Chuang Tzu*?", in H. ROSEMONT, Jr. (ed.), *Chinese Texts and Philosophical Contexts: Essays Dedicated to Angus C. Graham*, La Salle, Ill., Open Court, 1991, pp. 79-128, and LIU XIAOGAN, *Classifying the* Zhuangzi *Chapters*, Ann Arbor, Center for Chinese Studies, The University of Michigan, 1994.

31 The received edition of the *Laozi* is the one edited with a commentary by Wang Bi (226-249), which is very similar to the *Laozi* accompanying the commentary by Heshang Gong (II century BCE? – III-IV century CE?). All successive editions maintain the same structure: two main sections, *Daojing* (*Classic of the Way*) and *Dejing* (*Classic of the Virtue*), subdivided into 81 chapters. For this reason the *textus receptus* is also known as the *Daodejing*, or *Classic of the Way*

also a text like the *Guanzi* (*Master Guan*), a sort of collation of more or less eclectic essays whose only common feature is the fact that they were all compiled in Qi, at the so-called Jixia Academy.[32] The *Xunzi* could also be mentioned in this regard. In about 26 BCE, Liu Xiang (79 – 8 BCE) and Liu Xin (46 BCE – 23 CE), the two scholars heading the team of experts charged with the task of ordering the shelves of the immense imperial library, assembled the definitive text by selecting 32 bundles of bamboo strips and silk scrolls out of the 322 collected from all over the empire: recorded on freshly prepared bamboo strips, these became the thirty-two 'chapters' (*pian*) of the standard text from which, in turn, all subsequent versions of the text

and the Virtue. In 1973, at Mawangdui, a hillock on the eastern outskirts of Changsha, the capital of Hunan Province, in the tomb of the son of the Marquis of Dai, Li Cang, who died in 168 BCE when he was in his thirties, around thirty manuscripts were found, two of which, written on silk, are said to be copies of the *Laozi*. They can roughly be dated to about 200 BCE. The most considerable differences between these two versions of the *Laozi* and the Wang Bi edition consist in the chapters being ordered slightly differently and the order of the two sections being inverted. It is for this reason that the Mawangdui texts are also known as the *Dedaojing*, or *Classic of the Virtue and the Way*. In 1993, at Guodian, near Jingmen, in Hubei Province, in a grave dating back to the end of the fourth century BCE, thirteen philosophical texts were found (actually sixteen, if the four texts belonging to the collection modern scholars call *Yucong*, or *Collected Sentences*, are counted as one). Among these was a partially complete version of the *Laozi* (one-third of the *textus receptus*), which was neither subdivided into sections nor into chapters. A comparison of these editions, written centuries apart, shows that the arrangement of the text and its subdivision into sections and chapters belongs to the Han period. See R. G. HENRICKS, *Lao Tzu's Tao Te Ching. A Translation of the Startling New Documents Found at Guodian*, New York, Columbia University Press, 2000, and for an Italian translation of Mawangdui *Laozi* compared with the Guodian *Laozi* A. ANDREINI, *Laozi. Genesi del «Daodejing»*, with an Introduction by M. SCARPARI, Torino, Einaudi, 2004.

32 On the history, activities, and protagonists of the Jixia Academy, see BAI XI, *Jixia xue yanjiu: Zhongguo gudai de sixiang ziyou yu baijia zhengming* (*A Study of Jixia Academic Thought: Freedom of Thought in Ancient China and the Fighting of the Hundred Schools*), Beijing, Sanlian, 1998.

derive.[33] This meant that an enormous amount of material, i.e. nine-tenths of the total, was discarded, either because it was considered inauthentic or duplicate, or because it was considered of little interest or not entirely orthodox in nature. Or perhaps for other reasons we will never learn unless some lucky archaeological discovery brings to light an explanation. As it can well be imagined, the level of discretion employed by the editors was extremely high.

This particular way of producing written texts greatly influenced the intellectual climate of the ancient period. A consequence of this was the notion that

> the master was invented, or written as a character, in the text dedicated to him. This does not mean that some teachings were not enunciated by a historical Confucius or an actual Mencius, but such figures have left no writings of their own. All that we know of them was set down by disciples and disciples' disciples, so that we know them only as the figures who speak in the texts. They pronounce the words that the disciples attribute to them, and the latter had their own interests and programs that have left clear traces in the text.[34]

The majority of modern scholars agree that the so-called Hundred Schools of the Eastern Zhou period are in fact little more than a rhetorical artifice, in essence a response to the need for clarification and ordering which arose during the early imperial age. The only exceptions to this are the *Ru* and the Mohists, the only traditions to be organized and recognized as schools in Warring States writings.[35] In

33 On the genesis of the *Xunzi*, see the section "History and Authenticity of the *Xunzi*", in J. KNOBLOCK, *Xunzi: A Translation and Study of the Complete Works*, Stanford, Stanford University Press, 1988, vol. 1, pp. 105-128.

34 LEWIS, *Writing and Authority*, *op. cit.*, p. 58.

35 The term *baijia*, generally translated as Hundred Schools, appears once in the chapter *Qiu shui* (*Autumn Floods*) and three times in the chapter *Tianxia* (*Under Heaven*) of the *Zhuangzi* and refers to the philosophers of the Warring States period, but does not include the *Ru*, who are referred to separately as the "gentry of Zou and Lu" and experts in the *Odes* and *Documents*. It also appears once in the *Xunzi*. In around 100 BCE, Sima Tan (d. 110 BCE) used the term

the majority of cases, however, the intellectuals either acted independently or gathered in groups along with other intellectuals of different backgrounds and orientation around an acclaimed charismatic figure whose fame was almost legendary. These intellectuals were mainly engaged in the production of texts capable of sustaining and keeping alive the philosophical traditions to which they themselves belonged. As Mark Lewis has pointed out, the master, disciples, and text were elements in an interdependent relationship in which no single element could exist without the support of the others. The master was defined by his ability to attract disciples, but could guarantee the maintenance of his status only by being inscribed in his disciples' texts. In turn, the disciples became teachers in their own right by borrowing from the prestige of their master and his doctrine, both of which were preserved and disseminated through texts. The survival of these texts, consisting of bundles of bamboo or wooden strips, was dependent on active transmission and study. The constant addition and adaptation of material, favoured by their open format, meant that the contents of these texts were kept intellectually alive. These texts were constantly evolving and came to represent the spaces in which the factional tensions or splits within a tradition were inscribed and where basic doctrines were altered and adapted to meet new circum-

jia (literally "family", from which the term "school" derives meaning) in the last *pian* of the *Shiji* (*Records of the Grand Historian*) to mean the Six Schools, or *liujia*, in which he classified the philosophers of the Zhou period. This classification and Sima Tan's use of the term *jia* is inadequate, as convincingly argued by E. RYDEN in his "Was Confucius a Confucian? Confusion over the Use of the Term 'School' in Chinese Philosophy", *Early China News*, 1996, 9, pp. 5-9, 28-29. See also J. ØSTERGARD, "Which Books Did the First Emperor of Ch'in Burn? On the Meaning of *Pai Chia* in Early Chinese Sources", *Monumenta Serica*, 1995, 43, pp. 1-52, and M. CSIKSZENTMIHALYI and M. NYLAN, "Constructing Lineages and Inventing Traditions through Exemplary Figures in Early China", *T'oung Pao*, 2003, 89, pp. 59-99. Østergard suggests that the expression *baijia*, normally translated as "the hundred philosophical schools", should actually be translated as "the hundred (or many) persons", because the meaning of *jia* in this context is simply "person".

stances.[36] These groups of intellectuals were defined by loyalty to a common master and 'his' text to the extent that, as illustrated by the anonymous compiler of the chapter *Wu tu* (*False Followers*) of the *Lüshi chunqiu* (*Mr. Lü's Spring and Autumn Annals*), "teacher and follower share the same body".[37] They based their authority on quotation, incorporating

> earlier texts into later ones, and in collective writing and transmission, in the form of state-sponsored encyclopaedia, classics attributed to ancient or hidden sages, and the increasingly influential literary remains of the Zhou.[38]

This is the meaning underlying the following passages taken from the chapters *Wu tu* and *Zui shi* (*On Honouring Teachers*) of the *Lüshi chunqiu*:

> A good teacher […] regards his followers as akin to himself, puts himself in their place as he teaches them, and thus grasps the true nature of instruction. What he applies to others, he must have implemented in himself. When this is so, teacher and follower share the same body. It is an essential aspect of human nature to love those who are the same as oneself, to praise those who are the same as oneself, and to help those who are the same as oneself. The glorification of scholarly endeavour and the grand implementation of the arts of the Dao are caused by this.[39]

> When persuading and debating, the gentleman is certain to cite his teacher in order to explain the Dao. When listening to his teacher and implementing his teachings, the gentleman is certain to exert all his

36 LEWIS, *Writing and Authority*, *op. cit.*, pp. 94-95.

37 *Lüshi chunqiu* 4.4. J. KNOBLOCK and J. RIEGEL, *The Annals of Lü Buwei: A Complete Translation and Study*, Stanford, Stanford University Press, 2000, p. 127.

38 LEWIS, *Writing and Authority*, *op. cit.*, p. 95.

39 *Lüshi chunqiu* 4.4. KNOBLOCK and RIEGEL, *The Annals of Lü Buwei*, *op. cit.*, p. 127.

> energy so as to make them glorious and brilliant. Not exerting all one's energy when listening and implementing teachings is termed "forsaking"; and not citing one's teacher when persuading and debating is termed "rebelling". A man who "forsakes" or "rebels" should not be accepted at the court of a worthy ruler nor befriended by a gentleman.[40]

Thanks to archaeologists and their discovery of a great number of bamboo and silk manuscripts, the process by which philosophical texts were constructed is becoming ever clearer.[41] In turn, an understanding of this explains the substance of and reasons for the many contradictions inherent in the texts. Moreover, it provides us with an ideal standpoint from which to regard the complexity of a work like the *Lunyu*. The historical Confucius is seldom questioned; he is a kind of untouchable, sacred icon, and I certainly wouldn't want to be seen as being sacrilegious in my analysis of the figure.[42] Yet many academics have noted how the historical Confucius—the Kong Qiu born in 551 BCE at Zuoyi, in the small State of Lu, near the present-day city of Qufu, in Shandong Province[43]—has in fact very little to do with the mythical Confucius, "a product fashioned over several centuries by many hands, ecclesiastical and lay, Western and Chinese" according to Lionel Jensen.[44] As Mark Csikszentmihalyi pointed out in a recent

40 *Lüshi chunqiu* 4.3. *Ibid.*, p. 124.

41 Enno Giele has set up a database containing basic information on these manuscripts. It can be found on the *Early China* website: http://humanities.uchicago.edu/easian/earlychina. For an abridged version of it updated to 9.01.2000, see E. GIELE, "Early Chinese Manuscripts: Including Addenda and Corrigenda to *New Sources of Early Chinese History: An Introduction to the Reading of Inscriptions and Manuscripts*", *Early China*, 1998-1999, 23-24, pp. 247-337.

42 On the problems connected with the historicity of Kongzi, see the stimulating essay by L. M. JENSEN, "Wise Man of the Wilds: Fatherlessness, Fertility, and the Mythic Exemplar, Kongzi", *Early China*, 1995, 20, pp. 407-437.

43 According to his first biography, written around 100 BCE by the historian Sima Qian (145 – c. 86 BCE) and included in the *Shiji*.

44 JENSEN, *Manufacturing Confucianism*, *op. cit.*, p. 5.

study that reconstructs the socio-political context and psycho-cultural climate in which the myth took shape, it was precisely during the Han period that

> Confucius was thought to have possessed superhuman abilities, have displayed visible marks placed by Heaven that proved his destiny to rule as a king, have transmitted esoteric teachings and prophecies to his disciples, and have been sanguine about serving the ghosts and spirits. Because of these qualities, Confucius was seen and treated increasingly as a divinity.[45]

In 195 BCE, shortly before his death, Emperor Gaozi (r. 206 – 195 BCE) went himself to visit Confucius' birthplace during one of his inspection tours and offered the grand sacrifice of an ox, a sheep, and a pig (a high honour at the time), starting the custom of State-offerings and royal visits to Confucius' Temple, which continued down to the end of the Qing dynasty (1644 – 1911). In 1 CE, Confucius was canonized as Marquis of Completed Praise, Illustrious Duke Ni.

This was the period in which the *Lunyu* was edited, an undertaking which involved the distillation of a great quantity of texts, quotations, anecdotes, and maxims which had for the most part been created by Confucius' followers, the majority of whom had actually never met him. This varied material had been amassing over the centuries. The *Lunyu* should thus be seen as the culmination of a long journey undertaken by generations of intellectuals and followers who firmly believed in a set of common values and doctrines, transmitted in accordance with the changing political and social conditions, and in line with their own aims and aspirations. By re-elaborating their doctrines and disseminating them through texts that were 'open', 'provisional' and thus 'receptive'—capable, that is, of embracing new contributions and stimuli—they effectively guaranteed the survival and success of the tradition to which they belonged. Attilio An-

45 M. CSIKSZENTMIHALYI, "Confucius and the *Analects* in the Hàn", in VAN NORDEN, *Confucius and the* Analects, *op. cit.*, pp. 134-162: 135.

dreini's general definition of the classical text can be successfully applied to the *Lunyu*:

> The text becomes the medium through which the authority of the Master exists, is transmitted and recreated. It is the benchmark used to measure the level of subordination and fidelity of his disciples, the real author-compilers. But in conferring authority to the words and actions of the Master through the text, the disciple-author effectively denies his own existence. [46]

A great number of collections of anecdotes concerning Confucius as well as maxims attributed to him or to his disciples were almost certainly in circulation during the Han period. These collections were representative of the different traditions and currents of thought which were in clear competition with each other. Some of these were to find a place in the *Lunyu receptus,* others were lost, and still others were inserted into texts and anthologies thus providing a complement to the *Lunyu*. The most important of these works include the *Liji* (*Record of Ritual*), the *Da Dai Liji* (*Elder Dai's Record of Ritual*), the *Xinxu* (*New Preface*), the collection of moral tales and political admonitions *Shuoyuan* (*Garden of Persuasion*) attributed to Liu Xiang, and the *Kongzi Jiayu* (*School Sayings of Confucius*) ascribed to Wang Su (195 – 256). The great variety of maxims and anecdotes circulating during the Warring States and Han periods accounts for the high number of quotations present in pre-Han works albeit without counterpart in the *Lunyu receptus*.

The oldest *Lunyu receptus* manuscript in our possession was found in 1973 at Dingzhou, Hebei Province, in the tomb of Liu Xiu, who served as Prince Huai of Zhongshan during the reign of Emperor Xuan (r. 74 – 49 BCE). The tomb is dated to 55 BCE. Written on 620 bamboo strips and fragments, and consisting of 7,576 characters, this manuscript amounts to a bit less than half the length of the received text. It is thus representative of one of the 'winning' fac-

46 ANDREINI, "Scrivere, copiare, inventare", *op. cit.*, p. 280.

tions. Its discovery means that we can say without a shadow of doubt that by this date the *Lunyu* had already assumed its definitive form.[47]

Another manuscript, named *Rujiazhe yan* (*Words of the* Ru *Lineage*) by modern scholars, was found in the same tomb: it records conversations between Confucius and his disciples which are quite similar to those we find in the *Lunyu receptus* and other Han anthologies.[48] In three cases, the texts parallel some passages of *pian* 14 of the received text while two strips unfortunately destroyed in the 1976 earthquake are reminiscent of two passages of *pian* 3. Despite having been found in the same tomb, these strips do not have the same format as those belonging to the *Lunyu* manuscript, proving once more the existence of different collections.[49]

Two further discoveries in tombs dating back to the Han period are of great interest. The first concerns a list of the titles of forty-six narratives about Confucius, only three of which have been published up to now, found in a tomb dated 165 BCE and discovered in 1977 at

47 HEBEISHENG WENWU YANJIUSUO DINGZHOU HANMU ZHUJIAN ZHENGLI XIAOZU, "Dingzhou Xi Han Zhongshan Huaiwangmu zhujian *Lunyu* shiwen xuan" (*Selections from the Annotated Text of the Bamboo Strip* Selected Sayings [of Confucius] *from the Dingzhou Tomb of the Western Han Prince Huai of Zhongshan*), *Wenwu*, 5, 1977, pp. 49-54; ID., "Dingzhou Xi Han Zhongshan Huaiwangmu zhujian *Lunyu* jieshao" (*Introduction to the Annotated Text of the Bamboo Strip* Selected Sayings [of Confucius] *from the Dingzhou Tomb of the Western Han Prince Huai of Zhongshan*), *Wenwu*, 5, 1977, pp. 59-61; ID., Lunyu: *Dingzhou Hanmu zhujian Lunyu* (Selected Sayings [of Confucius]: *The Bamboo Strips from a Han Tomb at Dingzhou*), Beijing, Wenwu chubanshe, 1977. For an English translation of the *Lunyu* based on the Dingzhou fragmentary version, see *The Analects of Confucius*, *op. cit.* For an Italian translation, see Confucio, *Dialoghi*, Translated with an Introduction by T. LIPPIELLO, Torino, Einaudi, 2003.

48 HE ZHIGANG, "*Rujiazhe yan* lüeshuo" (*Brief Description of the Words of the* Ru *Lineage*), *Wenwu*, 8, 1981, pp. 20-22. For an annotated transcription, see "*Rujia zhe yan* shiwen" (*Explanations of the* Words of the Ru Lineage), *Wenwu*, 8, 1981, pp. 13-19.

49 CSIKSZENTMIHALYI, "Confucius and the *Analects* in the Hàn", *op. cit.*, p. 156, note 39.

Fuyang, Anhui Province.[50] The second and most relevant discovery is of one of the oldest extant versions of the *Yijing* (*Classic of Changes*),[51] though in a version quite different from the *textus receptus*.[52] Commentaries of it written on two pieces of silk unearthed in 1973 at Mawangdui, in the tomb of the son of the Marquis of Dai, have also been found. Li Xueqin suggests that these texts were copied during the Han but their compilation could be traced back to the middle and late Warring States period. The largest of these, which scholars have entitled *Ersanzi wen* (*Questions of the Various Disciples*), is transcribed onto the longer piece of silk, as an appendix to the *Yijing* text. The *Ersanzi wen* carries a series of elucidations, practically ignored by the editors of the *Lunyu receptus*, provided by Confucius for the benefit of a few of his disciples on the theme of the *Classic of Changes* and its mantic role. The second piece of silk carries five commentaries on the *Yijing*: the *Xici* (*Appended Statements*), the only text for which we have a received version, the Yi *zhi yi* (*Properties of the* Classic of Changes), the *Yao* (*Essentials*), the *Mu*

50 FUYANG HAN JIAN ZHENGLI ZU, "Fuyang Han jian jianjie" (*An Introduction to the Han Strips from Fuyang*), *Wenwu*, 2, 1983, pp. 21-23.

51 At present, the oldest extant version of the *Yijing* is the incomplete one found among the Shanghai manuscripts. It consists of 58 strips, 44 cm long, each containing up to 40 characters, for a total of about 1,800 characters. As a whole, the Shanghai *Yijing* includes 35 of the 64 *gua*, hexagrams, that make up the work; see MA CHENGYUAN (ed.), *Shanghai bowuguan zang Zhanguo Chu zhushu*, *op. cit.*, pp. 11-70, and pp. 131-260 for the annotated transcription by Pu Maozuo.

52 The main difference between the received version and the *Yijing* manuscript is the way in which the sequence of hexagrams is ordered. This differing order is due to the diverse reorganization of the material by the ancient classical masters, mainly decided on the basis of *yin/yang* principles. See LI XUEQIN, "Basic Considerations on the *Commentaries* of the Silk Manuscript *Book of Changes*", *Early China*, 1995, 20, pp. 368-380. Bibliographical information regarding the transcription, commentary, and translation of these texts can be found in an article by E. L. SHAUGHNESSY, "A First Reading of the Mawangdui *Yijing* Manuscript", *Early China*, 1994, 19, pp. 47-73 and in the volume *I Ching: The Classic of Changes*, Translated with an Introduction and Commentary by E. L. SHAUGHNESSY, New York, Ballantine, 1996.

He and the *Zhao Li*, both of which take their names from unidentified interlocutors. Some of these manuscripts contain explicit references to Confucius, particularly the *Yao*, a record of a conversation between an aged Confucius and his beloved disciple Zigong. Therefore, it can be said that these manuscripts are representative of one or more trends of specialist in the study of the *Yijing*—the texts of whom were clearly excluded from the *Lunyu receptus*—and its use for divination.

In his study of these manuscripts, Li Xueqin dedicates a short chapter, of central importance to the present analysis, to a discussion of the recurring use of the expression *zi yue* "The Master said..." in the *Yijing* commentaries, which he describes as a "puzzle" at the center of an argument which has been raging since the time of Ouyang Xiu (1007 – 1072). His conclusion is that the expression *zi yue* "could easily have been added to orally transmitted ancient texts" simply to avoid confusing "the citations of the classic with their appropriate commentaries, especially when the text was transmitted orally".[53] This hypothesis leads us to the next important issue—which is increasingly pertinent given the discovery of new material—i.e. the one concerning the oral transmission of ancient texts, and the processes of copying and transcribing in the Zhou period. Li Xueqin states that "the transmission of ancient texts was usually oral" and cites as examples the *Gongyang zhuan* (*Gongyang's Commentary*), the *Shangshu*, and the *Mozi* (*Master Mo*). Other texts also fall into this category, for example the *Shijing*, the *Zuozhuan*, the *Guoyu* (*Conversations of the States*)[54] and so on, not to mention the

[53] LI XUEQIN, "Basic Considerations", *op. cit.*, pp. 376-379: 377 and 378.

[54] For a close examination of the problems relating to the *Zuozhuan* and the *Guoyu*, see D. SCHABERG's stimulating essay "Orality and the Origins of the *Zuozhuan* and *Guoyu*", which appears in an appendix to his volume *A Patterned Past: Form and Thought in Early Chinese Historiography*, Cambridge, Mass., and London, Harvard University Asia Center, 2001, pp. 321-324. See also KERN, "Methodological Reflections on the Analysis of Textual Variants and the Modes of Manuscript Production in Early China", *op. cit.*

wealth of information contained in bronze inscriptions.[55] In my opinion, it would not be appropriate to limit Li Xueqin's hypothesis to the *Yijing* commentaries. On the contrary, it seems quite possible to extend it, though with the necessary caution, to the great part of the Chinese classical literary tradition.

Two important findings from the pre-Han period should be mentioned. The first concerns the manuscripts discovered at Guodian, which were written on 730 bamboo strips containing a total of 13,000 characters.[56] Part of the texts are attributed by modern scholars to Zi Si, Confucius' nephew who, according to Qian Mu, lived from 483 to 402 BCE,[57] and to his lineage (to which Mencius belonged). We knew very little about these texts; some were lost and nothing was known about them, and only the title was known about others. Yet in the third section of a hitherto-unknown collection of maxims and anecdotes called by modern scholars *Yucong*, there are some strips which display obvious similarities to the *Lunyu receptus*—in particular passages 7.6 and 9.4.[58] In 7.6 the *incipit zi yue*

55 The relationship between oral transmission and literacy in ancient China is too complex to be discussed in this article. On the oral transmission of classical Chinese texts, see David Schaberg's essay cited in the previous note as well as ZENG HAILONG, "Woguo gudai koutou shixue chuyi" (*Humble Opinions on the History of Ancient Oral Historiography in Our Country*), *Tangdu xuekan*, 1993, 1, pp. 91-94; GUO DONGMING, "Xian Qin shiguan wenhua ji qi wenxu yiyun" (*The Pre-Qin Culture of Historians and Its Literary Significance*), *Wenshizhe*, 1993, 2, pp. 60-67; ZHANG JUN, "Yu di chuanliu leibie he Churen songxi, zhizuo di yu" (*Transmission and Types of Legends, Recited and Created by the People of Chu*), *Hubei daxue xuebao (zhexue shehui hexue ban)*, 1991, 5, pp. 55-60. For an interesting treatment of oral composition, oral transmission, and oral performance of Chinese ritual texts, see KERN, *The Stele Inscriptions of Ch'in Shih-huang*, *op. cit.*, pp. 94-95, 104, 119-125.

56 See note 31.

57 QIAN MU, *Xian Qin zhuzi xinian* (*Chronology of the Pre-Qin Philosophers*), Beijing, Zhonghua shuju, 1985, 2 vols., pp. 172-176, 616 (reprint of the 1935 and 1956 editions).

58 JINGMENSHI BOWUGUAN, *Guodian Chu mu zhujian* (*The Bamboo Strips from a Chu Tomb at Guodian*), Beijing, Wenwu chubanshe, 1998. For passage 7.6 see strips 50 and 51 on p. 101, and their transcription into modern characters

"The Master said...", present in the received text, is absent in the manuscript.[59] In 9.4, although present in the received text, the first part (*zi jue si*, i.e. "There were four things the Master refused to have anything to do with") is absent from the manuscript version and the order of the four things listed *verbatim* is different.[60] What makes this collection particularly interesting for us is another of its passages, written on two strips, which is very similar to a passage found in the chapter *Quqie* (*Rifling trunks*) of the received *Zhuangzi*.[61] This is a good example of the above-mentioned construction process at work. The odd fact that at least three passages contained in the *Yucong* have parallels in two received texts belonging to such different traditions – the *Lunyu* and the *Zhuangzi* – brought Rao Zongyi to suggest the following: the *Yucong* could be a *zhongyan* (weighty words) collection, i.e. quotes and adages of ancient sages providing guidance in disputations. Such a text would have been widely available to all, regardless of one's cultural background.[62] When Confucius' followers came in possession of the *Yucong* maxims they simply added their own characteristic tags, one positive (*zi yue*: "The Master said..."), and one negative (*zi jue si*: "There were four things

on p. 211. For passage 9.4 see strips 64 *shang* and 65 *shang* on p. 102, and their transcription into modern characters on p. 212.

59 *Lunyu* 7.6: "The Master said, 'I set my heart on the Way, base myself on virtue, lean upon benevolence for support and take my recreation in the arts.'" *Confucius. The Analects*, *op. cit.*, p. 87.

60 *Lunyu* 9.4: "There were four things the Master refused to have anything to do with: he refused to entertain conjectures or insist on certainty; he refused to be inflexible or to be egotistical." *Ibid.*, p. 96.

61 Written on strips 8 and 9 of the fourth section of the *Yucong*. See JINGMENSHI BOWUGUAN, *Guodian Chu mu zhujian*, *op. cit.*, p. 105 for a reproduction of the strips, and p. 217 for a transcription into modern characters.

62 RAO ZONGYI, "Cong xin ziliao zhuisu xiandai qilao de 'zhongyan': ru dao xuepai shi lun" (*Former Sages' Adages as Seen from Newly Discovered Materials: A Tentative Discussion of the Confucian and Daoist Schools*), *Zhongyuan wenwu*, 1999, 4, pp. 60-62. The *zhongyan* are mentioned in another chapter of the *Zhuangzi*, the *Yuyan* (*Metaphors*), which describes three literary devices used at that time: *yuyan* (metaphor, allegory, fable), *zhongyan*, and *weiyan* (goblet words, words of warning).

the Master refused to have anything to do with"). In so doing, they attributed both to their Master, inserting them in their own textual tradition.[63]

The second discovery belongs to roughly the same period (around 300 BCE) and consists in several bamboo manuscripts of unknown origin now in possession of the Shanghai Museum. Some of these can be connected to Confucius or to his followers. Unfortunately, only four volumes in the series of six which will contain all the manuscripts have so far been published. In the first volume there is a text written on twenty-nine strips, which scholars call *Kongzi* Shi *lun* (*Confucius' Comments to the* Odes).[64] Some scholars have suggested, though to little effect, that the protagonist of these texts could have been Buzi (i.e. Zixia), one of Confucius' most beloved disciples alluded to in *Lunyu* 3.8. In this passage Confucius personally extols his great worth, recognizing his keen ability and sensitivity and praising his great knowledge of the *Odes*, which is equal, if not greater, to his own: "It is you, Shang [i.e. Zixia], who have thrown light on the text for me. Only with a man like you can one discuss the *Odes*".[65] This is evidently a self-referential passage, deliberately constructed in order to lend prestige to Zixia, possibly by his own followers, in an attempt to oppose the supremacy of the rival parties in the *Ru* tradition. It is no coincidence that a similar praise is directed towards Zigong, another disciple dear to Confucius and champion of one of the factions

63 Ancient Chinese literature was probably full of collections of maxims, anecdotes, and stories with a didactic background. Similar collections were found not only among the Guodian manuscripts, but also in the Mawangdui manuscripts, for example the *Chunqiu shiyu* (*Deeds and Sayings from the Chunqiu Period*). For a transcription, see *Mawangdui Hanmu boshu*, Beijing, Wenwu chubanshe, 1983, pp. 3-20. According to J. ØSTERGARD, the expression *baijia yu* "the sayings of the hundred persons" probably refers to "maxims of a moral or political nature voiced by 'wise men' of the past in stories of a didactic inspiration." See his "Which Books Did the First Emperor of Ch'in Burn?", *op. cit.*, pp. 2-5, *passim*.

64 MA CHENGYUAN, *Shanghai bowuguan zang zhanguo Chu zhushu*, *op. cit.*, pp. 119-169.

65 *Confucius. The Analects*, *op. cit.*, p. 68.

opposed to that of Zixia. In *Lunyu* 1.15, after having listened to Zigong's commentary on an ode, Confucius turns to him and says: "Ssu [Si, i.e. Zigong], only with a man like you can one discuss the *Odes*. Tell such a man something and he can see its relevance to what he has not been told".[66] As illustrated by Steven Van Zoeren and Mark Lewis, these stories

> reveal the *Lun yu* evolving over time as a text in which disciples not only preserve or elaborate the words of the master, but stake out claims for their unique percipience or closeness to their teacher, which enables them to act in turn as teachers.[67]

We are thus dealing with a rhetorical artifice, probably invented with the sole aim of excelling in a competition which, after Confucius' death, underscored the activities of his disciples. Such issues of prestige did not represent an end in and of themselves. The survival of these groups of intellectuals was partly based on the patronage and honours awarded to them by the powers of the time. As Steven Van Zoeren has observed, if these groups of disciples

> increasingly came to emphasize the study and exposition of the *Odes*, the question of which disciple's interpretations of the *Odes* had been certified by the Master would have become a particularly urgent and hotly disputed one.[68]

Michael Nylan was probably referring to the *Kongzi* Shi *lun* manuscript when she wrote the following:

> The Shanghai Museum apparently has in its possession an as-yet-unpublished text that purports to transcribe conversations between

66 *Ibid.*, p. 62.

67 LEWIS, *Writing and Authority*, *op. cit.*, p. 58. See also VAN ZOEREN, *Poetry and Personality*, *op. cit.*, pp. 25-51, especially pp. 32-35.

68 *Ibid.*, p. 33.

> Confucius and his disciples, many parts of which do not correspond with the *Analects*.[69]

If, on the other hand, she was referring to a different manuscript, written along the lines of the *Lunyu receptus*, we would have a completely new version of a *Lunyu*-like book (which almost certainly would not take the title *Lunyu*), edited around 300 BCE if not before, which would precede by at least one and a half centuries the editing of the *Lunyu receptus* in the Han era, and by about two and a half centuries the Dingzhou *Lunyu*, which is currently the oldest version in our possession, although incomplete.

I thus return to the question reflected in the title of this paper and which marked our departure: was what the Master said really said by him? Easy answers are not available. What is certain is that the degree of discretion of those involved in the elaboration of the texts was enormous, especially in the case of those disciples who were most distant in time from the Master and who certainly had never met him or heard him speak. A number of maxims attributed to Confucius were certainly created *ad hoc* by various generations of disciples. The propositions, though being written in the spirit of the Great Master's teachings, were dictated by the disciples' distinct goals and ambitions depending upon the changing historical context. Such maxims were meant to give greater credence and incisiveness to the disciples' own theories in the dialectic arguments that enlivened the intellectual debate in the Zhou and Han periods. It would, in fact, be more appropriate to discard the formula "The Master said..." in favour of expressions such as "According to the *Lunyu*, the Master said...".

So how important is it for the modern reader to know that not all texts attributed to Confucius actually originated with him, and that many were created by his disciples? In answer to this question let us consider the words of Zigong, the faithful disciple, who, having been

[69] M. NYLAN, *The Five "Confucian" Classics*, New Haven and London, Yale University Press, 2001, p. 364.

criticized for his excessive modesty before his Master's authority and superiority, is reported to have said:

> The gentleman is judged wise by a single word he utters; equally, he is judged foolish by a single word he utters. That is why one really must be careful of what one says. The Master cannot be equalled just as the sky cannot be scaled. Were the Master to become the head of a state or a noble family, he would be like the man described in the saying: he only has to help them stand and they will stand, to guide them and they will walk, to bring peace to them and they will turn to him, to set them tasks and they will work in harmony. In life he is honoured and in death he will be mourned. How can he be equalled?[70]

Zigong's absolute faith seems to be later echoed in Mencius' dedication to Confucius, if the conclusion to chapter 2A2 of the *Mengzi* can really be attributed to Mencius: "Ever since man came into this world, there has never been one greater than Confucius!"[71] In fact, what appeared to be the exaggerated enthusiasm of a faithful follower has lasted for more than two thousand years and will possibly endure in the future. Could Confucius have asked for more? Can we ask for more?

70 *Lunyu* 19.25. *Confucius. The Analects*, *op. cit.*, p. 157.

71 *Mencius*, Translated with an Introduction by D. C. LAU, Harmondsworth, Penguin Books, p. 80.

THE PARADOXICAL VIRTUE *(DE)* OF THE SAGE IN THE *LAOZI*

ATTILIO ANDREINI

> " I know", said Confucius to his disciples "that birds can fly, fish can swim, and animals can run. Whatever runs can be trapped with nets; whatever swims can be caught with fishing lines; whatever flies can be shot with arrows. But as for the dragons, I do not know how they ride the wind and the clouds and soar in the sky. Today I saw Laozi: is he not like a dragon?"
>
> (Sima Qian, *Record of the Historian*, 63)

Even the greatest Masters were once disciples. Or to put it differently, even the Sage has something more to learn. This is certainly true of Confucius. With such a premise I would seek to align myself with the views of Maurizio Scarpari, whose brilliant argument encourages us to reconsider the reliability of the sayings attributed to Confucius (ca. 551-479 BCE), the supreme "Master" according to Chinese tradition.[1] Without wanting to undermine the authority of the historical Confucius, nor indeed that of the centuries-old, near-indisputable hagiographical interpretation, I will begin by ana-

1 See the contribution of M. SCARPARI comprised in this volume.

lysing the meaning of a series of textual examples of the celebrated "Master of Lu" acting in his capacity as pupil. It will immediately become clear that by no means do I intend to reduce the paradigmatic importance of the role of Confucius by raising the status of the "Master's Master" above that of the "Master" himself. Rather, my intention is to test the authority of both.

Classical Chinese literary tradition attests to the way in which on a number of occasions Confucius, in his unrivalled love of study, welcomes the teachings of Lao Dan, Old Dan, who was consulted about the principles of ritual propriety (*li*).

What is clear, however, is that what we call a 'fact' often appears to lack intrinsic truth or precision, to the extent that its meaning can multiply or be dissolved, only to reappear enriched by a wealth of detail that radically alters the general picture. The event I intend to draw upon is a perfect example of this particular scenario.

There is always a certain systematic overlapping of historicity and hagiography as regards the thinkers of Chinese antiquity, and the case of Lao Dan is no exception. Best known as Laozi, the "Old Master" i.e. the presumed founder of Taoism (or "Taoist School", *daojia*) and the author of its 'Bible', the *Laozi* or *Daodejing* (*The Classic of the Way and the Virtue*),[2] this figure appears to be a 'conflation' of a number of different characters including, among others, the following: the keeper of the archives of Zhou, with whom Confucius consulted about the rites; the author of the *Laozi*, as well as the founder of Taoism; Historian Dan of the House of Zhou, who in 374 BCE predicted the supremacy of the state of Qin; and Lao Laizi,

[2] There is evidence to suggest that reports of the meeting between Confucius and the 'Taoist' Lao Dan and the journey of the latter towards the West, marked by the handing over of the *Laozi* to Yin Xi (usually identified as that equally obscure thinker Guan Yin, the Keeper of the Pass), did not take place before 280-240 BCE. In support of this hypothesis, see D. C. LAU, *Chinese Classics: Tao Te Ching*, Hong Kong, Chinese University Press, 1989, pp. 121-132. See also GUO MORUO, *Shi pipan shu*, Beijing, Dongfang chubanshe, 1996, p. 151.

a contemporary of Confucius who lived over 160 years, cultivating the *dao* and nurturing longevity.[3]

3 On the role of the legendary and historical figure of Lao Dan, see A. C. GRAHAM, "The Origins of the Legend of Lao Tan", in *Guoji Hanxue huiyi lunwenji*. Reprinted in *Studies in Chinese Philosophy and Philosophical Literature*, Singapore, National University of Singapore, Institute of East Asian Philosophies, 1986, pp. 111-124. In this essay, Graham argues that the biography of Laozi reflects a conflation of different persons. The oldest strata of the "legend" can be traced to at least the fourth century BCE and is based on the meeting of Confucius with Lao Dan; following this, during the first half of the third century BCE, Lao Dan was recognized as an authoritative thinker and started to be identified with the founder of a "Laoist" trend of thought. In the forties, there was a memorable exchange between two famous sinologists, Homer H. Dubs e Derk Bodde, which gave rise to a lively debate regarding the identity and historicity of Laozi. See H. H. DUBS, "The Date and the Circumstances of the Philosopher Lao-Dz", *Journal of the American Oriental Society*, 1941, 61, pp. 215-221; ID. "The Identification of the Lao-Dz: A Reply to Professor Bodde", *Journal of the American Oriental Society*, 1942, 62, pp. 300-304; D. BODDE, "The New Identification of Lao Tzu proposed by Prof. Dubs", *Journal of the American Oriental Society*, 1942, 62, pp. 8-13; ID., "Further Remarks on the Identification of Lao Tzu: A Last Reply to Prof. Dubs", *Journal of the American Oriental Society*, 1944, 64, pp. 24-27. According to Fung Yu-lan, Sima Qian had 'confused' the legendary Lao Dan with Li Er, who lived during the Warring States period (453-222 BCE), and was the actual founder of the Taoist school. See FUNG YU-LAN, *A History of Chinese Philosophy*. Translated by Derk Bodde. Princeton, Princeton University Press, 1983, 2 vols., p. 171 (vol. 1). The biography of Lao Dan is entwined with that of another thinker, Yang Zhu, a discussion of which can be found in A. ANDREINI, *Il pensiero di Yang Zhu (IV secolo a.C) attraverso un esame delle fonti cinesi classiche*, Trieste, Edizioni Università di Trieste, 2000, pp. 29-34. On Lao Laizi, see *Zhuangzi* 74/26/18-19, 74/26/21 and *Hanshu* 30/21a, where his book of sixteen chapters is mentioned. On the centrality of Laozi to religious Taoism, which started during the second century CE after the revelation of the *dao* to Zhang Daoling, the First Celestial Master, see A. SEIDEL, *La Divinisation de Lao Tseu dans le Taoisme des Han*, Paris, Ecole Française d'Extrême-Orient, 1969; L. KOHN, "Laozi: Ancient Philosopher, Master of Immortality, and God", in D. S. LOPEZ (ed.), *Religions of China in Practice*, Princeton, Princeton University Press, 1996, pp. 52-63. There are two recent volumes which broadly deal with issues concerning Laozi and the *Laozi*: L. KOHN –M. LaFARGUE (eds.), *Lao-Tzu and the Tao-te-ching*, Albany, State University of New York Press, 1998; M.

Such a complicated and contradictory profile emerges even in the bibliographical reports of the greatest Chinese historian, Sima Qian (ca. 145–86 BCE), who in his *Shiji* (*Record of the Historian*) tried to throw light on the identity of Lao Dan, twice mentioning the meeting between him and Confucius. In the biographical section on Laozi,[4] the narration reflects a markedly Taoist slant, whilst that appearing in the section on Confucius suggests that the famous historian consulted Confucian sources.[5]

It may be that Sima Qian's records form the basis for investigation into the identity of Lao Dan, yet the suspicion remains that what the author of the *Shiji* wrote probably amounts to "a confession that for the writing of such a biography no material existed at all" as Arthur Waley observes, with barely concealed disillusionment.[6] Or, in the words of William Boltz, it "contains virtually nothing that is demonstrably factual; we are left no choice but to acknowledge the likely fictional nature of the traditional Lao tzu [Laozi] figure".[7]

What becomes apparent on reading Sima Qian is, above all, the desire to reassemble in an organic whole those few but contradictory

CSIKSZENTMIHALYI – P. J. IVANHOE (eds.), *Religious and Philosophical Aspects of the Laozi*, Albany, State University of New York Press, 1999.

4 See *Shiji* 63/2a. "Laozi cultivated *dao* (the Way) and *de* (the virtue)", relates Sima Qian, "and his learning was devoted to self-effacement and not having fame. He lived in Zhou for a long time; witnessing the decline of Zhou, he departed". Once he reached the northwest border, Yin Xi, the official in charge of the border pass, asked him to put his thoughts into writing: the book he left before parting was composed of five thousand characters, divided into two parts, which discusses "the meaning of *dao* and *de*". No one knew where he had gone, according to Sima Qian's account. See CHAN WING-TSIT, *The Way of Lao Tzu*, Indianapolis, Bobbs-Merrill, 1963 and LAU, *Chinese Classics: Tao Te Ching*, *op. cit.*, X-XI, for the English translations of Sima Qian's report.

5 *Ibid.*, 47/4a.

6 See A. WALEY, *The Way and Its Power. Lao Tzu's* Tao Tê Ching *and Its Place in Chinese Thought*, New York, Grove Press, 1958, p. 108.

7 W. BOLTZ, "*Lao tzu Tao te ching*", in M. LOEWE (ed.), *Early Chinese Texts: A Bibliographical Guide*, Berkeley, The Society for the Study of Early China and The Institute of East Asian Studies, University of California, Berkeley, 1993, p. 270.

pieces of available information, which raises the suspicion that the Lao Dan consulted by Confucius was in fact none other than the author of the *Laozi Daodejing*, a work, we should remember, that is noteworthy for its anti-Confucian stance. The plot thickens.

Thus we should ask ourselves if such an approach can indeed be attributable to Sima Qian, whether a conclusion of this sort is justifiable and, above all, if Lao Dan or Laozi was (or were) identified from the beginning as the author of *that* book, the *Daodejing*.

The *Zhuangzi*, the *Book of Master Zhuang* (Zhuang Zhou, ca. 365-290 BCE), is possibly the oldest available source to attest to the fact that Confucius visited Lao Dan, and mentions the event at least eight times.[8] We should not forget that the anecdote, which reappears in excessively biased and often farcical terms, can only be found in the *waipian*, "Outer Chapters", which contain material probably compiled long after the death of Zhuang Zhou.[9]

In the *neipian*, "Inner Chapters", the oldest part of the *Zhuangzi* (which is possibly the only section attributable, at least in part, to Zhuang Zhou himself), Lao Dan appears in three episodes, of which only one[10] alludes to Confucius studying under the guidance of Lao Dan:

> Choptoes told Lao Dan: "As an aspirant to be the utmost man, Confucius has some way to go, wouldn't you say? Why did he bother to keep coming to learn from you?"[11]

The presence of the above passage in the oldest section of the *Zhuangzi* suggests the possibility that reports of the meeting between

8 See *Zhuangzi* 30/12/41, 35/13/45, 38/14/44, 39/14/56, 39/14/60, 39/14/74, 55/21/24, 58/22/28.

9 D. C. LAU has underlined the fact that none of the passages in which Zhuang Zhou is protagonist allude to Lao Dan or to the *Laozi*; see LAU, *Chinese Classics*, *op. cit.*, pp. 127-128.

10 See *Zhuangzi* 8/3/14, 13/5/29-30, 20/7/11-14.

11 *Ibid.*, 13/5/29. The translation follows A. C. GRAHAM, *Chuang-Tzu: The Inner Chapters*, London, Unwin, 1989, pp. 78-79.

Lao Dan and Confucius were already circulating between the fourth and third centuries BCE. But is this enough to confirm that the earliest reports of the event can be found in the *Zhuangzi*? And when exactly did the idea that Lao Dan taught Confucius gain credit? It must have been before the latter was identified as the leader of the Taoist School and before a text such as the *Laozi receptus*, attributed to him and with its anti-Confucian slant, started circulating.[12]

However, it would be difficult to believe that the reports of Confucius' visit to Lao Dan originate in Taoist sources, or at any rate in non-Confucian sources. Indeed, if it were true, how can we explain the inclusion of such an embarrassing episode (if Lao Dan really was the author of the *Laozi*) in the Confucian texts?[13] The only plausible reason is that, at least for a time, Lao Dan was not considered to be opposed to Confucian values. A likely hypothesis is that Zhuang Zhou or other Taoist thinkers wished to depict Lao Dan in this way

12 It should be noted that the Guodian *Laozi* (three texts on bamboo slips discovered in 1993 and dated to 350-300 BCE, which amount to two fifths of the *textus receptus*) does not include the passages contained in late editions which are openly critical of Confucian values. This led Guo Yi to conclude that the Godian *Laozi* can be traced back to Lao Dan, who met and instructed Confucius, while the Historian Dan of the House of Zhou is claimed to have been the author-editor of the *Laozi receptus*; see GUO YI, "*Cong Guodian Chujian «Laozi» kan* Laozi *qi ren qi shu*", *Zhexue yanjiu*, 7, 1998, pp. 47-55. The attribution of a text such as the *Laozi receptus,* characterized by anti-Confucian traits, to Lao Dan, has encouraged the crystallization of a reductive interpretation, based on the radical opposition between Confucianism and Taoism, which can no longer be upheld with as much conviction as it was in the past. Going by the Guodian *Laozi,* it might not be an exaggeration to claim that in the fourth century BCE the similarities between the two currents of thought were indeed noticeable and that thinkers who were close to Taoist ideas were not radically opposed to Confucius' doctrine.

13 A chapter of the Confucian *Liji* (*The Records of Rites*) entitled "The Questions of Zengzi" reports that a humble Confucius consulted Lao Dan on the proper performance of funeral rites; see *Liji* 7/16; 7/33. For details of other Confucian texts which attest to the fact that Lao Dan instructed Confucius, see the *Hanshi waizhuan* (5.28/40/13) and the *Xin xu* (5/1a).

in order to ridicule Confucius and his school, taking advantage of the fact that *that meeting* had by then become of public knowledge.

Scarpari throws light on the length and complexity of the process through which the canonical figure of the 'Master' was 'constructed' around Confucius, and discusses the way in which the definition of a *corpus* of canonical works representing his thought involved at times the instrumental alteration and interpretation of the original message.[14] As is the case with every great figure of the past, dehistoricizing is often the first step towards canonization, or the conferring of the highest degree of legitimacy and authority. If this was the case with Confucius, it was all the more so with Laozi, whom legend depicts as an elusive "dragon".

Yet, the authority and charisma of Laozi and the *Laozi* are partly based on 'derivative', almost 'parasitical' legitimising elements. There is strong evidence to confirm the fact that both the strict rivalry between Taoism and Confucianism, and the conviction that Lao Dan was the author of an anti-Confucian work such as the *Laozi receptus*, gained credence at a relatively late date, that is, around the third century BCE. Both factors were probably part of a scheme aimed at increasing the 'authority' of Laozi at the expense of Confucius. Works such as the *Zhuangzi* are full of clues which lead us to affirm the gradual growth of a tradition that moulded the figure of Lao Dan as the iconic image of the perfect Taoist. Such a tradition was scornful of Confucian humanism and was even prepared to humiliate the "Master of Lu" by depicting him as a dull-witted pupil.

It should no longer surprise us, therefore, that Taoist texts report the meeting between Confucius and Lao Dan, overtly implying the indebtedness or 'subjection' of the Confucian doctrine to Taoism. These works present Confucius as being hampered and exposed to ridicule by an implacable Lao Dan who, from the peak of his authority, demolishes one by one the foundations of Confucian ethics. Nor

14 See M. SCARPARI's article comprised in this volume.

then should we wonder at Confucian sources attesting to the fact that Confucius studied under the guidance of Lao Dan.

At this point, it should be said that we are probably in danger of losing the profile of Lao Dan (or simply Laozi), incapable as we are of capturing a dragon. However, what is important is that we have a text whose testament is beyond doubt.

So, in passing from Laozi to the *Laozi*, we encounter a voice, or rather a number of voices, which are anything but distinct and whose origins are, unfortunately, obscure.

Over the last twenty to thirty years, research into pre-Imperial Chinese thought has been bolstered by the great number of texts found in tombs dating from the fourth to the second centuries BCE. For the most part, these texts were totally unknown to us. The contents of some of them are so significant as to push back the boundaries of our research into Chinese classical thought, textual transmission, and epigraphy.

As regards the discovery of those manuscripts with transmitted counterparts, the most important piece of information to emerge appears to confirm the fact that the classical works which official historiography ascribes to the "Masters of the Hundred Schools" (*Zhuzi baijia*) were all subject to a long and troublesome genesis. The editions transmitted to us obviously exhibit various forms of *contaminatio* and the greatest difficulty faced by philologists lies in finding explanations for the proliferation of *variora* introduced by editors or copyists-interpolators, on some occasions merely mechanically or unconsciously, on other occasions voluntarily.

With the emergence of fresh evidence, we are now in a position to examine from an entirely new perspective certain aspects of pre-Imperial philosophical debate, which have been inaccessible for over two thousand years. The picture that is beginning to take shape is very detailed but not entirely clear, precisely because we have not yet been able to piece together the fragmented, disjointed, even partial data.

According to the information gained from recent archaeological findings, the *Laozi* did not spring *ex abrupto* from the pen of one single author. The *textus receptus*, a short work of about five thousand characters to which time has awarded a sacred status, can best be understood as the product of a lengthy process involving the sedimentation of disparate material. The majority of the 81 stanzas[15] of the *vulgata*, display the insertion at different times of units added onto a gradually expanding central nucleus, as well as 'imported' material which was opportunistically altered to fit the needs of the context.[16] The canonicity of the structure of the traditional text

[15] The Chinese term used is *zhang* "sections", "paragraphs", but given the poetic form of most of the *Laozi*, it would not be erroneous to refer to them as "stanzas".

[16] On the textual genesis of the *Laozi*, see A. ANDREINI, "Analisi preliminare del *Laozi* rinvenuto a Guodian", *Cina*, 28, 2000, pp. 9-26; ID., "Aporie di un classico taoista: il caso del *Laozi* di Guodian", in C. BULFONI (ed.), *Cina: Tradizione e innovazione*, Milano, Franco Angeli, 2002, pp. 141-152; W. G. BOLTZ, "The Religious and Philosophical Significance of the 'Hsiang erh' *Lao tzu* in the Light of the Ma-wang-tui Silk Manuscripts", *Bulletin of the School of Oriental and African Studies*, 45, 1, 1982, pp. 95-117; ID., "Textual Criticism and the Ma-wang-tui *Lao tzu*", *Harvard Journal of Asiatic Studies*, 44, 1, 1984, pp. 185-224; ID., "The *Lao tzu* Text That Wang Pi and Ho-shang Kung Never Saw", *Bulletin of the School of Oriental and African Studies*, 48, 1, 1985, pp. 493-501; ID., "Lao tzu *Tao te ching*", in LOEWE, *Early Chinese Texts: A Bibliographical Guide, op. cit.*, pp. 269-292; ID., "Textual Criticism *more sinico*", *Early China*, 20, 1995, pp. 393-405; ID., "Notes on the Authenticity of the So Tan Manuscript of the *Lao-Tzu*", *Bulletin of the School of Oriental and African Studies*, 59, 3, 1996, pp. 508-515; ID., "Manuscript with Transmitted Counterparts", in E. L. SHAUGHNESSY (ed.), *New Sources of Early Chinese History. An Introduction to the Reading of Inscriptions and Manuscript*, Berkeley, The Society for the Study of Early China and The Institute of East Asian Studies, University of California, 1997, pp. 253-283; ID., "The Fourth-century B.C. Guodian Manuscripts from Chu and the Composition of the *Laotzi*", *Journal of the American Oriental Society*, 119, 4, 1999, pp. 590-608; R. G. HENRICKS, "Examining the Ma-wang-tui Silk Texts of the *Lao-tzu*: With Special Note of their Differences from the Wang Pi Text", *T'oung Pao*, 65, 4-5, 1979, pp. 166-179; ID., "The Ma-wang-tui Manuscripts of the *Lao-tzu* and the Problem of Dating the Text", *Chinese Culture*, 20, 2, 1979, pp. 1-15; ID., "A Note on the Question of Chapter Divisions in the Ma-wang-tui Manuscripts of the *Lao-tzu*", *Early China*, 4, 1979, pp. 49-51; ID., "The Philosophy of Lao-tzu Based on the Ma-wang-tui Texts: Some Preliminary Observations", *Bulletin of the Society for the Study of Chinese Religions*, 9, 1981, pp. 59-78; ID., "On the Chapter Di-

visions in the *Lao-tzu*", *Bulletin of the School of Oriental and African Studies*, 46, 1982, pp. 501-524; ID., "The Ma-wang-tui Texts of *Lao-tzu* and Lines of Textual Transmission", *Chinese Culture*, 26, 2, 1985, pp. 29-43; ID., *Lao-Tzu Te-Tao Ching. A New Translation Based on the Recently Discovered Ma-wang-tui. Translated, with an Introduction and Commentary, by Robert Henricks*, New York, Ballantine Books, 1989; ID., *Lao Tzu's* Tao Te Ching*: A Translation of the Startling New Documents found at Guodian*, New York, Columbia University Press, 2000; LAU, *Chinese Classics, op. cit.*, pp. IX-XL, 121-184; R. G. WAGNER, "Wang Bi: 'The Structure of the Laozi's Pointers' (*Laozi weizhi lilüe*)", *T'oung Pao*, 72, 1986, 92-129; ID., "The Wang Bi Recension of the *Laozi*", *Early China*, 14, 1989, pp. 27-54; ID., *The Craft of a Chinese Commentator. Wang Bi on the* Laozi, Albany, State University of New York Press, 2000. For a detailed analysis of the *Laozi* in the light of the most recent archaeological discoveries, see S. ALLAN – C. WILLIAMS (eds.), *The Guodian* Laozi. *Proceedings of the International Conference, Dartmouth College, May 1998*, Early China Special Monograph Series no. 5, Berkeley, Society for the Study of Early China and The Institute of East Asian Studies, University of California, Berkeley, 2000. Chan Wing-tsit believes that the text "embodied" the teachings of Laozi (the historical Lao Dan), but was not written until the fourth century BCE; see CHAN WING-TSIT, *The Way, op. cit.*, p. 74. According to A. C. Graham, the *Laozi* was ascribed to Lao Dan around 250 BCE by some unknown author-editor, who took advantage of Lao Dan's reputation; see GRAHAM, *The Legend, op. cit.*, p. 119. This means that the whole book or parts of it could have existed before the middle of the third century BCE. In the light of this, we need to ask ourselves whether the *Laozi* was the work of a single author or not. D. C. Lau argued that the *Laozi* is an "anthology" (*Chinese Classics, op. cit.*, p. 14), Chad Hansen describes the *Daodejing* as an "edited accumulation of fragments and bits drawn from a wide variety of sources ... there was no single author, no Laozi"; see C. HANSEN, *A Daoist Theory of Chinese Thought*, New York and Oxford University Press, 1992, p. 201. This corroborates what is suggested by Bruce Brooks and Taeko Brooks, for whom the *Laozi* contains different layers of material spanning the period between 340 and 249 BCE, which means that "its long time-span precludes a single author"; see E. B. BROOKS - A. T. BROOKS, *The Original Analects*, New York, Columbia University Press, 1998, p. 151. In contrast, Rudolf Wagner's analysis recognizes a substantially homogenous "rhetorical structure" which would cast doubt on D. C. Lau's assumptions; see WAGNER, *Interlocking Parallel Style, op. cit*; ID., *The Wang Bi Recension, op. cit.*; ID., *The Craft, op. cit.* Some scholars have tried to develop the idea of an oral tradition behind the writing of the *Laozi*. One of them, Michael LaFargue, intends the *Laozi* as a (transmitted along with the commentary of Wang Bi, 226–249), seems to be thrown into question by the discovery of astonishing manuscript sources. For example, the sequence of the work's two sections – *Dao* (stanzas I-XXXVII) and *De* (stanzas XXXVIII-LXXXI) – is inverted in the two silk *Laozi* manuscripts found in 1973 in Mawangdui,[17] whilst the Guodian manuscript which dates back even further presents a completely subverted order of stanzas.[18]

The discovery of the Guodian bamboo manuscripts fixes the composition of the first layer of the work to at least the fourth cen-

reservoir of "aphorisms", which were circulated among "Laoist" adepts; see M. LaFARGUE, *The Tao of the Tao Te Ching*, Albany, State University of New York Press, 1992, p. 197. Victor Mair is another scholar who has dealt with the theme of the oral background of the *Laozi*; see V. MAIR, *Tao Te Ching: The Classic Book of Integrity and the Way*, New York, Bantam Books, 1980, pp. 119-130.

17 The division of the work into two sections (*dao* and *de*) is confirmed by one of these two manuscripts (the so-called "manuscript B") buried in 168 BCE in the tomb of the prime minister of Changsha, Li Cang, Marquis of Dai. It should be noted that "manuscript A", written in the style of *xiaozhuan* ("small seal"), was copied between 221 and 207 BCE, while "manuscript B", written in the style of *lishu* ("clerical script"), was copied between 206 and 194 BCE. The subsequent strict subdivision of the *Laozi* into 81 stanzas probably took place at a later date, and was possibly the work of Liu Xiang (79-8 BCE, the Confucian scholar who arranged and edited a large part of the classical texts kept in the Imperial Library during the Han Dynasty), who refers to the *Laozi* as having already acquired the status of a "classic" (*jing*) during the second century of the Christian era; see HENRICKS, *On the Chapter Divisions in the* Lao-Tzu, *op. cit.*, p. 502. Long before the discovery of the two Mawangdui *Laozi* copies, Hu Shi affirmed his belief that, originally, the work was not strictly divided into a precise number of sections and stanzas; see HU SHI, *Zhongguo zhexueshi dagang*, Shanghai, Shanghai guji chubanshe, 1997, p. 35 (reprint).

18 Beyond the marked structural differences with the *textus receptus*, the manuscripts in some instances present some important *variora* which offer new interpretations. The high frequency of diffractions (which occur when, along the line of its transmission, a text meets a hindrance, which either causes removal of the diffraction or the proliferation of variants distant from the original reading) is the reason why I have not directly analysed stanza XXIII of the *Laozi*, which is otherwise fundamental for an exploration of the term *de*, in that it describes the concept in great detail.

tury BCE (as Robert G. Henricks suspected),[19] leaving open Liu Xiaogan's suggestion that it might date back as far as the sixth century BCE.[20] In the absence of any precise indication regarding the title and author of these Guodian texts, it is difficult to say whether, at the time of their transcription, they were already recognized as belonging to the "*Laozi*". The most we can say is that sources relating to the *Laozi* are in fact older than what was originally suspected by the likes of Liang Qichao,[21] Qian Mu,[22] and Gu Jiegang,[23] and that it is no longer feasible to suggest that the text only took shape during the final phase of the Warring States Period, that is, after the composition of the *Inner Chapters* of the *Zhuangzi*.

With regard to content, it is still thought that the *Laozi* is the embodiment of Taoist ideals and gives voice to a profound mysticism, the expression of a theoretical approach resulting in meditative practices and psycho-physical self-cultivation aimed at achieving harmony with *dao*, the Way.[24] The *Laozi* would thus be seen as a man-

19 See his "The Ma-wang-tui Manuscripts of the *Lao-tzu* and the Problem of Dating the Text", *Chinese Culture*, vol. 20, no. 2, 1979, pp. 1-15.

20 See LIU XIAOGAN, *Classifying the* Zhuangzi *Chapters*, Ann Arbor, Center for Chinese Studies Publications, 1994, pp. 172-186. However, I believe that William H. Baxter's conclusions are more convincing. His analysis of the *Laozi* is focused on its structural features and on its phonological characteristics. According to Baxter, the *Laozi* preserves pronunciations which resemble those occurring in the *Shijing* (*Classic of Poetry*, a collection of material dating from about 1000 to 600 BCE), though the bulk of the text was probably composed around 400 BCE, thus after Confucius but earlier than the *Inner Chapters* of the *Zhuangzi*; see W. H. BAXTER, "Situating the Language of the *Lao-tzu*: The Probable Date of the *Tao-te-ching*", in KOHN - LaFARGUE, *Lao-Tzu*, *op. cit.*, pp. 231-253.

21 See LIANG QICHAO, "Lun Laozi shu zuo yu Zhanguo zhi wei", in LUO GENZE (ed.), *Gushi bian*, Beijing, Pushi chubanshe, 1933, vol. 4, pp. 305-307.

22 See QIAN MU, "Guanyu Laozi cheng shu niandai", in *ibid.*, pp. 383-411.

23 See GU JIEGANG, in *ibid.*, pp. 462-519.

24 An effective treatment of the meaning of *dao* in the *Laozi* is offered by R. HENRICKS, "Re-exploring the Analogy of the *Dao* and the Field", in CSIKSZENTMIHALYI - IVANHOE, *Religious*, *op. cit.*, pp. 161-173. Henricks takes the serene image of the "field, a 'natural' field, an untended field, one that is

ual for followers who, already familiar with specific macrobiotic, respiratory, and meditative practices, were fully able to make sense of a lexis whose reference is never conventional or literal, but anaphoric, metaphoric, and often paradoxical.[25]

A discussion on the role of the "Master" or "spiritual guide" in classical China focusing on the *Laozi*, the key Taoist text, is perfectly in line with traditional interpretive strategies pertaining to classical Chinese thought, according to which a focus on the "spirit" was the prerogative of the Taoists. The discovery of new textual evidence and a more detailed analysis of the sources have led some experts to question the validity of the category "Taoism" and even the preeminence of the *Laozi* within this particular system of thought.[26]

left to grow on its own" as a metaphor for the power of *dao*, which is assimilated into a bland soil in which the ten thousand things are grasses and wildflowers which cyclically take seed, grow, and die according to the seasonal cycles. *Dao* is the cosmic reality responsible for the laws of the universe and, as Mother Earth and creator of all things, it permeates all things in the form of energy or "power", *de*. The image of *dao* as "field" reflecting *de* ("virtue"/"power") as "focus", appears in numerous works by R. T. AMES (see his "Taoism and the Nature of Nature", *Environmental Ethics*, 8, 4, 1986, pp. 317-350) as well as by R. T. AMES – D. L. HALL (see their *Thinking Through Confucius*, Albany, State University of New York Press, 1986, pp. 238-239; *Anticipating China: Thinking through the Narratives of Chinese and Western Culture*, Albany, State University of New York Press, 1995, pp. 234-244, 268-278).

25 Several works by M. LaFARGUE focus on this precise theme: "Interpreting the Aphorisms in the *Tao Te Ching*", *Journal of Chinese Religions*, 18, 1990, pp. 25-43; ID., *The Tao*, *op. cit.*; ID., *Tao and the Method: A Reasoned Approach to the Tao Te Ching*, Albany, State University of New York Press, 1994.

26 See N. SIVIN, "On the word 'Taoism' as a Source of Perplexity", *History of Religions*, 17, 3-4, 1978, pp. 303-330; E. RYDEN, "Was Confucius a Confucian? Confusion over the Use of the Term 'School' in Chinese Philosophy", *Early China News*, 9, 1996, pp. 5-9, 28-29. When referring to groups of intellectuals sharing the same ideological assumptions and drawing inspiration from specific texts or Masters, we cannot always describe them as being 'schools' of thought. For a closer look at how in ancient China the transmission of teachings was teacher-based and text-based, see SCARPARI's article in this volume. See also M. E. LEWIS, *Writing and Authority in Early China*, Albany, State Uni-

Harold Roth has highlighted the way in which, far from exhausting itself in naturalistic mysticism or a vaguely anarchic quietism, the term "Taoism" (which was an unknown category in pre-Imperial China) in fact denotes disparate and incredibly complex phenomena.[27] Roth argues that we can no longer take the *Laozi* and the *Inner Chapters* of the *Zhuangzi* as standards to evaluate other Taoist sources. Moreover, the so-called Lao-Zhuang (Laozi and Zhuangzi) lineage was a label used from the third century CE, while during the Warring States period no thinkers referred to a set of basic Taoist theories as descending from a single founder, nor from canonical books. Taoism was not seen as an actual 'school' along the lines of the models provided by Confucianism and Mohism. It is significant that Roth prefers to speak in terms of *daoshu* "techniques of the Way" i.e. "a term that encompasses an apophatic inner cultivation practice aimed at a mystical realization of the Way and its integration into everyday life"[28] as the essential character of early Taoist thought. Basing his argument on such assumptions, Roth suggests that those doctrines founded on inner cultivation practices and enriched by a cosmological outlook centred on the *dao* and informed by more or less correlative practices - such as those present in the *Zhuangzi*, the *Lüshi chunqiu* (*The Annals of Lü Buwei*, ca. 240 BCE), the so-called *Huang Lao Silk Books* discovered at Mawangdui, up to the *Huainanzi* (*The Masters of Huainan*, ca.140 BCE) - did not descend from the *Laozi* but rather from other seminal texts, such as a

versity of New York Press, 1999, especially pp. 53-97; A. ANDREINI, "Scrivere, copiare, inventare: la trasmissione testuale nella Cina antica", *Annali di Ca' Foscari,* 2004, 43, 3, pp. 271-292.

27 ROTH highlights three orientations of early Taoism: Individualist, Primitivist, and Syncretist. He develops his thesis in various works, including "Psychology and Self-Cultivation in early Taoistic Thought", *Harward Journal of Asiatic Studies*, 51, 2, 1991, pp. 599-650; "Who Compiled the *Chuang Tzu*?", in H. ROSEMONT, Jr., (ed.), *Chinese Texts and Philosophical Context: Essays Dedicated to Angus C. Graham*, La Salle, Open Court, 1991, pp. 79-128; *Original Tao: Inward Training* (Nei-yeh) *and the Foundations of Taoist Mysticism*, New York, Columbia University Press, 1999, pp. 5-9, 173-203.

28 See ROTH, *Original Tao, op. cit.*, p. 185.

chapter from the eclectic *Guanzi* (*The Book of Master Guan Zhong*) called *Nei ye* or *Inward Training*, which dates to the fourth century BCE and which was neglected by scholars for centuries.[29]

The above argument smacks of an attempt to de-legitimise the authority of Laozi and the *Laozi*. What, then, is the nature of the Sage's Virtue (*de*) formulated in this work? The answer to this question must be preceded by some important philological definitions.

De is a concept with a wide semantic scope.[30] Translations of this term range from "ethical nature", "strength deriving from *dao*" to "spiritual strength", "potency", "charisma", "moral excellence", and also to "*virtus*" in an intrinsic, distinctly amoral sense.[31] In texts

29 Both the *Laozi* and the *Nei ye*, two works which are representative of a peculiar genre of early Taoist literature characterized by poetic prose, display a 'political' awareness, fully in line with the principle of *neisheng wai wang* ("interior wisdom and regal behaviour"). According to this principle, the participation in government activities is seen as necessary in order to put to test one's wisdom and virtue. This means that the Sage and the Master often take on the appearance of the virtuous ruler, the advisor, or the minister.

30 David L. Hall and Roger T. Ames have effectively revealed the complex meaning of the character *de*, utilizing the diverging interpretations provided by F. W. MOTE in his translation of HSIAO KUNG-CHUAN's *A History of Chinese Political Thought*; see D. L. HALL – R. T. AMES, *Thinking*, *op. cit*., pp. 216-217. Mote manages to find nine different ways of translating the character *de*.

31 We should consider the meaning of the late Latin word *virtutem*, "therapeutic property", "effect or quality typical of some plants". The *Zuozhuan* (*Zuo's Tradition*, ca. fifth-fourth century BCE.) also confirms a morally neutral value of *de* when it refers to the *de* of barbarians; see *Zuozhuan* 4:1548, 13:1667. The same work, as shown by Mark E. Lewis, displays a further usage of *de* "as a power that commanded through the act of preserving life and contrasted with 'punishments' or 'strength'... In other passages *de* was a general potency including both charismatic power and armed force", to the extent that those who submitted were spared, while those who were opposed to the hegemony were punished; see M. E. LEWIS, *Sanctioned Violence in Early China*, Albany, State University of New York Press, 1990, p. 274, note 50. The ambivalent nature of *de* also emerges in a passage in the *Shao gao* chapter (*Shao Gong Shi Pronouncement*) of the *Shujing* (*Classic of Documents*, ca. eighth century BCE), where it is attested that "The August Emperor... used the horror of his *de* to ter-

compiled during the classical period (from the sixth to the third centuries BCE), *de* tends to refer to an intrinsic quality by which a thing realizes certain specific and suitable ends, or to the "strength" or "potency" which leads to the revelation of one's nature and very often one's moral character. But *de* is not merely a category defining a form of self-expression, it is also the manifestation of a specific "form of kindness", typically derived from carrying out actions favourable to the deity or to other people, which results in the beneficiary of the action acquiring[32] a debt. This is why David S. Nivison, author of several brilliant articles on the meaning of *de*, has suggested that its meaning derives from the concept of "gratitude".[33] The idea is that a person responsible for a meritorious action induces the beneficiary to be 'attracted' by the moral strength he/she displays. This moral strength, as if it were some kind of magnetic energy, imposes a 'debt of gratitude', a pressing need to return the favour received. As suggested by Nivison, this notion should be intended, generally speaking, "as a moral-making property of a person ... conceived as giving the person psychic power or influence over others, and sometimes even over one's nonhuman surroundings".[34]

De is thus "power" and refers to a decidedly relational dimension.[35] As Vassili Kryukov has said, it "should be defined as a *ritual* category par excellence".[36]

rify and used the enlightenment of his *de* to enlighten"; see *Shujing*, 32/0603, 32/0708.

32 Thus we see the link with the cognate word *de*[a] "to get", "to gain", "to acquire".

33 See D. S. NIVISON, "'Virtue' in Bone and Bronze"; "The Paradox of 'Virtue'", "Can Virtue be Self-Taught", all in B. W. VAN NORDEN (ed.), *The Ways of Confucianism: Investigations in Chinese Philosophy*, Chicago and La Salle, Open Court, 1996, pp. 17-30; 31-43; 45-57.

34 NIVISON, *'Virtue' in Bone and Bronze*, *op. cit.*, p. 17.

35 This calls to mind the affirmation attributed to Confucius: "*De* is never isolated, but necessarily has neighbours" (*Lunyu* 4.25).

36 V. KRYUKOV, "Symbols of Power and Communication in Pre-Confucian China (On the Anthropology of *De*). Preliminary Assumptions", *Bulletin of the School of Oriental and Africa Studies*, 58, Part 2, 1995, p. 321.

According to the etymological dictionary *Shuowen jiezi* (*Explaining Single-component Graphs and Compound Characters*, first century CE), *de* is linkable to *sheng* "arising", "to rise up", "to ascend".[37] Although it has always seemed somewhat problematic, the phonetic and semantic proximity of *de* to *de*[a] "to obtain", "to get", has been used to justify this gloss. We find a passage in the *Gongyangzhuan*[38] (*Gongyang's Tradition*, ca. third century BCE) where the character *deng* "to climb", "to ascend", "to rise"[39] - a synonym of *sheng* - is supposed to mean *de*[a] "to obtain", "to get", following a peculiar use of this term in the ancient state of Qi. A specific link would then exist between *de*, *de*[a], *deng*, and *sheng*.

The structure of the character *de* consists of the elements *chi* "to take small steps", "to move ahead", "to walk", *mu* "the human eye", and *xin* "heart/mind" which indicates a psychological attitude or, in a broad sense, a mental activity.[40]

What is interesting to note is that the same dictionary, the *Shuowen jiezi,* sets out in a separate entry a graphic variant for *de*, *de*[b], which is made up of *zhi* "straight", "to grow straight", and *xin* "heart/mind". This character is explained as "upright heart/mind" or "upright dispositions", yet because of its connection with the cognate

37 In several sources *sheng* takes on the meaning of "to offer", which includes the notion of "sacrificial offering" (see *Lüshi chunqiu*, *The Annals of Lü Buwei* 4.1/7/22; 6.1/28/5; 7.1/33/22) or "cooking an animal as a sacrificial offering" (a typical example of the numerous passages in the *Yili*, *Etiquette and Rites*). As we will see later, there are obvious links between *sheng* and certain meanings of *de*, as focusing attention upon the deities or rising up offerings to Heaven.

38 See *Gongyangzhuan* 1.5.1/5/7.

39 On bone and bronze inscriptions, *deng* also signals the act of making a sacrificial offering, or rather the name of a specific sacrifice.

40 On the explanation of the presence of the element *xin* "heart/mind", centre of the emotional and intellectual activities, see KRYUKOV, *Symbols*, *op. cit.*, p. 316. The *xin* is seen as "receptacle of *de*", in that the manifestation of *de* directly affects *xin*. Furthermore, the process of enlightening the heart to which several sources allude to is very similar to the "comprehension of *de*" (*zhe de*).

de[a] "to get", it is also defined as "to get from oneself within and from others without".[41]

Donald J. Munro's opinion is that both entries in the *Shuowen jiezi* equally help to explain the complex meaning of *de*, a term which from the earliest usages had strong religious and politico-moral connotations. In both meanings reported in the *Shuowen jiezi*, *de* can be expressed by an 'upward' process, implying a consultation with the spirits of one's ancestors or a sacrificial offering to them. It can also imply the turning of one's attention towards Heaven's decree, often incarnated in exemplary figures who distinguished themselves through virtuous conduct. *De* links man to the deity and elicits "some benefit or reproach for man ... Frequently required was some form of bestowal of goods on others, in order to harmonise and glad-

41 See HALL - AMES, *Thinking*, *op. cit.*, p. 218. Donald J. Munro reports that the majority of commentators have followed Duan Yucai in interpreting the *Shuowen jiezi*'s definition of the character *de* as "the Way in which one gets himself in mind and body by self cultivation; the kindness which he has as a result of the cultivation he causes other men to get", yet a better reading would imply "externally achieving in man's hearts — i.e., causing the people to respect and obey one at heart" and "purifying one's own *te* [*de*] in accordance with the standard"; see D. J. MUNRO, *The Concept of Man in Early China*, Ann Arbor, Center For Chinese Studies, The University of Michigan, 2001 (reprint), especially the Appendix "The Origin of the Concept of *Te*", pp. 185-197 (quotation at p. 193). Munro suggests that *de*[b] derives from a rare Western Zhou bronze inscription, inclusive of the element *xin* "heart/mind". He also suggests that the use of this character marks the passage from "to consult" the ancestor about what should be done during the Shang to the Western Zhou "attitude or viewpoint toward Heaven-decreed norms, which, in the case of ideal *te* [*de*], revealed itself by regularly appearing conduct in accordance with them". While the Shang (ca. 1570-1045 BCE) antecedent of *de* involved "contact with deified ancestors through consultation and offerings" (see MUNRO, *The Concept*, *op. cit.*, p. 190), the meaning of *de* first attested during the Western Zhou (ca. 1045-771 BCE) involved "explicit assumptions about the actions prescribed for men to carry out" (*ibid.*, p. 191) in order to establish a communion between man and Heaven. Both texts and manuscripts attest to the fact that *de*[b] commonly occurs as a graphic variant of *de*; see the *Gu zi tongjia huidian*, Jinan, Qi Lu Shushe chuban faxing, 1989, p. 409.

den them; additionally, it elicited a response of obedience or good will".[42]

The oldest written evidence available to us, the oracle bone inscriptions from the Shang Dynasty (ca. 1570-1045 BCE) and the bronze inscriptions from the Western Zhou period (1045-771 BCE),[43] display several graphs which fix 'draft' stages of the character which subsequently took on the form we know today. According to Donald J. Munro,[44] such graphs are significant because of the presence of forms traceable to element **1** (an eye), which suggests the idea of "looking", "inspecting" or "consulting". At present, given the strong doubts regarding its existence during the Shang era, we can only observe the way in which the character *de* functions by examining inscriptions from the Western Zhou period.[45]

In searching to distinguish a set of possible Shang antecedents of the Western Zhou *de*, or "proto-*de*-forms", we might consider graph **2**, which corresponds (together with at least two other graphs) to the Western Zhou bronze inscription **3** "to look", "to focus attention on something", "to inspect". There is strong evidence to suggest that the notion of "to look" is indeed full of religious connotations, insofar as several specific occurrences can also be taken to mean "observe", "consult", "to raise (*sheng*) ones eyes", possibly towards Heaven, home of the ancestral deities to whom sacrifices must be made,[46] as

42 MUNRO, *The Concept, op. cit.*, p. 193.

43 Concerning these specific sources, Kryukov highlights the syncretic nature of *de*, and stresses its connections with certain related categories (such as "primordial integrity", "purity", "sacred awe") which make the common renderings as "power", "virtue", "charisma", "grace" partly appropriate; see KRYUKOV, *Symbols, op. cit.*, p. 321.

44 See MUNRO, *The Concept, op. cit.*

45 This idea is dominant among scholars, though Nivison argues that in bone inscriptions the proto-*de* forms have the same meaning as the Western Zhou character now known as *de*; see D. S. NIVISON, "Royal 'virtue' in Shang oracle inscriptions", *Early China*, 4, 1978-1979, 52-55, in particular p. 54. For a critique of Nivison's position, see KRYUKOV, *Symbols, op. cit.*, p. 322, note 23.

46 There is a strong temptation to link the "eye" element to the idea of "inspect", "scrutinize", "observe" in relation to the celebration of sacrifices, especially if

they are able to grant power, strength, and virtue. When this happens, the ruler, the ideal intermediary between the human order and the divine order and privileged recipient of *de*, is invested with such strength as to trigger emulation in his subjects, reciprocal trust, and social harmony. He who holds a position of absolute pre-eminence adheres fully to the rites and religious functions and fulfils his administrative and military obligations: such an individual possesses a sacred power which manifests itself as 'charisma'. Such charisma exerts a high level of psychological power, or 'influence', over others. But this can only happen with the backing of 'third persons' because the ruler, distinguishing himself by his actions, wins the favour of the ancestral spirits or, with the advent of the Zhou, of Heaven (*Tian*).[47] This might lead us to assume that *de* is closely linked to the

we examine certain graphic variants of *zhi*[a] in bone inscriptions, a few of which (not yet containing the element *xin* "heart/mind") could be understood as archaic forms of *de*; see *Jiaguwen zidian*, Sichuan cishu chubanshe, 1998, pp. 168-169, 372. The graph *zhi*[a] is not registered in the *Shuowen jiezi*, but appears in the *Yupian* (*Jade Leaves*, ca. 543), where it is assimilated with *shi*[a] "to dedicate oneself to someone", "give", "advance", "proceed"; *zhi*[a] is assimilated to *zhi*[b] (name of a sacrifice), a character which in bone and bronze also meant "offer in sacrifice", "go up", "rise", "promote" (see *Jiaguwen*, *op. cit.*, pp. 1509-1510), and, importantly, acts as a loan for *de*[a] "to get" and *de* (see *Gu zi tongjia huidian*, *op. cit.*, p. 409). The dictionary *Jiyun* (*Collected Rhymes*, ca. 1000), shows how *zhi* is equivalent to *deng* "ascend", "climb", "mount" and *zhi*[a], while the dictionary *Zihui* (*Lexicon*, ca. 1615) takes *zhi*[a] to be a synonym of *sheng* or *jin* "offer", "offer in sacrifice", "promote", "give". Kryukov interprets the ritualistic value among the "proto-pseudo-*de*" graphs in Shang inscriptions as referring to actions of sacred communications involving punishments or military campaigns in ritual or sacrificial contexts which required the use of a sacred form of violence. Kryukov accepts some of the interpretations forwarded by Munro, but holds that the shift from the Shang-proto-*de*-forms to the use of *de* in the Zhou period marks the rejection of the idea of power as authority and ritual violence in favour of the "universal power of ritual, the possession of which gave magical authority without resort to violent excesses;" see KRYUKOV, *Symbols*, *op. cit.*, p. 326.

47 *Tian* represents the supreme authority capable of presenting the ruler with the "decree", "command", "order" (*ming*) to govern, legitimising his guidance of the state by drawing inspiration from *de*. Recently, Yuri Pines has taken up

idea of "grace" or "gift from heaven". It is no coincidence that in many ancient sources *de* has been understood as the exclusive 'property' of Heaven or Shangdi, the supreme deity of the Shang pantheon. This latter one possesses *de*, together with the dead kings and royal ancestors, and it is for this reason that *de* can be sent down to the people and acquired by individuals. This justifies the close links existing between *de* and the ability to inspire sacred awe, since the ones possessing *de* resemble the source of supreme authority (Shangdi or Heaven) as well as the source of the highest terror in the eyes of all subjects.

De assumes a transpersonal quality because individuals cannot own it exclusively. It is a kind of 'communicative medium' which defines the relationship between the common people and the ruler and between the whole of mankind and the Gods. *De*, indeed, expresses a trait which is common to both mankind and the spirits, which is represented by a heavenly gift or heavenly favour and therefore possesses an 'external' character. However, its high level of immanence should not be overlooked. He who is touched by this heavenly 'grace' becomes a custodian of *de*, even if he does not entirely possess it. The granting of grace, but also its conservation, implies a form of nurturing or cultivation. The pact between Heaven and man should be unfailingly honoured and prolonged, and the

Kominami Ichiro's analysis, according to which in several pre-classical and classical sources *de* is essentially equivalent to *ming*; see KOMINAMI ICHIRO, "Tenmei to toku", *Toho gakuho*, 64, pp. 1-59. Pines highlights how Western Zhou sources present three distinct usages of *de*: as a religious category, with the meaning of "power" or "potency"; as "kindness" or "grace" exhibited by the ruler towards the subjects; as an ethical category, by which one acts according to what is morally appropriate. By the Chunqiu period (770-454 BCE), this third ethical dimension grew stronger and *de* became a characteristic of all superior men, extending beyond those charismatic-moral qualities which were formerly the privilege of the ruler, the aristocracy, and the ancestral spirits; see Y. PINES, *Foundations of Confucian Thought: Intellectual Life in the Chunqiu Period, 722-453 B.C.E.*, Honolulu, University of Hawai'i Press, 2002, in particular pp. 180-187.

temporary possessor of *de* must continue to deserve such attention. Here, then, we find the paradoxical nature of *de* being revealed.

As Nivison readily explains, "one must already have *de* if one is to do with things that would get it; and in particular one must have 'virtue' already if one is to heed the instruction that would lead one to it".[48] And that's not all.

The character *de* has been precisely defined as being a cognate of *de*[a] "to obtain", "to acquire", originally "obtain wealth". The assimilation of the two terms does not emerge in the oldest sources and thus it is probable that it occurred at a later date. Given the evident graphical distinction, such a process of assimilation was possibly aided by the homophonic relationship between the two characters as well as by the fact that both refer to a form of "acquisition" (*de* "virtue" insomuch as it represents "heavenly favour" or "restitution of a favour received", while *de*[a] effectively points to "earning", "conquering", "achievement"). However, *de* is better expressed as "loss" or "giving" rather than "acquisition". Nivison mentions many textual examples where a person offers his life or puts himself at risk on behalf of another before the spirits, and discusses the possibility that such acts might result in an increasing of *de*. Therefore, it would seem that the possession of *de* occurs when the subject refuses some sort of ostentatious manifestation of his own "power" or "virtue".[49]

A perfect example of this is to be found in the celebrated Duke of Zhou, the younger brother of King Wu. The Duke of Zhou is often portrayed as a model of virtue, especially in Confucian sources. It is said that when the King fell ill, the Duke ordered a divination rite to be held in great secrecy. He addressed the King's ancestors and offered his life to save King Wu. It was Heaven's will that the King be saved and the Duke be spared. All this would have remained cloaked in secrecy had it not been for a violent storm which took place many years later. The storm prompted the court dignitaries to open and check out the old divinatory documents. Once again, it was Heaven,

48 NIVISON, *The Paradox*, *op. cit.* p. 34.

49 *Ibid.* As we will see, this is a striking aspect of the *Laozi*.

according to the *Shujing*,[50] who sent the storm, in order to let everybody know of the Duke's *de*.

Contrary to what might be expected, the meaning of *de* in the *Laozi* is no different, conceptually speaking, from its meaning in many Confucian texts, the *Lunyu* included.[51] In fact, what we have before us are diverse perceptions of shared notions, already implicit in the archaic meanings of *de*.

What Confucius meant by *de* was the normative 'influence' exercised by the Sage who, himself an exemplary model of virtue, encourages others to share the tradition's ethical and ceremonial values, constantly following an irreprehensible line of conduct.[52] According to Philip J. Ivanhoe, for Confucius *de* was "less and less a matter of birth or one's relationship with powerful spirits ... it came to mean

50 *Shujing* 26/0433.

51 Philip J. Ivanhoe lists three characteristics shared by the Confucian and the "Laoist" conception of *de*: 1) the attractive power possessed by the one who has *de*; 2) the distinctive effect upon those who come into its presence; 3) the relationship between *de* and *wuwei* "non action, non interference" in government; see P. J. IVANHOE, "The Concept of *de* ("Virtue") in the *Laozi*", in CSIKSZENTMIHALYI – IVANHOE, *Religious and Philosophical, op. cit.*, pp. 239-257 (in particular, pp. 239-240).

52 Herbert Fingarette has highlighted the persistence of magical elements in Confucius' vision of *de*, which "always involves great effects produced effortlessly, marvelously, with an irresistible power that is itself intangible, invisible, unmanifest"; see H. FINGARETTE, *Confucius: The Secular as Sacred*, New York, Harper and Row, 1972, p. 4. In supporting his claims regarding such magical elements, Fingarette quotes the following passages from the *Lunyu*: "With correct comportment, non commands are necessary, yet affairs proceed" (13.6); "The *de* of the noble man is like wind, that of ordinary man is like grass: when the wind blows, the grass must bend" (12.19); "To govern by *de* is to be like the North Polar Star: it remains in place while all the other stars revolve in homage about it" (2.1). To this we might add the famous passage celebrating the virtue of the ruler Shun, who "merely placed himself gravely and reverently with his face due South: that's all!" (15.4). We might also consider *Lunyu* 7.22: when threatened by Huan Tui, Confucius said that he would be protected by the Heaven-bestowed-*de* which is in him.

something like moral charisma",[53] a moral force of gravity that "attracts and retains good, subordinates and subjects".[54] To be "fond of *de*"[55] means to act favourably towards the spirits or towards others and, in so doing, to increase one's moral power.

In Western Zhou inscriptions, *de* takes on the meaning of "Heavenly favour" or "Heavenly gift" that materializes in the subject invested with a magical or religious moral strength. But in the *Laozi* the divine prospect of the ancestral spirits, who the ruler invokes in order to receive *de*, is replaced by *dao*. Whilst retaining certain salient characteristics of its oldest meanings, the term *de* in the *Laozi* and other Taoist texts denotes, rather, a magical strength, that power directly emanating from the *dao* which is revealed in things, and which makes these things the material reflection of the *dao* itself.

But let us analyse this point in more detail. The *Laozi* refuses an anthropocentric perspective. This would explain the extolling of the notion of *wu wei*, generally translated as "non-action", which really means "non-assertive, non-coercive activity or action"; "non-meddling", "non-intervention", "non-interference".

The human perspective is grounded in desire (*yu*) which originates in the presumption of a unitary self (*wo, wu, ji*) or of a subject which deliberates and projects himself onto the world. The *Laozi* (and the *Zhuangzi*) counters this vain presumption with the following model: a non-subject (*wu ji / wu wo*)[56] who is without desire (*wu yu*) and who, consequently, does not deliberate (*wu wei*).

That said, *wu wei* has to be closely related to the idea of *de*. *Wu wei* expresses the attitude adopted by he who, strong with his own *de*, is able to achieve certain ends without actually imposing himself, without using coercion and without directing events in such a way as

[53] P. J. IVANHOE, *Confucian Moral Self Cultivation*, Indianapolis and Cambridge, Hackett, 2000, p. xiii.

[54] *Ibid.*

[55] See *Lunyu* 9.18; 15.13.

[56] For more on this theme, see W. BAUER, "The I and the Non-I in Laozi's *Daodejing*", in A. HSIA (ed.), *Tao: Reception in East and West*, Bern and Berlin, Peter Lang, 1994, pp. 73-91.

to further personal aims. *De* provides for the exercising of a 'power', but this power is of an occult nature. Whoever is possessed by this power abandons himself/herself unreservedly and almost unconsciously. *De* induces a form of 'non-interference' which gradually reduces[57] one's impact upon the world, or, as it also might be said, one 'listens' to the world and 'yields'. *De*, as we shall see, is always disinterested and is principally extolled by the "being without ulterior motives" (*Laozi* XXXVIII). The *dao* is by analogy the softest, the most pliable (*Laozi* XLIII), the speechless and silent, the weak, that which is "reversal" (*Laozi* XL) instead of "proceeding forward". *De* is thus the measure of one's own ability to harmonise with one's context through integration and, therefore, leads to shedding and depriving rather than acquiring.

There is also a strong link between *wu wei* and *de* in Confucian texts. Images such as that of the sage ruler who is like the North Polar Star, which "remains in place while all the other stars revolve in homage around it" (*Lunyu* 2.1), and also King Shun's portrait of "merely placing himself gravely and reverently with his face due South" (*Lunyu* 15.4) are certainly expressions of *wu wei*. And yet, according to Confucius, through the process of self-cultivation and observance of the rites, *de* can increase one's capacity to break down the barriers between self and other in order to attain a full social and cultural integration based on sharing and adhering to the traditional Zhou ideals. The accumulation of *de* consists in "doing one's best, living up to one's word, accommodating oneself to what is appropriate as one's most important concern".[58]

The need to overcome particularity is understood differently in Taoist sources since it aims at integration on a much higher and more radical scale, which involves the subject opening himself up to his whole environment, both culturally defined and natural, "so that the environment contributes to him, making him potent and productive,

[57] Consider stanza XLVIII of the *Laozi*: "Those who have heard the *dao* decrease day by day".

[58] *Lunyu* 12.10.

and he contributes to his environment, strengthening, enhancing, and interpreting its natural direction".[59] Moreover, to possess *de* is not the result of a voluntary act that can be imitated. Rather, it is total spontaneity and naturalness which lead to its bestowal.

How, then, is the figure of the Sage and his virtue, or 'charisma', depicted in the *Laozi*?

Granted that the Sage (*shengren*)[60] is really a "Master" in the true sense of the word, he embodies a paradox insofar as he "dwells in non-active affairs and practices a wordless teaching … the Ten thousand things come to light without him having created them, he acts on their behalf without exacting any gratitude for this, he accomplishes his tasks, but he doesn't claim any merit. It is only because he claims no merits that they therefore do not leave him" (stanza II); he "teaches without teaching" (or "teaches not to teach", or "learns not to learn"; stanza LXIV).

Perhaps the most emblematic image illustrating the definition of *de* in the *Laozi* is that of the newborn child (stanza LV). The latter does not distinguish himself from his context, and thus adheres to the *dao*:

59 HALL - AMES, *Thinking*, *op. cit.*, p. 225. On the differing perceptions of *de* in Confucius and the *Laozi*, see IVANHOE, *The Concept*, *op. cit.*, pp. 249-250, where he speaks of the force of *de* which is "centripetal" for Confucius (since it draws "people in and up in a common cause", i.e. the realization of a society based on Confucian moral values through the emulation of the Sage's virtue), while "the force of the *de* of Laozi's Sage is more centrifugal… it puts people at ease, brings them peace and allows them to settle down where they are". Indeed, according to stanza LVII of the *Laozi*: "I take non-action and people are transformed of themselves; I prefer stillness and the people are rectified of themselves; I am not meddlesome and the people prosper of themselves; I am without desires and the people of themselves become simple like an un-carved block". In the *Laozi*, we find a 'centrifugal' charisma which radiates from the Sage (or from the *dao*) towards all creatures and enables their dispersion in the *dao* by means of a return, a re-appropriation of primordial unity.

60 On the figure of the Sage in the *Daodejing*, see R. E. ALLINSON, "Moral Values and the Taoist Sage in the *Tao de Ching*", *Asian Philosophy*, 4, 2, 1994, pp. 127-136.

> One who embraces the fullness of *de* can be compared to an infant.
> Wasps, scorpions, snakes, and vipers do not sting him.
> Birds of pray and fierce beasts do not seize him.
> His bones and muscles are weak and pliant, yet his grasp is firm.
> He does not know about the union of male and female, yet his organ is aroused: this is because his essence is at its height.
> He screams the whole day, yet he won't become hoarse: this is because his harmony is at its height.[61]

Another passage that helps clarify the meaning of *de* in the *Laozi* is the following (stanza XXXVIII):

> The [person of] highest *de*, is not *de*: therefore has *de*.[62]
> The [person of] lowest *de*, does not lose (*shi*) *de*: therefore has no *de*.
> The [person of] highest *de* does not interfere and does not have ulterior motives.

In commenting on this passage it is necessary to go beyond the often-debated phonetic and semantic ambiguity between *de* "virtue" and *de*[a] "to get", and to reach out towards some of the 'earliest' meanings of *de*.

The first line has been traditionally interpreted as follows:[63] if we try to assimilate *de* into the albeit vague and inappropriate idea of "virtue", it follows that the person gifted with a superior virtue is already virtuous and thus has no reason to achieve anything. Such a reading would imply that the second occurrence of *de* "virtue" is in fact equivalent to *de*[a] "to get". This is echoed in passage 43/17/27 of

61 For more on the idea of the infant, see *Laozi*, stanza XXVIII.

62 In the *Kongcongzi* (*The Kong Family Masters' Anthology*) the line appears as follows: "The [person of] highest *de*, is not *de*: therefore he has no *de*". Yoav Ariel supposes that the replacement of *you* "to have" with *wu* "not to have" is an innovation of the author-editor of the *Kongcongzi* (ca. third century CE). As far as I know, no edition of the *Laozi* agrees with this reading; see Y. ARIEL, *K'ung-Ts'ung-Tzu*, Princeton, Princeton University Press, 1989, pp. 103, 174. I would like to thank Emanuela Franceschi for pointing out the different writing of this line of the *Laozi* in the *Kongcongzi*.

63 See XU KANGSHENG, *Laozi yanjiu*, Taibei, Shuiniu chubanshe, 1992, p. 5.

the *Zhuangzi* which reads *zhi de bu de*[a] i.e. "the highest *de* implies no acquisition". This indeed would justify saying that the man of highest *de* is not what he seems; he does not need to prove that he is virtuous, because he already is virtuous. His is an 'atypical' virtue, an unconventional virtue.

Further remarks can be made in the light of the content of the third line. The Sage must follow a conduct inspired by the *dao*, adapting himself to 'what' bestows favour on creatures and to 'what' establishes an infinite credit of gratitude. Here is that idea again: a credit of gratitude. Could we then interpret the first line, which reads "the highest form of *de* is not recompensed", as "the highest form of *de* is such because it knows it will not be recompensed"? Maybe "highest" does indeed refer to that virtue which is not recognized as such and thus does not put others, the beneficiaries of actions, in a position to feel obliged to return the favour received.[64]

In the second line, *xia de* "inferior virtue" seems to allude to a substantial absence of virtue. However, it is often the case that he who makes a show of possessing talents in fact possesses none. If the second occurrence of *de* "virtue" in the first line should be read as *de*[a] "to acquire", "to get", then there is a marked difference with the term *shi* "to lose", "to mislay", "to neglect". Thus, if superior virtue pursues no form of achievement, inferior virtue is never unaware of itself and trembles at the very thought of a lack of recognition or at the non-restitution of a bestowed favour.[65]

64 Let us remember the already mentioned episode in which the Duke of Zhou secretly consulted the ancestral spirits in order to offer his life in exchange for that of the ruler, and saw his *de* increase because his actions constituted a gratuitous offering, and, above all, because they were concealed from the world.

65 Stanza XXXVIII of the *Laozi* underlines the inexorable loss implied by the abandonment of the *dao* in favour of Confucian moral values: "When the *dao* is lost there is *de*; when *de* is lost there is benevolence; when benevolence is lost there is righteousness; when righteousness is lost there is ritual propriety. As for ritual propriety, it's but the thin edge of loyalty and trustworthiness, and the beginning of disorder".

Again, the issue of restitution comes up. The following is taken from stanza LXIII of the *Laozi* and is echoed in *Lunyu* 14.34:

> Act without interference.
> Pursue that which is not meddlesome.
> Savour what has no flavour.
> Regard the small as big and the few as many.
> Repay resentment (or "malice") with virtue (or "kindness", *bao yuan yi de*).
> Therefore, the Sage never attempts to be great and so he succeeds in becoming great.
> Therefore, even the Sage treats things as difficult and, as a result, in the end he has no difficulty.[66]

> "Someone said to use virtue to repay resentment (*yi de bao yuan*): how would that be?"
> The Master said: "How would you repay virtue? Use straightforwardness to repay resentment; use virtue to repay virtue".[67]

Should we take the allusion to the principle of "using virtue (or kindness, *de*) to repay resentment" in the *Lunyu* as a response to what is found in the *Laozi*? Or else, even though Confucius' interlocutor seems to allude to a doctrine already formulated by others, could the opposite be true? Indeed, it is hard to say. What is truly relevant is

66 *Laozi* LXIII. It is worth noting that the section of the Guodian *Laozi* corresponding to stanza LXIII of the received version omits a great part of the text, including the 'incriminating passage'. Huang Ren'er has suggested that the owner of the tomb, hypothetical keeper of the manuscript, or the editor of it were Confucian, and that they deliberately left out certain passages that were opposed to their own moral convictions, given that the *Lunyu* reports the need to "use straightforwardness [not *de*] to repay resentment". According to P. THOMPSON, the omission is due to an eye-skip of the copyist; see ALLAN - WILLIAM, *Guodian*, *op. cit.*, p. 132. The rejection of an ethical outlook which distinguishes the deserving one from the undeserving one, gains force in stanza XLIX of the *Laozi*: "Have faith in those who are of good faith; have faith also in those who lack good faith: by doing so, you gain good faith".

67 *Lunyu* 14.34.

that Confucius responds with great force, rejecting the principle of returning good for evil.[68]

At this point, it would be worth considering the meaning of the character *bao* in the above-mentioned passage taken from the *Lunyu*, which is clearly very different from the character *de*. If, in the light of its link with *de*[a] "to get", *de* "virtue" expresses "acquiring", "achieving" through some kind of "concession", a "granting", then *bao* indicates a form of "requite", "give", "confer" in the ritual sense of "remunerate", "repay", "recompense", "reinstate", "exact correspondence", "offer in sacrifice". *Bao* alludes to "offering as a sign of thanks", but also, as shown by the *Shuowen jiezi*, to the act of "repaying", and, if necessary, to the act of "sanctioning", "inflicting", "punishing the guilty" or "taking revenge". The overriding impression is that *bao* refers to a measured reaction that, insomuch as it signals a kind of "restitution", leads to some kind of expected response. What is certain is that this is a far cry from free concession or unconditional offering.[69]

Unlike that which is expressed by Confucius in passage 14.34 of the *Lunyu*, the content of stanza LXIII of the *Laozi* seems to invite us

68 For a detailed justification of Confucius' position, see *Liji* 37/2, where a series of relevant aphorisms linked to this topic appear:
These were the words of the Master: "(Humanity, of which the characteristic is) Benevolence, is the Pattern for all under Heaven; Righteousness is the Law for all under Heaven; and the Reciprocations (of ceremony, *bao*) are for the Profit of all under Heaven".
The Master said: "When kindness is returned for kindness, the people are exhorted (to be kind). When resentment is returned for resentment, the people are warned (to refrain from wrong-doing). It is said in the *Book of Poetry*: 'Answers to every word will leap / Good deeds their recompense shall reap [III, iii, ode 26]'".
The Master said: "They who return kindness for resentment are such as have a regard for their own persons, while they who return resentment for kindness are men to be punished and put to death".

69 D. SCHABERG offers an exemplary analysis of the concept of *bao* in his work *A Patterned Past: Form and Thought in Early Chinese Historiography*, Cambridge and London, Harvard University Press, 2001, pp. 207-221.

to do the following: distance ourselves from attitudes inspired by *bao* and repay those who display hostility with an action which surpasses the "restitution of a wrong received", and thus the logic of *do ut des*. The response to any wrong received is enhanced by the addition of some 'extra value'.

Unlike *bao*, *de* has no rigid boundaries, no solid moorings and, as such, can be said to be profoundly hazardous, markedly precarious or opaque. Far from being an irrevocable acquisition, *de* can be best explained as a 'provisional' gift, one which must be continually renegotiated on the basis of one's conforming to the *dao*. Thus, if *de* is taken to mean a debt of gratitude then, logically, this must imply some form of intrinsic insolvency and the need to 'honour' the debt *ad infinitum*. Such factors would indeed lead the contracting party to act according to a double aim: on the one hand, to repay the gift 'directly', and on the other to transfer onto others such favour through being magnanimous or benevolent. Both aims consist in a process of 'receiving', 'repaying' and 'extending'.

De is not only conferred in order that the debt of gratitude be extended; it is important for third parties to participate in this chain of action which consists in 'receiving-repaying-extending'. It is possible that in ancient times sacrifices to the ancestral spirits were understood to be primarily an attempt at 'repayment' or the paying-off of a debt, but it seems equally possible that Shangdi and Heaven were not necessarily the ultimate focus of such attentions. *De* was conferred by merit of clemency towards others, and was preserved with discretion, humility, and modesty.[70] It is precisely in this way that, as we have already seen, putting oneself in danger for the good of others implies a strengthening of support from the spirits, and thus a strengthening of one's own *de*. This means that the exposure to the

70 Taking passage 20:1415-1416 of the *Zuozhuan*, Pines shows that Heaven, spirits, and deities were responsive to human activities and particularly to the ruler's magnanimousness towards the people: it was thus the actions and not strictly prayers and offerings to determine the favour of divine forces; see PINES, *Foundations*, *op. cit*., pp. 81-84.

dao through a conferring of *de* necessarily implies the transcending of a partial outlook, marked by a merely quantitative understanding of the logic of 'gain and loss'.

Out of sheer arrogance, let us now try to assume the standpoint of the *dao*, the Mother of all things, the principle governing all cosmic processes which assures that everything is "that which it is". And, suddenly, we switch to a perspective which is 'human, too human', distinguished by a measured offering, by a 'giving in order to repay' (*bao*, precisely) and by a 'giving in order to receive'.

The beneficiary of the attentions of the *dao* or Heaven contracts an inextinguishable debt of gratitude. Thus, in imitating the *dao*, the Sage cannot but give more than he receives. The implication is that he has already received, he already lives in communion with all things. If it is true that *de* is "to get from *dao*", as suggested by Nivison,[71] we are dealing with the getting of that 'something' which makes a thing what it is and which renders it a docile instrument of the immeasurable power of the *dao*. Acquiring *de* consists in the muting of one's successes, in the non-imposition of one's pride, and in modestly concealing one's qualities. More importantly, it consists in the silent contracting of credits of gratitude from others without laying claim to anything, without even being perceived as a 'benefactor'. The continual experiencing of a sense of indebtedness highlights the infinite debt towards the *dao*. Precisely this debt inspires the Sage to extend towards others his care and attention, and to help all beings to become one with Ultimate reality.[72]

The Sage must remove all traces of subjectivity and unite himself with the *dao*, drawing from that power and strength which is "Mysterious, Obscure, and Profound" (*xuan de*):

71 NIVISON, *The Paradox*, *op. cit.*, p. 33.

72 See E. M. CHEN, "The Meaning of *te* in the *Tao te Ching*: An Examination of the Concept of Nature in Chinese Taoism", *Philosophy East and West*, 23, 1973, pp. 457-469, where the author finds in *de* a category which highlights "the original state of nature, a state when all is in all, when everything continues in everything else, when the whole universe is a continuous process of a single life process" (p. 469).

> *Dao* brings them to life and *de* nourishes them …
> Therefore, the Ten thousand things venerate the *dao* and honour *de*.
> As for their veneration of the *dao* and their honouring *de*,
> No-one orders[73] them to do it: it is constantly so on its own!
> *Dao* brings them to life, *de*[74] nourishes them, matures them, completes them, rests them, rears them, supports them, protects them.
> It gives life to them but doesn't try to possess them.
> It acts on their behalf but doesn't make them dependent.
> It matures them but doesn't rule them:
> This is what is meant by "Profound Virtue" (*xuan de*).[75]

Why would this virtue be described as "Profound, Obscure"[76] (*xuan de*)? Not because its origins are unknown, but rather because it is a form of virtue destined not to be perceived as such.

The Sage should function in a similar way, losing visibility so that everything takes place without him actively participating, everything being the result of a purely natural spontaneity.

But the Sage is fully conscious of the prodigious, silent power expressed by the *dao* in the form of favour and concession towards others. He is aware of having contracted a debt towards 'something'[77] which can never be directly repaid.

It is because of this unusual lack of proportion between 'giving and receiving' that, despite the favour he enjoys, the Sage must assume the role of the giver (which means "to lose", *shi*, since 'to lose is to possess' because 'to give is to have') rather than the role of he who acquires. He feels indebted rather than in credit towards others. This is confirmed by stanza LXXIX of the *Laozi*:

73 Both the Mawangdui silk manuscripts read "reward them (for it)" instead of "order them".

74 *De* is omitted in the Mawangdui manuscripts as it is in other editions.

75 *Laozi*, stanza LI.

76 The term *xuan* can also mean "mysterious", "obscure".

77 Though the *dao* isn't certainly a mere 'thing'.

> Therefore, the Sage holds the right tally[78] yet makes no demands of others.
> For this reason, those who have *de* are in charge of the tally.
> Those who are without *de* take charge of the collection of taxes.

Paradoxically, *de* signals the acquisition of a loss, a subtraction, a reduction. In stanza XLII we read, "with all things, some are increased by taking away, some are diminished by adding on". In full agreement, stanza XLVIII reads:

> The pursuit of studying is to increase day by day.
> The pursuit of the *dao* is to decrease day by day.
> Decrease and decrease, to the point of not interfering.
> Without interfering, there's nothing left undone.

Having been invested with a gift from the *dao*, the Master of authentic virtue, the Sage, is forever indebted. Thus the 'discredit' he throws upon himself is a sign of gratitude and respect towards that which made him such. This would explain the self-denigration typical of ancient rulers, who conferred upon themselves the most dishonourable epithets: "orphaned, widowed, having no grain" (*gu gua bu sou*, stanzas XXXIX and XLII). This can be explained by the fact that achieving uniformity with the *dao* means "taking the base as one's root", since "to be placed high, one must take the low as foundation" (stanza XXXIX). This is confirmed in stanza XLI of the *Laozi*:

[78] The so-called "manuscript A" from Mawangdui differs from the *vulgata* and reads "right" instead of "left". The right and left tallies represent the two halves of a contract, one kept by the buyer, the other kept by the seller. It is very hard to say which reading should be preferred. According to *Laozi*, stanza XXXI, the Sage is supposed to prefer the left because the left side is auspicious in all affairs, while in performing mourning ceremonies the right is better. Probably the reading in "manuscript A" is more subtle and must be preferred, especially if we remember that the virtue of the Sage is higher precisely because, despite playing a superior role (usually, it is the superior partner who takes the right tally) and the people owing so much to him, he claims neither rights nor merits.

> The highest *de* is [empty and low] like a valley.
> Vast *de* appears to be insufficient.
> Firm *de* appears to be thin and weak.

All this leads me to conclude that in the *Laozi de* seems to become the principle through which an element is identified as a reflection of the *dao*. Such an element must be dilated, open, it must make an offering of itself, it must yield itself, and thus dissolve in the *dao*. This is also true of the Sage, who acts according to the supreme model of unselfishness and indifference, the *dao*, and conforms himself to it. It has already been pointed out that the *dao* can never be fully compensated for how much it gives to 'things', and yet it always bestows its gifts without expecting any form of restitution. Couldn't it be that its infinite power lies precisely in this unconditional yielding?

Thus, if the Sage were not to offer himself as the *dao* offers itself to the Ten Thousand things, then the integrity of his *de* would inevitably be damaged. The highest extolling of his *de* necessitates therefore a final double sacrifice, that is, the renunciation on his part of all benefits resulting from the possession of *de*, and the non-recognition on the part of others of his 'sacred possession':

> The Way (*dao*) of Heaven is like the flexing of a bow.
> The top is pulled down.
> The bottom is pulled up.
> The surplus is removed.
> Where more is needed, it is added.
> Therefore, the Way of Heaven
> is to reduce what is excessive and increase what is insufficient.
> The Way of Man
> is to reduce what is insufficient and increase what is excessive.
> Now, who is able to **have a surplus** and use it to offer it to Heaven?[79]
> Only the one who possesses the Way!

79 Both the Mawangdui manuscripts read "Heaven" instead of "All under Heaven" i.e. "the world".

> Therefore, the Sage acts but does not possess his actions,
> accomplishes his tasks, but does not dwell upon them,
> and does not want to show his worthiness.[80]

What then is the meaning of the expression in bold, which corresponds to the characters *you yu*, literally "to have an abundance, a residue, an excess"? Couldn't it refer to that credit acquired from things in the form of 'power' or 'obscure charisma', deriving from a merit which the Sage refuses to take advantage of?

[80] *Laozi* LXXVII.

GLOSSARY

Main characters

bao 報 "remunerate, repay, recompense"
bao yuan yi de 報怨以德
chi 彳 "to take small steps, to move ahead, to walk,"
dao 道
Daodejing 道德經
de 德 "virtue, potency, charisma"
de[a] 得 "to get"
de[b] 悳
deng 登 "to climb, to ascend, to rise"
jin 進 "offer, offer in sacrifice, promote, give"
Lao Dan 老耽
Lao Laizi 老萊子
Laozi, *Laozi* 老子
mu 目/[illegible] "eye"
sheng 升 "arising, to rise up, to ascend"
shi 失 "to lose, to mislay, to neglect"
shi[a] 施 "to dedicate oneself to someone, give", "advance, proceed"
wu wei 無為 "non action, non interference"
xia de 下德 "inferior virtue"
xin 心 "heart/mind"
xuan de 玄德 "Profound Virtue"
yi de bao yuan 以德報怨
you yu 有餘 "to have an abundance, a residue, an excess"
zhi 直/[illegible] "straight, to grow straight"
zhi[a] 值
zhi[b] 陟 "offer in sacrifice, go up, rise, promote"
zhi de bu de[a] 至德不得 "The highest *de* implies no acquisition"

Special characters

1 
2 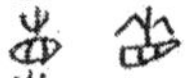
3 
4 
5 

The Master in *Dan* Taoism

Massimo Makarovic

I would like, first of all, to introduce some of the important terms related to the function of the master in China: *zhenshi* "true master", *mingshi* "master who sees clearly", *dashi* "great master", *fashi* "master of method", *dafashi* "master of the great method", *lianshi* "master of practice", *chanshi* "Chan master", *zushi* "founder master". It is noticeable that the term *shi* is common to all the above words. Furthermore, we have to consider terms like *zi*, *xiansheng*, *zhenren*. Even though these titles are used for a master, they do not originally refer to mastership but rather express a degree of attainment in which mastership denotes a function, consisting in the activities of initiation, teaching, and guidance. I shall now get into the details of the above activities.

Initiation: *kouchuanxinshou* ("transmission from mouth to heart") or *zhenchuan* ("the true transmission") is essentially the transmission of the *tianji* ("celestial heart") or *jingqi* ("spiritual influence"), which means the Way itself. In Taoism, this is usually done by the *duizuo*: seated, face to face or back to back. Also deserving mention is the Chan *moding* ("touching the top of the head"). In one document, the young He Xianggu, one of Taoism's eight immortals, states:

> He was qualified (*youyuan*), He gained initiation (*dedu*), He practiced the way of the immortals (*xiuxian*), He attained the Way (*dedao*).[1]

Here we find another term indicating initiation: *du*. *Du* represents initiation as a passage, a crossing. In addition to the above, initiation provides for the *chuanfa* or "transmission of a method" (also *daofa* or simply *fa*) and of a "technique" (*gongfa*) and, at the end, results in the assignment of a "name" (*daoming*) as the disciple dies to his previous state and is reborn as an initiated adept. For instance, we read:

> And the Wujidaoren master led me in front of the altar of the founder master and he allowed me to bow. When I got up, the master told me: 'Look at what is written on the ritual tablet (a wooden tablet that represents the dead)'. I got closer to have a look and saw my name. Then, the master added: 'Now you are another man, the previous one has died'.

These are the true words of a Taoist master who is at present living in northern China, describing the meeting he had with his own master more than thirty years ago. This virtual death, of course, is to be truly experienced by the disciple.

Teaching/instruction: Here, the master transmits a method, a technique (a technique which is chosen according to the disciple's nature). The master knows the correct way to recite the *zhou*-s and draw the *fu*-s, he knows the interpretation of the texts, interpretation that he enlightens with oral glosses which are never written (*zhenjue*, "true instructions"; *koujue*, "oral instructions").

The master is first of all a guide, the one who shows the path. He is the one who corrects, exhorts, but also the one who supports. On this subject, one of the present masters writes:

> Taoism speaks about the Way, the Books and the Master as the three treasures and states that you cannot transmit the Way without the

1 ZHENYANGZI, *Daodejing zhujie*, Dalian, Dalian chubanshe, 1994, p. 77.

> Books and that you cannot penetrate the Books without a Master. The word 'Way' means here the way of attainment. We referred to the personal practice that leads to the attainment of the Way. The word 'Books' means the reading of the Books, the reading of the founder masters' works that testify the realization. The word 'Master' means the transmission of the masters. The transmission of a true master (*zhenchuan*) enlightens the principles of the Way. True master means the master who actually holds the knowledge. Therefore, if you want to know the path leading to the mountain you must ask to the one who is coming from the mountain.[2]

Thus a master, to be truly identified as one, must have attained realization. This is the reason why he is called a *zi*, as it is clearly expressed by the corresponding ideogram: the one who attained or realized (*liao*) the Oneness (*yi*). In the same way, a great master can also be called *zhenren* "true man", or *xiansheng* "pre-born". Of course, this latter title must not be understood in a literal sense. A famous scholar of the Tang dynasty explains:

> Whosoever wants to learn, must have a master. A master is the one who transmits the Way, hands down the instructions and dispels all the doubts. Man is not born with wisdom and who in this world has no doubts! Whosoever has doubts and does not follow a master, will continue to have them and will never dispel them. The one who, born before me, heard the Way, is superior (i.e. pre-born) to me, I will follow him as a master. The one who, born after me, heard the Way, he too is superior to me and I will follow him as a master. I would be a very mean person if I distinguished people by elderliness. Actually, there is no difference between a noble man and a humble man, between an old man and a young man: the realization of the Way is the master's realization.[3]

2 QINGYANGZI, *Xiudao rumen*, Beijing, Zongjiaowenhua chubanshe, 1999, p. 33.

3 HAN YU, *Hanchangli quanji*, Zhongguo shudian, 1991, p. 185.

The use of the *xiansheng* title is widespread indeed. It is typically placed after the surname as a sign of respect; a wife uses it to call her husband. *Xiansheng* is an ancient term that originally indicated one who has attained realization. I take this opportunity to highlight that to consider it an exclusive title of the Confucian milieu does not correspond to reality, nowadays as in the past.

At the beginning of the nineteenth century, Min Yide, belonging to the eleventh generation of the *Longmen* school, gathered and edited the *Zhengdao xianjing* ("The Book of the Immortals that Testifies the Way"). A passage relative to the master's nature says:

> The *Liji* states: '[The title] *shi* (master) is given to one who practices his teaching by and through his realization'; and Nanjiaozi (a previous master) explained: 'That he practices his teaching by his activity means that he gathers the qualified beings so as to lead them to the Supreme Mystery (*taixuan*). [The expression] through his realization, means that he attained realization'.[4]

To gather disciples is not an easy task. Concerning this specific function, we must remember the fact that "a true master holding the true transmission must wait not only for other beings endowed with the qualifications (*yuan*) but also for the right moment (*ji*) to transmit."[5]

> The Heaven's Heart (*tianxin*) is what the three universal principles (i.e. Heaven, Earth, Man) have in common, It is what the books of Dan call *xuanqiao* (the Mysterious Cavity). Every man is endowed with That. The connoisseurs know how to open it and realize it, the dull ones close it and disregard it. If one opens it he will live, if one keeps it closed he will die. Since the primordial age, the immortals transmit this same Way from heart to heart because, as realization is one and the same, so is the transmission. The Reality of the Way is

4 MIN YIDE, *Zhendao xianjing*, V. Also quoted in XU ZHAOREN, *Quanzhen biyao*, Beijing, Zhongguo renmindaxue chubanshe, 1998, pp. 236-237.

5 See PANG YIDE, *Huayangdongtian xiuzhenvangshengfa*, Maoshan, Jiangsu Maoshandaojiaowenhuayanjiushi, 1994.

> certainly not hidden nor concealable, but the transmission of the heart is secret.[6]

Thus it is through the masters, through their realization, that tradition incessantly re-enlivens itself and continues to be transmitted. This line of succession is called *shichengfapai* or simply *shicheng*, "succession of masters".[7] One of these lines is the *Longmenpai*, of the *Longmen* school, from the place where the founder master Qiu Chuji, that is, Changchun zhenren, spent several years to test and improve himself. We are in the thirteenth century, in the Mongol domination period. Because of his many pilgrimages, he spent a large part of his life traveling. He once stopped for a long time in a village called "Dragon's door", that is, Longmen. He was one of the famous Wang Chongyang's seven disciples who later became "the northern seven founders", *beiqizu*. Their master, Wang Chongyang, was the great founder of the *Quanzhendao* ("The Way of Realization of Reality", one of the two ways of the present form of Taoism, the other one being called *Zhengyidao* or "The Way of Realization of Oneness"). Though the living schools are many, like many streams that flow into the same river (this is the meaning of *pai* or school), all of them meet in the *Taishanglaojundaodetianzun*, whose most well-known descent or bodily manifestation is Li Er, better known as Laozi.

In the third chapter of the *Zhuangzi* it is written:

> The Ancients compared man to a bundle that the Lord assembles (= birth) and destroys (= death). When fire extinguishes a bundle, it goes to another one. The fire, nevertheless, does not extinguish itself.

And one gloss explains:

6 LÜ DONGBIN, *Jinhua zongzhi*, I. Also quoted in XU ZHAOREN, *Quanzhen biyao*, *op. cit.*, p. 197.

7 Also, *shichuan* "The Transmission of Masters", *shengji* "The Succession of Knowers", and *Daotong* "The Succession of the Way".

> To know the doctrine of assembling and destroying (or, in other words, condensing and dispersing) means to understand birth and death. This is the prescription for 'nourishing the existence'. The fire spreads (*huochuan*) and does not extinguish itself. If the heart knows that Center which supports everything, it thus comes to the Will of Heaven and never stops to shine. Concerning the expression 'nourishing the existence', it is referred to the *Raison d'être* of existence. Time never comes back nor ceases; therefore, life is at one time acquired, and at another time lost. Who, in this world, knows of any extinction?[8]

Another gloss adds:

> The bundle is impermanent but of the propagation of the fire no one knows the end. The form goes away but the transcendent element remains. This is the investigation's sphere of the Principle which nourishes existence. The bundle is impermanent but the fire that extinguishes it never ceases.[9]

The *Zhuangzi* passage at hand speaks of permanence and impermanence, but, at the same time, in Taoism it bears witness to the master's symbol and function. The fee that in the past a disciple had to pay to his master for the teaching, was made up of a bundle that was used as firewood. The bundle corresponds to the disciple and the fire is the master's teaching. A teaching that inexorably brings the disciple to the final annihilation of his entire individuality. The *Xinhuo xiangchuan* ("The Bundle's Fire Transmission"), often abbreviated as *Xinhuo* ("The Bundle's Fire") or *Huochuan* ("The Fire's Transmission"), indicates, now as in the past, the initiating transmission.

Previously, I mentioned that the initiated person receives a new name i.e. *daoming*, a "Taoist name". The future master, as one who has achieved realization and is therefore able to transmit it and teach it, will also receive a new name, *daohao*, usually followed by the

8 GUO XIANG, *Nanhuazhenjingzhu*, *Guyi congshu*.

9 WANG XIANQIAN, *Zhuangzi jijie*, Shanghai, Shanghai shudian, 1987, p. 20.

suffix *zi* or *daoren* ("Man of the Way"), through a ritual of "registration in the register" (*denglu*). But a *zi* or *daoren* will not necessarily carry out the function of *shi*, the master. Although the master's function is one and perfect in and of itself, the individual beings who carry it out may have different degrees of realization. Therefore, one can say that 'this master is greater than that one', and a master - if required - can occasionally send one of his disciples to another master. Cases of jealousy, envy, or competition never happen, since this has nothing to do with the sphere of initiation nor with a true master. Both the initiation and the investiture of masters have names and forms which often change if we move to "the Way of realization of Oneness", the *Zhengyidao*. This, however, only concerns the forms and terminology and does not affect the essence of the ritual nor the essence of the function.

I would now like to propose a few brief considerations on the *shi* (= master) ideogram. Zhu Junsheng, a scholar of the last dynasty, in his *Yijing* commentary explains:

> *Shi* comes from *dui* [the ideogram's left element], that is, a heap of earth. It means to accumulate, to assemble, to get together a multitude. It comes from *za* [the ideogram's right element], that means everywhere, that extends everywhere. It is the armies' leader. In the *Zhouli* it is written that 2,500 men are a *shi*. Many are the armies but few are the leaders. *Shi* is a term wholly related to the idea of center (*zhong*). Considering the *Yijing*'s *Shi* hexagram, we can see the multitude (*zhong*) standing externally [this means the tri-gram *Kun*, which stands above] and the second line from below [the only *yang* or continuous line] which represents the lord of all hexagrams, the guide. The *Zhang* [lit.: "Man with a Staff"], which is mentioned in the hexagram's glosses, means guide or the one who is able to guide the multitude. The one *yang* line controls the five *yin* lines: this is the symbolic image.[10]

10 ZHU JUNSHENG, *Liushisiguajingjie*, Beijing, Zhonghuashuju chubanshe, 1990, p. 36.

The *Zhouli* passage: "2,500 men are one *shi*", which we can also read as "at the head of 2,500 men there is a *shi*", employs a military language. To understand such language, it is enough to know that the army represents the *yuanqi*, the causal *Qi* which pervades everything, and that the Supreme Commander is none other than the master who, from inside, carries out his own function of leading and guiding all beings. Yet, we should not forget another example, that is, the relationship between the Sovereign and the subject: in the human being, the lord symbolizes the *Shen*, the non-human and transcendent element, whereas the subject represents the *Qi*, his whole existence. We come across this language in Taoism's representative book, the *Daodejing*:

> This Lord (*zhu*) of the ten thousand war chariots mentioned in this chapter [= the twenty-sixth] is no one else but the transcendent Spirit who dwells in the human being's heart.[11]

This quote gives me the opportunity to consider terms such as *zhu*, *zai*, and *zhenzai*, the Lord, the true Lord, and the inner Lord, as well as *Yudi*, the Jade Lord. In other words, the human master in front of us is but a reflection of the inner one.

Without modifying the previous quotations, I would like to present a further explanation of the *Yijing*'s[12] and *Zhouli*'s passages. This is the interpretation of a master of the last century, who in turn quotes words of his own master:

> *Shi* means to accumulate, to assemble, to gather (*zhong*); it means that the master is the one who gathers in his own Center (*zhong*) all the inner virtues. *Zhong*, moreover, expresses an idea of fullness.

Regarding the second quotation, he notes the following:

11 HUANG CHANG, *Daodejingzhushi*. In ZHENYANGZI, *Daodejing zhujie*, *op. cit.*, p. 91.

12 It is also quoted in the *Erya*, under the voice *shi*.

> [The number] 2,500 must be understood as 25. This number expresses the master's fullness and completeness.[13]

Some further observations on the master's function.

The typical ideogram for master, *shi*, is read in the first accent. An ideogram which introduces us to a further aspect of the master figure is *shi* pronounced in the fourth accent, meaning "to examine", "to test". The master, before granting initiation and everything that follows it, examines the candidate repeatedly. Even if the candidate has already been initiated, the master will put him to test till the last minute before granting him the teaching. In the famous *Zhonglüchuandaoji*, the record of the transmission of the Way from Zhong Liquan to Lü Dongbin, the master never gets tired of admonishing the disciple, a future immortal, about the improper use or misuse of transmission. The teaching is not to be given to anyone but only to those who *yudaoyouyuan* i.e. "have affinity with the Way". Under certain circumstances, when the master tests a candidate, he can show harshness and say: "Go away, what do you have to do with the Way!". The literature is full of all sorts of tests that the master forced upon the pupil.

Finally, I would like to mention a celebrated and amusing example: the meeting of the immortal Huangshigong with Zhang Liang. Zhang Liang was a noble young man who, while crossing a bridge during a journey, happened to see an old man sitting on a rock nearby. Then, the old man threw his sandals down the bridge and, turning to Liang, said: "Hey lad, go and bring me my sandals!" Liang got angry but the stranger's old age forced him to obey and thus he went down, took up the sandals and brought them to him. Then the old man said: "And now slip my sandals on!" Liang got closer and, kneeling down, he slipped his sandals on. After this the old man smiled and, while departing, addressed Liang with a sentence that even today everybody knows: "*Ruzi kejiao* the lad can be instructed.

13 MIN YIDE, *Zhendao xianjing*, V. Also quoted in XU ZHAOREN, *Quanzhen biyao*, *op. cit.*, p. 237.

Let's meet here in five days at dawn!" So Liang obeyed, but when he came at the fixed time, the old man was already there waiting for him and looked at him angrily. "Go away and come here in five days, but this time come earlier!" said the old man. Five days later, Liang came earlier but the situation repeated itself in the exact same way, and thus he had to return back five days later. Not knowing what to do anymore, the young man decided to spend the night on the bridge. Early in the morning the old man arrived and with a smiling face said to Liang: "Just so!". Then the old man took out a book[14] and, giving it to Liang, said: "By reading this book one becomes a guide for universal monarchs!"[15]

14 The book symbolizes the transmitted knowledge.

15 See SIMA QIAN, *Shiji*, Beijing, Zhonghua shuju, 1994, pp. 2034-2035.

A Wordless Teaching: Native American Spiritual Masters

Francesco Spagna

A bright light flashed upon the banks of Lake Superior, that inland, restless sea which spreads on the border between the United States and Canada. I was staying in a Chippewa (Anishinaabe) reservation for one of my first researches on native American spiritual traditions. I had been welcomed in the small ranch of a local personality known as a medicine man, a shaman. His appearance could have been that of any Wisconsin fisherman or woodman. I will call him "Joe". Joe lived at the end of one of the reservation gravel roads, straight tracks running right in the middle of the woods and seemingly leading nowhere. To me, he looked like a simple and bashful man: he seemed quite reluctant to be considered as a spiritual guide.

After camping for several days near his house, I decided to talk to him. In times of *New Age* and after decades of Castaneda influence, I was feeling quite uneasy. It was difficult to find the right approach, the right words to establish a relationship. Actually, I didn't know exactly what I was looking for, whether I was doing an anthropological study or looking for a spiritual guide. Anyway, we managed to talk while he was cleaning birch bushes. I started to tell him some of my dreams and to discuss with him the interpretations of symbols. Joe was only vaguely interested by the different dream interpretations and the initiation symbolism of ancient Europe. He didn't say much about my dreams, something intimate he wouldn't come into: I would have to interpret my dreams by myself.

At that time, when the conversation was coming to an end, on a sandy track running along the lake bank some boys of the reservation came along on small beach go-karts, making an awful noise. I think one of them was Joe's son and Joe waved to him with his hand. They passed close to us breaking our quietness, but didn't seem to notice us, grasped as they were to their motors and wearing helmets. "Look, they didn't even notice us", Joe said, "they are below the threshold of consciousness". I was struck by these words and the entire scene. Also when compared to what we saw afterwards—once silence had returned—while walking together in the woods and meeting wild animals coming close to us and being surprisingly fearless.

The spiritual master is a pathfinder, one who shows the path and guides along the spiritual journey. This English word fits the native American thought quite well. It is also noteworthy that English allows two uses of the word "teaching", with both gerundive and substantive forms. To give a suitable example, "teaching" may as well refer to the famous *Teachings of Don Juan*—teachings given by somebody—as well as to something like the Teaching Rock, which is an important place for the native people of Ontario. The semantic ambivalence is shown in this place name: is it a rock where teaching is given or is it the rock which is teaching? The Teaching Rock is a large crystalline basement outcrop, typical of the Canadian Shield. On this rock are engraved sacred and mythological stone-glyphs, which are thousands of years old. Though it is an archaeological site, protected by the Canadian State and covered with a dome, the Teaching Rock is also a place where native traditionalists still come to hold ceremonies and give offerings to the engraved pictures. But, again, one might ask: "*Who* is in fact giving the spiritual teaching?"

On the opposite side, it's important to point out some general criteria of traditional native American *learning*. Whether there is a bark basket to be made or a spiritual teaching to be received, the way of learning in this cultural context is mainly visual. "Just watch!" was the only advice I was given by a Chippewa traditionalist, when I asked him how I should behave during a shamanic initiation ceremony I wanted to attend. *Learning by watching* without ever asking and *learning to watch*, again without asking, all this, and more, was included in this "just watch!". What would be regarded as a passive attitude in our educational system, actually stimulates very much one's attention and intelligence. While, in our system, the value of a pupil is bound to the question he or she is able to ask, it will be bound to his or her ability to remain silent in a traditional native American system. Another characteristic of this culture is that the learning capacity is always thought to depend on the pupil's interior life. One learns only what he or she is ready to learn and understand; besides that, nothing really matters. Therefore, it doesn't make any sense to measure the pupil's ability to learn with the teacher's ability to explain. The initiate's spiritual progress proceeds mainly by 'chance' or, better, through coincidences. In the shamanic initiation, as we shall see, the master only indicates a route—along which the candidate will have to individually face several trials. This aspect is particularly evident among native hunter groups of the Sub-arctic and other native groups of North America related with the Vision Quest complex, which entails temporary isolation in the wilderness and fasting. The initiation result—if I may call it this—will be different for each and every one. Revelation will be individual and secret.

Concerning the question "who are the teachers?", we are offered some clues from native cosmology and world representation: nature is animated and regarded as one whole living entity. Human beings, animals, plants, rocks, atmospheric phenomena, heavenly bodies, etc. are all shapes through which the life force manifests itself. On the earthly level, the exterior forms or coverings are made up of different skins, furs, scales, feathers, barks.

In this connection, especially interesting is a famous character of mythical narratives: the Trickster-Transformer. A demiurge, a cultural hero or 'divine rascal' as he has been called—he is particularly clever at changing his appearance into an animal, a tree or a rock in order to prepare his plots or to escape hitches.

I must here recall the importance attributed to the symbolical and ritual representation of external forms, whether they be feathers or furs. One thing that all coverings have in common is that they are transitory, ephemeral. Perhaps, their ritual significance lies precisely in this constitutive impermanence.

Every level of existence is ruled by the same principles. Rocks, stars, the wind and thunder are all viewed as endowed with personality. It is said that at the very beginning there was no difference between human beings and natural phenomena, all had a personality and communicated through a common language. According to shamanic thought, even nowadays we can find traces of this initial 'confusion' of all living species. In this anti-taxonomical philosophy, natural elements or events, taken as 'persons', can be regarded as teachers. That's how a rock can be a teacher.

In the Sweat Lodge ritual, stones are called "Grandfathers". The Sweat Lodge rite is an ancient ceremony occurring in different native groups of North America, and very likely it has circum-boreal origins. Each part of the ceremonial setting—the bent posts of the lodge frame, the East Door aligned with an outside fireplace and a sandy moonlike altar—has a precise symbolical and ritual order. I had personal experience of the Sweat Lodge during a meeting of the shamanic "medicine society" or Midewiwin, at a remote ceremonial site on Lake Huron, Canada.

After a walk around the sandy altar, officiants and guests came into the small and low hut and gathered on a mat of evergreen branches. The ceremonial stones and the outside incandescent fire were brought into the small well placed at the centre of the lodge. Then, the lodge canvas covering was closed and officiants started singing and beating the sacred drum. Water and herbs were thrown over the burning stones—the only light inside—generating strong steam springs: this is how the guests are thought to be 'cooked' into this kind of cosmic uterus, where all the elements melt together.

We came out of the lodge on our hands and knees, after a ceremony that lasted several hours and which is to be regarded as a metaphor of a new birth. Nothing of what happened or was said inside the lodge should ever be revealed. It must remain a secret among those who attended the ritual. I might call the officiants 'ceremony masters', although they regard themselves simply as mediums: very humbly and with a great sense of responsibility, they are called to infuse Life into all those who participated in the Sweat Lodge ritual.

In the Anishinaabe language, "life" is named with a quite complex concept—*bimaadiziwin*—which also means "well being" or "easy going". The Gift of Life is a most important shamanic concept. It is essential in the Midewiwin initiation rite, when the candidate is symbolically killed and then resuscitated as a new member of the shamanic group. The Gift of Life can be also conceived as a 'teaching' in the gift/offering relationship which starts with the teacher-shaman. One must never forget, when meeting a native spiritual leader, to offer him some tobacco, that he will afterwards offer to the spirits. So, in olden times as nowadays, one must offer a pinch of tobacco each time he or she receives a 'teaching'; whether it comes from a shaman or it is an eagle flying over him/her or the beauty of a waterfall.

Meeting with the spiritual powers of wild nature is the main point of the Vision Quest. In many native groups of North America young boys and girls, when puberty occurs, are sent fasting in the woods or in other remote places. This can last for several days. The candidate builds a small shelter and a fireplace from which he/she is not allowed to go away; the adept may also build a platform up in the trees, as Cree Indians do. Overcoming fear and getting purified through the fast are the main initiation trials. But what is most crucial is the special dream or visionary experience which occurs during these trials and which will bear fundamental importance in the life of each candidate. We find here the common categories of the rites of passage well known to us since the seminal work of Arnold Van Gennep: the parting from village social life; the 'liminal' phase, when the initiation experience takes place; the return and 're-aggregation' to one's previous life, with a new social role. However, there are some features of the Vision Quest which give it a special place among rituals. The 'separation' phase is sometimes represented as a symbolic death: the cheeks of the candidates are blackened with charcoal, as is usually done for the deceased. It is also important to notice how during the 'liminal' phase all values are in some way overturned, emphasizing nature's wild side. Especially in the Sub-arctic and Woodlands cultures, the forest is regarded as a place of absolute purity, contrasted to the human confusion and impurity of villages. It must be emphasized that the young people are completely alone when facing their initiation: the dreams or visions they will experience will remain the most important secret of their life.

The Vision Quest (*Waussaeyaubindumowin* in the Ojibwa-anishinaabe language) is also regarded as a typical shamanic rite and it can be practised by teenagers as well as by adults, anytime one feels it necessary. We could say it's a kind of setting inducing an eventual shamanic 'call'. Animals or natural events seen or dreamed during the Vision Quest might become spiritual assistants or tutelary deities of a future shaman. A shaman can also decide to go on a Vision Quest if he feels his relationship with the spirits is becoming weaker.

Among the hunters of the Sub-arctic, the Vision Quest is particularly important. The person who is undertaking the ritual is alone and helpless in the forest, and animals are supposed to come and take care of him. A situation which is the opposite of hunting: the candidate is in the position of becoming a possible prey, and his stomach is empty. His miserable state and cries are supposed to induce a kind of animal *pietas*. Usually aggressive or fearful, animals are believed to become helpful and tame.

In the Vision Quest the teacher/shaman acts only to set the ritual. He can only decide the times and places for the ritual and he will give just a few instructions about what to do or not to do during isolation. Here again, the teacher is only a medium. But the ritual he sets up is the necessary condition in order to receive the most precious and life-lasting spiritual teaching.

One could argue about modifications in one's state of consciousness caused by hypoglycaemia, but fasting must be regarded as essentially a metaphor. It is the means to escape what Lewis Hyde called "appetite traps". Fasting weakens the ties between humans and their need to feed themselves and to kill for this purpose: the everlasting cycle of full and empty stomachs, the 'gastro-enteric' relationship with the world. Fasting brings about a completely different point of view, it highlights an unconventional life level.

This new level of consciousness brought by the Vision Quest might be called 'trans-specific'. The identities of each species are altered: thus, animals are thought to be able to talk or bring messages. From our point of view, it is interesting to note how the cruel survival rules are in some way put aside. All that matters is the awareness of sharing a common destiny of existence, a common soul. To learn the teaching means to be able to transcend the ordinary limits of reality, to reach what Gregory Bateson called "third level learning".

As the Vision Quest is strictly personal and secret, there are no authoritative ethnographic descriptions of it. What is possible to know is that there are recurrent phases during the four 'canonical' days of fasting. On the first day, the spirits of nature or *manidoog* manifest themselves in different ways to the youngster or the shaman who is meditating alone. On the second day, they usually try to chase him/her away. If he or she resists—which is the most important initiation trial—the spirits will quiet down and be pitiful. They will then show themselves again, this time bringing a clear message through a dream or vision, or giving some kind of teaching.

We might argue about what kind of teachings these are: should they be classified as symbolical, mystical, archetypal? Indeed, it is very difficult to answer this question. By the way, through the Vision Quest a shaman is also believed to learn the healing properties of specific plants.

The 'dream visitors' are therefore the true teachers in the shamanic traditions of native Americans. They can be animals, plants, rocks, or even atmospheric entities, though they seem to be agents and 'speakers' of something much wider and comprehensive. It was about a century ago when historians of religion and anthropologists began to debate whether the concept of Great Spirit—*Kitchi Manido*—(akin to the Great Mystery—*Wakan Tanka*—in the Siouan language) is or is not a traditional native concept. In the traditions of the Micmac people of Atlantic Canada, very close to the Anishinaabeg, *Kinap* is a kind of monistic principle, a power which goes through and at the same time transcends the six cosmological levels of the world, giving energy and transforming the universe. As the myths of the Micmac tell us, the *Ki-*

nap principle acts through 'persons': animated forces such as human beings, animals, plants, minerals, atmospheric entities (Wind, Storm, the Seasons), parts of the landscape (Lakes, Mountains) or even astral bodies (Sun, Moon, the Stars).

If the visionary teaching is given by an animal, a whole life can be dedicated to it, studying and watching this particular subject with empathy and passion. It is one of the many forms of what anthropologists named a totemic culture. In which way can an animal be a teacher? I shall conclude by quoting the simple words of a Teton Sioux, Brave Buffalo, which sound like a piece of the eighteenth century English poet William Blake:

> Let a man decide upon his favourite animal and make a study of it, learning its innocent ways. Let him learn to understand its sound and motions. The animals wish to communicate with man.

Shall we call it 'the Way of Innocence'?

BIBLIOGRAPHY

Baesso, Agnese, *Digiuno e ricerca di visione presso gli Anishinaabeg dell'Ontario canadese*, BA Thesis, University of Turin, Faculty of Political Sciences, academic year 1997-98.

Bateson, Gregory, *Steps to an Ecology of Mind*, Chandler Publishing Company, 1972.

Benedict, Ruth F., "The Vision in the Plain Culture", *American Anthropologist*, vol. 24, n. 1 (1922): 1-23.

Benedict, Ruth F., *The Concept of the Guardian Spirit in North America,* Menasha (Wisconsin), Memoirs of the American Anthropological Association n. 29, 1923.

Bianchi, Ugo (ed.), *Transition Rites. Cosmic, Social and Individual Order.* Proceedings of the Finnish-Swedish-Italian Seminar held at the University of Rome "La Sapienza" 24th-28th March 1984, Roma, L'Erma di Bretschneider, 1986.

Brightman, Robert, *Grateful Prey. Rock Cree Human-Animal Relationship*, Berkeley, University of California Press, 1993.

Brown, Jennifer S. H. – Brightman, Robert, *The Orders of the Dreamed. George Nelson on Cree and Northern Ojibwa*, Winnipeg, The University of Manitoba Press, 1988.

Bruhac Joseph, *The Native American Sweat Lodge. History and Legends,* The Crossing Press, 1993.

Comba, Enrico (ed.), *Testi religiosi degli Indiani del Nordamerica*, Torino, Utet, 2001.

Duerr, Hans Peter, *Tempo di sogno. Sui limiti tra dimensione della natura selvaggia e processo di civilizzazione,* Milano, Guerini e Associati, 1992 (*Traumzeit. Über die Grenze zwischen Wildnis und Zivilisation,* Surkamp Verlag, 1984).

Flannery, Regina – Chambers, Mary E., "Each Man Has His Own Friends: the Role of Dream Visitors in Traditional East Cree Belief and Practice", *Arctic Anthropology*, 22, 1 (1985): 1-22.

Goulet, Jean-Guy, "Dreams and Visions in Indigenous Lifeworlds: An Experimental Approach", *The Canadian Journal of Native Studies*, vol. XII, n. 2 (1993): 171-198.

Hillman, James, *Animali del sogno,* Milano, Raffaello Cortina, 1991.

Hoffman, Walter J., *The Mide'wiwin or "Grand Medecine Society" of the Ojibwa*, Bureau of American Ethnology, Seventh Annual Report, 1885-86, Washington 1891.

Hultkrantz, Åke, *The Religions of the American Indians*, Berkeley, University of California Press, 1979.

Hultkrantz, Åke, "The American Indian Vision Quest. A Transition Ritual or a Device for Spiritual Aid?", in Bianchi, Ugo (ed.), *Transition Rites. Cosmic, Social and Individual Order.* Proceedings of the Finnish-Swedish-Italian Seminar held at the University of Rome "La Sapienza" 24th-28th March 1984, Roma, L'Erma di Bretschneider, 1986, pp. 24-43.

Hultkrantz, Åke, *Native Religions of North America. The Power of Visions and Fertility,* San Francisco, Harper & Row, 1987.

Hyde, Lewis, *Trickster Makes This World*, New York, North Point Press, 1998.

Johnston, Basil, *Ojibway Heritage*, Toronto, McClelland & Stewart, 1979.

Johnston, Basil, *Ojibway Ceremonies*, Toronto, McClelland & Stewart, 1982.

Landes, Ruth, *Ojibwa Religion and the Midewiwin*, Madison-London, University of Wisconsin Press, 1968.

Monaco, Emanuela, "La funzione iniziatica della visione presso gli Ojibwa", *Studi e Materiali di Storia delle Religioni*, Roma, vol. 50, n. 1 (1984): 71-99.

Monaco, Emanuela, "Considerazioni sulla visione puberale tra gli Ojibwa", in Bianchi, Ugo (ed.), *Transition Rites. Cosmic, Social and Individual Order.* Proceedings of the Finnish-Swedish-Italian Seminar held at the University of Rome "La Sapienza" 24th-28th March 1984, Roma, L'Erma di Bretschneider, 1986, pp. 199-204.

Radin, Paul, "Some Aspects of Puberty Fasting Among the Ojibwa", *Museums Bulletins of the Canada Department of Mines*, Geological Survey, n. 2 (1914): 69-78.

Ridington, Robin, "Telling Secrets: Stories of the Vision Quest", *The Canadian Journal of Native Studies*, vol. II, n. 2, 1982.

Rostkowski, Joëlle, "Spiritualité et affirmation identitaire", *Recherches Amérindiennes au Québec*, XXX, 1, 2000.

Spagna, Francesco, *L'ospite selvaggio. Esperienze visionarie e simboli dell'orso nelle tradizioni native americane e circumboreali*, Torino, Il Segnalibro, 1998.

Tanner, Adrian, *Bringing Home Animals. Religious Ideology and Mode of Production of Mistassini Cree Hunters*, New York, St. Martin Press, 1979.

Underhill, Ruth, *Red Man's Religion. Beliefs and Practices of the Indians North of Mexico*, Chicago & London, University of Chicago Press, 1965.

Vecsey, Christopher (ed.), *Religion in Native North America*, Moscow (Idaho), University of Idaho Press, 1990.

THE *GURU* AS MEDIATOR OF HEALING

LUCA CALDIRONI

Healing means daring to
step outside one's fence.
(H. Kalweit)

We must ask the question if it's legitimate to try to bridge the gap between Western and Indian culture and, more importantly, whether in doing so we should make use of the tools offered by psychoanalysis.

I'm convinced it is. Comparison doesn't mean assimilation. Building bridges is not synonymous with attempting to force one's own disciplines on others or to colonize areas of knowledge. It's rather an attempt to break down or 'melt' cognitive limits by using whatever tools help to encourage *thinking* and *thinking together*.

The aim of this effort is to offer different levels of interpretation to anthropological semantics – not through self-contained, exclusive models – but by taking an interdisciplinary approach to knowledge, warning against 'certainty' and working as far as possible towards a real *metanoia*.

The need for integration always stems from personal experience, especially when confronting 'internal' aspects of knowledge. This is also true in my case: I have a background in psychiatry combined with a passion for Indian culture.

INDOASIATICA 2/2004, [529-538]

Viewing landscapes that are so different to the point of being disorientating, helps see things from different perspectives and achieve what W. R. Bion has called "binocular" vision.[1] In particular, I use Indian culture as a dialectic counterpart not so much in order to borrow solutions from it but rather to encourage moments in which debate is suspended and our 'apparatus for thinking thoughts' is expanded.

It is not a question of compounding different hermeneutical strategies. It is an effort to make us more aware of the kind of ambivalence we feel when faced with anything 'other'. Sudhir Kakar reminds us that what we can learn from Indian culture is *not* how to solve problems but rather how to *suspend* our own viewpoints.

I believe that the psychoanalytic approach can help us carry out an in-depth investigation, limiting the risks of Western-centrism, in order to discover the deepest internal forces that determine who we are, not losing track of the complexity of human emotions.

In light of what Sigmund Freud referred to as "civilization and its discontents", we ethno-anthropologists, psychiatrists, and psychoanalysts must be willing to look beyond our particular areas of knowledge and study each others' disciplines if we wish to come up with hypotheses that take into account the extraordinary complexity of this phenomenon. This entails the opening of ourselves to other symbolic constellations of values, besides those of Judeo-Christian and Greek culture.

Indian civilization lends itself easily to psychoanalytic investigation. What is needed is a careful study of the underlying motivations of individuals and the cultures in which they live. We need to know how alienation is experienced and expressed – being very careful not to apply rigid psychopathological models or preconceived notions to what we study. Freud himself has paved the way for us, filling the gap between normality and abnormality by introducing the 'quantitative ' aspect of the workings of the psychic apparatus.

1 See W. R. BION, *Attenzione e interpretazione. Una prospettiva scientifica sulla psicoanalisi e sui gruppi*, Roma, Armando, 1973.

Besides the fact that Indian and Western cultures respond very differently to man's basic physiological needs, it is well-known that Indian culture has widely preserved its ancient mythical and ritual traditions.

Because of the steady process of 'world demystification' in Western society, public and private have been radically separated, relegating fantasy to the private, so that it can rarely be shared in public.[2]

It is important to avoid reductive psychological interpretations. Alongside an impulsive, individual psychic reality, we must envision a collective unconscious, forming a *continuum* of deeply-rooted osmotic phenomena.

One of our first tasks is to differentiate between the figure of the *guru* as imagined in today's society and the more ancient role of the *guru* as initiator of knowledge. The *guru* is a teacher or spiritual master. In particular, he/she is the one who gives initiation (*dikṣā*) to his/her disciples and carries *weight* (in Sanskrit *guru* is an adjective originally meaning *heavy*) in their lives.

Alain Daniélou, along the lines of a time-honoured tradition, highlights the symbolical interpretation of the two syllables of the term *guru* as offered in the *Advaya-taraka Upaniṣad*: *gu* = "darkness" and *ru* = "disperser", coming to mean *he/she who dispels darkness*.[3]

These are not the sole definitions of a *guru*. Initially, this figure seems to have functioned more as an *instructor* whose job it was to teach disciples how to perform sacrificial rites correctly.

The *guru* subsequently gained power and became a *model* for disciples to follow. This does not take place through any kind of 'divine' process, but happens when the *guru* incorporates those characteristics which are understood to be the attributes of a knowledgeable man: *bālya* or "childlike" mind (in a positive sense), entailing purity

2 On this issue, see G. OBEYESEKERE, *The Work of Culture*, Chicago & London, The University of Chicago Press, 1990.

3 See A. DANIÉLOU, *Yoga*. The *Method of Re-Integration*, New York, University Books, 1956.

and non-expansion i.e. a 'non-saturated' mind; *pāṇḍitya* or "wisdom", referring to the function of the qualified teacher who grants education and knowledge (*upadeśa*); *mauna* or "silence" of speech and mind. Indeed, in Indian culture silence is the pathway to *supreme union*.

It is at this level that the teacher-disciple relationship, although not symbiotic, becomes extremely intimate and filled with empathy. The teacher no longer bases himself/herself solely on doctrine but throws everything up for question, including his/her own authority. The *guru* encourages the disciple to test everything through constant, personal experimentation and verification.

Interestingly, as S. Kakar notices, while the *guru* progresses from a human status to a divine status, the disciple regresses from adulthood to childhood.[4]

A study of the *guru* figure necessarily leads to the thorny issue of the different conceptualisation of *time* in the Indian context. The West is where the sun dies ... and here time is clearly defined! In Hindī, on the other hand, there is only one word for both "yesterday" and "tomorrow": *kal*, the meaning depending upon the context and the verb used.

What I am interested in here is not the historical background of the *guru* as teacher and guarantor of true spirituality and philosophical doctrine, but rather his/her status as a 'mediator of healing', bringing about evolutive as well as cognitive change. The *guru* and similar figures in other cultures are more and more being called upon to intervene in psychic and somatic sufferings, in order to restore mental and physical health.

In the patient-therapist relationship in Western societies we have made the mistake of labelling regression as 'pathological', excessive submission as 'denial of hostility', and dependency as 'unresolved ties with the mother figure'. Well aware of these risks, I still think

4 On these patterns of transformation, see S. KAKAR, *The Inner World*, New York, Oxford University Press, 1981.

that the *guru* can offer patients the chance to engage in a relationship that may enable them to incorporate formative experiences.[5]

The *guru* links health with freedom i.e. liberation, so that the disciple may be both *sanus et salvus*. Herein, health is thought of in global terms: at once psychosomatic, moral, and spiritual.[6] It is therefore important not to try and apply rigid definitions to the figures of the *guru* and psychoanalyst (= therapist) but to look for similarities in their roles. For this reason, I purposely use the terms interchangeably, inasmuch as both the *guru* and the psychoanalyst are mediators of healing.

The *guru*'s first function is to guide the disciple through the initiation process and then through the process of self-awareness and introspection. He or she becomes a figure onto which the disciple, the patient, can project and transfer emotional needs as well as states of mind that have somehow marked his/her life. The mere presence of the *guru* may be enough to reawaken psychic states that prove to be highly curative, encouraging endogenous mechanisms of self-healing.

The benevolent, silent presence of the *guru*, sometimes experienced as a mirror in which the patient can reflect himself/herself, warm and comfortable, close, can trigger communication with deep levels of the psyche via pre-verbal emotional states. *Guru*-disciple interaction goes deeper, touching levels of the psyche usually reached only in rare and precious moments during psychoanalysis. The devotee comes in touch with the buried core of his or her depression, at the basis of his/her sense of self and life, beyond words.[7]

Human beings need attention and recognition. If they don't receive it they are often left with a deep sense of emptiness and psy-

5 See S. KAKAR, *The Analyst and the Mystic*, Chicago, The University of Chicago Press, 1991.

6 See V. LANTERNARI, *Medicina, magia, religione, valori*, Napoli, Liguori, 1994.

7 On the *guru*-disciple interaction, see S. KAKAR, *Shamans, Mystics and Doctors: A Psychological Inquiry into India and Its Healing Traditions*, Boston, Beacon Press, 1983.

chic pain that can alienate them from their very existence. The results of childhood neglect create situations – especially in Western society – in which we find extreme forms of self-sufficiency hand-in-hand with overwhelming feelings of inner emptiness, panic, and chronic spiritual hunger.

On the one hand, we must agree with Freud when he maintains that healing comes about through "awareness", "reclaiming" the area of the Es by expanding the Ego, but on the other hand we cannot underestimate how crucial the non-verbal master-disciple i.e. therapist-patient relationship is to this process.

D. Winnicott stresses this point, viewing the relationship between analyst and patient as much more important than any interpretations that may result.[8]

W. R. Bion, moreover, points out the enormous difference between a form of rational understanding and the kind of existential development which takes place when memory and desire (even the desire to understand and get better) are set aside, and the patient begins to experience what is actually going on in the relationship, enabling him/her to get in touch with the deepest recesses of himself/herself *and* the other. Once this "atonement" is achieved, the person is established in what Bion calls "O" (= the Ultimate Reality, the Thing in and of Itself).

This experience produces a highly emotional atmosphere – a preverbal mind-set – an intimate world enriched by everything the *guru* brings to it in terms of background, expectations, approach, and experience. The disciple's expectations play a fundamental part in this as well. I might say that people choose *guru*-s based on deep-seated, unconscious needs. Something similar takes place in Western therapy when people decide on the kind of treatment they want to undergo. In our Western cities, where all kinds of therapies are available, this kind of 'pre-transference' is even more evident. Thus, some people choose *marabout*-s, others prefer exorcists or even opt for

[8] See D. WINNICOTT, *Gioco e realtà*, Roma, Armando, 1990.

psychotropic drugs. Still others feel themselves 'destined' to psychoanalysis.[9]

Let's take a step back and say that the very symptoms a patient presents are an attempt at mediation, at resolving conflict. Freud considered symptoms a kind of compromise between two conflicting desires. We could then go so far as to say that *both* the *guru*-therapist *and* the symptom represent an attempt at mediating spontaneous recovery. The difference being that the *guru*-therapist, in taking on the symptoms – via the deeply emotional impact of his/her relationship with the disciple – offers a chance to change and grow emotionally.

The *guru*-disciple relationship becomes an important extension of the parent-child relationship for the disciple, offering him/her a second chance at experiencing the kind of nurturing needed for cohesion, integration, and self-strength. This can only take place through genuine involvement. There can be no artifice if one is to be successful.

This leads me back to the question of whether it is plausible to hypothesize a complementary approach to healing between Eastern and Western traditions. What are all these Westerners seeking when they go searching for *guru*-s in faraway lands?

It's well-known that Freud dismissed Indian culture in general and mystical phenomena in particular as the ghosts of regressive functions, encapsulated in what he referred to as the oceanic feeling (or the regression to ancient symbiosis i.e. *regressus ad uterum*). The correspondence between Freud and Romain Rolland on the subject is still famous. I will limit myself to cite a well-known passage from a letter Freud wrote to Rolland, who had been urging him to take more interest in the religious aspects of Indian culture:

> And now, under your guidance, I shall try to penetrate the Indian jungle from which a certain mixture of Hellenic love of proportion, Jewish sobriety and Philistine timidity have until now kept me at a

9 On these issues, see T. NATHAN, *La follia degli altri*, Firenze, Ponte alle Grazie, 1990.

> distance. I really should have confronted it sooner, as I am no stranger to the vegetation of that land, having dug deeply into it looking for its roots. But it isn't easy to exceed the limits of one's very nature.[10]

I am firmly convinced that the non-verbal in psychoanalysis enables us to reach the deepest recesses of the psyche, the previously unfathomable areas of the subconscious. I am also persuaded that meditation, total inner concentration, the listening to oneself, produces a state which puts people in touch with their emotions, even the most unpleasant and disturbing ones. This meditative awareness avoids the poisonous identification of the person with his/her own emotions. Even fear is transcended. The individual is then able to 'embrace' *all* emotions as precious and valuable tools for understanding.

This, and perhaps much more, can be learned from Indian culture. It's not a question of quenching our thirst for knowledge or finding answers to our doubts, but rather of learning how to suspend doubt, anxiety, and fear in a 'container' of constantly developing senses.

This is in agreement with the theories of those therapists who say that the ability to dissociate oneself from the specific contents of the mind is *basic* to psychoanalysis. Indeed, this is one of the tenets of Eastern meditation – the ability to become an observer of oneself, to view one's own mind 'from the outside'. Following this spiritual exercise, Easterners and Westerners should work together in an effort to uncover the analogies between the phenomenological and the mystical.

This is precisely what W. R. Bion advocates when he says that analysts must focus their attention on "O": the Unknown, the Unknowable. In fact, they must become It i.e. they themselves must become infinite by suspending memory, desire, and understanding. Perhaps, it's no accident that Bion was born in India!

At a seminar on dreams which was held in Rome in 1998, Parthenope Bion Talamo observed:

[10] S. FREUD, *Letter to Romain Rolland* (19 January, 1930).

> Bion entertained the idea of an unconscious flow, not in the sense of being unconscious, but in the sense of being unaware ... We could say that we are always dreaming, but are not always aware of our dreams....Bion theorized on a concept borrowed from the French idea of "*rêverie*" ... Bion took this idea (maternal *rêverie*) and applied it to psychoanalysis in the sense of working 'without memory or desire' ... [This has] something to do, I believe, with Bion's childhood in India and his contact with a culture having very different rhythms from our own, and in any case very different from the English culture of the time ... Bion's family was not strictly English, in fact hardly English at all ... it was a kind of Euro-Asiatic hybrid which turned out to be very influential in the development of a person who was a child at the time ... he certainly absorbed a great deal of Indian culture. We believe that when Bion speaks of thought that needs no one to think it, this in itself expresses that aspect of Indian culture that seeks perfect concentration and the "in–centring" of attention (*samādhi*).[11]

Mark Epstein argues that when Freud spoke of the oceanic feeling as the apotheosis of mystical sentiment, and when Fromm praised the sense of well-being resulting from Buddhist meditation, they were both overlooking a simple but very basic point. Meditation is not primarily intended to create states of well-being. Its fundamental aim is rather that of softening and eventually annihilating one's ego.[12] However, a person cannot 'dis-identify' himself/herself without first *becoming* himself/herself.

The *guru* facilitates this process by becoming a substitute ego for the disciple's distressed ego, developing metaphors that deeply touch the disciple's emotional realm and reawakening traumatized areas of

[11] P. BION TALAMO, "Sviluppi e cambiamenti nella teoria psicoanalitica del sogno con riferimento all'opera di W. R. Bion". In *Il sogno*. Atti del Seminario svoltosi il 10 giugno 1998 presso il Dipartimento di Scienze Neurologiche – Ambulatorio di Malattie Psicosomatiche dell'Università degli Studi *La Sapienza* di Roma (the article is available on the Internet: www.Psychomedia.it).

[12] On these issues, see M. EPSTEIN, *Pensieri senza un pensatore*, Roma, Ubaldini, 1996.

the disciple's psyche. This allows the disciple some room or space to think about himself/herself. And thought is *eros*, and it is precisely through *eros* that human beings establish ties. The master does not intervene in the area of *having*, but in the area of *being,* reactivating the ability to symbolize and expanding emotional life.

I can only briefly touch here on the benefits derived from sharing this process in a group situation. Groups, communities, as well as life in hermitages or *āśram*-s enhance emotional states. Herein, one's sense of identity tends to 'melt' and there is a progressive loss of control over impulses, leaving room for catharsis and change.

As a mediator of healing, the *guru*, just as the Western therapist, must use to advantage – and eventually sustain – all the disciple's idealistic projections as well as negative transferences. Accepting and understanding projection and idealization for what they are, but without identifying with them, is a complicated task which the *guru* is expected to have learnt during his/her long and strenuous initiation period.

The *guru* acts as a true 'catalyst', enabling the healing process. The disciple, the patient, is not considered sick. He is rather viewed as a person engaged in a difficult existential struggle. Therefore, it is not a question of changing him or her but of understanding and accompanying the person, since the process itself is the goal, and life is an unending, creative process.

Figure and Role of the Master Between East and West

Giangiorgio Pasqualotto

Don't try to identify me with anything,
don't even try to oppose me to something else.
I stand where there are no fear nor desires.
Nisargadatta Mahārāj

Whoever comes to reason with Socrates, as it happens, and dialogues with him, whatever is the argument, is led and invited to go on until he understands himself and the way he has lived.
Plato, *Lachetes* 187e

Generally speaking, any discussion about the transmission of knowledge always implies at least two basic prerequisites: a) the notion and use of a particular form of *temporality* – contents, quantity, and methods of teaching must necessarily take into account the way one understands the link between tradition and innovation; b) the notion and use of a particular form of *subjectivity*: contents, quantity, and methods of teaching must necessarily take into account what one means with the notion of 'self', both concerning the figure of the master and that of the disciple.

Therefore, in order to begin to understand the nature of the master-disciple relationship in Eastern traditions, it is necessary to remember that, first of all, the notion of time is expressed in a movement of *circularity*, not of linearity. Thus, what happens *after* never possesses the quality of absolute originality, but rather tends to exhibit the quality of repetition.[1] I say 'tends' because it's not a mere

1 This circular form of temporality is also found in the transmission of artistic skills; see G. PASQUALOTTO, *Yohaku. Forme di ascesi nell'esperienza estetica orientale*. Padova, Esedra, 2001.

INDOASIATICA 2/2004, [539-560]

repetition but rather a *relative repetition*, just as in the natural cycles, with the changing seasons or the alternation between night and day: there is never a night, day or season exactly identical to another. And in the same season there is never an event – an atmospheric or biological phenomenon – perfectly identical to another one. Likewise, in the teachings' transmission we never witness a pure and simple repetition. One cannot say there is a situation of absolute stillness, nor can one say there is a situation of drastic *innovation.*[2] A master's teaching, within a tradition, acts as a flower within a process of blooming that belongs to a particular season i.e. spring: a particular teaching does not claim it creates a new tradition, the way a flower does not create a new species or a new season. At the same time, this teaching doesn't simply repeat the contents of the doctrines worked out by tradition, the way a flower doesn't limit itself to duplicating without differences forms, colours, and smells of a flower of the same species, blossomed in a previous spring. This characteristic of 'difference in continuity' does not imply any evaluation, neither positive nor negative, of innovation compared to tradition: this would be as absurd as judging a flower in comparison with blossoming or spring. Similarly, it would be absurd to judge the wind that blows up the sail and compare it with the drift that stabilizes the hull. The knowledge built up by tradition, with the function of 'ballast', when compared to the 'bolts' produced by the innovative strength of the teachings does neither block nor exhaust them, but rather limits them in a positive way giving them measure and direction. Therefore, we cannot speak of *progress* or *regression* of the teachings, with reference to an assumed truth preserved by tradition: for instance, in a Buddhist milieu it would be ridiculous to say that the Vajrayana teachings should be considered better than the Madhyamika's just because they are more *modern*, just as it would be foolish to consider the Hinayana teachings better than the Mahayana's simply because they are *earlier*. This means, in general, that within each Eastern tradition one particular master's teachings may be differ-

2 See Confucius, *Analects* VII, 2. An interesting interpretation of Confucius is offered in F. JULLIEN, *Un sage est sans idée*. Paris, Seuil, 1998.

ent from another master's teaching, even in a quite radical way: nonetheless, all teachings must be considered potentially *equivalent* with regard to their truth contents. The differences of judgement depend upon the different evaluations expressed by the disciples. But these evaluations are superficial and flimsy as regards the kind of relation that the master has with his own tradition. In other words: from a peak, all peaks and paths to them are effective, independently of the different times and manners they have been traced. The different evaluations depend upon the different skills of the various individuals who walk along the paths.

The link between tradition and innovation in the experience of the teachings' transmission cannot be separated from the problem of understanding which kinds of subjectivity occur in this experience. Particularly interesting and original is the way of facing the problem used by the Buddhist tradition. It influenced most Asian civilizations except India. This tradition focuses special attention on the theme of *anattā* ("not-self"), deeply pondering over the impossibility of claiming the self-sufficiency of *whatever* reality, including that of the self which all individuals take to be permanent. Applied to the master-disciple relationship, this theory shows its disruptive strength with regard to the most common ways of thinking this relationship: its never discussed assumption is always the separation between the master, receptacle of all knowledge, on one side, and the 'empty' disciple, without any knowledge, on the other. The realization of *anattā* begins with the awareness – critically grounded – that there is no independent self separated from other selves. All objects or realities, including the self, are said to be produced by a plurality of conditions – physical, chemical, genetic, social, cultural – which can be compared to a geometrical point. This, however, should not be understood as an isolated monad but as the effect of manifold – virtually infinite – lines crossing each other i.e. as the 'focus' of a lens in which the light-rays are concentrated. In this perspective, it's simply unthinkable that the disciple's self can exist outside the relation with his master's self. Similarly, it's impossible to imagine the master's self as existing separately from his relation with the disciple. Moreover, there is no qualitative difference between the two individuals, such as a master's greater 'plenitude' opposing a disciple's 'empty' nature. If it were so, the consequence would be believing that the teaching is a mere indoctrination. On the contrary, the difference lies in the fact that the master is more powerful as he is more *empty* i.e. aware of the *relativity* of his knowledge. Socrates, like a Buddhist master, 'knows that he doesn't know', and thus lives every moment in the awareness that he finds himself in a condition of constant 'openness': openness to truth, which he considers not as a *possessed* object but as an object of infinite *search*; and openness to the disciple, considered not as 'inert matter' needing moulding or a void container but rather as a 'companion of adventure' in a *common*, unceasing quest for truth.[3] Thus the real master is he who is always willing to *learn*, even when he's transmitting particular teachings; who is always 'empty' whatever knowledge he has accumulated. The prototype of this figure of 'empty' master is the Taoist sage,[4] though similar figures can also be appreciated within the Sufi[5] and Jewish traditions.[6]

3 The great Tibetan master of the Kagyupa tradition, Chogyam Trungpa, spoke of the figure of the *guru* in terms of a spiritual friend; see C. TRUNGPA, *Cutting through Spiritual Materialism*. Berkeley, Shambala, 1973. On the 'common ground' on which master and disciple meet each other in the Buddhist tradition, see K. NISHITANI, "Die religiös-philosophische Existenz im Buddhismus", in R. WISSER (ed.), *Sinn un Sein. Ein philosophisches Symposium*. Tübingen, 1960, pp. 281-298.

4 See *Daodejing*, II, III, V, VII, XII, XV, XXII, XXVI, XXVII, XXVIII, XXIX, XXXI, XXXVIII, XLV, XLIX, LVIII, LXIV, LXV, LXVI, LXVII, LXX, LXXI, LXXII, LXXV, LXXVII, LXXIX, LXXXI.

5 See I. SHAH, *Learning How to Learn. Psychology and Spirituality in the Sufi Way*. New York, Penguin, 1981. If the disciple must learn to learn, the master is he who learned to learn, who has the quality of being always *open* to the process of learning. On the contrary, the person who hides himself in the shadow of his knowledge, proving his need for safety and protection, is still a disciple, even if he can formally exhibit the title of 'master.' On the figure of the master in the Sufi tradition, see E. PACE, "Il Maestro spirituale nella tradizione musulmana", in AA.VV., *Un padre per vivere*. Padova, Il Poligrafo, 2001, pp. 173-181.

6 On the figure of the *rabbi*, see H. SHACHS, "Origin of the Title 'Rabbi'", *Jewish Quarterly Review* 59, 1968: 152-157; R. DI SEGNI, "La sequela del Mae-

From these general characteristics of the Eastern master derives a whole network of specific behaviours which contribute to comprehend his figure more fully. First of all, from his inherent 'openness' one should not draw the conclusion that he doesn't transmit any specific contents, or that he transmits them in a weak or generic way. Nonetheless, the aim of this transmission is neither erudition nor indoctrination, but rather *shaping*. Here, 'shaping' doesn't mean 'imposing a form' upon a disciple. It would be better to say it is an *education*, in a literal sense, which indicates the activity of 'pulling out' the disciple's own nature, manifesting his qualities. A master never begins by exposing a general theory or doctrine, but by offering a particular *experience* of an empirical, psychological character. Sometimes he begins by telling a personal experience; he acts and speaks in a relaxed and detached way, almost neutral or objective, because too much participation could emphasize the centrality of one's own self, inhibiting the listeners. He may also choose to hear an experience told by a disciple, but also in this case he does not indulge too much in listening, avoiding too much involvement, and, above all, avoiding the temptation of the disciple to consider his own experience as unique and extraordinary. Sometimes, the master starts his teaching by showing some forms or movements related to his own discipline or way (*dō*, in Japanese) – be it an art as poetry or painting, or some form of fighting (*budō*): in this case, too, the master is careful to show his skill without any exhibitionistic straining, for instance by choosing to trace with the brush some of the *easiest* characters, or to execute some of the *less spectacular* movements: an impressive, flaunty, 'excited' demonstration would not only characterize a personality without measure and centre but would also bring the disciple to *imitate* such a behaviour. A proof of the master's quality

stro nella tradizione rabbinica", *Parola Spirito e Vita* 2, 1980: 71-80; R. NEUDECKER, "Master Disciple/Disciple Master. Relationship in Rabbinic Judaism and in the Gospel", *Gregorianum* 8, 1999: 245-261; M. M. MORFINO, "La Torah non si acquista a meno di quarantotto condizioni", in AA.VV., *Un padre per vivere, op. cit.*, pp. 75-172.

might be to verify if he acts or not in the opposite way: for instance, by using magical devices or by showing extraordinary powers.[7] This may indicate, in a quite infallible way, the master's will to gather followers, *quickly* and in great numbers, so as to increase his own power. Using powers with extraordinary effects causes the *closing* of the disciple's mind instead of its opening, since it determines *dependence* and emphasizes the hierarchical distance between disciple and master increasing the sense of submission the former feels towards the latter. In the end, the disciple cannot give up this sense of submission, so much so that sometimes – in pathological cases – he comes to annihilate himself. This dependence, brought about by the use of powers, is harmful not only from a psychological perspective, but also from a 'social' point of view. It works as a criterion to select a small circle of disciples, structured in a hierarchical way, and as a criterion to attribute, within such circle, the different hierarchical levels – assigned proportionally to the 'strength of belief' displayed by the pupils' belief in the 'special effects' exhibited by the master.[8] In this way, the sect strengthens itself by promoting the psychologically weakest disciples i.e. those who are more impressive and easily influenced. These become the 'strongest' disciples, in force of the master's recognition. Within the sect they are the most *authoritarian*, and outside of it they are considered the most *representative*. The cult of the master's personality, in which the display of powers is

7 Real masters always warned against the use of powers: see Patañjali, *Yoga-sūtra* 3.38. Concerning the Buddha's teachings, though he talks of "four constituents of magical powers" these have nothing to do with any supernatural faculty, since they are established by will, energy, purity of mind, and analytic skill; see *Dīgha Nikāya* XVIII, 22. The Buddha's critical position on the use of supernatural powers – even when aimed at a more effective exposition of the *dharma* – is explicit in the *Kevaddha-sutta* (*Dīgha Nikāya* XI). Confucius too observes that the master avoids using magical devices and esoteric forms of teaching; see *Analects* VII, 2 and 23.

8 The powers flaunted by the would-be masters are not only those of a supernatural kind: they are often more trivial, such as a boasted erudition, an intentionally eccentric dress, an intentionally extravagant house, a well-studied scandalous behaviour, a display of weird companions and esoteric readings.

crucial, produces 'epidemic' effects: all disciples, at different levels, feel themselves inferior, standing *below* their master, though at the same time they feel themselves as standing *above* individuals who are outside the sect.

Secondly, the master faithfully registers the *reactions* of the disciple to the various signs he has manifested and the various moves he has executed. If these reactions are minute or immature, he offers him the opportunity to increase them or even release them. On the contrary, if they are redundant he tries to lead him to restrain himself, using only a few words or even silence. This 'cultivation of seeds' which many Buddhist schools and masters speak about, lies just in this openness in the moulding process.

In this 'e-ducational' relationship the use of words is important, but not exclusive: it entails two modes. One mode is direct and personal, between master and a single disciple; the other mode is indirect and impersonal, between master and a community of disciples. In almost all Buddhist schools both ways are used: that of *public speech*, generally oriented toward an exposition of the teachings as objective as possible, and that of *private conversation*, aiming at a more personal, deep communication: for instance, in Zen Buddhism the first method is practiced in *teishō*, the second during *sanzen.*[9] It's important to stress the fact that in 'letting out' the disciple's nature, the master doesn't employ any pedagogical scheme i.e. he neither classifies the disciple's characteristics in a fixed typology nor interferes at one's aiming at any established goal. This attitude which renounces all prefixed schemes and targets, produces two important effects. First of all, the master, when using words in teaching, is able to modulate his talk in a very wide range of styles, conforming himself to the different intellectual and cultural levels of the disciples or,

[9] In the *Rinzai* school, the master offers the disciple a *kōan* (paradox) that breaks every logical and/or linguistic pattern and leads the pupil to a crisis, akin to the condition induced by the psychoanalyst in his patient; see J. R. SULER, "Paradox", in A. MOLINO (ed.), *The Couch and the Tree. Dialogues in Psychoanalysis and Buddhism*. New York, North Point Press, 1998.

in general, of his audience;[10] then, the master often teaches through examples[11] instead of words: in particular, he almost never *explains* what one should do, but does himself what he must do in the way he thinks best, in any given moment and situation. For this reason he never *urges*, even less he *shouts* orders. Rather, after performing signs or movements in a particular discipline, he *is present* when the disciple tries to imitate him. If the disciple makes a mistake, the master generally says nothing but repeats his movement, maybe after some time, and considers if the disciple has noticed the mistake by himself. The master, in short, doesn't 'lead' his disciples as a chief does with his followers, but acts as a 'truthful' *mirror* – clean, not deforming – helping them to find their own deficiencies.

The true master can be recognized by the fact that he's never tired of playing this role of 'mirror' (even if it can happen he must 're-

10 See in particular the famous Lotus *sūtra*, chapter II, all devoted to the "skill in means" (*upāya-kauśalya*). The skill of the master is presented in a very similar way in two texts belonging to very different traditions, that of Tibetan Buddhism and Sufism: see E. LO BUE (ed.), *La preziosa ghirlanda degli insegnamenti degli uccelli (Bya chos rin-chen'phreng-ba*). Milano, Adelphi, 1998; FARID AD-DIN ATTAR, *The Conference of the Birds*. New York, Penguin Books, 1984.

11 This is maybe the clearest difference between the Eastern and Western attitude. For this latter one, we may consider Plato's behaviour: even if he refuses the claims of excellence of the written word over the spoken word, he doesn't refuse the practice of talking (see *Phaed.* 276-277). In the Eastern traditions, on the contrary, silence is preferred to words; see *Bṛhadāraṇyaka Upaniṣad* IV, 22; *Daodejing* I, vv. 1-6; XIV, vv. 4 and 11; XXXII, v. 1; XXXVII, v. 7; XLI, v. 21; and, above all, LVI, vv. 1-2. A radical position is that of Zen Buddhism, in particular that of the *Sōtō* school, where the principle of *furyū monji* ("transmission beyond scriptures") is practised. However, the use of words is not entirely refused as testified by Dōgen (see *Master Dōgen's Shōbōgenzō*. London, Windbell, 1998). In the East the use of words is not rejected in an absolute way: words are intended as a *means*, to be utilized and then thrown away. One must be aware that truth always exceeds language. In the Western tradition too we find masters who value the use of silence, like for instance Pythagoras who requested from his disciples a *five-year* period of silence; see IAMBLICHUS, *Pythagorean Life* VII, 72.

flect' dull or fanatical disciples, with an ugly and excited mind). In other words, a genuine master always holds the capacity of *doing anew* the covered distance, even if he has progressed in the path of his art, discipline, or spiritual enterprise. This quality depends, one more time, on his 'consciousness of emptiness': indeed, if he maintained too strong an awareness of self and progress, he would be induced to give orders instead of educating. On the other hand, if this awareness didn't exist at all, he would only stand as a mute replica of the disciple.

The pupil, on his part, must trust the master until he *relies on* him. However, not in the sense of worshipping him, but rather in the awareness that just the emptiness of the master i.e. his playing the role of 'mirror' is basic to the learning of a discipline or art (much more than the master's strong personality' or imposed order). In this regard, we must notice that, while in the East – both in the Hindū[12] and Buddhist[13] traditions – one finds among disciples the tendency to rely *too much* upon the master, running the risk of losing oneself in an imitative process, in the West the opposite tendency prevails i.e.

12 In the Hindū tradition we find a real *worship* of the master; see W. DONIGER – B. K. SMITH (eds.), *Laws of Manu*. Harmondsworth, Penguin, 1991 (II, 144-154, 170-171, 225-235; IV, 130,162,179,182). In some radical forms, we find this also in Tantric schools; see ABHINAVAGUPTA, *Tantrāloka*. Berkeley, Asian Humanities Press 1985 (XV, 423b-434 and 534-591a). Traditional reverence toward the master is still prevalent in contemporary India; see P. YOGANANDA, *A Biography of a Yogi*. Los Angeles, Self-Realization Fellowship, 1958.

13 The unconditioned obedience to the master is evident above all in the Tibetan schools, as witnessed in the relations between Tilopa and Naropa and between Marpa and Milarepa. On the importance of the master-disciple relationship, see A. BERZIN, *Relating to a Spiritual Teacher*. Ithaca, Snow Lion, 2000 and M. FINN, "Tibetan Buddhism and Comparative Psychoanalysis", in MOLINO, *The Couch and the Tree*, *op. cit.* However, we must remember that in the Buddhist framework this relationship is intended in a reciprocal dimension: the symbolic "string" (*samaya*) binding master and disciple reveals two aspects; see LAMA GUENDUNE RIMPOCHE, *Maître et disciple*. Saint Léon-sur-Vézère, Dzambala, 1996. On the importance of the master in contemporary Buddhism, see *Duemilauno* XII, 61, 1997.

that of relying *too little* on the master, because of the fear of losing one's individuality. The consequence is that often, in the West, one tends to change master easily and quickly, in a frantic search to satisfy one's egotistic needs.[14]

Misunderstandings often arise because of the perverted way of comprehending and using the notion of 'personality', in particular when the disciple searches for a master with a 'strong personality' in order to achieve a similar one or even a 'stronger' one of his own. In these cases, some real distortions of reality can arise: for instance, the disciple can take the master's oddity or inaccessibility as a sign of excellence and imitate him. On the contrary, oddity and inaccessibility – if not devices contrived by a fraud – are symptoms of the master's detachment from his own self. So, if it's necessary to imitate, imitation must not have as object the *external signs* of detachment but rather the *internal discipline* leading to detachment. About the imitative practice, the Eastern disciple generally tends to mechanical repetition, forgetting the experience symbolized by what he imitates, while the Western disciple generally tends to avoid imitation, forgetting it is the basic means to diminish the claims of the self i.e. to begin to realize detachment.

The disciple must keep in mind that the imitation of the master's gestures, sentences, and thoughts is necessary to acquire basic notions and techniques, as it is necessary to study solfeggio in order to learn music: on the other hand, it is only a means to realize emptiness. In this regard, the meaning of the Japanese expression *shuhari* is very interesting: literally, *shu* means "to respect", *ha* "to break", and *ri* "to detach".[15] *Shu* refers to the respect of rules, the necessity of practicing imitation, being faithful to tradition; *ha* indicates the con-

14 No master exists to gratify one's needs but to testify, in the best way he can, the teachings of a tradition. In this sense it's good if a disciple softens his ego even *before* going to a master: otherwise, he will run the risk of establishing only an instrumental relationship with him.

15 See CHIBA EICHIRO, *Chiba Shusaku Iko* (*Posthumous Writings by Chiba Shusaku*). Okyo, Okasha, 1942, p. 41. Quoted in F. CHAMPAULT, "Apprendre par corps", *Daruma* 8-9, 2001, p. 73.

trary: the importance of going beyond the rules, of creating and innovating; *ri*, finally, hints at the necessity of detaching oneself from *shu* as much as from *ha*; whoever stops at *shu* is still attached to imitative models and to the master's personality, and whoever stops at *ha* is still attached to his own transgressing and creative skills and thus indirectly to the cult of his *own* personality. On the other hand, he who is able to reach *ri* shows he can incorporate the rules to the point of having the strength to break them and transcend them. He also proves he can detach himself from the very self that expressed that strength.

When a disciple exhibits the signs that prove his overcoming of the attachment to tradition, to innovation, and to their reciprocal opposition, he can be said to be a master.[16]

In the West, at the origin of the figure of the master lie the 'masters of truth' of ancient Greece,[17] among whom Epimenides and Parmenides stand out. If the former is referable to a circle of sages who passed on their knowledge as an already *owned* truth – in an oracular, apodictic way, without the possibility of replying and arguing – the latter opens the path to a *search* for truth which can be investi-

16 Interpreting these signs is an operation as important as difficult. In all traditions, the transmission of the title of master has always been problematic. In Zen Buddhism, for instance, there have been many misunderstandings, tensions, and controversies on the awarding of the *inka shomei* title. This title is used by the master (*rōshi*) to officially recognize the disciple who has attained a level of enlightenment (*kenshō*) which allows him to be called an "incomer of *dharma*" (*hassu*): the master can then pass on the doctrine to him. On the peculiar way of understanding the transmission of teaching in Zen Buddhism, see Th. and J. C. CLEARY (eds.), *The Blue Cliff Record*. Boulder, Shambala, 1977 (especially case XI devoted to Huang Po). On the problems relative to the transmission of teachings in general, see R. GUÉNON, *Aperçus sur l'initiation*. Paris, Etudes Traditionelles, 1992 (in particular chap. VIII, IX, XIV, XXX, XXXIV, XXXV, XXXVI). What is problematic is not only Guénon's naive belief that a traditionally ordered society may ensure to everyone the right rank and position according to his individual nature, but also the difficulty of ascertaining the specific traits which ensure one's qualification.

17 See the important study by M. DETIENNE, *Les maîtres de vérité dans la Grèce archaïque*. Paris, Maspero, 1967.

gated only through a series of logical arguments, culminating in the Socratic and Platonic 'widening', in which the dialogical method finds its origin and means of development.

However, it's in Heraclitus that we find real dialectics between some of the basic characters connoting the master: on one hand, when he claims that men do not listen to "this Speech, which is always",[18] and when he states that "not to me, but listening to the Speech is wise, saying that all things are one",[19] he seems to speak as the ancient masters i.e. as a *medium* of an eternal and transcendent truth, similar to that *vāc* ("voice", "word") which was heard and passed on by the seven great *ṛṣis* ("seers") of the Vedic tradition *in illo tempore*.[20] On the other hand, he insists on the fact that "common to all people is thinking",[21] and that "Speech is common, but most people live as having each one's own mind".[22] Thus, it seems that the oracular and sacerdotal attitude leave an open space to the possibility that *everyone* might have access to Speech, the *Logos* in which truth articulates and manifests itself. Of course, while it is true, in principle, that *all people* always have the *opportunity* to have access to Speech, it's also true that only *some of them* and only on some occasions realize this opportunity: "To the awakened person the world is one and common, but when they are sleeping they only consider their own particular".[23] This means that the master has the role of 'awakening' all those who think that the world and truth are reducible to their own world and truth i.e. to their own "particular" (*ìdion*): the

18 Heraclitus fr. I.

19 Heraclitus fr. VI.

20 See R. PANIKKAR (ed.), *The Vedic Experience: Mantramañjarī*. Berkeley, University of California Press, 1977. On the figure of the master in the Hindū tradition, see M. C. MINUTIELLO, *I guru. Maestri dell'India e del Tibet*. Milano, Xenia, 1999.

21 Heraclitus fr. X.

22 Heraclitus fr. VII.

23 Heraclitus fr. IX.

master, in short, shows to people the foolishness[24] which makes them blind, deaf, and dormant to truth. Truth reveals a unique, infinite system of interrelations: "Connections: whole and not whole, converging diverging, consonant dissonant: from all things one, from one all things".[25] Therefore "one is knowledge, knowing the mind that in the sea of the Whole signed the route of the Whole"[26] i.e. knowing that common *Logos* that binds together all things.

But Heraclitus, emblematically, attributes other basic characteristics to the teaching of a genuine master, characteristics which we find both in the Eastern[27] and Western traditions that followed him: first of all, it's not enough to know this structure of connections which rule the world and one's existence. One must practice in daily life the consequences of this knowledge: "Highest virtue is having judgement, and knowledge is telling the truth and living accordingly, as a man who knows and follows the nature of things".[28] Heraclitus, as many masters of all times and latitudes, warns against arrogance and illusion coming from erudition: "Knowing many things does not mean wisdom".[29] Moreover, Heraclitus – like all masters in the Buddhist tradition – warns against excesses in the imitation of the master, into which disciples often fall: "It is not to behave as sons of your father".[30] This advice doesn't mean that the masters' behaviours, words, actions, and thoughts are not to be followed, but that every disciple should consider them not as something to be imitated but as 'supports' and useful indications in order to build *one's own* way to

24 In this regard, a great master of truth in ancient times was also Dyogenes the Cynic; see S. VOLTOLINA, *Il Tao del cane. Filosofia cinica e filosofia taoista*. Lucca, Del Bucchia, 1998.

25 Heraclitus fr. XIX.

26 Heraclitus fr. XIII.

27 For a comparison between Heraclitus and 'philosophical' Taoism (*daojia*), see G. PASQUALOTTO, *Il Tao della filosofia*. Pratiche, Parma, 1989, chap. I.

28 Heraclitus fr. LXXV.

29 Heraclitus fr. LXXXII. See also fr. LXXXVI. Plato is also critic of erudition (*polymathia*); see *Laws* VII, 818-819a.

30 Heraclitus fr. XCV.

truth. At last, Heraclitus states: "I only investigated myself".[31] The direction and meaning of Heraclitus' words are similar to those we find in the Buddha's words: "Indeed, one's own self is the shelter."[32]

It will be Socrates who will investigate the way a master acts as an 'obstetrician' helping the disciple to 'give birth' to knowledge.[33] This role of spiritual 'obstetrician' means that the master lowers his claims of knowing i.e. applies to himself a radically ironical look:

31 Heraclitus fr. CXXVI. In the Buddhist tradition this attitude – assuming the doctrine and master who interprets it as "useful means" (*upāya*) to build up one's own way to enlightenment – finds in Lin-chi, master of the Chan school, a radical expression; see *The Record of Lin-chi*. Kyoto, Institute for Zen Studies, 1975, chap. XVIII. Here the genuine master's activity has nothing to do with any 'pedagogical project'.

32 *Dhammapada* 12, 4. One can value the difference between the Greek and Buddhist way, and, on the other hand, the Hindū way. In Hinduism it's not the disciple who comes to experience truth through his master's help but it's rather the master (*ācārya*) who brings to birth the disciple in the one Reality, making him a "twice-born" (*dvija*). Herein, the master is more important than the father himself; see DONIGER - SMITH, *Laws of Manu*, *op. cit.*, II, 144-148. On the importance of the master's figure, see also II, 170-171; II, 225-231; IV, 130, 162, 179, 182. On the different ways of understanding the relation between master and disciple, see P. MAGNONE, "Il maestro, il pupillo e la pupilla tra India e Grecia", *Avallon* 48, pp. 45-58. On the similarities between Socrates and Hindū masters, see the extraordinary essay by R. DAUMAL, *Les pouvoirs de la parole*. Paris, Gallimard, 1972, vol. II, pp. 9-32.

33 The originality of Socrates' pedagogy has been so important in Western cultural formation that many studies have been devoted to this subject: among others, see A. BANFI, *Socrate*. Milano, Mondadori, 1944; V. MAGALHAES-VILHENA, *Le problème de Socrate*. Paris, Puf, 1952; S. BLASUCCI, *Socrate. Saggio sugli aspetti costruttivi dell'ironia*. Bari, Levante, 1962; M. MONTUORI, *Socrate*. Firenze, Sansoni, 1964; H. MAIER, *Socrate*. Firenze, La Nuova Italia, 1970; G. VLASTOS (ed.), *The Philosophy of Socrates*. New York, Doubleday, 1971; F. SARRI, *Socrate e la genesi storica dell'idea occidentale di anima*. Roma, Abate, 1975; F. ADORNO, *Introduzione a Socrate*. Roma-Bari, Laterza, 1988; G. VLASTOS, *Socrates: Ironist and Moral Philosopher*. Cambridge, Cambridge University Press, 1992; H. BENSON (ed.), *Essays on the Philosophy of Socrates*. Oxford, Oxford University Press, 1992; F. TURATO, "Le *Nuvole* e la questione socratica", in ARISTOFANE, *Le Nuvole*. Venezia, Marsilio, 1995, pp. 9-61.

"My dear Critias, I said, you behave with me as if I knew the things about which I pose the questions, and as if I could agree if only I'd like to. But it's not this way: each time I examine what you propose since I myself do not know it".[34] The 'knowing of not knowing' is the foundation of the dialectical process in almost all Platonic dialogues. The dialogue is a means to reflect and reason about the relation between master and disciple: 'dialogue', in fact, is not a 'pouring off' of knowledge from the former to the latter,[35] nor is an exchange of opinions or a discussion confronting different theses. It requires that *both* interlocutors doubt the presuppositions of their opinions and knowledge: their only starting point is 'knowing they don't know'.[36] The dialogue requires that both should be prepared to 'empty' themselves of every certitude, prejudice, and assumption, reciprocally exposing this 'nakedness' without qualms or tricks: "Oh no!, I exclaimed, I do not need to discuss this 'if you want', this 'if it seems to you', but 'me' and 'you', and I say 'me' and 'you' because I am totally persuaded that only then the reasoning can be well discussed, when the 'if' is taken off".[37] The dialogue, then, is not a merely formal activity, but an activity that invests and transforms the speakers' life.[38]

From this special dialogical relationship between master and disciple emerges a critical attitude relative to all material goods, and money in particular. This attitude, in fact, doesn't consist in a generic and moralistic refusal of luxury and richness, but comes from the fact that dialogue is not a mere communicative situation but a means to a dialectical education, where no one claims to prevail upon the

34 Plato, *Carmides* 164d. See also *Apology of Socrates* 23b.

35 Socrates warns Teetetus that he's not a "sack of reasoning"; see Plato *Teetetus* 160a-b.

36 In this perspective, the meaning of Socrates' words in *Apology* 33a-b becomes clear: "I have never been the master of anyone. [...] I have never promised any teaching to anyone, and I haven't taught anything".

37 Plato, *Protagoras* 331c-d.

38 See P. HADOT, *Exercices spirituels et philosophie antique*. Paris, Études Augustiniennes, 1987.

other:[39] indeed, if the master doesn't presume he has 'something' to pass on to the disciple, but 'only' helps him to discover within himself the way to tread the path to truth,[40] there is no space for any material or economic interest. While the sophists asked for money to teach discussion techniques, with the only aim of making their disciple-clients win their debates, Socrates dedicates himself to dialogue in a free way because the goal is the searching for truth, and above all because it is a *common* search, in which *he himself* can profit: "But if you will pay attention to me, we two will study the subject together, and come to discover the matter".[41] There is another important reason which leads Socrates not to ask for money: it's because he does not choose to teach, but finds himself in the condition he cannot do anything else, because of the power of his *daimon* that makes him say: "I live in extreme indigence to serve the god".[42] Thus, when Socrates states: "I walk around doing nothing but trying to persuade you, young and old, not to lend too much importance to the body and wealth in comparison with the soul, so it becomes as perfect as possible",[43] he doesn't tribute any credit to himself, but observes that "to me, I repeat it to you, it was the god who ordered me to do this".[44] Socrates then cannot ask for money for his teaching because, literally, he hasn't got any given matter, any fixed truth to pass on: the only thing he is certain of, is 'knowing he doesn't know', and he offers this humility, this lack of knowledge, to all

39 It would be interesting to compare the Socratic dialogical function with the practice of *hossen* ("fight over the *dharma*") in Zen Buddhism. In Zen we witness a confrontation between two individuals who both attained enlightenment, and not between a master and a disciple. Here we do *not* see any *clash* to decide who is best, but rather a *debate* in order to investigate and clarify the requisites of a common path to knowledge.

40 See Plato, *Teetetus* 150c-d.

41 Plato, *Alcybiades* II, 140a. See also *Gorgias* 487e.

42 Plato, *Apology* 23c. Even for the Buddha the disciples' riches are of no importance: see the *Parabhāva-sutta* in *Suttanipāta* I, 6 and the *Vasala-sutta* in *Suttanipāta* I, 7.

43 Plato, *Apology* 30b.

44 Plato, *Apology* 33c. See also *Teetetus* 150c.

people who are willing to share it as an open space from which to begin the search for truth together.

The peculiar qualities stressed by Socrates' teaching contribute to spell out, both in the East and the West, in the past and in the future, the basic characteristics that distinguish a genuine spiritual master (not only from a fraud, but also from a simple instructor, an ordinary teacher, and even a traditional ('soul driver').[45] These characteristics are:

1) *unselfishness*, disregard for any form of material benefit that may derive from his teaching;
2) the *necessity* to be a master, established by the *lack* of a special choice to become a master – a lack accompanied by his *ignorance* of being one, when he really is;
3) *refraining* from imposing any form of pre-definite truth[46] and even the contents of a possible truth which he has found in himself;[47]

45 Among these 'soul drivers', teachers, and instructors sometimes an authentic master can be found: but we must exclude the idea that every instructor, teacher, or 'soul driver', simply because he has got a certificate, may be taken as a real master. Among the 'soul drivers' we may count psychoanalysts too. On the difficulties in order to understand how and how much the figure of the psychoanalyst differs from that of the master, see E. PERRELLA, "Pratica analitica ed orizzonte iniziatico", in C. DONÀ – M. MANCINI (eds.), *Tradizione letteraria, iniziazione, genealogia*. Milano, Luni, 1998. By E. PERRELLA see also *La formazione degli analisti e il compito della psicanalisi*. Pordenone, Biblioteca dell'Immagine, 1991, pp. 242-265, and *Il tempo etico*. Pordenone, Biblioteca dell'Immagine, 1992, pp. 285-288.

46 Here we find the problem of understanding if and to what extent the figure of the master is compatible with those religious traditions which are grounded on truths revealed by a transcendent God and on scriptures which preserve his word. St. Augustine claimed that no one should be revered as a master on earth, since everybody's sole master is in heaven; Augustine, *De Magistro* 46.

47 The truth the Buddha discovered is proposed to everybody not as a path to be copied or rerun, but as a way to walk independently. This is clearly born out in his speech to Kālāmas in the *Aṅguttara Nikāya*; see F. L. WOODWARD (ed.),

4) his *marginality* with respect to political life and, in general, public life;[48]
5) *life in common* with his disciples, implying not simply a verbal exchange, but a full communal existence.[49]

These criteria can be applied both *a priori* and *a posteriori*. It is possible either to *look for* a master with the right qualifications as well as to *verify* their occurrence in a known or casually come across master. In the first case, there is the problem of *where* to look for a genuine master. René Guénon, who devoted himself to this issue,[50] had no doubts: in the West the search must be limited to the two 'initiation organizations' that for a long time have granted a constant and controlled transmission of spiritual influence i.e. Freemasonry and the Roman-Catholic Church. Guénon himself is well aware that these two organizations cannot avoid the effects of a general decline, which involves the whole modern world, basically caused by the power of individualism. The critical thoughts set forth by Guénon on the possibility of finding genuine masters who may guarantee a spiritual transmission can be extended today to the cultural and religious worlds – such as the Islāmic world – which he considered not yet de-

The Book of the Gradual Sayings. Oxford, Pali Text Society, 1989, Vol. I, III, 7, § 65, p. 173.

48 See J. BROSSE, *Les maîtres spirituels*. Paris, Bordas, 1988.

49 See Plato, *Letter VII* 341c-d. In the Hindū tradition the disciple must live with the *guru* and his family, see DONIGER - SMITH, *Laws of Manu, op. cit.* On the condition of *brahmacarya*, see A. DANIÉLOU, *Les quatre sens de la vie et la structure de l'Inde traditionelle*. Paris, Editions du Rocher, 1992. In Buddhism, the importance of life in common is stressed by the fact that one of the three jewels i.e. the three basic elements that are a 'refuge' to whoever wishes to become a monk, is the community (*saṅgha*). On the importance of communal life, see the *Ratana-sutta* in *Suttanipāta* II, 13; G. PASQUALOTTO, "Il significato di 'essere Saṅgha'", *Paramita* 66, 1998, pp. 6-8. On the *saṅgha*'s relevance in the contemporary context, see A. KOTLER (ed.), *Engaged Buddhist Reader*. Berkeley, Parallax Press, 1996, part V.

50 Above all in GUÉNON, *Aperçus sur l'initiation, op. cit.*

clining.[51] This conclusion, applied to the relics of non-Western spiritual traditions, leads us to observe that the Western qualities and goals tend nowadays to place themselves as qualities and goals of *the world in its entirety*.[52] If this is true, the enormous diffusion in the West of extra-European, particularly Eastern, forms of spirituality, should not be interpreted as a sign of 'revenge' or 'rebirth' of these traditions, but quite to the contrary as a symptom of the relentless and unstoppable force of Western ideological (and economical) penetration, leading to the exploitation – widely and at the lowest merchandising levels – of the enormous heritages of images, symbols, ideas, and practices that have been produced and preserved by extra-European cultures.[53] From this wide and rapid process of 'cultural neo-colonialism' even the figure and role of the master can't be saved: the growing number of contacts that the West had, in the latest century's second half, with the masters of different religions produced of course a positive growth of the knowledge about spiritual realities, once known only to a small circle of specialists. But it has also produced a widespread application of an *utilitarian* approach to the master. He is addressed, in the worst cases, to satisfy a superficial curiosity by 'soul tourists', or in the best cases to solve *practical* problems, either physical (pain therapies, well-being cures, etc.) or psychological (therapies against fear, depression, insecurity, discon-

[51] Following these pessimistic conclusions, Guénon finally affiliated himself to an Islāmic *ṭarīqa*, believing that the Western world and culture were definitely incapable of offering warranties of a genuine spiritual transmission. Half a century after his death, it appears legitimate to ask whether Islām itself is not destined to succumb to the forces of Western globalisation.

[52] See S. LATOUCHE, *L'occidentalisation du monde*. Paris, La Découverte, 1989. On Westernisation, E. Zolla pithily noticed: "As the Akbar court shone, the India of villages prospered. Indigence would come later, with the West, as *The Capital* will meticulously demonstrate"; E. ZOLLA, *Aure*. Venezia, Marsilio, 1985, p. 64.

[53] The most recent and widespread example of this use is the galaxy of movements and enterprises that go by the name of *New Age*; see M. YORK, *The Emerging Network. A Sociology of the New Age*. London, Rowman, 1995.

tent, etc.).[54] There is no reason to express a negative judgement of these practical approaches, since their effects are often salutary. However, these approaches towards the master are *narrow*, since they neglect the basic function he has always held in all different traditions, either Eastern or Western. This basic function is that of showing – in different ways, according to the various schools – a path towards *deeper knowledge* (not necessarily opposed to erudition or technical 'know how'). The figures of Socrates and of the Buddha are emblematic: they did not pass on notions, or heal bodies, or teach some particular art and technique.[55] Rather, they enabled their disciples – via a preliminary emptying of doctrinal stiffness and prejudices – to build a 'method' to acquire meaningful knowledge for themselves. The general principles that more or less intentionally define and govern Western life conditions, which are spreading everywhere, impose ideologies and roles which prevent the development of any master-disciple relationship. They also prevent the possibility of the coexistence of different 'horizons of meaning', capable of challenging them.[56] If once the figure and role of the master had a central importance in producing the various 'horizons of meaning' in

54 One of the most efficacious presentations of the reasons which lead Westerners towards Eastern spiritual traditions can be found in G. COMOLLI, "I nuovi movimenti spirituali: la diffusione delle tradizioni orientali in Italia", in G. SANNA – A. CAPASSO (eds.), *Orienti e occidenti*. Farenheit 451, Roma, 1997, pp. 160-177. See also G. PASQUALOTTO, "Taoismo e buddhismo: risposte antiche a nuove domande", in P. FERLIGA (ed.), *Fine millennio. L'Occidente di fronte al sacro*. Grafo, Brescia, 1998, pp. 29-41.

55 This doesn't exclude that the master may use various notions and techniques as 'skilful means' to proceed on the path towards knowledge. Socrates used the technique of refutation (*élenchos*), which was also used in courts and assemblies of the time. The Buddha turned to the method of analysis (*vicāra*), which can also be found in the sacred texts of the brāhmaṇical tradition. Even the most innovative masters never completely break with tradition.

56 The current forms of consumerism can be traced back to the three causes of sorrow (*kilesa*) which Buddhism indicates by the names of *lobha* ("desire", "attachment"), *dosa* ("aversion"), and *moha* ("delusion", "blindness"); see P. HUTANUWATR, "L'educazione spirituale nella prospettiva buddhista", in AA.VV., *Sapienza d'Oriente e d'Occidente*. Il Cerchio, Rimini, 1999, p. 128.

any given culture, proposing educational systems and establishing the different levels in the articulation of knowledge, the present situation has deeply eroded these roles and functions: the different 'horizons of meaning' are more and more homologated – internally and among themselves – not only via the standardization of communication media, but above all by the standardized contents that these same media propose. The varieties of educational models increasingly tend to be reduced to a few elementary 'instruction strategies', aimed at producing small information 'packages' which are used in a polyvalent and undifferentiated way, independent from the historical and geographical peculiarities of the different cultures which are forced to 'open' and consume them. To produce these information 'packages' in the easiest way and in the shortest time – so as to obtain the largest benefits from them – it becomes necessary to drastically lower the level of knowledge that traditional cultures had originally worked out.

Nonetheless, this progressive eclipse of the figure and role of the traditional master in the contemporary world doesn't mean he's disappearing. Actually, his presence is more and more widespread: it's the meaning and form of his function that have undergone a thorough change. The master's traditional role is divested of all its deepest elements, especially those which might interfere with the utilitarian worldview. Only those exterior contents that can be sold as mass products[57] are restored and reworked, reducing them to their simplest terms – starting with the objects used in rituals and the many metaphysical symbols of the religious traditions to which the various masters belong. One of the clearest symptoms of this transformation and lowering of the figure and role of the master, is that Western culture – though not necessarily within its academic circles – appears to have completely forgotten its own tradition of masters, a tradition that can be traced back to the 'masters of truth' of ancient Greece and to the masters of the Hellenistic philosophical schools (leaving

[57] In an utilitarian perspective, secrecy and distance are valued as requisites to increase the aura of mystery surrounding a master.

aside the contributions offered by the three great religions of the Book). The reasons for such an oblivion are of course complex and stratified and I might mention two. One reason lies in the fact that the Greek tradition, which for centuries influenced the formation of Western culture with its myths and symbols, has lost all attraction in current mass society. And with the immense Greek heritage being forgotten, the West has discovered in the East – above all in India – a new 'field' of signs, words, and symbols even more attracting and charming, thanks to the increasing of rapid communication and inter-continental knowledge, raising popular interest in the Exotic.

Despite the consumerist aberration which has transformed the figure and role of traditional masters, the mass diffusion of information concerning them and their respective cultures – diffusion that lies at the core of these aberrations – may also represent a preliminary condition and suitable opportunity to open new access to knowledge. Of course, this may be possible only in the hypothesis, perhaps too naive, that the 'consumption of signs' still leaves an open space for the sincere search of a meaningful life.

Contributors

Attilio Andreini
Associate Professor of Classical Chinese
Department of East Asian Studies
University of Venice, Ca' Foscari
Dorsoduro 3462 – 30123 Venice, Italy
E-mail: attilio@unive.it

Stefano Beggiora
PhD Candidate in Indology
Department of Eurasian Studies
University of Venice, Ca' Foscari
San Polo 2035 – 30125 Venice, Italy
E-mail:
kuramboi@katamail.com

Pier Cesare Bori
Full Professor of Moral Philosophy
Department of Politics, Institutions and History
Via Strada Maggiore 45 – 40125 Bologna, Italy
E-mail: bori@spbo.unibo.it

Michele Botta
State Attorney
Avvocatura Generale dello Stato
S. Marco 63 – 30124 Venice, Italy
E-mail:
michele.botta@avvocaturastato.it

Luca Caldironi
Psychiatrist
Member of the International Psychoanalytical Association
Via Taglio 24 – 41100 Modena, Italy
E-mail:
lucaldir@caldironiluca.191.it

Piero Capelli
Associate Professor of Hebrew Language and Literature
Department of Eurasian Studies
University of Venice, Ca' Foscari
San Polo 2035 – 30125 Venice, Italy
E-mail: piero.capelli@unive.it

Claudio Cicuzza
Research Fellow in Indology
Department of Asian Studies
University of Naples, L'Orientale
Piazza S. Domenico Maggiore 12 – 80134 Naples, Italy
E-mail: c.cicuzza@iol.it

Chiara Cremonesi
Lecturer in History of Religions
Department of Antiquity Sciences
University of Padua
Piazza Capitaniato 7 – 35139 Padua, Italy
E-mail: chiara.cremonesi@tin.it

Thomas Dähnhardt
Lecturer in Urdu Language and Literature
Department of Eurasian Studies
University of Venice, Ca' Foscari
San Polo 2035 – 30125 Venice, Italy
E-mail: thomasda@unive.it

Fabrizio Ferrari
PhD in Bengali Studies
Department of the Languages and Culture of South Asia
SOAS, University of London
London WC1H 0XG, United Kingdom
E-mail:
fabrizio.ferrari@soas.ac.uk

Gian Giuseppe Filippi
Full Professor of Hindi Literature
Department of Eurasian Studies
University of Venice, Ca' Foscari
San Polo 2035 – 30125 Venice, Italy
E-mail: ggf@unive.it

Franco Macchi
President of the Cultural Center Palazzo Cavagnis
Castello 5170 – 30122 Venice, Italy
E-mail: fmacc@libero.it

Massimo Makarovic
BA in Chinese Language and Literature
Department of Eurasian Studies
University of Venice, Ca' Foscari
San Polo 2035 – 30125 Venice, Italy

Monia Marchetto
Lecturer in Hindi Language and Literature
Department of Eurasian Studies
University of Venice, Ca' Foscari
San Polo 2035 – 30125 Venice, Italy
E-mail: moniamar@libero.it

Giangiorgio Pasqualotto
Full Professor of Aesthetics
Department of Philosophy
University of Padua
Piazza Capitaniato 3 – 35139 Padua, Italy
E-mail: taotao@infinito.it

Gianni Pellegrini
Vedantashastri Candidate at the Sampurnananda Sanskrit Vishvavidyalaya
Hari Harshniketan
N/28 Nagwa, Lanka 221 005 – Varanasi, U.P., India
E-mail: paramatattva@yahoo.it

Cinzia Pieruccini
Lecturer in Indology
Department of Antiquity Sciences
University of Milan
Via Festa del Perdono 7 – 20122 Milan, Italy
E-mail: cinzia.pieruccini@unimi.it

Corrado Puchetti
PhD in Ancient Indian History, Culture & Archaeology, Banaras Hindu University
Via de' Rogati 52 – 35121 Padua, Italy
E-mail: prayagpuri@yahoo.com

Claudia Ramasso
PhD Candidate in Indian Art History
Department of Eurasian Studies
University of Venice, Ca' Foscari
San Polo 2035 – 30125 Venice, Italy
E-mail: ramasso@unive.it

Antonio Rigopoulos
Associate Professor of Sanskrit Language and Literature
Department of Eurasian Studies
University of Venice, Ca' Foscari
San Polo 2035 – 30125 Venice, Italy
E-mail: a.rigo@flashnet.it

Fabian Sanders
Lecturer in Tibetan Language and Literature
Department of Eurasian Studies
University of Venice, Ca' Foscari
San Polo 2035 – 30125 Venice, Italy
E-mail: fsanders@tiscali.it

Angelo Scarabel
Full Professor of Arabic Language and History of Islāmic Philosophy
Department of Eurasian Studies
University of Venice, Ca' Foscari
San Polo 2035 – 30125 Venice, Italy
E-mail: anscario@unive.it

Maurizio Scarpari
Full Professor of Classical Chinese
Department of East Asian Studies
University of Venice, Ca' Foscari
Dorsoduro 3462 – 30123 Venice, Italy
E-mail: scarpari@unive.it

Francesco Sferra
Associate Professor of Sanskrit Language and Literature
Department of Asian Studies
University of Naples, L'Orientale
Piazza S. Domenico Maggiore 12 – 80134 Naples, Italy
E-mail: fransfe@tin.it

Francesco Spagna
Lecturer in Cultural Anthropology
Faculty of Education
University of Macerata
Via Dante Alighieri 5 – 62100 Macerata, Italy
E-mail: immram62@yahoo.it

Aldo Tollini
Associate Professor of Japanese Philology
Department of East Asian Studies
University of Venice, Ca' Foscari
Dorsoduro 3462 – 30125 Venice, Italy
E-mail: tollini@unive.it

Giovanni Torcinovich
PhD Candidate in Indology
Department of Eurasian Studies
University of Venice, Ca' Foscari
San Polo 2035 – 30125 Venice, Italy
E-mail: gtor@inwind.it